Local Government
and Public Service
Reform Initiative

EUROPEAN CENTRE
FOR
MINORITY ISSUES

KW-448-948

MINORITY
GOVERNANCE
IN EUROPE

Edited by

KINGA GÁL

LGI Books

First edition published by
Local Government and Public Service Reform Initiative
Open Society Institute

Nádor utca 11
H–1051 Budapest
Hungary

Telephone: (+36 1) 327 3104
Fax: (+36 1) 327 3105
http://lgi.osi.hu

Design & Production by Judit Kovács/Createch Ltd.

OPEN SOCIETY INSTITUTE

ISBN: 963 9419 40 0
ISSN: 1586-1317

Printed in Hungary by Createch Ltd., October 2002

Local Government
and Public Service
Reform Initiative

Local Government and Public Service Reform Initiative (LGI), as one of the programs of the Open Society Institute (OSI), is an international development and grant-giving organization dedicated to the support of good governance in the countries of Central and Eastern Europe (CEE) and the Newly Independent States (NIS). LGI seeks to fulfill its mission through the initiation of research and support of development and operational activities in the fields of decentralization, public policy formation and the reform of public administration.

With projects running in countries covering the region between the Czech Republic and Mongolia, LGI seeks to achieve its objectives through:

- development of sustainable regional networks of institutions and professionals engaged in policy analysis, reform-oriented training and advocacy;
- support and dissemination of in-depth comparative and regionally applicable policy studies tackling local government issues;
- support of country-specific projects and delivery of technical assistance to the implementation agencies;
- assistance to Soros foundations with the development of local government, public administration and/or public policy programs in their countries of the region;
- publication of books, studies, and discussion papers dealing with the issues of decentralization, public administration, good governance, public policy and lessons learned from the process of transition in these areas;
- development of curricula and organization of training programs dealing with specific local government issues;
- support of policy centers and think tanks in the region.

Apart from its own projects, LGI works closely with a number of other international organizations (Council of Europe, Department for International Development, USAID, UNDP and the World Bank) and co-funds larger regional initiatives aimed at the support of reforms on the subnational level. The Local Government Information Network (LOGIN) and the Fiscal Decentralization Initiatives (FDI) are two main examples of this cooperation.

For additional information or specific publications, please contact:

Local Government and Public Service Reform Initiative
P.O. Box 519
H–1397 Budapest,Hungary
E-mail: lgprog@osi.hu • http://lgi.osi.hu
Telephone: (+36 1) 327 3104 • Fax: (+36 1) 327 3105

Introduction to the Series

Minority Governance in Europe is the first volume in the new ECMI/LGI Series on Ethnopolitics and Minority Issues. The Series is a joint venture of the European Centre for Minority Issues (ECMI) and the Local Government and Public Service Reform Initiative (LGI). ECMI conducts practice-oriented research, provides information and documentation, and offers advisory services concerning minority-majority relations in Europe; in addition, it engages in constructive conflict management through its action-oriented projects, particularly in the Balkans and the Baltics. LGI, a programme of the Open Society Institute, is a think tank specializing in improving governance practices and the provision of public services, especially at the local level.

The ECMI/LGI Series aims to provide a highly visible and accessible platform for ECMI's cutting-edge studies. These multi-author works are the result of the Centre's cooperative research projects, often lasting a number of years. While these projects were at times supported by conferences and seminars, the resulting books attempt to present a coherent and comprehensive picture of the area under investigation. In this way, the Series avoids the pitfalls of conference publications that often lack a clear focus and structure.

The Series will also make it possible for both ECMI and LGI to strengthen the link between their proactive work across Europe and the development of scholarly work that is geared towards influencing policy decisions. Through these studies, ECMI and LGI will raise awareness of crosscutting issues related to majority-minority relations and will analyze new issues and practices as they arise. In this way, the Series will advance the practical understanding of new challenges concerning minority issues while at the same time adding a dimension of theoretically based understanding.

The majority of countries in the former Eastern bloc, in particular in Central and Eastern Europe, feature multiethnic societies. Decentralization and the transition to a free market environment have made this characteristic of nation-states more visible and have raised the claim for a proactive approach toward multiethnic community management. The first step for countries that plan to solve ethnic conflicts in a peaceful way is to draft legislation on individual and collective minority rights. The second step is to implement these rules and manage the public sector in accordance with the accepted principles.

As there is a lack of relevant literature and research in this field, the ECMI/LGI Series intends to fill the gap by providing information and 'food for thought' for public officials and relevant professionals as well as practitioners. It is hoped that the ECMI/LGI publishing partnership will result in a significant addition to the study and practice of emerging policy issues related to minorities.

Marc Weller
European Centre
for Minority Issues

Petra Kovács
Local Government and
Public Service Reform Initiative

Contents

List of Contributors

Dr Florian Bieber is a Senior Non-Resident Research Fellow of the European Centre for Minority Issues. Before that, he was the Regional Representative for ECMI based in Belgrade. He previously worked in the same function in Sarajevo. He has taught at the Central European University in Budapest and the University of Sarajevo. He received his PhD in Political Science from the University of Vienna on contemporary nationalism in Serbia. He has published articles on nationalism and politics in South Eastern Europe in *Nationalities Papers, Third World Quarterly, Current History* and other journals. He has authored *Bosnien-Herzegowina und Libanon im Vergleich [Bosnia-Herzegovina and Lebanon in Comparison]* (1999) and edited, together with Džemal Sokolović, *Reconstructing Multiethnic Societies: The Case of Bosnia-Herzegovina* (2001).

Georg Brunner is Professor emeritus for Public Law and East European Law, and Director of the Institute for East European Law at the University of Cologne. He has authored numerous publications in the field of comparative law.

Douglas Chalmers is currently Researcher in the Economics of Gaelic Language Development at Glasgow Caledonian University, Scotland. As an activist in Scottish politics around the issue of Home Rule, he is a former secretary of the Campaign for a Scottish Parliament, and was an Executive Committee member of the Scottish Constitutional Convention (1989–95) which drew up the blueprint for Scotland's new Parliament.

Dr Gyula Csurgai is a Hungarian-born Canadian citizen. He received his BA in Political Science from Concordia University, Montreal, Canada, and his diploma in Political Science from the University of Toulouse, France. He has Master's degrees "Diplôme d'études supérieures" in European Studies from the Institute for European Studies, Geneva, and in "Nationalism, Cultural Identity and International Relations" from the University of Geneva. He wrote a PhD thesis on the *Geopolitical Approach of the National Question in Central Europe* and holds a doctorate degree from the University of Geneva. He worked as a scientific Collaborator at the Geneva International Peace Research Institute (GIPRI) and is currently Academic Director of SIT (School for International Training), International Studies Programme, Geneva. He is also Professor of Geopolitics at the International Centre for Geopolitical Studies, Geneva.

Farimah Daftary is Minority Protection Program Officer for the EU Accession Monitoring Program at the Open Society Institute in Budapest. Prior to that, she was a Senior Research Associate at the European Centre for Minority Issues (ECMI), Flensburg, Germany. She obtained her Master's in International Affairs with a specialization in

East Central Europe in 1991 from the School of International and Public Affairs (SIPA), Columbia University, New York. Her research concerns various aspects of majority-minority relations in East Central Europe as well as the OSCE's 'human dimension' and conflict prevention mechanisms. She is especially interested in autonomy as a means of conflict settlement. Her recent publications include: "Conflict resolution in FYR of Macedonia: Powersharing or the Civic Approach?", *Helsinki Monitor* 12: 4 (2001). Forthcoming publications include: "Insular Autonomy: A Framework for Conflict Settlement? A Comparative Study of Corsica and the Åland Islands", in: *Managing and Settling Ethnic Conflicts*. U. Schneckener and S. Wolff (eds.) (London: Hurst, 2002).

Ferenc Eiler, a historian, is Research Fellow at the Minority Studies Institute of the Hungarian Academy of Sciences, Budapest.

Dr Kinga Gál is Vice-President of the Government Office for Hungarian Minorities Abroad, Budapest, and Research Associate at the European Centre for Minority Issues (ECMI), Flensburg, Germany. She is a specialist in international human rights law and minority legislation in Central and Eastern Europe, as well as within the context of the UN, OSCE and Council of Europe. She is also an expert on bilateral treaties in Central and Eastern Europe, and coordinator of the project 'Minority Governance Concepts in Europe on the Threshold of the 21st Century'.

Dr François Grin, who holds a PhD in economics, is Adjunct Director of the Unit for Education Research (SRED) and Senior Lecturer at the University of Geneva. From 1998 to 2001, he was Deputy Director of the European Centre for Minority Issues (ECMI) in Flensburg, Germany, to which he remains affiliated as a Senior Fellow. His research focuses on the economics of language, the economics of education, and the evaluation of language and education policies. He is the author of some 150 publications in those fields.

Nóra Kovács, an anthropologist, is Research Fellow at the Minority Studies Institute of the Hungarian Academy of Sciences, Budapest.

Péter Kovács is Professor of International Law at the Faculty of Law of the Miskolc University and the Péter Pázmány Catholic University. He was a diplomat of the Ministry of Foreign Affairs between 1990 and 1994, and from 1998 to 1999. He is a former member of the intergovernmental expert group of the Council of Europe dealing with the preparation of the European Charter for Regional or Minority Languages, and the Framework Convention for the Protection of National Minorities. He was an invited lecturing professor at Montpellier University (2000) and Paris Sceaux University (2002). He is the author of *International Law and Minority Protection* (Budapest: Akadémiai, 2000) and *Le droit international pour la protection des minorités face à l'État-nation* (Miskolc: Miskolc University Press, 2000).

Dr Herbert Küpper, a lawyer, is Academic Assistant at the Institute for East European Law at the University of Cologne. His main fields of research are Hungarian law, law of the Central and South East European countries, comparative public law and minority law. He has authored various publications in these fields.

Dr Kristian Myntti is Senior Researcher at the Åbo Akademi University Institute for Human Rights, Åbo/Turku, Finland. His main reserach focus is on the rights of minorities and indigenous peoples, and he is a member of the Advisory Committee on the Council of Europe Framework Convention for the Protection of National Minorities.

Dr Claus Neukirch is a Political Scientist and works as Researcher at the Centre for OSCE Research in Hamburg. He served as Human Dimension Officer in the OSCE Mission to Moldova during 1996 and 1997, and has frequently served as an OSCE election monitor in Moldova between 1998 and 2001. He concluded his PhD thesis in 2001 on the topic "Conflict Management and Conflict Prevention in the Framework of OSCE Long-term Missions".

Dr Zsolt Gábor Pataki graduated in Economics and International Relations (MA in International Relations at the Budapest University of Economic Sciences, and MA of Geopolitics and MA of International Economics at the University of Paris). He worked as Researcher in the fields of international relations, geopolitics, security issues and ethnicity. He has taught at several universities in Hungary and as a Visiting Lecturer abroad (Montpellier, Paris) and was Research Associate in the programme of the Hungarian Academy of Sciences "Minority Protection in the European Union and in its Member States". He has a PhD in Political Science (Geopolitics) from the University of Paris. Author of one book and co-author of three books on the above themes, he has published in many Hungarian and international reviews.

Dr Karl Rainer graduated in political/judicial sciences and in literature and languages. He currently holds the positions of Director of the Department of EU Affairs and Interregional Cooperation within the Autonomous Province of Bozen, Director of the Presidential Department within the Autonomous Province of Bozen and of Vice-President of the Committee of Bozen for cooperation with developing countries and minority protection. He was a founding member of the European Academy and the Free University of Bozen.

Dr Ulrich Schneckener, a political scientist, is currently Fellow at the German Institute for International and Security Affairs (Stiftung Wissenschaft und Politik, Berlin). From 1996 to 2002, he was Lecturer and Researcher at the University of Bremen. His research interests are ethnic conflicts, international organizations and non-state actors in conflict management and prevention, and international terrorism. His recent publications include *Auswege aus dem Bürgerkrieg* (Frankfurt: Suhrkamp, 2002).

Dr François Vaillancourt holds a PhD from Queen's University (1978) and is Professor at the Department of Economics, and Research Fellow at the Centre de recherche et développement en économique (C.R.D.E.) at the Université de Montréal, and Fellow at the C.D. Howe Institute. He teaches, conducts research and has published extensively in the areas of public finance and the economics of language. He has conducted research and acted as a consultant for organizations such as the Canadian Tax Foundation, the Conseil de la langue française, the Department of Finance, the Economic Council of Canada, Statistics Canada, and the World Bank.

Balázs Vizi studied Law at the Lateran University in Rome in 1993–94, from 1994 at the Eötvös Loránd University in Budapest, and graduated in Law at the Faculty of Law of Eötvös Loránd University in 1999. In 1999–2000 he pursued pre-doctoral studies at the Katholieke Universiteit Leuven in Belgium. From 2000, he has been a PhD student at the Institute for European Policy of the Department of Political Science at the K.U. Leuven. He has participated on a regular basis in several projects of the Minority Studies' Institute of the Hungarian Academy of Sciences (Budapest).

Marc Weller is the Director of the European Centre for Minority Issues (ECMI), Flensburg, Germany. He is also an Assistant Director of Studies in the University of Cambridge, where he teaches International Law. He is currently working on a three-volume collection of documents and analyses on the Kosovo crisis.

List of Tables and Figures

Preface

There is no shortage of conference proceedings that end up thrown together, sometimes hastily, and published in the form of a book. Sometimes such ventures may be useful; on other occasions the urgent need of publication seems less persuasive. This book, it is hoped, manages to avoid the pitfalls of the latter scenario. The contributions contained in this volume are the result of a sustained, joint research effort, carried out over several years. The chapters in the main sections of this work were drafted according to a common methodology and a common structure. They were reviewed over time and exposed to critical examination at numerous pertinent workshops. Importantly, all of the contributions were written with a common purpose: to assess advances that have been made in the discourse on minority governance over the past decade.

This period has been turbulent indeed. Ethnopolitical conflict has dominated the political agenda of the wider Europe since the collapses of the Warsaw Pact, the Soviet Union, and the Socialist Federal Republic of Yugoslavia. A number of different approaches have been tried to address these tumultuous changes and challenges. The states of Central Europe have adopted minority regimes through networks of bilateral treaties embedded in the European Framework Convention on National Minorities. Autonomy systems are being introduced in places with wide-ranging circumstances, such as Corsica and Gagauzia. And adventuresome efforts are being made by international agencies to stabilize minority-majority relations in the Balkans, especially in Bosnia Herzegovina and in Kosovo.

This volume addresses many of these recent trends. It does so on the basis of a conceptual and theoretical foundation established in the first part of the book. Devolution and autonomy are then considered in some of the more well-established cases, as well as in relation to the attempt to utilize elements of minority self-governance for purposes of conflict management or settlement. In this way, an attempt is made to consider new developments against the background of tried and tested autonomous regimes.

An undertaking of this scope would not have been possible without significant support. Such support was made available by the OSCE Chairmanships of Norway and Austria. Their generosity is much appreciated. The kind hospitality provided for by the authorities in Bolzano/Bozen, South Tyrol, also deserves acknowledgement. In addition, ECMI received the cooperation of the Minority Studies Programme of the Hungarian Academy of Sciences. Its Director, Mr László Szarka, supported this project with unstinting vigour and effectiveness. The cooperation of the Ostrecht Institute at the University of Cologne and the European Academy at Bolzano/Bozen also merits acknowledgement.

However, the principal burden in carrying out this project fell on the shoulders of ECMI's Research Associate Dr Kinga Gál. She played the crucial role of conceiving this project, in the organization of the seminars and in pulling the contributions together in their present form. In the later stages, the editorial process was taken over by ECMI's publications officer, Ms Marita Lampe, with Ms Sabine Kozdon providing valuable assistance. To all of the above, ECMI is profoundly grateful.

This book also marks the launching of a unique joint publication endeavour between ECMI and the Local Government and Public Service Reform Initiative (LGI). This joint arrangement will greatly enhance the availability of this work, and of others that will follow. The splendid support of LGI, and especially of Ms Petra Kovács, director of the LGI Managing Multiethnic Communities Project, and LGI's production manager Tom Bass and his team, in the publication of this first volume in a series of studies, bodes well for the future of this venture.

As lies in the nature of collective works of this kind, the views expressed in this volume differ. They are attributable to the individual authors, and not to any particular institution. Taken together, however, it is hoped they will shed some further light on the often dramatic developments relating to minority governance in Europe at the beginning of the twenty-first century.

September 2002

Marc Weller, Director
European Centre for Minority Issues
Flensburg, Germany

Minority Governance on the Threshold of the Twenty-First Century

Kinga Gál

MINORITY GOVERNANCE—EFFECTIVE PARTICIPATION

The possibility for citizens to influence the decision-making process has always been a core issue within the democratic and pluralistic state structure. At the beginning of the twenty-first century, political, social and cultural rights of individuals are, for the most part, guaranteed and respected across the democratic states in Europe, regardless of their domestic governmental structure (i.e. whether they be of unitary or federal structure.)[1]

These issues become even more complex in the many European countries where another element is present: the existence of one or more ethnic groups different from the majority of the population, i.e. ethnic, national, religious, or linguistic minorities. A democratic system in itself does not automatically provide a solution for the problems of these minorities.[2] Democracy means the acceptance of the majority's decisions by the minority. However, the 'winner takes all' model cannot be the proper paradigm for societies with several national minorities. The voluntary acceptance of majority decisions by national minorities implies a strong sense of a common destiny, and this might be missing where the state structure is rather ethnicized. Here confrontation is likely to occur along ethnic lines; developments over the past few years have shown time and again that there is an urgent need to find solutions acceptable to opposing sides. Thus, protection of national minorities has become a question of security in Europe, with particular regard to Central, Eastern and South Eastern European regions of the continent.

Lasting solutions have shown to be the outcome of steps taken by governments to avoid zero-sum games and be better set for consensus. The effective representation of minorities on all levels of decision-making, the existence of strong self-governments with minority representatives or special minority self-governments, or even power-sharing within the institutional state structure, may ameliorate the deficiencies of democratic, multiethnic states. Minority governance in this context may range from accommodation of basic human/minority rights to the realization of certain types of autonomies.

Minority self-governance should be viewed as a practical solution to certain situations where the more conventional constructions may not prove sufficient. The term 'self-governance' is very elastic and interpretable in a multitude of social and legal relationships; it can thus be expected to become a solution in many political contexts and practices. Autonomy arrangements may in many situations be a compromise between the demands of one party and the initial position of another. Different models of minority self-government in general, and autonomy arrangements in particular, are related to the institutional organization of a country; within this structure could lie qualities that promote the protection of minorities. In this regard, they can be interpreted as an overall framework and mode of participation (by minorities) in public decision-making.

APPROACHES TO INSTITUTIONALIZATION OF MINORITY PARTICIPATION

The institutionalization and promotion of minority protection in international and domestic law has been developed primarily in three ways since World War II; today it continues to be redefined by recent developments.

(1) The promotion of minority rights through the general protection of individual human rights is the most commonly accepted principle under international law. This *human rights approach* guarantees the rights of national, ethnic, linguistic and religious minorities as part of the universally recognized human rights. The positive, individual rights of these minorities are generally related to, and derived from, the general non-discrimination clause and a whole set of specific human rights, such as the right to identity, linguistic rights, education, electoral rights and representation.[3]

On this level of the individual protection of minorities an important right emerged and developed in recent years, and may continue to do so as a reaction to the challenges of the new century: *the right to political participation of the persons belonging to national minorities.* This right, enshrined in the only legally binding international convention on minority rights (Council of Europe Framework Convention on the Protection of National Minorities, Art. 15) and in several legally non-binding, but politically strong commitments (OSCE Copenhagen Document, paragraph 35; UN Declaration on the Rights of Persons belonging to National or Ethnic, Religious and Linguistic Minorities, Art. 2), establishes the possibility to influence the decision-making by the minorities themselves. The right to effective political participation has been enlarged in some interpretations, such as the Parliamentary Assembly of the Council of Europe Recommendation 1201(1993). According to this interpretation, minorities may be entitled to establish their own self-governing institutions in certain circumstances.[4]

(2) The second approach envisages the protection of national minorities and the autonomous institution-building through another basic human right, the *right to self-determination.* Such an approach was delineated in Article 1 of each of the two UN Covenants.[5] The right of self-determination is granted only for peoples in international law; but because certain minority communities are treated as distinct entities but not as peoples in any legal sense, they were not entitled to this right. Hence, a new concept of self-determination was advanced by the representatives of minorities and policy-makers at the close of the twentieth century (especially due to the changes in Central and Eastern Europe): *the principle of internal self-determination.* According to this redefined principle, self-restriction is required both from the majority government and from the minority community. While the majority renounces the exclusive interpretation of state sovereignty as national sovereignty and accepts the distinct status of a minority, the minority community gives up radical demands that could endanger the integrity of the state and peaceful coexistence. They may be granted different forms of participation and representation through various autonomy arrangements depending on their needs, and they may be accepted as state constituents as well. Limited or internal self-determination can take various forms in the state structure, depending on a host of variables, needs, desires and restrictions.

(3) The third approach emphasizes the recognition of the fact that true protection of minorities can only be ensured within a democratic framework. In a functioning democracy, employing the *principle of subsidiarity*, the local and regional authorities enjoy a wide degree of autonomy in matters concerning the population under their jurisdiction. According to this principle, only matters that local and regional levels are not capable of dealing with should be conferred to superior authorities.

The Council of Europe has taken the first and most important steps in fostering the principle of subsidiarity and the role of local and regional authorities throughout Europe. One of the basic tasks of the Council was the promotion of the idea of democracy within communities, so as to support the active participation of citizens in the decision-making processes of society, especially at the local level. The idea of subsidiarity is reflected among others in the European Charter of Local Self-Government, the European Charter for Regional Self-Government, the European Charter for Regional or Minority Languages,[6] as well as several resolutions and recommendations of the Parliamentary Assembly of the Council of Europe, and the Conference of Local and Regional Authorities of Europe.

The idea of subsidiarity and the afferent institutions that provide self-determination, however, fit not only with the majority rule system, but allow for the promotion of specific minority interests. This has become an important argument in minority protection, with the local level being the closest to their specific problems as well as to their demands for equal opportunities.

The principle of subsidiarity is the basis of the *administrative autonomy with special status.* The key element of this autonomy regime is the division of power between the central government and the autonomous entity. Thus, the power transferred to the autonomous institutions can vary from an administratively enlarged authority through home-rule up to devolution. The highest possible degree of this 'special status' could be territorial autonomy, the most complex and wide-ranging type of autonomy for minorities compactly settled in a specific region.

ARRANGEMENTS OF MINORITY SELF-GOVERNANCE

According to the three approaches described above, minority self-governance may be one way of ensuring that all significant segments of a society are able to participate effectively in the political and economic decisions which affect their lives. Autonomy as an institutionalized form of participation in decision-making has appeared on all the above-listed levels to the same extent. In this regard, autonomy can be interpreted as an overall framework and mode of participation in public decision-making. It can exist within a wide variety of political structures, from federalism to consociation, devolution or decentralization.

The different autonomy arrangements can be classified by the level on which they are established, by the legal form of their establishment, by the field incorporated in the autonomy and by the subjects of that autonomy. This way a regime of autonomy can be established by treaty, constitution, statute or by a combination of these sources. These autonomies, as the comparative study by Professor Georg Brunner and Dr Herbert Küpper discusses, may then be divided into two main categories: territorial and cultural autonomy. Scholars also recognize the existence of 'in-between forms', such as: *personal autonomy,[7] administrative autonomy or self-government with special status,[8] as well as regional autonomy.[9]*

The particular form of self-governance adopted may depend on any, or any combination of the following factors: historical and political evolution (described in chapter by Balázs Vizi), geopolitical circumstances (analyzed by Gyula Csurgai), and economic factors (discussed by François Grin and François Vaillancourt). To the same extent it may depend on the characteristics of power-sharing between the central and autonomous government. The introductory comparative studies of the book discuss the above factors in detail and analyze the various forms of minority governance according to these factors.

The creation of the various autonomy arrangements does not follow any general pattern; it can be constructed in many ways and will either flourish or fail based on its framework and the myriad variables it will come up against. Autonomy or any other form of minority self-governance should be viewed as a practical solution to a practical problem that may be harnessed in situations where other, more conventional, constructions may be deficient.

The case studies on the arrangements of minority governance included in this book are described from both a dynamic and static viewpoint. The authors address the most important factors influencing the outcome of a particular arrangement (reflecting on factors such as history, existence and influence of a kin-state, involvement of the international community, the political environment and economic conditions). Other factors that will be considered on a case-by-case basis as well are: the legal basis of the model; the subject of the special right; the institutional framework; the mandate, power and duties of the self-governing institutions (relations to the public institutions, central government, regional government, international organizations, kin-state); financial issues and economic viability. Each case study contains certain assessments of the role these models play in ethnic conflict management and of the degree of national consensus attained or needed in each particular arrangement, i.e. their acceptance by the state and civil society of the majority, as well as by the minority community.

In addition, these studies stress the importance of state resources for autonomy durability and for the degree of national consensus regarding the arrangement. The role of international actors in the implementation of effective autonomies will also be analyzed.

While emphasizing both the characteristics and the environment of 'successful' models, the book also explores the problems and shortcomings of the cases where the utility of minority self-government is still largely debated in the society and faces difficulties to be accepted by the governments concerned.

The three approaches to the institutionalization of minority protection can be discovered in the different arrangements of ethnic accommodation.

The first approach, the institutionalization of minority representation and participation through the relevant human/minority rights, is the most typical solution. The implementation of the right of effective political participation could lead to one or even all of the autonomy structures discussed in this book. Nevertheless, the most eloquent cases of the practical implementation of this right are the Sami self-governments in the Nordic countries (described and analyzed by Kristian Myntti) and the minority self-governments in Hungary (of which an overview of these complex solutions is presented by Nóra Kovács and Ferenc Eiler).

The autonomy concepts based on internal self-determination of minorities (which were more desired as mere participatory rights and envisaged minority governance within the existing state structures without any hint of the classic principle of self-determination) became especially popular in Central and Eastern Europe. Well elaborated and analyzed legal drafts of the institutionalization of minority governance, prepared by representatives of the Hungarian minorities in Central Europe, are discussed in Zsolt Gábor Pataki's study. The case study on Vojvodina by Tamás Korhecz is based on the recent autonomy drafts prepared by the representatives of the Hungarian minority in Vojvodina that also combine the principles of internal self-determination and of subsidiarity.

These concepts are mainly based on the models offered by existing and 'functioning' European autonomies, such as the Catalan autonomous community in Spain or the regional autonomy in South Tyrol. The case of South Tyrol is considered by Gyula Csurgai, in his comparative study on geopolitical aspects of minority governance, as one of the most appropriate models for minority accommodation in Central and Eastern Europe.

However, the classic model of the South Tyrol autonomy will be discussed in this book from a slightly different perspective, focussing on the practical issues related to the functioning of this arrangement. Karl Rainer, being in charge of the implementation of this regional autonomy from its conception, will refer to the most relevant and debated issues of this model within the society of South Tyrol. In order to reflect the complexity of this case often referred to as 'the model arrangement', the concluding study of the book by Ulrich Schneckener will also analyze the South Tyrol arrangement from the perspective of shared-rule in practice.

The Gagauz territorial autonomy, 'Gagauz Yeri' in Moldova, is another exciting example of the realization of the theory of internal self-determination. This unique autonomy arrangement in Eastern Europe will be discussed in detail by Claus Neukirch, who will present both the positive and negative elements of this particular model.

Less difficult is the interpretation of participatory rights through the other basic principle related to democratic state structure and rule of law—that of subsidiarity. This would help lead to minority self-governance through the institutionalized devolution of power, either by providing an additional mandate for normal self-governments or through different autonomy arrangements, without being based exclusively on an ethnic basis. The best example of the practical realization of the principle of subsidiarity without ethnic features is the devolution of Scotland. Douglas Chalmers gives a detailed explanation of this long-lasting process which led to the establishment and functioning of the Scottish Parliament.

The very recent developments in Corsica are also based on the implementation of the subsidiarity principle through decentralization and devolution of power analyzed by Farimah Daftary. In Corsica it is not clear whether the achieved model will be more an administrative autonomy with special status or a regionalization of this island.

While the concepts of autonomy arrangements that appeared in Central and Eastern Europe may be regarded as combinations of all three above-mentioned approaches, the case of Bosnia, presented in its complexity by Florian Bieber, and of Kosovo, analyzed by Marc Weller, are less easy to define or place into any single category of autonomy arrangement. Kosovo, according to Marc Weller, accepted for an interim period a complex power-sharing arrangement featuring a highly fragmented layering of authority from local communes up to the federal level. These cases evidence a combination of the principles of internal self-determination, effective participation and subsidiarity, but also introduce further elements related to external self-determination, and in relation to the latter that of violence and war.

Within the different forms of minority self-governance, autonomy in general is the institution where there are no clearly defined borders between the two basic theoretical approaches of rule, i.e. shared-rule and self-rule. While *shared-rule* (i.e. different forms of power-sharing) may use autonomy as one of the implementing mechanisms, *self-rule* (i.e. the theoretic definition of the classic autonomy concepts based on a certain form or level of separation) is using power-sharing mechanisms during the implementation[10] of the classic autonomy concepts. Therefore, it is almost impossible to establish clear borders between the two concepts of political theory, as autonomy models will routinely mix the existing theoretical concepts whenever realized in practice.

Most of the comparative and case studies of this book concentrate on the autonomy models in their classic meaning, although without clearly delimiting self-rule and shared-rule when referring to the establishment, structure and implementation of the models. The concluding study by Schneckener will refer to these differences and to the complexity of both theories while analyzing minority governance between self-rule and shared-rule.

The practical functioning of all the models analyzed in this book proves that even the 'classic' arrangements face formidable challenges on the threshold of the new century. Further improvements are predictable both in Western Europe (Corsica, Scotland, Northern Ireland) and in Eastern Europe (Vojvodina, Kosovo, Bosnia). The cases of Corsica, Bosnia, Kosovo and Vojvodina are so topical that their arrangements continue to be debated. This makes these special cases more difficult to assess but at the same time more exciting to unravel.

CONCLUSION—CHALLENGES

Questions of minority self-governance and possible forms of minority participation currently generate a lively exchange of opinions in the international community. The various autonomy models offer constructive methods of solving ethnic conflicts through providing means for political participation of minorities.

The powers accorded to the different minority self-governments vary from case to case according to the aims sought. The creation of the various autonomy arrangements does not follow any general pattern; it can be expected to flourish as well as to fail depending on the relevant political contexts and practices.

Several paradigms of minority governance can be found in the world.[11] Each minority–majority relationship differs from country to country, as the minority communities themselves are very different. Each minority situation presents its own particular characteristics.

The means and tools used by the parties involved in mutual ethnic accommodation, as well as the range of models that can be considered to this end, depend to a large extent on the current developmental stage of the society and, more precisely, on the democratic strength it embodies. The reconciliation process depends on the political culture and will of the majority and minority communities, as well as the political culture of politicians and policy-makers. When addressing these issues, the choice of terminology is crucial, not just in analytical terms but also in the context of public debate about possible minority regimes.

As noted, there is no standard method of resolving the numerous concrete problems associated with the creation and improvement of minority governance. Models that could be transferred from one context to another are extremely difficult to find. Yet any model or concept can serve as a source of inspiration and indeed insight for the international community which is currently grappling with many questions and concerns within this domain.

As there are no clear borders between the different models of minority protection, the different solutions are largely interrelated, and this must be kept in mind when analyzing them. The different self-governance arrangements in Europe, including forms of autonomy, have been analyzed from several perspectives thus far. This project focuses on a category of issues where more in-depth research is needed, in particular as regards the implementation of some of the aforementioned models and their practical implications.

The comparison of existing drafts for minority self-government and corresponding specific arrangements in Central and Eastern Europe on the one hand, and existing and functioning autonomy models in Western Europe on the other hand, can be useful for both governments and minorities, particularly with a view to clarifying differences and similarities. Another goal of such a comparison is to shed light on the legal and socio-economic environment of these models.

During the implementation period of the various minority government models, care must be taken not to extrapolate and apply information haphazardly; seemingly identical events may have quite different causes and may lead to different results in different places. The protection of minorities and the management of ethnic tensions require a healthy degree of historical, political geographical and cultural awareness. These are the issues under which people construct their identities.

International standards have improved in an unpredictable way over the last years. The international institutions took huge steps forward in identifying key problems and trying to provide answers to questions that had been considered taboo some years ago. Nevertheless, even these steps can be considered a slow reaction to the fast developing realities in the field of ethnic accommodation. A legal framework exists today in which the adequate protection of minorities could become a reality. But international law can only lay down a minimum set of standards and general orientation points. The foundation has been provided; now the emphasis should be on implementation at the international and national levels, as well as on the realization of the declared principles in practice.

NOTES

[1] Unitary states comprise the large majority of states. Here, central authorities are the representatives of the state, and can be located in the centre (ministries), or at local or regional level (prefect in France or equivalent). Although the unitary states are more centralized, at the end of the twentieth century almost all of them went through a modernization process which altered their administrative structure, consisting of three levels: municipalities, regions and central authorities. Unitary states with decentralized state structure are, among others, France, the United Kingdom and the Netherlands. States with traditional federal state structures are Germany and Austria. Federal states with 'federalist' or regional state structure are countries where the system of relations and supervision is twofold, central and regional (Spain, Italy). Belgium is a special case where different levels of decentralization existed during the several administrative reforms. These range from the decentralized state, regional state structure to the federal state system.

[2] There is no standard definition for minorities in international law. One widely accepted definition is by Capotorti prepared for the UN. Another is enshrined in the Council of Europe Parliamentary Assembly Recommendation 1201(1993). For more on the question of definition, see the study by Vizi, or the study by Brunner and Küpper in this book.

[3] Enshrined in the United Nations International Covenant on Civil and Political Rights (1966) and the International Covenant on Economic, Social and Cultural Rights (1966), in the International Convention on the Elimination of All Forms of Racial Discrimination (1965); in the European Convention for the Protection of Human Rights and Fundamental Freedoms (1950). During the last decade of the twentieth century important developments took place in this particular field of international law: There have been documents adopted dealing exclusively with minority protection based on the human rights approach, such as the UN Declaration on the Rights of Persons belonging to National or Ethnic, Religious, and Linguistic Minorities (1992), the Council of Europe Framework Convention for the Protection of National Minorities (1994), as well as the CSCE Document of the Copenhagen Meeting of the Conference on the Human Dimension (1990). All these legally binding and non-binding documents of the international community (UN, OSCE, Council of Europe, EU) perceive minority

rights as individual rights. Nevertheless, throughout the 1990s, also due to the changes (such as) in Central and Eastern Europe, slowly a slight shift emerged in this concept with the acceptance of the idea of collectively practiced individual minority rights, leading to the still debated and partly accepted principle of collective minority rights.

4   For a more detailed analysis on the international legal framework, see the studies by Vizi, as well as Brunner and Küpper in this book.

5   See endnote 3.

6   The Charter sets out to protect and promote regional or minority languages, not linguistic minorities. Nevertheless, the obligations enshrined in the Charter will have an effect on the situation of the communities concerned.

7   *Personal autonomy* applies to all the members of a certain group within the state, irrespective of their place of residence. It is adequate for minorities which live dispersed in the country but have a strong political will for self-government and articulate their claims as such. The community is entitled to different, wide-ranging rights in political, economic as well as social life, although these rights have so far usually been limited to matters of culture, language, religion and education.

8   If in a given administrative unit a national minority constitutes the numerical majority of the population, the local self-administration coincides with a higher degree of administrative autonomy; that is, a higher degree of administrative decentralization. This administrative autonomy may involve a special status related to such questions as education, social assistance or welfare, by the enlargement of the powers and competencies of the existing local authority.

9   *Regional autonomy* can be a result of the association of local governments with special status and greater complex competencies.

10   For more details on the theoretical approach and the difference between *self-rule* and *shared-rule*, see the concluding study of this book by Schneckener.

11   As stated by Gianfranco Martini, Special Rapporteur for the Congress of Local and Regional Authorities of Europe in Strasbourg, 26–28 May 1998, in the explanatory memorandum of the report on "Territorial autonomy and national minorities":

> The geographical boundaries of the self-governing region may not be based on exclusively ethnic criteria but must also take into account historical and economic ones. The forms of territorial self-government may be highly diverse, ranging from federalism to regionalism as well as to special status combining the principle of self-government with the principles of participation and interdependence. (…) Territorial self-government is not the answer to every problem: it may, for example, require integration with a system of cultural autonomy. It is up to the minorities themselves to make the most appropriate choices (p.6).

PART I

Minority Governance Concepts in Europe: Theory and Practice

European Options of Autonomy: A Typology of Autonomy Models of Minority Self-Governance

Georg Brunner and Herbert Küpper

European Options of Autonomy: A Typology of Autonomy Models of Minority Self-Governance

Georg Brunner and Herbert Küpper

1. INTRODUCTION

The concept and notion of autonomy as a means of giving a certain group within the human race the right to decide and administer certain affairs essential to their well-being is very old in European political and legal culture. As such, autonomy is not necessarily linked to the question of national and ethnic minorities. In fact, the 'classical' forms of autonomy can be found in different contexts, such as the local autonomy of towns and villages, as the academic autonomy of universities or, in the more modern area, the functional autonomy of public broadcasting.

In the field of minority rights, autonomy is only one possible solution. It forms a part of a large variety of legal instruments designed to help minorities to survive and prosper. Therefore, this chapter will first give an overview of the possible legal forms of minority rights and the position of the autonomy in this system. This is followed by a detailed analysis of the specific legal and conceptual questions of minority autonomies.

2. PRE-LEGAL REQUIREMENT: AWARENESS

All minority rights presuppose the existence of a minority. This may sound banal but it is important. A minority only exists if the members of the minority are aware that their group is different in an essential aspect. If the characteristics that constitute the difference between a minority group and the majority are socially quite irrelevant, the acknowledgement of the existence of a minority situation may be lacking. Religion provides a good example: in modern Western Europe, religion is considered predominantly a private matter of little societal relevance. For this reason, a group that is different only in terms of its religious beliefs will find it much more difficult to be acknowledged as a minority—both by its own members and by the majority—than would have been the case two centuries ago when religion was essential for individual and collective identity.

The corresponding awareness on the part of the majority population is not a *conditio sine qua non* for the existence of a minority. A minority group may well go unnoticed by the majority and still have the consciousness of being different in an essential feature. However, in modern European democratic systems, it is the majority of citizens and the majoritarian public opinion that have a decisive influence on the creation of constitutions, laws and rights. This is ensured by deciding directly in referenda, by determining the legislative majority in the parliaments and by threatening not to vote the present parliamentary majority back into office. For this reason, awareness on the side of the majority may not be a necessary element for defining a minority; but for the creation of adequate minority laws it is essential that the majority is aware of the difference of the group in question, i.e. of the existence of the problem, and that it agrees that some sort of protection of that difference is fair, just or practical.

It was mentioned before that the factor of difference must be one of social relevance. Here we are speaking of national and ethnic minorities—distinguishing features vitally important all across Europe nowadays. Yet, in some countries being a member of the state nation (which is generally conceived as the political nation) prevails over the purely ethnic factor. In France, national identity is predominantly defined as being a citizen of the French Republic; one's legal status is linked to the French state, not his ethnicity. The fact that one may belong to a non-French ethnic group is considered of little importance—a feeling that is shared by many members of the Flemish, Breton, German, Basque, Italian and Catalan-speaking communities in France. This concept of nation makes it hard for French citizens of non-French ethnicity to consider themselves, and to make themselves considered by the majority, as ethnic minorities within the overall French nation.[1]

A similar situation can be found in Switzerland. Here, ethnic and linguistic differences are not ignored or judged irrelevant. However, the notion of a Swiss nation embraces these differences and constitutes a multiethnic state nation comprising of all Swiss citizens. Ethnic differences find their place in this notion, and for this reason all four language groups are equally constituent parts of this Swiss nation. This is true not only for the larger German and French communities, but also for the smaller Italian and Rhaeto-Romance language groups. They are not minorities because they are accepted as a part of the multiethnic majority.[2]

It is not only the prevailing definition of a state nation that may prevent the awareness of a minority situation. Close similarities between minority and majority groups may also make it difficult to arrive at a minority status. One example of this is the Frisians, both in the Netherlands and in Germany. Although their idiom, in linguistic terms, is unequivocally a language onto its own and not a dialect of Lower German or Dutch, its resemblance to both Lower German and Dutch is acute. Frisian customs and folklore differ little from that of the surrounding Dutch or German populations. Hence, the awareness of a distinct Frisian ethnic identity was and still is weak both among the Frisians and the majority populations. Only in the last few decades did the conscious work of Frisian minority activists awaken the sense of being a distinct ethnic group. This occurred first among the Frisians and later among the majorities, beginning in the Netherlands and followed in Germany. Similar situations exist with the Kashoub minority and the Polish majority, with the Sard minority and the Italian majority, and with the Ruthenian minority and the Ukrainian majority, to cite a few examples.

3.   THE DEFINITION OF MINORITIES

Once awareness exists that a certain group is a national or ethnic minority, the question of certain rights for this group arises. If a right is conferred to a group or to its members on the basis of their belonging to this group, the group as well as the fact of belonging to it will have to be defined in legal terms in order to determine who is the bearer of the right conferred and who is not. This means that the law granting minority rights must provide for at least some minimal delimitation of its personal scope, i.e. a minimal definition of the national or ethnic minority or minorities in question.

There is no universally valid definition of a national or ethnic minority. There have been many attempts to formulate a definition, but so far none has been generally accepted. Even in just the European context the forms of national and ethnic minorities vary to such an extent that it is virtually impossible to find a broad definition which could cover all minority situations, in their most basic sense. Yet, the more widely accepted definitions, especially Francesco Capotorti's, may serve as a useful guideline:

> a group numerically inferior to the rest of the population of a State, in a non-dominant position, whose members—being nationals of the State—possess ethnic, religious, or linguistic characteristics differing from those of the rest of the population and show, if only implicitly, a sense of solidarity, directed towards preserving their culture, traditions, religion, or language.[3]

Jules Deschênes later tried to reformulate this definition in a more precise way to avoid some of the complications that had arisen with Capotorti's definition:

> a group of citizens of a State, constituting a numerical minority and in a non-dominant position in that State, endowed with ethnic, religious, or linguistic characteristics which differ from those of the majority of the population, having a sense of solidarity with one another, motivated, if only implicitly, by a collective will to survive and whose aim is to achieve equality with the majority in fact and in law.[4]

Leaving the universal level and turning to European legal instruments, one finds documents for the protection of minorities in comparatively large numbers, but only one attempt at definition. In its 44th Session on 1 February 1993, the Parliamentary Assembly of the Council of Europe adopted the famous Recommendation 1201, which contains in Article 1 the following definition of a national minority:

A group of persons in a state who:
a) reside on the territory of that state and are citizens thereof;
b) maintain long-standing, firm and lasting ties with that state;
c) display distinctive ethnic, cultural, religious or linguistic characteristics;
d) are sufficiently representative, although smaller in number than the rest of the population of that state or of a region of that state;
e) are motivated by a concern to preserve together that which constitutes their common identity, including their culture, their traditions, their religion or their language.[5]

It should be noted that none of these definitions formulated in international law is binding upon any state. They may serve as guidelines, but are by no means compulsory, neither in law nor in logic. Given this situation, it is advisable that in a given state a definition is found that serves the needs of the specific minority situations in this state. This definition should include all groups that can justifiably be considered a national or ethnic minority; it should exclude all other groups that do not constitute a minority on a national or ethnic basis. In 1990, the Jewish community as well the intellectual élite in Hungary protested against—by intention benevolent—government plans to include Jews in minority legislation,[6] and since then it has been clear that Jews do not see themselves, nor are they seen by the majority, as a national or ethnic minority. The subsequent minority legislation took account of this fact. In Germany, a legal definition of minority would have to exclude the various regional forms of German ethnicity, or *Landsmannschaften*. Saxons, Bavarians and Rhinelanders are not ethnic minorities, whereas Frisians, Danes, Sorbs and the various Gypsy groups are. There are and will always be, of course, borderline cases of groups which are difficult to identify as a mere *Landsmannschaft* or as an ethnic entity different from, though very close to the majority. The Occitan population in France provides a good example of this.

So far, Hungary is one of the few states in Europe that has tried to incorporate in their legislation an abstract definition of a national or ethnic minority. According to the Hungarian Minorities Act, minorities are:

> all ethnic groups having lived on the territory of the Republic of Hungary for at least one century, that are in a numerical minority among the population of the State, whose members are Hungarian citizens and different from the rest of the population in terms of their own language, culture, and traditions, and that give proof of such a conscience of belonging which is directed towards the preservation of all this, to the expression and the protection of the interests of their historically evolved communities.[7]

§2 makes it clear that refugees, immigrants, foreign and stateless residents do not fall under the scope of the definition, and §61(1) enumerates the thirteen groups that fulfilled the criteria of the abstract definition at the time when the Act was passed. The Estonian Cultural Autonomy Act contains a similar definition, shaped on the definition in the Council of Europe Recommendation 1201:

> A national minority in the sense of this Act is deemed to consist of Estonian citizens who:
> - reside on the territory of Estonia;
> - maintain long-standing, firm and lasting ties with Estonia;
> - are different from the Estonians by their ethnic belonging, their cultural characteristics, their religion or their language;
> - are motivated by the wish to preserve together their cultural traditions, their religion or language, which form the basis of their common identity.[8]

§2 of the Cultural Autonomy Act prescribes a minimum number of 3,000 members of a minority in order to enjoy the privileges of that legislation; the traditional minorities of Germans, Jews, Russians and Swedes being *ex lege* exempted from this numerical requirement.

In an act of law, it would of course suffice to enumerate the groups concerned instead of trying to formulate an abstract definition. This is what various German *Länder* did in their constitutions and minority acts: Schleswig-Holstein names the Danes and the Frisians; Brandenburg and Saxony name the Sorbs. However, the Estonian and Hungarian solution of an abstract definition, combined with an enumeration of the groups falling under the definition at the time the act was passed,[9] serves the interests of the minorities better because it allows the acknowledgement of subdivisions of a given group as a separate minority if this subdivision wishes so. This could happen, for instance, within the highly fragmented Gypsy population in countries like Hungary; but it would also allow the Csángó groups east of the Carpathians to create a minority identity and structure different from that of the local Hungarians if they feel the necessity to do so. An abstract definition also remains open towards immigrant groups that may become a minority after a given time of residence in their state of immigration, provided that they obtain the citizenship of this state and preserve their ethnic differences.

It is not necessary to use the term 'minority' in the definition. If a given group feels unhappy with this expression, as is often the case when a part of the former majority population becomes a minority due to border changes (i.e. the Russians in the non-Russian successor states to the Soviet Union or the Serbs in Slovenia, Croatia and Macedonia), another term that is more acceptable to them may be adopted, such as 'language group', 'cultural group' or 'community', 'nationality', 'nation', etc.

4.   THE 'HIERARCHY' OF MINORITY RIGHTS

Once the awareness of a minority situation exists, and it is agreed how to define the minority group, there are various legal instruments to assist in the process. The aim of all these minority rights is to stabilize the minority, and allow them to preserve their differences. Thus, if the aim is assimilation (which may be quite justified if the minority members themselves wish so), no minority rights are needed. If, however, the minority's goal is to maintain its customs and beliefs, certain minority rights must be chosen, granted and implemented, according to the situation.

The various forms of possible minority rights form a hierarchy in the sense that they range from minor to comprehensive. Yet, this purely quantitative qualification must not be confused with a qualitative assessment: More rights are not necessarily better; it all depends on the specific features of the situation that is to be regulated.

At the bottom of the hierarchy of minority rights is the principle of non-discrimination and of equal rights. The next step are special rights, which may or may not be accompanied by affirmative action. These special rights, which take into account the differences of the minority members, can be granted as individual or collective rights. If the collective rights reach a certain level of self-determination, they become an autonomy. Thus, autonomy is at the top of the hierarchy and constitutes the maximum legal status a minority may achieve within a state.

4.1 Non-Discrimination and Equal Rights

The very basis of the legal status of a minority is the principle of non-discrimination. This means that the law must not attach any negative consequences to the fact that an individual belongs to a minority.

If the principle of non-discrimination is converted from its negative outlook (no negative consequences) into a positive formula, it says that minority members must not have fewer, but the same rights (and duties) as any other citizen. Thus, the principles of non-discrimination and equal rights are closely linked.

However, the principle of equality can be more than mere non-discrimination: it may be interpreted in a way suitable to specifically serve the interests of a minority and thus go beyond mere prevention of discrimination. Equality does not have an absolute value; it is relative and can only be determined in comparison to someone else's situation. This comparison and the formulation of the relevant factors can be done in various ways and thus leaves room for a minority-centred application of the principle of equality. One example of the rule of equality is that all pupils have the right to receive their schooling in the state language. This rule does not take into account the minority's special needs. If, however, the rule is altered in a minority-centred way, it would read: All pupils have the right to receive their schooling in their mother tongue. Both rules create formal equality. The minority-centred approach creates material equality as well.[10]

In this respect, it is worthwhile mentioning that in Europe all countries are parties to the Convention for the Protection of Human Rights and Fundamental Freedoms of 4 November 1950 (CPHR), which contains in Article 14 the principle of equality. Its relevance for minority issues in the practice of the European Court for Human Rights is low. The lessons that can be drawn from these decisions are far from being unequivocal, but one can state that Article 14 forbids arbitrary differentiation only, whereas different treatment within an overall concept which takes into account demographic facts and can as such be taken as just and justified (such as the present Belgian concept of dividing the state's territory into monolingual areas with only very small areas of transition), is not arbitrary and hence does not contravene Article 14.[11]

4.2 Special Rights

Non-discrimination and equal rights—even in a minority-centred approach—do not normally suffice to enable the minority to maintain a distinct collective identity. The special features of their identity are, by the very fact of being different, threatened numerically, socially, economically and culturally by the surrounding majority. The majority identity—or, as one could put it, the majority culture—exercises a certain pressure for assimilation, which is the stronger the more a minority is integrated into the overall society, the more dispersed its members live and the more exposed they are to the majority culture. Maintaining a distinct minority identity thus entails a fight against the pressure of the majority culture. Special rights serve to equip the minority with the necessary means of defence. Thus, special rights go further than mere equal rights (even in their minority-centred approach): They give the minority and/or its members rights which are different and more extensive from those of the majority. These special rights are designed to account for the cultural differences of the minority.

The basic form of special minority rights are individual rights. The bearer of these rights is the individual member of the minority. Individual rights include such rights as to use one's native language in private, public and official communication; to establish media businesses in the minority language; and to create, in communion with other individuals, organizations that serve minority purposes. Individual rights are closely linked to a human rights approach since human rights, too, centre on the individual. Apart from general human rights, which can also serve the purpose of the members of a minority, there are few special individual human rights that are aimed exclusively at the protection of minority interests. One could cite the right to use one's language in private, public and before authorities and courts unconditionally,[12] or the right to have and to use one's name(s) according to the traditions of one's group. On a more factual level, the freedom of religion is a right typically relevant for minorities because the members of the large majority religions will find their opinions expressed in general legislation. The conditions of coeducational school sports in Europe remain within the morals of the Christian (or religiously indifferent) majority, but may violate the tenets of religions such as Islam. The imposition of a general duty to wear a helmet on a motorcycle does not interfere with persons belonging to the majoritarian religions, but may conflict with the customs of someone whose religion demands that a *kippa*, veil or *turban* also be worn while participating in road traffic.

Individual rights cannot take into account the basic truth that minority identity can only be lived and maintained in a group. There is no point in talking Frisian or dressing in Sorb costume while sitting all alone in one's room. This is unsatisfactory both for the individual and for the Frisian or

Sorb community respectively. Only when Frisian is spoken or Sorb costume is worn in the community can it serve as an expression of the identity of a minority group. To a certain extent, though, the individual rights of minority members can create a space where minority identity can be expressed.

However, many minorities feel the need to be granted rights which address the minority as a group. The bearer of these collective rights is the minority 'as such'. This means that the bearer of the collective rights is no more the individual alone or together with others, but some legal entity representing the minority. This can be a private organization, a public body or any number of other entities. Whatever form or combination of forms is chosen, there is always the question of whether the entities can legitimately speak for and represent the minority. In this respect, internal democracy is important to prevent the minority organizations from monopolizing minority issues and thus violating the individual rights of the minority members who may wish to exercise their rights of individual self-determination not only against the state and the majority institutions but also against the institutions of the minority.

The rights conferred to minority institutions—both private and public—typically centre on cultural issues. The establishment, maintenance and administration of minority schools (perhaps even including the drafting of teaching plans) are a typical example; the same is true for infant schools, theatres, publishing houses, broadcasting services or language education. These institutions the operation of which normally go beyond the means of an individual minority member or a small private organization; they require a solid financial and organizational background. However, culture is not necessarily the only field of collective rights. A minority institution may, to give one example, be charged with policing minority institutions or events, the way the organizers of large sports or cultural events police football stadiums or concert halls.

4.3 Autonomy

Collective rights may encompass a wide range of issues important for minority life. If collective rights amount to some form of essential self-determination (political, cultural or other) they become an autonomy. A minority autonomy is vested with the jurisdiction over a substantial number of minority issues and exercises this jurisdiction in its own responsibility. Thus, it is the maximum legal position minorities may achieve in a state. Since autonomies are discussed in detail below, it suffices here to say that they may be based on persons or on territory.

4.4 Affirmative Action

When talking about minority rights, the term 'affirmative action' is nowadays mentioned more and more often. This, however, does not denote a special class of rights such as the ones discussed above, but rather describes an attitude a state may take towards its minorities. Affirmative action means that the state does not only tolerate and accept the minority, but actively feels responsible for it and its well-being. Sometimes this attitude is enshrined in a country's constitution by pronouncing it as an objective principle without conferring subjective rights as such. Examples of this can be found in Article 6 of the Italian Constitution of 27 December 1947 and in Article 68(2)1 of the Hungarian Constitution, as established by the amendment Act XL of 1990 dated 25 June 1990. On the international level, the concept of affirmative action underlies many of the more recent legal instruments, such as the European Charter for Regional or Minority Languages of 5 November 1992, the Framework Convention for the Protection of National Minorities of 1 February 1997 or the United Nations Declaration 47/135 on the Rights of Persons Belonging to National or Ethnic, Religious, and Linguistic Minorities of 18 December 1992.

This responsibility, be it mandated by the constitution or not, may be legally codified. This takes place when the granting of special rights to minority members allots them more rights in fact than majority members legally have. The exemption of minority parties from suffrage thresholds in the electoral system is just a form of active care of the state as is the reservation of certain quotas for minority members in the public service. Most forms of affirmative action, however, take place outside the legal sphere, especially in the distribution of public funds for minority issues or in efforts to teach the spirit of tolerance and acceptance in state schools.

4.5 Duties

The picture would be incomplete without a word about the duties of minorities and their members. Naturally, under the principles of equality and territorial state sovereignty, members of the minority are subject to the same duty of obeying the law of the land as any other citizen or resident of the state. The question of whether the peculiarities of a given minority may exempt its members from obeying a certain legal duty is more prone to arise in the case of religious minorities (e.g. in the question of compulsory military service); but it is also conceivable in the case of national or ethnic minorities as well. In such a situation it would be advisable to find a legal regulation which takes into account the special situation and needs of the minority; such a regulation may compensate for the exemption from one duty with the imposition of an alternative duty which is acceptable to the minority, e.g. community service instead of military service.

Sometimes it is argued that minority members have a general duty to be loyal to their state. It is hardly conceivable, however, what elements such a duty to loyalty encompasses that are not already contained in the duty to obey the laws of the land, including the constitution.[13] A certain aspect of this duty to loyalty can be seen in the obligation to prevent too strong an influence of a kin-state on the decisions of a minority's autonomy, at least as long as this autonomy exercises public powers: in this case, the influence of the kin-state would amount to an interference within the internal affairs of the minority's resident state.

Special duties, such as the duty to learn the state language laid down in the Bulgarian Constitution, certainly make sense on a practical scale (and are, for this reason, contained in the school laws of many countries with a view to minority education), but it is questionable for symbolic reasons whether they ought to be pronounced by the constitution as a special duty for minority members.

5.   AUTONOMY AS A SOLUTION TO MINORITY PROBLEMS

As previously noted, autonomy is the highest form of minority rights in the 'hierarchy' outlined above, and its constituent element is a certain degree of self-determination. Autonomy may relate to a given territory (territorial autonomy) or to the members of the minority (personal autonomy).

Below, we will analyze both territorial autonomy and personal autonomy. This will be followed by a comparison of two forms of minority rights.

5.1 Territorial Autonomy

In territorial autonomy, a certain territory inhabited by the minority is defined and vested with a special status. This special status is designed to serve the interests of the minority. Since territorial governance in modern Europe cannot be but that of a majoritarian democracy, territorial autonomy only makes sense if the given minority forms the majority in the territory in question. If this precondition is not met, the minority remains a minority in the territory as well and cannot profit from the democratic institutions created therein.

5.1.1 The Subject of Autonomy Rights

In territorial autonomy, the subject of autonomous rights is a public body governing a given part of a country's territory. The delimitation and the definition of that territorial unit may fit into the overall administrative structure of that country, i.e. it can be one or several local authorities (such as the Gagauz territorial autonomy in Moldova, the autonomous districts designed for the Serbs in Croatia and the autonomous communities of the Italians and Hungarians in Slovenia); it can be a province (such as Frisia in the Netherlands or the Val d'Aosta and South Tyrol in Italy), or it can be a state in a federal system (such as the non-Russian republics in the Russian Federation). A local authority, province or federal unit can only be considered a minority's territorial autonomy if it has substantially more (or special) rights than a parallel local authority, province or federal unit inhabited by the majority population. One such special feature may be that in the autonomous city, province or state, the language of the minority becomes the official or co-official one along with the majority's state language.

This does not mean that a minority cannot make use of the rights and competencies any other local authority, province or federal unit may have in a given system, without an extra element of autonomy. If the minority is the majority in that territorial unit, it can profit from the powers this level of administration has in the state system through the normal mechanisms of majoritarian democracy. However, there is not much sense in referring to such an entity as territorial autonomy; since its powers are not specific, there is no surplus of rights for the minority which could justify the use of the attribute 'autonomous'.

It is also possible to create for the minority territorial entity distinct from the rest of the country. Classical examples of this were the autonomous provinces of Vojvodina and Kosovo within the Serbian Republic in socialist Yugoslavia and the higher forms of territorial autonomy in the Soviet system (the lower forms belonging to the model described first: regular administrative units are given extra powers in order to serve the purposes of the minority).[14] These examples follow the Leninist and Stalinist concept of minority policy which exclusively concentrated on territorial rights.

More modern examples of special entities outside the general administrative structure of the state are the Åland Islands (Finland), the Færøer Islands (Denmark), Corsica (France), Crimea (Ukraine) and to a certain extent, the state of Jersey, the Isle of Man, Scotland and Wales (United Kingdom).

All these are political entities which do not fit into the general administrative pattern of the state's administration, but form units of their own under a special legal regime. One could also mention the territory of Athos (Greece); yet, this is a very special case which does not necessarily allow lessons to be drawn from it but may illustrate what can be achieved if a certain degree of political will exists. These examples show that often a special form of territorial autonomy is particularly practical in the case of islands and peninsulas due to their geographical delimitation.

5.1.2 Representativeness, Legitimacy and the Relationship between the Autonomous Body and the Individual

Participation in autonomy rights is granted by virtue of residence in a specific territory. As with any territorial unit with certain rights to self-government, the minority's territorial unit will need to have a representative organ (a 'parliament') capable of making important decisions and controlling the executive. This parliament will have to be elected by all residents of the respective territory with the right to vote under the general rules. The minority can avail of territorial autonomy if they form the local majority in the territory in question. By making use of the general mechanisms of majoritarian democracy, the minority can realize its interests in the autonomous territory through its organs.

Any territorial unit, even if it is a territorial autonomy for the benefit of a given minority, should serve the interests of all its inhabitants. In a minority territory, minority schools have to be maintained; theatre performances in the minority language have to be financed; all children will have to be provided with schooling; streets and other public works will have to be built and maintained; building permits will have to be issued (irrespective of the ethnic background of the applicant); and the use of chemicals in agriculture will have to be controlled. These are just a few examples of regular territorial administration. The autonomous territorial unit exists for all its residents, and it is open to participation for all its residents who do not fall under some general category of disqualification. It draws its legitimacy—just as any local autonomy or federal unit does—from the local community as a whole, not just from the minority community.

As its name would suggest, the delimitation of territorial autonomy takes place in terms of territory and not in terms of people. Therefore the question of who belongs to the minority does not arise, either for the autonomy's authorities or for the individuals concerned. If a special minority or special minorities are to be granted territorial autonomy,[15] the territory will have to be defined in a way that guarantees the minority's majority and, ideally, that comprises as many minority members as possible.

It is impossible, however, to draw the boundaries of the autonomous territory in such a way that it encompasses all members of the minority and no members of the majority. Such a clear-cut delimitation can only be achieved by expulsion or at best peaceful exchange of members of that state and can only be maintained by infringing on the human right of free choice of residence within a state's territory (CPHR Article 2 of Protocol No. 4). For this reason, territorial autonomy will always have residents belonging to the majority population or to third ethnic groups, and there will always be members of the minority residing outside the autonomous territory. Since a territorial unit is the legitimate representation of the local community of residents, a territorial autonomy cannot legitimately administer the minority members who live outside its territory, and, on the other hand, it has to deal with the majority members and eventually members of third ethnic groups residing within its territory. The latter ones might have to be granted minority rights on a non-territorial basis (i.e. individual or collective rights or a personal autonomy) in the autonomous territory.

Assuming the autonomous territorial unit is the legitimate representation of its inhabitants, which should consist mostly of minority members, also makes this unit a form of political representation of the minority on a national level. The constituency system for the national parliament could therefore be shaped in such a way that the MPs elected in the autonomous territory are representatives not only of the territory but also of the minority (if indeed they belong to it). If the state has a second chamber with representation of territorial or local units, the minority may be represented here through its territorial autonomy. On a general level, the territorial autonomy, which will be experienced as a political institution of the minority (even if a certain proportion of its inhabitants belong to the majority or to third groups), can be accepted as the representation of the issues of that minority as a whole. Hence the Spanish autonomous region of País Vasco/Euskadi is generally accepted as the mouthpiece of the entire Basque minority in Spain irrespective of their place of residence although it is, in a stricter sense, only representative of the persons residing in its territory, regardless of their ethnic background.[16]

If the demographic situation is such that it is difficult or impossible to define a contiguous territory or if the political situation is such that the creation of a well-defined territorial autonomy appears unacceptable to the majority, it is also possible to assemble the local and, in certain cases, regional authorities relevant to the minority in a specialized organization. Membership in such an organization need not be limited to the local (regional) authorities where the minority forms the majority; it may also be open to the local authorities where the minority has a certain demographic centre even without forming the local majority. This organization may be granted certain powers relevant to the minority (e.g. with regard to schools). Examples of organizations with (compulsory or voluntary) communal membership established to serve certain purposes that are beyond local in nature are the German *Zweckverbände* and the Hungarian *önkormányzati társulások*. In the Netherlands, the *rijkswaterstaat* is an example of an elaborate hierarchical system of this type of specialized organization designed, in membership and scope, according to the special needs of each individual situation.[17] In its classical form, such communal organization is governed by a board representing the members, both the local and regional authorities. This organizational form can represent the minority only if the local and regional authorities are governed by a majority of minority representatives. If this condition is not met, i.e. if the minority does not have the local or regional political majority, its representation in the organization could be guaranteed in a different manner. For instance, the local and regional authorities could delegate minority councillors (if these exist) as their representatives to the organization's board. Instead, or in addition, representatives of minority organizations or associations may be granted a seat on the board or even membership in the organization, thus mixing forms of personal and territorial autonomy and transcending the classical form of an institution exclusively composed of, and governed by, units of territorial admin-istration. However, purity of principle or form ought not to be a reason for refusing solutions to special situations if they are operable.

A special form of territorial autonomy can be chosen for multiethnic regions. If one region of a state—which in general consists of more or less monoethnic areas—does not have a local majority of a given minority, but shows a patchwork of ethnic groups, then this region can be endowed with a special multiethnic regime to manage its territorial autonomy. This arrangement would be the legitimate representation of all groups involved, including the majority members who reside there. In socialist Yugoslavia, the autonomous province of Vojvodina exemplified a multiethnic regime functioning even though the state's majority formed the local majority as well.[18] Today the bilingual status of Brussels is such an exception, for elsewhere in Belgium there is a strict separation of languages.

5.1.3   The Scope of Rights

Territorial autonomy is an integral part of the administrative apparatus governing the territory of a given state. It would be sensible to endow territorial autonomy with all the competencies and powers parallel units enjoy in other regions of the state. There is not much sense in granting autonomous regions powers only in relation to minority issues, as that would mean that the general functions of territorial administration would have to be taken over by special state agencies which do not have any function in other areas of the state. The result would be less, instead of more, autonomy and a closer attachment to the central government in all matters other than minority related issues.

Apart from the general functions of territorial administration, of such a territorial unit, the minority's territorial autonomy will need to have all the powers necessary to ensure its cultural survival. For this reason, a territorial autonomy would need to oversee: schooling (including the right to determine lesson plans, at least for minority schools); cultural affairs; and, where required, the relationship between public and religious authorities. The power to regulate and promote small enterprises, traditional industries and agriculture can help to preserve and modernize the minority's economic standing and can enable the autonomy to promote economic wealth in its territory in accordance with the needs of the minority. The organs of a self-government will be much more sensitive to the problems of promoting larger economic projects. This can result in changes in the demographic situation due to the likely movement of labourers, especially among the majority population. A self-government would be more conscious of its effects on the local demographic situation and its impact on the minority's chance to survive than a regular state organ.

A territorial autonomy may also be empowered to control immigration not only from foreign countries, but also from other areas of the state. This arrangement exists on the Åland Islands or in the state of Jersey.[19] This power enables the territorial autonomy to maintain the minority's local majority situation, but also means a restriction on the constitutional right to freely choose one's residence.[20] For this reason, a territorial autonomy should be empowered with such rights by the state's constitution and not by norms of a lower level. However, intra-state migration control may prove to be a sensitive issue, and this power should be granted only if political acceptance among the majority can be achieved. Immigration control is probably not as important as competencies in schooling, cultural affairs and general territorial administration; thus a lack of acceptance in that area should not be allowed to jeopardize the realization of overall minority autonomy.

All powers granted to an autonomy must be accompanied by a corresponding financial regime to provide the autonomous body with the necessary means to implement economic policy. This can be achieved through the right to levy taxes, although this carries the risk of causing economic distortions if the tax system or interest rates vary considerably from the rest of the state. A constitutional guarantee of an appropriate allocation of the central state's financial resources to the autonomy might therefore be a better solution which, however, causes additional dangers by linking the region's budget more closely with that of the central government's.

The autonomy's territorial governance can be limited to some administrative functions in the fields that are relevant to the minority (with the rest of public functions being exercised by state organs). But it can also be as far-reaching as to encompass all of a state's functions, like federal units in a federal system. This means that a territorial autonomy can be endowed with functions from all three state powers: legislation, government and administration, and court jurisdiction. In a federal system, autonomous powers can include policing and perhaps even military jurisdiction. Soldiers from an autonomous territory can form separate units within the armed forces of the state, as was the case with regiments from some *Länder* in the German armed forces between 1871 and 1914.

Territorial autonomy is not a solution to all minority problems. It cannot regulate the protection and local representation of minority interests elsewhere, such as the use of minority languages outside its territory. For these problems, individual and/or collective rights, or personal autonomy may offer an adequate remedy.

5.1.4   Conflict Settlement

Minority situations are often associated with conflict. Therefore, one important role of minority rights is conflict settlement. With a view to minority autonomy, two types of conflict can be distinguished: first, disputes between the minority and the state; and second, conflicts between the citizen and the autonomy's organs or agencies. In principle, conflicts may be settled legally (by courts of law), politically (by direct negotiations) or by mediation (by, for example, an ombudsperson).

Since the territorial autonomy is a public body of territorial governance, conflicts between the autonomy and the state can be settled judicially in the same manner that conflicts are settled between any other official bodies, i.e. between local authorities and the state. In questions of detail, the administrative courts can help. If no such courts exist, ordinary courts may offer protection for the autonomy's rights if they are given the power to do so. If the right of autonomy as such is violated and if this right is enshrined in the constitution, legal remedy may be sought before the constitutional court, if one exists. Many Western European and practically all Eastern European countries have a constitutional court, and most of them are competent to protect the right of local authorities to self-government. This procedure will sometimes closely resemble the protection of individual human rights.[21] A legal protection for the rights of a territorial autonomy can be shaped according to these existing and functioning models. For an effective judicial protection of minority rights, these rights have to be formulated as subjective rights of the autonomous body—and not only as objective principles—and they need to be formulated in a sufficiently precise way.

As far as political conflict settlement is concerned, the most important aspects, as outlined above, deal with questions of representation. In the case of a conflict between the minority and the state, the territorial autonomy can represent the minority's interests in negotiations with the central government in a comprehensive way. Agreements reached in such negotiations may be codified by a subsequent law, but they can also be implemented by a treaty between the autonomy and the state. Contractual agreements between central government agencies and lower territorial units are quite common in modern Europe, especially if the territorial unit has some form of autonomy. An extreme example is the 'negotiated federalism' in Spain and Russia. More commonly, in many countries local authorities and central state agencies conclude contracts and treaties to resolve matters of dispute.

When a conflict arises between a territorial autonomy and the state, it may be helpful to involve a neutral institution, such as an ombudsperson. In this case, both procedure and solution may follow more formal rules than in direct negotiations, but they are less binding than a court decision. In some countries, special committees exist within the public administration to mediate disputes between local authorities and the state. If any of these non-binding mechanisms of conflict settlement fail, it may be sensible to seek judicial settlement. That said, it is advisable to make some form of mediation compulsory before involving the courts. However, these are general questions of judicial protection in administrative matters and not limited to minority autonomies.

Not only the minority and its territorial autonomy may need protection against the state. Individual citizens could, on occasion, need protection against the territorial autonomy. After all, it exercises public power, and public power needs to be controlled if it violates individual rights. This control is normally exercised by administrative courts, although sometimes by ordinary courts as well. If the rights violated are constitutionally protected, additional protection can be provided by a constitutional court. There is, of course, a certain danger that the state may interfere through the courts in the free exercise of autonomous rights; but this problem also exists, and is regulated, in connection with local authorities enjoying some form of autonomy. As long as control is limited to legal control (as opposed to political control), it will not harm the autonomy which is a public body and as such bound to observe the law and the individual rights of persons resident in the autonomous territory. Thus, a purely legal control will not result in a reduction of competences.

The ombudsperson may offer additional protection of citizens' rights against abuse by the territorial autonomy. Here again, the solution is not binding, and it does not follow legal norms but common sense and a spirit of compromise. In many cases of conflict between individuals and public authorities, these latter strategies may be of greater help to the individual than a formal court decision. The ombudsperson may also be given the right to assist an individual in court proceedings if mediation fails.

Direct negotiation between a citizen and the territorial autonomy may, in rare cases only, be a suitable instrument to settle conflicts. This is because the autonomy exercises public authority and is thus in a superior position. This is true for the exercise of all public authority, and is not a special feature of minority territorial autonomy. In many West European countries, however, there is a tendency for negotiations between the public authority on the one hand, and the individual concerned on the other, to replace unilateral authoritative action by the authority in order to harmonize interests from the very beginning and thus avoid the emergence of hostilities. A territorial autonomy can, of course, make use of these techniques the same way any other public authority can.

5.2 Personal Autonomy

Personal autonomy does not relate to territory, but to all members of the minority. Thus, the crucial factor is not residence in an autonomous territory but membership of the minority. This membership, however, is difficult to define. Another problem is that personal-based autonomy seems to be an alien element in a world where governance is normally based on territory. However, churches are one example that personal based authority is still able to function today. Thus, personal autonomy can be defined as a form of self-government granted to a group, with organs or organizational structures that exercise the various rights and powers of the autonomy.

5.2.1   The Subject of Autonomy Rights

Since personal autonomy relates to the individuals belonging to a minority, the subject of autonomy needs to be an institution that comprises and thus organizes its members into a legally sizeable forum. The classical example of a non-territorial legal entity that consists of individuals and represents their interests is the association, which may exist in private law (e.g. a philatelist's club or a trade union) or in public law (e.g. a chamber of commerce or religious establishment).

Unlike in the case of territorial autonomy, the subject of personal autonomy does not necessarily have to be a public body. The autonomous rights of personal autonomy can also be vested in an organization of private law. Since many legal systems in Western Europe allow public authority to be transferred to private individuals or institutions under specified conditions (such as the *beliehene Unternehmer* in Germany, the *mandaat* in the Netherlands or the *organ employant prérogatives de puissance publique* in France), personal autonomy created and operated under private law can be endowed with public functions. Thus, a minority parents' association may operate a minority school which is granted the right to graduate its pupils the same way as schools run by the state or by the local authorities can.

The subject of personal autonomy need not be restricted to one single organization or association only. It is possible to give autonomous powers in different fields to different specialized associations, organizations and institutions, just as the powers of territorial autonomy can be conferred to various authorities that may be independent of each other. There can be, for example, a different association for each minority school, comprising the parents or a group that maintains a minority theatre or runs a publishing house for books in the minority language. If, however, autonomy rights are granted to various specialized associations, it is important to create an umbrella organization with the double function of internal coordination of the minority's affairs and of outward representation so that the minority speaks with 'one voice' in spite of the decentralized nature of the personal autonomy's powers. An autonomy has by definition a certain degree of self-governing power, and it is hard to conceive of how a minority can be represented and its affairs be administered by various competing autonomies. For this reason, autonomy should have a monopoly which is vested either in a centralized structure or in an umbrella organization as discussed. Since the main problems and advantages of an umbrella organization lie in the fields of representativeness, legitimacy and inner democracy, these questions will now be discussed in detail.

5.2.2   Representativeness, Legitimacy and the Relationship
between the Autonomous Body and the Individual

Personal autonomy is organized in the form of an association (or a variety of associations). Membership in an autonomous association can be restricted to members of the minority. Ideally, all members of the minority should be members of the personal autonomy. As this membership is independent from the place of residence, problems of territorial delimitation do not arise. However, the question of delimitation of the autonomy's scope arises in two other respects. First, there has to be a way to establish who belongs to the respective minority and who does not. Second, those judged as belonging to the minority have to become members of the association(s) that is/are the bearer of the personal autonomy.

The first question of whether an individual belongs to a given minority must not be confused with the definition of a minority. It may well be clear that the Armenians form a minority in Hungary or the Basques in France and Spain. The next step is to define who among the citizens of the Hungarian or French Republic or the Kingdom of Spain belongs to the Armenian or Basque minority. Since personal autonomy defines its scope by the fact that a given individual belongs to a certain minority, it is important to know who the individuals are that form the minority.

One solution to this problem would be the registration of every citizen within an ethnic group. This can be done, for example, at birth, or when the person comes of age and is included on the lists of voters. Such compulsory ethnic registration was operated in the Soviet Union with little success in relation to the congruence of registered and 'true' identity. A more flexible version of this registration system would to have a procedure to alter the group registration if an individual changes his or her ethnic identity by assimilation or dissimilation. In the case of double identity (which may occur with the children of mixed marriages or with the members of highly integrated small minorities as in Hungary) there would have to be the possibility of double registration. This represents a flaw in the seemingly so unequivocal character of the system. It is also doubtful whether the mandatory ethnic self-definition of every individual is not too strong an infringement on human rights such as the right to privacy (CPHR Art. 8) and, more specifically, to freely declare or not to declare one's ethnic belonging (Art. 3 [1] European Framework Convention for the Protection of National Minorities).

Similarly, in a national census questions directed at ethnic belongings, language, etc. would often unearth ethnic identity. Being that a census cannot be anonymous, this would again raise question of human rights infringement.

The problems mentioned above can be avoided through the establishment of a list that everybody who considers themselves to be a member of the minority may register and by virtue of this act may be included under personal autonomy status.[22] It is conceivable to impose the duty to register as such by law (disregarding the human rights problems such a measure would involve), but it is hard to see how such a duty could be controlled efficiently. For this reason, registration would have to be voluntary. This causes, however, two problems. First, personal autonomy which relates only to those who have registered does not reach the less conscious, less aware and less active members of the minority. In order to keep the minority identity alive, though, it is important to include such persons because they will generally constitute the bulk of the minority. However, once minority autonomy is established and has developed attractive activities, it may enhance awareness and the desire to participate.

The second problem is even more difficult to solve. There needs to be a specific mechanism to ensure that the individuals joining the minority list really belong to the minority; that the minority autonomy is not 'infiltrated' by members of the majority who want to take advantage of funds or privileges reserved for the minority; and that those involved do not want to sabotage or discredit minority autonomy or simply make themselves 'interesting' by purporting to belong to a minority.[23] There is no single factor that unequivocally differentiates between members of a minority and those of the majority. Where language is important, the mother tongue can serve as a guideline. Yet there are minority situations (e.g. in Hungary) where linguistic assimilation is more or less complete but a special minority awareness continues to exist. Another factor can be religion; for instance, the Armenian church for the Armenian minorities and the various orthodox national churches for minorities originating from orthodox countries. However, minority members who have converted to a different religion or have given up all religious ties but still feel that they belong to that specific minority again pose a problem. There needs to be some protection against abuse by a control mechanism on the basis of outward—one could also say objective—criteria to be certain whether an applicant for inscription on the list belongs to the minority in question.[24]

Once the members of a given minority have been identified, the problem arises whether membership in a personal autonomy can be imposed on the basis that one has confessed to belonging to a minority. If the subject of the autonomy is a legal entity under public law, compulsory membership appears possible (as it is in the case of compulsory membership in autonomous professional chambers); but the case is different if the association is under private law. If, for example, the autonomous association runs a school, it is conceivable to demand that the users, i.e. the pupils and their parents, become members of the autonomous association; but this solution is inoperable for institutions with only occasional users such as theatres or libraries or with no users at all such as a publishing house for minority literature.

Only if a personal autonomy is derived solely by professional specialists who run the minority institutions and who can offer the services of these institutions to everybody who wishes to avail of them (e.g. a minority teachers' board responsible for the minority schools), does the question of membership become irrelevant. But even in such a model, professional specialists would only have the power to administrate these institutions; within the framework of a democracy it is hard to conceive of these specialists as having the legitimacy to regulate the basics of these institutions, such as the modes of access to a minority school. These regulations would have to be enacted by a legitimate representative body or some form of direct democracy such as a referendum. This representative or directly democratic forum could be taken from the general state structure (in which case the minority would not be autonomous anymore because that would involve majority participation in the regulation of minority institutions), or they could be formed by the members of the minority only, in which case it becomes important again to create structures which draw their legitimacy from their membership, which gives rise to the all the questions connected with membership.

In practice, the result will nearly always be that the more active, more aware members of a minority will be the ones to register voluntarily or to formally join some association that is the subject of personal autonomy. This poses certain problems for the representativeness of their organizational structure because it will speak for the entire minority. However, those who did not join the association can hardly complain if the more active 'happy few' speak in their name, being that they had the option to participate in the association. (This argument is similar to the discussion about referenda and their representativeness.) As long as the structures are open to every member of the minority and if there is inner democracy in the autonomous organization(s), then the inactive portion of the minority can be deemed to be represented by the personal autonomy.

The question of the freedom of individuals to leave the autonomous organization can only be answered in the context of the form of membership. If membership is mandatory, then the individual cannot easily be given a right to repudiate involvement. If membership is a consequence of the inscription into an ethnic list, then there will have to be a procedure to annul that inscription. In an organization with voluntary membership there will have to be rules regarding leaving the organization: if nobody can be forced to join then nobody can be forced to stay.

As mentioned before, decentralized structures of personal autonomy call for an umbrella organization for all other minority organizations, associations and institutions. Any organization, or institution—be it private or public—purporting to be a minority organization or institution may be given the right to apply for membership in the umbrella organization. Alternatively, it may acquire membership therein by virtue of law, provided that it meets certain conditions such as that no organization or institution can name itself a minority organization under false pretences (e.g. in order to obtain funding reserved for minority purposes). Membership in the umbrella organization is reserved for the organizations or insitutions respectively (as opposed to membership of individuals), and their representatives form the 'parliament' of the umbrella organization. If the members, i.e. the organizations and institutions, are organized in a democratic way, then the umbrella organization has a democratic legitimation as well, though 'only' in an indirect way. A more practical problem, connected with legitimacy, is the question of how to weigh the votes of the various member organizations and institutions in the 'parliament'. The number of members an organization has or the proportion of its financial contribution to the umbrella organization's budget may be regarded as sufficiently objective criteria.

Since the umbrella organization ideally encompasses all organizations associated with the minority, it has true legitimacy in representing the minority. Indeed, if the various organizations are corporate members of the umbrella organization and if the latter follow a democratic pattern of governance, the structure is open to new grass-roots activities, which enhances its democratic legitimacy.

Since the personal autonomy speaks for the entire minority (and ideally has a corresponding membership) it represents the minority as a whole in the political process. However, the minority as a whole is not a homogeneous body, but a society of individuals with diverging interests. The autonomy, having a monopoly in representing the minority as a whole, needs to express this diversity of interests in some way. Inner democracy is one, though it is not a sufficient way to meet this need. There have to be safeguards within the political structure of personal autonomy so that the interests of the political minorities within the autonomy can be expressed and, as far as it is practical, be taken into account.

One problem of personal autonomy is parliamentary representation at the national level. As discussed, a territorial autonomy can speak also for the minority as such through the MPs elected in that territory and/or by its own representation in a second chamber. Personal autonomy, not being based on the general territorial organization of the state, does not have these channels of access to parliamentary membership. Therefore, if the minority is to be represented in the national parliament, other ways have to be found. The problem is easily solved if the minority is strong and homogeneous enough to vote their own MPs into parliament under the general election rules, perhaps with exemption from minimum percentage requirements in systems of proportional representation. If, however, the minority is too small or too fragmented, there may be a guaranteed seat in parliament for a representative of the personal autonomy, or several minorities may share a reserved seat, as in the Croatian Parliament, where there are between five and seven seats for more than ten small minorities.[25] Special minority MPs elected on the basis of minority privileges may be endowed with the right to speak and, perhaps, with the right to vote. MPs who are allowed to speak but not allowed to vote are an anomaly but not inconceivable.[26]

5.2.3   The Scope of Rights

Similar to territorial autonomy, personal autonomy is established with the aim to serve and promote the interests of the minority. For this reason, the autonomy needs to be given powers in important areas, especially culture and education.

Personal autonomy will normally operate institutions such as schools, cultural and social institutions, and affiliated associations. Its governance is therefore related to institutions and people, not to territory. For this reason, the powers of a personal autonomy will concentrate on administrative questions, whereas it is harder to conceive of powers of legislation beyond the internal regulations of the institutions, or of court jurisdiction, being granted to a personal autonomy. However, this is not entirely impossible. The ecclesiastical courts are an example of a jurisdiction based on personal membership instead of territory. And the autonomous subordinate legislation of universities and of chambers of certain professions and industries are other examples of non-territorial legislation. A personal autonomy can also be authorized to police its buildings, events and institutions. There is no reason why personal autonomy should not be as sovereign as territorial autonomy, even if it appears unusual in the context of the territory-based sovereignty of the state.

A personal autonomy can be granted rights in the social sphere as well. The Russian Indigenous Peoples Act[27] concentrates on special measures of a social nature which are to be dealt with by personal autonomies designed to cope with the peculiarities of nomadic or semi-nomadic societies. The most crucial question for indigenous peoples, i.e. land rights and land use as well as the preservation of the natural environment and the fight against pollution, cannot be addressed by a personal autonomy, even if it contains certain territorial elements, as the Russian legislation does. However, the structures for indigenous personal autonomies try to reflect the special needs of an indigenous population, and the same is true for the rights granted to these autonomies.

It would probably not be practical to allow a personal autonomy to tax minority members. This additional financial burden would make membership in the autonomy and thus in the minority quite unpopular and would deter members of the minority from seeking membership. As a consequence, a personal autonomy would have to rely on state grants and thus depend strongly on the national parliament's budgetary decisions. A constitutional guarantee (as in the case of judges' salaries in connection with judicial independence) could reduce the autonomy's dependence on the government of the day and their political priorities.

5.2.4   Conflict Settlement

The problems of conflict settlement are in principle the same for an autonomy based on territory and an autonomy based on persons. In the relationship between the autonomy and the state, all the mechanisms outlined above apply here as well: the autonomous body may seek protection of its rights before ordinary, administrative or constitutional courts. It may also negotiate directly with state organs to solve existent or prevent future disputes. Ombudspersons or other mediation committees can also help to solve conflicts.

A personal autonomy can be given the right to assist individual members of the minority before a court in the defence of his or her minority rights against state organs and, eventually, against private parties such as an employer. The autonomy may even be granted the right of representative action in procedures where an individual's minority rights are at stake. There are models for this in various European countries, e.g. in the field of consumer protection where the appropriate organizations are given the right to sue to protect individual consumer rights. For individuals who want to assert their rights, such assistance may be of considerable help.

Conflicts between the personal autonomy and individual members of the minority can be settled in the same way as conflicts between a territorial autonomy and an individual citizen.

Judicial protection against the personal autonomy can be granted irrespective of the nature of the autonomy in public or private law and irrespective of the public or private nature of the powers in question. These differences may at best have an influence on which court to address (administrative or ordinary). Conflicts between a personal autonomy and an individual are of course open to mediation—by ombudspersons, for example—and contracts between private individuals and the organs of the autonomy are suitable instruments to coordinate interests and prevent or settle disputes.

6. ASPECTS OF CHOICE

Territorial and personal autonomy are merely abstract models for possible solutions in concrete situations. Some of their respective positive and negative aspects have been discussed. These, however, are not the only factors important in a situation when a decision has to be made regarding how to grant a given minority certain rights. It is quite difficult to discuss the advantages and disadvantages of different models and solutions in the abstract. The case studies in this book will explore the evolution of a number of minority autonomies and will assess how well each paradigm has functioned.

As said before, a territorial autonomy only makes sense if the minority forms the majority in a certain territory. If this condition is not met, personal autonomy is the better option. Other aspects are less unequivocal. Yet, the demographic factor is important beyond the local majority question in the context of territorial autonomy. If a minority lives in extreme dispersion this may cause serious problems—e.g. in communication—which would have to be taken into account in the search for solutions. However, modern forms of communication offer new possibilities and perspectives, especially to person-based organizations by making distance and place of residence more and more irrelevant for participation.

Another aspect is the maturity of political culture in both the majority and the minority communities. An autonomy structure that is too complicated and too integrated might easily fail in surroundings that are unfamiliar with the existence of interlocking spheres of public authority. In a patriarchal society, proposed solutions must not isolate the patriarchs; instead they must include them although, of course, the policy may strive to develop more democratic forms of societal organization and then gradually adapt to social progress the solutions found for the minorities. The Russian Indigenous Peoples Act is an example how clan-like structures of nomadic and semi-nomadic populations can be transformed into a personal autonomy.

The traditions of statehood and autonomy in the majority and minority populations are also an important factor. Territorial autonomy—perhaps within a federal system—may compensate a minority for the loss of the statehood it may have previously enjoyed. Scotland is an example of how modern autonomy may offer compensation for the loss of past independence, although here the ethnic factor is rather weak.[28] The closeness to statehood can also be a disadvantage of territorial autonomy because it may give rise to fears of secession among the majority, especially where the memory of former irredentism within the minority is still alive, as is the case with the Slovak majority and the Hungarian minority in the border areas of the Slovak Republic. Even in Romania, where the Hungarian minority lives far away from the Hungarian border, these fears exist and prevent a territorial autonomous solution. Yet the autonomy of South Tyrol was possible although similar fears existed in Italy.

If the majority is accustomed to a special status for certain territories it may not object as strongly to the idea of territorial autonomy as the majoritarian population in a traditionally unitarian state might do. This is especially true for the successor states of the Soviet Union, where Russia chose a sort of ethnically asymmetrical federalism to organize the state, where the Ukraine gave autonomy to Crimea and where the Republic of Moldova granted the Gagauz minority territorial autonomy as a solution to ethnic tensions.[29] Socialist Yugoslavia also had long traditions of territorial autonomies as a form of minority rights, but in Serbia these institutions were deliberately destroyed and would now, after a decade of anti-minority propaganda, be difficult to reestablish. In contrast, Slovenia and Croatia (the latter state on paper only) chose territory-based models as one form of minority (self-)governance after gaining independence so that in these countries the traditions serve as a basis for new solutions. Traditions of a special personal status for members of minority religions (Jews, Armenians, Muslims) can make the idea of personal autonomy for an ethnic minority appear more familiar in the eyes of both minority and majority.

Not only the traditions of statehood and autonomy are relevant, but also the traditions of cooperation or separateness of both groups in everyday life. If there is a deep psychological gap between majority and minority, solutions which require close cooperation run a high risk of failure. In Kosovo, to name the most poignant example, relations between Albanians, Gypsies and Serbs are so deeply disturbed that any form of cooperation and even coexistence is refused. Forms of personal autonomy may be more appropriate in a climate of mistrust because they are better designed to keep the governance of minority issues apart from those of the majority, thus avoiding the need to cooperate on a wider scale.

Resources, both public and private, available for minority purposes are an important factor which should not be forgotten. A solution that would cost more than a given country and society can reasonably afford, must be considered inappropriate under the given circumstances. However, one must keep in mind that often minority rights and forms of autonomy do not cost more—or much more—than the administration of the same areas by the majoritarian state: a teacher's salary remains the same whether they teach in the majority or in the minority language, and the minority children have to be taught in any case. The administration of state territory must be organized at any rate, and the administration of a given territory by a minority authority instead of a state authority does not entail much extra cost.[30] Thus, the question of the costs of minority rights is relevant in fewer situations than is generally assumed, but where it really makes a difference, the availability of resources does matter.

Although the various models of ethnic autonomy were presented here in their pure form, they cannot be implemented as such. There are many examples of mixed or differentiated models, like in Croatia, Hungary and Slovenia. The fact that they combine various principles may make them appear complicated at first, but in fact they are better adapted to the special needs of the specific situation than a methodically pure solution would be. From an abstract legal perspective, there are no reasons against combining various models to best meet local needs.

The decisive factors are the interests, desires and aims of both the majority and the minority. There is not much point in granting a minority more, or different, rights than they wish for themselves. It would also be difficult to implement a solution that is entirely unacceptable to both or either of the two sides. A compromise that serves both sides equitably (and especially the minority, which is in the more vulnerable position) is better than an arrangement that favours the minority in the short-run but contains the seeds of future contention and ultimate failure.

NOTES

1   For the situation in France cf. the chapter by Daftary in this book; Jörg Polakiewicz "Die rechtliche Stellung der Minderheiten in Frankreich", in *Das Minderheitenrecht europäischer Staaten*, 2 vols., Jochen Frowein, Rainer Hofmann, Stefan Oeter, eds. (Berlin: Springer, 1993–94), vol. 1, pp.126–131; Norbert Rouland, Stéphane Pierré-Caps, Jacques Poumarède, *Droit des minorités et des peuples autochtones* (Paris: PUF, 1996), pp.307–328.

2   The situation in Switzerland is described by Dagmar Richter in Frowein, Hofmann, Oeter, *op.cit.*, vol. 1, pp.308–320; Wolf Linder, *Schweizerische Demokratie* (Bern: Haupt, 1999), pp.36–47.

3   Francesco Capotorti, *Study on the Rights of Persons belonging to Ethnic, Religious and Linguistic Minorities*, UN Doc E/CN.4/Sub.2/384/Rev.1 (1979).

4   Jules Deschênes, *Proposal Concerning a Definition of the Term 'Minority'*, UN Doc E/CN.4/Sub.2/1985/31, par. 181 (1985).

5   Parliamentary Assembly of the Council of Europe: Text of the proposal for an additional protocol to the Convention for the Protection of Human Rights and Fundamental Freedoms, concerning persons belonging to national minorities, in: Recommendation 1201 on an additional protocol on the rights of national minorities to the European Convention on Human Rights, 1 February 1993.

6   Report of the President of the Parliament, György Szabad, to the House, of 18 June 1990, published in *Országgyűlési Napló* [Parliamentary Minutes], 18 June 1990, column 863. It should be noted, however, that a small fraction within the Jewish community supported the government's plans, but they did not find any backing among the majority of the Hungarian Jews.

7   § 1 (2) Act LXXVII of 1993 on the Rights of the National and Ethnic Minorities (Minorities Act), *Magyar Közlöny* (1993), p.5273. For details cf. Brunner in *Der Minderheitenschutz in Ungarn und in Rumänien*, eds. Georg Brunner, Günther Tontsch (Bonn: Kulturstiftung der deutschen Vertriebenen, 1995), pp.32–33; Georg Nolte in Frowein, Hofmann, Oeter, *op.cit.*, vol. 1, pp.510–512; Herbert Küpper, *Das neue Minderheitenrecht in Ungarn* (München: Odenbourg, 1998), pp.89–101.

8   § 1 Act on the Cultural Autonomy of the National Minorities of 26 October 1993 (Cultural Autonomy Act), Riigi Teataja I (1993) no. 71, Art. 1001. For details cf. Henn-Jüri Uibopuu in Frowein, Hofmann, Oeter, *op. cit.*, vol. 2, pp.45–46; Boris Meissner, "Die Kulturautonomie in Estland. Ein Modell?" in *Kontinuität und Neubeginn. Festschrift für Georg Brunner aus Anlaß seines 65. Geburtstags*, Mahulena Hofmann, Herbert Küpper, eds. (Baden-Baden: Nomos Verlagsgesellschaft, 2001), pp.484–491; Carmen Schmidt, *Der Minderheitenschutz in den baltischen Staaten* (Bonn: Kulturstiftung der deutschen Vertriebenen, 1993), pp.17–19.

9   Such a combination can be found in Austria as well: The more general framework, the Federal Act on Ethnic Groups (Volksgruppengesetz) of 7 July 1976, Bundesgesetzblatt no. 396/1976, contains an abstract definition—which, due to a conceptual weakness, is apt to cause some problems—whereas the more concrete (e.g. school) legislation of the federation and the federal units, the *Bundesländer*, normally names the minorities. It refers to, e.g. the Federal Minority Official Language Act for Carinthia of 1959, Bundesgesetzblatt no. 102/1959 (in favour of the Slovene minority), the Federal Minority Schooling Act for Carinthia of 1959, Bundesgesetzblatt no. 101/1959 (in favour of the Slovene minority) or the Burgenland Infant School Act since its reform by an amendment act of 16 October 1989, Landesgesetzblatt Burgenland no. 12/1990 (in favour of the Croatian and the Hungarian minorities). The legal situation of minorities in Austria is discussed by Thilo Marauhn in Frowein, Hofmann, Oeter, *op.cit.*, vol. 1, pp.225–257; Rainer Hofmann, *Minderheitenschutz in Europa* (Berlin: Gebrüder Mann, 1995), pp.115–119.

10   The question of a minority-centred approach to equality is discussed in detail with view to the Dutch Equal Treatment Act (Algemene wet gelijke behandeling) of 1994, Staatsblad 1994/334, in *Gelijk behandelen*, A. W. Heringa, A. K. Koekkoek, Louise Mulder (Zwolle: W.E.J. Tjeenk Willink, 1991).

11   The leading case is the decision of the European Court of Human Rights of 23 July 1968, officially published in Série A, vol. 6, 1; it was upheld in the so-called Fouron case by the report of the commission of 30 March 1971 (*Europäische Grundrechte-Zeitschrift* [*EuGRZ*]1975/443) and the decision of the committee of ministers of 30 April 1974 (*EuGRZ* 1975/423). On the situation in Belgium cf. Hervé Bribosia, Jean-Louis van Boxstael, *Le partage des compétences dans la Belgique fédérale* (Namur: Faculté de Droit, 1993), pp.99–113; Christian Hillgruber, Matthias Jestaedt, *Die Europäische*

Menschen-rechtskonvention und der Schutz nationaler Minderheiten (Bonn: Kulturstiftung der deutschen Vertriebenen, 1993), pp.24–33.

[12] If such a right is granted only under the condition that the individual does not understand the language of the authority or the court, it is not a minority right proper, but a typical right for aliens.

[13] The question of loyalty is discussed in detail by Otto Luchterhandt, *Nationale Minderheiten und Loyalität* (Köln: Verlag Wissenschaft und Politik, 1997).

[14] An example of the higher form was the Autonomous Socialist Soviet Republic, an administrative unit created for minority purposes only; it did not exist in the regions inhabited by the majoritarian population. On the lower level, one could mention national villages or national districts: villages and districts were administrative units throughout the country, but in units inhabited by a minority they were declared 'national' in favour of the minority in question.

[15] It is not impossible to shape an autonomous territory in such a way that it accommodates not only one minority, but two or more neighbouring minorities. Within the Republic of Italy, the autonomy of South Tyrol serves the interests of both the German and the Ladin minorities, as the chapter by Rainer in this book explains in detail. In the German *Land* of Schleswig-Holstein, the Danish and the Frisian minority are represented by a single political party, the Südschleswigscher Wählerverband, and these examples show that a close cooperation, especially of small minorities, is possible and has its advantages.

[16] This example sheds light on another problem: if the minority forms the majority in several territorial units of one state, it is questionable which unit may represent the majority on a national level. As for the Basque minority, it is quite clear that the province of País Vasco/Euskadi can serve as a representative, but which of the Catalan-speaking provinces of Aragón, Baleares, Catalunya and Valencia may act as a legitimate representative of all-Catalan interests on the national level?

[17] On the German *Zweckverbände*, cf. H.-W. Rengeling, "Zweckverbände," in *Handbuch der kommunalen Wissenschaft und Praxis*, ed. G. Püttner, 2nd ed. (Berlin: Springer, 1982), vol. 2 (Kommunalverfassung), pp.385–415. On the Dutch rijkswaterstaat, cf. Thom Holterman, *Recht betreffende decentrale rechtsgemeenschappen*, 3rd ed. (Deventer: Tjeenk Willink, 1998), 6-8; J. M.de Meij, *Inleiding tot het staatsrecht en het bestuursrecht*, 6th ed. (Groningen: Wolters–Noordhoff, 1996), pp.227–230.

[18] Also in Vojvodina, the majority of the population was Serbian, and there were dozens of other ethnic groups of varying size. On this, cf. the paper by Korhecz in this book.

[19] In Jersey, the immigration restrictions—exercised mainly through housing law since the accession of the United Kingdom (including the Crown's European possessions) to the European Community—are designed not for ethnic reasons but to protect the natural environment because low taxes make this small island an attractive place of residence in the eyes of many British citizens. The preservation of the rural character of most of the island has had the side effect that the French patois of the village population was given a habitat where it has been able to survive until today. The European Court of Human Rights found the Jersey laws in principle in accordance with the CPHR in the Gillow case. For details cf. Stanley de Smith, Rodney Brazier, *Constitutional and administrative law*, 8th ed. (London: Penguin, 1998).

[20] This right is not only enshrined in most constitutions, but also in the principal international human rights instruments. These instruments, however, allow for certain restrictions of this right. Art. 12 (3) of the International Covenant on Civil and Political Rights names national security, public order, public health or morals or the rights and freedoms of others as possible grounds for restrictions, and according to Art. 2 (3) of Protocol no. 4 to the CPHR, restrictions are possible if necessary in a democratic society in the interests of national security or public safety, for the maintenance of public order, for the prevention of crime, for the protection of health or morals or for the protection of rights and freedoms of others.

[21] An example is the German communal constitutional complaint (*Kommunalverfassungsbeschwerde*): Articles 28 (2), 93 no. 4b German Constitution of 23 May 1949, as amended by the Act of 29 January 1969.

[22] An example for a minority list system is Estonia where registration in the list establishes the right to take part in the cultural autonomy: Articles 8, 15 Cultural Autonomy Act. In Slovenia, registration in the minority list entitles to vote for the minority candidates in general elections: Articles 2, 3, 8, 20, 23 Act on the Elections to the State Assembly of 1992, *Uradni List* no. 44/1992; Articles 2, 4 Act on the Establishment of the Constituencies for the Elections to the State Assembly of 1992, *Uradni List* no. 45/1992; Articles 2, 19, 21, 22 Act on the Registers of the Right of Suffrage of 1992,

35

Uradni List no. 46/1992. On the Italian and Hungarian minorities' representation in the Slovene Parliament cf. Joseph Marko, *Der Minderheitenschutz in den jugoslawischen Nachfolgestaaten* (Bonn: Kulturstiftung der deutschen Vertriebenen, 1996), pp.146–148.

[23]   An example for the alienation of minority autonomy structures by persons not belonging to the minority is the elections of the Romanian self-government in Hungary in 1998, fuelled by the principle of free choice in Hungarian minority law. This case is dealt with in the chapter by Eiler and Kovács in this book.

[24]   An example for this control is the definition of Sami in Finnish law, as described in the chapter by Myntti in this book.

[25]   Art. 18 (2) Constitutional Law on human rights and freedoms as well as on the rights of ethnic and national communities or minorities in the Republic of Croatia of 4 December 1991, newly promulgated on 3 June 1992, *Narodne Novine* 1992, no. 34, item 896, amended by the Constitutional Law of 11 May 2000, *Narodne Novine* 2000, no. 51, item 1127.

[26]   Until 1990, the special status of Berlin demanded that the MPs from West Berlin in the West German Parliament did not have the right to vote on bills, but had the full right of speech and were allowed to vote in non-binding decisions.

[27]   Federal Act of 20 July 2000 no. 104-FZ on the general principles of the organization of the communities of the small indigenous peoples of the North, of Siberia and of the Far East of the Russian Federation (Indigenous Peoples Act), *Sobranie Zakonodatel'stva Rossiyskoy Federacii* no. 30/2000, item 3122. As a contrast, see the Sami autonomies in the Scandinavian countries as presented in the chapter by Myntti in this book.

[28]   On Scotland, cf. the study by Chalmers in this book; de Smith and Brazier (*supra*, footnote no. 19), 48, 62; Gerry Hassan, Chris Warhurst, eds., *The New Scottish Politics* (Norwich: The Stationery Office, 2000).

[29]   On the Gagauz minority in Moldova cf. the chapter by Neukirch in this book. In the same small state, the case of Transdnistria, where so far territorial autonomy could not solve the ethnic problems, shows the limitations of that model when political will is lacking.

[30]   These questions are discussed in detail in the chapter by Grin and Vaillancourt in this book.

Minority Groups and Autonomy from an International Political Perspective

Balázs Vizi

Minority Groups and Autonomy from an International Political Perspective[31]

Balázs Vizi

1. INTRODUCTION

The present paper focuses on minority groups, especially politically organized ones, and seeks to provide a general overview of the political position of minorities on the international scene, with special emphasis on the legal institution of autonomy. However, the observations below can be chiefly interpreted in a European context. Today it would be impossible to provide a global and universally acceptable analysis of this issue as the different political and legal approaches to the 'question of minorities' show an immense variety even in Europe, not to mention the rest of the world. Thus, exceptions can always be found and will always be present.[32]

Furthermore, the problems discussed below are more closely related to the present realities of Central and Eastern Europe than to minority questions emerging in other parts of the continent. The reason for this lies primarily in the different European regional international legal instruments on minority protection, which emerged over the past decade partly as international reactions to the problematic situations in Central and Eastern Europe, while Western European minority issues seem to be less present on the international agenda.

It also has to be stressed that the acknowledgement of the political character of minority groups or the establishment of legally institutionalized autonomous bodies for minority groups cannot solely be regarded as a general solution for the problems associated with minorities. Other legal structures and political solutions may be equally appropriate for guaranteeing minority rights, according to the position of the minority concerned.

Nevertheless, acknowledgement of minority groups as political entities and the establishment of adequate self-governing institutions can, in many cases, represent a pragmatic and appropriate solution for the problems existing between minority groups and their states.

After briefly analysing various features of the political mobilization of minorities, an overview of the political position of minorities in international relations theory and practice will be presented. The third issue that will be discussed is the international legal environment of minority rights, especially regarding the question of collective rights. A fourth point considered deals with the problem of self-determination and a potential right to autonomy under international law: two of the most important legal institutions with regards to the political rights of minorities. Before proceeding, however, some important terminological comments shall be made.

2. TERMINOLOGICAL REMARKS

Most attempts to discuss national minorities in an international context are faced with the terminological problems that exist in this field. The term 'minority' is widely used in political science and in international relations to describe different phenomena on a relational basis. This term, without any complementary qualifications, describes merely a numerical disproportion between two or more groups of people. However, such a disproportional relation does not necessarily reflect a political issue on the international scene. As Bíró underlines:

> The question of minorities generally becomes an issue when groups, numerically inferior within a state, claim rights that are politically sensitive to grant. In practice, sensitive means prone to real or perceived offences to representations whose characterization is overloaded with symbols, like national dignity, honour, or national feelings. The stakes in debates becomes more tangible when minority claims give rise to the devolution of power, or to power-sharing schemes and the process involves actors from the international arena, thereby affecting the foreign relations of the concerned state.[33]

The minority groups referred to here are organized along these lines; political organization along their ethnic or national identity generally raises the concern of their state on politically sensitive arguments. These include issues related to "the rights of persons belonging to national, or ethnic, religious and linguistic minorities".[34]

So far, there is no universally accepted definition of 'minority', and in international documents other terms such as 'people' and 'nation' are widely used interchangeably, without being clearly defined.[35] Nevertheless, similar views are emerging in the relevant literature (explicitly) and in international documents (implicitly) as well.

From the various existing interpretations of national, ethnic, religious and linguistic minorities, a few general statements can be derived: minority groups generally have a sense of community (organized around a well definable group identity), a common will to preserve that group cohesion and usually, but not always, a territorial concentration.[36]

In this paper, three main aspects of group identity that play a central role in politically manifested group cohesion are taken into account. These are ethnic, national and cultural identities, which refer to the perception—often mythical—of a common ancestry (ethnic identity), to the loyalty or disloyalty to a nation-state (national identity) and to a language, religion, or a cultural tradition in the broad sense of the word (cultural identity).

Nevertheless, even within this limited concept of minorities, their political mobilization is often described with further contentious terms such as nationalism, national revival, ethno-nationalism, or ethnocentrism, etc. Until now these terms have neither in theory nor in practice reached a universally accepted definition. The reasons for such political mobilization, especially from an ideological point of view, are widely discussed in the vast literature on nationalism,[37] but, again, no universally accepted definition of the phenomenon exists.

As this brief overview of terminological problems shows, no general agreement on even the most basic terms has been reached yet. In this paper I prefer to accept the existing great variety of often contentious terms, without attempting to introduce further definitions or new terminology.

3.   POLITICAL MOBILIZATION AND GROUP COHESION

Turning to the political aspects of minorities it has to be stated that minorities have to possess specific features in order to be political subjects or actors in general. The mere difference in ethnicity, language or religion of one group from another does not necessarily constitute a political issue. These differences may not raise political questions in the related groups or remain unnoticed by the majority population. Furthermore, it should be underlined that not all minorities want or are willing to articulate themselves in political terms.[38] Self-awareness of a common need to preserve, maintain and articulate group identity is thus of outstanding importance if minority status and rights are desired.[39]

This paper focuses on those minorities which articulate their political goals along the lines of their religion, ethnicity, culture or language. In group-identity formation, such distinctive features have an outstanding role. Religion, ethnicity or any other factors which may concern the group identity are deeply rooted components of individual identity as well. It is also often disputed whether the feeling of belonging to a national or ethnic group is the result of social development or whether it represents a natural tendency of human nature. Both constructivism and primordialism are widely accepted and significant approaches in nationalism studies.[40]

Generally, in the eyes of minority representatives, the individual is seen as having been born into a given group which they later consciously accept, reaffirm and strengthen. The important factor is how the persons within a group perceive of their group identity. When political mobilization is made along these lines, provided that such components of personal and group-identity are perceived as unchangeable, given features, the political mobilization is made on absolute terms. The representatives of the minority group can hardly put these issues up for negotiation. If a person's belongingness—to an ethnic group, for example—is viewed as an unalterable reality, then such a person can never refuse their affiliation. This concept can be applied also at a group-level. These minority groups sometimes formulate politically irreducible claims on their expressed will to preserve, maintain and develop their ethnic, national or cultural identity. In such cases, religion, ethnicity and language are politically non-negotiable. On these issues no compromise can be made with the other political actors or with the state. In democratic structures it also implies that political mobilization on these grounds can never achieve the primary political goal of most actors: to obtain power. "Groups politically organized along these lines, soon find themselves in the role of structural minority on the political scene, whatever the extent to which the members of the group regard their claims to be irreducible. They can participate in various power-sharing schemes, but never become a political majority through democratic elections".[41] As a result, their role is more the reinforcement of consciousness in their group identity than obtaining actual political power in a country.

When identity becomes a political issue, its importance and role in group cohesion will likely increase and tend to emphasize the existing differences between the group and others. Consequently, this process may result in serious political or even violent conflict.

Studies of nationalism often express a deep concern regarding the idea of the national state, particularly with respect to interethnic relations within a state. When the term 'national identity' or 'national minorities' is applied, it expresses a certain relation of that minority group to a state in terms of their loyalty or disloyalty to this state. States have usually been established as the nation-states of the ethnic majority or dominant ethnic group. In recent times, the overlapping interpretation of ethnic nation and state has been widely criticized in literature. However, governmental practices in most countries still show that an ethnically homogeneous state is considered to be preferable to a multinational one.[42] In this perspective minorities are often seen as a possible danger by undermining state sovereignty, claiming rights which could limit the central government and, above all, representing a threat to the territorial integrity of the state. This is especially true if they live in a compact community or have a neighbouring kin-state. As a result states usually emphasize the importance for minority groups to be loyal to the state. Without exploring the delicate and complex question of loyalty in detail, it shall be noted that in legal terms loyalty exclusively refers to the respect of laws and the accomplishment of civic duties by all citizens. That said, many states require something more of their minorities. Expanding upon the definition of loyalty, they seek a certain additional 'loyalty' (or self-identification with) the majority nation not only in legal but also in political or in cultural terms. In this case, the state is usually identified with the ethnic majority. Such a vague interpretation of loyalty usually 'justifies' governments' labelling of minority groups' behaviour offensive and ultimately serves as an excuse to restrict or oppress minority claims. However, it would be very difficult to find, either in internal legal regulations or in political terms, any definition for such a broadly defined use of the word 'loyalty'. In this vague sense of the word, minorities usually cannot declare an exclusive 'loyalty' to their state, as they possess a different identity not necessarily represented by that state, and possibly represented by another kin-state. On the other hand, almost all politically organized minorities, except those claiming secession, accept and declare their loyalty to the state in which they live, in the generally accepted legal sense of the word.

Until political actors accept the distinction between state and nation, the competing and contradictory claims of minorities and states always presents a potential source of conflict.

The strengthening of group cohesion as a response to increasing threats from the state may lead to drastic means and claims being adopted during the process of political mobilization of minority groups (e.g. the use of violence or pronouncements of secession).

Certainly—taking into consideration the dissolution of the former Federal Republic of Yugoslavia in the past decade—such threatening sentiments may also be manipulated by politicians or groups in their competition for power (e.g. persons participating in 'ethnobusiness', the so-called 'ethnic entrepreneurs'). However, it may be difficult to identify hidden political interests beyond the actual ethnic conflict. Manipulations may appear both in the minority and majority realms of society. But while the manipulators of the majority usually can be identified among those in power, the situation is often not so clear in minority groups. When we talk of the political mobilization of minorities, this also raises the question of the legitimacy of political leaders of the minority group and whether they represent the entire community or just specific political groups within it.

Considering that the question of leadership within the minority group is an important element for increasing group cohesion, a further brief comment shall be made here on this point. In the process of political mobilization of minorities there is a normal need for certain forms of 'formal' leadership, which can manifest and represent the group-identity both towards the outside world and within the community. This role can be played by:

- traditional institutions, which are based on their own autonomous hierarchy (e.g. a church or a 'council of elders', etc.);
- formal, legally established institutions as the representative bodies of any level of self-government or the representatives of political organizations functioning on the legal

basis accessible within the legal system of the state (i.e. elected MPs, local authority councillors, etc.);

- charismatic individuals who are highly regarded in the community and are accepted by an overwhelming majority of the group, without a formal electoral process.

As a result of a growing political mobilization of minorities, the representatives and decision-makers of the group will have a more influential political role. When minority groups enter in the political field—at a national or international level—the role of its leaders will change. Decisions taken by them will directly affect the everyday life of the group and that of the individuals who belong to the group. Nevertheless, representation and decision-making will not always coincide. According to Kellas, three important elites can represent national groups: the representative role of cultural, political and economic elites can be equally important.[43]

When the leadership becomes more contested politically—if, for example, self-appointed leaders emerge—inherent dangers may arise. The political rule within the group may become authoritarian if there are no agreed mechanisms to select its political leadership. However, if there are legally regulated measures and mechanisms to control the group's internal political structure, then such an outcome is less probable.

When appropriate legal channels are not available for selecting political elites within the minority group, competing elites may emerge, articulating a large scale of different, possibly contradictory, political goals as claims of the minority group. Such a situation can further complicate the representation of the group and the possibilities to accommodate their real needs in the future.

In those states which do not recognize their minorities or refuse them the needed means for political mobilization—for example by prohibiting organizing parties on an ethnic basis—minorities will probably become more radicalized and increase the chances of authoritarian rule coming to power

4. MINORITIES IN INTERNATIONAL RELATIONS—AN OVERVIEW

As referred to above, minorities formulating sensitive claims on national issues may face the suspicion and reluctance of the state in which they live to acknowledge and meet their wishes. As these political goals may include power-sharing schemes or decentralization of political power, the issue becomes even more delicate. The potential involvement of third actors in the dispute, namely international organizations or another state, can also seriously affect the foreign relations of the concerned state. In this case minority groups can strongly influence their political, international environment, even without having any appropriate international formal or legal channels to do so.

It has been impossible to develop a generally acknowledged and universal paradigm for the political mobilization of minorities and how that efects international relations. Each case is unique and many complementary or even contradictory observations can be made.[44] In the following, some core questions in relation to formulating a general model of the position of minorities in international relations will be presented.

4.1 Historical Theoretical Remarks

For most of the Cold War period the question of minorities was a predominate issue in international politics. The League of Nations system, which had provided a certain level of protection for minority groups in Europe (only in Europe and only in the defeated and new states) had collapsed and the experiences of the Second World War almost erased minority issues from the international agenda. In the *travaux préparatoires* of the United Nations Charter the problem of minorities was thought to be resolved by the general prohibition of discrimination on ethnic, national or racial grounds and by the reaffirmation of peoples' right to self-determination. In the bipolar world of the Cold War period, minority issues were considered to be almost exclusively a matter of domestic concern. In the fragile balance between the two great powers, the inviolability of state sovereignty and respect for the territorial integrity of states superseded minority considerations. However, from 1966, following the reappearance of the protection of persons belonging to ethnic, religious or linguistic minorities (as referred to in Article 27 of the United Nations International Covenant on Civil and Political Rights, or ICCPR), the idea of individual rights to preserve minority identity was generally accepted. But for a long time this assertion was not more thoroughly elaborated. The question of minorities clearly started to receive more attention from international organizations only after 1989.

Within the United Nations, serious concerns lead to the approval of the Declaration on the Rights of Persons belonging to National or Ethnic, Religious, and Linguistic Minorities in 1992. Although the Declaration is an international legal instrument which does not prescribe any specific obligations under international law, it was an important development in the universal acknowledgement of the rights of minorities.

In Europe serious attempts have been made to establish a consistent and detailed framework of minority protection in the past decade by such international organizations as the Council of Europe (CoE) and the Organization for Security and Cooperation in Europe (OSCE).[45] But state practices regarding their implementation have been varied.

Considering these recent developments in Europe, it can be stated that a dual approach emerged in relation to the international protection of minorities: firstly, the accommodation of minorities is regarded as relevant to international security; and secondly, the protection of minorities is derived from the universal protection of basic individual human rights and freedoms. However, this individualistic approach does not reflect the community character of minority groups.

Similar approaches are reflected in international legal or political theories as well. Until 1989, the main contentious issue in academic debate was how the rights of minorities (usually formulated as rights of persons belonging to minorities) can be implemented in the general framework of human rights.[46]

In another mainstream theoretical approach the question of ethnic-based conflicts was widely analyzed.[47] The protection of minorities as an issue of international security first emerged in international documents within the CSCE/OSCE in 1975. Dispersed ethnic conflicts in Africa, Asia and the Middle East also drove scholars to investigate why ethnic-based conflicts emerge and how they can be managed or settled. Besides different theoretical considerations on the correlation between ethnic identity and security, Ted Gurr and Barbara Harff recently tried to set up a quantifiable assessment of different criteria which can lead to open conflicts in ethno-political mobilization, from permanent interethnic cleavages to the rise of exclusionary ideologies.[48]

Existing realities usually follow a similar trajectory described by Gurr and Harff. But persisting cleavages between ethnic groups, or the rise of exclusionary ideologies in a society, can be noticed well before a conflict erupts, which could make ethnic-based conflicts quite foreseeable and could enable the international community to find different measures to prevent their escalation. From early warning to military intervention at different phases there is a wide scale of possible actions at the disposal of the international community. However, the success of these actions cannot be assured from the outset, and in most cases the main international actors are reluctant to take appropriate actions immediately.

Liberal approaches failed to foresee the difficulties associated with the supposed universal victory of human rights and democracy after the collapse of the communist world. Humanitarian interventions have not always been successful in terms of stopping human rights abuses (e.g. in Somalia) and usually do not take place at all. The peaceful cooperation of nations to protect human rights and minorities is not a worldwide reality, and minority issues usually deepen, rather than bridge, existing gaps and conflicts between states.

Realist theories of international relations, which focus on the pre-eminence of the state, maintain that the question of minorities is strictly a matter of domestic concern. However, in recent times a number of states were split along their ethnic cleavages as they failed to establish a democratic and stable, political community on a multiethnic basis. This implies that formal international recognition and respect of a state does not in itself secure the survival of that state.

World-system theories focusing on the questions of central and peripheral areas cannot provide a universal explanation for the political mobilization of minorities either, as it turns out that economic development or uneven distribution of resources is not the general (but a possible) cause for rising ethnic tensions.

Despite some achievements in Europe regarding the international legal protection of minorities, a coherent international regime (including, for example, also sanctions or a judicial forum to settle disputed cases) is not likely to be established in the short term. In a more global perspective, such issues have not even been raised so far by the international community.

University textbooks also mostly ignore the issue, usually referring to minorities as non-formal, non-state actors of international relations and failing to explain their role or their activities at an international level.[49]

Sovereign nation-states are still the most important actors of international relations. International legal regulations are almost exclusively designed and implemented by nation-states and they are the most influential in setting the international agenda. In this context, minority groups have a very firm interest in presenting their claims to the international community to receive attention and possibly support from another state, group of states or international organization. External actors can apply serious pressure on a government which cannot always be achieved by a minority alone. This was certainly the case in Kosovo and East Timor.

Minority groups can become political actors at the international level and may be able to influence the international environment without being formally recognized by states or other potent actors. But the preponderance of the state still seems to be solid and strong despite the strong challenges coming from non-state actors, of which minorities are but one group.

It can be concluded that although minorities play a considerable role on the international scene as political actors (politically organized groups), the influence and possible results of their political mobilization are still unexplored in theory. This incomplete overview on some current ideas on minorities in international relations is intended to show that the emergence of minority issues (or rather the re-emergence) over the past decade has not yet received a generally accepted response.

4.2 International Law and Collective Rights of Minorities

If minorities can and do articulate their will to preserve their identity in the political field, what kind of legal measures can be applied for realizing their collective will?

Will Kymlicka's self-proclaimed "liberal theory of minority rights"[50] remarks that liberal fears of collective rights as threatening the primacy of individual rights are practically without foundation. He argues that collective rights in inter-group relations of minorities belong to the "external protection" of minority rights and serve to resolve the otherwise existing unfairness in minority–majority relations.[51] Accordingly, minorities with access to collective rights would come to enjoy widely assured and accepted individual rights of persons belonging to minorities. Asbjorn Eide expresses a similar idea in a deductive analysis of non-minority specific individual human rights that is relevant to minority groups as well:

> Human rights are essentially individualistic. They deal with the rights of the human person as an individual. Many persons belonging to ethnic, religious or linguistic groups feel, however, that they need a protection of their group identity. The core elements of that identity is the right to organize themselves as a group, to use their own language, to be able to preserve, to reproduce, and to develop their own culture, and therefore to control or have a significant impact on the content of the education of their new generations. A part of this concern is to be able effectively to influence political decisions affecting themselves.[52]

However, among international organizations this approach is not universally recognized. Rather—as was briefly mentioned above—the individual character of minority rights is emphasized in the interpretation of legal instruments. On the other hand, by the mid-nineties the rights of minorities became universally acknowledged as forming an integral part of the human rights regime. Although Ragazzi notes that nowadays respect for human rights can be regarded as a part of the general international obligations *erga omnes*,[53] it evidently does not mean that their universal obligatory status is guaranteed, as many state practices and governmental approaches show.

The actual protection of minorities regime is a relatively recent development in international law. The first basic documents on human rights, like the UN Charter, the Universal Declaration of Human Rights (1948) and the European Convention on Human Rights (1950) did not contain any reference to minority rights. Until the late1960s, the anti-discrimination provision[54] was the only existing measure which was specifically relevant to minority populations. States were often reluctant to confer these human rights such a broad interpretation. (It is noteworthy that the 1948 Convention on the Prevention and Punishment of the Crime of Genocide, without mentioning minority groups, implicitly reaffirmed their right to existence.[55]) The first explicit step towards the international legal protection of minorities was made with the introduction of a minority Article in the UN International Covenant of Civil and Political Rights (1966). Article 27 of the Covenant states:

> [i]n those States in which ethnic, religious or linguistic minorities exist, persons belonging to such minorities shall not be denied the right, in community with other members of their group, to enjoy their own culture, to profess and practice their own religion, or to use their own language.

This section clearly distinguishes the special status of the rights of minorities among other human rights. The free enjoyment of one's own culture, faith and language describes the living identity of a minority group. The expression "in community with other members of their group" refers to the fact that the individual who constitute such groups cannot avail of these rights as individuals. However, the expression that "persons belonging to such minorities shall not be denied the right..." signals that only individuals shall be entitled to this right; the community itself is not intended to be the right-holder. This duality characterizes most of the documents in international legislation concerning minorities. The individual approach refers to the members of an undefined community (as there is no universally accepted legal definition of 'minority' in international law). This ambiguity opens up wide possibilities to states not to recognize their minorities as minority groups.

At the international level, as states have strong fears of minorities claiming secession (and in their internal conflicts political cleavages are often constituted along ethnic divisions), besides the recognition of minority rights, stable norms limit the extent of minority mobilization. For example, the UN General Assembly Declaration on the Rights of Persons Belonging to National or Ethnic, Religious and Linguistic Minorities formulates in Article 8: "Nothing in this declaration may be construed as permitting any activity contrary to the purposes and principles of the United Nations, including sovereign equality, territorial integrity and political independence of States".

This and other similar vague formulations leave ample room for state interpretation when defining, for example, what kind of action is regarded as contrary to the territorial integrity of a state. The implementation of these international documents is the responsibility of the signatory states, and—as there are no agreed mechanisms to clear discordance on interpretation—each government is free to interpret such regulations as it desires. Regarding the violation of the rights of minorities, no formal, institutionalized international forum has yet been established.

Different instruments adopted by European regional organizations, though, contain the first steps towards introducing a coherent protection of minorities. These legal instruments also handle minority rights on an individualistic basis, by making reference to "persons belonging to national minorities". Most of the rights encompass linguistic and cultural aspects but only few explicit references are made to explicitly collective or political rights of minority communities, if any are made at all. Within the frameworks of the CoE and OSCE, influential developments have taken place over the past ten years. New measures of international protection of minorities were approved such as the Articles 30–47 of the CSCE Copenhagen Document on Minority Rights (1990) and the CoE Framework Convention for the Protection of National Minorities (1995). Another important action of the CSCE/OSCE was the establishment of the monitoring institution of the CSCE High Commissioner on National Minorities by the 1992 Helsinki Document *The Challenges of Change*. To date, this is the only international institution which is entitled to monitor the situation of minorities in the field; it maintains contacts with both representatives of minorities and of governments in an effort to warn of any possible conflicts at the earliest possible stage. The High Commissioner's mandate includes providing an "early warning", being able to take "early action" when needed.[56] "He thus has a two-fold mission: first, to try to contain and de-escalate tensions and, second, to act as a 'tripwire', meaning that he is responsible for alerting the OSCE chief organs whenever such tensions threaten to develop to a level at which he cannot contain them with the means at his disposal."[57] It is crucial that the High Commissioner has free movement in the field, the ability to visit countries at will and the capacity to receive information from different sources, including various minority and civil organizations. It should be underlined that this is the first international institution with a mandate that gives it direct contact with the representatives of minorities, hence implicitly recognizing the political character of minority groups. Over the past years the High Commissioner, widely broadening the limits of his mandate, was also able to exercise a certain 'control' over the accommodation of minority rights. The institutionalized position of the High Commissioner[58] is an important contribution to the management of ethnic non-violent conflicts in Central and Eastern Europe.

The integration of minority rights in the system of individualistic human rights does not solve, but rather reaffirms, the problems emerging from the consistent, collective group character of minorities. There are, though, some attempts to codify at an international level a wider range of collective rights of persons belonging to minorities. The CoE Parliamentary Assembly Recommendation 1201/1993 (referred to hereafter as the Recommendation) needs to be mentioned here. This document raised serious debates between Hungary, Romania and Slovakia in the mid-nineties on the right of autonomy for the respective minorities in these states. The realities today, and Romania's and Slovakia's final interpretation of this document, clearly show that states (especially in Central and Eastern Europe) are still far from being open to such notions, even though Article 11 of the Recommendation makes clear reference to the possibility of establishing territorial autonomy for minorities.[59]

The Recommendation is not a legally binding document under international law. However, it received considerable international attention, emerging as a key issue during the Hungarian–Slovakian and Hungarian–Romanian bilateral negotiations on the treaties on good-neighbourly relations and friendly cooperation (also called Basic Treaties) in the mid-nineties.[60] In both cases, one of the most delicate issues was the minorities' right to autonomy, proposed by the Hungarian party to be included in both documents in the form of a reference to the Recommendation. In the treaty with Slovakia, the Recommendation was included in a list of international documents under Article 15, paragraph 4(b) of the Treaty. It declared that the "norms and political commitments laid down" in these documents are accepted by the parties as "legal obligations". However, the Slovak delegation, just before signing the document, presented a unilateral restrictive interpretation denying any collective minority rights and also any right to autonomy[61]—an interpretation which was reinforced by the Slovak National Council before it ratified the document. Similarly, in the Basic Treaty stipulated between Hungary and Romania almost the same international documents were applied as "legal obligations".[62] However, in this case the list of documents appeared in a separate Annex to the Treaty, including a restrictive endnote on the Recommendation, declaring that "the Contracting Parties agree that Recommendation 1201 does not refer to collective rights nor does it impose upon them the obligation to grant to the concerned persons any right to a special status of territorial autonomy based on ethnic criteria". Furthermore, even the article on the rights of minorities is legally not as strong as in the Hungarian–Slovakian Basic Treaty, it can be also noted that the implementation of the article has neither been completed yet in Romania. The outstanding importance in the negotiations of any possible reference to the minorities' right to autonomy and the following governmental interpretations, however, show a deep concern of states on the collective rights of minorities. Both Romania and Slovakia clearly wanted to avoid even the idea of ethnic-based self-government.

These two examples of attempts to include, in general terms, the rights of minorities to autonomy in international legal documents may well illustrate the delicacy of the question not only in the wider international community but also with bilateral relations. It underscores the inevitable necessity of introducing adequate regulations in internal legislation in order to provide a concrete legal framework for the implementation of similar international obligations.

Noting that under universal and regional international law there are no agreed upon institutions for the collective political rights of minorities, it will be interesting to see how different and far-reaching autonomy regimes are developed in the internal legislation of many European states. Considering the diversity of the case studies presented in this volume, it is obvious that no universal formula will be possible. The existence of well-functioning autonomy models show that it is not *a priori* impossible to grant collective political rights to minority groups, while at the same time respecting the principle of state-sovereignty and territorial integrity. Nevertheless, for the introduction of such political institutions a strong and deeply rooted political will is needed on all sides. As the great variety of existing arrangements show, appropriate legal solutions can generally be found, if indeed the political will exists.

4.3 Self-Determination and Minorities

Most minority rights are derived from individual human rights. Cultural or personal autonomy is also explained from this perspective. However, the relevance of the delicate question of peoples' right to self-determination cannot be neglected. Territorial autonomy is generally perceived as a certain level of self-determination.[63] States often see territorial autonomy as the cradle of future secession. As a result, most of them ignore or refuse to grant autonomy rights to minorities. The existing examples of territorial autonomy have usually been the result of long negotiations and are often enforced by international agreements.

Since the end of the First World War, the right of peoples to self-determination has been among the cornerstone arguments in international politics. Today, the right to self-determination is embedded in international documents as one of the most basic human rights. It appears in the UN Charter and explicit reference is made to it in both of the 1966 UN Covenants on human rights. Article 1 of the International Covenant on Civil and Political Rights is identical to Article 1 of the International Covenant on Economic, Social and Cultural Rights: paragraph 1 in both texts reads as follows: "All peoples have the right of self-determination. By virtue of that right they freely determine their political status and freely pursue their economic, social, and cultural development".

Self-determination, first and foremost, describes the process whereby a people freely determines its own political status. In a broad sense it may extend to the definition of the political system, in which people want to live, or to the creation of an independent state.

Among the different interpretations of self-determination in Western political culture, it could generally mean the process by which people regularly elect a representative government. In many ethnic communities throughout the world self-determination is thought to exist whenever an ethnic group can form its own nation-state. In most parts of post-colonial Africa and Asia, the concept has been officially equated with the process of decolonization. However, the first or second interpretation would be unacceptable to many Third World countries, and an ethnic-based self-determination would be refused by most of them. As such interpretations exist simultaneously, states tend to selectively define how such norms apply to it. Decolonization has been the only generally accepted formula for interpreting peoples' right to self-determination. The extent to which self-determination has become a legal right can still not be established, as the crucially important term 'people' has never been defined in a precise legal manner and international practice has been inconsistent regarding the implementation of the right to self-determination. At present, states are not likely to accept ethnic groups as the holders of the right to self-determination. Today, it is generally understood that the ultimate goal in achieving any level of self-determination or self-government is secession, and the creation of a nation-state on their own.

However, in political and legal theory, attempts have been made to extend this legal right to ethnic groups as well and to separate the concept of self-determination from that of secession. Thomas Musgrave, at the end of his investigation of the present position of self-determination in international law, concluded that "international law neither sanctions nor prohibits secession within a particular state. Ethnic self-determination is simply a political act which occurs outside the jurisdiction of international law and is not governed by its principles".[64] It is also problematic to escape the exclusive exposition of self-determination as a full, indivisible right. As Antonio Cassese emphasized:

> If the concept of self-determination comes to represent a range of choices and options rather than solely the 'ultimate goal' of independence, the gap between legal right and political reality could be considerably narrowed. Self-determination, divisive by its very nature, would still mean a contest for power, control, and authority. However, envisioned as a concept permitting a range of solutions, it would render the gulf between States and the groups asserting their rights easier to bridge. If a right to self-determination also meant something less than a right to sovereignty, the concept would generally quell nationalism, which, if carried to the extreme, can cause immense suffering.[65]

The previously quoted paragraphs of the UN international human rights covenants on the right to self-determination do not exclude such a limited, divisive interpretation. Self-determination does not have to necessarily connote the right to establish an independent state.

In this perspective, the relation between the right of minority groups to maintain their identity and peoples' right of self-determination could be reexamined. The right to maintain one's identity can also be extended to other derived, practical rights. Eide offers some examples of the possible extensive interpretation of the UN Declaration of Human Rights:

> Relevant to minorities and group accommodation are for instance, the provisions which oblige states to respect freedom of thought, conscience, and religion (Universal Declaration Article 18). Members of any religious groups are entitled to manifest, in public as well as in private, their religion or belief in teaching, practice, worship and observance. Equally relevant is the right to freedom of opinion and expression (Universal Declaration Article 19), which includes the right also to seek, receive, and impart information and ideas through any media and regardless of frontiers. This right clearly includes the right to use one's own mother tongue and to receive and give information in that language; on this basis minority groups can assert their right to protect their own language. Also of relevance is the right to freedom of peaceful assembly and association (Universal Declaration Article 20): minority groups are entitled to organize for the promotion of their interests and values by forming their own associations. Furthermore everyone has the right to participate in the cultural life of the community (Universal Declaration Article 27). This implies, also, that members of minority groups can carry on their particular group culture.[66]

In a similar way the peoples' right to self-determination could be reversely interpreted: instead of denying ethnic groups this right, they can limit it. This would reaffirm the territorial integrity of states at the same time.

If the group-character of minorities as well as their right to preserve their own identity is accepted—as it appears in different international legal measures—then they shall have the right to have their own institutions to promote and control the preservation (transmission from one generation to another) of such identity. Appropriate technical, legal and institutional schemes have already been developed, and applied and implemented in some countries.

The continuous existence of group identity includes its transmission between generations. To express such continuity and to assure the development and transmission of identity, minority groups have to be in a position to make decisions and create and maintain institutions in the relevant areas. A coherent structure of different levels of self-government can be established where the exercise of the right to (external) self-determination of the majority does not exclude the same right of minority groups within the state. "Self-determination does not give the resulting majority the right to impose its will in such a way that the rights of others are violated...".[67]

The different regimes of autonomy merely reflect some possible solutions. Personal, cultural and territorial autonomies may cover such in-between accommodations of self-determination and minority rights. Territorial autonomy, which stands the closest to the classical meaning of self-determination, is usually referred to as a form of internal self-determination. It denotes an autonomous legal-political alternative institution of the right to self-determination. According to Hannum, the basic issues, of which some or all shall be under the exclusive jurisdiction of the (territorial) autonomous bodies, are the following: language, education, social and personnel affairs (access to police, governmental services, etc.), land and natural resources, and representative local government structures.[68]

However, at the present stage of international law, it would be hard to claim a right to autonomy on the basis of customary international law. As actual cases show, usually the option of autonomy is offered by states on a unilateral basis as a self-limitation of their sovereignty and there is no international instrument which could force states to establish autonomous bodies for their minorities. At times the legal foundations of autonomies may be rooted in bilateral international agreements. The existence of an international legal background is very positive, as such contractual undertakings cannot be unilaterally abolished. Moreover, an international organization or the kin-state of a minority will hardly give its consent to a similar amendment. In the absence of international legislation, the autonomy should be inscribed in the constitution or in another legal act that takes precedence over the ordinary laws of the state. As Hannikainen points out, the formal consensus of minorities (e.g. in the form of a referendum) is not a necessary requirement in establishing autonomy; therefore the minorities have no possibility to veto any attempts to abolish the autonomy. As even constitutions can be amended by certain procedures, the danger of abolishment of such a regime can never be excluded.

Further legal solutions that could be implemented by states to realize internal self-determination are described by Hannikainen in regard to the concrete experiences of the autonomy of the Åland Islands:

> If the language of the autonomous region is different from the dominant language of the State, it should have official status in the region, perhaps together with the dominant official language of the State. ...
>
> It is inevitable in practice that there arise disagreements over the powers of the autonomous region. It would be preferable that such disagreements were not solved simply by the decision of State organs. There should exist a special organ, composed of the representatives of the State and of the autonomous region, to settle disagreements.
> ...
> The autonomous region should have the possibility to be party to the decision-making process at a national level in those matters which affect its interests. ...

The local courts should preferably be a part of the autonomous machinery but should naturally enjoy in their work the independence from the executive and legislative power.[69]

This list would certainly include further elements. But as this selected assessment shows, minority desires can be secured in an international legal perspective: in the absence of a consistent international legal background, states are free to make decisions in this field as they see fit.

On the other hand, a raft of various state practices has resulted in a variety of possible legal settlements of autonomy which could be examined and adapted, with some modification, by other states as well, for the crucial legal elements of autonomy already exist in one country or another; .they just need to be adapted to other country's specific circumstances. Although models exist and references can be made to them, the existing self-governmental and autonomous bodies are so different that despite their quite frequent occurrence in different European countries autonomy cannot be regarded as forming a coherent legal point of reference under customary international law.[70]

5. CONCLUSIONS

What political and legal choices do minorities have at an international level in their quest for preserving their group identity and 'living their own lives'? As was briefly presented above, their position in international relations is still uncertain, and the international legal instruments available at the threshold of the twenty-first century leave a considerable space for different governmental interpretation, which usually try to exclude group rights or the right to autonomy. (The international community has not yet established any forum for controlling and sanctioning violations of minority rights.)

On the other hand we are witnessing a deep concern of the international community for the political mobilization of minority groups. The rise of minority claims to preserve their identity, articulated as well-defined political and legal goals and as requests presented to the state in which they live, raises governmental as well as international attention.

The claims formulated certainly depend largely on the position (population, settlement, the degree of political mobilization within minority society, etc.) of the minority within the state. Possible choices can vary from claiming secession by violent means to participating in democratic structures to negotiating with state authorities. These choices and the claims formulated by minorities may change over time. Governmental attitudes often determine the reactions of minorities.

In this perspective some minority groups appear to have a strong interest in presenting their claims at an international level as well, in order to increase foreign pressure on their governments. Appeals can be made to the international community in general or to the kin-state in particular, and foreign reactions may influence governmental policies toward minorities.

If a state recognizes its minorities as distinct communities, wider possibilities may be opened up for the accommodation of contradictory ideas and aims between the state and its minorities. State sovereignty and the respect of territorial integrity may be well compatible with a minority's claim to have appropriate political institutions for preserving its identity. The legal institutions of different forms of autonomy can be considered as a suitable and appropriately adjustable normative framework for the different situations. Among the existing political agreements, a large number of institutionalized compromises can be found in the different state practices and the different international legal measures applied.

NOTES

31   A special thanks is due to Dr Gáspár Bíró who read the first draft of this article and provided valuable comments on it. Many arguments reproduced here—especially with regard to international relations—are based on his observations. Naturally all the shortcomings of this paper are of my exclusive responsibility. In the academic year 2000/2001, I followed my PhD studies at K. U. Leuven with the help provided by the joint scholarship of the Katholieke Universiteit Leuven (Belgium) and the Soros Foundation (Hungary).

32   Cf. Gáspár Bíró, "Minorities in International Relations", in Klaus Segbers and Kerstin Imbusch, eds. *The Globalization of Eastern Europe: Teaching International Relations without Borders* (Hamburg: LIT, 2000), p.297.

33   Bíró, *op.cit.*, p.298.

34   As recent United Nations documents usually refer to them. (See, among others, the UN General Assembly Declaration on the Rights of Persons belonging to National or Ethnic, Religious, and Linguistic Minorities, 1992).

35   For the legal problems regarding the definition of 'minority', see the chapter by Brunner and Küpper in this book.

36   As the Council of Europe Parliamentary Assembly Recommendation 1201/1993 defines under Article 1:
For the purposes of this convention the expression "national minority" refers to a group of persons in a state who a) reside on the territory of that state and are citizens thereof; b) maintain long standing, firm and lasting ties with that state; c) display distinctive ethnic, cultural, religious or linguistic characteristics; d) are sufficiently representative, although smaller in number than the rest of the population of that state or of a region of that state; e) are motivated by a concern to preserve together that which constitutes their common identity, including their culture, their traditions, their religion or their language.

37   As nationalism is not only an ideology, but also a form of behaviour and a programme of action, this political character was also underlined in the classic works on nationalism. A condensed and critical overview on these theories is given by James G. Kellas, *The Politics of Nationalism and Ethnicity* (London: Macmillan, 1998), pp.43–65.

38   Cf. Brunner and Küpper in this volume.

39   Cf. *Ibid.*

40   See, for example, John Hutchinson and Anthony D. Smith, eds., *Nationalism—A Reader* (Oxford: Oxford University Press, 1994); Tom Nairn, *Faces of Nationalism* (London: Verso, 1997) or Craig Cahoun, *Nationalism* (Buckingham: Open University Press, 1997).

41   Bíró, *op.cit.*, p.299.

42   See among others, Josep R. Llobera, "The Future of Ethnonations in a United Europe", in Hans-Rudolf Wicker, ed. *Rethinking Nationalism and Ethnicity* (Oxford and New York: Berg, 1997), pp.43–57.

43   Kellas, *op. cit.*, pp.92–97.

44   Cf. Bíró, *op.cit.*, 297 and John T. Ishiyama and Marijkee Breuning, *Ethnopolitics in the New Europe* (Boulder Co.: Lynne Rienner, 1998), Preface, pp.viii–x. See also Janusz Bugajski, *Ethnic Politics in Eastern Europe: A Guide to Nationality Policies, Organizations, and Parties* (New York: Sharpe Armonk, 1993).

45   Before 1994 it was known as the Conference for Security and Co-operation in Europe.

46   See Patrick Thornberry, *The Rights of Minorities and International Law* (Oxford: Clarendon, 1991), pp.385–395.

47   Already in the 1980s, considerations on ethnic-based conflicts emerged in theory, first of all from a sociological perspective, see Donald L. Horowitz, *Ethnic Groups in Conflict* (Berkeley: University of California Press, 1985).

48   These include: "1) Persisting cleavages exist among ethnic groups, 2) elites have a history relying on repression to maintain power, 3) elites use their power to reward groups differentially for their loyalty, 4) the society has recently experienced a political upheaval, for example a revolution or a defeat in war, and 5) exclusionary ideologies arise that define target groups as expandable. When all these five factors are present, ethnopolitical concept is likely to have genocidal consequences", in Tedd Robert Gurr and Barbara Harff, *Ethnic Conflict in World Politics* (Boulder: Westview Press, 1994), p.79.

[49]   Robert Jackson and Georg Sorensen, *Introduction to International Relations* (Oxford: Oxford University Press, 1999); Daniel S. Papp, *Contemporary International Relations* (New York: Macmillan, 1992); or P. A. Reynolds, *An Introduction to International Relations* (London: Longman, 1994) to just mention a few of the widely used textbooks.

[50]   Will Kymlicka, "Introduction", in *Multicultural Citizenship* (Oxford: Clarendon, 1995), pp.4–9.

[51]   *Ibid.*, pp.34–37 or see Will Kymlicka, ed., *The Rights of Minority Cultures* (Oxford: Clarendon, 1996).

[52]   Asbjørn Eide, "Minorities in a Decentralized Environment," paper presented at the International Conference on Human Rights "All Human Rights for All" in Yalta, 2–4 September 1998—available at: http://www.riga.lv/minelres/publicat/Eide_Yalta98.htm.

[53]   Maurizio Ragazzi, *The Concept of International Obligations Erga Omnes* (Oxford: Clarendon, 2000), pp.135–145.

[54]   Art. 2 of the Universal Declaration of Human Rights states: "Everyone is entitled to the rights and freedoms set forth in this Declaration without distinction of any kind, such as race, colour, sex, language, religion, political or other opinion, national or social origin, property, birth or other status."

[55]   See Thornberry, *op. cit.*, Chapter 6.

[56]   OSCE Copenhagen Document (1992) Section II Paragraph (3).

[57]   Cited from the brief introduction to the mandate of the High Commissioner on the official homepage of the HCNM at http://www.osce.org/hcnm/mandate.htm.

[58]   The first High Commissioner was the Dutch diplomat Max van der Stoel. His mandate ended in June 2001.

[59]   "In the regions where they are in majority the persons belonging to a national minority shall have the right to have at their disposal appropriate local or autonomous authorities or to have a special status, matching the specific historical and territorial situation and in accordance with the domestic legislation of the state."

[60]   On the bargaining on the 'territorial clause' (on inviolable territorial integrity, which was strongly emphasized by the Slovak and Romanian governments) and on the rights of minorities (of outstanding importance for the Hungarian governments) as well as on the political environment of the negotiations, see Gáspár Bíró, "Bilateral Treaties between Hungary and its Neighbors after 1989," in Béla Király and Ignác Romsics, eds., *Geopolitics in the Danube Region* (Budapest: CEU Press, 1999), pp.357–373.

[61]   "The Government of the Slovak Republic emphasizes that it has never accepted and has not enshrined in the Treaty any formulation that would be based on the recognition of the principle of collective rights for minorities and that would admit the creation of autonomous structures on ethnic principle..." cited in Bíró, "Bilateral Treaties...," *op. cit.*, p.376.

[62]   Art. 15, paragraph (b).

[63]   For more details, see the study by Brunner and Küpper in this book.

[64]   Thomas Musgrave, *Self-Determination and National Minorities* (Oxford: Clarendon, 1997), p.258.

[65]   Antonio Cassese, *Self-Determination of Peoples—A Legal Reappraisal* (Cambridge: Cambridge University Press, 1995), p.351.

[66]   Eide, *op. cit.*

[67]   Hurst Hannum, *Autonomy, Sovereignty, and Self-Determination—The Accommodation of Conflicting Rights* (Philadelphia: University of Pennsylvania Press, 1990), p.455.

[68]   For more detail, see Hannum, *op. cit.*, pp.458–468.

[69]   Lauri Hannikainen, "Self-Determination and Autonomy in International Law", in Markku Suksi, ed. *Autonomy: Applications and Implications* (The Hague: Kluwer Law International, 1998), p.92.

[70]   See Hans-Joachim Heintze, "On the Legal Understanding of Autonomy", in Markku Suksi, ed. *op.cit.*, pp.7–33.

Geopolitical Aspects
of the Minority Question
in Central and South Eastern Europe

Gyula Csurgai

Geopolitical Aspects of the Minority Question in Central and South Eastern Europe

Gyula Csurgai

1. INTRODUCTION

While the question of borders and minorities in Eastern Europe was essentially frozen during the Cold War due to its bipolar status quo logic, the end of the Cold War and the crumbling of the communist regimes in Eastern Europe has given rise to the reemergence of the national question in the region.

With the reunification of Germany and the withdrawal of the Soviet army from Central Europe the bipolar geostrategic equilibrium evaporated. Moreover, the violent disintegration of Yugoslavia and the separation of Czechs and Slovaks into two states has questioned the validity of the territorial status quo, as defined by the peace treaties concluded after the First World War and by the 1975 Helsinki Final Act.

The reemergence of the question of borders and national minorities[71] has, at times, meant the opening of Pandora's box in the region situated between Russia and Germany. As Kosovo has illustrated, movements of national emancipation which affect multiethnic and multinational states and their neighbours are confronted with a crucial geopolitical question: what sort of political sovereignty is sought and how will it be realized—through negotiation, attribution or conquest?[72] The precarious and unresolved situation in Kosovo—whereby everyone is waiting to see if independence or autonomy will be the outcome—will likely have a direct impact on other multiethnic regions in South Eastern and Central Europe.

The existence of minority groups influences the internal geopolitical structure of a state in terms of its territorial organization. It also affects external geopolitics in terms of inter-state relations. The fact that a nation is divided by political frontiers can have serious implications for state relations, in particular if sub-groups of the nation are situated in neighbouring states. This is the case with the Albanian, Hungarian and Russian minorities, to name a few.

Multiethnic states have to satisfy the growing demands of ethnic groups for autonomy, and maybe even secession in some cases. These demands can lead to open conflicts in which the territorial dimension plays an important role. However, multiethnic situations do not necessarily lead to territorial conflicts. Different mechanisms for peaceful coexistence have been found in many countries in forms of power-sharing between the majority and minorities that lead to satisfactory territorial arrangements. The case of Switzerland, the autonomous regimes in South Tyrol, Italy, and Catalonia, Spain are examples of reconciling unity and diversity within a democratic framework.

Globalization did not eliminate nationalism but rather put it in a new context. On the one hand the process of globalization favours regional integration that reduces state sovereignty through the emergence of supra-national power centres, such as the EU, with transnational flows. On the other hand, a process of fragmentation has accompanied this integration. The search for identity on the basis of religion, ethnicity and nationality—forces that shape the geopolitical map of the international system—exemplifies this fragmentation.

The situation of contemporary Europe is characterized by this double logic of the globalization process. National sovereignty and political borders are losing importance in the countries of the European Union. Contrary to this integration process, Eastern Europe and the Balkans has undergone a process of fragmentation since the end of the bipolar equilibrium in Europe, as with the violent break-up of Yugoslavia and the more peaceful 'Velvet Divorce' in the former Czechoslovakia. But forces of integration also exist in Central and South-Eastern Europe with the prospect of future accession to the European Union.

From a geopolitical point of view, the main causes of the problem of national minorities originate from two factors: first, the application of the concept of a unitary nation-state which cannot satisfy the aspirations of minorities for power-sharing territorial arrangements. Second, the actual process of self-determination and the application of the principle of territorial integrity do not allow for a middle path between these two opposing principles of international law in order to find peaceful solutions for the problem of minorities. Moreover, in most cases the modification of political frontiers according to an ideal design is impossible; new nation-states cannot satisfy the aspirations of national communities because of the mixed geographical distribution of ethnic communities.

As integration becomes a major driving force in the international economy, the process of fragmentation based on ethno-cultural and religious factors does not favour the emergence of integrated geo-economic zones in the East and in the Balkans. A new strategy of territorial organization should be developed in order to improve the possibilities for integration in this region.

This study focuses on the following issues:

- What type of territorial organization can satisfy both minority demands for self-governance and respect for the territorial integrity of the state?
- To what extent and according to which criteria could self-determination serve as a guide in restructuring territorial order that meets the demands of ethnocultural minorities and conflict prevention and favours regional integration dynamics?
- What type of territorial organization could be envisaged for the minorities in Central and South Eastern Europe?
- Which aspects of the South Tyrol–Alto Adige autonomy regime in Italy could be used to guide autonomy models for minorities in Central Europe?

2.   GEOPOLITICAL ASPECTS OF THE MINORITY QUESTION

2.1 Geopolitics: A Multidimensional Reasoning

Geopolitics is the policy necessitated by the constraints and rewards of geography.[73] The study of geopolitics examines the relations between geographic space and political actions. Geopolitical analysis is concerned with the control of a given space by a power.[74] Until the end of the Cold War, geopolitics was regarded as the examination of the relationship between the conduct of power politics in the international system and the geographical framework in which it was applied.[75] This theoretical framework places the rivalry between states at the centre of the analysis. However, the proliferation of geopolitical questions since the end of the Cold War necessitated an evolution of the geopolitical approach.

First, geopolitical situations, such as the demands of minorities for greater autonomy and the emergence of regions in the European Union have been occurring within state borders. These questions are related to internal geopolitics as Yves Lacoste states.[76] Second, non-state actors are playing a larger role in contemporary international relations. Prominent examples include the strategies of non-governmental organizations (NGOs), the influence of major oil companies in Central Asia and extensive economic penetration by multinational enterprises. Third, in many cases traditional power rivalries over the control of territories have been gradually replaced by geo-economic competition. According to Edward Luttwak, Cold War ideological rivalries have been replaced by world-wide economic competition, in which trade and finance overshadow military power.[77] Considering these new dimensions, the study of geopolitics can be defined as a multi-dimensional method that analyzes the conflicting strategies of the different competitors (state and non-state) for the control of a given space. These strategies are often influenced by geopolitical representations. These can be considered as a subjective dimension of a given territory in the collective mentality of a human group ('mental maps') connected to national myths, symbols, religion and a specific interpretation of history.

Geopolitical reasoning takes into consideration the geographical dimension which should be considered not only in its physical sense, but in terms of demographic, cultural and economic aspects as well. Furthermore, the external and internal factors related to the geopolitical situation in question need to be taken into account. These factors can be divided between constants and variables.[78] Permanent factors refer to the geographic position and configuration of a given territory and to enduring elements of cultural identity such as language and religion. Variable factors are those that change on both the internal level (inside of state borders) and external levels (interstate and global level). These variable components refer to demography, socio-political structure, alliance configuration, strategic motivations, geo-economic interests, technological factors, etc.[79] An analysis of the interrelations of these factors necessitates an interdisciplinary approach that has to be carried out on the national, regional and global level.

The study of historical factors is a key element in a geopolitical analysis. Starting with an examination of the evolution of the spatial dimensions of a given territory through history, the historical retrospective approach allows us to understand the different territorial changes that have affected the life of a nation or state.[80] The territorial losses or gains in a certain period of history often relate to geopolitical representations and play an important role in national identity. This fact is particularly relevant in Central Europe where a great number of territorial changes have shaped the state building process. Historical arguments based on subjective territorial representations may be reinforced by geographical, economic and strategic ones.[81] The second important factor in the historical context is the study of the demographic and political evolution of human groups occupying a given territory. The study of the historical input is not a merely descriptive approach but rather an analytical one, based on the examination of the role of forces behind the geopolitical changes in a given period. For instance, the system of frontiers set up in Europe after the end of the Second World War, was determined by the bipolar power structure that divided Europe in to Soviet and American spheres of influence.[82] The international distribution of power influences the dynamics of a given territorial order.

This study does not intend to analyze either the question of geopolitical representations or the impact of the international distribution of power on the minority question in South Eastern and Central Europe. The analysis is focused instead on territorial arrangements which can prevent ethnic conflicts and may serve to define a new approach to interpreting both the self-determination principle and state sovereignty with regard to territorial integrity. Moreover, this territorial strategy should take into consideration the importance of regional integration and globalization.

The examination of the autonomy model of the South Tyrol region in Italy is particularly useful for developing proposals for minorities and states in South Eastern and Central Europe. The South Tyrol model of autonomy has proved that a viable solution for peaceful and democratic multiethnic coexistence can be found which satisfies the demands of ethnic groups for participation in political life while maintaining their collective identity and respect the territorial integrity of the Italian state. Moreover, South Tyrol has proven to be successful in the development of interregional and transborder cooperation that shows the important role that multiethnic border regions can play in the European integration process. Therefore some elements of the South Tyrol situation are included, without assuming that Western European systems of autonomy can be copied and implemented in Central Europe.

2.2 Geopolitics and Minorities

The affirmation of the identity of minorities and of their claims is related to the internal geopolitics of states in terms of territorial organization i.e., whether they be unitary states, federal structure, regional autonomies, etc. In this case, a geopolitical analysis concerns the administrative subdivision of states in the context of two issues closely connected to each other: territorial division and the sharing of political responsibilities.[83]

Minority issues can affect relations between states where territorial claims and border problems are concerned. In particular, this may occur when a national minority group is dispersed throughout different countries; Albanians in Serbia and Macedonia, and Hungarians in Romania, Slovakia and Serbia are examples. The fact that one part of a nation is under the sovereignty of another state can lead to the phenomenon of a 'support state' or 'kin-state'. In this arrangement the kin-state gives different kinds of support to the parts of its nation that are separated from it by state borders. This part of the nation, often defined as a national minority, can receive educational, cultural, media, political and economic support from the nation-state of its origin. In extreme cases this help can even take the form of military support, as in the 1999 Kosovo conflict when the Kosovo Liberation Army used Albanian territory for military training purposes.

Another example of a kin-state is Hungary. Its political strategy toward its neighbouring countries is influenced by its 'support state' role. The fact that about three million Hungarians reside in neighbouring countries has been a major foreign policy consideration in the region since the collapse of the communist system. Budapest accepted *de facto* that its borders do not coincide with the ethnic boundaries of Hungarians in the Carpathian Basin. The renunciation of territorial claims and boundary rectification has been facilitated by the integration process of Hungary into the European Union and NATO. This policy of integration has been supported by the Hungarian minorities living in countries neighbouring Hungary.[84]

Conflicting territorial claims are often related to the rivalry of 'geopolitical representations' of a given territory in the collective mentality of ethnocultural groups. These representations, as discussed, are connected to national myths, symbols, religion and a specific interpretation of history and have a significant impact on strategies for the control of a given territory sought by two or more ethnic groups. (For instance, to understand the roots of the Kosovo conflict one has to consider the rivalry of geopolitical representations of Serbs and Albanians with relation to the same territory.)

The question of minorities can be exploited indirectly—by powers seeking to extend their influence in a given geopolitical zone. This reality was evidenced throughout the war in the former Yugoslavia. Germany backed Croatia and Slovenia, Russia and Greece supported the Serbs and the United States assisted Bosnia.

2.3 Territory, Nation-State and Borders

In South Eastern and Central Europe[85] almost every state is composed of different ethnocultural communities. Secession and the creation of a new state in the name of self-determination could occur without major effects of regional destabilization only in a very few states and only if two major geopolitical conditions are met. First, successor states must be able to negotiate and accept new political borders. Second, the question of national minorities must not pose a problem for the relations of these states. Examples include Slovenia's recently gained independence from Yugoslavia and the separation between Czechs and Slovaks.

However, in most cases, the delineation of new sovereign entities by altering political borders (guided by one of the major principles of the nation-state that claims that nation and state should coincide) cannot be envisaged. It is almost impossible to draw borders along ethnic lines because of the very mixed spatial distribution of the different ethnic groups. A modification of political frontiers would simply create new minorities in the newly independent states. Therefore, in most cases a change of boundaries cannot resolve the minority question. This geopolitical problem stems from the fact that nation and state do not always coincide in the geographical space; a state can cover one part of a neighbouring nation at the same time that one or more parts of the nation belonging to the first state can be under the sovereignty of another state or group of states.

In the multiethnic states of Central and South Eastern Europe there is a conflicting relationship between two identities: civic and ethno-cultural. The first refers to the Western concept of the nation-state: all persons living in a given territory defined by state sovereignty, are citizens of that state regardless of their ethno-cultural origin. This concept is frequently defined as 'civic-nation'. The second refers to the ethno-cultural origin of a national community, often called 'ethnic-nation' or 'Kulturnation'. The mixture of these two concepts of nation frequently creates tension in these regions.

Due to the reality that nation and state are often juxtaposed geographically, ethno-cultural identity does not coincide with political frontiers. For instance, a Hungarian from Transylvania is a citizen of Romania but has strong emotional identification with the Hungarian nation. The opposite is a unitary nation-state where the majority of the population represents one nation. However, this type of state is based on the sovereignty of the majority, which in the case of multinational states leads to the domination of the largest ethnic group over the less numerous communities and sometimes cannot provide a framework for peaceful coexistence among various ethnic groups. Unitary nation-states cannot reconcile the conflicting nature between ethno-cultural and political identity. Aspirations of national minorities for autonomy are often considered by the state to be a challenge to its unity. On the other hand, the frustration of minorities with highly centralized state structures by which they feel oppressed can lead to the radicalization of their demands; they may opt for violence and seek secession.

As mentioned, unitary nation-states are highly centralized. The administrative division of state territory does not favour regional or other kinds of autonomy for minorities. Indeed, this kind of state aggravates tension caused by the rivalry of geopolitical representations because it does not take into consideration the perception of a given territory by groups other than the majority.

2.4 Self-Determination and Territorial Integrity

Latent and open conflicts are occurring in many parts of the world, caused by secessionist movements demanding the right to have their own statehood in the name of self-determination. Opposing these claims, many states in which these movements occur are defending their rights to uphold territorial integrity and national unity.

Facing the multiplication of demands for independence, the international community is confronted with a dilemma: which one of the two antagonist principles, the respect of territorial integrity or the right to self-determination, should be privileged? The first principle aims for the preservation of the status quo by respecting the territorial integrity of states, while the second one favours the changes that could often lead to a total disintegration of central authorities and catalyze the fragmentation of states.

Guy Héraud defines five stages of self-determination: self-affirmation, self-definition, self-organization, self-government and secession.[86] Among these five steps, the right of secession poses the biggest problem in Central Europe. It can be used by sub-national groups to seek the recognition of their own statehood, or in the case of national minorities, to achieve unification with their kin-state.

Within the generally recognized procedures of the international community, secession can easily become a cause of destabilization for the following reasons: first, states from which an ethno-cultural group wants to secede often defend their territorial integrity by using military force. Second, minorities might be created in the newly independent states. These new political units will themselves have to deal with minority issues. (The case of the Serb community in Krajna, Croatia, illustrates this problem.) Third, all aspirations of minorities for autonomy and political power-sharing within the framework of the state (with respect to its territorial integrity) are frequently considered by central authorities as a first step towards eventual secession. This problem is especially evident in the case of national minorities who live in border regions where they constitute the majority of the population and belong, in ethno-cultural terms to neighbouring state. (The Hungarian minority in southern Slovakia is a good example of this.)

Some questions need to be raised concerning the actual procedure of self-determination. Who decides whether an ethnic community seeking secession and statehood should legitimately be recognized as an independent nation? Should the right of a nation to establish its own state be recognized without a *proviso* granting rights to the minorities living in the territory of the newly created state? Finally, should the new status of minorities and borders be negotiated before the recognition of a new state by the international community? A major weakness of the international community's response to self-determination claims has been the lack of consensus on a reasonable set of principles to which a self-determination movement should commit before being granted support or recognition.[87]

The question of political borders cannot be separated from minority issues. Borders have been changed countless times in Central Europe, and often by external powers that took little or no consideration of ethnic, economic, cultural and historical factors.[88] In many cases national communities are separated by political frontiers from their kin-states. Moreover, arbitrary delineation of borders led to the disruption of former common economic zones, thus creating obstacles to regional integration.

With the signing of the Helsinki Final Act, states promised to respect the inviolability of current boundaries and territorial integrity. Specifically, they renounced the the use of force when considering territorial alterations.[89] But the Helsinki Final Act does not exclude the possibility of territorial modifications achieved through negotiation.

The possible disintegration of Belgian and Basque demands for self-determination in regions of Spain and France may create geopolitical concerns in the future.

2.5 Geopolitical Factors in the Kosovo Situation[90]

To illustrate the influence of geopolitical factors in a minority situation the impact of some of these factors—geographic distribution of ethnic community, demography, geopolitical representations, political boundaries and geostrategy—on the Kosovo situation will be briefly presented. Serbs and Albanians both claim the territory of Kosovo. While Albanians represent the overwhelming majority of the Kosovar population, Serbs view Kosovo as their spiritual and historical homeland and are loath to see it detached from the rest of their state.

The territory of Kosovo is 10,887 square km. The border between Albania and Yugoslavia is 486 km long. Albania's borders were defined by the 1913 London Conference. As a result, about two-thirds of the Albanian population found itself outside of Albania. Today, Albania has 3.4 million inhabitants and a further 2.6 million Albanians live in neighbouring countries.[91] This fact has serious 'kin-state' implications for the foreign policy of Albania, which directly influences regional (in)stability.

It is important to note that the Albanian population forms a geographically compact zone outside the borders of Albania including areas of Kosovo, the Former Yugoslav Republic of Macedonia, Serbia and Montenegro. That is why the situation of Kosovo has a direct impact on the stability of other states that have large Albanian populations. This is especially true in the Former Yugoslav Republic of Macedonia, where the estimated 430,000 Albanians represent 21 per cent of the country's total population.

In 1945 Kosovo was incorporated into Yugoslavia, but unlike other federal units it did not have the right to secede from the federation. Kosovo was granted an autonomous status. The 1969 and 1974 constitution considerably enlarged the competencies of the autonomy it enjoyed. This status, however, was abolished by the Milošević regime in 1989.

The total population of Kosovo is approximately two million. The demographic evolution of Kosovo over the last decades drastically altered the ethnic composition of the region. In 1981, Albanians composed 81 per cent of the population and Serbs 14.8 per cent. Due to higher birth rates among the Albanian population and Serb migrations from Kosovo to other parts of Yugoslavia and abroad, the ratio increased to 90 per cent in favour of the Albanians by the end of the 1990s.[92] After the 1999 NATO intervention, Serbs left the province of Kosovo in large numbers. Hence, Albanian claims for independence have been bolstered. Meanwhile, the insecurity of the Serb population remaining in Kosovo has worsened.

The geopolitical representation of Kosovo plays an important role in the collective mentality of Serbs. As noted, it is perceived as a holy land and the cradle of the Serb nation. National myths and symbols of Serbs are closely linked to Kosovo. Moreover, the presence of a great number of orthodox churches and monuments in the region contribute to the crucial importance of Kosovo for Serb national identity.

Another important geopolitical aspect to be considered is the geostrategic situation of Kosovo. The Balkan region, as the French geopolitical expert Alexandre del Valle[93] points out, is a key connecting region because it is situated between Western Europe, the Caucasus, Central Asia, the Middle East and North Africa. Control of the Balkan region is essential not only for geo-strategic but also for geo-economic reasons. The transport of goods and energy (oil and gas) in the region is of major economic concern.

From 1989 to 1999, Albanians sought the independence of Kosovo. The 1999 military intervention by NATO against Yugoslavia, officially based on humanitarian grounds, allowed the Atlantic Alliance to have a permanent presence in Kosovo. The construction of an enormous American military base called 'Bondsteel' in Kosovo proves the strategic interests of NATO in the region.[94] These motivations have influenced the Kosovo situation.

The internationalization of the conflict with the NATO military intervention left the future status of Kosovo uncertain. On 10 June 1999, NATO bombing was suspended and UN Security Council Resolution 1244 soon after established a United Nations protectorate. Resolution 1244 was an explicit recognition that Kosovo would remain within the Federal Republic of Yugoslavia. Its objective was the implementation of substantial autonomy and meaningful self-administration for Kosovo.

The two contradictory aims—self-determination of the Albanian community and the respect of the territorial integrity of Yugoslavia claimed by the Serbs—are in competition and raise a number of questions: will Albanians be considered the rightful administrators of Kosovo based on their right of self-determination, or should they form a national minority in Yugoslavia? Based on the definition of their status, do they have the right to self-determination? Will Albania accept the territorial status quo? What kind of territorial restructuring, if any, can assure stability and peaceful multiethnic coexistence in the region?

The evolution of the situation in Kosovo may lead to a *de facto* independent state. A large portion of the Serb minority, as noted, has left the province.[95] The euro has become the main means of payment. The UCK largely controls Kosovo's administration, security and economy. And there is little sign of peaceful coexistence between Serbs and Albanians.

On 17 November 2001, Kosovars voted for a new Assembly. Formally, this election and the formation of institutions of self-government was a step forward in the implementation of Security Council Resolution 1244, which recognized self-government and autonomy but rejected the granting of full independence to Kosovo. Today Kosovo remains an international protectorate administered by the UN.

The result of the elections confirmed the desire for independence by the Albanian majority of Kosovo. All political parties representing the Albanian population in the newly elected Assembly proclaimed the goal of independence for Kosovo. The existence of a democratically elected Assembly, in which the overwhelming majority of the elected representatives want independent statehood, will make it very difficult to maintain the status quo. The Albanian political parties of Kosovo might organize a referendum on independence in the near future.

On the other hand, the secessionist tendency of Montenegro could be reinforced should the re-negotiating of constitutional ties between Serbia and Montenegro fail. Montenegrin authorities announced their intention to create an independent state if Belgrade does not approve a radical transformation of Yugoslavia into a confederation of sovereign states.[96] An eventual secession of Montenegro would mean the end of Yugoslavia. In that case Kosovo might become an independent state and the fate of the Hungarian minority of Vojvodina would be uncertain. An independent Kosovo might also result in the disintegration of Macedonia. Albanians in Macedonia would probably opt for their unification with Kosovo. Then, this new independent state could unite with Albania, creating a 'Greater Albania'.

Furthermore, the independence of Kosovo and Montenegro, with the eventual reunification of all Albanians in the same state could lead to the further disintegration of Bosnia-Herzegovina. New armed conflicts could occur which would further destabilize the Balkans.

2.6 Internal Dynamics of Yugoslavia: Integration Versus Fragmentation

The situation of Serbia heavily influences the geopolitical dynamics of Central and South Eastern Europe. There are two major possibilities for the future evolution of Serbia: integration or fragmentation. A redefinition of relations among the various entities in Serbia-Montenegro and the central authority of Belgrade is inevitable, and if a consensus can be reached on this matter, a process of integration can be envisaged. Indeed, the recent change of the political system can be expected to lead to a new distribution of power among the different territorial constituents of Serbia-Montenegro.

In this process of decentralization, Vojvodina, Montenegro and Kosovo could gain a new status within a framework of regional autonomy, be it within a federation or confederation. Internal integration within the framework of a new federal state of Yugoslavia would help its external integration both on a regional and European level.

An eventual settlement with regards to the status of Kosovo should not only define the political and legal status of this province but also that of Vojvodina and Montenegro. Moreover, it should be part of a political and economic integration process for the entire region of South Eastern Europe. Otherwise, destabilization with serious consequences for the entire region could take place in the near future.

3. TOWARDS A POSSIBLE SOLUTION FOR STATES AND SUBNATIONAL ENTITIES

3.1 Internal Self-Determination

From a geopolitical point of view, both the actual process of self-determination and the rigid application of the principle of territorial integrity should be reexamined in order to develop a new framework for dealing with the question of national minorities in South Eastern and Central Europe.

External self-determination includes the right of secession and independence; a given national group can establish a new state or it can unite with the nation-state of its ethnic origin. The recognition of internal self-determination, on the other hand, does not necessarily mean the modification of the territorial integrity of the state. In this case a subnational entity can obtain a special status within the framework of autonomy, regionalization or federalism within the existing state borders. In this scenario, the right of secession is renounced by the subnational group.

Therefore, the use of internal self-determination could be a middle way between the two antagonistic principles in international law: self-determination and territorial integrity. This solution supposes a compromise between national groups composing the state; a subnational community renounces the right of secession, thereby protecting the territorial integrity of the state, while the state guarantees the constitutional and political framework necessary for the different forms of minority self-government.[97] Expanding the political options offered by the interpretation of the principle of self-determination with the different forms of cultural and political autonomy would provide an effective instrument for conflict prevention and resolution.[98]

Internal self-determination can coincide with a state's interest because the state can maintain its sovereignty and territorial integrity and simultaneously delegate more power to regions in order to improve the country's capacity to compete in a globalized geo-economic system. As Philippe Moreau Defarges affirms, states in geo-economic competition should have a different vision of their territory. Contrary to the traditional role of protection and differentiation, states should open their territories and improve their conditions to confront the challenges of geo-economic rivalry.[99]

Internal self-determination linked to regional autonomy has been put into effect in several Western European states. Catalonia in Spain is a good example of the implementation of internal self-determination, which could be considered "as the assertion that nations have the right to negotiate their position within the state and international order".[100] The autonomy solution of South Tyrol is also an example of internal self-determination. Territorial integrity of the Italian state is respected; neither Austria nor the majority of the German-speaking minority want territorial modifications.

3.2 Implementation of Autonomies

One of the major problems concerning the concept of autonomy is that it does not have an exact definition.[101] Besides, there is no universal model of autonomy which could be implemented everywhere. In order to develop an appropriate form of autonomy, political actors should take into consideration historical, geographical, cultural and economic factors. Moreover, the implementation of autonomy should be a gradual process in order to respect the equilibrium of the society concerned and ensure the emergence of a strong civil society. An autonomy project should be supported by civil society, both of the majority and the minority, and should not be based exclusively on ethno-cultural affiliation. As Michael Keating affirms, one of the imperatives of any autonomy regime is to remain open to external influences, in particular to cultural ones.[102]

Autonomy is best defined as the provision of all necessary means (legal, political, institutional, economic and cultural) for the preservation and development of minority identity with respect to the territorial integrity of the state in which they live.[103] Autonomy is a form of power-sharing, based on a consensus between the minority and the majority, which reflects the principle of subsidiarity. According to this principle, when local and regional authorities can decide and elaborate policies more efficiently than the central government, they should have the power to do so. The use of subsidiarity can improve minority participation in the political decision-making process. This principle is an important contribution to democracy in Europe because it promotes the legitimate interaction among various levels of power: local, regional, national and supranational (European).[104]

66

Moreover, an autonomous regime should seek to achieve the following objectives: develop the economic performance of the region for effective participation in geo-economic competition, promote social integration, provide an open and democratic political system, and find an equilibrium between national interest and regional interest in a larger framework.[105]

There are different forms of autonomy which often overlap each other. A basic distinction can be made between two major categories:

- territorial autonomy;
- personal (non-territorial autonomy).[106]

The first includes regional autonomy, territorial autonomy of special status and local autonomy. The second consists of cultural and administrative autonomies. The best approach is to combine these different forms of autonomy according to the socio-cultural, economic and geographic characteristics of the given region and the minority group in question.

Territorial autonomy could be implemented in areas of the state where minorities form the majority of the population. These regions should have a special status that is defined in the constitution. This status should include:[107]

- constitutional definition of the status of autonomy;
- legal recognition of the language status of the region;
- an educational system and cultural facilities that correspond to the needs of the given community;
- legal, administrative and political structures of self-government;
- fiscal autonomy;
- implementation of international (bilateral or multilateral) supervision mechanisms;
- a system of 'positive discrimination' in favour of the persons belonging to other ethno-cultural groups than the majority in the autonomous region.

Local autonomy refers to the auto-administration of a minority living in small areas. The degree of autonomy is less than in the previous case; it aims at assuring the full application of democratic principles through the participation of members of the local collectives in public life.[108]

The concept of personal or non-territorial autonomy was developed by two Austro-Marxists, Otto Bauer and Carl Renner in 1907 to find a solution for the nationality problem in the Austro-Hungarian Empire at the beginning of the twentieth century.[109] It was not based on the notion of territory, but rather on the ethno-cultural identity of a person. It can be applied:

- in areas where the geographic distribution of ethnic groups is mixed and therefore territorial autonomy cannot be implemented;
- in regions where minorities are geographically dispersed in small communities;
- if a territorial autonomy is already implemented for a community representing the majority in the area, then personal autonomy could protect the minority group that lives in the same zone but does not benefit from the advantages of territorial autonomy; and
- for minorities who do not live on a fixed territory, such as the Roma.

The implementation of personal autonomy is not incompatible with the different forms of territorial autonomy. Decentralization processes can proceed together with both principles.

In order to implement autonomy, the concept of the unitary nation-state might have be redefined. The different ethno-cultural communities living in a state could be recognized as constituent nations within that state. The concept of a multinational state based on shared sovereignty might be an option to replace the unitary nation-state model.

3.3 Transborder Cooperation and Regional Integration

The existence of a border region with a minority population can be considered in two different ways. From a unitary nation-state's point of view these areas are dangerous because they can challenge the idea of homogenous state structure and can represent cause for border readjustments. On the other hand, these border regions, like in Western Europe, can act as a catalyst for a transregional integration process. As Remigio Ratti states, "according to historical situations and contingencies, a frontier can be a separating line, or, on the contrary, a contact area".[110]

The modification of state borders cannot solve the minority question in Central Europe due to the geographic distribution of ethnic communities, as mentioned earlier. The solution would be to open state borders in order to eliminate their 'border-barrier' effects. Border regions in Central Europe should become a contact area, as has happened in the European Union.

Transborder cooperation could serve this purpose; it could lay down a framework for relations between the political-institutional and socio-economic subsystems of the bordering countries to create open-border areas. This could reduce tensions in multiethnic regions, such as Vojvodina in Serbia and Transylvania in Romania, and could give impetus to regional integration.

The territorial decentralization within the Italian state considerably enlarged the ability of Italian regions, such as South Tyrol, to participate in interregional cooperation on a European level.[111] Cultural, economic, ethnic and geographic factors have played an important role in the development of transborder cooperation in South Tyrol, but the fact that both Austria and Italy are part of the EU greatly facilitates cross-border and inter-regional relations. The political border dividing Tyrol between Austria and Italy has lost much of its significance. South Tyrol also actively participates in multilateral, transborder and inter-regional cooperation processes in the framework of the ARGE ALP and Alps-Adria initiatives.

3.4 Euro-Region Projects: Towards a New Geopolitical and Geo-economic Integration Dynamics

The successful implementation of different Euro-region projects can have a very positive impact on multiethnic regions in Central Europe. Within the framework of these projects, important geopolitical and geo-economic zones situated in border regions of two or more countries can be reconnected.

The Tyrol Euro-region project illustrates this point. Artificially divided by political frontiers, the northern part of Tyrol is situated in Austria while the southern portion lies in Italy. They will essentially be reconnected by the Tyrol Euro-region project. The creation of Euro-regions does not, however, mean the secession of regions from their respective states as some authors claim.[112] Rather, it follows the logic of European integration and worldwide geo-economic competition. The logic of geographical proximity and pressures of economic interdependence have contributed to a strong movement toward regionalization. Globalization has led to the blurring of national and international boundaries, at least in Europe. Moreover, globalization has also resulted in the erosion of state sovereignty and the transmission of a global, universalistic subculture through a worldwide mass communication network. A counter-tendency of these processes has been a more profound search for identity, which many have found in religion, ethnicity and culture. This tendency has reinforced regional identity in Europe.

The traditional concept of sovereignty based on a Westphalian conception of the state system has altered significantly over the last few decades; sovereignty is more recently diffused among different power centres. The emerging geopolitical and geo-economic world system has four levels:[113]

- a global regime with international organizations (UN, IMF, OSCE, etc);
- continental blocs (European Union, NAFTA, MERCOSUR, etc.);
- states;
- regions.

Integration dynamics have been shaped by the interrelations between these power centres. This emerging system with the previously noted factors (search for identity, regionalization, geo-economic competition, erosion of state sovereignty) will contribute to the growing importance of regions not only in the EU but in Central and South Eastern Europe as well. Regional integration, often called 'micro integration', can complement 'macro integration' on a continental European level.

Let us briefly mention the Carpathian Euro-region project conceived in 1993. Five countries participate: Hungary, Poland, Slovakia, Romania and the Ukraine. The regional integration process of the Carpathian Euro-region project can provide positive support for the long-term integration of these countries into EU structures.[114]

Frontiers can gradually open and the objective of free movement of persons, goods and capital can be promoted within different time frames. The Carpathian Euro-region is an initiative that promotes cross-border, inter-regional economic, scientific, cultural, educational and sporting relations among participant border states. It also supports common cross-border projects and the intensification of collaboration with different international organizations and institutions.[115]

This regional integration process through the Carpathian Euro-region project can be beneficial for all minorities in the region. Exchanges between minority groups and their home country can become more frequent and cultural exchanges and other forms of collaboration can improve mutual understanding among all ethnic groups living in different border regions.

Regionalization necessitates a significant decentralization of power. Central state authorities must delegate part of the decision-making process to the local or regional level. This power-sharing between regional and central authorities can provide a good framework for the implementation of different autonomy structures that would be beneficial to minorities.

4. CONCLUSION

The sudden reemergence of the national question after the end of the Cold War has created an incredibly complicated geopolitical situation in South Eastern and Central Europe. The problem of national minorities there (closely connected with border issues) has shown that its implications affect not only the respective region, but European and international security as well.

From a geopolitical point of view, the main problems associated with national minorities originate from two factors: first, the application of the concept of the unitary nation-state which cannot satisfy the legitimate claims of minorities to preserve their identity; and second, that the process of self-determination and the application of the tenet of territorial integrity do not allow for much leeway in working out peaceful solutions to the structuring of multiethnic states. Moreover, in Central Europe it is nearly impossible to modify political frontiers to perfectly correlate to nationalities. New nation-states cannot satisfy the aspirations of national communities due do their mixed geographical distribution.

A new strategy of territorial organization should be developed in order to foster stability in the region. The implementation of different forms of autonomy based on internal self-determination with the creation of 'open-border' regions can provide a new framework for the peaceful coexistence of multiethnic states in South Eastern and Central Europe.

As the South Tyrol region indicates, a well-developed framework that includes different levels of autonomy can provide the conditions to generate stability, democratic participation and economic well-being of multiethnic communities. The autonomy of South Tyrol is a concrete example of European regional integration based on peoples with different languages and cultures living together in the name of common interest in a power-sharing management of territory.[116]

A long-term solution for minorities in Central and South Eastern Europe should follow the same path. The implementation of regional, territorial and personal autonomies for minorities could assure the basis of a strategy of regional integration.

NOTES

[71]   The term 'national minority' was defined by the Council of Europe in 1993 in Recommendation 1201 "as a group of persons in a state who: reside on the territory of that state and are citizens thereof; maintain longstanding, firm and lasting ties with that state; display distinctive ethnic, cultural, religious, or linguistic characteristics; are sufficiently representative, although smaller in number than the rest of the population of that state or of a region of that state; are motivated by a concern to preserve together that which constitutes their common identity, including their culture, their traditions, their religion or their language".

[72]   Michel Foucher, *Fronts et Frontières* (Paris: Fayard, 1991), p.12.

[73]   Pierre Behar, *Une nouvelle géopolitique pour l'Europe* (Paris: Desjonqueres, 1992), p.163.

[74]   Gérard A. Montifroy, *Puissances et Conflits* (Montréal: Editions du Fleuve, 1990), p.22.

[75]   Saul B. Cohen, *Geography and Politics in a World Divided* (New York and Oxford: Oxford University Press, 1973), p.25; Pierre M. Gallois, *Géopolitique. Les voies de la puissance* (Paris: Plon, 1990), p.37.

[76]   Yves Lacoste, "Préambule", in *Dictionnaire de géopolitique* (Paris: Flammarion, p.3).

[77]   On the relations between geo-economics and geopolitics, see Edward Luttwak, *The Endangered American Dream* (New York: Touchstone, 1994); Edward Luttwak, *Turbocapitalism. Winners and Losers in the Global Economy* (London: Weidenfeld & Nicolson, 1998); Pascal Lorot et al., *Introduction à la géoéconomie* (Paris: Economica, 1999).

[78]   Aymeric Chauprade, *Introduction à l'analyse géopolitique* (Paris: Ellipses, 1999).

[79]   Gérard A. Montifroy, *Puissances et Conflits* (Montréal: Feluve, 1990), pp.48–58.

[80]   François Thual, *Méthodes de la géopolitique* (Paris: Ellipses,1996), p.65.

[81]   John Coakley, "Introduction: The Territorial Management of Ethnic Conflict", in *The Territorial Management of Ethnic Conflict*, John Coakley, ed. (London: Gainsborough House, 1993), p.2.

[82]   Ekkehard W. Bornträger, *Borders, Ethnicity, and National Self-Determination*, Ethnos, N°52 (Wien: Braumüller, 1999), p.22.

[83]   André L. Sanguin, *La Géographie Politique* (Paris: PUF, 1977), p.7.

84   Statement issued by the "Conference of Hungary and Ethnic Hungarian Communities Beyond the Borders", Budapest, 20 February 1999.

85   While during the Cold War the term Eastern Europe was attributed to a very heterogeneous group of communist countries, since 1989 different geopolitical blocs have been emerging in the zone situated between Russia and Germany (the Baltic region, the group of Orthodox Slav nations, the countries of the former Habsburg empire and so on). Debates are continuing about the exact delimitation of these geopolitical regions. For the purpose of this study the geographic zone situated between Russia and Germany is meant when South Eastern and Central Europe are referred to.

86   Guy Heraud, *L'Europe des ethnies* (Paris: Bruylant LGDJ, 1993), pp.190–192.

87   Morton H. Halperin and David J. Schiffer with Patricia L. Small, *Self-Determination in the New World Order* (Carnegie Endowment for International Peace, Washington, D.C., 1992), p.84.

88   On this subject see Michel Foucher, *Fronts et Frontières* (Paris: Fayard, 1991).

89   Victor-Yves Ghebali, *La Diplomatie de la Détente: la CSCE d'Helsinki à Vienne (1973–1989)* (Bruxelles: Bruylant, 1989), p.83.

90   For more details on Kosovo, see the study by Weller in this book.

91   Yves Lacoste, *Dictionnaire de Géopolitique* (Paris: Flammarion, 1995), p.88.

92   Michel Roux's analysis of the impact of the demographic evolution on the geopolitical situation of Kosovo is pertinent. Michel Roux, *Les Albanais en Yugoslavie* (Paris: Edition de la Maison des Sciences de l'Homme, 1992).

93   Alexandre del Valle, *Guerres contre l'Europe* (Paris: Syrtes, 2000), pp.176–177.

94   Donald William, *Le Choc des Temps* (Montréal: Frison Roche and Paris: Science Culture, 2000), pp.186–198.

95   According to an estimate of the UNHCR, more than 140,000 Serbs had already left Kosovo by July 1999.

96   *The Economist,* 14–20 August 1999.

97   The Barcelona Conference "The Implementation of the Right to Self-Determination as a Contribution to Conflict Prevention", Catalonia, 1999, organized by the UNESCO.

98   Dr. Pau Puigi Scotoni, *The Implementation of the Right to Self-Determination in the European Union—A Strategic Approach*, presented at the 55th session of the UN Commission on Human Rights, United Nations, Geneva, 20–24 March 1999.

99   Philipe Moreau Defarges, *Introduction à la géopolitique* (Paris: Seuil, 1994), pp.165–179.

100 Michael Keating, "Self-Determination, Multinational States, and the Transnational Order", p.172, presentation at the Barcelona Conference "The Implementation of the Right to Self-Determination as a Contribution to Conflict Prevention", Catalonia, 1999, organized by the UNESCO.

101 For more details on this, see the studies by Brunner and Küpper, as well as by Vizi in this book.

102 Michael Keating, *Les défis du nationalisme moderne. Québec, Catalogne, Ecosse* (Montréal: Les Presses de l'Université de Montréal and Bruxelles: Presses Interuniversitaires Européennes, 1997), p.72.

103 Gyula Csurgai, "La question des minorités en Europe centrale et balkanique sous l'angle géopolitique", in *L'Europe en formation,* 303 (CIFE, NICE, France, 1997), p.58.

104 Various documents points out the importance of subsidiarity: European Charter of Local Self-Government, European Charter for regional Self-Government, European Charter for Regional and Minority Languages, Conference of Local and Regional Authorities of Europe among others.

105 Keating, *Les défis, op.cit.*, p.73.

106 For a more detailed discussion, see the general comparative study by Brunner and Küpper in this book.

[107] On this matter it is useful to study the competencies of South Tyrol autonomy to elaborate a more detailed list. See *L'Autonomia dell'Alto Adige, Provincia Autonoma di Bolzano-Alto Adige 1994*, Giunta provinciale, Bolzano, Italy.

[108] *Déclaration finale de la Conférence sur la régionalisation en Europe*, Geneva, 3–5 June 1993, p.3.

[109] Otto Bauer, *Die Nationaltätenfrage und die Sozialdemokratie* (Wien: Ignaz Brand, 1907).

[110] Remigio Ratti and Shalom Reichman, *Theory and Practice of Transborder Cooperation* (Basel: Helbing & Lichtenhahn, 1993), p.23.

[111] "South Tyrol: A European Border Region", (Budapest: Minority Protection Association, 1998), p.23.

[112] Bruno Luverà, "L'Internazionale Regionalista Tra Maschera e Volto", *LIMES Rivista Italiana di Geopolitica*, 3 (1996): pp.35–58.

[113] Allen J. Scott, "La nouvelle géoéconomie des regions", in *Introduction à la géoéconomie*, Pascal Lorot, ed. (Paris: Economica, 1999), p.71.

[114] Attila Gergely, "Integráció, Globalizáció, Regionális fejlődés", (Budapest: Teleki László Institute, Centre for Foreign Policy, 1999), p.16.

[115] Süli-Zakar István, "A határokon átnyúló (transznacionális) regionalizmus az Európai Unióban és Kelet-Közép Európában", in *Alföld és Nagyvilág* (Budapest: Magyar Tudományos Akadémia, Földrajztudományi Kutató Intézet, 2000), p.115.

[116] Francesco Palermo, "Self-Government (and Other?) Instruments", in *The Constitutional and Political Regulation of Ethnic Relations and Conflicts*, Mitja Zagar, Boris Jesih, Romana Bester, eds. (Ljubljana: Institute for Ethnic Studies, 1999), p.311.

Minority Self-Governance in Economic Perspective

François Vaillancourt and François Grin

Minority Self-Governance in Economic Perspective

François Vaillancourt and François Grin[117]

1. INTRODUCTION

The purpose of this paper is to provide an introduction to the main analytical tools used by economists in examining models of governance and to apply them to issues of self-governance as they appear in the debate on the legal and political position of minorities. This problem is of interest: firstly because minority issues have, in recent years, taken on increasing geopolitical saliency, thereby increasing the relevance of various forms of power-sharing arrangements, with the attendant questions of distribution of competencies in economic matters, and secondly because the rationale of the economic approach has remained relatively under-utilized in the predominantly legal and institutional approaches usually brought to bear on the comparison between models of minority self-governance.

This paper is divided into three parts: the first reviews the economic literature on 'federalism' (the blanket term used by economists working on these questions), as developed by classical authors in the field of public economics. The second proposes a brief reinterpretation, in economic perspective, of some of the key distinctions between models of self-governance found in the work of legal and political scholars. The third part uses the concepts reviewed in the first part, together with some concepts developed in the economics of language, to analyze core questions in the governance of linguistic diversity. A brief conclusion will outline priorities for further research.

2. THE ECONOMICS OF FEDERALISM

One of the long-established areas of economic analysis is 'public economics,' also referred to as 'public finance'. Economists working in this field were first and foremost concerned with establishing the theoretical foundations of the role of the state; milestones in this literature are contributions by the founding fathers of contemporary economic theory, in particular Adam Smith and John Stuart Mill, in the eighteenth and nineteenth century respectively. However, little work was done on what level of government should carry out what function until the second half of the twentieth century. Today, most countries are organized with at least two levels of government institutions, namely, central government (CG) and local government (LG), and often three with subnational governments (SNG) also present. Considerable differences exist between the powers of SNGs in different countries. In some states, there are no SNGs, with just administrative divisions of the CG instead, while in others, SNGs are strong and highly autonomous units. International differences also exist regarding the extent of the competencies exercised by LGs, but in most countries they are responsible, like municipalities, for a core group of activities such as the maintenance of parks and streets, garbage removal, etc. In some countries, the functions of LGs are more diverse and include the provision of education and health services. In these cases, LGs may include not only municipalities, but also, for example, school boards with jurisdiction over specific geographical areas or other types of specially created districts. Even though the context within which these various manifestations of decentralization occur is not necessarily one of 'federalism' in the legal or political sense of the word, this is, as noted earlier, the term commonly used by economists, which justifies its use in the title of this section.

The first attempt at establishing, in economic perspective, what level of government should carry out what function was Musgrave's 1959 treatise on public finance. This work shifted attention away from the then dominant concern for macroeconomic management issues towards micro-economic concerns. The former, which includes, for example, monetary and fiscal policy, were then the primary focus of economic works on the role of government, partially attributable to the popularity of Keynesian theory.[118]

Musgrave proposed the following distribution of powers, based on a fundamental distinction between stabilization policies, income redistribution and the allocation of services.

1) *Stabilization policies:* since monetary and fiscal policy should be closely coordinated and since monetary policy is always a central government responsibility, fiscal policy must also be set at the central level. This implies that the CG should have a sufficient size in terms of expenditure, particularly capital ones, and be able to collect enough tax revenue to influence the level of macroeconomic activity. SNGs, however, can act as implementers of CG policies. To this end, they may be guided by a system of grants from the CG. The relevance of this prescription has decreased with the reduction in macroeconomic interventions by CGs since 1980, owing both to the increase in the sophistication of markets (reflected in the 'rational expectations model', where actors are assumed to anticipate the evolution of key economic variables, thereby depriving most forms of macroeconomic policies of their effectiveness) and to the decreasing capacity of CGs to influence increasingly open economies.

2) *Income distribution:* the CG should be responsible for programmes that redistribute income between individuals (social security, welfare, unemployment insurance, etc.), since individuals would have a general incentive to migrate from the least to the most generous SNG within the state. This recommendation was implicitly made for single labour-market countries with no internal barriers to labour mobility. If there are such barriers, like those that arise in multilingual countries where members of minority language groups reside in specific areas and may not be as mobile as members of the majority group because they do not know the majority language as well (or because they fear to lose their linguistic or cultural identity if they move to a majority language area), SNGs have more scope to play a significant role in income redistribution.

3) *Allocation:* the CG, SNGs and LGs all have a role to play in carrying out this function, which covers the provision of public services ranging from agricultural support to the provision of education, health and transportation, among others.

The exact role to be played by each level of government can be better established by turning to the criteria developed by Oates. Wallace Oates[119] puts forward four criteria to assign specific roles to specific levels of government. These four criteria are economies of scale, heterogeneity of preferences, externalities and emulation (or competition).

1) *Economies of scale:* economies of scale occur when the unit cost of producing a particular good (or service) goes down as the number of users (or consumers) goes up. One example in which economies of scale is significant is television broadcasting, where unit cost per viewer drops by half when the number of viewers of a given programme doubles. On the other hand, economies of scale are negligible in the provision of individualized health services such as surgical treatment. The existence of significant economies of scale constitutes an argument for the provision of a particular good or service by a larger government; that is, by the CG rather than the SNG, or by the SNG rather than some LG.

2) *Heterogeneity of preferences:* economics is, at heart, a theory of the efficient allocation of scarce resources that have alternative uses, as well as a tool for implementing such allocations. This raises the question of people's preferences for allocating scarce resources to certain uses over others, and also explains why preferences play such a central part in economic analysis, no matter what the topic being considered may be.[120] If groups living in different parts of a country display strong heterogeneity of preferences regarding, for example, the language in which public services are delivered, the amount provided of such services, or the nature of public intervention, then decentralization to SNGs or LGs is appropriate—if their jurisdications are separated by borders that correspond with those separating groups of people with differentiated preferences.

3) *Externalities:* externalities arise when the action of one actor (be it an individual, a firm, or a level of government) affects (positively or negatively) the situation of other actors,[121] without the latter being compensated for it (in the case of *negative externalities*) or contributing to it (in the case of *positive externalities*). A classical example of negative externality is air pollution: the environmental damages caused by smoke emissions from an industrial plant decreases the quality of life for people who live in the area, but the latter are not compensated for this loss. A classical example of positive externality is bees and apple trees, with bees needing pollen to make honey, and trees needing bees to pollinate them. The owner of the orchard benefits from the fact that his or her neighbour keeps beehives; the owner of the beehives benefits from the fact that his or her neighbour has apple trees. Both types of benefits arise without any matching contribution being paid by the person gaining from it to the person whose activity gives rise to the benefit; in this example, benefits are mutual, but they may also flow in one direction only.[122] If some of the activities of a government have important 'external effects' (positive or negative externalities) on others actors, then these activities should be more centralized; that is, they should be located at the level of the CG rather than SNGs, or a SNG rather than an LG; at the very least, the action of lower-level authorities should be well coordinated.

4) *Emulation or competition:* in order to increase or introduce best practices in government, one needs at least two, and probably more, units involved in a given activity; further-more, citizens and civil servant must be able to acquire the relevant information.[123] This is a general argument for decentralizing governmental activities.

The reader should note here that we have not, thus far, explicitly defined the concept of decentralization. This concept covers three different choices, namely, deconcentration, delegation and devolution.

1) Deconcentration occurs when the CG retains responsibility for a given action but transfers execution of it from central government offices in the capital city to field offices.

2) Delegation occurs when the CG retains a responsibility but transfers the execution to SNGs or LGs with or without appropriate funds—that is, entrusting lower-level authorities with funded or unfunded mandates respectively.

3) Devolution occurs when the CG transfers responsibility for a given activity to SNGs or LGs.

The reader should note that Oates's is a top-down model where the CG is assumed to have authority over all fields of jurisdiction and to be in a position to decide which ones should be decentralized. However, the situation also arises, particularly in federal states, where sovereignty rests with the SNGs, who may then cede some powers to the CG when the federal state is created and as subsequent constitutional amendments are adopted, resulting in further competence transfers.[124]

Finally, it is useful to introduce the 'club model' proposed by Buchanan in 1965.[125] This model was developed from a local government perspective. It states that individuals with similar preferences will regroup by moving geographically or by joining common institutions in order to jointly consume some goods and services that are costly to provide at the household level. For example, tennis players (or swimmers) can either move to a city which is known for the quantity and quality of its tennis facilities (or swimming pools), or they can remain in their city of residence and join a private tennis (or swimming) club, incurring higher costs to it to enjoy the facilities. In this manner, private clubs can act as substitutes of governments in the provision of certain quasi-public services.

Once the issue of 'who does what' is clarified, the next issue to turn to is how the provision of those services is financed. In general, economists recommend that each level of government should finance itself by an appropriate mix of taxes and user fees. In the case of federations, the degree of mobility of the tax base is the main criterion for allocating various tax fields between various levels of government as shown in Table 1.1.

Table 1.1
Allocation of Tax Fields

Tax base	Capital	Consumption and labour	Property
Mobility of tax base	High	Medium	Low
Government level	Central (CG)	Subnational (SNG)	Local (LG)

Economists generally agree that it is preferable for tax fields to be solely occupied (that is, for only one level of government to levy a certain type of tax), but this is not usually feasible in practice for personal income and goods and services taxes. In the case of 'joint occupation' of a tax field, the usual prescription is for SNGs to be allowed to set their own tax *rate* on a common (CG/SNG) tax *base*, with taxes collected by one level of government and remitted to others; collection by each level of government increases costs.

In most countries, CGs collect an excess of revenue over expenditure needs, and are, therefore, in the position to transfer financial resources to SNGs or LGs. This then raises the issue of how these transfers are managed. Transfers and grants can be tied to the resources and/or to the needs of the recipient units; the rationale for tying the former with the latter can be a concern for equalizing the conditions between SNGs or between LGs. Furthermore, transfers may be tied to a specific type of spending, and they may be conditional on a certain spending effort by the recipient. In general, untied or unconditional grants give more freedom to recipients than tied or conditional grants. Block grants are a typical example of transfers which afford the highest degree of freedom to the recipient units.

3. MODELS OF SELF-GOVERNANCE FOR LINGUISTIC MINORITIES: AN ECONOMIC INTERPRETATION

In this and the following section we discuss the case of linguistic minorities, in which language issues can be expected to be more salient features of autonomy. Consequently, language is a dimension that needs to be accounted for in the assessment of the operations, benefits and costs of the corresponding autonomy arrangement.

Much of the literature on the self-governance of linguistic minorities is rooted in the disciplines of international law, international relations or political science. A brief review of this literature, however, suggests that the joint questions of the allocation of duties and their financing is hardly ever addressed. For the most part, this literature does not yield a typology of self-governance models. What regularly emerges, however, is the distinction between the personality and the territoriality principles of language legislation, which of course carries certain consequences for governance. This apparent disregard for the issues of service provision and their financing may result from the fact that much of the political and academic discourse about minority governance rests on the notion of rights. For example, one major question seems to be whether minorities have an unqualified right to self-determination—or whether it is merely an internal right that applies solely within the boundaries of the nation-state into which they are currently integrated.[126]

From an economic perspective, however, these questions are not very relevant. Economists view rights as parameters or constraints affecting the behaviour of individuals, firms and states, which then make decisions given those constraints; in other words, the examination of the nature of rights and how those rights emerge is clearly placed outside of the range of questions that economics should study. However, a few economists go further in the analysis of the economic meaning of rights. From an economic standpoint, the only 'rights' that exist are those that can be enforced. This ultimately means that not only the beneficiary of those rights, but also the entity which has the capacity to enforce them, must find an interest in the existence of those rights. Consequently, whatever 'rights' actually exist only reflect the convergence of the interests of different groups of actors in society, and the notion of rights could, from an analytical perspective, be dispensed with almost entirely, since even if they are treated as given parameters (analytically, operating as constraints), they hark back to deeper, presumably more relevant factors ('more relevant', that is, from the standpoint of mainstream economics).[127]

Economists usually view the world as one whose guiding organizing principle is market exchange, but after property rights have been allocated. Of course, at its origin, a system of property rights often arises as a result of force, and in this sense, economics is deeply Hobbesian. However, the role of economic analysis is usually assumed to begin once that stage of brute force has passed and conflicts have been resolved (or are now solvable) through legal means. What initially allows the emergence of an alternative to brute force (including the establishment of the state to guarantee so-called 'rights') is nothing but the fact that the strong see an interest (self or altruistic) in protecting the weak. Jeremy Bentham famously summed this up by stating that it is in the wolf's interest that the sheep be fat and numerous. Economic, social and cultural rights[128] then only exist as part of a progressively complex social contract which the strong find it advantageous to support. The precise extent of the rights enjoyed by given individuals and groups can be seen as a function of their position in society but will also depend on the governance arrangements. In a democratic society, the relative strength of various groups will depend on their absolute size, their voting patterns, the type of democracy (parliamentary or other) and the role of SNGs.

If the only rights that exist are those that can be enforced, and if rights will be enforced by those who do so only if it is in their interest to do so, then economic analysis will have little to say about rights themselves, beyond the fundamental analysis of the nature of rights just sketched out. However, economic analysis is useful in the treatment of two questions which arise 'downstream' with respect to the question of rights: first, how to evaluate, economically, the consequences of rights—which amounts to the identification and measurement of those consequences; and second, how to choose, economically, between various policy alternatives, each of which is associated with a certain set of rights for all or for some—which amounts to the adoption of a rationale for making choices at the societal level. This procedure requires consideration of allocative and distributive aspects.

Before a more in-depth discussion of these topics let us briefly assess the economic consequences of adopting one or more of the following models:[129]

1) *The personality principle* to minority language rights (and governance) is conceptually similar to the club model introduced in the preceding section. Members of a minority are given access to certain services in their language, whatever their place of residence in the country, or perhaps in certain parts of the country, even if they do not constitute a majority there. The key difference is that they do not fund these services directly by paying fees to the service provider (as would be the case for a tennis club), but by paying taxes to the CG or to the SNG. Through their vote, they may influence the latter's policies, under more or less strict constraints imposed by legal and constitutional requirements at the national level, or by international norms. This electoral influence remains, of course, contingent on their absolute and relative numbers in the overall population. Thus, they do not have direct control over the amount of resources devoted to their language or the way in which those resources are spent.

2) *Weak territorial autonomy*, as an approach to minority language rights, is conceptually similar to deconcentration, delegation or devolution with conditional transfers. In the first two cases (deconcentration and delegation), the policy choices are still made by the CG (while SNGs and LGs implement them in the second case). In the third case (devolution), policy choices are likely to remain influenced by funding arrangements controlled by the CG.

3) *The strong territorial autonomy* approach to minority language rights is conceptually similar to devolution with self-financing or unconditional/untied grants.

4. CHOOSING LINGUISTIC GOVERNANCE ARRANGEMENTS: TOWARDS A SET OF GUIDELINES

From an economic analytical standpoint, the choice of governance arrangements in multilingual contexts should be guided by the following considerations, which draw not only on the economics of federalism discussed in the first section, but also on the economics of language,[130] in which particular emphasis is placed on linguistic diversity in society, and on the way in which this diversity can be managed.[131]

1) The possibility of using territorially based arrangements, which depends on the geographic dispersion of the language minority, is of crucial importance. If such arrangements are politically possible, they are preferable to club arrangements since it is easier for minority language groups to exercise some control in federal-type structures. It follows that the selection, design, implementation and ex-post evaluation of policies can be expected to match more closely the needs of linguistic minorities, particularly in the presence of preference heterogeneity.

2) The use of 'special districts' can be considered in order to insert some elements of strong territoriality in an otherwise weak territoriality environment. This is certainly true for schooling, since the provision of a school system in which minority languages can be effectively taught is a prerequisite for the long-term survival of such languages.[132]

3) Self-financing should be encouraged as much as possible; this implies, however, that linguistic minority SNGs should have the right to levy additional taxes, namely, to set their own tax rates while maintaining, together with existing tax authorities, a common tax base and collection procedures in order to minimize collection costs. Additional revenue generated by higher tax rates at SNG or LG level can serve to finance the extra costs they may incur in order to provide special language-related services. Such higher tax rates may even be preferable to alternative forms of financing such as subsidies from the CG in order to clearly identify the additional costs of providing such services to minorities.

4) The preceding general rule, however, should be replaced in the broader context of the value of linguistic diversity for society as a whole. In the same way as environmental quality, the long-term vitality of smaller languages may contribute to the quality of life of all members of society, including non-users of the languages concerned. A strong case can be made, on analytical grounds, that optimal diversity, from the standpoint of society as a whole, is probably finite (or, more to the point, not infinite); but that it is certainly positive—that is, higher than zero, which means that linguistic uniformity is certainly suboptimal, as a logical consequence of the result that some degree of nonzero (positive) diversity is optimal.[133] In this case, cofinancing by the majority of the costs associated with the preservation of minority languages is economically justified. In an economic perspective, however, the justification for the financing (at least in part) of minority language policies out of general tax revenue should be based on these allocative considerations (that is, on regard for aggregate welfare) rather than by invoking notions of rights.[134]

5) The logical framework within which the above principles should be applied is one of comparison between alternatives. A model of governance is only ever 'good' in the sense that it is 'better' than at least one competing option. This requires us to move on to the terrain of policy evaluation, to which the rest of this section is devoted.

First, any model of minority governance entails benefits as well as costs; in principle, all must be evaluated. The theoretical tools provided at this time by the literature, as well as the range of data available in practice, will typically fall short of the needs of a full-fledged evaluation of costs and benefits. However, as a stepping stone towards an extensive identification (which logically precedes measurement) of costs and benefits, it remains useful to make a distinction between market (or quasi-market) costs on the one hand, and non-market costs on the other hand. The former are reflected directly in terms of monetary values which are usually revealed by the interplay of supply and demand on a market. Alternatively, they give rise to relatively easily observable monetary consequences. Choosing a certain mode of governance has an impact on the volume of tax revenue generated and on the level of state expenditures at various levels of government; the different sets of policies that ensue can also impact price and salary levels.[135] The latter, however, also need to be taken into account from a welfare perspective. For example, there are symbolic costs to the non-recognition of minority languages. For the most part, this symbolic cost is borne by speakers of these languages. The fact that this does not give rise to market effects does not imply that they are non-economic (in the same way as welfare loss resulting from environmental damage is an economically relevant element of cost, despite the fact that no market effects arise). The complete evaluation of costs and benefits usually starts at the private level, and appropriate aggregation procedures must then be applied to move from the private to the social level, in order to assess total benefits and costs.[136] When evaluating economic models of minority governance in practice, an exhaustive identification and measurement of benefits and costs is near impossible. The narrower the policy, the more likely it is that a reasonable attempt to evaluate its effects precisely can be made; the broader the policy, the more likely it is that analysts will have to be content with a partial estimate—or with a set of partial estimates.

The general rationale of a comparative investigation would then be to establish a set of indicators belonging to three categories, and to examine how these indicators are related to each other. The blueprint for an economic study of models of self-governance would therefore contain the following set of ingredients.

First, in order to characterize models of self-governance, it is helpful to arrange them in terms of some indicator of their respective degree of autonomy. Given the extreme variance of minority situations, this indicator will be a rather partial one. One possible procedure is to use a quantitative indicator, j, based on the share of public spending per capita under the authority of a decentralized or autonomous government. For example, if total per capita spending on all services provided by the state, directly or indirectly, is EUR 10,000, and if EUR 2,500 of this total is made up of educational and cultural expenditures under the control of the minority community, then the value of the indicator will be j=0.25. In principle, all models can be described in terms of this indicator j.[137] Of course, the degree of autonomy in financing the expenditure also matters, and subnational units that finance their expenditure through taxes which they set and collect themselves are arguably more autonomous than subnational units that are dependent on transfers from the central government. Consequently, it would be possible to refine this indicator, and to multiply the indicator j by another one, denoting the percentage of self-financing of the local or regional community through its own tax regime (this other indicator could be given by the ratio of locally-governed taxes and locally-determined expenditure).

Second, a set of *success indicators* would be required. This can include classical indicators such as per capita income, unemployment rates or, perhaps more relevantly, survey data on people's general satisfaction. A successful autonomy model should score high on such indicators, and one would also expect public expenditure to be, in principle, more thoughtfully and appropriately targeted by an autonomous government—with its more acute awareness of local needs—than by the national government.[138] Ideally, such data should allow for a comparison of an 'ex ante' (before autonomy) and 'ex post' (after autonomy) situation. In the absence of relevant data, these may be collected using what is called the 'contingent valuation' method, in which people's willingness to pay for autonomy (or the compensation they would require for giving up an existing autonomy) would be surveyed. This method is used for the evaluation of environmental commodities;[139] however, we are not aware of any applications of this method to matters of linguistic, cultural or minority policy. Such application is likely to be methodologically difficult, which suggests that resorting to surveys of resident satisfaction is an acceptable, if far from perfect, fall-back solution.

Another likely benefit from introducing minority self-governance (yet one which it is exceedingly hard to circumscribe, let alone to evaluate) is that by meeting the needs and aspirations of the people concerned, it can prevent or reduce tensions and make a marked contribution to peace in the long term. While this point is inductively a very convincing one, it is difficult to demonstrate on theoretical grounds or to prove empirically.

Third, some indicator of the costs that can be associated with different models has to be developed. In this case, the indicator can well be a monetary cost. At the time of writing, a methodology for the extensive identification and measurement of costs of policy options remains undeveloped. However, some general principles are already well established. In particular, it is important to remember that the relevant costs of a policy choice are limited to those that would accrue in addition to those that accrue under another policy choice (such as that of 'doing nothing'). For example, the added cost of an education system that is run by the minority (and which uses the minority language as a language of instruction) is almost zero, because those children would have to be educated anyway, whether in a centralized or decentralized system, whether through the majority or the minority language. The extra cost induced by a shift to a minority-specific education system is confined to short-term investments that would be quickly amortized, such as the development of teaching materials and curricula, the setting up of minority-language teacher training, etc. Autonomy arrangements typically carry some extra costs derived from the additional administrative or other structures that need to be set up, but these amount to a moderate sum, particularly if seen in relation to aggregate public expenditure. However, the net cost in terms of education, health and social services is generally minor. In other words, what a current centralized government and what a future autonomous government would be spending, per capita, may not be very different.

One potentially major factor, but one which it would be difficult to express in money terms, is the fact that decentralization, and in particular autonomy arrangements, may be more likely to weaken people's sense of national unity. The long-term evolution (since the mid-1960s) of the attitudes of the Québécois regarding the sovereignty of Québec could be interpreted as such. However, should an evolution of this type be interpreted as a cost or as a benefit? The answer to this question is one that economics cannot answer. It will be a benefit for some, a cost to others, and hence a matter of preferences, ideological or other. However, all economic analyses (except in the very specialized subfield of endogenous preference modelling) take preferences a given, relying on other disciplines, such as sociology and psychology, in particular, to tell what these preferences are.

5.   CONCLUDING REMARKS

This brief foray into the economic perspective on models of minority governance has shown some of its limitations but has also shed light on its usefulness.

With regards to the limitations of this approach, it should be clear that economics can tell us relatively little about why an observed model of minority governance presents particular features. An economic approach can also not determine whether minority governance (for example, in the form of autonomy) is 'good' or 'bad'. If actors consider a particular arrangement to be good, they will pay what it costs; and if actors demonstrate a willingness to carry these costs (including, where necessary, some compensation for those who lose out when these policies are put into place), then the economist has no grounds for branding this behaviour as economically inefficient.

The usefulness of an economic approach rests on its methodological and informational contents. It provides a helpful methodological contribution, in that it offers a structured and systematic method of comparing options. Such a comparison is not sufficient to dictate policy decisions, but a strong case can be made that it would be difficult to make sound decisions without, at some stage, comparing options—and their consequences. To a large extent, this is what economics is about. Further, economics offers a methodology for filling some of the blanks—more precisely, for evaluating with some degree of precision some of the important consequences of different policy options. The evaluation is not exhaustive, and its precision is far from perfect; but when faced with major policy decisions, some information (as long as one is aware of its incomplete nature) is better than no information at all.

Future work on these questions ought to prioritize two different directions. First, there is a need to carry out fundamental research as to how best identify and measure levels of value of different policy arrangements. The conceptual and empirical difficulties are major and this undoubtedly amounts to a long-term research endeavour, but even limited progress can make a significant contribution to the clarity and transparency of policy choices. Second, there is room for a systematic, yet simplified presentation of possible or actual procedures, in the form of a set of homogeneous and coordinated indicators. Such simplified procedures may be derived from the more in-depth developments just advocated; at the same time, some may also be identifiable by evaluating select aspects of experience in various cases of decentralized governance.

NOTES

[117]   Respectively Department of Economics, University of Montreal, Canada; Non-Resident Senior Fellow of European Centre for Minority Issues (ECMI, Flensburg, Germany) and University of Geneva, Switzerland.

[118]   So named after John Maynard Keynes, perhaps the single most influential economist of the twentieth century, whose work emphasized the role of the central government in maintaining macroeconomic equilibria. Since this paper does not contain a general presentation of the evolution of economic thought, the interested reader is referred to textbooks like Mark Blaug, *Economic Theory in Retrospect* (1ˢᵗ ed. 1961) (Homewood, IL.: Richard Irwin, 1985) or Michel Beaud and Gilles Dostaler, *La pensée économique depuis Keynes* (Paris: Seuil, 1993).

[119]   Wallace Oates, *Fiscal Federalism* (New York: Harcourt Brace Jovanovich, 1972).

[120]   Gary Becker, *The Economic Approach to Human Behaviour* (Chicago: Chicago University Press, 1976).

[121]   What sociologists and political scientists usually call an 'actor' is generally referred to as an 'agent' by economists. More specific assumptions are made about the behaviour of an agent than about that of an actor. For the purposes of this paper, however, the distinction between these terms is not essential.

[122]   The absence of a compensation or contribution is precisely what sets externalities apart from goods and services traded on a market.

[123]   This point raises the question of the meaning of 'best practice'. From an economic perspective, such a definition should be based on a concept of economic *efficiency* which rests, in turn, on a triple condition of 'efficient production', 'efficient consumption', and 'efficient product-mix'. Given the theoretical complexities of the concept of 'efficiency', we shall assume 'best practice' to be captured, to a large extent, by *cost-effectiveness*, implying that any particular policy objective is achieved, *all other things being equal*, with the lowest possible expenditure. An additional requirement is that the range of publicly provided goods and services is defined as the outcome of a democratic process.

[124]   A classical example of such a system is Switzerland; see e.g. Hanspeter Kriesi, *Le système politique suisse* (Paris: Economica, 1995).

[125]   James Buchanan, "An Economic Theory of Clubs," *Economica* 32 (1965), pp.1–14.

[126]   This literature will not be further discussed here, and its main contents are examined at closer range in other chapters of this volume; see e.g. Hurst Hannum, *Autonomy, Sovereignty, and Self-Determination* (Philadelphia: University of Pennsylvania Press, 1990); Catherine Brölmann, René Lefeber and Marjoleine Zieck, eds., *Peoples and Minorities in International Law* (Dordrecht: Martinus Nijhoff, 1995); Christian Tomuschat, ed., *Modern Law of Self-Determinaton* (Dordrecht: Martinus Nijhoff, 1993); Patrick Thornberry, *International Law and the Rights of Minorities* (1st ed. 1991) (Oxford: The Clarendon Press, 1994); Fernand de Varennes, *Language, Minorities and Human Rights* (The Hague: Martinus Nijhoff, 1996); or Péter Kovács, *Le droit international pour les minorités face à l'État-nation* (Miskolc: Miskolci Egyetemi Kiadó, 2000); for a linkage with sociolinguistic perspectives, see e.g. Tove Skutnabb-Kangas and Robert Phillipson, eds., *Linguistic Human Rights. Overcoming Linguistic Discrimination* (Berlin: Mouton de Gruyter, 1994); Hervé Guillorel and Geneviève Koubi, *Langues et droit* (Bruxelles: Brylant, 1999) or Miklos Kontra, Robert Phillipson, Tove Skutnabb-Kangas, and Tibor Varády, eds., *Language: A Right and a Resource* (Budapest: Central European University Library, 1999).

[127]   Philippe Simonnot, *Trente-neuf leçons d'économie contemporaine* (Paris: Gallimard, 1998).

[128]   Asbjørn Eide, Catarina Krause, and Allan Rosas, eds., *Economic, Social and Cultural Rights* (Dordrecht: Martinus Nijhoff, 1995).

[129]   This emphasis on *linguistic* minorities reflects the authors' view that concepts of 'ethnicity' can only be operationalized in reference to some attributes thereof. Language is probably the most common and *empirically* least controversial of such attributes. Much of the discussion that follows, however, also applies to minorities defined with attributes other than linguistic ones.

[130]   François Grin, "Economics", in *Handbook of Language and Ethnic Identity*, J. Fisherman, ed. (Oxford: Oxford University Press, 1999): pp.9–24.

[131]   François Grin, "On the Economics of Diversity Governance", in *Governance of Cultural Diversity*, J. Dacyl and C. Westin, eds. (Stockholm: CEIFO & Swedish UNESCO Commission, 2000), pp.355–378.

[132]   François Grin and François Vaillancourt, *The Cost-Effectiveness of Minority Language Policies. Case Studies on Wales, Ireland and the Basque Country* (Flensburg: European Centre for Minority Issues, 1999).

[133]   François Grin, "Conflit ethnique et politique linguistique", *Relations internationales* 88 (1996), pp.381–396.

[134]   Grin and Vaillancourt, "On the Financing of Language Policies and Distributive Justice", *op.cit.*

[135]   For example, applying the personality principle, which implies that minority language, goods and services will be available throughout the national territory, will typically drive up the labour market value of bilingualism and hence the wage premia that accrue to bilingual as compared with monolingual civil servants.

[136]   The application of this procedure to language policies is sketched out in François Grin and François Vaillancourt, "The Economics of Multilingualism. Overview of the Literature and Analytical Framework", in *Multilingualism and Multilingual Communities*, ed. W. Grabe (Cambridge, MA.: Cambridge University Press, 1997), pp.43–65 and may be generalized to other forms of policy comparison.

[137]   Another useful indicator is the VFI (vertical fiscal imbalance), given by the ratio (or the difference) between two ratios: first, central government tax revenue over total tax revenue (rc/R); second, central government spending over total spending (gc/G). This is typically high for Australia (where the values of these two ratios are around 0.8 and 0.6 respectively), and somewhat lower for Canada (where they stand at about 0.6 and 0.5 respectively), indicating that Australia is more centralized than Canada.

[138]   There are some counter-examples, though. For example, the transfer of responsibility for vocational training from Ottawa to Québec in 1996 resulted in a temporary decline in the satisfaction of Québec francophones, because of egregious mismanagement of the programme by the Province.

[139]   Robert Mitchell and Richard Carson, *Using Surveys to Value Public Goods. The Contingent Valuation Method* (Washington: Resources for the Future, 1989).

PART II

Functioning Autonomies in Europe

The Autonomous Province of Bozen/Bolzano–South Tyrol

Karl Rainer

■

Autonomy and Conflict Transformation:
The Gagauz Territorial Autonomy in the Republic of Moldova

Claus Neukirch

■

Scotland Year Zero—From Words to Action

Douglas Chalmers

■

The Sami Cultural Autonomies in the Nordic Countries

Kristian Myntti

■

Minority Self-Governments in Hungary

Ferenc Eiler and Nóra Kovács

The Autonomous Province of Bozen/Bolzano–South Tyrol

Karl Rainer

The Autonomous Province of Bozen/Bolzano–South Tyrol

Karl Rainer

1. BACKGROUND

The Provincial Government of South Tyrol has started to give way to a more autonomous governmental structure, accepted by Rome under the definition of 'dynamic autonomy'. The South Tyrolese Government's ambition to extend its autonomy and to establish new competencies for its administrative structures has been successfully realized. The introduction of some new competencies in the last few years, such as the reduction of the state control functions (court of account), the extension of administrative jurisdiction, new prospects in the energy sector, recognition of competencies in the EU sector (Europe-Office), and the founding of the Free University Bozen/Bolzano, has increased the self-assurance of the South Tyrolese population. As the state of the Provincial Government of South Tyrol has shown, autonomy is not a static concept, but is capable of development. A very important measure for South Tyrol was the fixing of its name, Südtirol, in the Italian Constitution by the March 2001 constitutional law on federalism. It is the first time that 'Südtirol' appears in the Italian Constitution. Today's Autonomy Statute provides the Province of South Tyrol with far-reaching independence from the region and the state.

In the following essay a detailed analysis is provided of the decisive factors influencing the development of the Autonomy Statute, including its legal basis, the subjects involved, the power and duties of the institutions and financial issues. This is followed by an investigation of the more practical aspect of how the Statute can be used as a conflict-solving mechanism. The study concludes with a brief consideration future developments.

The autonomy regulation of South Tyrol is characterized by the following:

The region has three official linguistic groups, Italian, Ladin and German, the last two forming linguistic minorities within Italy. The equality of rights for all citizens regardless of linguistic group is recognized, safeguarding citizens' respective ethnic and cultural characteristics. In order to achieve effective equality of rights, the Autonomy Statute and its implementing regulation require affirmative action, granting special rights to the two linguistic minorities. Some of these special rights enacted since the 1972 Autonomy Statute are intended to offer reparation for ethnic discrimination by the Fascist government in cooperation with the Nazi regime, and not completely repealed by the Italian Republic in the years following the Second World War.

The German linguistic minority forms the majority in the territory of the autonomous province. However, all the provisions belonging to territorial autonomy are applied without distinction to the whole population of the territory, aiming for the best possible economic and social progress of the region.

The main force for a dynamic autonomy is the European Union and its rules for free movement and integration in a constantly increasing number of areas. On the one hand, the implementation of the Common Market and the following of internal borders in most cases favours linguistic minorities. On the other hand, the European Union has put into force no special provisions for the protection of minorities until now. The official draft of the Charter of Human Rights has no explicit minority protection provision, although the Committee of Regions had proposed a specific text for the matter. Still, the autonomy regulations for South Tyrol have a few extremely static elements thought to guarantee 'forever' the survival of the minorities. They follow:

- The international anchorage of the main cultural and linguistic rights as well as the territorial autonomy guaranteed by the so-called Paris Agreement of 10 February 1946, Annex IV of the Treaty of Peace with Italy. This agreement recognizes that Austria has a protective function towards the German-speaking minority in South Tyrol. This new autonomy provision was officially acknowledged by the Austrian Parliament in 1992, and can be changed only by the approval of all interested parties: the Italian Republic, the Austrian Republic and the minorities themselves.
- The Italian Republic has a duty to protect linguistic minorities under Article 6 of the Constitution which stipulates that the Republic has to protect them by special measures. An important step towards an open-minded implementation of this article with respect to all historical linguistic minorities is Italian state law no. 482 of 15 December 1999. It provides for financing in vital fields like teaching minority languages and utilizing it in public relations, media and local autonomy.
- Autonomy provisions and rules have to be in harmony with the principles of the juridical system of the state and must respect international obligations and interests, as well as the fundamental principles of the economic and social reforms of the Republic, but safeguarding local linguistic minorities is a national interest. This is a very significant recognition of minority rights involving measures to guarantee and promote rights and to support minority integration into majority society, without assimilation.

1.1 Historical Overview

A deeper understanding of these facts and principles of the autonomy of South Tyrol requires some consideration of the local history and the geography. The 'South Tyrolese question' arose in 1919 following the annexation of South Tyrol by Italy. This is a region in the heart of the Alps, and had been part of Austria for nearly 600 years. Throughout the nineteenth century, Italian irredentists sought the area in order to gain the strategic Brenner Pass. At that time the overwhelming majority of the inhabitants were German-speaking. In 1910, Italian-speakers constituted less than five per cent of the population. Any promises by the Italian Government to respect the rights of the German-speakers became worthless with the assumption of power by Mussolini in 1922. Throughout the inter-war period, a programme of de-nationalization was enacted in order to make Italy's state border constitute a linguistic border. In addition to the suppression of the German and Ladin language and culture, massive immigration of Italians was enforced.

The tragedy was worsened by the cooperation between Fascism and Nazism, which culminated in an agreement between Hitler and Mussolini and gave the South Tyroleans the option to vote either for the German Reich, thereby leaving their homeland, or to remain in Italy and be fully Italianized.

Although impressive initiatives by the population pressed for the return of South Tyrol to Austria following the Second World War (according to the principle of self-determination), the

Peace Treaty of 1947 confirmed the 1919 Italian border. However, due to diplomatic activities by former Austrian and South Tyrolese personalities who had opposed Fascism and Nazism, the Allied Forces supported international protection for South Tyrol, and in 1946 the Paris Agreement was signed between the Italian and Austrian representatives De Gasperi and Gruber.

According to this agreement, the linguistic minorities of South Tyrol are assured complete equality of rights with the Italian-speaking inhabitants and given teaching in their mother tongue, as well as promised parity of the German and Italian languages in public offices, and a proportion of public sector employment. Furthermore, the agreement obliged Italy to grant the population of the area autonomous legislative and executive power.

Following this agreement, Italy adopted the first Autonomy Statute for the Region of Trentino-Alto Adige in 1948, uniting the provinces of Bolzano-South Tyrol and Trento, so as to create a substantial Italian majority of nearly two-thirds in the resulting autonomous region. Therefore the region could not qualify as a minority protecting entity, as designed by the Paris Agreement. In a democratic system, territorial autonomy can achieve its goals for minorities only if they have a majority in the territory itself.

The resentment which this and the continuing discrimination in public employment and housing aroused within the German-speaking community led to an outbreak of violence in the 1950s, which continued through the 1960s. Austria raised the issue before the United Nations in 1960 and 1961, while also presenting complaints against Italy under the relevant provision of the European Convention of Human Rights. The dispute was continued for many years, but finally the United Nations' call for negotiations led to a 1969 agreement on the so-called 'Package', and an Operational Calendar for its implementation.

The main part of the 'Package' found its legal framework in the approval of a new Autonomy Statute in 1972 by constitutional law no. 1 of 10 November 1971, and in the adoption of more than seventy implementing regulations, in the form of decrees of the President of the Republic over the following 20 years. In 1992 Austria declared to the United Nations that the dispute with Italy over South Tyrol was settled.[1]

The Autonomy Statute of 1972 along with its regulations constitutes one of the most complex yet efficient system of minority protection and, furthermore, a very successful model of territorial autonomy in a plurilinguistic area.

2. MINORITY PROTECTION WITHIN THE AUTONOMY ARRANGEMENT OF SOUTH TYROL

According to the 1991 census, the total population of the province of Bozen/Bolzano is 462,542 persons, the German-speaking group representing 67.99 per cent, the Italian group 27.65 per cent and the Ladin-speaking group 4.36 per cent. The Italian-speakers live mainly in the towns. The total population of Italy is 57,000,000.

2.1 Language Use

Language use, education and the principle of proportionality are major minority rights concerns. In the region, the German language has parity with the Italian language, which is the official language of the state. Parity is applied:

- in relationship with the organs and offices of public administration situated in the province or having competence for the whole region of Trentino-South Tyrol;
- to public services in which effectiveness requires the use of both languages (i.e. not *every* employee is bound to be bilingual);
- in relationship with the courts and police;
- in the internal affairs of the above-mentioned offices;
- in the external affairs of the army;
- in public, notarized and equalized documents;
- in documents concerning obligatory assurances;
- to former public enterprises like Italian Railways or Postal Offices which are now joint-stock companies.

The joint use of the two languages is laid down as well for the followings:
- documents concerning the general public and those bound to be published (all provincial laws and decrees); state laws concerning directly the autonomous province are translated and published in the regional law gazette;
- individual documents for public use like identity cards, concessions, diplomas, etc.;
- documents intended for more than one office.

In documents, the two languages are one beside the other and have the same layout. The above-mentioned offices use the language requested by the citizen. If the citizen's preferred language is not known to the office, it uses the presumed language of preference.

Ladin-speaking citizens have the right to use their language in relationship with the above-mentioned offices and organs situated in their valleys, or outside, if these offices have chief or exclusive competence for the Ladin population. Ladin citizens also have the right to use their language in judicial proceedings. Within elected organs, like the Provincial Parliament and municipal councils, all members have the right to use their mother language. However, politicians are not required to be speakers of more than one language, as simultaneous and written translations are provided.[2]

Particularly difficult was the regulation of bilingualism within the courts. For years the so-called monolinguistic proceedings issue was a serious point of dispute. Now legal proceedings and trials must be conducted in the declared mother tongue of the accused.

The executive measures relating to language use also contain various other regulations to ensure the use of the mother tongue. Thus, for example, in South Tyrol medicine labels have both a German description and an Italian one.

The implementation of the right of all citizens to use their mother language in oral and written relationship with public offices, as well as the principle that proceedings are considered annulled if language rules are violated, can be considered as the most important language protection rule. The Autonomous Province is following the observance of these rules with great attention and takes complaints by citizens in this regard very seriously. Experience in this area so far show that most complaints by Italian citizens regard local authorities, whereas most cases involving German people have problems with central administrations. Efforts in improving language knowledge are therefore still needed in many public services.

Language use has an uncalcuable psychological impact on a minority. Previously, the violation of language rights had been one of the main hurdles for cooperation among the linguistic groups in South Tyrol. The minorities were compelled to struggle with an unknown language in everyday life, and therefore had a feeling of being foreigners in their own homeland. Another consequence was a deep mistrust of state institutions. How much the situation has changed following the improvement of language regulation is shown by the results of a 1998 inquiry carried out by the renowned CENSIS foundation of Rome. More than one-third (35.6 per cent) of those interviewed trusted the police forces, a figure unimaginable in previous times when police forces were considered by the minorities as an expression of state power rather than protector of minorities. Banks and political parties obtained only 8.2 per cent and media 6.6 per cent of respondents' trust.

Today, members of minorities are proportionally represented in police forces and are guaranteed work within the province. Article 22 of the Autonomy Statute indicates that to ensure observance of provincial laws and regulations, the President of the Provincial Government may request the intervention and the assistance of the state police or of the local, urban and rural police. The practical implementation of this regulation created deep psychological mistrust among German-speakers against the Statute in its first years, when town planning reforms connected to expropriations went forth with the use of public force.

In order to guarantee the right of the use of the mother tongue, proof of an acceptable knowledge of German and Italian and partial knowledge of Ladin is obligatory for applicants for the public services posts. This knowledge its ascertained by a special Commission through a bilingualism/trilingualism examination geared towards four different career levels. In order to guarantee equal chances for all EU citizens to compete with public sector jobs, the examination texts and precise criteria were published and placed on the Internet. Nevertheless, the European Court of Justice's 6 June 2000 judgement ruled as follows:

> Article 48 of the EC Treaty (now, after amendment, Article 39 EC) precludes an employer from requiring persons applying to take part in a recruitment competition to provide evidence of their linguistic knowledge exclusively by means of one particular diploma issued only in one particular province of a Member State.

The language rules of South Tyrol also aroused the attention of the European Court of Justice in another matter relating to a 1996 criminal proceeding and the right of EU citizens to use their mother tongue. It is worth reporting the conclusions of the Court in the following judgement of 24 November 1998:

> The right conferred by national rules to have criminal proceedings conducted in a language other than the principal language of the State concerned falls within the scope of the EC Treaty and must comply with Article 6 thereof.
>
> Article 6 of the Treaty precludes national rules which, in respect of a particular language other than the principal language of the Member State concerned, confer on citizens whose language is that particular language and who are resident in a defined area the right to require that criminal proceedings be conducted in that language, without conferring the same right on nationals of other Member States travelling or staying in that area, whose language is the same.

The above examples show the importance of the influence of European integration on the minority protection system and the relevance of the concept of dynamic autonomy. In the long term, minority protection very often has a positive impact on international relations and benefits human rights generally.

More important for South Tyrol is the fact that bilingualism has become a main factor for economic competition, due to its strategic geographic position. Together with the benefits of territorial autonomy, plurilingualism has been decisive for the creation of highly specialized jobs, for the settlement of a large number of promising modern enterprises and also for increasing scientific research, particularly after the foundation of the European Academy and the Free University of Bozen/Bolzano.

2.2 The Principle of Proportionality

Another fundamental principle recognized and implemented by the new Autonomy Statute is that of proportional representation, which must be seen in a historical prospective. It was designed to ensure adequate proportional representation of German- and Ladin-speakers in the public sector. This principle had a strong reparational character, and in order to understand all its delicate implications one has to take into account the time preceding the new autonomy regulation. In 1972, only 643 of 6,784 jobs in state administration were held by German-speakers. In the field of social housing the situation was no more balanced.

The implementing regulations of 1976 introduced the principle that the recruitment of public employees for services in South Tyrol had to be carried out on a provincial level in order to avoid the competition between local inhabitants and non-locals. The number of jobs had to be determined in a way that by 2002 it would be possible to achieve appropriate representation of all linguistic groups in all areas.

For a long time the principle of proportionality has been at the centre of criticism and was viewed as a particularly heavy burden by the Italian-speakers. This is understandable if one takes into account that due to the immigration politics in previous times, public service was a main employment destination for Italian-speakers. In the early years of Autonomy, this discomfort was particularly strongly felt, as the German-speaking group, not professionally prepared for the assumption of all these jobs within a relatively short time (due partly to the abolition of German schools during the Fascist period), was not able to furnish a sufficient number of interested applicants. Many competitions had to be repeated several times owing to the lack of German-speaking candidates, whereas Italian-speaking candidates could not participate because of their ethnicity. However, these difficulties have been nearly overcome and there is a move towards normalization in the sense that proportional representation is applied nearly everywhere. This principle is more and more considered a basic rule to avoid discrimination, but leaves enough flexibility to choose the right person (that is to say the person with the best qualifications) for a job, apart from his/her linguistic grouping.

Directly connected with the principle of proportionality and other minority rights is the personal declaration of belonging to one of the three linguistic groups. Most linguistic minorities consider it of greatest importance to have the possibility to declare themselves as such in order to gain protection as a group. The German and Ladin minorities in South Tyrol have always had strong feelings about this. This is emphasized by the unique political compactness of the minorities. The South Tyrolese People's Party (SVP) has represented as a collective party all social classes of the overwhelming majority of German- and Ladin-speakers since 1948. Of the 35 members of the actual Provincial Council elected in 1998, 22 belong to the SVP, another party has three seats, two other parties hold two seats each and seven parties have one seat each. The influence of the

SVP is often felt by the other parties as too heavy, leaving little space for a more pluralistic decision-making in matters of inter-linguistic relations and autonomous life. This lack of a strong and compact opposition does not favour continuous and deep democratic discussion of the various subject matters within the SVP itself. The South Tyrolese People's Party has indeed worked to achieve minority protections and autonomy rights, but now is in danger of becoming bound to specific lobbies. The declaration of belonging to one linguistic group or the other has been criticized as undermining integration and cooperation among the groups and for privacy concerns. Also, several persons had no clear ethnic belonging. The problem was mitigated when the declaration became a less binding formula, asking no longer for an ethnic or linguistic confession, but only for an indication to which linguistic group a citizen would like to be counted when taking advantage of rights connected with the proportional system.

2.3 The Educational System

The educational system is closely linked to minority rights. Article 19 of the Autonomy Statute rules states:

> In the province of Bozen/Bolzano, instruction in the nursery, elementary and secondary schools is given in the Italian or German mother tongue of the pupils by instructors for whom that language is also their mother tongue. In the elementary schools, starting from the second or third class, as it is established by Provincial law on the basis of a binding proposal by the language group concerned, and in the secondary schools, the instruction of the second language is obligatory and is given by instructors for whom that language is the mother tongue.
>
> The Ladin language is used in the nursery schools and is taught in the elementary schools of the Ladin areas. Likewise that language is used as a medium of instruction in schools of each type and level in these areas. In these schools, instruction is given in Italian and German on the joint basis of hours and final achievements.

The enrolment of the pupil in the schools of the province of Bozen/Bolzano is made by simple request of the father or a person acting for him. An appeal against the denial of enrolment is authorized on the part of the father or the person acting for him, to the Autonomous Section of the Regional Court of Administrative Justice in Bozen/Bolzano.

Education in the mother tongue, together with the promotion of cultural interests, is vital for every linguistic minority. Remembering the disastrous consequences of the Fascist dictatorship, the German- and Ladin-speaking minorities have attached great importance to a flourishing educational system, starting with adequate training of teachers to providing curricula and teaching tools at all school levels.

The teaching of the second language from the second class of elementary school onwards can be considered as an attempt to promote integration and mutual understanding for the groups living in South Tyrol. Nevertheless, the use of separate educational systems for each linguistic group has been criticized. Many are convinced that mixed schools could facilitate the learning of the two main languages, and in this way also promote interethnic understanding. It would be an advantage to avoid the rigidity of a separate school system.

The Province spends a considerable amount of money for linguistic exchange programmes, i.e., Italian classes visiting Germany or German classes in other Italian regions. Why not proceed with such exchanges within South Tyrol? It is understandable that linguistic minorities fear assimilation by plurilinguistic classes in a more open school system for linguistically integrated classes or full-immersion methods. However, the present situation of the German-speaking group in South Tyrol, seen against the background of European integration and the *de facto* abolition of borders, should lead to a reexamination of the whole situation, not only to facilitate the learning of the second language for Italian children, but also to improve methods of learning Italian for German-speakers. This aspect is often neglected.

Local customs, cultural institutions and artistic, cultural and educational events have a particular significance for each linguistic group. For the two minorities it is advantageous to utilize radio and television for cultural life.

The Province was authorized by a 1973 implementing rule to run a technical network for receiving radio and television programmes from broadcasting corporations of the German- and Ladin-speaking cultural area. This provision was and is of decisive importance for the two minorities and contributes to their feeling of security. Furthermore, these programmes offer the Italian citizens great opportunities to learn a second language, and to better understand the cultural background of the majority population in the province.

The above-mentioned minority protection instruments have been successfully employed to create a feeling of security, faith in the future and the chance for cultural survival within Italy. However, all these provisions would have failed if they had not been accompanied by the implementation of territorial autonomy, which allowed the development of real self-determination in the most important social and economic sectors of everyday life.

3. LEGISLATIVE AND EXECUTIVE POWERS OF THE AUTONOMOUS PROVINCE

Article 8 of the Autonomy Statute enumerates a long list of 29 areas where the Province has the power to enact legislative norms within the so-called 'primary competence'. This means that these provincial laws have the same juridical strength as ordinary state laws and are therefore approved by the provincial parliament in harmony with the Constitution, the principles of the juridical system of the state, international obligations, national interests and the fundamental principles of the economic and social reforms of the Republic. In order to guarantee to the provincial parliament a genuine expression of democratic decisions by the local population, Article 25 rules that to exercise the right to elective franchise, four years of uninterrupted residence in the regional territory is required.

In order to ensure this harmony, bills approved by the provincial parliament are sent to the central government. Bills are promulgated 30 days after notification, unless the central government sends them back to the provincial parliament with the observation that they go beyond provincial competence or conflict with national interests. When the provincial parliament approves the bill again—without taking into account the observation of the central government—the bill is promulgated if the central government does not raise the question of illegitimacy before the Constitutional Court or the question of conflict of interests before the national parliament.

A characteristic aspect of South Tyrol autonomy should be highlighted. All powers at each level are allocated in a system of continuous communication, mutual information and constitutional verification. It is an autonomy system of integration, not separation, based on the principle of subsidiarity and of respect of the single spheres of competence. This principle finds significant expression in the rule that the composition of the provincial government, of commissions, of municipal bodies not directly elected by the people must correspond to the relative numerical strengths of the linguistic groups. This is parallel to the language rule, where we saw that languages have to be used together, one *beside* the other and not one *before* the other. Here the authors of the Statute thought of the necessity of bringing together people of different languages, involving all linguistic groups in decision-making.

Accounting for the fact that within the Autonomous Province the German group has a large majority, the Statute provides guarantees for the smaller groups. Article 56 rules as follows:

- If a proposed bill should be considered to violate the equality of rights of citizens of the different language groups or of the ethnic and cultural characteristics of those groups, the majority of the members of one of the language groups in the Regional Parliament or in the Provincial Parliament of Bozen/Bolzano may call for a vote by language groups.
- In the event that the call for separate voting is not accepted, or should the proposed bill be passed in spite of two-thirds of the members of the language group that formulated the demand voting against it, the majority of that group can impugn the law before the Constitutional Court within 30 days of its publication, for the reason stated in the preceding paragraph. The appeal does not suspend the force of the law.

A similar guarantee is foreseen for the approval of the provincial budget. Continuous communication should also be the guideline for the relationship between the central government and the Autonomous Province. Examples of this principle being put into practice are the participation of the President of the Province in the Conference of the Presidents of the Regions and the right of the President of the Province to attend meetings of the Council of Ministers when questions concerning the Province are under consideration. These interactions are becoming even more important and frequent due to the participation and cofinancing of European programmes and initiatives which require common strategies for regional development.

However, in the fair handling of relationship between the German and Italian groups the Statute has gone too far by stating that half of the president's term has to belong to the German group and half to the Italian one, precluding Ladin candidates from this high office. A proposed constitutional bill is going to remove this discriminatory requirement along with others, including the difficulties facing the Ladin group to be represented in the provincial government.

The primary powers listed in Article 8 of the Statute are, among others, the following:

- *Culture and education:* place naming, protection and promotion of historic, artistic and ethnic heritage, local customs and local institutions, schools at all levels, academic assistance, professional education and vocational training.
- *Economy:* rights of shared use of properties, regulation of the minimum cultivated property, handicraft, fairs and markets, public works of provincial interest, tourism, agriculture and forestry.
- *Social services:* public welfare and social security, social housing and assistance of workers in arranging employment.
- *Natural resources:* town and country planning, protection of the landscape, preventive measures and first aid for public disasters, hunting and fishing, alpine pasturage, parks for the protection of flora and fauna and expropriation for public use.

Article 9 adds provincial powers within the limits of primary competence and the limits of fundamental principles of state laws, which normally consist of basic directives and guidelines, in the following fields: commerce, industrial production, utilization of public water supplies, public health and recreational activities. Furthermore, the province has the power to integrate provisions of state laws, for example, in the field of allocation of employment.

Without entering into the details of all these legislative areas, one can see that the Province disposes of the natural resources, has competence for planning and protection of the countryside and is largely responsible for economic and social development. Thus, the local population largely controls its own destiny.

Economic and social figures of the Autonomous Province can give an idea of how promising the results of enacted subsidiarity in the framework of the proceeding European integration can be. The outstanding characteristic of South Tyrol's economy is the very dominant structure of small-to-medium-sized enterprises, which are run primarily by families. This development, together with the enacted principle to bring work to people and not vice versa, has always been a main pillar of economic policy. Attention has also been paid to creating appropriate living conditions for the rural population.

Another outstanding characteristic of South Tyrol's economic and social situation is the non-existent unemployment, whereas in Europe, it reaches 12 per cent, in Italy itself is 12.8 per cent and some Italian regions have a 25 per cent rate of unemployment. All this success would hardly be imaginable without the contribution of the autonomous institutions and without a good financial framework. Before having a look at the provincial budget, it is important to mention that this settlement does not include—except for a few cases of limited tax sovereignty— powers of taxation. The state introduces and administrates taxes and charges, assessing and collecting them on behalf of its own offices and according to state laws.

With regard to finances the Autonomy Statute lays down three important principles.

1) The Province receives nearly all tax revenue collected by the state in South Tyrol, as well as that collected outside it in so far as the income or expenditure involved relates to activities somewhere within the territory of the Province. One-tenth of the revenue is retained by the state to cover the collection costs, etc.

2) The allocation of financial resources to the Province must take place at regular intervals and for the most part is in no way earmarked. As regards expenditure, the Province has complete autonomy.

3) The financial system of the Autonomous Province cannot be altered without the agreement of the Province itself.

In addition to the funds from state tax revenue, the Province is also entitled to the contributions collected in the territory of the Province by welfare institutions for the financing of the health service. Furthermore, the Province receives money for the implementation of European programmes and initiatives in various social and economic sectors. For the period between 1994 and 1999, some of the following contributions from the structural funds of the EU were allocated to South Tyrol.

- Objective 3 and 4—directed to long-term
  unemployment and workers assistance   32.5 million EUR
- Objective 5B—directed to the promotion of rural areas   44 million EUR

- LEADER—directed to the rural development
  of three specially defined areas   5.7 million EUR
- INTERREG—directed to the transregional cooperation   6.6 million EUR
- EMPLOYMENT   nearly 7 million EUR

Since 1998, the demand of the South Tyrolese politicians for tax sovereignty of the Province has become louder.

4. PROVINCIAL BUDGET

In 1999, the Province had a budget of 3.88 million EUR at its disposal, while the budget for the year 2000 is 3.76 million EUR. The economic aid distributed each year to single economic actors has a decisive multiplication effect on investments and economic initiatives in general.

Due to the vast fields of decision-making, the considerable budget and the elimination of competence centres in various fields, the Autonomous Province has had a great impact on the economy and the employment situation. It supplies services involved in legislative and administrative powers. The provincial and local administration plays a central role within the labour market of the province. With a total population of 462,000, South Tyrol counts 241,000 employed persons, slightly more than 40,000 of them civil servants. The Autonomous Province is the largest employer in the province and has a decisive influence on the social and economic life. It therefore carries the greatest responsibility for the quality of life, sustainable development, environmental protection and territorial planning. It is the heart of the autonomy and also of minority rights and of fair cooperation among the linguistic groups.

The Autonomous Province—especially on an administrative and management level—has provided good answers to all these challenges. This is evident in the results reported in the above-mentioned study by CENSIS: the Province obtained the highest percentage of confidence by those interviewed, precisely 43.2 per cent. The figure becomes even more significant if one considers that the study was conducted with the purpose of examining the reasons for a certain discomfort reported by the Italian group.

The same study underlines a general satisfaction of all linguistic groups with the performance of autonomy, with the Italian group making interethnic relationships a priority. Environmental protection, problems with youth and housing and immigration are perceived as concerns by all groups to a certain degree.

For the German and Ladin minority, autonomy is of course considered a guarantee for survival. Together with European integration and increasing contacts and cooperation with all neighbouring regions, especially within the European initiative, INTERREG, the autonomous bodies headed by the Autonomous Province have provided the basis for a feeling of freedom, and a sense of compensation for the loss of the former belonging to Austria. The success of the Province demonstrates that the common European house will be a union of diversity and a mosaic of language and culture, within which linguistic minorities can contribute to tolerance, understanding and peace.

5. CONCLUSION

To summarize, the autonomy and minority regulation of South Tyrol is characterized by the following main facts:

Type of Autonomy

Constitutional Autonomy including regional legislative powers and minority protection measures in linguistic, educational, social and economic fields, accompanied by an international guarantee.

Important Factors Influencing the Arrangement

The struggles of the 1960s had their origin not only in ethnic, but also to a large extent in economic and social discrimination of the minorities. It is of the greatest importance to analyze the social and economic situation of minorities in relation to the majority when models of minority protection are being developed.

The Most Relevant Characteristics of the Arrangement

a) Autonomy and minority protection are based on a special Statute with implementing regulations approved by constitutional law and which can be changed only on the basis of an agreement with the minority representatives.

b) The rights concern primary legal competencies for the autonomous body in all main fields of social, economic and cultural life, as well as land planning and environmental protection.

c) It is an autonomy with strong instruments of minority integration but not assimilation, and with specific arrangements of consultations foreseen at all levels. The most significant consultative feature is the right of the President of the Autonomous Province of Bozen/Bolzano to take part in meetings of the Council of Ministers when matters concerning South Tyrol are discussed. The South Tyrol arrangement is a model of power-sharing at all levels, based on participation by all linguistic groups. This may be considered a model of internal self-determination, on the basis of respect of constitutional principles, national interests and international obligations. It has to be emphasized that minority protection is constitutionally regarded as a national interest.

d) The most expressive self-governing institution is the Autonomous Province with its organs, the Provincial Council and the Provincial Government, which, by a sentence of the Constitutional Court, have an expressive role for protection and fair relationship among the linguistic groups. The organs of the Autonomous Province have an institutionalized relationship with the European Union, especially on the basis of participating in programmes and initiatives cofinanced by the Structural Funds. Representatives of the minority communities have periodic information meetings with the Austrian authorities because of Austria's function as kin-state.

e) It is important to stress that one pillar of the autonomy construction is the financial provision which assures the autonomous local bodies of nine-tenth of the tax income of the area.

The Role of This Arrangement in Ethnic Conflict Management

In the nearly 30 years of its implementation, the arrangement has given proof of its conflict-solving capacities. The Italian-speaking group had to renounce former privileges in order to eliminate minority discrimination. It was not easy to reach the special majority necessary for the approval of the constitutional autonomy law within the Italian Parliament, owing partly to a strong Fascist political movement in South Tyrol. The acceptance of the whole arrangement by the Italian-speaking group is increasing as the reparation measures will soon be fulfiled (for instance, proportional representation of all groups in public offices is expected to be reached by 2002) and the benefits of autonomy are enjoyed to the same extent by the whole population of the province without difference.

Outcome of the arrangement:

a) The South Tyrol model is assured long-term success, as it is based on a principle of fair integration of minorities into the majority state without any attempt at assimilation and characterized by far-reaching self-determination within the autonomous territory and by special measures, like for instance the financial arrangement that benefit the entire area.

b) Problems mainly concern the self-declaration of people to belong to a certain linguistic group. While not an ethnic confession, the declaration is often perceived as a violation of privacy. Another subject matter waiting for a solution accepted by all groups is place naming, which should be bilingual according to the Autonomy Statute, but is considered by many as a direct recognition of Fascist topographic inventions.

The South Tyrol arrangement, due to its particular historical and geographical connections and its complex provisions, cannot be copied as a model in every aspect by other minorities or plurilinguistic realities, but it can surely provide interesting information and practical input for other areas where minority protection is a concern.

All the linguistic groups in South Tyrol have good reasons to look to the future with confidence. The present situation can be maintained and adapted to future needs only if all proceed in co-operative efforts and proceed with mutual respect. This is not an easy task as there are always those who attempt to gain political capital out of the shadows of the past, rather than working for the future. One should never forget that in multiethnic regions balances are always delicate and therefore need continuous attention and, above all, commitment at all levels.

NOTES

[1] Austria's role as kin-state, giving priority to the support of the interests of German and Ladin minorities in the economic and political relationship with Italy, has to be underlined. An in-depth study of this role would be an interesting subject for analysis within the context of the development towards European integration and peaceful cooperation of nations formerly in conflict.

[2] After thirty years of language rules, one could expect at least passive bilingualism from politicians, but that reality is still far away. For example, in the Municipal Council of Merano/Meran the simultaneous translation of German into Italian was newly introduced instead of abolishing the existing system of Italian–German translation.

Autonomy and Conflict Transformation: The Gagauz Territorial Autonomy in the Republic of Moldova

Claus Neukirch

Autonomy and Conflict Transformation: The Gagauz Territorial Autonomy in the Republic of Moldova

Claus Neukirch

1. INTRODUCTION

Gagauz-Yeri, the land of the Gagauz, is a relatively young autonomous territorial unit situated in the southern part of the Republic of Moldova. Following tense conflicts in the late eighties and early nineties between the Gagauz and the independence-seeking Government of the then Moldovan Socialist Soviet Republic (MSSR), an agreement on an autonomy statute was reached in 1994. In the meantime, Moldova had achieved independence and suffered through a bloody civil war with the separatist regime in its eastern Transdniestrian region. The Autonomy Statute for Gagauzia, which entered into force on 14 January 1995, was aimed not only at bringing the area around Comrat, the Gagauz capital, back under the control of the central government, but also at serving as a model solution for the conflict with the separatist Transdniestrian regime.

Whereas some international observers regard the Gagauz autonomy as an encouraging model that can be applied elsewhere in Eastern Europe and the CIS, others consider it to be too liberal, claiming that it grants too many rights to the small Gagauz minority.[3] Another point of debate is the 'leopard skin pattern' of Gagauzia. The territory of the autonomous region is not contiguous but is divided into three parts by areas populated mainly by Moldovans and Bulgarians. In any case, it soon became clear that some crucial details had not been resolved satisfactorily by the Autonomy Statute and that further agreements and regulations were necessary. To that end, the Statute was buttressed by a tax distribution agreement in 1997, by the adoption of the Basic Law Code of Gagauz-Yeri in 1998, and by the Moldovan territorial-administrative reform initiative of 1998–1999. These additions to the Statute's framework nearly completed the legislation regarding the Gagauz autonomy. Following the 1999 local elections in Gagauzia, however, discussions arose between the newly elected Gagauz leadership and the central government in Chişinău focusing on, *inter alia*, economic matters.

The main purpose of this study is to analyze how the legal propositions of the Autonomy Statute and related legislation are implemented and, on that basis, to develop recommendations of how to optimize the design of the Gagauz autonomy. To achieve this aim, the study consists of three parts. First, the socio-historical background of the Gagauz conflict and its solution through the Autonomy Statute will be discussed. Second, the legal framework will be analyzed with the purpose of isolating and evaluating the salient features of the Gagauz autonomy. Special emphasis will be put on the political system, the economic dimension, the relationship between Gagauz and non-Gagauz in Gagauzia, and on the protection and development of the

Gagauz identity in the framework of the autonomy. The final part will summarize the findings made in the first two sections and will develop the envisaged policy recommendations.

2. THE GAGAUZ CONFLICT

The Gagauz are a Christian-Orthodox Turk people located primarily in the southern part of what is today the Republic of Moldova. According to the 1989 Soviet census, 153,458 Gagauz lived in Moldova, while some 45,000 others resided in the immediate region, primarily in the Ukraine.[4] Smaller Gagauz settlements can also be found in Romania, Greece and Bulgaria. Thus, some Gagauz leaders argue that the Republic of Moldova is as much their homeland as that of the Romanian-speaking Moldovans.[5]

The Gagauz ethnogenesis is still subject to debate.[6] It is, however, generally accepted that the Gagauz lived under Ottoman rule in Bulgaria around Varna and Balchik, together with Muslim inhabitants and Bulgarians.[7] Like many Christian Bulgarians they fled to Bessarabia during the Russo-Turkish wars and they settled alongside Bulgarian, German and other settlers in the southern Bugeac region. The area often changed hands between Romania and Russia, respectively the Soviet Union; periods of Romanian rule are remembered by the Gagauz as having been particularly oppressive and corrupt. Gagauz peoples had little or no conflict with the local Moldovan population, Bulgarians or any other groups.

Modernization, albeit in small measures, reached Bessarabia, and therefore Gagauzia, only under Soviet rule. Collectivization and the mechanization of agricultural production was introduced, as well as standardized education. Except for the short period of 1958 to 1962, this education took place in Russian instead of Gagauz. As a result, the Gagauz language was almost only used for oral communication in local communities. Between 1957, when the Cyrillic alphabet was introduced for the Gagauz, and 1989, only 37 books were published in the Gagauz language.[8] All official communication took place entirely in Russian. Therefore, "Gagauz national awareness was initially activated as a struggle to save the Gagauz language and thus (sic) population from disappearing during Soviet rule".[9] One of the goals of those who were engaged in identity politics was to create a literate population in their native tongue. The policies of *glasnost* and *perestroika* gave the small circle of Gagauz intellectuals more room to voice their ideas resulting in a small cultural awakening in the mid-1980s.[10]

During the same period, a Moldovan national movement came into being in Chişinău, which was united in the Popular Front of Moldova in the summer of 1989. At first, the Front embraced opposition forces from different nationalities—especially Ukrainians and Gagauz who had also suffered under Soviet-style Russification, for the Moldovans perceived them as potential allies. However, a nationalistic agenda quickly supplanted more general demands for democratization and transparency. The effort to make Romanian in the Latin script the official state language won large support in the spring of 1989. The first splits between reform-minded Moldovan-speakers and more conservative Russian-speakers became apparent soon after. On 31 August 1989, the Supreme Soviet of the Moldovan Soviet Socialist Republic (MSSR) collapsed under public pressure and passed a new language law, declaring Moldovan in the Latin script to be the official state language of the MSSR. This was a compromise solution. The language was called 'Moldovan' and not 'Romanian', and Russian retained an official status as the language for interethnic communication. Nevertheless, the Russian-speaking part of the population, including the Gagauz, perceived the new language law as an outright threat. The crucial point was Article 7, which stipulated that everybody working in a position in which they had to communicate with customers had to speak both languages. In order to enforce these provisions, compulsory language tests were foreseen within five years. After decades of intense Russification, everybody in Moldova could speak Russian to some extent, but nearly nobody besides the Moldovans themselves could communicate in the new state language. According to the 1989 census, only 4.4 per cent of the Gagauz were fluent in Moldovan, but 73 per cent used Russian as a second language. In fact, Russian was their language in the political field in this period of "national awakening".[11] Demands for Moldova and neighbouring Romania to unite stirred fears even further, considering how brutal Romanian rule had been in the inter-war period when it ruled Moldova. The result was reactive nationalism[12] on the part of the non-Moldovan segments of the population. In the case of the Gagauz, this reactive nationalism was further strengthened by a proactive nationalism, which concentrated on demands for control over local resources and the revival of indigenous culture.[13] Communist elites in the region, who reckoned they could improve their situation by mobilizing national sentiments, worked together with the Gagauz nationalists during this period.

The *Gagauz Halki* (Gagauz people) movement, which had also been founded in 1989 and which had sided with the Popular Front of Moldova early on, had consequently changed sides quickly. The Gagauz leadership under Stepan Topal, a nationalist turned communist, was seeking closer relationships with pro-Soviet forces, including the Transdniestrians. On 12 November 1989, a 'Gagauz Autonomous Soviet Socialist Republic' was proclaimed by an assembly in Comrat. This step was regarded as unlawful by the Moldovan Supreme Soviet, but a real dialogue between Moldovans and Gagauz was not initiated. In reaction to the Moldovan declaration of sovereignty, on 19 August 1990 the Gagauz leadership proclaimed a 'Gagauz Soviet Socialist Republic', which would be independent from Moldova, but part of the Soviet Union. Gagauz elections were scheduled for 28 October. Three days before they were to take place, approximately 40,000 Moldovan volunteers mobilized by the then Prime Minister Mircea Druc travelled to Gagauzia in order to prevent these illegal elections. Moldovan police and Soviet Interior Ministry troops managed to stop the volunteers and ward off the impending violence. This showdown between the lightly armed Moldovans and paramilitary Gagauz formations did not result in large-scale violence, but it alienated the Gagauz further from the Moldovans. The central authorities lost *de facto* control of the Gagauz area around Comrat and lingering violence—a small number of Moldovan policemen were killed in 1991 and 1992 by Gagauz rebels—kept tensions high between the two groups.

The first compromise proposals to establish some form of self-governance in the Bugeac region had been voiced in the spring of 1991 by the Moldovan Supreme Soviet as well as by moderate Gagauz nationalists.[14] But official negotiations between the Moldovan Government and the leaders of Gagauz-Yeri started only in September 1992, when President Snegur travelled down to Comrat for a meeting with Gagauz 'President' Stepan Topal. In the summer of 1992 Moldova again found itself involved in a civil war, this time in Transdniestria. This had a decisive influence on the Gagauz conflict. The bloodshed of Bender—a town actually on the right bank of the Dniestr, but controlled by Transdniestria—in June 1992, where at least 200 people were killed in the course of three days, acted like a healing shock. The civil war in Transdniestria as well as the experiences in Gagauzia of October 1990 strengthened moderate, compromise-seeking forces on both sides. Another important factor that favoured a compromise solution in Gagauzia is the fact that, unlike Transdniestria, it is an extremely poor region which has always depended on the help of the central government. Decisive for a political settlement were, however, the political developments in Chişinău. The pro-Romanian unionist parties lost power step-by-step to centre-left parties, which supported Moldova's independence.

The unionist forces opposed any form of political-territorial autonomy for national minorities or any federalization of Moldova. As a compromise solution, they promoted the idea of a new county which was to include all settlements of southern Moldova, regardless of whether they were populated by Moldovans, Bulgarians or Gagauz. This county should receive a special status directed at the development and preservation of their culture and identity. Special sub-prefects, located in Comrat and Taraclia, the centres of the Gagauz and the Bulgarian minorities, were to be appointed.[15] Although the unionists were ready to accommodate the non-Moldovan population to a certain degree by offering them some element of cultural autonomy, the general attitude of the right wing forces towards the minorities remained mixed. From within the more radical parts of the Popular Front, today represented by the Christian Democratic Popular Party, the view is still expressed that the minorities living in Moldova are a result of the colonizing policy of the Russian and Soviet Empires aimed at the de-nationalization of Bessarabia.[16] In contrast, however, the majority of the Moldovan population believes that the harmonious accommodation of the demands of ethnic minorities is integral for the healthy consolidation of Moldovan statehood.[17] Moreover, facing harsh socio-economic conditions, most Moldovans became more and more preoccupied with the question of daily survival and did not show much interest in the political peculiarities of Gagauzia.

The 1994 parliamentary elections yielded a clear victory for the centre-left Agrarian Democrats. With some 43 per cent of the vote they received an absolute majority of the seats. Together with the Socialist Unity Bloc, they were even strong enough to pass a new constitution without the consent of the unionist parties, which together gained only 17 per cent of the vote. This new constitution finally opened the road for an autonomy statute for Gagauzia, which had already been drafted to a large extent by the negotiations underway since 1992. Article 111 (1) reads: "The places on the left bank of the Nistru river, as well as certain other places in the south of the Republic of Moldova may be granted special forms of autonomy according to special statutory provisions of organic law".[18] After further negotiations with Gagauz politicians and discussions in Parliament as well as consultations with experts from the Council of Europe, on 23 December 1994 the Moldovan Parliament passed the Act on the Special Juridical Status of Gagauzia (Gagauz-Yeri), which is referred to here as 'Autonomy Statute'. To safeguard the compromise, two stipulations were included in the legal framework. First, any change to the law would require a three-fifths-majority vote in the Moldovan Parliament. Although the opinion of the Gagauz authorities does not have to be heard officially before introducing such changes, this provision gives them a certain assurance. Second, and more importantly, enactments by the central authorities which infringe on the powers of Gagauzia shall be annulled by the Moldovan Constitutional Court. Consequently, the Moldovan Parliament passed a resolution the same day, calling on the Moldovan Government to bring its own enactments into accord with the law and to submit to the Parliament suggestions on actions necessary for introducing conforming legislation. According to Gagauz officials, however, this promise has gone largely unfulfiled.

Nevertheless, the near-violent conflict between the central government and Gagauzia has been successfully transformed into a political discussion based on a commonly accepted legal framework. The negotiations which led to the Autonomy Statute were the first important step in this transformation process, as suspicion on both sides gave way to a certain degree of confidence.[19]

However, as Gurr mentions, "Transformation of secessionist conflicts is decisively achieved only when political trust in autonomy arrangements has been established on both sides, and tested in the peaceful resolution of subsequent disputes".[20] The following discussion on the legal nature of the Autonomy Statute and how it is used in practice will explore how conflicts can potentially be handled.

3. THE AUTONOMY STATUTE OF GAGAUZ-YERI AND ITS APPLICATION IN PRACTICE

3.1 The Political System of Gagauzia

The Autonomy Statute defines Gagauz-Yeri—the Gagauz Land—in Article 1 as an autonomous territorial unit, with a special status as a form of self-determination of the Gagauz, which constitutes an integral part of the Republic of Moldova. As Chinn has noted: "The title itself has significance. From the outset the law recognizes both the people and their land".[21] Gagauzia is entitled to resolve, within the limits of its competence, questions of political, economic and cultural development. In case of a change in the status of the Republic of Moldova as an independent state (for example, if it merges with Romania), the people of Gagauzia are even granted the right of external self-determination. This provision, laid out in Article 1, paragraph 4, is one of the most controversial of the Statute and is anathema to the right-wing elements in Moldova. However, for the Gagauz it was a central, non-negotiable provision that had to be included in any overall settlement. The fundamental rejection of Article 1, paragraph 4 by unionist forces, which continues today,[22] motivated them to challenge it at the Constitutional Court—without success. The significance of the controversial article for the present is, however, merely symbolic: for one, the unification debate in Moldova has cooled off considerably. Additionally, the odds of forming a viable independent state out of the scattered parts of underdeveloped Gagauzia is judged extremely low.

From the outset, it was the aim to include as many Gagauz as possible in the new entity without including too many non-Gagauz. In order to decide on the disputed territory of the autonomous unit, a referendum was held on 5 March 1995 in 36 localities in which the Gagauz either constituted more than 50 per cent of the population or in which the referendum was initiated by one third of the population. As a result of this procedure, Gagauzia today consists of 1,848 km², comprising three towns and 29 villages from the former districts of Basarabeasca, Ceadîr-Lunga, Comrat, Taraclia and Vulcăneşti. Twenty-eight of these localities are inhabited mainly by Gagauz; the other four have a Bulgarian or Ukrainian majority with a strong Gagauz minority. In total, Gagauz represent 78 per cent of the region's 175,000 residents. Of this total, Bulgarians account for 5.5 per cent of the population, Moldovans 5.4 per cent, Russians 5 per cent and Ukrainians 4 per cent. The territory of Gagauzia is not contiguous. Three Gagauz 'islands' lie between Bulgarian and Moldovan villages in southern Moldova. The administration of this dispersed territory remains difficult in practice. The whole infrastructure used to be concentrated in and maintained by the district centres. This structure has now been partly destroyed. For example, in Vulcăneşti the district centre joined Gagauzia but most of the surrounding villages did not. On the other hand, villages which originally belonged to the Bulgarian-dominated Taraclia or some other district whose centre was not incorporated into Gagauzia, had to be served via another town. Although the administration on both sides acted quite pragmatically and flexibly and, for instance, allowed people from nearby villages to still use 'their' hospital, some tension arose, especially in Vulcăneşti. There remained a Moldovan and Gagauz district administration in this town and it was not always clear who had to finance and control what. However, the socio-economic problems of the region ranked higher in importance than these questions.[23] After the whole territorial administrative structure of Moldova had been reformed in February 1999, the Moldovan villages in the region were incorporated in the Cahul county, whereas the Bulgarian ones now form the quite small Taraclia county. The territorial-administrative structure of Gagauzia was brought in line with the new Moldovan one in late 1999 by dissolving the districts. A solution of the administrative nightmare seems now to have been reached, as the administrative subordina-tion is clear today and the structures do not differ as they have done between 1995 and 1999.

Fulfiling the idea of subsidarity, Gagauzia is entitled within the limits of its competence to resolve questions of political, economic and cultural development. (Article 1 [2]). In Article 12, the local parliament was granted the right to adopt local laws in the areas of:

- science, culture and education;
- public utilities and services and urban planning;
- health services, physical culture and sports;
- local budget, financial and taxation matters;
- economy and ecology;
- labour relations and social security.

Moreover, the People's Assembly of Gagauzia was also vested with power to deal with the internal territorial and administrative organization, local elections and referenda. Finally, a state of emergency can be declared on Gagauz territory only on the initiative of the Gagauz legislative.

The Assembly is not restricted in its competence by ordinary Moldovan laws; however, Gagauz enactments that conflict with the Moldovan Constitution can be declared null and void. This is also true for stipulations of the Statute itself: on 6 May 1999 the Moldovan Constitutional Court annulled Article 20 of the Autonomy Statute which it judged to contradict the Constitution. The article allowed the Gagauz People's Assembly to recommend to the President, with the concurrence of the Supreme Magistracy Council, the judges of the judicial bodies of Gagauzia. According to the Constitution, however, they are to be appointed by Moldovan presidential decrees based upon proposals by the Supreme Magistracy Council.

The political system of Gagauz-Yeri resembles the mixed parliamentary-presidential system spelled out by the Moldovan Constitution. The Gagauz People's Assembly (Halk Toplushu) and the Governor (Bashkan) are both elected for a four-year term. The legislative powers are vested in the Gagauz People's Assembly. It consists of 35 deputies who are directly elected for a term of four years. The respective rules are laid down in the Autonomy Statute, the Code of Gagauzia and the local election laws. In most respects similar to the national system, one of the particularities of the Gagauz election system is that every single locality, irrespective of its size, elects at least one deputy for the People's Assembly. While this ensures that every village is represented in the regional parliament, it produces some problems with regard to the equality of the vote. Whereas in the smallest circumscription only 383 voters are registered, 5,100 are entitled to vote in the largest.

Moreover, the Gagauz election system favours independent candidates and thus political parties did not play a major role in the most recent local or regional elections in Gagauzia. This is true even for the Communist party, which received 70 per cent of the votes in Gagauzia in the 1998 Moldovan Parliamentary Elections. Of the current 35 deputies, 25 are independent, only four belong to the Communist Party and the six remaining represent various centrist parties. The fact that there exists no special Gagauz party is nevertheless striking. This was not always the case and is mainly due to changes in the Moldovan Law on Parties and Socio-Political Organizations. In its revised version the law effectively bans regional parties by stipulating that to register a party, a minimum of 5,000 of its members must come from half of the Moldovan counties. In addition, the Autonomy Statute does not authorize the Gagauz to adopt their own law on parties. That said, the Gagauz Vatan Party seems to have its structures informally still in place. About half of the 25 formally independent deputies actually belong to this party, which has won ten seats in the 1995 elections. Although the Moldovan Law on Parties and Socio-Political Organizations does not violate the Autonomy Statute, it nevertheless fails to take the particular situation of the Gagauz region into account. Exceptions, allowing smaller non-nationwide parties to run in local or regional elections, would certainly be an improvement.

The *Bashkan* is entitled to direct the activity of the public administrative authorities and is responsible for exercising the powers vested in him by law. He is directly elected for a one-time renewable four-year term according to the rules stipulated in the Autonomy Statute, the Code of Gagauzia and the local law on the Bashkan elections. He is also an *ex officio* member of the Moldovan Government, which creates a power-sharing system that is actually based on separation. The *Executive Council (Bakannik Kometeti)*, as the permanent executive authority, fulfils the functions of a government. It is approved by the People's Assembly on the proposal of the *Bashkan* and is led by him. The directors of the corresponding branch departments become members of the board of ministries and of the departments of the Republic of Moldova. This provision was meant to ensure the participation of Gagauzia in the internal policy of Moldova. In practice, however, it is reported not to be very efficient.[24] The prosecutor of Gagauzia and the heads of the departments of Justice, National Security and Internal Affairs are appointed and dismissed by the respective central authorities on the recommendations of the People's Assembly and the Bashkan.

Apart from the broad autonomy powers Gagauzia has been granted for handling its own internal affairs and the right to participate in the internal policy of the Republic of Moldova, it has also been granted the right to participate in the external (foreign) policy of the country. This is generally done by including representatives from Gagauzia in Moldovan delegations. The Gagauz are also active themselves, especially in economic matters. Cooperation agreements touching mostly on cultural and economic issues were signed, for example, with Moscow and Tartastan, and representatives were dispatched to Ankara and Tiraspol (Transdniestria). According to the interpretation of the Moldovan Ministry of Foreign Affairs, such representatives can tackle only questions of a cultural, scientific or economic nature.[25] Thus, Gagauz-Yeri had to revoke its representative to Transdniestria after he introduced himself as "the Gagauz ambassador".[26] However, the fact that the person in question resumed his duties after several weeks proves that Gagauzia had reached a certain degree of *de facto* autonomy in the area of 'foreign affairs'.

On 14 May 1998 the Gagauz People's Assembly passed a Basic Law for Gagauzia to bolster the provisos of the the 1994 Autonomy Statute. This Code of Gagauzia or *regulament*, as it is officially called, was originally intended to specify the more broad-based regulations delineated in the Statute. Plans to conduct a referendum on the Basic Law during the March 1998 parliamentary elections in Moldova were blocked by the Moldovan Supreme Court for formal reasons as well as for reasons of content. The document was finally approved by Moldovan and international experts, but still seems to be in contradiction to the original statute as well as to the Moldovan Constitution and other republican laws.[27] This is especially true with regard to various stipulations related to Gagauz-Yeri territory and property. Other stipulations, too, show some disregard for the Autonomy Statute and the Moldovan legislation and suggest that the People's Assembly tried unilaterally to expand the powers of Gagauz-Yeri. Moreover, the Code adds few specifications to the existing legislation and therefore plays more of a symbolic role (as the Gagauz 'Constitution') than a practical one. The Code is certainly an important symbol for Gagauz identity. Given its constitutional character, which, unlike the law on the special status, has been developed by the Gagauz themselves, it completes the list of the basic symbols of statehood which have been introduced before: a parliament, a 'president', a flag and an anthem. To be sure, these symbols as such can be found in other autonomous regions in Europe as well, but the fact that some provisions of the Code run counter to the Moldovan Constitution and to the Autonomy Statute is worrisome. The following discussion on property, territory and administration will show, however, that the Moldovan central government has also introduced legislative acts after 1995 that are not fully in accordance with the terms and spirit of the Autonomy Statute.

Contrary to the Autonomy Statute, Article 8(6) of the Code restricts the right to leave Gagauz-Yeri to localities where the Gagauz constitute less than 50 per cent of the population. Only in these settlements might a referendum to leave Gagauzia be organized. Moreover, in Article 8, Gagauzia claims the right to decide in a local referendum not only the question of secession, but also that of inclusion if the referendum is initiated by at least one third of the population. Although the Code vests this right with the People's Assembly, the Autonomy Statute does not actually suggest that the regional parliament should be entitled to do so. It is true that Article 12 of the Autonomy Statute empowers the People's Assembly to organize local elections and referenda in Gagauzia, although not in localities outside the unit. To summarize, the conflicting stipulations notwithstanding, the People's Assembly might decide on a referendum to be held on the question of secession, which might be initiated in every locality of Gagauz-Yeri by at least one-third of the population. As for the question of late inclusion to Gagauz-Yeri, the new Moldovan Election Code added some confusion to the mix by ruling out, in Article 178 (e), any local referendum regarding the modification of the territorial administrative subordination of any locality. Considering the special status of the Autonomy Statute in the Moldovan legal system, this stipulation cannot be considered valid in cases dealt with by Article 5 of the Autonomy Statute. As the changes and amendments to the Statute require a three-fifths majority of the elected deputies, it cannot be changed by the respective provision of the Election Code. Both the Electoral Code and the Code of Gagauzia should be applied only to the extent that they do not run counter to the Autonomy Statute.

These considerations are not purely academic. There are voices in Gagauzia which claim that some villages from the Cahul county would actually like to join the autonomy and demand a referendum to be held there. At the same time, most political forces in Chişinău would rather support the secession of any locality from Gagauz-Yeri rather than allow a referendum on joining the autonomy in another. The fact that Moldova's leading right-wing newspaper, *Flux*, published a map of Moldova, showing Gagauz-Yeri even smaller and more dispersed than it actually is, expressed this attitude well.

Irritation among the Gagauz arose also in connection with the new Moldovan Law on Public Administration. The law foresees the nomination of a prefect not only for every county, but also for Gagauz-Yeri. The prefect should function as the representative of the central government and his duty would be to supervise whether the actions of the local authorities are in compliance with the Moldovan legislation. Each prefect should also lead the public services of the ministries and central departments in the counties. In Gagauzia these powers are vested in the *Bashkan* and the Executive Committee. Thus, virtually all political forces in Gagauzia regard the nomination of a prefect for Gagauzia as a violation of the Autonomy Statute and as an attempt to downgrade Gagauzia to a regular county. Indeed, it is hard to understand how a prefect could fit into the current Gagauz scheme of government and which functions he could carry out without infringing on the autonomous rights of Gagauz-Yeri. Strictly speaking, the prefect would basically be confined to reporting to Chișinău or initiating legal proceedings if it is believed that certain actions taken by Gagauz authorities conflict in some way with Moldovan legislation. Although the prefect is not entitled to give orders to the regional administration, his function as supervisor does not fit into the autonomy concept. This is even more so considering the Bashkan is an *ex officio* member of the central government to which the prefect is supposed to report. Some juridical problems which might occur because of the concurrence of different and unclear legal stipulations might have to be cleared by the Constitutional Court. However, dealing with such disputes when they arise, instead of pre-emptively, is not sound policy. This may have been the reason why the Moldovan Government on 29 March 1999 announced that prefects were to be appointed to all counties except Gagauzia.

3.2 The Economic Dimension

The economic stabilization of the autonomy is the chief concern after political stability. Efforts to attract foreign investment to the region, especially from Turkey, have been made, but the pro-Russian and post-Soviet character of the former leadership sometimes hindered such intentions. It took nearly five years of negotiations before a Turkish-financed water supply project was started in January 1999. Given the chronic lack of drinking water in the region, this project is of utmost importance. Another vital issue is land reform. Until 1999, only 4,000 of 55,000 residents who were entitled to a land share received their plots. Under the new administration, however, the attitude towards land reform and privatization changed radically. In November 1999, the administration announced plans for an agricultural reform initiative which would reorganize the state and collective farms by privatizing the land and establishing holding companies to improve cooperation between producers and their corresponding processing industries.[28]

Control of local resources and the development of the region have always been at the top of the Gagauz agenda. The Autonomy Statute, however, did not elaborate in detail on the questions of finance and economics. Article 6 vaguely states that the "land, mineral resources, water, flora and fauna, other natural resources, movable and real property situated on the territory of Gagauzia shall be the property of the Republic of Moldova and at the same time shall represent the economic basis of Gagauzia". Gagauzia was also granted the right to introduce its own taxes. As additional taxes would hardly have fostered the much needed investment in the region, this stipulation was not a major concession. Thus, the revenues of the autonomy come mostly from transfers from the national budget, including foreign aid, and a quota of the national tax revenues collected in Gagauzia: 30 per cent of the Value Added Tax, 70 per cent of the profit tax and 100 per cent of the land tax. The region is allocated a larger portion of the former two taxes than ordinary districts, but the transfers it receives from the state budget and from international grants tend to be comparatively low.[29] Moreover, all excise taxes have to be transferred to the central budget. The speaker of the People's Assembly, Mihai Kendighelan, is not alone in asserting that Gagauzia could improve its social and economic situation if it received the right to draft its own budget on the basis of the taxes and duties collected on its own territory.[30] In 1999, the budget of Gagauz-Yeri amounted to 42 million lei (USD 5 million), of which 12.4 million came from the central budget. On the other hand, all excise duties and 70 per cent of the VAT collected in Gagauzia had to be transferred to Chişinău. Given that tobacco and wine are the staple products of the Gagauz economy, the local authorities believe they could increase their budget as high as 120–150 million lei, if they could keep all the taxes and duties they collect. With this kind of budget, they argue, Gagauzia would be able to spend more money on schools and culture in order to maintain and develop the Gagauz language and identity. Indeed, the 2000 Gagauz budget was set at 81.7 million lei (USD 7 million) and no transfer of taxes was envisaged.[31] The question is whether this system is the best method for financing the autonomy. The central authorities have pointed out that the debt of Gagauzia already amounts to more than 143 million lei and that after the implementation of the new budgetary law Gagauzia would have to bear all the expenses for education, health and cultural institutions which are now financed by the central budget.[32] An exact breakdown of the direct financing from the state budget, including the myriad transfers that flow back and forth between Chişinău and Gagauzia, does not seem to exist.

The latest row on economic matters escalated in early 2000 when the Moldovan authorities started to privatize several enterprises located in Gagauz-Yeri, including the southern electricity distribution enterprise and the Ceadîr-Lunga tobacco factory. This took place without the consent of the local authorities.[33] Although the inclusion of the Bashkan and the heads of the branch departments in the central governmental structures should ensure, at least in theory, that the regional government is informed about the plans of Chişinău, the Gagauz side claimed that they were not consulted. In the same period, the Gagauz People's Assembly voted for its own property law and held a special session on the issue of privatization. According to the local law, following the respective stipulation of the Code of Gagauzia, the entire property in the region belongs solely to Gagauzia and the money earned in the privatization process should remain in the local budget.[34] But no money earned in the privatization process has thus far been transferred to Gagauzia. The central authorities uphold the position that the process of privatization has to be conducted by the respective ministry in Chişinău and that the local law contradicts the Moldovan Law on Privatization. Thus, in conformity with Article 12(6) of the Autonomy Statute, the Gagauz property law has to be considered null and void.[35] The Gagauz authorities, on their part, stress that according to the Autonomy Statute, the property in the region forms the basis of the Gagauz economy (Article 6), and thus has to be managed by them.[36] On its special session in March 2000, the Popular Assembly demanded from the Moldovan leadership to pass over to Gagauzia ownership of the state-held parcels in enterprises located in Gagauzia and to prohibit the sale of such enterprises without prior agreement with the local parliament.[37] According to Kendighelean, the property question touches on the basis of Gagauzia's existence and the future of the Gagauz people, as a privatization process as organized by Chişinău would likely result in the exploitation of the region's raw materials.[38] The socio-economic strategy for Gagauzia, however, foresees exactly the opposite: integral production lines within Gagauzia in order to assure that the agricultural products are processed by the local industry. Thus, the question at stake here is not only "Who gets how much?" but indeed to which degree Gagauzia can conduct its own economic policy.

3.3 The Gagauz/Non-Gagauz Relationship on the National and Regional Level

Considering the above, the relationship between Comrat and Chişinău since 1995 might at best be characterized as mixed and complex. Both sides have interpreted the division of competencies quite differently in some regards and have also undertaken certain unilateral actions which are not in conformity with the spirit of the Autonomy Statute.

The relationship between the central government and Gagauzia has ebbed and flowed, depending on a number of intervening factors. The first Gagauz elections, held in the spring of 1995, yielded a clear victory for moderate left-wing forces which were more inclined to cooperate with the central authorities than was the former secessionist leadership. The first *Bashkan*—former Comrat party secretary Grigorii Tabunshik—did not make 'Gagauziation' of Gagauzia a priority, which resulted in relatively cordial relations with the central government. The Gagauz leadership elected in 1995 used its power primarily for the promotion of particular goals rather than for the development of Gagauz identity. Even after a reform-oriented government was installed in Chişinău in early 1997 under Ion Ciubuc, economic reforms were not forthcoming in Gagauzia. This lack of economic reform and the authoritarian way the Gagauz leadership treated the opposition within Gagauzia could even give rise to concerns that an autonomy introduced in order to safeguard the rights of a national minority was used to hinder economic and democratic reform in the region. For instance, in 1997–98, the regional authorities for several months prevented the rightfully elected mayor of Comrat, Konstantin Tavsanci, from taking office. Tavsanci had been politically active in Gagauzia since the late 1980s and was considered to be a moderate. He even supported the Moldovan president Mircea Snegur and his centre-right coalition during the 1996 and 1998 national elections. Thus, next to the regional/central cleavage, a cross-cutting ideological cleavage can be identified in the Gagauz-Moldovan relationship which might ease the solution of future conflicts. However, it can be noted that when both cleavages reinforce each other, relationships between Chişinău and Comrat might become even more strained. This was the case in 1998–99 when a reform-minded central government had to deal with a pro-Communist regional government. The second Gagauz elections in the summer of 1999 produced mixed results in this regard. The People's Assembly was now dominated by the Gagauz nationalist forces of Mihai Kendighelean, who was speaker of the 'Gagauz Supreme Soviet' from 1990 to 1994. The new *Bashkan*, Dumitru Croitor, however, is a moderate centrist who used to be Vice-Minister of Foreign Affairs of the Republic of Moldova.

As complicated as the relationship between the regional and central authorities may be, the interethnic relations as such do not seem to be strained. As far as the majority of the titular nation on a nationwide level is concerned, it is preoccupied with other socio-economic questions and does not show much interest in the southern region. Given the dearth of media coverage of the Gagauz situation, one might doubt if people living in other parts of Moldova are even fully aware of the potential for conflict that lies in its southern realms.

Although the Gagauz remember Romanian rule of Bessarabia in negative terms, there does not exist historical enmity between the Gagauz and Moldovans. Relationships between Gagauz and Bulgarians, who often live in the same villages, are also traditionally constructive and peaceful, although some incidents strained those relations during the lawless period from 1990 to 1994.[39] Although most villages with Bulgarian majorities preferred to remain outside the Gagauz Autonomy in 1995, the Bulgarian population in some mixed villages, like Chirsova, voted in favour of their inclusion in Gagauzia. As Demirdirek noted, the borderline between being Gagauz or Bulgarian was often blurred in the past and it was common to 'change' ethnicity after marriage.[40]

After 1995, no conflict has arisen between the Gagauz and the minorities in the autonomous region. The provision in the Autonomy Statute that at least one of the deputy speakers of the Popular Assembly has to be non-Gagauz also assured minorities a certain degree of political influence. Between 1995 and 1999 the two deputy speakers were Moldovan and Bulgarian, since 1999 one of them is Russian. Besides, 17 per cent, or six out of the 35 deputies elected in 1999, are non-Gagauz and represent all the major minorities of the region. Moreover, since Russian still functions as the *lingua franca* in Gagauzia, no Gagauzization threatens the non-Gagauz in the region. On the contrary, even Romanian-language education was introduced in 1999. Such an arrangement will not only please the Moldovans in Gagauzia, but will also safeguard the career chances of all children in the region, as a proper knowledge of the state language is required today on the national level.

3.4 Language, Culture and Identity in Gagauzia

Although in 1989 over 90 per cent of the Gagauz claimed that Gagauz was indeed their mother tongue, Russian has remained the chief language of communication, especially for official affairs. In fact, even studies elaborating on Gagauz issues have been published in Russian. Efforts to support the development of Gagauz language and culture started only in the late 1980s and were partially supported by the central government. Although strictly opposed to granting the Gagauz any form of political or economic autonomy, the Popular Front of Moldova was ready to provide them with the right to develop their language and culture. The aim of the afore-mentioned 1989 language law was to achieve a Romanian/mother tongue (i.e. Gagauz) bilingualism among the national minorities and thereby to break the dominance of the Russian language in the Republic. A weekly Gagauz-language newspaper, *Ana Sözü* (mother tongue), was founded in 1988 but ceased to exist in 1995 due to financial reasons.[41] As a result, the vast majority of media coverage today is done in Russian. This is also true for the state-owned and private TV stations operating in Gagauz-Yeri. There are minor exceptions to this rule; the national radio and television stations transmit programmes in Gagauz once a month and specialists from the State Department for National Relations have tried to revive the traditional Gagauz festivals and folk culture. However, as King observes: "These efforts sometimes met with little interest on the part of Gagauz villagers, whose distinctive music, dress, and folk art in large part disappeared under the Soviets".[42]

A sceptical attitude towards Gagauz language and culture could also be found among the leaders who were elected to power in the 1995 elections. They stressed the importance of Russia for Gagauzia and were worried about the Islamic influence which might spread to the region from Turkey. In the 1995 socio-economic programme for Gagauzia, the development of language, culture and identity was not especially pronounced. Although Article 3 of the Autonomy Statute foresees that Moldovan, Russian and Gagauz are the three official languages of Gagauz-Yeri, and the Code of Gagauzia and the Local Law on Languages repeat this stipulation, the only language used in official communications in Gagauz-Yeri is still Russian. All local laws are published in Russian only and the Code of Gagauzia was translated into Gagauz and Moldovan only after the intervention of the Moldovan Supreme Court. The 1999 election campaign was also conducted mainly in Russian; ironically, even the nationalist Gagauz parties used primarily Russian in their campaign in order to be understood by the bulk of the population.[43]

Although Gagauz as a language is today taught in the region, there is no single school that teaches its entire curriculum in Gagauz. The language of education at Comrat University, which was founded in 1991, is also Russian. The former regional government did not show much interest in changing this situation and respective efforts by the Moldovan Ministry of Education were met with a cool response.[44] Moreover, a Gagauz library, organized by the opposition, was harassed for political reasons.

As a result, the development of Gagauz language, culture and probably also identity did not develop as one should have expected during the first years of the autonomy. This might change over the next years, as the new leadership has a fundamentally different attitude in this regard.

4. A CASE OF SUCCESSFUL CONFLICT TRANSFORMATION? CONCLUSIONS AND POLICY RECOMMENDATIONS

The Gagauz autonomy can clearly be put into the category of territorial autonomy arrangements. The breakup of the Soviet Union not only paved the way for Moldovan independence, but the turmoil of the early 1990s also gave leeway to local leaders within Moldova and enabled them to block attempts by the new Moldovan central leadership to impose its notion of a unitary state. By creating a Gagauz Republic, these leaders established facts that, notwithstanding their economic weakness, gave them a certain degree of bargaining power with Chişinău, which itself was severely weakened after the *de facto* secession of the eastern Transdniestrian region. History's influence on the territorial configuration of the Gagauz autonomy—which, as a result of the 1995 referenda, followed the settlement structure created in the second half of the 19th century—cannot be underestimated. This is especially so with regard to the right of external self-determination in event that Moldova unites with Romania to form one independent state. The latter is a direct result of the negative historical memories associated with Romanian rule in southern Bessarabia. The involvement of the Council of Europe and the OSCE, as representatives of the international community, helped to streamline the final draft of the Autonomy Statute and assured the supervision of the referenda and elections in the region. However, this influence, like the economic assistance of Turkey, which could be described as a quasi-kin-state, while helpful was not decisive for the concrete layout of the Autonomy Statute.

Article 111 of the Moldovan Constitution can be seen as the legal basis of the autonomy. The concrete rights and fundamental structures of the autonomy, however, can be found in an organic law which can be changed only by a three-fifths majority vote of the elected deputies. The consent of the Gagauz People's Assembly—which, next to the Governor and the Executive Council of Gagauzia, represents the subject of the autonomy rights—is, however, not needed in order to change this law.

The institutional framework of Gagauzia resembles partly the Moldovan parliamentary-presidential system on the national level as well as the administrative structures of ordinary counties and, thus, fits quite well into the overall administrative structure of Moldova. Theoretically at least, the integration of the autonomy into the state structure is also assured by the inclusion of the Bashkan and local heads of departments into the structures of the central government. Thus, a power-sharing system that is actually based on separation is balanced by an interesting element of inclusion in the Gagauz case. The representation of additional minorities in the region is also assured both in theory and practice.

As mentioned, the Gagauz conflict was transformed in the course of the years from a hot conflict—where the use of force and threat of violence prevailed—to a process of negotiation based on a commonly accepted legal framework. Thus, the Gagauz Autonomy can indeed be regarded as a successful conflict resolution model. At the same time, as we have seen, certain problems and conflicts of interest remain. The main problem today remains that neither the existing legal framework, the Moldovan Constitution nor the Autonomy Statute, provide clear answers for all the practical questions that have arisen during the autonomy's implementation process. These documents provide solely a broad framework for the autonomy's structure and evolution; a more comprehensive legal guide, with concrete stipulations, is vital to the state-autonomy relationship. And furthermore, some controversial issues were left unresolved in 1994, so as not to risk the total collapse of negotiations at that point. This is especially true for the delimitation of powers and duties. While the idea of an autonomy for the Gagauz is rejected only by certain right-wing forces who represent less than 15 per cent of the population, an extension of powers for the Gagauz authorities does not seem to be acceptable for the majority of the Moldovans. Conflicts remain with regard to the following issues:

1) Political and legal system:
   - the extent to which ordinary Moldovan laws take the special status of Gagauzia into account (Act on Public Administration, Act on Parties and Socio-Political Organizations, Election Code, etc.);
   - the extent to which the local laws of Gagauzia respect the Autonomy Statute and the Moldovan Constitution (Local Law on Property, Articles 8 and 12 of the Code of Gagauzia etc.);
   - the extent to which the Gagauz can conduct their own 'foreign policy'.
2) Territory:
   - Who is responsible for deciding future territorial changes?
3) Economic Dimension:
   - Who controls locals resources, taxes and the privatization process?
   - Does Gagauzia have the capacity to conduct its own economic policy?
4) Gagauz/Moldovan relationship:
   - What is the proper equilibrium regarding the use of Russian and Moldovan in official affairs and in the education sector?

The preservation and development of Gagauz culture and identity does not represent a dispute as such between Comrat and Chişinău. In fact, cleavages in this regard are deeper among the Gagauz themselves. Also ethnopolitical conflict between Gagauz and non-Gagauz is not an issue. However, control over local resources presents a serious lingering problem. This issue is strongly related to the present socio-economic crisis. Moldova, in general, and Gagauzia, in particular, are facing and thus can only be resolved by employing an integrated strategy that includes:

1) a development programme for Gagauzia; and
2) an effective conflict resolution system.

The need for a development programme is self-evident. The region is underdeveloped, even by Moldovan standards. It lacks economic viability and is totally dependent on its agrarian sector, which has hardly been invested in thus far. Investment in the infrastructure specifically for the wine, tobacco and food-processing industries is strongly needed to give the autonomy the economic basis it needs in order to function. A lesson learned from the Gagauz case should be that the peaceful resolution of a conflict pays off also in economic terms. People in Gagauzia today have the impression that the international community forgot them after the conflict abated. Creating the conditions that will allow for long-term stability in Gagauzia will require a healthy and sustained effort to increase development and investment in the region. Then, and perhaps only then, will the potential of this autonomous arrangement be realized.

This long-term approach to address the background factors of the conflict has to be complemented by short-term measures that address the conflict resolution capacity of the region. As mentioned, successful conflict transformation requires the peaceful resolution of subsequent disputes, something that is currently not functioning very efficiently in Moldova. Although the legal framework set up in 1994 seems to be commonly accepted as far as its basic structure is concerned, the interpretations regarding certain stipulations differ in a manner that is hardly acceptable in the long run. Both sides have introduced new legislation which is not always entirely in conformity with this framework and both have employed very liberal interpretations of the Autonomy Statute in their day-to-day policy. At the same time, no effective conflict resolution system seems to be in place which would handle such disputes. An effective conflict resolution system should settle conflicts mostly by recognizing the main interests of the parties concerned and should recur to legal and power positions only as substitutes.[45]

Thus, although a step forward in comparison to the way conflicts were dealt with between 1990 and 1994, utilizing the Moldovan Constitutional Court to arbitrate disputes cannot be regarded as ideal either. This is because the Court, from a Gagauz point of view, is a central institution and thus might not be totally impartial. What is needed for Gagauzia today is a transparent political structure that encourages interest-oriented negotiations which aim at finding mutually agreeable solutions. The current practice, whereby case-by-case talks are conducted in different frameworks (within the government or ministries/between representatives of the local and regional parliaments or departments) does not seem to be effective. To tackle this issue, the following is recommended:

1) An office of the Gagauz People's Assembly should be opened next to the Moldovan Parliament to ensure that both sides keep each other informed about legal projects and the other side's opinions.

2) A Gagauz–Moldovan Roundtable, under the auspices of the OSCE Mission to Moldova, should be created in order to provide for an institutionalized conflict resolution system. It should consist of plenipotentiary representatives from the regional and the central government as well as from deputies of the two legislative bodies. Experts from the ministries should be invited as necessary. The Roundtable should be convened at the request of either of the two parties and should tackle only issues which could not be solved in the framework of previous bilateral talks.

3) Moldova should become a full member of the Stability Pact for South-Eastern Europe.

4) An international economic workshop under the auspices of the Stability Pact should be organized in the region. In the first round, representatives of Gagauz-Yeri and Moldova should discuss their main ideas and interests regarding economic policy in southern Moldova. The main aim would be to determine responsibilities for finances, as well as to stress common interests and to look for compromise solutions to address issues of conflicting interests. In a second round, concrete development and investment projects for the region should be discussed, taking the results of the first round into account. The workshop should be followed by a development programme for Gagauzia that stresses the idea that peaceful conflict resolution pays off.

121

As for the areas of conflict identified in this article, the following recommendations are made:

1) The Moldovan Act on Political Parties and Socio-Political Organizations should allow for regional parties, which, however, should be banned form taking part in national elections.

2) The Moldovan Election Code and the Code for Gagauzia should be amended, stipulating clearly that a referendum on the question whether a locality would like to leave or join Gagauz-Yeri will be held without further restrictions if it is lawfully initiated by one-third of the respective population and that it will be conducted by the respective local authorities.

3) Transparency should be introduced, specifically pertaining to the amount of transfers from the central budget to Gagauzia as well as with regards to the transfer of taxes and earnings from the privatization process or other sources from Gagauzia to the central budget.

NOTES

[3] Paula Thompson, "The Gagauz in Moldova and Their Road to Autonomy", in Magda Opalski ed., *Managing Diversity in Plurar Societies—Minorities, Migration and Nation-Building in Post-Communist Europe* (Ontario: Nepean Forum Eastern Europe, 1998), pp.128–147; Vladimir Socor, "Gagauz Autonomy in Moldava: A Precedent for Eastern Europe?" *RFE/RL Research Report* 3 (1994), 33, pp.20–28.

[4] Charles King, *The Moldovans. Romania, Russia and the Politics of Culture* (Stanford, Ca.: Hoover Institution Press, 1999), p.209.

[5] *Ibid.*

[6] Thompson, "The Gagauz in Moldava", *op.cit.*, pp.129–131; Hülya Demirdirek, "Reclaiming Nationhood through Renativization of Language: The Gagauz in Moldova", *Nationalismus in den nationalen Gebietseinheiten der osteuropäischen Gesellschaft*, Nationalismus, nationale Bewegungen und Nationalstaatsbildung in der spät- und postkommunistischen Gesellschaft 3 (Oslo: [manuscript], 1998); King, *The Moldovans*, op.cit., pp.210–211.

[7] Demirdirek, "Reclaiming Nationhood through Renativization of Language", *op.cit.*, p.3. Some scholars even maintain the position that the Gagauz are actually Bulgarians, see for example Emil Peitschev Boev, "The Scientific Problem Gagausians", *South East European Monitor* 2 (1995), 5, pp.60–72.

[8] Charles King, "Gagauz-Yeri and the Dilemmas of Self-Determination", *Transitions* 1 (1995), 19, pp.21–25.

[9] Demirdirek, "Reclaiming Nationhood through Renativization of Language", *op.cit.*, p.1.

[10] Thompson, "The Gagauz in Moldava and Their Road to Autonomy", *op.cit.*, p.132.

[11] Demirdirek, "Reclaiming Nationhood through Renativization of Language", *op.cit.*

[12] William Crowther, "The Politics of Ethno-national Mobilization: Nationalism and Reform in Soviet Moldavia", *The Russian Review* 50 (1991), 2, pp.183–202.

[13] King, *The Moldavans*, *op.cit.*, p.217.

[14] Thompson, "The Gagauz in Moldova", *op.cit.*, p.135.

[15] Interviews with Vasile Nedelciuc, and Ion Neagu and Marin Beluta, September 1999.

[16] Interview with Ion Neagu and Marin Beluta, September 1999.

[17] Thompson, "The Gagauz in Moldova", *op.cit.*, p.137.

18 Constitution of the Republic of Moldova at http://www.ifes.md/constitution/03/11.html as of 16 December 2001.

19 Rudolf Mark, "Das Gesetz über die besondere Rechtsstellung von Gagausien (Gagauz-Yeri)", *WGO-Monatshefte für Osteuropäisches Recht* 37 (1995), 5, pp.291–297.

20 Cited after Connie Peck, *Sustainable Peace: The Role of the UN and Regional Organizations in Preventing Conflict* (Lanham, Md.: Rowman & Littlefield, 1998), 50.

21 Jeff Chinn and Steve Ropers, "Territorial Autonomy in Gagauzia", *Nationalities Papers* 26 (1998), 98.

22 E.g. Eugen Patras, *Minoritale nationale in Ucraina si Republica Moldova*, 2nd ed. (*Statutul juridic*, Cernauti, 1999), Glasul Natiunii, 21 October 1998.

23 Interviews with the heads of both sides, Constantin Ion Caraghiaur and Gheorghe Ivan Ivanoglo, September 1997.

24 Randolf Oberschmidt, "Neue Satzung für Gagausien (Gagauz-Yeri) in der Republik Moldau", *WGO-Monatshefte für Osteuropäisches Recht* 41 (1999), 1, pp.13–21.

25 *Infotag*, 11 January 2000.

26 *Infotag*, 11 January 2000; *RFE/RL Newsline* 12 January 2000.

27 Randolf Oberschmidt, "Neue Satzung für Gagausien (Gagauz-Yeri) in der Republik Moldau", *op.cit.*

28 *Basa Press*, 19 November 1999.

29 See Budget Act 1999 and Monitorul Oficial, 17 November 1999, No. 128–129, 7.

30 *Infotag*, 14 September 1999, Interview Mihai Kendighelan, 21 October 1999.

31 *Infotag*, 24 January 2000.

32 *Basa Press*, 19 November 1999.

33 *Basa Press*, 19 January 2000; *Infotag*, 14 March 2000.

34 *Basa Press*, 19 January 2000; see also Article 16(22) of the Local Law on Property, in *Vesti Gagauzii* Nos. 12–13, 21 March 2000.

35 *Basa Press*, 19 January 2000.

36 *Infotag*, 20 January 2000.

37 *Vesti Gauzii*, 21 March 2000.

38 *Ibid.*

39 Stefan Troebst, "Die bulgarische Minderheit Moldavas zwischen nationalstaatlischem Zentralismus, gagausischem Autonomismus und transnistrischem Separatismus (1991–1995)", *Südosteuropa* 49 (1995), 1, 562–584.

40 Demirdirek, "Reclaiming Nationhood through Renativization of Language", *op.cit.*

41 Sylvie Gangloff, "L'émancipation politique des Gagaouzies, turcophones chrétiens de Moldavie", *Cahiers d'étude sur la Méditerrannée orientale et le monde turco-iranien* 23 (1997), 256.

42 King, *The Moldovans, op.cit.*, p.214.

43 Interview Mihai Kendighelean, August 1999.

44 Interview with Tatiana Stoianov, August 1999.

45 See William Ury, Jeanne M. Brett, and Stephen B. Goldberg, *Konfliktmanagement* (Frankfurt am Main: Heyne Verlag, 1998) and Roger Fisher, William Ury and Bruce Patton, *Das Harvard Konzept*, 17th ed. (Frankfurt am Main: Campus Verlag, 1998).

Scotland Year Zero—
From Words to Action

Douglas Chalmers

Scotland Year Zero— From Words to Action

Douglas Chalmers

"We were appointed because, in the opinion of the Campaign for a Scottish Assembly, Parliamentary government under the present British Constitution had failed Scotland and more than Parliamentary action was needed to redeem the failure. We share that view and in this report set out what we consider must be done if the health of Scottish government is to be restored".[46]

"The first and greatest reason for creating a Scottish Parliament is that the people of Scotland want and deserve democracy. Their will is powerful and clear. It has been expressed calmly and consistently over a period of decades, and has strengthened rather than diminished with the passing of time. In a responsive and effective democracy, this would be reason enough for change. But present constitutional circumstance denies Scotland responsive and effective democracy".[47]

"Post-devolution, political Scotland is behaving like a newly formed volcanic island, its topography still heaving and shifting so rapidly that only a fool could attempt to map it".[48]

"The new political environment requires a shift in emphasis away from a singular concern with *institutions* to a renewed engagement with *ideas*".[49]

1.   INTRODUCTION

Pierre Trudeau, the Canadian Premier, once said that for Canada, having to share a continent with America was like an individual having to share a bed with an elephant. It is an experience which can be dangerous or very uncomfortable and lead to pressures which are difficult to resist. The elephant can use its sheer bulk and weight to flatten resistance altogether. This can happen even by accident without any malicious intention. If there is a conflict of interests or of tastes, weight is liable to predominate. In many ways this is a fitting metaphor for Scotland's situation *vis-à-vis* England within the United Kingdom.

The relationship between Scotland and England can be traced back at least 700 years. In fact, the border that divides them today has its roots in Roman times, and coincides with the remains of 'Hadrian's Wall'. The Wall, constructed under the rule of the Emperor Hadrian, marked the outlying areas of Roman domination in earlier centuries. How that division stands today is the focus of this chapter.

The first real signs of any national consciousness of Scotland can be found in the important Declaration of Arbroath of 1320, drawn up by notable royal families in Scotland following defeat of the English army by the Scots at the battle of Bannockburn in 1314. This is in many ways a remarkable document which seeks to outline early principles upon which the embryonic Scotland would be governed. Although historians traditionally consider the French Revolution to have spawned the ideas of national self-determination and sovereignty residing with the people, these tenets were espoused in the Declaration of Arbroath over 400 years before Rousseau's ideas filled the cafes of Paris and beyond.

Within this document emerge two inter-related ideas—that the distinctiveness of a national community is worth defending for its own sake, and that rulers exist to serve the community and not the reverse. This latter principle—of sovereignty residing with the people—(as opposed to the principle of 'Divine right', or of sovereignty residing within an institution such as the 'Crown-within-Parliament'),[50] has by and large shaped the modern movement for constitutional change in Scotland, and specifically the movement for the foundation of a modern, devolved parliament, which eventually saw its realization with the inauguration of Scotland's new Parliament in Edinburgh on 12 May 1999.

Almost 700 years after the Declaration of Arbroath, the United Kingdom has therefore embarked on an exciting period of constitutional change within which Scotland is seeking to bring together the best elements of its own historical traditions with a forward-looking approach to extending democracy in the twenty-first century.

1.1 The Scotland Act of 1998

The Scotland Act of 1998 was one of the most important constitutional acts ever passed by the modern British Parliament. For Scotland it meant steps were taken to establish a parliament, with the power to make laws over a wide area of competence, together with additional (albeit limited) tax-varying powers. The act was part of a wider devolutionary approach involving the transfer of a lesser package of powers to a Welsh Assembly and to an Assembly in Northern Ireland. In the longer term, this significant transfer of power from England could also lead to regional government within England itself.

1.2 Historical Echoes

On opening the first session of the new parliament on 12 May, Winnie Ewing, the Scottish Nationalist MSP (Member of the Scottish Parliament), who, as the oldest of the newly elected MSPs had been designated 'Mother of Parliament', stated: "The Scottish parliament adjourned on 25th March 1707 is hereby reconvened". In her choice of words, she was drawing attention to the previous existence of an independent parliament within the country which operated until its voluntary amalgamation with the English Parliament in 1707.

Until 1707, and the Act of Union between Scotland and England, both countries had had separate parliaments and governments which ceased to exist following the passing of individual acts within each parliament, signifying their amalgamation into the British, Westminster Parliament. At that time the Act of Union was undoubtedly unpopular with the people of Scotland and resulted in a period of rioting and disturbance in the streets. That said some commentators viewed amalgamation as a necessary step in order for Scotland to overcome trade barriers imposed on it by its larger neighbour, and thus gain economic advantage through expanded markets.

Although the individual parliaments were now subsumed into a new, ostensibly all-British parliament, expressly guaranteed within the Act of Union were the continuing independence of three key aspects of Scottish life: its separate legal system (based upon Roman Law and differing—as it continues to do today—in some fundamental aspects from its English counterpart); its separate educational system—seen at the time to be in advance of the low level of educational provision in England; and its own national church—the Church of Scotland, which was independent of the state (unlike the 'established' church in England).

Although the words of Winnie Ewing quoted above make claim to continuity with the old Scottish Parliament, in practical (rather than symbolic) terms, there is little in common between the two bodies, save the name. The parliament of 1707, reflecting its times, was not a democratic body, unlike today's equivalent which has sought to turn its face 'violently towards the present' in aiming to adopt best practice relevant to modern realities.

1.3 From 1707 to the Present—The Process of Achieving Change

Like its English and Scottish predecessors, the new British Parliament established in 1707 made no pretensions to being a democratic body. Even one hundred years later, the electoral system remained so corrupt that in 1823 it was estimated that fewer than 3,000 Scotsmen were entitled to vote for members of parliament. Women were not entitled to vote at all in parliamentary elections—a situation only partially resolved in 1918 and fully so in 1928, following a long and hard-fought campaign by women themselves.

Such were the anomalies and demands for increasing democracy in the nineteenth century that several acts were passed to enfranchise a greater number of voters. In 1832, the vote was extended to middle class males, with subsequent acts in 1867 and 1884 then granting all men 21 and over the right to vote.

With the increasing (albeit limited) democratization of Westminster's Parliament, it was natural that discontent would grow about Westminster's lack of interest in Scottish affairs. This lack of interest is perhaps best encapsulated by a reported conversation in 1886 between a prominent Scottish academic and Benjamin Jowett, Vice Chancellor of England's Oxford University: after the Scottish academic commented to Jowett: "I hope you in Oxford don't think we hate you", Jowett's reply was, "We don't think about you".

Because of this inattention and lack of interest grew increasing demands for new structures to better deal with the specific aspects of Scottish life, inadequately dealt with under the centralized Westminster system. The first practical movement towards this evolution was the agreement in 1885 to appoint a Secretary for Scotland (with a seat in the British Cabinet granted in 1892), an office which was upgraded to the more important level of Secretary of State in 1926. In 1939 the Scottish Office was moved from Westminster, London, to St Andrews House in Edinburgh, Scotland.

These gradual changes were in many ways a concession to growing extra-parliamentary agitation around Scotland's interests, illustrated for instance by the establishment of the Scottish Home Rule Association in 1886. This was also a period of great upheaval in British politics with regards to the Irish question, where agitation for Home Rule in Ireland was taking a more radical turn. Although Home Rule for Scotland was often discussed in parliament, it did not result in the passing of legislation (unlike the Northern Ireland Act of 1920 brought about as a result of the 1918–21 Irish War).

1.4 Towards the Modern Movement for Home Rule

While the Liberal Party had long been seen as a party of Home Rule, it was soon supported in this cause by the Labour Party, from its inception in 1896, and then by the much smaller but very active Communist Party from 1920. However, the first political party dedicated to Scottish independence— the National Party—was formed in 1928. In 1934, the National Party merged with another pro-independence party to form the Scottish National Party (SNP), which is today the second largest party within Scotland's new Parliament.

Although the SNP was to win a by-election in 1945 (subsequently lost at the General Election of the same year), it was only in the 1960s that it began to make a significant breakthrough, winning an important by-election in the former safe Labour seat of Hamilton in 1967, a year after the SNP's sister party for independence for Wales, Plaid Cymru (PC), had also won a Westminster by-election.[51] In 1968, the SNP went on to win 30 per cent of the vote in the Scottish municipal elections, resulting in 108 council seats overall.

Undoubtedly concerned about the rise of nationalist feeling in the UK, the Labour Government of Harold Wilson appointed a Royal Commission of Enquiry to examine the UK Constitution in 1969. In 1973 the commission finalized the 'Kilbrandon Report' in which Lord Kilbrandon rejected separatism and federalism and recommended a limited Assembly for Scotland, elected under a system of proportional representation.

However, in the following general election of 1974, it was notable that neither of the two main parties, Labour or Conservatives, mentioned devolution in their manifestos. This apparent disregard of the national question by the Westminster-based parties was answered by the winning of seven seats (out of 72 Scottish seats) by the SNP, and two by Plaid Cymru in Wales. The seven seats won by the SNP were not a true reflection of the party's support, which was much higher in terms of the percentage of the popular vote which it represented than the seats achieved would suggest—the lower seats being due to the unrepresentative nature of the 'first-past-the-post' electoral system under operation in Westminster.

1.5 Labour as a Minority Government

The result of the General Election forced Labour to operate as a minority government and to bring forward measures to address the national issue. This was seen in a hurried White Paper entitled *Democracy and Devolution: Proposals for Scotland and Wales*, which proposed directly elected Assemblies for Scotland and Wales, with Scotland having legislative but not tax-varying powers. Wales was to have administrative powers only. A second general election in October 1974 saw a surge forward for the SNP in the British Parliament, with 30 per cent of the popular vote achieved, resulting in 11 seats.[52]

The years 1975 and 1976 saw several attempts made by the government to gain support for their limited devolutionary proposals. This finally resulted in separate parliamentary bills being proposed for Scotland and for Wales, which were to be put to separate referenda in each country. Despite the bills having emanated from a Labour administration, there still existed great opposition to any form of devolution from many parliamentary MPs of the Labour Party (from Scotland, Wales and England), leading to attempts to weaken the proposed scheme to the utmost.

The Bills were also opposed by the Conservative Party, despite a previous period in which it had also envisaged the possibility of a greater degree of Home Rule in Scotland. Now, however, it projected itself as the 'Party of the Union' and opposed Labour's proposals, which predictably were also given a rough reception by the SNP due to their limited nature.

A controversial and crucial flaw of the Bill as published was a Labour-sponsored amendment imposing a minimum voting threshold for the referenda that would require a 40 per cent vote of the total electorate in favour of constitutional modification before change could come about. On 1 March 1979, the majority of Scottish voters taking part in the referendum on the establishment of the Assembly cast their votes in favour: 32.9 per cent voted 'Yes' while 30.8 per cent voted 'No' in a 63.9 per cent poll. However, this was stated as insufficient due to the provision that 40 per cent of the electorate must vote in favour before the government would proceed with the establishment of the Assembly.[53] On the same day, the Welsh people decisively voted against the proposals for their assembly.

The referendum therefore obtained its majority of approval, but failed to satisfy the restrictions attached to it by politicians hostile to the proposed change. As some commentators pointed out, however, this was despite the fact that no British Government had been elected on a majority vote of the populace since 1918—and for local elections the percentage turnout in terms of 'legitimacy' was even worse.

As part of the fallout from what was widely perceived as both a debacle and a profoundly undemocratic measure by Labour, a no-confidence motion in the Callaghan (Labour) government was successfully moved in parliament. It passed by one vote and led to the fall of the Labour government. In the subsequent general election in October a Conservative administration headed by Margaret Thatcher was elected into power (albeit with less than one in four votes in Scotland). She repealed the Scotland and Wales Act the following month.

1.6 The Political and Social Effect of Thatcherism on the National Question

In Scotland, the 1980s saw an intensification of the feeling that democratic rights were being withheld by the government in Westminster.

A widespread feeling existed that Scotland, with its different legal, educational, administrative and local government systems, with a wide range of separate state and voluntary organizations, with a four-party system, and with a substantially different press, was being misgoverned by a political party representing less than a quarter of the Scottish electorate. This situation was aggravated by the government's determination to push ahead with a radical rightist agenda in Scotland despite its questionable legitimacy.

The clash of political culture was more intense in Scotland than elsewhere. The Thatcherite brand of competitive individualism never truly came into fashion in Scotland with collectivist values continuing to be broadly acceptable across all social classes.[54]

It was within this political context that an initiative was taken to try and change the nature of the constitutional debate and to broaden its scope. The debate over the Scottish Government had gone on for over twenty years in its modern phase and had suffered from being stuck in a groove of *independence versus a rather restricted devolved assembly versus the status quo*. Some of those favouring reform had spent more time fighting each other than they did in opposing the Conservative position.

1.7 The Formation of the Campaign for a Scottish Assembly

Early in 1980, a group of Home Rule campaigners came together in order to assess the possible avenues for democratic change, given the setbacks of the election and its implications. This grouping was a remarkably broad set of individuals, ranging from the Communists and Labour on the left, through members of the Liberal Party and SNP to even some members of the Conservative party (which had also historically had a small 'Home Rule' wing which was now under threat from the discourse of Thatcherism).

Crucially, in addition to these members of political parties, this fledgling organization—which went on to call itself the Campaign for a Scottish Assembly (CSA)—also had the support of prominent church figures, and the still powerful Scottish Trade Union Congress (STUC), a body independent of, but allied to the larger British TUC. Later on, the newly formed Green Party in Scotland was also to join the group.

What linked these groups together was a particular Scottish tradition of cross-party activity and broad coalitions. On many previous occasions following the Second World War, cross-party and broad coalitions had been formed, usually around the core of the STUC and the churches, in order to put a consensual Scottish case (where it existed) to a Westminster Government. This had happened in the past over such issues as unemployment, the Peace Movement, expanding women's rights (regarding abortion and other issues) and, on many occasions, over demands for better and more appropriate governance in Scotland.[55]

With the formation of the CSA, a semi-permanent vehicle was therefore created to continue this tradition and to unite those in favour of constitutional change, irrespective of any other differences that might normally divide them.

One of the immediate results of Labour's shock defeat in 1979 was a tendency by the parliamentary Labour Party to relegate the issue of devolution again to minor status. For the majority of the next decade it would be regarded as only one of the issues upon which Labour and Conservatives differed. Indeed for some, devolution and the national question was now an abhorrent issue, given that the SNP was perceived to have helped Labour's downfall in the parliamentary vote of no confidence. However, with the re-election of the Conservative administration in 1983 and 1987, together with the increased stridency and radicalism of its policies (all of which were prefigured on a centralized unionist state), a growing sense of urgency arose among Labour activists in Scotland regarding the centrality of devolution for democratic advance. The marked decline in electoral support for the Conservative Party in Scotland during this period was also matched by a tangible increase in nationalist sentiment and support for independence.

Within the CSA, there had been a growing interest since the early eighties in trying to resolve the demand for a Scottish legislature by establishing a 'Constitutional Convention' to devise a consensus scheme around which reformers could rally. This gained momentum after the 1987 election, when the CSA decided to initiate such a convention, using the Scottish tradition of a 'Claim of Right'.

1.7.1   The Claim of Right

The concept of a 'Claim of Right' arises from the Scottish constitutional perception that sovereignty lies with the people.

On two previous occasions, in 1689 and 1842, Scots had acted against misgovernment by issuing a 'Claim of Right' to redress wrongs. Both times Scots were reacting to constitutional infringements and concerns related to power and sovereignty. In reviving this tradition, the Campaign for a Scottish Assembly insisted that Scotland had the right to articulate its own demands and grievances, rather than having them articulated by a government now seen utterly unrepresentative of Scots.

In order to issue the Claim of Right, a committee of prominent Scots was brought together by the CSA as a 'Constitutional Steering Committee' to draw up the document. This committee was remarkable for its broad-based composition, which included representatives of: the National Federation of Small Businesses; the Catholic, Methodist and Scottish Churches; numerous academic fields including constitutional law and sociology; the Scottish Trade Union Movement; Scottish cultural organizations; the local government; and the Labour, Liberal Democrat and Scottish Nationalist parties.

The Committee was chaired by Sir Robert Grieve, previously the chairman of the Highlands and Islands Development Board, the main economic agency for developing the Scottish Highlands. Its secretary was Jim Ross, a retired Civil Servant who had played a prominent role in drawing up the previous bill for a Scottish Assembly prior to 1979. On 6 July 1988, the report of the Committee, after having been sent to the Convenor of the Campaign for a Scottish Assembly, was published to widespread interest.

1.7.2   The Case for a Constitutional Convention

The Constitutional Steering Committee had been given three terms of reference to report on:
- all aspects of the case for reinforcing parliamentary action by setting up a Scottish Constitutional Convention for the express purpose of securing the creation of a Scottish Assembly;
- the practical steps required to set up such a Convention on an effectively representative basis;
- the tasks it should be prepared to undertake in order to achieve an Assembly.

The committee report's epilogue stated the case for change in dramatic terms:

Scotland faces a crisis of identity and survival. It is now being governed without consent and subject to the declared intention of having imposed upon it a radical change of outlook and behaviour pattern which it shows no sign of wanting. All questions as to whether consent should be a part of government are brushed aside. The comments of Adam Smith are put to uses which would have astonished him, Scottish history is selectively distorted and the Scots are told that their votes are lying; that they secretly love what they constantly vote against.

Scotland is not alone in suffering from the absence of consent in government. The problem afflicts the United Kingdom as a whole. We have a government which openly boasts its contempt for consensus and a constitution which allows it to demonstrate that contempt in practice. But Scotland is unique both in its title to complain and in its awareness of what is being done to it.

None of this has anything to do with the merits or demerits of particular policies at particular times, or with the degree of conviction with which people believe in these

133

policies. Many a conviction politician contemptuous of democracy has done some marginal good in passing. Mussolini allegedly made the Italian trains run on time. The crucial questions are power and consent: making power accountable and setting limits to what can be done without general consent.

These questions will not be adequately answered in the United Kingdom until the concentration of power that masquerades as 'the Crown-in-Parliament' has been broken up. Government can be carried on with consent only through a system of checks and balances capable of restraining those who lack a sense of restraint. Stripping away the powers of politicians outside Whitehall (and incidentally increasing the powers of Ministers inside Whitehall) restores power not to the people but to the powerful. The choices we are promised in consequence will in practice be the choice the powerful choose to offer us. Through effectively answerable representative institutions we can edit the choices for ourselves.

It is a sign of both the fraudulence and the fragility of the English constitution that representative bodies and their activities, the lifeblood of government by consent, can be systematically closed down by a minority Westminster Government without there being any constitutional means of even giving them pause for thought.[56]

Following an examination of why the present constitutional settlement did not fulfil the needs of the Scots, the steering committee recommended the establishment of a much broader and representative 'Constitutional Convention' to further the case for better governance in Scotland.[57]

The aim of the Scottish Constitutional Convention (which of course did not have the Conservative government's blessing or sanction) was to bring together Scotland's elected representatives in Westminster and local government with churches, trade unions, political parties, women's organizations and ethnic groups in order to see how much agreement could be reached. All but a few local authorities participated, as did 63 of the 78 MPs and MEPs. So did Scotland's churches, trade unions and many other organizations. Representatives of Scotland's small businesses took part, although the main employers organization, the Confederation of British Industry, declined the invitation. Predictably, the Conservatives did not take part. After initial support for the Convention proposal, the Scottish National Party withdrew before the first meeting. Several different reasons were given but the most important was probably the fear of compromise blurring their image.

The Convention initiative was a genuine attempt to move the constitutional debate away from the uncooperative sectionalism that had plagued it for the previous twenty years. It brought groups representing important interests into active dialogue with the political parties. It opened up a debate not just about the relationship between Scotland and England but also about the nature of Scottish democracy. This distinguished the Convention's work from most of the constitutional debate that had taken place over the previous two decades. Electoral reform, the participation of women, a Bill of Rights, a democratic parliament and greater public access to government were all issues addressed in the Convention proposals.

The remit of the Convention was outlined at its first meeting on 30 March 1989, where all present signed the following Claim of Right:

> We, gathered as the Scottish Constitutional Convention, do hereby acknowledge the sovereign right of the Scottish people to determine the form of Government best suited to their needs, and do hereby declare and pledge that in all our actions and deliberations their interests shall be paramount.

We further declare and pledge that our actions and deliberations shall be directed to the following ends:

- to agree a scheme for an Assembly or Parliament for Scotland;[58]
- to mobilise Scottish opinion and ensure the approval of the Scottish people for that scheme;
- to assert the right of the Scottish people to secure the implementation of that scheme.[59]

Over the next seven years the Scottish representatives pushed ahead with the painstaking job of creating a model of modern governance from scratch.[60] Their strength lay in their diversity, but it was that diversity that also presented them with many potential pitfalls and difficulties towards achieving consensus.

1.8 A Democratic, Not an Ethnic Question

One issue which favoured the successful outcome of the project was the reality that the struggle for better governance within Scotland had been seen from the outset as a *democratic* issue, with no vestiges of ethnicity connected to it. This was mirrored in the presentation of the scheme, where strategy documents were pointedly named "Towards *Scotland's* Parliament", rather than "Towards a *Scottish* Parliament". By doing so, it was emphasized that the parliament would be democratically structured for all those who lived within the geographical boundaries of Scotland, irrespective of ethnicity, race, religion or nationality.

1.9 The Process of Achieving the Scheme

In order to create a scheme from what was essentially a virgin canvas, working groups were formed after the initial full meeting of the Convention in order to examine specific topics: finance, power distribution, the situation of the outlying Scottish islands and making the parliament truly representative.

These committees reported regularly to the Executive Committee, a body of approximately 30 people, which in turn presented reports to the Convention for debate at its following nine full meetings (of approximately 160 people). Drawing upon agreement reached at these meetings, the Executive prepared a draft scheme for a parliament in Scotland, which was approved on 28 September 1990. "Towards Scotland's Parliament," the Convention's first report to the people of Scotland was launched at a civic and cultural event in Glasgow on 30 November 1990.[61] Further work was then undertaken on two important areas: the electoral system and gender balance; and the parliament's practices and procedures.

1.9.1   Electoral Reform and Gender Balance

Electoral reform was obviously the most difficult issue. The Labour Party gained substantially from the existing first-past-the-post electoral system in Scotland; everyone else lost out. Change, therefore, required one party to sacrifice for the benefit of others. Without the desire to make the Convention work, it is unlikely that there would have been any possibility of reform. The trade unions played a crucial role in this process, as did the fact that the churches and other groups as well as the Liberal Democrats favoured change.

After much discussion it was agreed that the Additional Member system should be used to elect a future Scottish Parliament. Under this system, 73 members of parliament would be elected from the existing Westminster constituencies (an extra constituency being created by splitting the Westminster Island constituency of Orkney and the Shetlands into two separate seats) by the first-past-the-post arrangement. Additional seats would be allocated to parties in accordance with the proportion of votes cast for each in each region. The final size of the parliament including the additional members would be 129 MSPs.

Linked to the issue of the electoral system was the recognized problem of women's under-representation in Scottish political life. This was accepted by the convention as a central issue, thus stimulating a number of women's groups in Scotland such as the Scottish Convention of Women and the STUC Women's Committee to produce proposals for inclusion in a new constitutional settlement.[62] The most radical of these was a proposal for a statutory requirement for gender balance among MPs in any future Scottish Parliament.[63]

Although no final agreement could be reached on the above-mentioned statutory element, action by the parties themselves, in furtherance of the broad aim of equality resulted in the new parliament being comprised of 38 per cent women MSPs overall—reportedly (at the time of writing) the third highest parliamentary representation for women in the world.

Other key proposals put forward regarding women-friendly and family-friendly hours of work, care facilities and gender balance in public appointments were also readily accepted by the Convention and saw light of day in the consultative steering groups proposals.

Various recommendations related to these issues were approved by the Convention on 27 February 1992. The next important step came in November 1993 when the Convention established a Constitutional Commission.

1.10   The Constitutional Commission

The Commission's main purpose was to develop further proposals on a number of key areas, including finalizing the issue of gender balance, the electoral system and parliament's relationships with Westminster, the European Union and local government. The Commission's report was discussed by the Convention on 2 December 1994.

This led to what was undoubtedly the more challenging phase of the Convention's work, and certainly the most innovative. The various partners in the Convention spent some (difficult) months discussing the Commission's proposals. They derived a common position on each issue before them. It should be stressed that throughout the seven years of its operation, *all* decisions arrived at by the Constitutional Convention were adopted on the basis of *consensus*, with voting (which would have divided the Convention) being rejected as a means of achieving a workable scheme.

Having reached an agreement, the Labour and Liberal Democrat parties committed to implement the scheme in their respective manifestos. The Scottish National Party, while arguing for Scottish independence, also made it clear that it would regard the consensual scheme as a useful progression from the status quo.

1.11   The 1997 General Election and the Referendum

Following their commanding return to power in the 1997 general election, Labour published a White Paper—called *Scotland's Parliament*—within three months as promised. In addition, a new Referendums Act was quickly passed, leading to referenda on the proposals. These took place in Scotland and Wales in September 1997.

Although no wrecking amendments (such as the previous forty per cent rule) were put forward, the Blair government surprised some by insisting on two questions, rather than one, being put on the ballot paper in Scotland. The first was simply whether parliament should be set up based on the Convention's scheme and the published White Paper. The unexpected second question asked whether (as all parties to the Convention's scheme had already agreed) the parliament should in fact have tax-varying powers (the power to vary income tax up or down by three per cent). In the run up to the referendum it was clear that the new Labour government, while in favour of the first vote, was far from enthusiastic about the second.

As expected, 74.3 per cent of those who voted (1,775,045 voters) supported the creation of a new parliament in Scotland. To the government's surprise, however (and much to its dismay in the view of some commentators), 63.5 per cent voted in favour of tax-varying powers (1,512,889 voters).

The results were confirmation of what the supporters of the Convention's scheme had long argued: that the introduction of a parliament for Scotland was "unfinished business" and "the settled will of the Scottish people".[64] Moreover, Scotland was a nation able to handle the responsibility of a parliament which had financial powers among its remit.

Following the majority support shown for constitutional change, the Scotland Bill (and a similar one for Wales where the referendum had also resulted in a narrow majority for an Assembly) was introduced into the Westminster House of Commons in December 1997 and received Royal Assent on 19 November 1998.

1.12   Shaping Scotland's Parliament—From White Paper to Reality

While the post election referendum clearly demonstrated support for the principle of constitutional change, and while the powers and remit of the parliament had been largely agreed by the cross-party consensus during the years of Thatcherism, much detailed work remained to be done in establishing how the parliament would operate in practice. One thing that was clear was that all the main bodies subscribing to the model outlined by the Scottish Constitutional Convention in their final document *Scotland's Parliament, Scotland's Right* wished for a parliament whose mode of operation would be fundamentally different from the outdated, unsatisfactory and confrontational Westminster model.

To oversee this matter, the Consultative Steering Group *on the Scottish Parliament* was created by the incoming Labour government with a threefold remit:

- to bring together views on and consider the operational needs and working methods of the Scottish Parliament;
- to develop proposals for the Rules of Procedure and Standing Orders which the Parliament might be invited to adopt; and
- to prepare a report to the Secretary of State by the end of 1998, to inform the preparation of draft Standing Orders.

Again, the group itself consisted of a broad range of academic, legal, cultural and political figures from Scottish life, and operated in an open and inclusive manner.

More than 800 organizations were canvassed on their opinions, and copies of the papers and minutes of the group were put on the Internet for easy access. Research was also commissioned on the working methods of national and regional parliaments in the European Union and elsewhere. Targeted focus groups were also set up, particularly those normally excluded from consultations such as young people and people in rural and remote areas. Finally, a series of open forum meetings were held across Scotland to allow views to be heard by the panel first hand. This allowed the group to claim, without exaggeration, that their exercise had been the most transparent and open within Britain to date and could stand as a model for good, modern governance.

1.13 The Significance of Scotland's Parliament as an Example of Good Governance

By the time the parliament opened in May 1999, its initial structure and method of operation had been worked out in some detail, firmly based on cross-party committee structures, learning from the perceived disadvantages of existing Westminster practice.[65]

Some key points are worth highlighting here, however. In its report, the Consultative Steering Group included comprehensive proposals for the functioning of the new parliament, identifying four key principles:

- *Sharing the power:* The Scottish Parliament should embody and reflect the sharing of power between the people of Scotland, the legislators and the Scottish Executive.
- *Accountability:* The Scottish Executive should be accountable to the Scottish Parliament, and the Parliament and Executive should be accountable to the people of Scotland.
- *Access and participation:* The Scottish Parliament should be accessible, open, responsive and develop procedures which make possible a participative approach to the development, consideration and scrutiny of policy and legislation.
- *Equal opportunities:* The Scottish Parliament in its operation and its appointments should recognize the need to promote equal opportunities for all.[66]

Thus, stress was put on the rejection of a model of government *above the people*, in favour of a model of governance where the concepts of *sharing, accountability, access, participation and equal opportunities* were paramount. That did not mean, though, that all possible future causes of tension were adequately dealt with. These issues will be examined below, following a brief consideration of models of legislative devolution.

2. MODELS OF LEGISLATIVE DEVOLUTION

The parliament established in Scotland remains part of the United Kingdom, with power voluntarily transferred from Westminster, London, to Holyrood, Edinburgh.

It is useful to consider two approaches to legislative devolution:

- *The Retaining Model:* This exists when all powers are devolved to the new body apart from those retained centrally. This implies that a devolved parliament can do everything which is not specifically prohibited.
- *The Transferring Model:* This model spells out the specifics of what the devolved parliament is permitted to do.

Interestingly, the original plan of the Constitutional Convention was for a Transferring Model, which in many ways is the weaker of the two options. In the event, however, the White Paper produced by the incoming Labour government accepted arguments for the former and more powerful Retaining Model, leaving Westminster only the specific powers outlined on such issues as:

- defence;
- social security benefits;
- foreign policy;
- immigration and nationality;
- employment;
- equal opportunity.

The issue of which powers have been retained is interesting, and will undoubtedly be a source of future debate and contestation as Scotland's Parliament gains more experience and thus more confidence in its own abilities. A case in point which caused debate at the time was the retention of the ability to legislate on matters relating to Equal Opportunities. Similarly powers over abortion provision were retained, indicating a difficulty with aspects of the feminist critique of central parliament.

3. POSITIVE ACHIEVEMENT AND POSSIBLE FUTURE TENSION

Several points should be highlighted as very positive aspects of the parliament which have begun to show their advantage already, together with several possible sites of tension which may sharpen in the future:

3.1 New Procedures and Structures

3.1.1 *Keeping the Executive in Check*

An innovative and potentially crucial aspect of the new parliament is its design around committees in order to empower 'ordinary' (i.e. backbench) members of the Scottish Parliament and avoid the centralization of executive power seen at Westminster.

This is assisted by the new electoral system which, given Scotland's voting patterns, has ensured the need for coalition government (at present between Labour and the much smaller Liberal Democrats). The electoral system has also allowed the breakthrough into parliament of two smaller parties—the Scottish Socialist Party (a formerly Trotskyist grouping) and the Green

Party, who gained one MSP each and were also joined by an independent, former Labour Party MSP who defeated the official labour candidate 'imposed' on the area by the party.

The importance of the culture shock brought about by coalition politics and the need to reach consensus cannot be underestimated in the British parliamentary system. Evidence arises every day of the steep learning curve of the largest party, Labour, and to a lesser extent of the Liberal Democrats, in readjusting to the real need to consult, work across party boundaries and respect the integrity of the individual backbench MSPs in the main body of parliament.

This was illustrated by the first defeat of the Executive by the body of the Parliament as early as May 2000. This arose over a private members Bill[67] initiated by the sole representative of the Socialist Party. The Bill examined procedures for debt collection in Scotland and sought to outlaw the particularly offensive practice of 'Warrant Sales'—the last resort enforced selling of an individual's household possessions to pay off the individual's debt.

This Bill, coming from an MSP on the floor of the parliament in consultation with a broad range of anti-poverty organizations, had been properly scrutinized by the three necessary parliamentary committees, which had approved it after amendment. It was then, however, opposed by the Coalition executive who sought to defeat it, but who had to accept defeat on the floor of parliament, given that the clear majority of their own backbenchers supported it. The role of women MSPs—vocal critics of their own coalition Executive—was also a notable issue in the above matter.

This may seem a small first measure of success. Nevertheless, such an outcome would have been absolutely impossible to achieve in the Westminster Parliament where such a bill would be talked out of time. The real significance of the defeat of the Executive was that it was seen as symbolic of the 'Parliament coming of age' by the majority of Scotland's media and commentators.[68]

A further indication of its importance is the fact that current opinion polls suggest 11 per cent of voters will now be willing to change their voting patterns and vote for smaller parties, given the demonstrable possibilities of this having a tangible impact.

The defeat of the Executive was repeated again in January 2001, over the question of financial charges for elderly people in residential care. This followed the Executive's proposal to only partly accept the recommendations of its own enquiry into the issue.

While its own enquiry had recommended free provision of such care, and acceptance of this had been implied by Executive spokespersons on several occasions, the final proposals fell well short of this on grounds of costs. The prospect of a looming defeat led to a last minute acceptance of the full package, the costing of which would now be brought to the full parliament at an early date. Ironically the ostensibly improved provision has raised voices of protest in England and Wales, where a more market-oriented approach has led to a less adequate package being offered to elderly people in care.

3.1.2   Living in Coalition

Coalition has never been seen by the major parties as a normal part of British politics. The situation in Scotland therefore causes some difficulties for members of parties accustomed to representing absolute majorities.

Again, the practice and experience in Scotland's Parliament must be counted as positive. This can be shown by the overturning of one of Labour's key pre-election policies—that of tuition fees. In their election manifesto, Labour supported the payment of tuition fees by university students (a newly introduced and controversial approach which appeared to emanate from the increasing neo-liberal approach of the Westminster-based Labour establishment). This standpoint was unacceptable to Labour's coalition partners (and similarly to the other Parties represented in the Edinburgh Parliament). A compromise was therefore struck, resulting in the abolition of fees for students in Scotland (while they continue for students elsewhere in the United Kingdom). The result for British Labour (similar to the case with elderly residential care outlined above) has been learning to live with the difficulty of two different policies—one for England and Wales, and the other for Scotland. It is perhaps the first example of the foreseen 'multi-layered politics' where political parties working within a diverse constitutional settlement will now have to get used to acting differently at different layers of government.

There are other symbolic examples of the steep learning curve. While to form a majority it was necessary for Labour to create a parliamentary coalition with the considerably smaller Liberal Democrats, the reality is that for more 'chauvinistic' elements in Labour, they would prefer to govern alone. From time to time this opinion is aired publicly—particularly by Labour MPs serving at Westminster, where all notions of coalition governments are regularly discounted.

The tensions which still existed were soon illustrated due to the unexpected hospitalization (within the first year of the parliament) of the Labour 'First Minister'[69] of the coalition government. This position endured for several months and meant that the representative of the coalition partner, the Liberal Democrats, became the main spokesperson and figurehead of the coalition government for that period—something which was obviously a grave difficulty for some in the Labour Party, as reported in the press.

4. UNRESOLVED ISSUES FOR TODAY AND THE FUTURE

4.1 The Relationship between the Westminster Government and the Scottish Government

Although measures have been enacted to help resolve tensions if and when they may arise between both levels of government, the practice of the first months of the parliament's existence has revealed some of the fault lines which still exist. Not all of these are clearly government-to-government. Some are based on the power structures within the parties in government at these different levels of Westminster and Scotland. Two examples will serve to illustrate this.

4.1.1   The Position of Secretary of State

The Westminster Cabinet position of 'Secretary of State for Scotland',[70] while long fought for, and extremely necessary before the establishment of the new structures in Edinburgh, is clearly a position that needs reassessment. Given the previous importance accorded to the office, the position itself has always been a sought after appointment by members of the governing party at a British level.

Rather than the position being downgraded immediately after Scotland's Parliament was created, the first post-devolution Scottish Secretary immediately set about doubling the number of civil servants under his control in Scotland in the departments remaining under the remit of Westminster (major parts of the Economy, etc). Public interventions were also made into issues of economic restructuring in Scotland, apparently without the full involvement of representatives of the Scottish Executive or MSPs. This led to well-publicized reports of these differences in the media and a suggestion that the Scottish First Minister had told the Scottish Secretary of State to "Get your tanks off my lawn".[71]

Reports at the time of writing (May 2001), however,[72] suggest that the anomalous position of Secretary of State for Scotland may be soon replaced by a more general position—possibly called Secretary of State for Devolution or Constitutional Affairs Minister—with a remit that covers Wales, Northern Ireland and Scotland.

4.1.2   Investigating the Costs of a Scottish Government

A second example that may be quoted here concerns the costs of building a new permanent home for the nascent parliament to replace its temporary venue. Following a debate over the site of the new building, growing estimates of the final cost led to concerns being raised in Westminster. Because of the concern raised in Scotland and elsewhere, the Scottish Parliament announced an independent inquiry into the proposed costs, and politely but very firmly rebuffed the suggestion by the Westminster Accounts Committee that it should play a role in the investigation.

4.2 The Changing Nature of 'Britishness'

One of the clear results of the devolutionary settlement is a sharpening of the discussion on the concept of 'Britishness'. It is clear that the idea of Britishness is entering some kind of crisis, not only in Scotland, but all across the UK. Labour in Westminster, and indeed historically, has had no tradition of articulating a positive, non-jingoistic image of Britain. Following the devolutionary settlement, most Scots under the age of thirty-five now say that they do not feel at all British, not even as a subsidiary identity. Ironically a similar process may also be taking place in England, where it is notable that English football fans have recently taken to sporting the St George's Cross[73] at football matches, rather than the Union Jack.[74]

This is not to suggest that a reversal to the four basic national identities of the United Kingdom—English, Scottish, Welsh and Irish—can constructively foreshadow the future for the UK, as is seen most pointedly in the complex peace process in Northern Ireland. A failure to recognize the complexity of modern identities, and the reality, for instance, of the extant Catholic-Irish and British Unionist identities, would lead to a setback, not a step forward, in the process of extending democracy in the United Kingdom.

In addition, the misgivings of Britain's Black citizens—who find themselves reasonably comfortable with the broad idea of Britishness, but uncomfortable with the idea of themselves as English—need to be noted here. Although the concept of Britishness is undoubtedly in crisis, and there is still a tendency to regard pluralism or dualism of identity as an 'untidiness' to be suppressed, rather than as a positive quality to be celebrated, progressive politicians of all political persuasions now need to consider how a modern concept of 'Britishness' can regain democratic relevance in the rapidly changing constitutional situation of the United Kingdom.

Salutary attention also needs to be paid by Scotland's new politicians to the fact that post-devolution Scotland remains predominantly white, English-speaking and Protestant, with an un-warranted complacency on racial issues and multiculturalism. This is reflected in one of the notable failures of the devolutionary process: to elect a single Black or Asian Scot to the new parliament.

5.   AREAS OF POSSIBLE FUTURE TENSION

5.1 Finance

Finance is the area of greatest potential disharmony in relations between future Scottish governments and their Westminster counterpart, particularly if the governments in power in Westminster and in Edinburgh are of a different political complexion.

In outlining its proposed scheme of financing the parliament, the Westminster Government final White Paper outlining proposals for the establishment of the parliament stated that "Scotland will continue to benefit from an appropriate share of United Kingdom public expenditure" and also established that the existing block grant arrangements would remain in place, adjusted annually by the 'Barnett Formula' (see below). Originally the Convention had proposed a 'reverse block grant' scheme, where all tax revenues levied in Scotland would remain in Scotland, with payments being made to London from Scotland for issues such as UK defence and other 'reserved' matters (matters of retained central responsibility).

This scheme was eventually rejected in favour of a variant of the existing funding arrangement between the Westminster Government and Scotland.[75] This arrangement is known as the Barnett formula where spending is based on a needs assessment exercise, then allocated on the basis of population.

Identifiable public spending in Scotland in 1996/97 was £24.7 billion, of which £14.9 billion came within the Secretary of State's responsibility. The 'Scottish block'[76] comprised £13.8 billion of this and it is only to this latter figure that the Barnett formula is applied.

The principle of the formula as it has been applied for the last twenty years has meant that for every £80 of public spending in England, £10 should be spent in Scotland and £5 in Wales. In the event, this has led to a higher level of spending per capita in Scotland than in England (due to higher needs assessment and differing social, economic and geographical conditions). Figures for 1995–96 indicate that per capita spending in Scotland is 125 per cent of the average per capita spending in England overall.[77]

While this has caused consternation in some areas of the English popular press, common sense has prevailed among most politicians who realize that much of the financial interaction between Westminster and other areas of the United Kingdom is difficult to quantify and that debate on fiscal transfers alone is inadequate to portray the contributions which different parts of a multinational state such as the United Kingdom respectively produce.

Behind much of this debate, however, is a failure to find agreement on whether Scotland would have a viable economy if independent, and the direction in which the revenues flow between England and Scotland. The SNP claim that England is a benefactor of the Union while the Westminster Government claims that Scotland is a net benefactor. The complexity of the argument is increased by the lack of consistent statistics. This is largely attributable to the Conservative Party which, while in office, took measures to stop the collecting of relevant comparative statistics disaggregated at the Scottish (rather than all UK) level.

This is therefore obviously an area where more long-term and clearer thinking needs to be developed to avoid further clashes. Experience to date suggests that this should also draw upon a broad range of sources and approaches.

5.2 Scottish Representation at Westminster

Another area of importance for future relationships is the claimed post-devolution 'over-representation' of Scottish MPs at Westminster. At present, 72 MPs continue to represent Scottish constituencies in the British Parliament. For geographical and historic reasons,[78] the average size of a Scottish constituency remains smaller than that of the average English one, leading to the claim that Scotland is over-represented in the House of Commons. At present, a Boundary Commission is examining future changes and it is thought that it may soon recommend a cut in Scottish representation to perhaps 57 or 58 MPs.

The reason that this may become an issue of contention is that an attempt may be made by the Westminster Government to force the Scottish Parliament to similarly cut the number of directly elected constituencies in order to retain uniformity of Westminster and Holyrood boundaries.[79] Any such attempt would be resisted fiercely as it would at a stroke destroy the proportionality offered by the current unique Additional Member Voting System in the Scottish Parliament and would thus undermine perhaps the key unique feature of Scotland's Parliament, from which all other changes are emanating.

The tardiness of the Blair government in implementing its own proposals for electoral reform at Westminster, however, suggests that major elements of the Westminster-based Labour establishment would not find this change unattractive.

A final issue of contention in regard to Scotland's representation at Westminster (and an ironic result of the uneven nature of the devolutionary process) is the continuing ability of Scottish MPs to vote on matters affecting only English constituencies while their English counterparts can no longer do the same in regard to matters devolved to Scotland. Thus, a Scottish MP can vote on the issue of English education, whereas an English MP is prevented from doing the same with regard to education in Scotland. While during the previous Conservative administration it was commonplace for English Conservative MPs to vote on Scottish matters (the 1993 General Election having seen the total disappearance of conservative MPs from Scottish constituencies), the current ability of Scottish MPs to do the same on English matters is now raised as a growing constitutional issue (by the Conservative opposition). It is clear that a process must be developed to remove what is an anomaly (albeit one that seemed to be acceptable under the previous political regime).

6.   CHALLENGES FACING THE PARLIAMENT

6.1 Extending Democracy to a Local Level

An issue currently before the Scottish Parliament and within its remit for action is the present structure and function of local government.

Given the low participation in elections for local government in Scotland and its heavy domination in many areas by single parties, a commission was set up prior to the Scottish Parliament inauguration to look at how to modernize local government and make it more responsive to the needs of the twenty-first century. This commission—the McIntosh Commission—has recommended the introduction of proportional election to local government elections. It has also suggested the need to reinvigorate the decentralized system of Community Councils which is set up at a very localized level in most parts of Scotland, and recommends a whole range of measures to make the practice of local government more accountable and accessible. To date, these suggestions have been received coolly by Labour, the majority party in most of Scotland's councils. It will be a measure of the parliament how seriously it promotes root and branch change at this lowest level of government.

6.2 Taking Civic Scotland Seriously

Parallel to the process which helped bring about the construction of the parliament was a similar increase of cooperation and coordination among Scotland's civic organizations in order to ensure their voice was always taken seriously by politicians. From this process has arisen a semi-permanent civic body, the Scottish Civic Forum, which periodically brings together representatives of 650 of Scotland's civic organizations to debate many of the same issues which are arising in the new Parliament, or are about to do so. Among the issues already discussed have been those of sustainable transport in Scotland, the situation facing the elderly and the question of fighting poverty.

It has long been proposed that the new parliament needs to take the deliberations of the Civic Forum seriously and listen to its views as a body representative of Scotland's grass-roots organizations. Again, this will be an issue upon which the new parliament is tested as it matures.

6.3 Dealing with Quangos

One of the more disturbing aspects of the eighteen years of Conservative administrations was their undermining of locally elected bodies such as municipal councils. Filling the power void were Quangos,[80] whose members were not elected but appointed by the prevailing governmental authorities. Such was the extent of this practice that in Scotland for every one individual elected to local government, four people were appointed to other positions of power over services. In many instances the agenda of the 186 Quangos in operation is still 'pre-May', that is, they do not fit in with the trajectory of the elected Scottish Government. Hence, civil service is to a large degree driven with little regard to local accountability.

Again there appears to be a reluctance to carry out the pre-election pledges of a 'bonfire of the Quangos', the current Scottish Executive seeming more willing to replace current appointees with others of a different persuasion, rather than subjecting these individuals and bodies to public scrutiny.

6.4 Dealing with the Senior Civil Service

The devolution transition within the Civil Service tended to be seen as a period of maintenance rather than a time of opportunity. Commentators have seen this as the result of the failure of the

145

Constitutional Steering Group to be able to spend the time necessary for the root and branch examination of Civil Service practice which was being afforded to the other elements of the parliament's functioning.

Where the Constitutional Steering Group laid down details of good practice, it has tended to be followed. Nevertheless, several policy advisors to the current Executive[81] have castigated current practice, which they allege is not keeping up with the type of imaginative changes seen elsewhere in the governance of Scotland. The first criticism was voiced by John Rafferty, the former Chief of Staff to the First Minister. In a speech to the Executive secretariat shortly before his departure from office, he stated that officials gave their Ministers "servility but not an imaginative consideration of what Ministers are trying to do". Officials in his view were the masters of the technicalities of the game, but did not come to grips with the way that policy outputs were to be achieved and real differences made.

In a more cutting criticism, Brian Fitzpatrick, who headed the St. Andrews House (Scottish Executive) policy unit for its first 17 months, has severely criticized the top level Civil Service who have staffed the Scottish Executive since its inception. Fitzpatrick in fact told the *Sunday Herald* in January 2001 that officials acted as if they were running a colonial administration and wished that the ministers would go off to London and leave them to run the country. Claiming that they failed to give adequate administrative backup to the First Minister and that they were hostile to ministers and advisors who brought a progressive agenda and a different mindset, he claimed: "On reaching office, we encountered a 'can't do' philosophy in the senior Civil Service, ... this might be a result of politicization and management structure shaped by men who had risen up the career ladder under Tory (Conservative) Scottish secretaries". He continued to say that "senior officials seemed to be looking towards their retirement packages and are unwilling, or unable, to accept the political priorities of the administration".

Traditionally theorists of the left have tended to emphasize the innate conservatism of the state and of the Civil Service. Evidence suggests that the issue is one that the new Scottish Executive cannot afford to ignore if it is to proceed with the type of fundamental change it has championed in the new parliament.

7. OVERALL ASSESSMENT OF THE SCOTTISH MODEL

In assessing any model of minority governance, authors (particularly those who have been intimately connected with the process of achieving change) need to tread warily when generalizing. Drs Brunner and Küpper in their earlier chapter do an admirable job in teasing out the many steps between principles and practicability, and the pragmatic nature of much current change.

Every model is unique, as is the Scottish model. As a type of territorial autonomy based on a long held, clear and uncontested geographical border, it escapes many of the complexities which those dealing with forms of personal or ethnically based autonomy have to grapple with daily. Like all other models, it is a product of its own particular history and political background, but importantly, it has a constitutional basis which is still developing as new issues are encountered for the first time, thus setting a precedent for future reference. Likewise, its relationship with local government is still in a formative period, with reform of local government an early item upon its agenda.

It has been fortunate in that its creation was part of a bigger change in British politics, and thus the political complexion of the Executive in Scotland, while not identical, is similar to that in

Westminster. A true test of the real power of the devolved parliament will surely only come when parties of a different political complexion occupy the British and Scottish levels of government.

On its side, however, it continues to have the acceptance of the vast majority of Scottish citizens, including a growing amount of those within Scotland who have tended to vote to preserve the Union. As in the rest of the British state, there has been a growing recognition of the new constitutional realities within the UK—with this recognition sparking off demands in England for a new approach to deal with the increasingly pluralistic demands of the English regions, including the special needs of the capital, London. The catalyst for this has partly been the increasing awareness of the differential policies (such as on student loans, elderly care, etc.) which the Parliament in Scotland is adopting, and which are being seen as perhaps more positive than those adopted elsewhere.

While this model is unique, there might still be general lessons to be learned. It would appear that the element which has given the Scottish experiment in better governance its apparent strength and stability, whatever its shortcomings will turn out to be, was undoubtedly the *process* of bringing the scheme to fruition. Building upon Scottish historical precedent (the Claim of Right) and Scottish legal tradition (sovereignty lying with the people), the consensual nature of the process of starting anew and excluding no one from the discussion (although some parties and organizations excluded themselves), together with the very difficult (and time-consuming) approach of seeking to move forward through consensus, resulted in the overwhelming vote in favour of the change (the 'settled will' of the Scottish people), as shown in the result of the referendum in September 1997.

7.1 Future Prospects

The Chinese politician Chou-En Lai, when asked his views on the impact and importance of the French Revolution on its two-hundredth anniversary, is alleged to have replied that it was far too soon to tell.

Likewise, Scotland's Parliament is a new arrival on the political scene in a rapidly changing Europe. A window of opportunity has clearly opened for the people of Scotland, and it is offering an opportunity which others may be able to learn from. Whether like the French Revolution it will stand the test of time and have significance in years to come is still a moot point. However, the first signs are certainly positive.

NOTES

[46]   Constitutional Steering Committee, "A Claim of Right for Scotland", in *A Claim of Right for Scotland*, Owen Dudley Edwards, ed. (Edinburgh: Polygon, 1988), p.13.

[47]   Scottish Constitutional Convention, *Scotland's Parliament. Scotland's Right* (Edinburgh: Scottish Constitutional Convention, 1996), p.6.

[48]   Joyce McMillan, "Britishness after Devolution", in *A Different Future—A Moderniser's Guide to Scotland*, G. Hassan and C. Warhust, eds. (Glasgow: The Centre for Scottish Public Policy and The Big Issue in Scotland, 1999), p.266.

[49]   G. Hassan, "Tomorrow's Scotland", in *A Different Future—A Moderniser's Guide to Scotland*, G. Hassan and C. Warhurst, eds. (Glasgow: The Centre for Scottish Public Policy and the Big Issue in Scotland, 1999), p.2.

[50]   The latter principle being the basis upon which English constitutional law has rested.

[51]   Ironically, the first SNP member who made the breakthrough into the 1960s Westminster Parliament was the same Winnie Ewing who opened Scotland's Parliament in 1999.

[52]   It may be noted that given the vagaries of the 'first-past-the-post' system of voting, a popular vote of 34–35 per cent could conceivably have led to a *majority* of the 72 Scottish seats going to the SNP, had it received that slightly higher level of public support.

[53]   Ironically, as pointed out by pro Assembly campaigners, this had the effect of counting the votes of the dead (if their names remained on the register) as among the opposition to the Assembly.

[54]   Evidence suggests that this tendency also appears to continue within the new Scotland, with the first piece of research to be published by the Central Research Unit of the new Scottish Executive confirming the view that the Scots continue to have a closer affinity to public services than their counterparts elsewhere in the UK. M. Smith, "Re-Energising the Public Sector", in *A Different Future—A Moderniser's Guide to Scotland*, G. Hassan and C. Warhurst, *eds., op.cit.*

[55]   James Mitchell, "Consensus, Whose Consensus?", in *A Different Future—a Moderniser's Guide to Scotland*, G. Hassan and C. Warhurst, eds., *op.cit.*, however, suggests that it would be unhelpful to label this approach solely as "consensus … since it tends to lump too much together. It would be well to recognise that Scottish politics involves shifting coalitions of minorities", p.28.

[56]   The reference here is to the abolition by the Conservative government of the Greater London Council—the elected body which had formerly represented the interests of the people in London. This was despite evidence in a London-wide referendum that this was against the wishes of a clear majority of Londoners.

[57]   Few examples existed of similar constitutional conventions, although the Constitutional Steering Committee mentioned three: the 1975 Northern Ireland Convention—set up as a 'legitimate' body by the British Government, and the much earlier examples of the German *Vorparlament* of 1848 and the French *Assemblée Consultative* (both of which had begun clandestinely, the latter having begun work in illegality in Algeria in 1944 before later being transferred to France and enlarged after the recovery of Paris).

[58]   Importantly, the word 'Assembly' was to be later unanimously dropped, in favour of the word 'Parliament' to signify the qualitatively new nature of what was coming into shape within the Convention's deliberations. In Wales, where no similar convention met, the scheme finally put forward by the Labour government in 1997 was limited to an assembly with a much lesser package of powers than was the case in Scotland.

[59]   Cf. Scottish Constitutional Convention, *Scotland's Parliament. Scotland's Right, op.cit.*

[60]   The Convention was commonly held to represent 75 per cent of the Scottish people and their organizations.

[61]   30th November is 'St Andrews Day', the day of the patron saint of Scotland, and has always held a significance for the Home Rule movement in Scotland.

[62]   A useful series of writings upon this is brought together in the publication *A Womens' Claim of Right*, published during this period of debate. Alice Brown, *A Womens' Claim of Right*, Determinations (Edinburgh: Polygon, 1986).

[63]   More than one commentator has stressed that the prominence of the issues of gender balance and women's representation in Scotland's politics historically was not by any act of goodwill by male dominated organizations. Rather the placing of women's issues on the agenda was a hard fought result of years of consistent campaigning and the action of women themselves. Esther Breitenbach, "Changing Gender Relations in Contemporary Scotland", in *A Different Future—A Moderniser's Guide to Scotland*, G. Hassan and C. Warhurst, eds., *op.cit.*

[64]   The words of John Smith, the former Labour leader whose death had ushered in Tony Blair's period as Labour leader.

[65]   Very useful outlines of how the parliament works in practice can be found on the Scottish Parliament Website: http://www.scottish.parliament.uk.

[66]   The Scotland Act referred to the need to remove discrimination based on marital status, race, disability, age, sexual orientation, language, social origin, religious beliefs and political opinions.

67 See the procedures for introducing legislation outlined on the Scottish Parliament Website.

68 Cf. G. Hassan and C. Warhurst, eds., *A Different Future—A Moderniser's Guide to Scotland* (Glasgow: Centre for Scottish Public Policy, 1999).

69 Equivalent to the Prime Minister.

70 Traditionally seen as Scotland's person in the British cabinet.

71 A phrase which gained currency in the 1960s when Labour government ministers told Trade Union officials to stop meddling in issues not seen as directly of their concern, i.e. the running of the economy.

72 *Glasgow Herald*, 8 May 2000; *Sunday Herald*, 28 May 2001.

73 The emblem of St George, the patron saint of England.

74 There is quite a significance here because a common complaint of Scottish football fans (and the Scottish media) was that while Scots sported the Scottish flag (saltire) and had adopted a recognizably Scottish song, 'Flower of Scotland', as Scotland's anthem to be sung at international games, until the recent change mentioned above, English fans would sport the United Kingdom's official flag, the Union Jack, and sing the UK's national anthem 'God Save the Queen', although their team represented only one of the UK's four nations.

75 The author, who was a member of the Scottish Constitutional Convention working group on Finance, can attest to this as an example of the 'real politique' which still surfaced from time to time in the nine years of the Convention's work during which a consensus was being forged on the constitutional blueprint. Three detailed and long meetings of the subgroup had taken place and had so far led to unanimous support for the reverse block grant approach (even from Labour), when at the last meeting a totally new draft was produced by Labour which reversed this position, and was presented as a 'non-negotiable' bottom line by Labour. It was popularly supposed that this was the 'price' of Labour accepting the move towards a form of proportional representation in the voting field, which was the Liberal Democrats' 'bottom line'.

76 Short for 'block grant'.

77 This figure is identical to the 125 per cent spending in London per capita when compared to the English average. Gavin McCrone, "Scotland's Public Finances from Goschen to Barnett", *Fraser of Allender Quarterly Economic Commentary* 24 (1999), pp.2, 35.

78 Some of these are obvious, such as the rural nature of the Highlands, where one would expect constituencies of necessity to consist of fewer people to allow a manageable electoral unit. Historically, however, there also remains the effect of the 'Unionist consensus' where Scotland was over-represented partly as a compensation for its subordinate position in the Union and to help dispel nationalist sentiments.

79 With the exception, of course, of the extra Island Seat representing Orkney and Shetland.

80 Quasi autonomous non-governmental organizations.

81 Ironically (or perhaps understandably), on leaving office, or being about to leave office.

The Sami Cultural Autonomies in the Nordic Countries

Kristian Myntti

The Sami Cultural Autonomies in the Nordic Countries

Kristian Myntti

1. INTRODUCTION

1.1 The Sami—An Indigenous People and a Minority

The Sami (in Sami: *Sápmi*)[82] are the indigenous people of Northern Scandinavia. There are altogether around 65,000 Sami in four countries: some 40,000 in Norway, 17,000 in Sweden, 7,000 in Finland and 2,000 in Russia.[83] *Sápmi* also means Samiland, i.e., the northern region that for one thousand years has been inhabited by the Sami people. Although *Sápmi* crosses the borders of four nations, the Sami have had a common flag and a national anthem since 1986.

The language, culture and way of life of the Sami differ from those of the majority populations.[84] Above all, the culture of the Sami reflects their traditional livelihoods, such as reindeer-herding, fishing and hunting. Although most Sami earn their living from sources other than the traditional Sami livelihoods, these are still of great importance for the Sami culture as a whole. Reindeer-herding requires—as do fishing and hunting—large unpopulated areas and an unspoiled nature. This means that the interests of Sami livelihoods may easily conflict with those of others or with other forms of the use of land and water, such as agriculture, forestry and tourism.

The Sami are no longer a homogeneous group. There are, for instance, reindeer-herding Sami and non-reindeer-herding Sami. Although the majority of the Sami still live within their heartland in the north, a considerable number of them have settled down in other parts of their countries, many in the Nordic capitals. Nearly all Sami know and use the majority language and most of them have received their education in this language. Today, only a minority of the Sami speak the Sami languages. Mixed marriages between persons of Sami ethnic origin and persons belonging to the majority populations are common.

1.2 Why Cultural Autonomy?

Within the Nordic countries there are three internationally well-known autonomous territories: the *Åland Islands*, which belong to Finland, and *Greenland* and the *Færøe Islands*, which belong to Denmark. The autonomy of the Åland Islands was established in 1921 as a part of the minority regime of the League of Nations. The Home Rule of the Faeroe Islands dates back to 1948, and the Greenland Home Rule to 1979. All of the Nordic territorial autonomies have far-reaching independent legislative and administrative powers.

The Åland Islands, the Færøe Islands and Greenland are all islands, and, consequently, clearly separated from the rest of the territories of the states to which they politically belong. Another common denominator is that their populations consist of linguistic or ethnic groups which form an overwhelming majority within each of the autonomous territories.

The Sami do not have a corresponding territorial autonomy, but they enjoy various forms of cultural autonomy. This is not because they would not be in need of any far-reaching self-governance, or because they, in contrast to the Åland Islanders, Færøe Islanders and the Greenlanders would not be entitled to claim territorial autonomy. The main reason is the dispersed nature of their settlements. Although the majority of the Sami lives in the northernmost parts of their countries, the Sami territories cover several provinces and a number of municipalities in Norway and Sweden. In most of these the Sami are in a minority. This is also the case in Finland where the Sami form a majority only in one of the four municipalities that together form the so-called Sami Homeland in the Province of Lapland.[85] In one of these municipalities their proportion amounts to only 1.5 per cent.

Today, there are so-called Sami Parliaments in Finland, Norway and Sweden. The first Sami Parliament was established in Finland in 1973 and the second in Norway in 1989. The most recent one, the Swedish Sami Parliament, was founded in 1993. The Sami Parliaments show some common features. A main characteristic is that their members are elected by and among the Sami populations in the respective country. Nevertheless, they have a history of their own and differ from each other from a legal-institutional as well as a functional point of view. They also have differing material and territorial competences.

The Sami Parliaments in the Nordic countries with a Sami population are studied in greater detail below.

2.   THE CULTURAL AUTONOMY OF THE NORWEGIAN SAMI

2.1 The Alta Conflict

The largest Sami population of the Nordic countries is found in Norway. It is estimated that some 40,000 Sami live in Norway. Today, the situation of the Norwegian Sami is probably the most satisfactory of the Nordic Sami. In recent years, there have been relatively few problems between the Norwegian Sami and the government, or between the Sami and the majority population.

This has not always been the case. For a long time, the Norwegian Sami were subject to a policy now commonly referred to as Norwegianization. This was a policy of assimilation legitimized by increasing Norwegian nationalism in the nineteenth century. From the 1850s onwards, the objective of the government was the establishment of Norwegian as the language of instruction for the Sami.[86] Later this policy was transferred to other sectors as well, such as agriculture, defence, communication and the media. It is worth mentioning that the 1902 Land Act stipulated that real property could only be transformed to Norwegian citizens who could speak, read and write Norwegian. Although in 1930 the Sami language was again allowed as a secondary language in some school districts, but Sami was in practice banned in many Norwegian schools right up until the 1950s. The policy of assimilation continued to influence Sami life after the Second World War, but at that time its motives were mostly of a socio-economic character.

The time after the Second World War was a time of political mobilization of the Norwegian Sami. In 1948, the first of the two principal Sami national organizations in Norway, the Confederation of Norwegian Reindeer Herders (NRL), was founded. The second one, the National Association of Norwegian Sami (NSR), was founded in 1968. Of these, the NRL, which promotes the economic, professional, social and cultural interests of Sami reindeer herders, has had a semi-official status since 1976.[87] In a framework agreement concluded between the NRL and the Norwegian government in that year, the NRL was given the exclusive and official competence to conduct annual negotiations with the state on reindeer-herding agreements. Based on these annual agreements, state subsidies are directed to this significant Sami livelihood.

In 1979, the Norwegian government decided to commence a major hydroelectric power project in the Alta-Kautokeino water systems. The project included the building of a 100-metre high dam across the Alta River in the northern Province of Finnmark, the very heartland of the Norwegian Sami. It also involved the construction of a road across Sami reindeer grazing land. The Sami conceived the project as a serious threat to their livelihoods in the area and to the vulnerable arctic nature in general.[88] The Sami and the environmentalists joined forces in demonstrations and civil disobedience actions directed against the project. These actions were not always peaceful, but entailed repeated clashes between the demonstrators and the police. In order to support the protests a number of Sami activists began a public hunger strike in front of the Parliament building in the capital of Oslo.

The protests had no impact on the hydroelectric power project itself. The dam and the road were constructed regardless of the resistance. The Alta controversy, which attracted much negative attention in Norway as well as abroad, nevertheless became the turning point for the official Norwegian Sami policy. The government now realized that the interests of the Sami had to be taken into consideration in major decisions that affected them directly. One immediate effect of the Alta controversy was the appointment of an *ad hoc* Sami Rights Commission in 1981 with, *inter alia*, the task to analyze the need for special legal rights for the Sami in Norway, and to draw up the guidelines for a future Norwegian Sami policy.[89] The Commission submitted a voluminous report in 1984.[90] One of its proposals was that an amendment to the Norwegian Constitution (*Grunnloven*) be adopted on the rights of the Sami as an indigenous people.

The proposed amendment, Section 110(a) of the Constitution, was adopted by the Norwegian Parliament (*Stortinget*) in 1988. It provides that "[it] is the responsibility of the state to create conditions enabling the Sami people to preserve and to develop their language, culture, and way of life". It is the task of the Norwegian Sami Parliament to implement the principles and aims of Section 110(a).

2.2 The Norwegian Sami Parliament

2.2.1 The Tasks and Competences of the Norwegian Sami Parliament

The Norwegian Sami Parliament (*Sametinget)* was founded in 1989 by an Act of Parliament ("Lov om sametinget og andre samiske rettsforhold [sameloven]"). King Olav IV declared its first session open on 9 October 1989. At the same time, it took over the tasks and duties of the Norwegian Sami Council.[91]

The Norwegian Sami Parliament has two major functions. Firstly, it is the representative political institution of the Norwegian Sami population in relation to the state, regional and local administration. Secondly, it is the administrative body of the Sami cultural autonomy in Norway.

Although it is subject under public law and financed directly from the state budget, the Sami Parliament is not a state authority. This means, for instance, that the government cannot direct its decision-making in concrete cases. It can also freely pursue its own policy in Sami issues even if it is not in line with that of the Norwegian government. The Sami Parliament has the competence to engage in all matters that, according to its own judgement, particularly concern the Norwegian Sami. Within its jurisdiction it may take initiatives, make petitions and issue statements to public authorities and to private parties. All public authorities must provide the Sami Parliament with an opportunity to be consulted before they take any action in matters that fall under its competence. It is not, however, a body to which a proposed measure is referred for mandatory consideration. In addition to these functions, it has been given some restricted decision-making powers regarding its own affairs. Under the Act, decision-making powers can be delegated to the Sami Parliament also through other legislation.

The office of the Sami Parliament, which is situated in Karasjok, has a staff of some 40 persons, including a full-time President and Vice-President. Its budget for working expenses amounts to roughly 30 million NOK.

The special Sami administration consists of four *Sami Councils* working under the auspices of the Sami Parliament: one for Sami cultural affairs *(Samisk kulturåd)*, one for the Sami languages *(Samisk språkråd)*, one for the Sami livelihoods *(Samisk næringsråd)* and one for Sami memorial monuments *(Samisk kulturminneråd)*. The Sami Councils employ some 20 persons and decide annually on the distribution of some 84 million NOK in state subsidies to Sami livelihoods, languages and culture. This task has in fact become one of the primary roles of the Sami Parliament.

2.2.2   Elections of the Sami Parliament

The Norwegian Sami Parliament consists of a total of 31 members who are directly elected from 13 constituencies. Entitled to vote at the elections of the Sami Parliament are those who have the right to vote at municipal elections and who have been registered in the Sami electoral roll of their own municipality. In order to be entered in the Sami electoral rolls a person must be a Sami. Under the law a Sami is a person who, according to his own declaration, considers himself a Sami and who 1) has Sami as his home language, 2) has had at least one parent or grandparent, who had Sami as his home language,[92] or 3) is a child of a person who is entered or has been entered on the Sami electoral roll. The voting age is 18.

At the elections held in 1997, 12 of the 39 members of the Sami Parliament were elected from the list of candidates of the Norwegian Labour Party *(Arbeiderpartiet)*, two from the Norwegian Centre Party *(Senterpartiet)*, 19 from the list of the National Association of Norwegian Sami (NSR)[93] and six from various Sami lists of candidates (electoral associations). From time to time the participation of political parties in the elections has been criticized. For instance, in the view of the Chairman of the NSR genuine Sami self-governance becomes impossible if the political parties dominate it. The Chairman of the Sami Parliament (also former Chairman of the NSR) defends the current system. Generally, those who are in favour of the current system argue that the participation of the political parties in the work of the Sami Parliament in fact reinforces—through their close contacts to the legislator, government and the central administration—the political influence of the Sami Parliament in public life.

2.3 Assessment of the Norwegian Sami Cultural Autonomy

During the past years, the Norwegian Parliament has established itself as the principal political institution of the Norwegian Sami. The government and the central, regional and local public authorities have recognized its status and importance. As a whole, the establishment of the Sami Parliament seems to have had predominantly positive effects. It has contributed to the political awareness of the Sami and consolidated their will to protect and promote their language and culture. For the government the Sami Parliament is a natural contact in all Sami issues, with the exception of reindeer-herding, which is still in the hands of the Confederation of Norwegian Reindeer Herders.[94] Generally speaking, the relationship between the Sami and the Norwegian majority population is probably better today than it was during the decades preceding the establishment of the Sami Parliament. To what extent the latter may have contributed to this development is, however, difficult to assess.

One problem that the Norwegian Sami Parliament needs to address is its lack of political legitimacy. In 1993, only 5,613[95] of an estimated total number of 40,000 Norwegian Sami participated in the elections of the Sami Parliament. The low voter participation has been attributed to the fact that many Sami have lost their language and therefore do not consider themselves Sami any more.[96] At this time the legal definition of a Sami entitled to participate in the elections was strictly linked to the Sami language. Before the 1997 elections, this definition was slightly amended on the initiative of the Sami Parliament.[97] In these elections, however, only 6,222 Sami used their right to vote. The figures show that the amendment of the Sami definition only had a marginal effect on the voting activity. Today, a fairly common opinion in the Sami Parliament is that the definition should be based solely on the principle of self-identification.

From this voting activity it could be deduced that many Sami have, in fact, a rather indifferent attitude towards their own representative organ. The parliament's lack of independent decision-making powers may be one possible explanation for this attitude. It has, for instance, no control over the lands that the Sami have traditionally occupied and used for their livelihood. Despite the unsolved Sami land rights question, Norway was one of the first states to ratify the 1989 International Labour Organization (ILO) Convention No. 169. At the time of ratification the government argued that the Convention does not require that indigenous peoples are given a legal title to the lands traditionally occupied by them, but that a strongly protected usufruct was sufficient for fulfilment of the Convention.

In January 1997, the Sami Rights Commission submitted its final report on Sami land rights.[98] In the report the Commission proposed the establishment of a new authority (*Finnmark grunnforvaltning*) for the administration of land and non-renewable natural resources in the Province of Finnmark. This authority was to have a Board consisting of eight members, four of which were to be appointed by the Provincial Government of Finnmark, and four by the Sami Parliament. The Commission further proposed that hunting, fishing, the collection of bird eggs and down, as well as the picking of cloudberries were to be rights of all the residents in the municipalities of Finnmark, regardless of ethnicity. The proposal is now subject to a broad political debate in Norway. If implemented it may make the Sami Parliament more interesting in the eyes of the Sami.

157

3. THE CULTURAL AUTONOMY OF THE FINNISH SAMI

3.1 Its Constitutional Basis

In contrast to the Norwegian Sami, the Finnish Sami have never had any national Sami associations to defend their interests in relation to the government and the state authorities. This is probably why their Sami Delegation was founded already in 1973 (by a decree). The Finnish Sami Delegation was an elected and representative Sami body. It consisted of 20 members who were chosen in free elections held among the Sami every four years. It had a duty to monitor and promote the economic, social and cultural rights of the Sami and to submit initiatives, make petitions and, since 1976, issue statements to the authorities regarding such matters within the Sami homeland. Its legal position was, however, rather unclear. For instance, it was not authorized to represent the Finnish Sami population nationally or internationally, nor had the state any express legal obligations to finance its activities.

In 1995, the status of the Sami as an indigenous people as well as their right to maintain and develop their language and culture was recognized following an amendment of Section 14 of the 1919 Constitution Act. The Constitution Act was repealed by the new Constitution on 1 March 2000. Today, Section 17, Sub-section 3 of the new Constitution provides on their rights: "The Sami as an indigenous people and Romanies and other groups shall have the right to maintain and develop their languages and cultures. The right of the Sami to use the Sami language before authorities shall be prescribed by an Act of Parliament".

Since 1 January 1996, the Finnish Sami have also enjoyed cultural autonomy, based on Section 51a of the 1919 Constitution Act. In the new Constitution, the legal basis for their cultural autonomy is provided by Section 121, Subsection 4, which states: "The Sami have, in accordance with what is prescribed in the law, cultural autonomy in respect to their language and culture within their Homeland". This constitutional provision was followed by an Act No. 974 of 1995 on the Sami Parliament. The Sami Parliament, which is an elected and representative Sami assembly, governs the Sami cultural autonomy.

3.2 The Finnish Sami Parliament

3.2.1 *The Tasks and Competences of the Finnish Sami Parliament*

The tasks, competences and organization of the Finnish Sami Parliament resemble those of its Norwegian counterpart. Its decision-making powers are limited. In practice, the Sami cultural autonomy is implemented through the right of the Sami Parliament to participate in public decision-making and administration. It is therefore more of a policy organ than an administrative organ.

Like the Norwegian Sami Parliament the Finnish Sami Parliament is a public law body. It works under the auspices of the Ministry of Justice and is financed from the state budget. However, it does not form part of the ordinary state administration, which means, for instance, that the government cannot give instructions to it on individual matters. The Sami Parliament also appoints its own staff, on which the legislation on civil servants is only partly applicable.

Under the law, the Sami Parliament represents the Finnish Sami population nationally and internationally. Its other principal task and duty is to promote the Sami language and culture and to take care of matters relating to the status of the Sami as an indigenous people. In such issues it may take initiatives, make proposals and issue statements to the authorities. The central, regional and local authorities also have an obligation to negotiate[99] with the Sami Parliament regarding all far-reaching and important measures which may directly and in a specific way affect the status of the Sami as an indigenous people, and which concern the following matters in the Sami Homeland:

1) community planning;
2) the management, use, leasing and assignment of state lands, conservation areas and wilderness areas;
3) applications for licenses to stake mineral or mine claims patents;
4) legislative or administrative changes in the occupations belonging to the Sami form of culture;
5) the development of teaching of and in the Sami language in schools, as well as social and health services; and
6) any other matters affecting the Sami language and culture or the status of the Sami as an indigenous people.

The decision-making powers of the Sami Parliament are likely to be extended in the future.[100] Today, the Sami Parliament has already assumed full responsibility for the production of Sami language textbooks and other teaching materials.

In 1999, the Sami Parliament received 4.3 million FIM from the state budget to cover its working expenses. In the same year it decided on the use of some 2.6 million FIM in state subsidies to the Sami culture and Sami language teaching material. The office of the Finnish Sami Parliament is situated in Inari and has a small staff. The Chairman of the Sami Parliament is employed full-time.

3.2.2   Elections of the Finnish Sami Parliament

The members of the Finnish Sami Parliament are elected by and among the Sami. For the purpose of these elections the country constitutes a single electoral district. The right to vote is given to all Sami, irrespective of domicile, who have reached the age of eighteen before the elections and who are either Finnish citizens or who, as citizens of some other state, have had their domicile in Finland for a period of two years prior to the election year. Today, the Sami election register comprises little more than 5,000 persons.

A person who is entitled to vote is also eligible to stand as a candidate at the elections of the Sami Parliament. Three persons entitled to vote may together nominate one candidate for the elections. In the elections the electors vote on individual candidates. In Finland there are no Sami parties, and the national political parties do not have the right to nominate candidates for the elections of the Sami Parliament.[101] At the 1999 elections, a total of 2,941 votes were cast. This amounted to 57.4 per cent voter participation.

3.3   Who is a Sami?—The Question of Sami Community Membership

The definition of a person entitled to vote and to stand as a candidate at the elections of the Sami Parliament differs from that in Norway. For the purposes of the Act on the Sami Parliament, Sami means a person who considers himself a Sami, provided:

1) that he himself or at least one of his parents or grandparents has learnt Sami as his first language; or
2) that he is a descendant of a person who has been entered in a land, taxation or population register as a mountain, forest or fishing Lapp; or
3) that at least one of his parents has or could have been registered as a voter for an election to the Sami Delegation or the Sami Parliament.

This definition of a person entitled to vote at the elections of the Finnish Sami Parliament has caused many debates in Finland and is discussed in greater detail below.

The establishment of the Finnish Sami Parliament had a rather unexpected negative impact on the relationship between the Sami and the majority population in northern Finland.

Already the legislative proposal of a Sami cultural autonomy was fiercely opposed by some groups of local residents within the Sami Homeland, such as non-Sami reindeer herders, who feared that a Sami cultural autonomy would be a first step towards exclusive Sami rights within the said territory. The reason for their fear was a proposal submitted by an *ad hoc* Sami Rights Commission in 1990. According to this proposal the land managed by the state within the Sami Homeland should be handed over to the Sami with ownership. Furthermore, it was proposed that reindeer-herding, fishing and hunting within this area would become exclusive Sami rights.[102] Despite the protests, the legislation on a Sami cultural autonomy was adopted, but with some adjustments as regards the beneficiaries of the right to cultural autonomy.

The earlier legal definition of a Sami was a linguistic one,[103] while the new definition includes 'descendants of Lapps' as beneficiaries of the political rights pertaining to the Sami cultural autonomy. *Lappalainen* ('Lapp') is the old Finnish language term for a Sami, which in turn is a Sami language term in use since the 1960s. This means that all individuals who were Sami under the earlier linguistic Sami definition are descendants of Lapps, too. One of the differences between the present 'descendants of Lapps' and the [linguistic] 'Sami' is that the former have already lost their contact with the Sami language several generations ago.

Due to certain amendments decided by the Parliament it was a common belief at the coming into force of the Sami cultural autonomy that the reference to the descendants of Lapps in the Act meant that an individual who can prove that he or she is a direct descendant of a person who has once been registered as a Lapp—be that two centuries ago—qualifies as a descendant of a Lapp and is, for the purposes of the Act, a Sami with the right to vote and to be elected at the elections of the Sami Parliament.[104]

After the legislation on the Sami cultural autonomy came into force in 1996, the conflict continued, centring on the definition of a Sami. Now many of the local inhabitants who had originally opposed the legal proposition required—claiming to be descendants of Lapps—to be registered as Sami with the right to participate in the elections of the Sami Parliament. This was strongly rejected by the Sami Parliament. It requested an immediate amendment of the new Sami definition. According to the Sami Parliament the definition of a Sami must be based solely on the Sami language, as the characteristics and culture of the Sami are strongly tied to that language. It was feared that the provisions on the descendants of Lapps might result in the domination of the Sami Parliament by persons who had lost their ties to the Sami language and culture several generations ago.

However, the Sami definition was not amended, and in 1999, a total of 1,128 persons filed an application to the Electoral Board of the Sami Parliament to become registered voters in the elections of the Sami Parliament (in September 1999) on the grounds that they were descendants of Lapps. The Sami Parliament rejected all of the applications. Of those rejected, over 600 appealed to the Supreme Administrative Court. In its decision, the Supreme Administrative Court rejected all but ten of the appeals. The Court noted that the linguistic part of the definition of a Sami stretches four generations back in time. According to the Court, the same rule shall apply in regard to descendants of Lapps. The debate on the definition of a Sami nevertheless continues.

3.4   Assessment of the Finnish Sami Cultural Autonomy

Compared to its predecessor, the Sami Delegation, the establishment of the Sami Parliament represented a positive development from a Sami point of view. This is far from saying that the new body would have solved all the problems. For instance, the public subsidies to the Finnish Sami Parliament are still modest, particularly compared with those of the Norwegian Sami Parliament. The lack of real independent decision-making powers for the Sami Parliament has also been criticized. The obligation of the central, regional and local authorities to negotiate with the Sami Parliament in all far-reaching and important measures which may directly affect the Sami has in practice too often proved to be more of a formal consultation than real negotiations. Often, the time limit set by the authorities for the Sami Parliament to react has been too short. On the other hand, it is stated in the Government's Bill that the Act only gives the framework for Sami cultural autonomy, and that it is the task of the Sami themselves to develop it further.

The conflict between the Sami and the local majority population regarding the definition of a person entitled to participate in the elections of the Sami Parliament was a very unfortunate result of the new legislation. However, it must be underlined that the conflict does not concern the Sami cultural autonomy as such, but certain economic matters such as the right to herd reindeer within the Sami area.[105] The situation is fomented by the fact that the national and international pressure on the government to ratify the 1989 ILO Convention No. 169 concerning Indigenous and Tribal Peoples in Independent Countries has increased. Article 14 of the ILO Convention recognizes a right of ownership of the lands traditionally occupied by indigenous peoples. The Finnish Sami claim—with reference to history—that they are the legitimate owners of the land within the Sami Homeland that is now administered by the state. Again, the local non-Sami reindeer herders fear that a Finnish ratification will have as a consequence that reindeer-herding, together with fishing and hunting, will become exclusive Sami rights. This debate is still continuing.

4.   THE CULTURAL AUTONOMY OF THE SWEDISH SAMI

4.1   The Taxed Mountain Case

The Sami population of Sweden is often estimated at some 17,000. Of these, fewer than 2,500 are members of a so-called Sami Village and engaged in reindeer-herding.[106] Those Sami who are members of a Sami Village have a usufructuary right to practice reindeer husbandry within the reindeer breeding area, including the right to hunting and fishing. Most Swedish Sami are not members of a Sami Village and, consequently, not permitted to exercise the aforementioned rights.

In Sweden a major political mobilization of the Sami took place in the late 1940s and the 1950s. At that time a number of Sami organizations were founded, including two national Sami organizations: the *Same Ätnam*, founded in 1945, and the Swedish Sami National Union (SSR), founded in 1950. *Same Ätnam* represents the interests of non-reindeer-herding Sami, while the SSR is the umbrella organization for the Sami Villages and the reindeer-herding Sami.[107] The time after the Second World War was also a time of rapid industrialization in Sweden. Hydroelectric power plants were constructed and forests were logged for the needs of the fast growing Swedish forest industry. Such measures were also taken within the reindeer-herding areas of the Sami, which caused tension and conflicts between the Sami and the government. In the 1970s, the Sami defended their rights and interests by taking legal action. In particular, the SSR was actively engaged in the so-called *Taxed Mountain Case*, which was decided by the Supreme Court of Sweden in 1981 after fifteen years of proceedings. In this case the parties were a number of Sami Villages and the Crown, and the issue at stake was the legal title to the so-called Taxed Mountains in the north of the Province of Jämtland. The Sami parties lost this case.[108]

4.2 The Swedish Sami Parliament

4.2.1   The Tasks and Competences of the Swedish Sami Parliament

After the failure to reach a satisfactory legal solution on Sami land and water issues, the reindeer-herding Sami too were ready to try to reach a political solution in these matters. In 1983, the government appointed an *ad hoc* Sami Rights Commission with the task to assess the need of a representative political Sami body in Sweden. The Commission submitted two reports, the first in 1986[109] and the second in 1989.[110] In its second report the Commission elaborated three alternative models: (1) the fusion of the three existing central Sami organizations into one national Sami organization, (2) the establishment of an elected Sami Parliament, and (3) the establishment of an umbrella organization for the existing national Sami associations. The Commission decided to recommend the establishment of an elected and representative Sami Parliament.

In 1993, the Swedish Sami Parliament was established by an Act of Parliament (1992:1433). However, already the *travaux préparatoires* show that it was not the government's intention to create a Sami self-governance or to grant any special political rights to the Sami. The new Sami body was not supposed to restrict the competence of the already existing democratic institutions of society. The government emphasized that the Sami Parliament should not be in a superior position in relation to other authorities, and that the interests of the Sami should not necessarily prevail in a possible conflict of interest. Nor was the government prepared to introduce any special constitutional guarantees for the Sami culture or language. The Swedish Constitution (Chapter I, Section 2) only includes a general provision on the right of ethnic, linguistic and religious minorities to maintain and develop their cultural and social life, but does not specifically mention the Sami.

Under the Act the Swedish Sami Parliament is not a representative Sami organization or an organ for a Sami cultural self-governance but an administrative state authority with a Sami

representation with the task to promote a living Sami culture and to protect the cultural interests of the Swedish Sami population. In particular it should:
1) decide on the distribution of state subsidies to the Sami culture;
2) appoint the Board of the Sami School;
3) direct the work for the promotion of the Sami language;
4) contribute to the societal planning and monitor the interests of the Sami, among them, the interests of the reindeer breeding in relation to the exploitation of land and water;
5) provide information on Sami conditions.

The task of the Sami Parliament is thus limited, with very few exceptions, to taking of initiatives in certain Sami cultural matters. It has no voice as regards new legislation. It is not, for instance, a body to which proposed measures are referred for consideration. Legally, the Sami Parliament is a state authority under the direct control and jurisdiction of the Swedish government. This means, for instance, that it is bound by the ordinary administrative legislation and that its members and employees are civil servants. State authorities and civil servants are generally expected to be loyal to the government and to implement its official policies. In strict legal terms the Sami Parliament seems to have limited possibilities to pursue policies of its own, such as Sami land rights claims.

The office of the Sami Parliament is situated in the town of Kiruna and has a staff of some nine persons. The President of the Board of the Sami Parliament is a full-time civil servant. The working budget of the Sami Parliament amounts to some 14 million SEK. In addition, it decides annually on the distribution of some 20 million SEK in state subsidies for Sami culture and language, and some 40 million SEK in compensation to reindeer owners for damage caused by predators.

The Sami were from the beginning dissatisfied with their new organ. It was not the representative Sami organ they had hoped for. It may also be noted that on the establishment of the Swedish Sami Parliament there was a simultaneous decision by the Swedish government to allow public hunting of small game within the Sami reindeer-herding area, a decision which greatly upset the Sami, in particular those engaged in reindeer-herding.

4.2.2   Elections of the Sami Parliament

The 31 members of the Swedish Sami Parliament are elected by and among the Sami. For the purposes of the elections, the country constitutes a single electoral district. The elections are held every four years. A person who is entitled to vote is also eligible to stand as a candidate. In order to be entitled to vote a person must be registered in the Sami electoral register. A person is entered in the electoral register on application, provided that he is a Sami, has reached the age of eighteen before the elections and is a Swedish citizen or a foreign citizen, provided he has had his legal domicile in Sweden for a period of three years prior to the elections.

The Sami Parliament meets in plenary sessions three times a year. The Parliament appoints a Board with seven members. The Act on the Sami Parliament includes a definition of a Sami entitled to be registered in the Sami electoral register. Under the Act a 'Sami' is a person who considers himself a Sami, and shows:
1) that it is likely that he has or has had Sami as his home language;
2) that it is likely that at least one of his parents or grandparents has or has had Sami as his home language,
3) that at least one of his parents is or has been registered in the Sami electoral register.

The Swedish definition of a Sami entitled to vote at the elections of the Sami Parliament is thus in principle based on the Sami language but is not necessarily a linguistic definition. The definition speaks of a person who "has or has had Sami as his home language". It is not required that the person in question actually knows the Sami language, or that it was his dominant language during his childhood and adolescence. Before the 1997 elections of the Sami Parliament, the Election Committee decided that Sami spouses have the right to be registered in the Sami election roll regardless of their language and ethnicity. In practice, the Election Committee without any investigations approves all applications for registration, whether or not the applicant actually fulfils the stipulated linguistic criteria. The third criterion of the definition, that is that at least one of his parents is or has been registered in the Sami electoral register, has the effect that a child of a registered person is always entitled to be registered as a Sami, regardless of the language requirements of the Sami definition. In the 1997 elections of the Sami Parliament the number of persons entitled to vote amounted to a total of 5,990. Of these 3,803, or 65 per cent of those entitled to vote, participated in the elections. Taking into account that the total number of Sami in Sweden is estimated to amount to 17,000, voting activity is rather low.

At the elections, the candidates are nominated by Sami parties representing various Sami groups and interests, such as the reindeer-herding Sami, the forest Sami, the fishing and hunting Sami, etc. The Sami parties with a representation in the Sami Parliament receive public subsidies amounting to some 470,000 SEK per year. The national political parties in Sweden have so far not participated in the elections of the Sami Parliament, although they have a legal right to do so.

4.3 Assessment of the Swedish Sami Cultural Autonomy

After seven years of operation the Swedish Sami Parliament has not quite come up to all Sami expectations. What the Sami had hoped to see was the beginning of a new era of increased Sami influence and self-governance in important Sami issues. What they got was state authority with almost no independent powers, the work of which is characterized by internal disagreements, particularly between the Sami Parliament and its Board, as well as by conflicts with the Swedish government.

One reason for the current situation is the Swedish reindeer-herding legislation which divides the Swedish Sami population into reindeer-herding and non-reindeer-herding Sami. The interests of these two groups are not always easy to reconcile. But the main reason is apparently the Sami Parliament's dual role as a state authority under the government and a representative Sami assembly. It is expected to be loyal both to the government and to the Sami electors. Furthermore, the division of work, powers and responsibility between the Sami Parliament and its Board seems unclear. Under the Act on the Sami Parliament the Board must reflect the political composition of the Sami Parliament. Therefore, the members of the Board are proportionally selected, which means that the Sami parties have seats in the Board in proportion to their number of representatives in the Sami Parliament. The principle of parliamentarism is not applied. Soon after the 1997 elections, some members of the Board defected from their 'parties', with the consequence that the Board no longer reflects the political composition of the Sami Parliament, a fact that has deepened the internal political discord.

Several attempts to correct the situation have been made. Already in 1996, an internal *ad hoc* organization committee of the Sami Parliament proposed the Board be selected with a majority of the votes. According to another internal proposal put forward in 1998, the Sami political representation and the Sami administration should be separated from each other.

In October 2000, after an unsuccessful effort to mediate between the parties,[111] the Minister responsible for Sami Affairs appointed an official administrator with the task to submit a proposal for the separation of the two functions of the Sami Parliament (state authority and elected Sami organ). This work continues.

Another source of frustration among the members of the Sami Parliament, and in particular among the members of Sami Villages, is that Sweden has not ratified the 1989 ILO Convention No. 169 concerning Indigenous and Tribal Peoples in Independent Countries. The obstacle for a Swedish ratification of the Convention is its Article 14 on indigenous peoples' land rights. In 1999, a Special Rapporteur appointed by the Swedish government estimated that Sweden could accede to the ILO Convention within approximately five years, provided that a number of steps related to Sami land rights are effected.[112]

5. THE NORDIC SAMI CULTURAL AUTONOMIES— SUMMARY AND CONCLUSIONS

5.1 The Sami Parliaments Compared

This brief presentation of the Nordic Sami cultural autonomies shows that the situation and problems of the Sami as well as the minority policy vary from one Nordic state to the other. For this reason, the measures taken by each state in regard to the Sami differ. The Nordic Sami cultural autonomies have different backgrounds. The Norwegian and the Swedish Sami Parliaments are at least indirect results of concrete problems in the relationship between the Sami and the national governments and/or the majority populations. In contrast, the establishment of the Finnish Sami Delegation in 1973, and later the Finnish Sami Parliament, seems more like an attempt to put the Sami on the same footing as the Åland Islanders and the Swedish-speaking minority on the Finnish mainland.

There is little evidence that the existing cultural autonomy arrangements of the Nordic Sami as such would have prevented any concrete ethnic conflicts. On the other hand, the Norwegian and the Finnish Sami Parliaments have clearly improved the possibilities of the Sami to participate in decisions that affect them directly. Improved participatory rights of minority groups usually reduce the risk of ethnic conflicts. This does not mean that the Norwegian and Finnish Sami are entirely content with their respective cultural autonomy. In particular, the Finnish Sami have criticized the narrow decision-making powers and the modest economic resources of their Sami Parliament.

The work of the Swedish Sami Parliament has not been equally successful. So far the work of the Swedish Sami Parliament has not fully satisfied the Sami community. Nor does it seem to have contributed substantially to the improvement of the relationship between the Sami minority and the majority population. The primary reason for its relatively modest performance is found in the Swedish government's principal reluctance to recognize special Sami rights, in particular special political rights. Sweden has been a country of immigration for a long time and has therefore pursued a policy of integration, rather than one of minority protection.

Unfortunately, new sources of conflict have emerged between the Sami and the majority population during recent years as well. One is the opening up by the government of the Sami reindeer-herding areas for public hunting of small game. The second new source of conflict is the legal protection of large predators such as bear, wolf, wolverine, lynx and eagle within the reindeer-herding areas. The Sami see the ever-rising number of large predators in these areas as a serious threat to their livelihood, while the environmentalists accuse them of obstructing nature conservation in northern Sweden. In recent years the Sami have often been accused of poaching.

It is evident that the Swedish Sami Parliament needs some reorganization. These measures should aim at the strengthening of its role as a democratic and representative Sami political organ. In no case should it be transformed into a purely administrative state authority. Such a development would not be consistent with Article 6 of the 1989 ILO Convention No. 169, according to which indigenous people shall have their own representative institutions.

Normally, the question whether or not a person belongs to a minority group is determined following the principle of self-identification. According to this principle an individual identifies him or herself with a certain group of people and decides to become one of its members.

In the case of the Sami, self-identification is one, but not the only definition criterion. Only those persons who fulfil the stipulated objective Sami criteria have the right to participate in the elections of the Sami Parliaments. In Sweden and Norway the legal Sami definitions have been interpreted broadly. Today, there is a common understanding in the Swedish and the Norwegian Sami Parliaments that the legal definition should not prevent anybody who feels that he or she is a Sami from taking part in the work of the Sami Parliaments. Even so, in particular the Norwegian Sami Parliament suffers from a low voting activity.

In Finland the situation is quite the opposite. The Finnish Sami emphasize the importance of a strict interpretation of the criterion of the Sami definition. In their view the definition of a Sami should be based solely on the Sami language, as characteristics and culture of the Sami are strongly tied to that language.

In Norway and Sweden the right to herd reindeer and the right to hunt and fish within the reindeer-herding areas are rights of certain Sami families only. The subjects of these rights are defined in the Norwegian and Swedish reindeer-herding legislation. The rights are transferred from one generation to the next. Therefore, any additional land or water rights that may be granted to the Sami in the future, for instance, as a consequence of a possible Swedish ratification of the ILO Convention No. 169, will be exclusive rights of the reindeer-herding Sami. In any case, they would not become rights of all those defined in the Acts on the Sami Parliaments.

In Finland, the corresponding rights are not exclusive Sami rights, but rights of all local inhabitants within the Sami area. The Sami therefore hope that a future Finnish adherence to the ILO Convention would make the said rights exclusive Sami rights, that is to say, rights of persons fulfiling the definition in the Act on the Sami Parliament.

Another difference between the Nordic Sami cultural autonomies lies in the different roles of the political parties in the work of the Sami Parliaments. In Norway, two parties are currently represented in the Sami Parliament. In Sweden, only Sami parties so far participate in the elections of the Sami Parliament, and in Finland the electors cast their votes on individual Sami candidates. Obviously, the participation of the political parties in the work of the Sami Parliaments could have negative as well as positive effects. It is a known fact that Sami issues can rarely be solved on a classical left–right political scale. If the political parties gain too much influence in the Sami Parliaments, there is a danger that they might produce solutions to problems involving Sami culture, language or way of life that are not necessarily consistent with the collective interests of the Sami population but rather reflect party interests. Those who defend the participation of political parties in the work of the Norwegian Sami Parliament often underline the importance of the Sami Parliaments having direct political links to the government and legislator.

5.2 The Sami Parliaments in the Light of the Common Criteria and Factors for the Comparison and Analysis of Minority Self-Governance in Europe

The Sami cultural autonomy arrangements in the Nordic countries are in many respects typical examples of personal autonomy solutions. For instance, all Sami, irrespective of their place of residence in their countries, have the right to vote and to stand as candidates in the elections of their own Sami Parliaments. The Sami cultural autonomies are not entrusted with any independent legislative or administrative powers, but their decision-making competence is restricted to a limited internal self-administration. On the other hand, their jurisdiction, particularly that of the Finnish Sami Parliament, is partly territorially defined, and covers certain matters within the traditional Sami areas. The geographical borders of this area are defined in the legislation.

There are Sami electoral rolls in all the three Nordic countries. Only a person who fulfils the legal definition of a Sami may be registered in these rolls. A personal application, or at least a written consent, is a further requirement for such a registration.

Being an indigenous people, the Sami differ from most other minorities in Europe. Unlike many European national minorities they have no kin-state. They are also dispersed on the territories of four nation-states. In each of these states they form a very small minority.

In Finland, the establishment in 1973 of the predecessor to the current Sami Parliament, the Sami Delegation, was most likely inspired by the autonomy of Åland, on the one hand, and the special constitutional and legal guarantees for the protection and promotion of the Swedish language and culture on the Finnish mainland, on the other. Again, the establishment of the Norwegian and Swedish Sami cultural autonomies appear to have been consequences of efforts to solve conflicts of a more concrete and immediate nature between the Sami and the governments—the Alta controversy and the outcome of the Taxed Mountain Case. However, in this context one should not underestimate the influence of the Nordic democratic traditions either.

In Norway and Finland the Sami cultural autonomies have a strong constitutional basis. Special statutes establish the Sami Parliaments themselves. In Sweden, the Sami cultural autonomy does not have a constitutional ground, but there is nevertheless an Act on the Sami Parliament. All Sami Parliaments are thus bodies under public law. They are financed directly from the state budgets. Legally, the Swedish Sami Parliament is a state authority with a Sami representation, while the Norwegian and Finnish ones are clearly Sami bodies and are relatively independent from the government and the state administration.

The primary tasks and duties of the Sami Parliaments are to protect and promote the Sami culture and language. Although the arrangements are called cultural autonomies, their main role, particularly of the Norwegian and the Finnish Sami Parliaments, is to be the representative political institutions of the Sami minority in relation to the government, the legislator and the state, regional and local administration. In other words, they are basically bodies for political participation. The Swedish Sami Parliament is a political body, too, but with a more limited competence. As a result of their characteristics the Sami cultural autonomies are more designed to prevent than to solve interethnic conflicts. It is also important to note that the majority populations have not opposed the establishment of the Sami cultural autonomies. In Finland, the negative reactions by a relatively limited number of local inhabitants of non-Sami origin had mainly economic reasons.

As the Nordic Sami cultural autonomies are still developing, it is too early to assess their final successfulness. Naturally, a number of problems and shortcomings remain to be solved and corrected. Some of them can obviously be overcome relatively easily, for instance, through technical re-organizations or by providing the economic resources required, while others may prove to be of a more complex character. Among these is the lack of control by the Sami—through ownership and possession—over the lands traditionally occupied by them. Collective land rights claims are, however, normally not claims of ethnic or linguistic minorities. On the whole, the Nordic Sami cultural autonomy concepts appear to be both viable and reasonably successful arrangements, which could, with certain modifications, be applied to other small and dispersed minorities as well.

NOTES

82   Sami, or *Sápmi*, is a Sami language term that has been employed since the 1960s. Earlier, the Sami were often called 'Lapps'.

83   This article does not deal with the Russian Sami, as they do not yet have a representative political assembly of their own. For an overview of the Sami of the Kola Penisula see, for instance, Hans-Erik Rasmussen, "The Sami on the Kola Peninsula", in *The Barents Region,* Ingvar Björklund, Jakob J. Möllerand and Per K. Reynert, eds. (Tromsö: University of Tromsö), 1995, pp.48–55; and Leif Rantala, "The Russian Sami of Today", in *The Barents Region, op. cit.,* pp.56–62.

84   Some indigenous peoples speak of themselves as peoples, nations or first nation and deny that they constitute minorities even if they are in a numerical minority in a state. It may nevertheless be noted that there is no commonly recognized definition of an indigenous people or a minority in international law. For instance, the Human Rights Committee has not seen any obstacles for persons belonging to indigenous peoples to claim the rights of persons belonging to minorities under Article 27 of the International Covenant on Civil and Political Rights. In practice the Committee has received and decided a number of complaints under Article 27 by such persons. It may therefore be concluded that at least an indigenous people in a numerically inferior position in a state is—objectively speaking—a beneficiary of minority rights. This is, however, not to say that a state would have the right to define or treat—not even by referring to objective criteria such as a numerically inferior position—an indigenous people as a minority against the will of the group in question.

85   Geographically, the Sami Homeland covers some ten per cent of the total area of Finland.

86   See, for instance, Eivind Bråstad Jensen, "Norwegian Policy towards the Sámi in a Historic Perspective", *Interskola Conference* (Bodø: Nordland County Director of Education, 1992), pp.132–138.

87   In Norway, reindeer-herding is an exclusive Sami right within the reindeer-herding area. Some 95 per cent of the reindeer in the country are owned by Sami. Over-grazing of the pasturelands is a serious problem also in Norway. As the highest number of animals which can be grazed within the reindeer-herding is limited, only a small minority of the Norwegian Sami, some 2,000, have the right to herd reindeers. Within the reindeer-herding Sami families the right is transferred from one generation to the next. The right to herd reindeers is a usufructuary right and can be exercised within the reindeer-herding area regardless of ownership or possession of land.

88   On the Alta/Kautokeino controversy see Odd Terje, Brantenberg "The Alta-Kautokeino Conflict: Saami Reindeer-herding and Ethnopolitics", in *Native Power*, Jens Bröstedt et al., eds. (Bergen: Universitetsforlaget, 1985), pp.23–48; Ole Henrik Magga, "Are We Finally to Get Our Rights", in *Native Power, op. cit.,* pp.15–22; and Robert Paine, *Dam a River, Damn a People? Saami (Lapp) Livelihood and the Alta/Kautokeino Hydro-Electric Project and the Norwegian Parliament* (Copenhagen: IWGIA, 1982), Document 45.

[89]   See Carsten Smith, "The Development of Sami Rights Since 1980", in *Loven og livet* (Oslo: Universitetsforlaget, 1996), pp.223–232.

[90]   *Om samenes rettstilling*, Norges offentlige utredninger (NOU), 1984, p.18.

[91]   The *Norwegian Sami Council (Norsk Sameråd)* was already founded in 1964. At first this non-elected public law body had some advisory functions in matters that especially concerned the Norwegian Sami's economic, social and cultural matters. In 1980, the Norwegian Sami Council was reorganized and became an advisory body under the auspices of the Ministry for the Municipalities and Labour for the state, provincial and municipal authorities in Sami matters. The 18 members of the Council were appointed by the king on proposal of the Sami central organizations, the municipalities within the Sami area and some organizations representing the Norwegian fishermen and farmers.

[92]   While the Finnish definition speaks of 'first' language, the Norwegian and Swedish definitions use the concept of a 'home' language. According to the law, for instance, a person has Sami as his 'home' language if his wife and children speak Sami in his home.

[93]   NSR (*Norske Samers Riksforbund*) asserts the rights of the Sami people as a separate ethnic group and as an indigenous population and endeavours to improve the social, cultural and economic position of the Sami.

[94]   The fact that reindeer-herding and non-reindeer-herding Sami in Norway may have different interests in certain matters made the Confederation of Norwegian Reindeer Herders (NRL) to decide not to participate in the work of the Sami Parliament.

[95]   77.6 per cent of those registered in the Sami electoral rolls.

[96]   Another possible explanation of the low voting activity is that the number of persons in Norway identifying themselves as Sami is simply notably lower than the often-estimated figure of 40,000.

[97]   See above on the new definition.

[98]   *Naturgrunnlaget for samisk kultur*, NOU (1997), p.4.

[99]   Although the text of the Act on the Sami Parliament speaks expressly of an obligation of the authorities to 'negotiate' with the Sami Parliament, and not, for instance, of an obligation to 'consult' it, the Act nevertheless provides that in order to fulfil its obligation to negotiate with the Sami Parliament, the authority in question has a duty to provide the Sami Parliament with the opportunity 'to be heard' and 'discuss' matters. However, a failure to use this opportunity does not prevent the authority from proceeding in the matter.

[100]   Already in Bill No. 248 of 1994 the government recognized that the Act only provides a framework for the Sami cultural autonomy and that it is the task of the Sami themselves to develop it further.

[101]   The rules in the Act on the Sami Parliament on the nomination of candidates for the elections of the Sami Parliament are not very detailed. However, in the Government Bill (No. 248 of 1994) it is confirmed that the electors must cast their votes on individual candidates nominated by electoral associations. A possible participation of the political parties in these elections is not discussed in the Bill.

[102]   In Finland reindeer-herding is not an exclusive Sami right. A non-Sami may also own and herd reindeer, provided he or she lives within the reindeer-herding area. This area covers most of the Province of Lapland and the northern parts of the Province of Oulu. Within the herding area reindeer may be grazed regardless of ownership or possession of land. Although most Finnish Sami today earn their living from sources other than the traditional livelihoods, most reindeer in Finland are still owned by the Sami. In the Province of Lapland the local inhabitants have the right to hunt and to fish freely in state-owned land and water regardless of ethnic origin.

[103]   According to the earlier (1973 to 1994) Sami definition, a Sami was a person who considered himself a Sami, provided that he himself or at least one of his parents or grandparents had learnt Sami as his first language.

[104]   Originally, the initiative to introduce the concept of 'descendants of Lapps' into the legislation came from the Sami themselves. But it was not their intention to extend—at least not considerably—the group of persons qualifying as Sami beyond those who already fulfilled the requirements of the former (linguistic) definition of a Sami. The idea was to include a provision in a separate Decree on the Sami Parliament, stating that only land, taxation and population registers

drawn up in 1875 or later should be taken into account when determining whether a person is a descendant of a Lapp and, for the purposes of the Act, a Sami. The Constitutional Committee of Parliament decided, however, that it was not appropriate to refer to any particular land, taxation or population register. The Act was therefore adopted by Parliament with no reference to any precise year or register.

[105] The background to the discord is to be found in the 1990 report submitted by an *ad hoc* Sami Rights Commission.

[106] In Sweden, reindeer-herding is an exclusive Sami right. In practice, however, only those Sami who are members of a Sami Village have both the right and opportunity to practice reindeer husbandry, including the right to hunting and fishing. A Sami Village is both a geographical area and a subject of law. In its latter capacity it promotes the rights and interests of its members.

[107] In order for a Sami to be a member of a Sami Village he must have reindeer-herding as his main livelihood. If he takes up another profession he loses his membership. The right to belong to a Sami Village has also been an issue for the Human Rights Committee in the case of *Ivan Kitok v. Sweden*, Communication No. 197/1985. Views adopted on 27 July 1988. Report of the Human Rights Committee, GAOR, Forty-third Session, Supplement 40 (A/43/40).

[108] See Tom G. Svensson, *The Sámi and Their Land. The Sámi vs the Swedish Crown. A Study of the Legal Sstruggle for Improved Land Rights: The Taxed Mountain Case* (Oslo: Novus, 1997) and Tomas Cramér, *Skattefjällsmålet* (Stockholm: Bloms, 1975).

[109] *Samernas folkrättsliga ställning*, Statens offentlige utrendniger (SOU), (1986), p.36.

[110] *Samerätt och sameting*, SOU (1989), p.41.

[111] One of the mediators was the former Chairman of the Norwegian Sami Parliament, Prof. Ole Henrik Magga.

[112] According to the report the following measures need to be taken: a) the Sami lands must be identified and b) the scope of Sami hunting and fishing rights on the land that they traditionally occupy must be identified. In addition, it is recommended that these initial steps be followed by further measures:

- Protection against restrictions on the Sami reindeer breeding rights should be strengthened. On lands which are traditionally occupied by the Sami, they should be granted the right to transmit their hunting and fishing rights to others in exchange for payment. The Sami Parliament should be empowered to submit its views before matters of national interest for reindeer breeding are defined and before exploitation of such land is permitted. Explicit protection against exploitation of such land should be incorporated into the resource management provisions of the Environmental Code along with a provision giving the Sami Parliament the right to state its views before exploitation is permitted.

- On lands which the Sami traditionally use parallel with other groups increased protection against restrictions on reindeer breeding rights is needed. The Sami Parliament should have the right to state its opinion before areas of national interest for reindeer breeding are defined and before exploitation of such lands is permitted.

- Measures should be taken to ensure that the Sami have sufficient land to enable them to continue with reindeer breeding.

- It should be possible to receive compensation from the state for legal costs incurred in connection with important [court] cases of principle involving Sami land rights.

- A national information campaign about the Sami as an indigenous people and about the Sami culture should be launched.

See *Samerna—ett ursprungsfolk I Sverige. Frågan om Sveriges anslutning till ILO:s konvention nr 169. Betänkande av Utredningen om ILO:s konvention nr 169*, SOU (1999), pp.30–31 (Summary in English).

Minority Self-Governments in Hungary

Ferenc Eiler and Nóra Kovács

Minority Self-Governments in Hungary

Ferenc Eiler and Nóra Kovács

The Parliament of the Hungarian Republic approved the Act LXXVII on the Rights of National and Ethnic Minorities in 1993. The national and international reception of the system of minority self-governments based on this law and introduced in 1994–95 was fundamentally positive.[113] Today, based on the experience gathered during the past years, a first assessment of it can be made. Since this topic is a very complex one, we shall focus on the most important problems related to minority self-government after giving an overview of the rules and regulations that apply to them. Parliament is going to modify the law on the rights of national and ethnic minorities and also the law on the election of minority self-government representatives in the near future, which makes this issue particularly relevant.

1. MINORITIES IN HUNGARY TODAY

The proportion of national and ethnic minorities within the entire population of Hungary has not been established with certainty. According to the official data of the 1990 national census, 232,751 persons (2.24 per cent) preserved their national or ethnic identity, while 137,724 persons (1.33 per cent) out of the 10,374,823 inhabitants of Hungary declared one of the minority languages as their mother tongue. Minority organizations have a considerably higher estimate (8.1–10.2 per cent). Like most statistical data, the figures of the 1990 census have to be viewed with certain reservations.[114] The same considerations apply to the estimates of several minority organizations that are based on descent and disregard losses due to assimilation. Several of these estimates seem rather exaggerated. Reality probably lies halfway between the official figures and the estimates. Since there are and will be no inventories of those belonging to the national and ethnic minority groups, one has to rely on the data of censuses and scientific research as well as on the minority groups' own estimates.

Minority groups in Hungary have reached an advanced level of assimilation. Most of them are dispersed, and most of them can be characterized by a double ethnic identity often accompanied by language loss.[115] Modernization and urbanization acted as natural factors of assimilation as early as the nineteenth century and this tendency became even stronger during the course of the twentieth century. The rural population moved to the cities, leaving their local communities behind. In a matter of a few decades minorities became Hungarianized, a process which enabled upward social mobility. Internal migration and the large number of ethnically mixed marriages led to the dissolution of local communities in a few generations' time. Moreover, governments of the inter-war and post-war period intended to fortify the rather strong spontaneous assimilation process by political means.[116]

The social and economic integration process of national minorities in Hungary has been successful. Generally, the majority society expresses a benevolently neutral attitude towards minorities and their organizations. This positive attitude, however, does not apply to all minority groups in Hungary. The situation and social acceptance of the Hungarian Roma, defined as an ethnic minority, and largely assimilated from a linguistic point of view, is much less favourable than those of the twelve other Hungarian minoritie groups:

> The social structure of Gypsies [Roma] has preserved several elements of their position on the periphery of society, they do not all have a shared language and culture, and their ethnic identity is still in formation. Their internal cultural differences hinder their assimilation, while there are several obstacles to the formation of a Roma community, such as their linguistic and cultural differences, their geographic dispersion, their social problems, and the small number of Roma intellectuals needed for the moulding of a common Roma identity.[117]

Negative stereotypes rooted in the majority society and the practice of discrimination frequently encountered at workplaces, in the administration, in police action and in the education system further obstruct the integration possibilities of this minority group.[118]

2. MINORITY RIGHTS BEFORE THE CHANGE OF REGIME

As far as the aims and methods of the official state policy on minorities are concerned, the four decades of socialism cannot be regarded as a unified period. The Constitution of 1949 prohibited discrimination, declaring the national minorities' right to education in their mother tongue and preservation of their national culture. However, no serious attempts were made to actually fortify the minorities' national identities before 1989. It was only in 1968 that the Party abandoned the plan of the rapid assimilation of minorities; however, not even after this did it face the challenge of the gradually accelerating natural assimilation process.[119] During the mid-seventies, a new element was included in the official minority policy. Unsettling developments in the situation of the Hungarian minority groups in the neighbouring countries and some basic principles of minority protection accepted at international conferences (the Helsinki UNESCO Conference, the UN seminar in Ohrid, the 1975 Helsinki Document of the CSCE) forced minority policy-makers to launch the concept of minorities as connecting elements. It essentially meant that by making use of the minorities' natural cross-border connections and by suggesting the principle of mutuality, tensions generated by the minority policies of neighbouring countries that considered minority questions as strictly internal affairs could and should be eased. This attempt, however, failed due to the uneven numbers and proportions of minorities on the two sides of the border, i.e. there are far more Hungarians living in Hungary's neighbouring countries than ethnic minorities living in Hungary, compounded by deeply rooted fears and prejudices which the communist propaganda of proletarian internationalism did not manage to change.

Officially, the interests of the 'Southern Slav', as well as of the Slovakian, Romanian and German minorities were supposed to be represented by the so-called national associations established between 1945 and 1955. These associations, however, were created from above by the highest political circles and were kept under their strictest control. Instead of representing the minorities' interests they conveyed governmental (Party State) policies towards national minorities. Although minority primary and secondary schools, integrated into the national educational system, existed throughout the entire period, they could not stop the process of assimilation. (Until 1960, there were three types of institutions: schools teaching in the minority language exclusively, schools teaching in both the minority language and Hungarian, and schools teaching the minority language as a foreign language; between 1960 and 1985, only the last two types existed, whereas since 1985, all three types have operated again.)[120]

As a result of the new international political situation and the radical transformation of national political relations, a new era started in national minority policies as well.[121] In accord with the political and social transformations of the country, the last communist government approved the Act XXXI of 1989 on the Constitution, which prohibited discrimination and guaranteed educational, cultural and language rights to the state-forming components of minorities as well as their collective participation in public life. During the summer of 1990, the first democratically elected parliament modified the Constitution again, thus defining the main directions for the legal regulations concerning the situation of minorities in Hungary. The Constitution specified local and national minority governments as the future organizational framework for minorities. At the same time, it admitted the—not precisely circumscribed—right of national and ethnic minorities living in Hungary to political representation and it declared the necessity for a law concerning minority rights.[122]

Although the unregulated situation did not threaten to cause social upheaval, an exemplary regulation was important to the Hungarian political elite, mainly due to foreign policy considerations.[123] The direction of Hungarian foreign policy was expected to change radically after 1989–90. Priority was given to the rapid establishment and consolidation of economic, political and (later) military relations with Western Europe and to supporting the Hungarian minorities living in the neighbouring countries as much as possible. The legislature decided to guarantee minorities the possibility of establishing cultural autonomy in a separate law. This decision was motivated by Hungarian responsibility felt for the minorities living in the neighbouring countries and also by the decades-long internal reparation owed to the national and ethnic minorities living in Hungary.[124]

Once free from the suffocating state control, minority organizations soon discovered the possibilities of democratic social development. They needed real, well-functioning organizations to represent their interests, and therefore wanted to participate in the preparation of the law on minorities, which had been in progress from September 1989. Thus, in early 1991, the Minority Roundtable, a consultative moderator forum, was formed, comprising representatives of all organizations of the thirteen minority groups in Hungary.[125] Due to the great number of conceptual differences, the negotiations between the Office for National and Ethnic Minorities in Hungary, the respective Ministries and the Minority Roundtable did not reach an end until the summer of 1993. Consensus was finally reached, and the Parliament passed the Act LXXVII of 1993 on the Rights of National and Ethnic Minorities (Minority Act) on 7 June 1993 with a 96.5 per cent majority.[126]

3.   THE LEGAL REGULATION OF MINORITY SELF-GOVERNMENTS

The Minority Act occupies a peculiar place in Hungarian jurisdiction. It departs from the basic right referring to minorities included in the Constitution and defines specific details of it, while it directly changes those parts of the Hungarian jurisdiction that have regulated this issue. The Act itself can be called a 'skeleton law' since its applicability depends on the numerous other specific laws that it refers to in several places.[127]

The Act departs from the principle of *free choice of identity*,[128] according to which "[t]o admit and to acknowledge that one belongs to a national or ethnic group or minority (hereafter minority)

175

is the exclusive and inalienable right of the individual. Nobody is obliged to make a statement concerning the issue of which minority he or she belongs to".[129] The prohibition of registration demanded by minorities led to a unique legal resolution of the definition of the subject of the law. The subjects of the law are determined by a definition that takes into consideration Capotorti's suggestion. Besides, the law enumerates thirteen local minorities and their languages that are automatically covered by it and defines the procedure through which new members can be included in the enumeration.

The legislation defines the right of national and ethnic minorities to their identity as part of universal human rights, while their individual and collective rights (*Gemeinschaftsrechte*) are seen as basic rights to freedom. Thus, one of the main characteristics of the Minority Act is that it is based on a dualistic concept of minority rights. In accordance with this, it specifies individual and collective rights in separate chapters. The collective rights cover the most important areas of collective minority identity preservation. Minorities have the right to preserve their language and traditions, to organize their feasts and events, to preserve their architectural, cultural and religious heritage, and to use their symbols. At the same time, the law guarantees their rights to education in their mother tongue and to the establishment of a national network of educational, cultural and scientific institutions. Public radio and television are obliged to prepare and transmit minority programmes regularly, while the state is called upon to facilitate the reception of radio and television programmes transmitted from the minorities' motherlands. Minorities have the right to form social organizations as well as local and national minority governments, and these are entitled to establish direct international relations. The law mentions the possibility of minorities' parliamentary representation, too. Finally, it enacts the institution of the ombudsman for the rights of national and ethnic minorities.[130]

The explicit aim of the Minority Act is the establishment of a person-based cultural autonomy.[131] The organizational consequence of this—and thus the essence of the entire regulation—is a system of minority governments endowed with legal status. As far as self-organization of minorities was concerned, during the preparation of the Minority Act the Ministry of Justice held the view that minorities could enjoy full rights under the general democratic legislation so that their self-organization based on the right to form civil associations could guarantee minority identity preservation in Hungary. This view, however, was shared neither by the Minority Roundtable nor by the Office for National and Ethnic Minorities, and finally the legislature decided to integrate minority governments into the system of local governments and modelled minority representation on the regulations for local self-governments.[132]

The system of minority self-governments consists of two levels, the local and the national. The law outlines three possible local minority government models. If more than half of the members of a local self-government board are representatives of a particular minority group, the local self-government can transform itself into a local minority self-government. In this case the minority government is granted all the necessary rights to achieve cultural autonomy, and at the same time it performs all regular legal duties of a local self-government. If thirty per cent of the board of the local representatives have been elected as representatives of the same minority group, they as a minority may form *an indirectly created local minority self-government,* whose area of competence coincides with that of the third type, the most frequent *directly created local minority self-government.*[133] (The last type of minority government is elected by voters directly, that is votes cast for the minority government. In villages with a population of less than 10,000, fifty valid votes are necessary to do this. In villages with more than 10,000 one hundred valid votes are needed.)

Local minority self-governments are legal entities, and they fulfil their duties in close coordination with the local self-government. Since minority governments are elected at the same time as local governments, both the principle of concession and the free choice of self-identification are met.[134] Minority candidates can present themselves for election with as few as five recommendations. Since minority group citizens are not registered in Hungary as such, the legislation has decided to entitle all Hungarian citizens to both active and passive voting rights for minority self-governments. The minority candidates themselves do not have to make a declaration about their minority affiliation; they merely have to give a written declaration that they take charge of the representation of the minority group in question. Depending on the size of a particular municipality, minority self-government bodies consist of three representatives in municipalities with a population of no more than 1,300 people, five in larger villages and towns, and nine in the capital.

A local minority self-government has the power to establish cultural autonomy.[135] It may approach the head of the board of the competent public body with a request concerning any issue affecting the minority. It may ask for information, make a proposal, initiate measures and object to a practice or decision related to the operation of institutions that violate the rights of the minority. The minority self-government can define within its authority: the use of the property set aside for it as part of the total property of the local government; its budget; its closing balance sheet; the circle of its protected monuments and memorial sites; its organizational structure and operational system; its own name and insignia as well as its medals and decorations and the holidays and festivals of the minority they represent. The local minority self-government may establish and operate an institution within its authority, it may invite tenders and establish scholarships, and it has the right to establish and run a company or other business organization. Concerning the issues of basic education, media, promotion of tradition and culture, and the language used by the community, any act of the local government affecting the minority population in their capacity as such may be passed by the board of representatives only with the approval of the minority self-government representing the population.

A local minority self-government may assume control of an educational institution from the local self-government if the two can reach an agreement about it and if the former can ensure the maintenance of the same standards of education as the latter.

The legal supervision of local minority self-governments is performed by the regional offices of public administration, while the lawful use of the subsidies provided by the government may be supervised by the National Audit Office.

The Minority Act makes it possible for local minority self-governments to integrate on a national level: each minority group can establish one national minority self-government or national assembly.[136] These represent the interests of local minority self-governments on the county and on the national level. The local level is not subordinated to the national level, nor are local minority self-governments obliged to report to the national one.

The national minority self-government is elected by the minority electors.[137] A quorum is constituted by fifty per cent of all electors at the national assembly. The national minority self-government can have a minimum of 13 and a maximum of 53 members. Similarly to local minority self-governments, the lawful use of the subsidies provided by the government is supervised by the National Audit Office. Nevertheless, unlike in the case of local minority governments, no state organ is legally entitled to the legal supervision of national minority self-governments.[138]

The national minority self-government has the same rights to send memoranda as local minority self-governments (except for remonstrance). The national council decides independently on the location of its headquarters, its form of organization, its operational mode, its budget, its closing balance sheet and an authoritative statement of its asset inventory. Similarly, it can decide independently on the principles governing the use of the radio and television channels at its disposal. It can establish and maintain different types of institutions (libraries, theatres, museums, publishing companies, secondary and higher education institutions) with a national scope. The national council may also state its opinion on bills concerning the minority represented by it, including the regulations issued by the general meetings of counties and the capital. The national council has a right of veto in the course of legislation on the preservation and conservation of the historical settlements and architectural monuments of the minority as well as in regard to the development of the core curriculum of minority education.[139]

The infrastructural background to the operation of local minority self-governments has to be provided by the local self-government. They have to be provided with a separate building or room (as possible) and with the use of technical facilities necessary for their operation. National minority self-governments are entitled to a self-contained building or part of a building with a net area of 150–300 square metres. The fixed assets do not become properties of the minority self-governments, but are transferred to them only for usage. If the minority self-government terminates its activities, they have to be returned to the local self-government. The state compensates all losses for local self-governments in connection with accommodating the local minority self-governments. Besides the fixed assets the state provides national minority self-governments with a one-off allocation of property.[140]

The financial conditions of the operation of minority self-governments are created by an annually changing standard financial assistance from the central budget.[141] They may, however, obtain financial assistance from other sources, too. Local and county-level self-governments, foundations, national and foreign organizations, and individuals can also support them financially. They may participate in enterprises in which their liability does not exceed the total value of assets demanded by such an enterprise.

The assistance to the operational costs of minority self-governments is only part of the multi-channel system through which national and ethnic minorities are supported. The largest part of the central budget assistance for minorities is the additional standard assistance promoting minority education.[142] Minority civil associations may apply for support from the Human Rights and Minorities Committee of the Hungarian Parliament. Minority public foundations are equally indispensable elements of the financial support system financing programmes and activities.

4. MINORITY SELF-GOVERNMENTS: RESULTS AND DILEMMAS

During the six years after the local elections of 1994, the basic principle of the system of minority self-governments proved to be fundamentally correct.[143] In spite of the deficiencies of the legal regulations pointed out as early as the first electoral cycle, according to the representative survey of 1996–97, most people concerned found the recently introduced system necessary and a step towards the representation of minority interests.[144] The number of local minority self-governments almost doubled after the local elections of 1998, which confirmed this impression. At the same time, it demonstrated the majority's positive attitude towards this issue since the number of sympathy votes in 1998 was much higher than at the previous elections.[145]

Table 2.1
The Number of Local Minority Self-Governments as a Result of the Two Elections[146]

Minority	1997	Number of Votes	1999	Number of Votes
Bulgarian	4	2,882	15	21,998
Roma	421	888,279	754	1,092,044
Greek	6	10, 635	19	61,605
Croatian	56	98,005	75	102,956
Polish	7	3,220	33	82,743
German	163	560,620	272	966,324
Armenian	16	32,052	25	72,725
Romanian	12	19,844	31	36,430
Ruthenian	1	1,323	10	7,117
Serbian	19	37,319	35	34,642
Slovak	49	114,460	75	163,110
Slovenian	6	5,660	10	9,558
Ukrainian	—	0	5	6,670
Total	760	1,774,299	1,369	2,657,922

Experiences of the first four years have thrown a sharp light on the weak points of the minority self-government system. This was the reason the parliament decided to modify the Minority Act and the Law regulating the election of minority self-government representatives on several points in 1998. At the same time, the question of parliamentary representation of minorities was also raised.

4.1 Minority Self-Government Elections—The Trap of Free Identity Choice

During the parliamentary debate on the Minority Act, the *ad hoc* committee of experts formed by the Human Rights and Religion Committee of the Hungarian Parliament sent the bill to the Council of Europe for evaluation. The Rights and Human Rights Committee of the Council of Europe gave a positive evaluation of the bill, emphasizing especially that the principle of free identity choice would be included in the legislation of a country for the first time.[147]

While preparing the Minority Act it became evident that minority organizations would object categorically to any kind of minority registration—primarily because of negative historical experiences. Thus the complete freedom of the assumption or expression of identities became the cornerstone of the preparatory debates and of the system of minority self-governments as a whole. When it became clear that minority self-governments would be integrated into the existing system of local self-governments and that they would be financed permanently from the central budget, a new electoral system respecting these ideas had to be developed. Its realization, however, faced legal experts with a serious dilemma because they had to validate two opposing articles of the Constitution that were very difficult to reconcile. While Article 68(4) of the Constitution states that it is national and ethnic minorities that can form local and national minority self-governments, Article 70(1) guarantees active and passive electoral rights to all Hungarian citizens in the elections prior to the formation of self-governments. Finally, the legislature decided to give priority to the principle of free identity choice. The legislation also decided that elections for minority self-government representatives should take place on the same day as elections for local government representatives.

During the first term of office of minority self-governments, fears of possible electoral abuse were related primarily to Article 70(1) of the Constitution. Theoretically, it is possible that the majority votes for persons who are not authentic leaders of the particular minority community and in this way they may intervene—out of lack of information or driven by political goals—in the minority community's power relations, with the potential of seriously threatening their possibilities to represent their interests.

The local elections of 1998 verified the reservations about the possible abuse inherent in the electoral system. Four years after the first elections, the opportunities for abuse became well known among all those who wanted to take advantage of the weaknesses of the electoral system. The so-called ethno-business phenomenon was born. Although the financial position of minority self-governments is still far from ideal, there is enough money in it to induce some persons to run for minority representative who do not belong to any minority group, or who belong to a different group from the one they intend to represent. Since voters of the majority usually do not know minority candidates, sympathy votes have, in some cases, helped several such persons to get into local minority self-governments.[148] One might have serious moral reservations about these self-candidates; nevertheless, their behaviour is completely lawful. At the moment nobody is authorized to question a candidate's minority identity. The sympathy-voters' lack of information can also be abused by the fact that the names of minority candidates appear in alphabetical order on the electoral list. The electoral behaviour of majority voters during the second elections showed that due to their lack of information they tended to give their votes to those candidates who appeared on the top of the alphabetical list. As it is legally permitted in Hungary to change one's surname once, certain candidates changed their family names in order to obtain a better position on the alphabetical list of candidates. They were quite efficient in doing so and became minority self-government representatives while several actual minority leaders did not.[149] These problems have generally occurred in larger towns, and mostly in the capital. On the other hand, in small villages which provide the mass-basis of most minority groups in Hungary there is a natural social control that makes this type of abuse more difficult.

Local election results obviously influence the election of the national minority self-governments since local minority self-government representatives become electors automatically. It may cause serious problems in the formation and operation of the national minority self-government, too, if several non-minority representatives get elected on the local level. The best example for this is the scandal concerning the election of the Romanian National Minority Self-Government that broke in 1998. The number of Romanian local minority self-governments increased by 250 per cent after the second local elections. Leaders of the Romanian minority in Hungary, however, noted that a considerable number of the representatives elected in Budapest did not actually belong to the Romanian minority group. These representatives (and electors) decided not to take part in the election of the Romanian National Minority Self-Government. As a consequence, the representatives who were present in the assembly and genuinely belonged to the Romanian minority did not reach the 75 per cent of all the representatives required by law and the Romanian National Minority Self-Government could not be formed.[150] Due to the principle of free identity choice present in the law, the odd ones out could not be made responsible, and it was only by lowering the 75 per cent threshold to 50 per cent that this problem, generating also some diplomatic complications, could finally be solved.[151]

The free choice of identity can also be abused in the elections for local self-government.[152] The Act LXIV of 1990 regulating the election of local self-government representatives and mayors allows minority candidates to enter the local self-government as representatives even if none of the minority candidates obtains the necessary minimum of votes. If a minority candidate gets half as many votes as the local representative who has got in with the smallest number of votes, he or she automatically becomes a full member of the local minority self-government board.[153] It should be noted here that this article of the law has been received with serious reservations by members of the public administration. According to their views, it is minority self-governments that are expected to achieve cultural autonomy. If no minority self-government is formed, a minority spokesperson is expected to represent the minority's interests. Moreover, if a particular national or ethnic minority forms the majority in a specific village or locality, the local self-government can transform itself into a local minority self-government. It is for this reason that this advantage is found redundant.[154]

After the minority self-government elections of 1998, minorities and government officials alike found it necessary to modify the Minority Act and also the law regulating the election of local self-government representatives, primarily in order to avoid the abuse of the electoral system. There would be several ways to do this without harming substantially the principle of free identity choice.

First, it has to be accepted that the active franchise should not in any way be restricted in the future. The twelve national minorities in Hungary reject registration unanimously.[155] This leaves only two ways left to resolve the problem. First, the passive franchise could be restricted, which means that only those candidates would be included in the minority electoral lists whose candidacy has been consented by a competent authority, such as the respective national minority self-government. Most minority leaders would find this alternative acceptable.

The second proposal, prepared by the Ministry of Internal Affairs in July 2000, discards this alternative and would only oblige minority candidates to declare that they belong to the minority they intend to represent.[156] The Ministry's solution, which in some way could be combined with the first one, is a legal-technical solution and would separate local elections from local minority self-government elections by six weeks. This would increase the probability that only the people concerned go to vote who naturally know which candidates are genuine members of their minority group. In this case sympathy votes cast by the majority would not influence the election results considerably.

Most minority leaders do not find this idea acceptable for several reasons. It would decrease dramatically the number of sympathy votes that give—among other things—vital feedback on the acceptance of the minorities by the majority. A more serious and substantial reason against the second procedure is that the identity of minority communities is not yet strong enough to mobilize its members for minority elections held on a separate day. They find the six-week pause between the two elections particularly unacceptable.[157]

4.2 Operational Problems of Minority Self-Governments

4.2.1 Cooperation of Minority Self-Governments and Local Self-Governments

Minority self-governments are integrated into the self-government system and do their tasks in coordination with the self-government of the village or locality. Some of their powers are similar to those of civil law associations (e.g. petition), and they have others that they can exercise together with the local self-government (e.g. the right of consent). At the moment, the operational efficiency of minority self-governments depends largely on their relationships with the local self-government because several operational and infrastructural aspects of minority self-governments are still unregulated,[158] and because minority-protective sanctions are almost completely absent from the Minority Act. Moreover, the right of consent, an actual veto right and the strongest power in the hands of minority self-governments, can only be used if the local self-government wishes to settle an issue by passing a decree. Most issues concerning minorities are decided upon by decrees and not by regulations.[159]

The results of the above-mentioned survey of 1996–97 show that the majority of minority self-governments find cooperation between the two types of self-governments satisfactory. Nevertheless, five years after the introduction of the system of minority self-governments the minority ombudsman still receives formal complaints frequently. The majority of these complaints draw attention to the exclusion of minority self-governments from joint decision-making with the local self-governments.[160] These offences are extremely important because they affect the most basic interests of entire minority communities. The right of consent in the nomination and removal of minority institution leaders, for example, has been ignored several times. Numerous minority self-governments have sent petitions in this matter to the Ombudsman for National and Ethnic Minorities.[161]

Minority education in Hungary today is integrated into the public education system—except for the so-called Sunday schools maintained by the national self-governments of some smaller minorities and financed by the Ministry of Education. Schoolchildren may receive their education in three different types of schools according to the language of instruction: instruction in the minority language; instruction in the minority language and Hungarian; instruction in Hungarian with minority language classes. Roma students may also participate in remedial education. Most schools concerned belong to the language-teaching type, with very few schools where the minority language is the language of instruction.[162] The positive statistical indicators of minority education are due to the increased prestige of the German language in Hungary.

The state provides these schools with additional standard assistance.[163] The distribution of this assistance with a precisely defined purpose has been a frequent element of minority self-government complaints. Schools are financed from the national budget and from the budget of the local government. A large proportion of local self-governments in Hungary, however, is in a very difficult financial situation and some of them do not actually transfer the additional standard assistance to the school that it has actually been allocated to. Instead, they decrease their own contribution to the budget of the school by the amount of the additional standard assistance.[164] Since most schools have to be operated with very limited financial resources, it seems a great achievement in the present economic situation if a school does not have to be closed down. The infringing local self-governments therefore often argue that priority has to be given to basic school functions over perfect conditions for minorities.[165]

The legal background to this has changed from the beginning of the academic year 2000–01 since the financial assistance allocated to minority education in the Central Budget has been re-qualified as additional standard assistance with no obligatory purpose. The institutions maintaining schools in villages with a population of less than 3,500 inhabitants receive double the standard assistance for each student who participates in minority education. Moreover, they may apply for additional standard assistance if less than 80 per cent of the local self-government's expenses on minority education are covered from the Central Budget.[166]

Local self-governments could only be prevented from ignoring the right of consent if the relationship between local self-governments and local minority self-governments was regulated in much more detail in the Minority Act, and if efficient control mechanisms and sanctions against the violation of the law were also included.

Besides the competence of joint decision-making, the law allows minority self-governments to take over the maintenance of cultural and educational institutions from the local self-government, with the latter's approval. However, in practice, the takeover of institutions by minority self-governments is made impossible by the incomplete legal regulation and by its unclear financial consequences. Moreover, such a change is not necessarily in the interests of the employees of the institution to be taken over because in cases of public education institutions they would loose their civil servant status.[167] In order to give the idea of cultural autonomy real meaning, minority self-governments should have the possibility of maintaining their own, primarily educational, institutions. As the financial situation of local minority self-governments generally does not allow for more than their daily maintenance, they are unlikely to establish new institutions using their own economic resources. It is for this reason that the takeover of existing institutions is so important. Nevertheless, no mass takeover of institutions can be expected as a result of the improved conditions (after a possible modification of the law) neither on the local nor on the national level. Preliminary enquiries have also shown that it is primarily national assemblies that would use this possibility and take over schools that accept students from larger regions or from the entire country.[168] Once the law is modified and defines the conditions of takeover, the effective functioning of the institutions concerned could be guaranteed by an agreement on specific details. The overwhelming majority of local minority self-governments are satisfied to participate in the direction of minority institutions by making joint decisions with the local self-governments.

4.2.2   Roma

While the principal objective of the 12 national minorities today is to stop the process of assimilation and to fill the framework of cultural autonomy with actual content, the greatest challenge for Roma minority self-governments is the social and economic integration of the Roma minority.[169] Although the Minority Act defines minority self-governments as the tools to achieve cultural autonomy, fundamentally, most of the resources and energy of Roma minority self-governments are spent on urgent social and employment-related problems.[170] The results of the national survey of 1996–97 on minority self-governments provided empirical data on this allocation pattern. According to the survey, Roma minority self-governments have to attend to social problems much more frequently than other minorities (they make up 26.3 per cent of all their cases).[171] This tendency can also be observed in the takeover of tasks and duties. Several local self-governments have handed over tasks related to social work and social benefits to Roma minority self-governments, arguing that they know the internal situation of their community and can therefore identify the persons in need much better and make more adequate decisions.[172] Although generated by good will to help, this procedure is problematic and raises constitutional questions. The Minority Act only promotes the takeover of tasks in the areas of education and culture. Social issues are set clearly within the competence of local self-governments. Instead of handing over these tasks, this issue could be treated more adequately by involving Roma minority self-government representatives in the work of the local self-government's decision-making bodies.

4.2.3   Financing of Minority Self-Governments

The efficient operation of the self-government system would be guaranteed not only by unambiguous legal regulation but also by sufficient financial resources. The financial aspect of minority self-governments is very complex; it includes national and local governmental subsidies and is related to the infrastructural background as well as to the distribution and use of the available financial resources.

Local minority self-governments receive an annual amount of additional standard assistance from the national budget. Although the amount is slightly increased each year, in most cases it is only enough to cover operational costs.[173] Local self-governments can also contribute to the budget of local minority self-governments, but as most of them struggle with their own difficult financial situation, they can either not support the minority self-governments at all or provide only very small subsidies.[174] The financing system of governmental subsidies has been criticized repeatedly because it does not take into account the proportions of minorities. Minority self-governments representing a less numerous minority community receive the same amount as those uniting larger groups. Opinions differ within the particular minority groups as to how this problem should be addressed. A more proportional support system would be quite difficult to establish due to technical reasons because the prohibition of registration will always hide the actual size of the minority communities. The population of a particular village obviously cannot be taken as the basis for subsidy distribution. On the other hand, the votes cast for a minority self-government also include sympathy-votes and thus do not necessarily reflect the actual proportions. Therefore, a fair proportional distribution of financial support remains a problem whose solution can only be achieved—if at all—by the active involvement of national assemblies. For this to happen, however, the relationship between the two self-government types should be redefined and their complete independence from each other abolished.

Minority self-governments differ considerably according to their infrastructural background. Most of them are accommodated, although few of them enjoy ideal conditions. Generally, they have a room in the building of the local self-government. In more fortunate cases they have access to this room seven days a week; in others they can only hold their office hours in it. In some of the worst cases, the mayor's office does not provide minority self-governments with the most essential technical conditions of administration either. On the other hand, the legal requirements to accommodate and to provide technical conditions cannot be fulfiled beyond the possibilities of the local self-governments.

4.2.4   Levels of Minority Self-Government

In the future, the structure of the self-government system will have to be adjusted to the needs expressed by some minority groups. At present, it is the national assemblies that represent minorities on the county level as well. They give their opinion on the minority-related decrees issued by county self-governments. However, experience has shown that it would be very useful to construct a separate county level of minority self-governments. The new level could provide a framework of communication for local minority self-governments and, at the same time, cut short the distance between the local and the national levels, facilitating the flow of information. Even more importantly, county level minority self-governments as legal entities could become constant and legitimate partners of the county self-government, thus influencing the processes at this level. Whether or not the county level is organized would depend on the number of local minority self-governments. Even today, there are German, Roma, Croatian and Slovakian county federations initiated by the local minority self-governments themselves.[175] They have been established in accord with the law of association, and this is why their communication with county self-governments, the administrative bodies responsible for minority-related tasks, depends on the willingness of the county self-government to cooperate. The terms of organization and operation of several county self-governments state that the county minority federations may participate in the assembly sessions with a right to consultation.[176] The proposal presented to the government by the Ministry of Internal Affairs in July 2000 on the election of minority self-government representatives suggests that regional minority representatives should be elected in the system of electors and that nine should be the maximum number of local minority self-government representatives.[177]

Based on the experiences gained during the past few years it can be stated that the Minority Act has to be modified in order to make minority self-governmental work more efficiently. The relationship between local self-governments and local minority self-governments requires more detailed and specific regulations, and the tasks, tools and internal operational rules of minority self-governments should be clearly defined. Also, punitive sanctions should be included in the Act. Preferably, all these modifications should be included in the Minority Act, thus minimizing the possible interpretational problems arising from the simultaneous interpretation of rules and regulations in different laws. However, the modification of the law should by no means reduce the autonomy of minority self-governments.

4.3 Parliamentary Representation

Although no international law existed that obliged states to guarantee parliamentary representation to minorities, the Hungarian government undertook this obligation voluntarily with the Minority Act of 1993. Seven years later, the issue of the parliamentary representation of national and ethnic minorities in Hungary remains unsettled.

In each parliamentary term since 1990, proposals were prepared suggesting the modification of the election law to ensure the parliamentary representation of national and ethnic minorities in Hungary.[178] Due to the lack of political consensus, however, the proposed bills have never received the support of two-thirds of all parliamentary representatives and have never become laws.[179] The legal arguments of political party experts reflect conceptual differences, but in fact there is a lack of political will to resolve this problem. Parliamentary representation has never been an issue of primary political importance neither in internal nor in foreign affairs. The political parties have also ignored this issue because parliamentary minority representatives may appear as an 'unsettling force' in politics and outside the power relations of the purely political parties. This new force could also tip the scales in crises of political struggles.

Article 68 of the Constitution of the Hungarian Republic states:
(1) The national and ethnic minorities living in the Republic of Hungary share the power of the people; they are constituent factors in the State. ... (3) The laws of the Republic of Hungary ensure representation for the national and ethnic minorities living in the territory of the country.

Legal experts dedicated to this problem and knowledgeable about the standpoint of the Constitutional Court have not reached an unanimous opinion on whether or not the soft legal norm obliges Parliament.[180] The legal interpretation of the Ombudsman for National and Ethnic Minorities—also supported by the resolution of the Constitutional Court—states that the Constitution has been neglected.[181] Although this professional debate has started out from a significant issue, the actual achievement of parliamentary representation is not of primary importance at the moment. If real political willingness existed, Article 20(1) of the Minority Act would have been enough to stimulate action.[182]

If we take into account the preparation of the Minority Bill, this is the fourth time since 1990 that the Parliament has attempted to resolve the question of the parliamentary representation of minorities. Several plans have been proposed during the last ten years and today there are no alternatives that have not been analyzed comprehensively by experts in the subsequent phases of the preparation of the bill.[183]

The problem of parliamentary representation of minorities must be solved in the existing single-chamber system. Theoretically, representation may also be achieved in a two-chamber system; however, political reality makes one abandon this alternative. Most political parties prefer the one-chamber system.

Some political parties have insisted on the introduction of the two-chamber system since 1990 and can imagine the realization of minority representation only in this framework.[184] While it is true that the issue of minority representation could be most easily handled in a two-chamber system, this does not mean that it could not be achieved within the framework of the one-chamber system. In European constitutional systems minority politicians tend to be members of the House of Representatives, rather than of the second chamber.

If the legislation wants to achieve the political representation of minorities, some basic issues need to be settled before details can be elaborated. Is full parliamentary representation of political minorities intended or will minority representatives have only the right of consultation? If full representation of minorities is envisaged, the question needs to be addressed whether it should be granted to representatives of all the minorities with parliamentary seats or only to those who have obtained a considerable number of votes.

Theoretically, there are two ways to achieve the parliamentary representation of all thirteen minority groups. The first possibility is that all minority groups get into Parliament automatically. The list of parliamentary representatives would be drawn up by the simultaneous application of the election and the delegation procedures. In this case—according to the existing plans—the representatives would only be entitled to the right of consultation. While the minorities—quite rightfully—see this alternative as a pseudo-solution, the political parties think of it as a temporary solution in case the modification procedure of the electoral law fails.[185]

The alternative option, the election-based, full-right representation of all national and ethnic minority groups in Hungary, can only be achieved if the majority is not excluded from the election of minority representatives by any legal-technical means.[186] This means that all Hungarian citizens could cast three votes in the elections. They could vote for one national deputy candidate, for one political party list and, optionally, for one minority list. This solution raises the problem of legitimacy already known from previous elections for the minority government. In this case the principle of proportionality between minorities would not be validated. The 400,000 Roma would have one parliamentary representative just like the smallest minority groups who have a population of no more than one thousand people. This solution could be a legal possibility, but for the time being it does not have the support of political parties in Parliament.

If the political parties do not intend to provide all minorities with automatic parliamentary representation, they have several means to choose from during the elaboration of the electoral regulations. If the three-vote system is put into practice voters will not receive the minority ballots automatically but will have to ask for them. Alternatively, all Hungarian citizens could cast their vote for a minority list, but they would have to choose between a political party list and a minority list. This would be the so-called 'two-vote system'. The majority would probably give their votes to political parties. No doubt it would be the two-vote system that guarantees the highest level of legitimacy to the minority representatives in Parliament because it would be their community that has supported their candidacy. Several of the thirteen minorities would have no chance at all of getting into Parliament, not even if the minimum threshold of votes was lowered to one thousand. Raising the threshold could also reduce the circle of minorities with parliamentary representation. The national assemblies of less numerous minorities obviously would not like this solution, whereas the larger groups would find it acceptable.

At the moment, the majority of the political parties are inclined to accept the 'two-vote system' in principle.[187] The electoral threshold is most likely to be defined between 3–5,000 votes. The minority that receives the prescribed number of votes for the minority electoral list would automatically achieve full-right parliamentary representation. The concession would apply to the election of one minority representative only. The second candidate would need as many votes to get into Parliament as a political party candidate needs to get on the national party list. According to preliminary estimates, four to five minorities could obtain full-right parliamentary representation in this way in 2002.[188] Although the opinions expressed by the largest political parties have drawn closer recently, the chances of reaching an agreement are diminished by the fact that the biggest of the governing parties connects the solution to this problem with their political goal of reducing the number of parliamentary representatives. At the time of writing, the largest party in opposition objects categorically to the solution preferred by the biggest governing party and without the votes of the opposition the two-thirds majority cannot be reached.[189] So it may well happen that the minorities will only have delegated representatives entitled to the right of consultation after 2002.

5.   EVALUATION—A POSSIBLE TREND OF DEVELOPMENT

The international reception of the Hungarian model has been positive. According to experts of the Council of Europe, "the proposal takes into very high consideration the latest results of the international debate on human and ethnic rights ... and intends to achieve the most modern minority protection".[190] They have declared as a great merit of the proposal that it enlists the collective as well as the individual rights of minorities. This is particularly important, since international law has not recognized collective rights yet. They have found the planned system of minority self-governments "very original" and "a precedent in international law".[191]

187

The Act LXXVII of 1993 is situated in the progressive trend of state legislation regulating the situation of minorities. The otherwise detailed law acknowledges the collective rights of minorities and lays down the organizational framework, i.e. the local and national minority self-governments, to exercise these rights. It guarantees the minorities' right to use their mother tongue and regulates the legal pre-conditions of minority education. It is a fact, however, that the "regulation of the systems of tasks and tools of minority self-governments does not follow the theoretical requisites of self-governance; and based on their actual tasks and tools minority self-governments are self-governments from a formal-organizational but by no means from a real functional point of view".[192] This can be illustrated by the fact that only occasionally have minority self-governments taken over cultural and educational institutions from local self-governments. These would be some of the typical functions of cultural autonomy. So the Minority Act needs to be modified. Based on the experiences gathered during the past five years a corrected version could be prepared, a version that better reflects the legislature's original intentions and that is closer to the minorities' expectations. The political will to achieve this is not absent.

The sub-committee to modify the law on the rights of national and ethnic minorities was formed in September 1998 and prepared its proposal by May 2000.[193] This proposal does not refer to the issues of parliamentary and self-government elections because these areas are regulated by separate laws.[194] The main aim of the modification is to fill the framework created with actual content to achieve cultural autonomy.

In order to do this the proposal suggests a more detailed regulation of certain areas so that minority self-governments can actually make use of their already existing rights without any obstacles.

According to the proposal, the Minority Act should be complemented by explanatory regulations defining some concepts that are vital during the application of the law.[195] Their unambiguous definition would minimize the risk that certain regulations are not validated in practice because of their different interpretations.

Based on reports by the public administration offices responsible for lawfulness, the legal specification of the regulations concerning the internal relations of minority self-governments is also necessary.[196] The remuneration of self-government representatives, the occupational incompatibility of minority self-government presidents or their dismissal, the committee-formation and by-elections have all raised questions impossible to answer without the simultaneous interpretation of several regulations. Besides, from 2002 onwards the self-government system is planned to be complemented by an additional level, the county level, should the minority groups request it.[197]

The proposal re-regulates the relationship between local self-governments, minority self-governments, national minority self-governments and governmental organs. Minority self-governments would not obtain new rights as compared to the rights guaranteed in the 1993 Minority Act. However, the specification of deadlines and the introduction of sanctions would hopefully ensure that in the future they could validate their rights guaranteed by the law.[198] To achieve practical, functional cultural autonomy, joint decision-making has to be fostered and the actual possibility of taking over cultural and educational institutions needs to be promoted. The proposal takes a great step forward in this direction, which is the most significant merit of the reform. According to the plan of the sub-committee, the takeover of institutions would not be accompanied by a reform of the financial system. As a new element, local self-governments would be obliged to hand over the maintenance right of cultural and minority education institutions if certain prerequisites are met. In the case of educational institutions, the change would apply to those schools and boarding schools which have a regional or nationwide scope and which perform minority duties exclusively.[199]

National minority self-governments would be entitled to take over these institutions. If the founding document of a cultural institution verifies that it has been established to serve minority cultural purposes exclusively, local self-governments can also be obliged to hand over their maintenance right to the *local* minority self-government.[200] The takeover in the latter case has to be initiated by the national minority self-government.

Those involved with minority self-government have expressed mixed opinions about the system in place. In general, its existence has been seen as positive, while there have been serious reservations about the legal and financial conditions of its operation. The annual reports by the minority ombudsman have also supported these reservations. Thus, the modification of the Minority Act and the law regulating the election of minority self-government representatives has become indispensable.

6.   SUMMARY

1)   The Hungarian autonomy model can be classified as personal autonomy. Its main goal is to foster the ethnic identity of minority groups already rather assimilated by providing them with cultural autonomy. The legislation has also included certain elements of territorial autonomy that can be achieved on a municipality level.

2)   The international political situation of 1989–1990 made political and social changes possible in Hungary, too. Preparations for the long-absent Minority Act had been started four years before the changes of 1990. The task was finally accomplished by the first democratically elected Hungarian parliament.

On the national level the legislature was motivated by the historical debt to minorities. The international political aspects of this issue were seen as equally important. The attempt for an adequate legal regulation of the situation of Hungarian national and ethnic minority groups was a positive signal for the neighbouring countries and for the international— primarily the Western European—political community. Hungary would do its best to improve the minorities' chances in the gradually consolidating democratic system in spite of its limited financial resources. This was what Hungary would expect from its neighbouring countries' policies towards their ethnic minorities. As far as mutuality was concerned, these hopes proved to be illusory. On the international level, however, the Minority Act created a very positive impression and contributed significantly to enhancing Hungary's international reputation.

3)   The 1993 legal regulation of the minority issue in Hungary was an original legal-dogmatic experiment. For the first time a law aimed at the right-resolution of relatively small minority groups living in geographical dispersion. The Hungarian Constitution defines minorities in Hungary as state-forming components, prohibits their discrimination and guarantees them educational, linguistic and cultural rights as well as the right to participate collectively in public life. At the same time, it defines local and national minority self-governments as the organizational framework to exercise these rights. The Minority Act passed by the Hungarian Parliament in 1993 contains the detailed regulations concerning these rights.

The election of the minority self-governments integrated into the national system of local governments is not based on a minority inventory. Since minority leaders had objected categorically to any form of minority registration during the preparations of the Minority Act, giving priority to the principle of free identity choice, the legislation decided to restrict neither the active nor the passive franchise in any way. Thus, local minority self-governments are elected by the residents of a particular locality regardless of whether or not they belong to a minority group.

Local minority self-governments can exercise the right of consent to local government decrees related to local public education, local media, preservation of traditions and culture, and collective language use. The consent of the local minority self-government is also needed for the nomination of minority institution leaders and for any local government decision affecting the education of those belonging to minorities. According to the Minority Act, the local minority self-government may take over the maintenance of educational institutions from the local government in case they can reach an agreement about the takeover.

Although national minority self-governments are elected by the members of local minority self-governments, the two levels of minority self-governance actually work independently and none of them is subordinated to the other.

Although the entire self-government system is financed by the national government, self-governments and the motherland of the particular minority may also contribute to the improvement of the financial conditions.

4) Based on the experiences of the past six years, it has become evident that the system of minority self-governments needs to be reformed since in its present form it does not guarantee the achievement of the goals set down by the Minority Act.

The regulation of the election of minority self-governments needs to be changed so that only representatives of the particular minority group may become members of the self-governments. Since minority registration is prohibited, this can be achieved only through restriction of the passive franchise and/or through the separation of local elections and local minority self-government elections.

The relationship between local governments and local minority self-governments should be re-regulated, too. At present, the Minority Act includes no sanctions for those cases when local governments ignore the veto right of local minority self-governments. The internal operational regulations of minority self-governments concerning the remuneration of repre-sentatives, by-elections, committee formation, etc., must also be specified and elaborated. The conditions for the actual takeover of educational and cultural institutions also have to be created. Since minorities have scarcely intended to do this, the regulations will have to be made more specific to make this possible.

There are great deficiencies in the area of financial support. The Minority Act gives no specific method of budget planning and the sum delivered to minorities is always dependent on negotiations over the national budget. More predictability would be needed in this area, too. It has to be noted as well that the financial assistance given to minority self-governments is generally insufficient. An adequate budget should be provided in order to cover more than merely the representatives' pay and operational costs.

The parliamentary representation of minorities has not been achieved since the first democratic elections in 1990. As this issue primarily depends on negotiations between the political parties, it is unlikely to be resolved in the near future.

5) There are mixed opinions about the Hungarian minority self-government model. Its mere existence is seen as positive because it has created a framework of self-organization for minorities on the verge of assimilation. Another positive result is that the Minority Act guarantees not

only individual but also collective rights with constitutional support. The system was well received by the minorities and by the majority.

Much criticism, however, has been levelled towards its implementation. It has to be reformed in order to secure more adequate functioning. Not only the Minority Act has to be modified, though, but also the law on local governments. The national minority self-governments and the ministries concerned received the two modification-proposals for evaluation in May and June 2000. Six years after the first minority self-governments the possibility has opened to correct the minority self-government system by including the feedback from minorities and taking into account the needs of those concerned.

Table 2.2
National and Ethnic Minorities in Hungary[201] (1990 National Census Data)

Minorities	Ethnicity (as appears in census)	Mother Tongue	Estimates of the Minority Organization
Roma	142,683	48,072	400,000–600,000
German	30,824	37,511	200,000–220,000
Slovak	10,459	12,745	100,000–110,000
Croatian	13,570	17,577	80,000–90,000
Romanian	10,740	8,730	25,000
Serbian	2,905	2,953	5,000
Slovenian	1,930	2,627	5,000
Armenian	*	37	3,500–10,000
Greek	*	1,640	4,000–4,500
Bulgarian	*	1,370	2,500–5,000
Polish	*	3,788	10,000
Ukrainian	*	**	2,000
Ruthenian	*	**	6,000
Total	232,751	137,724	843,000–1,062,500

* All other minorities. Total: 19,640 persons. This number includes the ones marked by * whose exact number cannot be stated.

** The two languages appeared in the same question of the questionnaire. Altogether 647 persons.

NOTES

[113] The proposal was presented at the Rights and Human Rights Committee of the Council of Europe in 1992. The two experts of international reputation, Christoph Pan and Jean-Pierre Worms, gave a positive evaluation of it at the Committee's meeting in Venice. See Judit Bodáné Pálok, "A magyar kisebbségi törvény megszületésének körülményei (The Birth of the Hungarian Minority Act)", *Acta Humana*, 12–13 (1993), pp.42–43.

[114] Hungarian minorities are characterized by a double identity. The census questionnaire did not allow for the selection of Hungarian identity and a minority identity simultaneously. Moreover, the elder generations keep vivid memories of the fact that the majority of Hungarian Germans were forced to migrate to Germany after the Second World War based on the data of the 1944 census. The Hungarian–Czechoslovakian Population Exchange Agreement also contributed to the older generation's lack of confidence in and cooperation with the national census.

[115] On the situation of minorities in Hungary, see Erzsébet Forgács, "Ungarn und seine Minderheiten", *Österreichische Osthefte* 2, 1992, pp.195–217; Edwin Bakker, *Minority Conflicts in Slovakia and Hungary* (Capelle: Labyrint Publication, 1997), pp.139–243.

[116] On the minority politics of Hungary, see Gerhard Seewann, "Minderheiten in der ungarischen Innenpolitik 1949–1989/ 90", in *Nationen, Nationalitäten, Minderheiten*, Valeria Heuberger, ed. (Wien, 1994), pp.105–114; Lóránt Tilkovszky, *Nemzetiségi politika Magyarországon a 20. században* (Debrecen: Csokonai Kiadó, 1998); Gizella Föglein, *Nemzetiség vagy kisebbség? (Nationality or Minority?)* (Budapest: Ister, 2000).

[117] István Schlett, "Nemzetek és nemzeti kisebbségek (Nations and National Minorities)", in *Mi a politika? Bevezetés a politika világába*, János Gyurgyák, ed. (Budapest: Osiris, 1996), p.197. See also István Kemény, ed., *A magyarországi romák (Roma in Hungary)* (Budapest: Útmutató Kiadó, 2000).

[118] The Annual Report of the European Committee on Hungary's development emphasizes the frequent occurrence of the discrimination of the Roma. The problem is analyzed in detail in *Beszámoló a Nemzeti és Etnikai Kisebbségi Jogok Országgyűlési Biztosának tevékenységéről, 1999. január 1–december 31.* (Report on the Activity of the Ombudsman for National and Ethnic Minority Rights, 1 January–31 December 1999) (Budapest: Országgyűlési Biztosok Hivatala, 2000), pp.113–152.

[119] Gizella Föglein, *Nemzetiség vagy kisebbség?* (Budapest: Ister, 2000), p.82.

[120] Ágnes Vámos, *Magyarország tannyelvi atlasza/Atlas of languages of instruction in Hungary/Atlas der Unterrichtssprachen in Ungarn* (Budapest: Keraban Kiadó, 1998).

[121] Róbert Győry Szabó, *Kisebbségpolitikai rendszerváltás Magyarországon* (Budapest: Osiris, 1998).

[122] The Constitution of the Hungarian Republic, Articles 68–70/A.

[123] Herbert Küpper, *Das neue Minderheitenrecht in Ungarn* (München: R. Oldenbourg Verlag, 1998), p.3.

[124] For the "national liberal" and the "autonomist" concepts, see in detail: Gáspár Bíró, "A magyarországi nemzeti és etnikai kisebbségek jogairól szóló törvénytervezet elkészítésének tapasztalatairól", in Gáspár Bíró, *Az identitásválasztás szabadság* (Budapest: Századvég, 1995), pp.36–42.

[125] One of the Hungarian Jewish organizations also participated in the negotiations. Finally, however, the Hungarian Jewry decided not to be included in the 13 minorities enlisted in the Minority Law. See Küpper, *op.cit.*, pp.96–98.

[126] The minority law does not differentiate between national and ethnic minorities. The term 'ethnic' refers to the fact that the Roma have no mother country.

[127] The minority law is described and analyzed by Küpper, *op.cit.*; Jenő Kaltenbach, "Die Rechtstellung der Minderheiten in Ungarn", in *Ethnos-Nation* 1–2, 1997, pp.115–128; Jenő Kaltenbach, "Hungarian Report", in Jerzy Kranz, ed. *Law and Practice of Central European Countries in the Field of National Minorities Protection After 1989* (Warszawa: Center for International Relations, 1998), pp.61–131.

[128] The theoretical background of this problem is described and analyzed in Gáspár Bíró, "Az etnikai elvű csoportautonómia néhány elméleti kérdése", in Gáspár Bíró, *Az identitásválasztás szabadsága* (Budapest: Századvég, 1995), pp.177–211.

[129] Minority Act (LXXVII) of 1993 on the Rights of National and Ethnic Minorities (Minority Act), Article 7(1).

[130] Minority Act, Articles 15–20.

[131] Due to the dispersion of the minorities, territorial autonomy was completely out of the question.

132 Some minority leaders were afraid that local minority self-governments might become too dependent on local self-governments. Cf. Judit Bodáné Pálok, "A magyar kisebbségi törvény megszületésének körülményei", in *Acta Humana* 12–13, 1993, p.38.

133 If no minority government is formed at a particular locality, minority rights are represented by a minority spokesperson. Minority Act, Articles 40–41.

134 The election of national and ethnic minority self-government representatives is regulated by the Act LXIV of 1990 on the election of local government representatives and mayors (Articles 48–50/D).

135 Minority Act, Articles 25–30.

136 The Ruthenian and Ukrainian minorities formed no national minority self-governments in 1995. In 1999 all thirteen traditional national and ethnic minorities became integrated on the national level as well.

137 Every local government representative who has been elected as a minority representative is a minority elector, and so are the minority self-government representatives and spokespersons. If in the municipality the minority concerned does not have a minority self-government, the election of the elector may be initiated by three citizens who are entitled to vote, who are residents of the municipality, and who declare themselves to be members of the minority concerned. Minority Act, Article 31(2).

138 Minority ombudsman Jenő Kaltenbach has pointed out this deficiency several times. *Beszámoló a Nemzeti és Etnikai Kisebbségi Jogok Országgyűlési Biztosának tevékenységéről, 1997. január 1–december 31.* (Report on the Activity of the Ombudsman for National and Ethnic Minority Rights, 1 January–31 December 1997) (Budapest: Országgyűlési Biztosok Hivatala, 1998), p.53.

139 Minority Act, Articles 35–39.

140 The national self-governments (in the year 1995) received shares in the following values: the Roma National Minority self-government: 60 million HUF (250,000 USD); the German, the Slovak, the Croatian and the Romanian national self-governments: 30 million HUF (125,000 USD); the others: 15 million HUF (62,500 USD). Minority Act, Article 63(4) (1 USD = 240 HUF in 1 May 2000).

141 The standard financial assistance received by local minority self-governments was 300 million HUF (1.25 million USD) in 1997, 350 million HUF (1.46 million USD) in 1998, and 730 million HUF (3.04 million USD) in 1999. In J/1397sz. Kormánybeszámoló a Magyar Köztársaság területén élő nemzeti és etnikai kisebbségek helyzetéről 1999. június. In Mária Demetre Zayzon ed., *Kisebbségek Magyarországon* (Budapest, 1999), p.172.

142 In 1997 3,246.8 million HUF (13.528 million USD), in 1998 3,924 million HUF (16.350 million USD), in 1999 4,941 million HUF (20.588 million USD). Zayzon, *op.cit.*

143 The minority self-government system is discussed by Csaba Tabajdi, "Minderheitenselbstverwaltung in Ungarn", in *Ethnos-Nation* 1–2,1996, pp.129–136; Bakker, *op. cit.*, pp.181–189; Ferenc Csefkó and Ilona Pálné Kovács, *Kisebbségi önkormányzatok Magyarországon* (Budapest: Osiris–MTA Kisebbségkutató Műhely–MTA Regionális Kutatások Központja, 1999).

144 Csefkó and Kovács, *op. cit.*, p.138. The legal regulation has been criticized frequently because it guarantees minority self-governments few real powers and because it contains many merely permissive, conditional regulations. Those concerned have found it a very serious deficiency that there are contradictions between the Minority Act, the self-government law and the public education law. Csefkó and Kovács, *op cit.*, pp.132–144.

145 The term 'sympathy vote' refers to the votes cast for minority self-government representatives by the majority. The legal prohibition of registration makes it impossible to find out the exact ratio of minority votes and sympathy votes. In the case of most minorities, however, sympathy votes are considerably higher than minority votes. According to the 1990 national census, 232,751 persons declared themselves members of ethnic minority groups. According to the estimates of minority organizations, on the other hand, a minimum of 843,000 and a maximum of 1,062 5000 minority citizens live in Hungary. If one compares these data with the votes cast for minority representatives, one can see that the majority supports the institutions of minority self-governments as well.

146 *J/1379 számú Kormánybeszámoló* (Government Report No. J/1397), pp.42–43.

[147] The Parliamentary Assembly of the Council of Europe, Strasbourg, 1992. The Legal Affairs and Human Rights Committee's remarks on the bill concerning the rights of national and ethnic minorities. The statement of Jean-Pierre Worms is cited by Bodáné, *op. cit.*, p.42.

[148] Although several minorities had to face this problem, the largest scandal occurred about the election of the Romanian Minority Self-Governments in the capital. The president of MRDSZ (*Magyarországi Románok Demokratikus Szövetsége*, Democratic Federation of Romanians in Hungary) formed just before the elections had been the president of the Roma Minority Self-Government of the 16th district of the capital four years before. (The law permits this.) "Román választás (Romanian Election)", in *HVG* 27 (1995), 5, pp.89–90. There were Roma candidates who ran for Romanian self-government representatives and there were also Hungarian candidates who had previously moved from Romania to Hungary. (Several of the latter had obtained their Hungarian citizenship more rapidly because they had formally claimed to be ethnic Hungarians.) Riba István, "Vita kisebbségi önkormányzati szabályokról", in *HVG*, 1998/8 pp.105–106. The general context of this problem is presented in Sándor Palásti, ed., *A kisebbségi önkormányzatok kézikönyve*, (Budapest: Nemzeti és Etnikai Kisebbségi Jogok Országgyűlési Biztosa, 1999) pp.104–106.

[149] *A Kisebbségi Önkormányzatok kézikönyve, op. cit.*, p.107.

[150] The Romanian National Minority Self-Government could not be formed in Gyula because of the absence of the MRDSZ. Forty per cent of the electors are MRDSZ-members. It was unwilling to participate in the election unless the authentic leaders of the Rumanians in Hungary participated, too, thus making possible the election of the Rumanian minority self-government in the capital which would logically have fallen under MRDSZ control. Moreover, the MRDSZ wanted to be represented in the presidency of the Romanian National Minority Self-Government according to the number of its electors. Their requests were turned down. "Román választás (Romanian Election)", in *HVG* 31 (1999), 8, pp.105–106.

[151] Romanian Prime Minister Radu Vasile met Prime Minister Viktor Orbán in February 1999 and urged for measures so that the Romanian National Minority Self-Government could be formed. The Hungarian Prime Minister promised to take measures. Public speech held by political the Under-Secretary of the Foreign Ministry, Mr Csaba Hende, at the national self-government electing reunion of the Rumanian minority of Hungary in the town of Gyula on 18 September, 1998.

[152] *Beszámoló a Nemzeti és Etnikai Kisebbségi Jogok Országgyűlési Biztosának tevékenységéről, 1998. január 1–december 31.* (Report on the Activity of the Ombudsman for National and Ethnic Minority Rights, 1 January–31 December 1998) (Budapest: Országgyűlési Biztosok Hivatala, 1999), Chapters 2, 4, 5.

[153] *A kisebbségi Önkormányzatok kézikönyve*, pp.103–104.

[154] Sándor Makai, "Az önkormányzati választási törvények módosításához", in *Magyar Közigazgatás* (2000),1, p.58.

[155] Although several Roma minority leaders would find registration acceptable, the other minorities reject this alternative. Greek National Minority Self-Government director Jorgosz Dzindisz stated in an interview for the weekly *HVG* that small minority groups living in geographical dispersion would have to face serious difficulties when trying to form their minority self-governments. Péró Lásztity, director of the Serbian National Minority Self-Government feared that minority self-governments would be financed according to their size and not according to the tasks they performed. Riba, "Vita a kisebbségi önkormányzatokról", *op. cit.*, p.106.

[156] *6-Á-568/2000. sz. Előterjesztés a Kormány részére a kisebbségi képviselők választásáról szóló törvénytervezetről* (Proposition for the Government on the Bill on the Election of Minority Representatives, No. 6-Á-568/2000).

[157] The reservations about the proposal were summarized by Péró Lásztity in an interview given to ETNONET. He emphasized that the proposal would make the formation of minority self-governments in several places and primarily in larger towns impossible. In this case intellectuals would be excluded from minority self-governments. http://etnonet.hu/archiv/inter/interpero.htm.

[158] The law has not regulated the remuneration of minority representatives and has given instructions neither on the incompatibility of different functions nor on the possibility to remove the president of minority self-governments. It has been unclear who should finance by-elections if the local minority-self government terminates its activities. The possibility to take over institutions from the local self-government has already been pointed out; nevertheless, it has been unclear how the institution would be financed in the new situation.

159　A regulation is a legal norm issued by the self-government in its own area of competence. A decree is a decision made by the self-government board.

160　Csefkó and Kovács, *op. cit.*, p.120.

161　The vice-director of a Slovak Minority Self-Government in the county of Nógrád complained to the minority ombudsman that the permanent director of the local cultural centre was removed from his post by the self-government of the municipality because of his lack of ability to carry out this task. The local self-government did not ask for the opinion of the local minority self-government; moreover, the opinions they expressed were ignored. The ombudsman found the complaint well-grounded. *Beszámoló a Nemzeti és Etnikai Kisebbségi Jogok Országgyűlési Biztosának tevékenységéről, 1997. január 1–december 31.* (Report on the Activity of the Ombudsman for National and Ethnic Minority Rights, 1 January–31 December 1997) (Budapest: Országgyűlési Biztosok Hivatala, 1998), pp.59–61.

162　Minority kindergarten education in the academic year 1997–98 took place in minority language kindergartens (69 groups) and in language-teaching minority kindergartens (860 groups). At primary school level 174 groups participated in minority language education, 446 in bilingual education, and 3,019 in the language-teaching type of education. The German National Minority Self-Government questioned the statistical data based on the auto-classification of minority education institutions because they found them exaggerated. There are 19 minority language and bilingual secondary schools, there is one Roma secondary school and there are four secondary level technical schools providing minority education. In *J/1379 számú Kormánybeszámoló* (Government Report No. J/1397), pp.7–72.

163　The additional standard assistance in the 1999 national budget (Ft/person) amounted to: kindergarten: 25,000 HUF (104 USD), minority language as a foreign language: 26,000 (108 USD), Roma remedial schools: 27,000 HUF (113 USD), normative supplement for kindergartens and schools: 20,000 HUF (83 USD), boarding school for Roma students: 22,000 HUF (92 USD). In *J/1379 számú Kormánybeszámoló* (Government Report No. J/1397), p.172.

164　*Beszámoló a Nemzeti és Etnikai Kisebbségi Jogok Országgyűlési Biztosának tevékenységéről, 1998. január 1–december 31.* (Report on the Activity of the Ombudsman for National and Ethnic Minority Rights, 1 January–31 December 1998) (Budapest: Országgyűlési Biztosok Hivatala, 1999), Chapter 7.4.

165　The ombudsman studied in detail the situation of minority education. He found that some of the local self-governments did not use the state assistance for the purposes it was intended. The study by the National Audit Office reached the same conclusions. *Beszámoló a Nemzeti és Etnikai Kisebbségi Jogok Országgyűlési Biztosának tevékenységéről, 1999. január 1–december 31.* (Report on the Activity of the Ombudsman for National and Ethnic Minority Rights, 1 January–31 December 1999) (Budapest: Országgyűlési Biztosok Hivatala, 2000), pp.60–61.

166　About the new legal background and its application possibilities, see the interview to ETNONET with Nándor Torba, director of the Public Education and Minority Relations Department of the Ministry of Education, at http://www.etnonet.hu/archiv/inter/torba.htm.

167　*Beszámoló a Nemzeti és Etnikai Kisebbségi Jogok Országgyűlési Biztosának tevékenységéről, 1997. január 1–december 31.* (Report on the Activity of the Ombudsman for National and Ethnic Minority Rights, 1 January–31 December 1997) (Budapest: Országgyűlési Biztosok Hivatala, 1998), p.79.

168　Interview with Mr János Hargitai, president of the subcommittee preparing the modification of the Minority Act. 2 March 2000. AKM Sound Archives. Tape 1. Side A.

169　The Roma situtation is presented in "Zur Lage der Zigeuner in Ungarn. Ein Untersuchungsbericht", in *Ethnos-Nation*, 2 (1994), pp.49–60. See also István Kemény, ed., *A magyarországi romák* (Budapest: Útmutató Kiadó, 2000); István Kernény "Cigánykérdés a 20. század végi Magyarországon", *Regio* 4 (1993), 1, pp.84–102.

170　The situation of the Roma in Hungary cannot be improved merely within the scope of the Minority Law. As opposed to national minorities, the primary objective of the Roma minority is not the achievement of cultural autonomy. Minority self-governments cannot resolve social problems on their own. Although the new government has taken over the middle-term Roma programme from the Horn Government and there is an Inter-Ministerial Roma Committee, too, serious doubts have been raised about their efficiency. Flórián Farkas, Director of the Roma National Minority Self-Government, has noted several times that ministries spend only a fraction of the assistance at their disposal on the improvement of the Roma's situation. János Dobszay, "Hazai cigányügy", in *HVG* 32 (2000), 31, p.8.

[171] Csefkó and Kovács, *op. cit.*, 102. The operation and problems related to Roma minority self-governments are analyzed in the case study by Erno Kállai, "The Operation of the Roma Minority Self-Government of Abony", *Regio* 9 (1998), 4, pp.99–111.

[172] According to the survey by the Regional Studies Centre of MTA, 55.6 per cent of the takeover of duties by Roma local self-governments concern social issues. This rate is particularly high. Other local minority self-governments generally take over cultural duties. Csefkó and Kovács: *op. cit.*, pp.97–98.

[173] Local minority self-governments received 450 thousand HUF in 1997 and 550 thousand HUF in 1999 from the Central Budget.

[174] Most municipalities receive only government assistance. Several minority self-governments may receive financial support from the local self-government depending on the economic situation of the municipality. The amount of this support varied from 777 HUF up to several million HUF in 1997. Minority self-governments may also apply to public foundations (e.g. The Public Foundation for Minorities) for financial assistance. Csefkó and Kovács, *op. cit.*, pp.78–89. The national minority self-governments have also supported the local minorities, although generally with very small amounts. This support, however, does not go to the minority self-governments but to the local cultural and folklore groups. See Ferenc Eiler, "Az országos német, szlovák és horvát kisebbségi önkormányzatok első négy évi működésének tapasztalatai", *Regio* 9 (1998), 4, pp.62–63.

[175] Csefkó and Kovács, *op. cit.*, pp.135–137

[176] The county federation of Germans, Croats and Gypsies can participate in the sessions of the county assembly of Baranya. Interview with János Hargitai. AKM Sound Archives. Tape 1. Side A.

[177] *6–Á–568/2000. sz. Előterjesztés a Kormány részére a kisebbségi képviselők választásáról szóló törvénytervezetről (Proposal for the Government on the Bill on the Election of Minority Representatives, No. 6–Á–568/2000)*, Chapter 3. According to the proposal, the rules of the national self-government election would be changed, too. The existing system of minority electors would be replaced by a three-step system, and 700 would be the maximum number of electors electing the national minority self-government, *6–Á–568/2000. sz. Előterjesztés a Kormány részére a kisebbségi képviselők választásáról szóló törvénytervezetről (Proposal for the Government on the Bill on the Election of Minority Representatives, No. 6–Á–568/2000), op. cit.*, Chapter 5.

[178] Borók "A nemzeti és etnikai kisebbségek országgyűlési képviseletének szabályozási modelljei Európában és Magyar-országon", *Társadalmi Szemle* 1998, 4, pp.68–85.

[179] In principle, the national assemblies of the German, Croatian and Slovak minorities backed up the Minority Forum formed in a rush before the parliamentary elections of 1998. The Minority Forum accepted the general conditions that applied to political parties. It managed to set a national electoral list, but it had no chance whatsoever to get into Parliament.

[180] György Borók, *op.cit.*, pp.78–80.

[181] *Beszámoló a Nemzeti és Etnikai Kisebbségi Jogok Országgyűlési Biztosának tevékenységéről, 1995. július 1–1996. december 31.* (Report on the Activity of the Ombudsman for National and Ethnic Minority Rights, 1 July 1995–31 December 1996) (Budapest: Országgyűlési Biztosok Hivatala, 1997), pp.95–97.

[182] It states that minorities have the right—as determined in the Minority Act—to be represented in the National Assembly.

[183] Some aspects of this problem are summarized by János Hargitai, in *A kisebbségek parlamenti képviselete és részvételük a politikai döntéshozatali folyamatban*. Budapest, 1999. október 15–16. Nemzeti és Etnikai Kisebbségi Jogok Országgyűlési Biztosa, Budapest, 2000, pp.60–68.

[184] The Smallholders' Party: FKGP, and the Hungarian Truth and Life Party: MIÉP.

[185] This solution may seem simple from a political point of view, but its legal-technical resolution is more difficult. To implement it, the Constitution would also need to be modified.

[186] The minimum threshold of 5 per cent would not apply to the minority lists in the elections.

187   In spite of the reservations by the Smallholders' Party (FKGP), all government parties would prefer to resolve the problem of the minorities' parliamentary representation in this form. The Hungarian Socialist Party (MSZP) prefers the three-vote system but it does not reject the two-vote system categorically either. The Alliance of Free Democrats (SZDSZ) would also find this system acceptable.

188   Joint minority lists could be one of the possible solutions. In this case minorities should reach an agreement on candidates.

189   Both parties support the reduction of the number of parliamentary representatives. The difference is that one party would decrease the number of individual deputies while the other the number of those who enter from the political party lists. F.K.: "Bizottsági patt", in *Magyar Nemzet*, 26 April 2000.

190   "A magyar kisebbségi törvény megszületésének körülményei", in *Acta Humana*, 12–13 (1993), p.42.

191   Christoph Pan's statement about the proposal on the rights of national and ethnic minorities in Hungary, September 1992, cited by Judit Bodáné Pálok.

192   Ferenc Csefkó, "A kisebbségi önkormányzatok közjogi státusa, működésük meghatározó területei", *Regio* 9 (1998), 4, p.43.

193   The minorities would have preferred the modified Minority Law to regulate their parliamentary representation as well. They fear that they will have no parliamentary representation in the next electoral term either. The ombudsman has also prepared a proposal about the rights of minorities in Hungary. *Beszámoló a Nemzeti és Etnikai Kisebbségi Jogok Országgyűlési Biztosának tevékenységéről, 1999. január 1–december 31.* (Report on the Activity of the Ombudsman for National and Ethnic Minority Rights, 1 January–31 December 1999) (Budapest: Országgyűlési Biztosok Hivatala, 2000), pp.168–220.

194   The bill on the election of minority self-government representatives was prepared in July 2000.

195   The interpretative regulations apply to the following concepts: minority public affairs; minority self-government; educational institutions of minority public education; employees of minority public education; minority cultural institutions; cultural institutions; minority media; minority settlement with historical traditions; part of a settlement; official documents. Cf. *Törvényjavaslat a nemzeti és etnikai kisebbségek jogairól szóló 1993. Évi LXXVII. Törvény módosításáról. Tervezet.*

196   Sándor Puskás, "A helyi kisebbségi önkormányzatok működésének tapasztalatai Bács-Kiskun megyében", in *Magyar Közigazgatás* (1997), 4, pp.223–227; László Hajdú, "Cigány kisebbségi önkormányzatok működése Jász-Nagykun-Szolnok megyében", in *Magyar Közigazgatás* (1998), 9, pp.554–563; Csilla Kiss, "A fővárosban megalakult kisebbségi önkormányzatok törvényessége 1995. évben," in *Magyar Közigazgatás* (1996), 6, pp.375–380.

197   *Törvényjavaslat a nemzeti és etnikai kisebbségek jogairól szóló 1993. évi LXXVII. törvény módosításáról. Tervezet.* Article 30(P–R).

198   As it stands in Article 47(b). "If the law guarantees minority self-governments the right of evaluation or the right to consult about any decision concerning public education issues, they have 15 days to make a declaration unless another regulations specifies it otherwise. After fifteen days they lose their right to do so. If the minority self-government does not agree and if the local self-government and the local minority self-government do not reach an agreement during the subsequent fifteen days, both parties have five days to initiate a legal case. After five days they loose their right to do so. A court tries the case exclusive of turn".

199   Modification bill of the 1993 Act on the Rights of National and Ethnic Minorities. A Proposal. Article 47(4).

200   Article 49(3).

201   J/1397 sz. kormánybeszámoló a Magyar Köztársaság területén élő nemzeti és etnikai kisebbségek helyzetéről, 1999. június. In Mária Demeter Zayzon, ed. *Kisebbségek Magyarországon 1999* (Minorities in Hungary) (Budapest, 1999), pp.35–36.

PART III

Self-Government: A Framework for Conflict Settlement?

Insular Autonomy: A New Approach to Conflict Resolution in Corsica?

Farimah Daftary

∎

Overview of Proposals for Minority Self-Goverments of Hungarian Minorities in Central Europe

Zsolt G. Pataki

∎

Chances for Ethnic Autonomy in Vojvodina: Analysis of the Latest Autonomy Proposal of Hungarian Political Parties in Vojvodina

Tamás Korhecz

∎

Substantial Self-Administration for Kosovo: From Rambouillet to the Adoption of a Constitutional Framework Document

Marc Weller

∎

Governing Post-War Bosnia-Herzegovina

Florian Bieber

Insular Autonomy: A New Approach to Conflict Resolution in Corsica?

Farimah Daftary

Insular Autonomy: A New Approach to Conflict Resolution in Corsica?

Farimah Daftary

1. INTRODUCTION

Despite decentralization in 1982 and the establishment of administrative autonomy in 1991, Corsica has been plagued by under-development, political instability and, since the mid-1970s, by political violence. Neither institutional reform nor repression have been successful until now and the Corsican crisis has become ever more entrenched.

Against the backdrop of efforts undertaken throughout Europe over the past decade to find innovative solutions to ethnic conflicts, France stands out as having remained very conservative in its approach to the Corsican conflict. Indeed, France has been traditionally very reluctant to recognize regional diversity and to grant collective rights. Institutional reform in Corsica has been further limited by the fact that it is considered to be one of the 22 regions of 'Metropolitan France' (*France métropolitaine*). Indeed, when it comes to the administrative structure of the French Republic, the Constitution (1958) allows for very little regional variation. The Constitutional Council's interpretation of the Constitution has also been very strict. Thus, although unique in the context of mainland France, Corsica's special statute lags behind those of some of the French overseas territories.

In recent years, we have witnessed a slow transformation of the French state. The intense debates concerning the European Charter for Regional or Minority Languages and on reform in Corsica are a testimony to this evolution. The murder of the Prefect of Corsica on 6 February 1998 and the fiasco of the government's subsequent strong-handed policy of 're-establishing the rule of law' led to the realization by Socialist Prime Minister Jospin that a new approach to the 'Corsican Question' was warranted. On 13 December 1999, discussions with elected representatives from Corsica on reforming the 1991 Special Statute were launched. The so-called 'Matignon Process' resulted in a set of compromise proposals by the government on 20 July 2000; they were approved by a majority of the regional Corsican Assembly on 28 July.

Although weak compared to recent developments in other conflict regions of Europe, the proposals are innovative in the context of the French mainland regions and constitute the most significant effort to date to settle the Corsican conflict. Not only the agreement but also the political process behind it merit further analysis. If the measures are fully implemented, Corsica's administrative autonomy will be significantly expanded but stop short of full political autonomy.[1] Implementation is likely to be slow and entails overcoming significant political and legal obstacles. A law modifying the current statute is due to come into force at the beginning of 2002 (Phase 1). However, the most interesting measures which will result in a new statute for Corsica, its third, can only be introduced after 2004 once the Constitution has been revised and pending the 'durable re-establishment of civil peace' (Phase 2).

After an introduction to the 'Corsican Question', an overview of past attempts at resolving the conflict and the current arrangement based on the 1991 Special Statute will be provided. In the analysis of Corsica's past experience with institutional reform, problem areas as well as elements of success will be highlighted. In a third section, the broad outlines of the proposals of 20 July 2000 and the determining factors in the process leading up to it will be analyzed. The drafting process for the law on the first phase of reforms (2002–04) will also be presented, with references to the important provisions of the government's bill (December 2000) as well as to the draft law adopted by the National Assembly (May 2001). Finally, the potential of the 'Matignon Process' to durably resolve the Corsican conflict will be assessed. We shall also place the recent developments in Corsica in comparative perspective by referring to other French regions and overseas territories where relevant.

2.   BACKGROUND: WHAT IS THE 'CORSICAN QUESTION'?

A matter of self-determination at heart, independence is not the desire of the majority of Corsicans; according to polls, only about six to ten per cent of them favour it.[2] However, as much as 46 per cent of the population of France now supports independence for Corsica, an increase from 40 per cent a few years ago, reflecting increasing lassitude regarding the fate of this island perceived as a source of constant trouble and a guzzler of state funds.

Although often reduced to a problem of violence, political corruption and nationalist racketeering *(dérive mafieuse)*, the Corsican Question[3] is quite complex. While Corsica's problems are usually attributed to specific social, economic and cultural features related to insularity, in Corsica itself the poor economy and widespread violence are seen as a consequence of the refusal of the French state to search for the roots of the crisis and to take the island's specific character into account. Indeed, while local actors share responsibility for the crisis, its roots also lie in neglect and inconsistent development policies of the central government. The Corsican Question is also the product of the history of relations with the state, characterized to this day by misunderstanding and mistrust.

2.1 Considerations Related to Language, Culture and Identity

The existence of a separate Corsican people has never been officially recognized by the French government, although there is a consensus that Corsicans possess a distinct identity based on a specific history and distinct culture. Most of the island's inhabitants consider themselves simultaneously Corsican (in the ethnic sense) and French (in the civic sense).

Territory is the primary reference point in determining Corsican identity. The population of barely 260,000 consists of a dominant group of Corsicans (70 per cent), a minority of the French titular nation (20 per cent), as well as smaller immigrant communities (10 per cent of non-citizens, mostly from North Africa and Southern Europe).[4]

Another vector of identity is the Corsican language or *Corsu*. Spoken by about 65 per cent of the total population of the island,[5] and for a long time considered by the government as a dialect of Italian,[6] it has no official status. The administrative and legal role of Corsican is therefore minimal. It is now used on a voluntary basis by teachers in kindergartens and is taught as an optional subject for about three hours a week at the primary and secondary levels. There is also a limited presence of Corsican in the print media state radio, and television.

2.2 Considerations Related to the Economy

Corsica is one of the most under-developed regions of France, with a GDP 23 per cent below the national average, and an unemployment rate a few percentage points above the national average. It is the least populated region of France (the decrease of the population was only reversed in recent decades due to immigration).

In order to compensate for the handicaps linked to insularity, peripheral location, a seasonal economy and a high cost of transportation, the Corsican economy is heavily subsidized by the French government and the EU. The economy is also highly dependent on public sector employment (25.7 per cent of jobs are in state administration) and on revenues from tourism (15 per cent of GDP), making it vulnerable to nationalist violence.

2.3 Considerations Related to History

Due to the island's strategic position in the Western Mediterranean, Corsican history has been a succession of rebellions against domination by foreign peoples (Romans, Pisans, Genoese, Italians and, finally, the French).[7] A leading figure in the history of Corsican nationalism is Pascal Paoli, leader of the rebellion against the Genoese after 1755 and under whom Corsica enjoyed a period of partial independence (1755–69). After Corsica was sold by Genoa to France in 1768, the competition between French and Italian influences was won by the former, leading to a slow integration into French polity.[8] A period of cultural revival starting in 1896, followed by political opposition to the French (by the *Partitu Corsu d'Azzione* founded in 1923 and renamed *Partitu Corsu Autonomistu* in 1927) ended with the Second World War. Expecting independence, Corsica found itself again under French rule.

The post-war period was marked by economic, demographic and cultural decline. A 1957 development plan (*Programme d'action régional de la Corse*) based on the expansion of tourism and the agricultural sector failed to bring any benefits to the local population, for it was used to facilitate the relocation of 17,000 *pied noir* colonists from Algeria who were given preference in obtaining land in the Eastern Plain of Corsica, much to the frustration of the local population.

2.4 The Emergence of Corsican Nationalism and State Responses

The modern phase of the conflict can be traced to the mid-1960s when various environmental and autonomist movements emerged demanding that the French government design adequate policies for the development of Corsica while respecting its specific identity, rather than try to forcibly assimilate it. Since the publication of a document entitled *Autonomia* (1974) by Corsican autonomists, demands for a special status and the recognition of the Corsican people have been closely linked.

The events in Aleria in August 1975[9] and the appearance one year later (5 May 1976) of the separatist Corsican National Liberation Front (FLNC) marked the radicalization of protest against the 'colonial oppressor', it also indicated a split between 'separatist nationalists' and 'autonomist nationalists'. Although these two groups still share a number of common aims, autonomists have largely abandoned the use of violence whereas separatist nationalists systematically resort to it. According to some interpretations, the cycle of terrorist violence and state repression could have been avoided by the French government had it granted Corsica and other French regions more powers in the late 1960s and early 1970s when regionalist movements were sweeping Europe.[10]

Despite the outlawing of the FLNC by the government in 1983, separatist organizations proliferated and the nationalist movement became increasingly crippled by fragmentation and infighting.[11] Clandestine activities are often funded by means of 'revolutionary taxes' and illegal business, making it difficult to draw a clear dividing line between nationalists and the local mafia. At the same time, nationalists have sought to exert influence through political fronts with a certain success. This can be explained by the fact that they are an instrument for the articulation of disparate interests, thereby capturing the discontent of very diverse sectors of the electorate. At the centre of nationalist demands is the recognition by the state of the existence of a distinct historical and cultural community: the Corsican people (*peuple corse*) as well as the protection of the Corsican language and culture. While local politicians were originally very hostile to the nationalist discourse which also attacked the power of the 'clans', they adopted elements of it because of their mobilizing potential.[12] The local political elite also stands to benefit from the expansion of autonomy which reinforces their power and control over resources.

State responses to the Corsican conflict have varied (at least on the surface) depending on the parties in power. Right-wing RPR interior ministers (Pasqua 1986–88; 1993–95; and Debré 1995–97) have practiced 'double diplomacy': dealing with the mainstream Corsican political actors while at the same time conducting negotiations with clandestine movements or with their political fronts and playing one against the other; secret negotiations thus alternated with open repression with no success. Left-wing (Socialist Party) interior ministers (Defferre 1981–86; Joxe 1988–93), on the other hand, have sought to devise institutional solutions.

3. THE DEVELOPMENT OF ADMINISTRATIVE AUTONOMY IN CORSICA (1982–1991)

In this section, the two attempts at resolving the Corsican conflict through institutional reform will be presented, paying particular attention to the current arrangement based on the 1991 Special Statute.

3.1 The Unitary French State

A determining feature of institutional arrangements in Corsica is that it belongs to the traditionally centralized and unitary French Republic based on the Jacobin conception of the state. The two founding principles of the French state are the equality of all French citizens before the law and the indivisibility of the Republic (Article 1 of the 1958 French Constitution).[13]

France has been particularly reluctant to recognize regional diversity and to develop asymmetric solutions or grant any collective rights which it believes contradict the founding principles of the Republic and its legal and political traditions. France is one of the few Council of Europe members not to have signed the Framework Convention for the Protection of National Minorities. It signed the European Charter for Regional or Minority Languages on 7 May 1999 but has not ratified it because the Constitutional Council ruled that this would violate the Constitution.[14] Thus, French is the only official language in the territory of France.

Two institutions play an important role in ensuring respect of the Constitution and entrenchment of the rule of law (l'État de droit). If so requested, the Constitutional Council (Conseil Constitutionnel), which is not a supreme judiciary court but a permanent consultative court,[15] will issue an opinion on the conformity with the Constitution of Acts of Parliament—the latter consisting of the National Assembly (Assemblée nationale) and the Senate (Sénat). Its decision is binding and may lead to either total or partial censure of a proposed law (but not its annulment as decisions are made before promulgation). Consultation of the Council of State (Conseil d'État)[16] can prevent such an outcome, for, in addition to its function of supreme administrative organ, it acts as advisor to the government by examining bills before they are adopted by the Council of Ministers (Conseil des Ministres) and submitted to Parliament.

In addition to the strict limits imposed by the Constitution, there are also mental obstacles for Corsica is considered not an overseas territory, but an integral part of 'Metropolitan France' (France métropolitaine), a distinction not explicitly made in the Constitution. Thus, Corsica is the only Mediterranean island not to enjoy political autonomy today. Still, the Constitution allows for a limited degree of variation. Article 34 recognizes the possibility of self-administration of territorial units while Article 72 foresees the creation of territorial units other than communes, departments and overseas territories, and which are "self-governing through elected councils and in the manner provided by statute".

It should also be stressed that this has always been an internal conflict. The lack of a kin-state as well as the refusal of France to recognize the existence of any minorities on its territory means that there can be no international mediation nor can one refer to the application of international norms on minority or even linguistic rights. The right to internal self-determination cannot be invoked either, for this is a right granted to the peoples inhabiting the French overseas territories only (preamble of the Constitution).

3.2 The 1982 Special Statute and Decentralization

The victory of the Socialist Party in 1981 marked a new phase in state policy towards Corsica. In keeping with a promise made by François Mitterrand before he was elected president, Corsica received its first special statute on 2 March 1982.[17] Although it was expected to be similar to those of Sicily and Sardinia, the new statute was much less significant in the form of a simple law.[18] Still, this was the first attempt to recognize the specific character of Corsica and to grant it a degree of autonomy to administer its own affairs through specific institutions.[19]

The impact of the reforms was diluted by the process of decentralization (1982–86) which extended the same measures to mainland France.[20] Corsica and the mainland regions now had similar institutions with the exception that Corsica's elected body was called the 'Corsican Assembly' (Assemblée de Corse) rather than the 'regional council' (conseil régional). Still, although the Corsican Assembly was given no legislative powers, its administrative competencies were more extensive than those of other regions in a few areas relevant to the specific needs of the island (culture, transport, planning and education). Also, Corsica received not one but two consultative councils—

one dealing with economic and social matters, the other with cultural and educational issues.

3.3 The 1991 Special Statute

3.3.1   The Result of a 'Top-down' as well as of a 'Bottom-up' Process

The 1988 reelection of Mitterrand led to renewed debates and a second attempt to lay the institutional foundations for the development of Corsica while respecting its special identity.[21] On 29 September 1988, an inter-ministerial committee on Corsica was set up by Interior Minister Pierre Joxe with the task of formulating a new approach. His policy of dialogue with local representatives paved the way for including the nationalists.

On 13 October 1988, the Corsican Assembly adopted a historic resolution affirming the existence of a living historical and cultural community, the Corsican people.[22] Joxe promised to incorporate this resolution in the new statute which he hoped would not only enhance the effectiveness of regional institutions but also establish peace through the recognition of identity claims. These reforms were to a certain degree the result of a bottom-up process, the Corsican deputies having had some influence over the content of the agreement.

3.3.2   A New Territorial Entity

On 12 April 1991, the National Assembly adopted by a narrow margin a bill establishing a new statute for Corsica.[23] However, Article 1 of Act no. 91–428 of 13 May 1991 (also called the Joxe Statute)[24] which referred to the "Corsican people, component of the French people", had to be deleted, depriving the statute of its very political foundations.[25] However, the Constitutional Council ruled that granting Corsica a special arrangement did not contravene the Constitution. The 1991 Special Statute established Corsica as a *collectivité territoriale de Corse*—an administrative entity combining elements from the French Overseas Departments (DOMs) and Overseas Territories (TOMs)[26]. This enabled further decentralization in Corsica, granting it expanded administrative autonomy within the confines of the Constitution.

3.3.3   Specific Institutions and Competencies

The new statute was innovative, reinforcing the powers of the Corsican region, giving it specific institutions (separate deliberative and executive bodies were established) as well as more competencies than in other French regions.

The Corsican Assembly in Ajaccio manages the affairs of Corsica and controls the Executive Council. It is composed of 51 members elected for six years and is headed by the Assembly President. The new system of two ordinary sessions of three months each year enforced the parliamentary nature of this body (in the rest of France, regional councils meet only when convoked by the council president). Although the Corsican Assembly still has no legislative powers, it possesses a *residual regulatory power* to implement national laws and decrees; it also defines and implements policies within its spheres of competence. The establishment of administrative autonomy was accompanied by the transfer of new areas of competence including education, media, culture, the environment ("Cultural Identity of Corsica", Arts. 50–57 of the 1991 Statute), economic development, agriculture, tourism, housing, transportation, training and energy (Arts. 58–77). A separate section is devoted to resources (Arts. 78–82). The Assembly adopts the budget and sets the medium-term objectives for Corsica's economic, social and cultural development as well as an outline of the financial means necessary ("Plan de développement de la Corse"). The Assembly also adopts a plan for the teaching of the Corsican language and culture, establishes the broad outlines of agricultural development and tourism, and manages transportation between the island and the continent. If it cannot function normally (e.g. if it fails to adopt the budget), it can be dissolved by a decree of the central government (Art. 27).[27]

The Executive Council (Conseil exécutif) implements the policies of the Corsican Assembly mainly in the spheres of economic and social development, education and culture and regional planning. It is a collegial body composed of a president and six councillors selected from the Assembly (who must resign from it); four of the councillors preside over the offices which are mixed state-region technical bodies for implementing policies in the fields of agriculture, water management and distribution, transportation, the environment and tourism.

The Economic, Social and Cultural Council (Conseil économique, social et culturel, CESC), a fusion of the two consultative councils established under the 1982 Statute, is a consultative body at the service of the Corsican Assembly and the Executive Council. It assists, inter alia, with preparing the development plan for Corsica and the plan for the teaching of the Corsican language and culture.

3.3.4 The Electoral System of the Corsican Assembly and Corsican Political Parties

The 1991 Statute sought to remedy the problem of weak and unstable political institutions by introducing a special electoral system for the Corsican Assembly aiming to produce a stable majority.[28] It reinstated a single electoral district, reduced the number of seats from 61 to 51, and awarded a special bonus of three seats to the electoral list with the most votes. The Assembly is now elected in a two-round proportional voting (unless a list obtains an absolute majority in the first round). The threshold for entering the second round was raised from three to five per cent in June 1984.

Political parties in Corsica may be divided into local branches of French parties and specific Corsican parties which are more or less nationalist (separatist or autonomist) in orientation. The Corsican Assembly has traditionally been dominated by the right (both the President of the Assembly and the President of the Executive Council belong to right wing parties, albeit different ones).[29] However, political affiliation counts less than the leading personalities due to the predominance of clans within traditional parties in Corsica.

The current Corsican Assembly was elected in 1999 (Table 3; see also Table 2) and is dominated by the right-wing coalition RPR-DL (17 out of 51 seats); the second political force is the 'plural left' coalition gauche plurielle (which is in power in Paris) (11 seats). Although divided, nationalists have become an important political force in Corsica (see Table 3.1). Separatist nationalists constitute the third largest group. Corsica Nazione, the only nationalist movement to make it to the second round in the 1999 elections, received eight seats with nearly 17 per cent of the votes (the best result obtained by nationalists since 1992). The growth of the separatist vote has occurred at the expense of autonomists who have paid the price for the failure of successive statutes. This outcome can also be explained by the great number of nationalist lists in regional elections,[30] as well as by protest votes following the strong-handed government policy of 're-establishing the rule of law'.

3.3.5   Economic Development and Financial Issues

The 1991 Statute also sought to promote economic development and to give the new institutions the financial means connected with the additional transfer of powers. Resources are to a large extent provided by the state on the basis of a contract negotiated with the region ("*Contrat de Plan État-Collectivité territoriale*") which is one means of implementing the development plan adopted by the Corsican Assembly.

Additional means were also put into place, including a development fund financed by taxes on passenger transport to and from Corsica and a special fiscal regime to compensate for the high cost of transportation of goods to the island, termed '*dotation de continuité territoriale*' (Act of 15 November 1994). In addition to reduced value added tax on certain items, a special free trade zone (*zone franche*) was created in December 1996. Finally, Corsica receives the product of taxes levied on local sales of tobacco and alcohol. France had to request derogations from the EU for the special fiscal regime as well as for the special measures concerning the Corsican agricultural sector.

3.4   A Right to be Consulted

The 1991 Statute incorporated a provision from the 1982 Statute (Article 27c) giving it the capacity to communicate directly with the French government regarding existing or draft laws and decrees concerning Corsica. The Corsican Assembly could thus suggest the modification or adaptation of existing or draft texts on Corsican institutions and their competencies as well as those affecting the economic, social and cultural development of the island. It could make such proposals of its own initiative or be consulted by the Prime Minister. The procedure was slightly modified in the 1991 Statute (Art. 26d) so that it could also be initiated by the Executive Council. This mechanism did not function well due to the fact that the government was *not* obliged to act upon these proposals and was eventually abandoned.[31]

This mechanism was reinforced by a new provision which made consultation of the Corsican Assembly mandatory in the case of *draft* laws and decrees containing measures affecting Corsica (Art. 26a). The Assembly must issue an opinion within one month (or 15 days, in case of an emergency); again, its opinion is non-binding. It was thus intended that Corsica be involved in debates concerning its own affairs and future, although the final decision rests with the French government.

3.5   State-Region Relations: Corsica Today within
the French System of Multi-Layered Governance

As a result of significant changes over the past twenty years, relations between the centre and the periphery have been redefined with the emergence of a new system of local government while respecting the principle of the unitary French state.[32] We can speak today of multi-layered governance in France, accomplished by decentralizing in a uniform fashion, with some local variation.[33]

There are three levels of local government: regions (26, including Corsica and four overseas regions/DOM), departments (100, including the four overseas departments) and communes (36,763). French governance is based on the principle of co-administration of the territory which has resulted in a high level of institutional pluralism. Regional administration consists of the superimposed decentralized regional institutions and a 'deconcentrated' state administration.[34] Decentralization (1982–86) was carried out in accordance with Article 72 of the Constitution which refers to the necessity of a specific decentralized administration, and the constitutionally recognized right of free administration of regions (Article 34). Normative powers are the exclusive competence of the central government (Article 34 also states that "statutes shall be passed by Parliament"), while regional institutions have residual regulatory powers.

In addition to the specific regional institutions described above, Corsica, like any other region of France, is divided into departments with similar accompanying departmental institutions and state administration. The law of 15 May 1975 divided Corsica into two *départements*: *Haute-Corse* (North Corsica) and *Corse-du-Sud* (South Corsica)—each with its own directly elected general council (*Conseil général)* and a president who also acts as the executive of the department. The state is represented by the Prefect—a political and administrative instrument for ensuring respect of public order and facilitating dialogue between the centre and the periphery. He is nominated by the French President following a proposal by the Prime Minister and the Interior Minister. There is one prefect for the Corsican region (who is simultaneously the prefect of South Corsica where the regional capital Ajaccio is located) as well as one prefect for North Corsica. Corsica, like other regions, is under the administrative supervision of the state (via the prefect who verifies the legality of the acts of the region) as well as judiciary control (via the administrative judge). The regional accounts chamber controls local public finances.

Corsica participates in political life at the national level through four directly elected deputies at the National Assembly (two for each department); it also has two indirectly elected representatives in the Senate (one for each department).[35] Other mainland regions and overseas departments and territories have a similar representation which is related to the number of departments and the size of each department in terms of inhabitants.[36]

Although Corsica has no international status, there is an increasingly important European dimension which confers Corsica some degree of influence. Until the latest European elections in 2000, Corsica had one representative at the European Parliament in Strasbourg, the President of the Executive Council of Corsica Jean Baggioni (RPR), but not in his capacity as a representative of Corsica. Corsica is, however, entitled to one of France's 24 seats in the EU Committee of the Regions. Corsica is also a member of an interest group uniting the islands of the Western Mediterranean (IMEDOC).

3.6 An Assessment of Administrative Autonomy in Corsica

An assessment of administrative autonomy in Corsica today, resulting from two waves of reform in 1982 and 1991, reveals persistent problems in those areas which reform sought to address. Political and other forms of violence were on the increase,[37] although on a lower scale than in other conflict regions of Western Europe. Little improvement was seen in the political and economic situation. Although the survival of the Corsican language relies heavily on the commitment of parents to transmit it to their children, the situation is not yet critical, as Corsica is one of the regions of France with the strongest linguistic and cultural identity. Further, excessive urbanization has been prevented thanks to a French law protecting coastlines (*loi littoral*). Seventy per cent of Corsica's coastlines are still in the natural state and massive urbanization may have been curbed by terrorist violence.

Although this is a difficult exercise, one can attempt to distinguish between problems related to the institutional arrangement and those due to external factors affecting its functioning.

3.6.1   Problems with the Arrangement Itself

- *Unstable institutions with weak powers.* There were no less than four elections to the Corsican Assembly between 1982 and 1991. Although the changes introduced in 1991 improved the functioning of the Assembly by reducing the number of seats and adjusting the electoral system, it still lacked sufficient responsibility and was unable to exert much influence on the adaptation of national norms and decrees to its specific situation.
- *Unclear division of competencies.* Another problem was related to the division of competencies between the decentralized authorities of the region and the state administration of the departments. There has been much overlap and inefficiency. Corsica is also an over-administered region with the highest number of elected state officials per capita in France.
- *Lack of entrenchment of Corsica's autonomy.*[38] No special mention is made of the autonomy of Corsica in the Constitution, which is entirely defined by a separate, ordinary law. The administrative autonomy established in 1991 was a simple delegation of state authority which could be modified without the approval of Corsican institutions, by a simple majority in Parliament. The provision on mandatory consultation of the Corsican Assembly on laws and decrees affecting Corsica (1991 Statute, Article 26a) was only a first step towards regional entrenchment since the Assembly's opinion is non-binding.

3.6.2   Political, Economic and Social Factors

- *Increase of political and other forms of violence.* Increased violence was both a cause and an effect of problems with the autonomy regime. Violence is deeply entrenched in Corsican society and has become a means of conflict settlement. Much of this violence is due to nationalist infighting, with a particularly violent period from 1993–96.
- *A fragile and fragmented political environment.* Fragmentation is also due to infighting between mainstream parties as well as between various nationalist tendencies. Political fragmentation has been enhanced with each new statute which divides those in favour of experimenting with institutional reform and those against.
- *Electoral fraud.* The 1991 Special Statute sought to reestablish the foundations of democracy by reforming the electoral registers in an attempt to eradicate electoral fraud (the number of registered voters thus dropped from 200,000 to 158,000). Still, problems persisted: the Assembly elected in 1998 was dissolved and reelected in 1999 due to complaints of electoral fraud.[39]

- *Persistent Problems of Corruption.* Decentralization brought increased control over local resources, fuelling clientist networks and possibilities for corruption. This phenomenon discredits not only the regional government but also the state for insufficient enforcement of the rule of law in Corsica.[40]

4.   THE 'MATIGNON PROPOSALS' OF 20 JULY 2000: EXPANSION OF CORSICA'S AUTONOMY?

The 'Matignon Proposals' of 20 July 2000 represent the third attempt to resolve the Corsican conflict through institutional reform. They merit further study not only from the perspective of the contents of the agreement but also from that of the political process leading up to it.

4.1 The Matignon Process (13 December 1999–20 July 2000)

4.1.1   The Context

Over recent years, an increasingly strong movement in favour of recognizing regional diversity has been emerging in France. Disagreements between the regionalist and the Jacobin/'National-Republican' visions intensified in 1999–2000 over the European Charter for Regional or Minority Languages and especially over Corsica.

The assassination of the Prefect of Corsica, Claude Erignac, on 6 February 1998, was a turning point in the conflict, for, until then, violence had not claimed the life of a representative of the state. The fiasco of the government's strong-handed policy of 're-establishing the rule of law', implemented by the Prefect's successor Bernard Bonnet, further discredited the actions of the state in Corsica. It also led to the realization by the French Government that reducing the Corsican Question to a problem of restoring order was insufficient and that serious discussions about Corsica's statute were again warranted.

Calls for a solution to the crisis had also been increasing within Corsican institutions as well as among the population, especially since the nomination of a Socialist Prime Minister on 2 June 1997 (the premature dissolution of Parliament by President Jacques Chirac (RPR) and the holding of new elections had ushered in a renewed period of 'cohabitation' between a right-wing president and a left-wing government). Indeed, hopes were high in Corsica that the new socialist government would reconsider Corsica's status. The two main proposals which emerged from a working group of the Corsican Assembly established in April 1999 were a revision of the 1991 Statute in order to devolve legislative power to the Corsican Assembly and simplification of the institutional setup by abolishing the two departments. A few days prior to a visit to Corsica by Prime Minister Lionel Jospin in September 1999, the President of the Corsican Assembly, José Rossi, of the centre-right party *Démocratie libérale* publicly called for (political) autonomy.

At the same time, significant developments were occurring in the nationalist movement. On the one hand, new fringe groups, such as the one which claimed responsibility for the Prefect's murder, were calling for a return to the 'pure' nationalism of the 1970s. On the other hand, a process of unification was officially initiated in May 1999 by the main separatist groups with the

213

aim of putting an end to violence between them. On 4 November 1999, an umbrella organization, *Unità*, was formed by nine nationalist organizations, including *A Cuncolta naziunalista*. This sent a message to the government that the nationalist camp (or at least a major part of it) [41] was ready for dialogue.

The prospect of the 2002 presidential and parliamentary elections also motivated potential presidential candidates such as Chirac, Jospin and perhaps also (now former) Interior Minister Chevènement to preempt Corsica as a campaign issue.

There was also heightened concern in Corsica regarding the island's economic future due to a 1999 decision by the EU that it would no longer be eligible for 'Objective 1' structural funds reserved for peripheral and underdeveloped regions since Corsica's GDP had marginally surpassed 75 per cent of the EU average.

Although the Prime Minister had clearly stated in an address to the Corsican Assembly on 6 September 1999 that for a dialogue to begin there must be an open condemnation by all of terrorist violence, what triggered the process of dialogue, paradoxically, were two bomb explosions in broad daylight in Ajaccio on 25 November 1999. Thus, only five days later, the Prime Minister announced that he was willing to meet with elected Corsican representatives.

4.1.2   The Negotiations

The Matignon Process (named for the Prime Minister's office in Paris) was launched by the Prime Minister on 13 December. As he himself later explained, it was motivated by the political will to find a political solution to the Corsican Question. [42] It consisted of two major meetings in Paris between the Prime Minister and elected representatives from Corsica on 13 December 1999 and 6 April 2000, [43] followed by technical working meetings held every Monday in Paris starting on 15 May. These working meetings were attended by 22 deputies from the Corsican Assembly while the French Government was represented by three persons: Jospin's advisor for Corsica, Alain Christnacht, who had been involved in developing a new statute for New Caledonia, the new Prefect of Corsica, Lacroix, and the head of Interior Minister Chevènement's office.

The choice of regional deputies as negotiation partners had one major implication: the government would also be dealing with the separatist *Corsica Nazione* (the only nationalist group represented in the Corsican Assembly). [44] *Corsica Nazione* presented five short-term demands: strict application of the *loi littoral*, protection of the wild areas in Corsica, total cessation of the 'inquisition-style' practices of the French administration and justice system, an end to the 'de-Corsicanization' of jobs [45] and the regrouping of 'political prisoners' in Corsica until the declaration of an amnesty.

The Corsican Assembly was split between an 'Autonomist' faction in favour of a transfer of legislative power and a 'Republican' one which agreed that more decentralization was needed but did not support legislative powers which would necessitate a revision of the Constitution. Both factions, however, requested mandatory teaching of the Corsican language. Having reviewed the two proposals submitted on 10 March by the Corsican Assembly (the autonomist one obtained a relative majority with 22 votes, while the republican one obtained an absolute majority of 26 votes), [46] the Prime Minister stressed on 6 April 2000 that the Corsican Assembly had to reach a compromise.

The discussions focussed on six main issues raised by the Corsican side: questions related to Europe; fiscal matters; economic development; language and culture; institutional reform (simplification of Corsica's administrative organization) and the devolution of legislative power. The latter two proved to be the most difficult.

On 10 July, having already submitted a synthesis of the discussions to the Corsican deputies and before they had time to react, the government made a first set of proposals in order to establish limits. On 12 July, Rossi managed to enlist the support of a majority of the deputies for a set of counter-proposals. In a closed vote at the Assembly that evening, 42 of 51 deputies expressed the wish to see the Matignon Process result in a revision of the Constitution. Thus, as a result of Rossi's efforts to reconcile the two factions of the Assembly while ensuring the continued support of the nationalist deputies as well as a collective learning process extending over two months of meetings, a consensus had emerged between the Corsican deputies.

The seventh months of talks resulted in a set of proposals (in fact counter-counter-proposals) on 20 July 2000 by the French government to the Corsican deputies gathered in Paris. These proposals were approved by an overwhelming majority of the Corsican Assembly on 28 July (44 in favour with 2 votes against and 5 abstentions).

4.1.3   Facilitating Factors

Several factors facilitated the process. First, both the government and the Corsican deputies were willing to compromise. The Jospin Method marked a new approach of the government to the Corsican Question based on transparent dialogue with elected representatives of the Corsican population, thereby sending the message to the clandestine organizations that it would no longer engage in secret negotiations which had failed in the past. Furthermore, Jospin stressed the importance of reaching a consensus on any decision. Another feature of his method was to listen and draw up a list of all ideas set forth and then react. His political opponents, however, accused him of making promises which he could not keep beyond the end of his term in 2002. The good will demonstrated by the Prime Minister was backed by that of his ministers who endorsed the proposals due to be presented to the Corsican side on 20 July. There was one exception, Interior Minister Jean-Pierre Chevènement (MDC), who opposed the reforms from the start and finally resigned in August 2000 was replaced by a Jospin associate, Daniel Vaillant (PS).

The Corsican side too developed a willingness to compromise. This included the nationalists who did not place recognition of the Corsican people on their list of demands (which would have resulted in a legal dead-end) and also agreed to put off for some time the question of the political prisoners. Finally, Jospin waived the precondition of a condemnation of violence. He later sought to justify his decision by his determination to initiate a dialogue, underlining that the government would continue to fight violence in Corsica.

4.1.4   The Strategic Use of Political Violence

Violence, which triggered the initiation of dialogue, played a key role throughout the negotiations, leading to criticisms that the government had been blackmailed by the nationalists (although some acts of violence were most probably committed by radical elements seeking to derail the process). The nationalists did indeed pursue a double strategy of engaging in political discussions while also using the threat of violence. *Unità* exerted continuous pressure on the nationalist deputies to obtain concrete concessions, especially on the regrouping of the political prisoners, and threatened several times to withdraw its support for the negotiations.

In December 1999, one day before the first meeting in Paris, several bomb attacks took place in Corsica. The *FLNC-Canal historique* showed its support for political dialogue by declaring a ceasefire on 24 December and announced that it had fused with three other clandestine organizations[47]— an unprecedented event in the history of Corsican nationalism. Responsibility for four bombs in June, one of which was found in Paris, was claimed by the 'new FLNC' (which, paradoxically, claimed that the ceasefire still held). Seen by some analysts as a warning sign to the government, it was interpreted by others as an attempt to placate the more impatient nationalists within *Unità*.

4.2 The Proposals of 20 July 2000

4.2.1 A Compromise Document

The document of 20 July 2000, "Propositions du gouvernement soumises aux représentants des élus de la Corse" ("Proposals of the government submitted to the elected representatives of Corsica")[48] was a politically-binding compromise incorporating most of the proposals worked out by Corsican side within the confines set by the government. It was very ambiguous, especially concerning an essential demand of the nationalists: the devolution of legislative power. This led to diverging interpretations concerning the proposal for new powers to be transferred to the Corsican Assembly which seemed to satisfy both supporters and opponents of legislative powers. Assembly President Rossi hailed the government's proposal for the power to adopt national laws, calling it an innovation between regulatory and legislative powers, while the nationalists seemed satisfied that their demand for legislative powers had been fulfiled. Even legal experts were divided as to whether this consisted of a devolution of legislative power.[49]

4.2.2 A Two-Phased Approach to the Reforms

The general aims of the reforms are to better take into account the specificity of Corsica within the French Republic based on its insularity and history and draw upon the lessons from the implementation of the statute. The reforms also seek to clarify responsibilities concerning the management of the island's affairs, promote economic and social development, and establish a durable 'civil peace'. There is no mention of the *peuple corse*.

The rest of the document is divided into five sections: (1) administrative organization of Corsica and competencies of regional institutions; (2) fiscal and economic matters; (3) teaching of the Corsican language; (4) public investment in Corsica and (5) a timeframe for implementation.

An interesting feature of the proposed reforms is the two-phased approach to the devolution process:

- *A transitory experimental phase (2002–2004) (Phase 1)* during which a maximum number of measures not requiring revision of the Constitution would be introduced.
- *A second 'constitutional' phase (after 2004) (Phase 2)* once the Constitution has been amended to allow for implementation of the remaining measures. A major precondition

for embarking in this second phase is the 'durable reestablishment of civil peace'. Also, the phase can only be initiated if the parties in power after the 2002 national elections agree, since a constitutional revision may only be undertaken with the approval of the President.

4.2.3   A New Regional Organization with New Institutions after 2004

The proposal to replace the current overlapping structure of one region plus two *départements* by a single region was one of the most significant measures for Corsica as it would become the only region of Metropolitan France without any departments. It would also entail a significant reduction of state administration associated with the competencies of the departments. It was a significant victory for the Corsican side that the government had accepted their preference for abolishing the two departments, even though the government had indicated its strong preference for a Corsican region with a single department formed by the fusion of the current two, with a single assembly alternating as a regional and a departmental council. The advantage of this second solution in the government's eyes was that no revision of the Constitution would have been necessary.

Administrative simplification will be carried out in Phase 2 since it necessitates a revision of the Constitution. The future institutional structure of Corsica will have to be clarified in a separate law.

4.2.4   New Powers and Additional Areas of Competence

Perhaps the most interesting and certainly most complex element of the reforms was the proposal for new powers to adapt national laws and decrees. Designed as an improvement of the mechanism contained in Article 26 of the 1991 Statute (on the capacity to suggest modifications to existing or draft laws and decrees), the Corsican Assembly would be granted two types of powers (a distinction is made between the procedure for regulatory and normative texts):

i) *Extended regulatory powers* of the Corsican Assembly or the power to adapt national decrees to the specific situation of the island through its deliberations, rather than having to submit proposals for modifications to the Prime Minister without any guarantee that they would be accepted.[50] This further delegation of regulatory powers should not necessitate a revision of the Constitution, provided it does not infringe upon the regulatory competence of the Prime Minister.

ii) *The power to adapt national laws (faculté d'adaptation de mesures législatives)* through its deliberations, in its areas of competence.
   • In Phase 1, a complex and experimental mechanism was proposed based on Decision no. 93–322 of 28 July 1993 of the Constitutional Council regarding the autonomy of educational institutions whereby it had found that such institutions could derogate from national norms due to their particular situation.[51] The request for such a power would have to be justified by difficulties in applying certain national norms to the particular situation of Corsica. This delegation of power to adapt national laws (in fact, a power to derogate from national norms) would be temporary and revocable and under the strict control of Parliament: any decision to modify the

application of a national law would have to first be authorized by Parliament and would be effective for a certain period of time only. Parliament would then decide whether or not to ratify the adaptation to make it permanent. This was a genuine *coup de théâtre* by Jospin who claimed to have found a way to grant additional powers without revising the Constitution.[52]

- In Phase 2, the new Corsican institution established after administrative simplification would have the possibility to adapt existing or draft French laws *without* the systematic evaluation/ratification by Parliament.[53] This power to introduce permanent adaptations would still be under the general supervision of Parliament which could at any time decide to evaluate a particular decision of the Corsican Assembly and cancel it through a simple law. This power to adapt legal norms without *a posteriori* evaluation by Parliament calls for a revision of the Constitution because it falls outside the mechanism foreseen by the 1993 decision.

Already in Phase 1, new areas of competence were to be devolved to Corsica including regional planning; economic development; education; professional training; sports; tourism; environmental protection; local infrastructure and services; and transportation (these areas were to be further specified by law). A major area left out was social policy. Following protests by labour unions in Corsica, meetings were organized in September 2000 with advisors of the Prime Minister and with the Prefect.

4.2.5   Measures Concerning the Corsican Language and Culture

Regarding the mandatory teaching of Corsican, the government again demonstrated political acuity by making a proposal designed to satisfy the Corsican Assembly (and the nationalists) while avoiding a clash with the Constitutional Council.[54] The expression used was "generalization of the teaching of Corsican" in kindergartens and primary schools during normal hours unless parents are opposed (so that the coverage of students, currently about 80 per cent at the primary level, would be extended to 100 per cent). The Corsican Assembly would accordingly be tasked with developing a revised plan for the teaching of the Corsican language and culture. Additional measures would be introduced to ensure a sufficient supply of primary school teachers without, however, making knowledge of Corsican a requirement for employment.[55] No measures were proposed concerning the teaching of Corsican at the secondary level nor was the question of an official status for the language raised.[56]

4.2.6   Economic and Fiscal Matters and Resources

A whole series of economic and fiscal measures were also worked out. Economic development was in fact a priority area, with a 15-year public investment plan for Corsica to be financed jointly by the state (70 per cent) and Corsica, in order to catch up with other French regions; sectors to receive special support include road and rail infrastructure. A special investment fund will also be established by the Corsican authorities to help local enterprises. The government also proposed a new system of tax credits over a period of ten years to encourage investment in certain sectors, namely tourism, new technologies, industry and energy. These measures, which are also designed to spur economic growth in the least developed areas inland, would replace the free trade zone starting in January 2002.

Regarding the special inheritance tax regime, the transitory period for maintenance of full exemption was extended for ten years; after that, for a further period of five years, only 50 per cent tax would be levied; again, this was more than what the government had originally offered on 10 July.[57]

4.2.7   The European Dimension

As to the European dimension, the head of the European Affairs Commission of the Corsican Assembly, Jean-Guy Talamoni (*Corsica Nazione*), was put in charge of a working group to draft a list of dispensations to be presented to the European Commission as soon as possible.

4.3   Implementation of Phase 1 (2002–2004)

Due to come into force on 1 January 2002, the law on Phase 1 will not grant Corsica a new statute but will modify the existing one. It therefore does not address the new institutional make-up or extended powers which will follow once the Constitution has been revised. The drafting process[58] has been long and complicated. Some of the important provisions will now be discussed.

4.3.1   Clarifications Offered by the Government Bill on Phase 1

A government bill on the first phase was drafted starting in September 2000 by the new Interior Minister, Daniel Vaillant, and a working group of the Legal Affairs Commission of the National Assembly. In November, members of the Commission visited the island, the first time that an information mission had been organized *prior* to the debate of a draft law by Parliament. Vaillant also sought to involve a broader spectrum of representatives from Corsica than during the Matignon Process. Thus, on 16 November, the heads of the political groups of the Corsican Assembly were joined in Paris by the four deputies and two senators from Corsica in a preparatory meeting in view of the debates at the Corsican Assembly.

In conformity with Article 26a of the 1991 Statute, the Corsican Assembly was consulted on the first draft of the government bill.[59] After extensive discussions, it adopted the bill on 9 December (with 42 votes in favour, 4 abstentions and 5 against). The overall position of the Assembly was that the bill was in conformity with the proposals of 20 July 2000. However, further clarifications were requested, especially regarding the division of competencies in the areas in which regulatory powers would be exercised. The Corsican Assembly requested certain additional spheres of competence[60] while rejecting others deemed too costly. A total of 56 'opinions' (in fact, suggested amendments, despite a cautionary note to the Corsican Assembly by the Interior Minister not to engage in the type of debate reserved for Parliament) were forwarded to the government. Further-more, a popular consultation in Corsica before entering Phase 2 was requested (by the deputies opposed to autonomy).

- *Aims*
Perhaps the most interesting section of the government bill presented to the Corsican Assembly in December[61] is in fact the preamble ("*Exposé des motifs*") in which the aims of the proposed measures were outlined and reference was made to the second phase; this preamble disappeared in the draft law of the National Assembly.

- *On the new powers envisaged*
Article 1 of the bill sheds some light on the nature of the experimental powers in Phase 1. First comes a provision identical to that of Article 26d of the 1991 Statute according to which the Corsican Assembly, upon its own initiative or upon the request of the Executive Council or the Prime Minister, may present a proposal to modify or adapt legislative or regulatory texts already in force or which are being discussed (Article 1[1]). Concerning the power to adapt decrees, the bill specifies that they apply only to the areas of competence of the Corsican Assembly and that no prior permission from Parliament would be needed (Article 1[2]).[62] Concerning the power to adapt national laws, a complex mechanism is proposed whereby the Corsican Assembly may request from the government that it be authorized to adapt a law through its deliberations (Article 1[3]).[63] The government will decide whether the request is justified.

    Requests to adapt a national law are transmitted to the Prime Minister via the president of the Executive Council (same as in the 1991 Statute) and to the Prefect (this is new) (Article 1[5]). Every year, the government must present to Parliament a status report on the adaptations made by the Corsican Assembly. In case of a dispute, the adaptation will be suspended and submitted to the administrative judge who must rule within two months; otherwise, it becomes effective again (Article 2).

    Finally, the mechanism making it mandatory to consult the Corsican Assembly on proposed laws and decrees affecting Corsica is significantly improved by adding an *obligation on behalf of the government to give an answer*. Indeed, although the opinion of the Corsican Assembly is still non-binding, the Prefect must inform it on the response of the government (Article 1[5]). The Assembly's opinions are transmitted to the government through the same channels de-scribed above.

- *On the teaching of the Corsican language*
The commitment to extend the teaching of Corsican to all children in kindergartens and primary schools was translated literally from the document of 20 July (Article 7).[64]

- *Additional areas of competence include:*
    - *Education and language* (Arts. 4–7): including full responsibility for training, higher education and research.
    - *Culture:* full responsibility for developing the cultural policy of Corsica, while the state preserves the competence to implement national cultural policy (Arts. 8–10). The ownership of historic monuments and archaeological sites is transferred to Corsica.
    - *Transportation:* the ownership of all ports and airports is transferred to Corsica which was previously responsible for their management only.
    - *Tourism and the environment:* Corsica will decide on the designation of protected sites and the classification of tourism facilities; it will also be responsible for construction and urbanization policy (Art. 12[10]) (meaning that it can authorize the construction of

temporary service facilities for tourists such as the infamous *paillotes* or beachside restaurants like the one involved in the scandal with Prefect Bonnet in April 2000). This new area of competence is subject to the strict control of public authorities and is also limited by national regulations (*loi littoral*).

4.3.2   The Opinion of the Council of State

A slightly modified government bill taking into account some of the proposals by the Corsican Assembly was submitted to the Council of State for its opinion which it rendered on 8 February. Four problem areas were identified which could lead to a censure by the Constitutional Council:[65]

1) *On the power to modify national decrees:* The Council of State highlighted the lack of specification of the areas in which these powers could be exerted.

2) *On the power to adapt national legislation:* The power to adapt national laws based on the 1993 decision of the Constitutional Council concerning the autonomy of universities was deemed by some members of the Council of State to be inapplicable to a region of France. They also found that the spheres in which these powers would be granted had not been defined clearly enough. One particular point of concern was the new competence of the Corsican Assembly to authorize construction on protected coastal areas (Art. 12[10]).

3) *On the generalized teaching of the Corsican language:* The phrasing was found to be problematic due to concerns that parents might be afraid of requesting that their child be exempted from Corsican classes (a similar phrasing in the 1996 statute of French Polynesia encountered no problems because such concerns apparently did not exist). The Council of State therefore judged that Article 7 would make Corsican classes *de facto* mandatory and was therefore anticonstitutional.

4) *On the special fiscal regime:* The prolongation of the grace period for the abrogation of the 'Miot Decrees' and the establishment of a normal common law regime in Corsica was found to be too long and constituted a violation of the principle of equality of all citizens.

The Prime Minister decided to leave it to Parliament to make the necessary changes to make the bill compatible with the Constitution, stressing that this bill was the result of a political agreement which he did not have the authority to modify. The unaltered bill was adopted by the Council of Ministers on 21 February 2001 and submitted to the National Assembly[66] as well as to the Corsican Assembly and the Executive Council.

4.3.3   The Draft Law Adopted by the National Assembly (22 May 2001)

The government bill was debated by the National Assembly starting on 15 May, together with over a hundred amendments. On 22 May, a draft law on Corsica was adopted with 287 votes in favour (including 23 favourable votes from opposition deputies) and 217 against.[67] In this draft law, the changes made in order to take into account the opinion of the Council of State included the following:

1) *Changes to the provision on regulatory powers in Article 1:* This provision was modified to state that the Corsican Assembly would first have to ask Parliament to authorize it to modify a national decree. It was also specified that the exercise of these regulatory powers would respect Article 21 of the Constitution (on the regulatory competence of the Prime Minister) and that it was possible only in the areas of competence transferred to Corsica.

2) *Changes to the provision on the power to adapt laws in Article 1:* this provision was considerably modified to avoid any ambiguity concerning whether the Corsican Assembly would be authorized to pass laws of its own, even for a limited period. There is no more reference to "adapting laws" but rather to "experimenting" and "derogating" from national regulations. It is also stated that Parliament will subsequently adopt the appropriate legislative measures[68] and that the conditions and duration of this experimentation will be fixed by law (i.e. Parliament will also decide how long the derogations will be effective).

3) *Changes to Article 7 on the teaching of Corsican:* This article was watered down by removing the mention "unless parents are opposed" so that it simply stated that Corsican would be taught in kindergartens and primary schools during normal school hours.[69]

4) *Other changes:* Another significant cluster of amendments concerned the social and fiscal measures. The special regime for inheritance dues (the Miot Decrees) contained in Article 45 would end in 2012 rather than 2015 as proposed by the government but the free trade zone would end in three, rather than two years.

While the Interior Minister was satisfied with the clarifications made to Article 1, he stated his preference for the government's original phrasing of Article 7. He also defended the provision allowing for derogations to the *loi littoral*, expressing his confidence in the capacity of the Corsican Assembly to make the right decisions.

4.3.4   Modifications by the Senate

The draft law adopted by the National Assembly was then forwarded to the Senate (where the opposition centre-right and right hold about 200 of the 321 seats). Following debates on 6–8 November, the Senate made drastic modifications putting into question whether its implementation would result in any changes at all.[70] These modifications concerned primarily Article 1 where the provisions on the experimental powers were simply deleted, for despite the clarifications made by the National Assembly, they were still deemed to be against the Constitution. Article 7 was modified to read that Corsican language classes would not be taught but "offered", in order to stress their optional nature. Safeguards were also added to Article 12 to allay fears that the Corsican coastline would be exploited.

On a positive note for the Corsican side, the Senate reverted to the government's original proposals of 20 July 2000 concerning the Miot decrees; it also extended the tax credits to additional sectors suggested by the Corsican deputies.

4.3.5   Further Steps in the Drafting Process

A mixed commission consisting of seven members each from the National Assembly and the Senate meeting on 15 November 2001 failed to reach a compromise between the two versions.

At the time of writing (end of November 2001), the Senate bill was being examined by the National Assembly. While it seems unlikely that the law will be adopted by the end of the year, the government still hopes that the process will be completed before the elections.

4.4 Type of Arrangement

The type of arrangement envisaged by the French government for Corsica hinges on the nature of the powers which will be granted. It is therefore necessary to clarify whether the power to adapt national laws in Phase 2 will amount to legislative or broad regulatory powers. Despite speculations to the contrary, based on the document of 20 July 2000, the latter is envisaged. It is true that it is stated that the deliberations of the Assembly will be executory and that no subsequent ratification by Parliament will be necessary.[71] It is also specified that the deliberations of the Corsican Assembly will take effect immediately as *administrative*, not legal acts, and that they will be subject to the authority of the administrative judge rather than the Constitutional Council, which further de-legalizes them. The government has also insisted that, even though the so-called 'adaptations' will affect the legal domain, they will be regulatory. This interpretation is confirmed, at least for Phase 1, by the government bill and the draft law adopted by the National Assembly.

Even in Phase 2 when the delegation of the power to adapt laws will become permanent, there is still the possibility of *a posteriori* censure by Parliament through an ordinary law. The future powers of the new Corsican institution will be simply delegated and therefore remain weaker than those transferred permanently to the Overseas Territories through an organic law.

To summarize, if the proposed reforms are fully implemented, Corsica will enjoy at most a significantly expanded administrative/regulatory self-government, albeit in a broad range of fields, accompanied by a unique power in the context of Metropolitan France to adapt national norms and decrees to its specific situation. Corsica's autonomy will be under the control of Parliament and of the administrative court system. After 2004, following the abolishment of the two departments, a new institutional structure will be introduced based on a single regional assembly. There will be a reduction in state administration due to the transfer of the competencies of the departments to the region as well as of the number of areas of shared competence with the centre. There will probably also be a single, regional prefect rather than two. A reduction of the number of representatives from Corsica in national institutions following the abolishment of the two departments is doubtful.

5.   ASSESSMENT OF THE MATIGNON PROCESS AND PROSPECTS FOR A DURABLE RESOLUTION OF THE CORSICAN CONFLICT

The following section seeks to assess the prospects for successful conflict resolution in Corsica through the expansion of the autonomy arrangement. Success will be related to whether it is believed that the conflict can be contained as well as whether some of the root causes, such as concerns about the minority identity or economic under-development, are being addressed. We will also point out some of the shortcomings and potential obstacles to implementation which can be identified already at this point.

5.1 Autonomy Success Factors?

What are the factors on which an effective and successful implementation of autonomy depends? Based on a large set of case studies from various parts of the world, Lapidoth derives sixteen "ingredients" which might enhance the chances of success (Table 3.4). While this table seeks only to provide a guideline, one can see that very few of these factors were present in Corsica for the administrative autonomy established by the 1991 Statute (Column B). Although implementation of the new arrangement will represent an improvement, many of the autonomy success factors are still lacking (Column C).

5.2 Issues of Concern Related to the Arrangement

5.2.1   The New Powers and Division of Competencies

In defence of the proposed reforms, one can say that they demonstrate a genuine effort to clarify the division of competencies between the state and the region and to grant Corsica a greater degree of control over its own affairs. Concerns regarding the division of competencies between regional and departmental institutions should be allayed to a degree when the latter are abolished. As with the law on Phase 1, the new powers granted by the new statute must be carefully defined and be effective; otherwise they will be abandoned, as in the past.

Not much can be said at this point on the stability of the new institutions to be established as no details are provided.

5.2.2   Possibility of Evolution

Another positive feature is the two-phased approach to implementation, with an assessment foreseen at the end of the experimental phase. This gradual approach, credited to the president of the Corsican Assembly, was instrumental in enlisting the support of the nationalists who eagerly await Phase 2. It was also requested by the Corsican deputies who preferred to wait until their mandate expires after 2004 before new institutions are created. The Prime Minister also noted that the political environment was not yet favourable to a revision of the Constitution.

The experience of other autonomous regions has shown the benefit of the gradual establishment of autonomy and of evaluation over time in order to fine-tune the arrangement. It would also be desirable to propose a calendar in the new statute for further steps in order to allow for improvement, with the close involvement of representatives of the autonomous entity.

5.2.3   Mode of Establishment and Entrenchment of Autonomy

The mode of establishment of the new arrangement represents an improvement compared to the debates preceding the 1991 Statute (and even more compared to the previous one) in that elected local representatives were closely involved in the debates.

Due to the opposition of a significant segment of the French political class to autonomy, the issue of the entrenchment of Corsica's new statute is crucial. The first and most likely option would be to incorporate the main elements of the reforms into the Constitution. Such semi-general entrenchment would make them compatible with the Constitution and, for the first time offer a degree of protection to Corsica's autonomy. However, some experts argue that this is not a desirable solution for it has been used too often, thereby undermining the Constitution's coherence.[72]

Another option would be to grant all overseas territories as well as Corsica and maybe even other French regions rights going beyond self-administration. As this would entail substantial revisions to the first three articles of the Constitution as well as to those defining the competencies of the main institutions of the state (Arts. 20, 34, 72ff), a new constitution would be needed.[73]

A third option would be to stipulate through an organic law that Corsica constitutes an overseas territory; the argument that the reforms violate the principles of indivisibility and equality would no longer hold.[74] Until then, Corsica will be considered a region of Metropolitan France by default. However, this would be a highly unlikely solution, for, whereas there is a consensus that special measures are justified for the overseas territories due to their great distance from the mainland and colonial history, the situation of Corsica is not deemed special enough to justify major derogations (even though the EU has recognized that insularity as such justifies special measures). It would also be controversial because, if Corsica were designated as an overseas territory, then the Corsican people would be entitled to (internal) self-determination and the door to independence would be slowly opened.

5.2.4   Dispute Settlement

The lack of adequate dispute settlement mechanisms beyond the administrative court system is a potential problem area, as disputes are likely to arise concerning adaptations made by the new Corsican institution in Phase 2. Problems similar to those arising in French Polynesia under the 1996 statute (disputes were frequently referred to the administrative court in Papeete which was ill equipped to settle them, resulting in the great frustration of the local government) should be expected.

While other mechanisms already foreseen under the 1991 arrangement, such as the Prefect or even the Council of State acting as the supreme administrative judge, could be involved, no joint organ for mediation has been suggested. (The mechanism providing for the consultation of the Corsican Assembly regarding draft laws and decrees could also function as a conflict prevention mechanism, provided that its recommendations are taken into account.)

5.2.5   Protection of the Rights of Included Minorities

The extended powers and areas of competence as well as measures concerning the Corsican language and culture should not represent a threat to individual rights and freedoms. Still, the human rights of individual members of Corsican society are protected by the anti-discrimination principle in the Constitution (Art. 1). The jurisdiction of the Constitutional Council is also clear on this point: fundamental freedoms may not be dependent on the authority of local territorial units.[75] Article 1 of the government bill also clearly states that the powers of the Corsican Assembly may not be exerted when a "public freedom" ("individual freedoms or fundamental rights", in the draft law of 22 May 2001) is affected.

As the Corsican Assembly has no competence regarding employment policy, fears that it might introduce preferential measures for the employment of local residents are unfounded. In any case, particular attention will be paid to the rights of the approximately 400 state employees of the 'offices' who might be transferred to the regional authorities (although the Corsican Assembly indicated in December 2000 that it did not wish this to be done for the time being). One could eventually foresee that the Corsican Assembly would introduce a (temporary) regulation making the Corsican language official, along with French.[76] Any violations by the local authorities may always be referred to a local administrative court.

5.3 Issues Related to Implementation

5.3.1 Constitutional and Other Legal Hurdles

The constitutional and other legal obstacles to the implementation of the government's proposals have been very significant in the case of the law on Phase 1 which was supposed to contain the least controversial measures. Despite the modifications made by the National Assembly and the Senate, there is still a possibility that the Constitutional Council will be called upon. However, it is the new statute that is likely to face the greatest legal obstacles.

5.3.2 A Fragile Political Environment

The Corsican political class is highly fragmented and has shifted positions during the Matignon Process, suggesting a high degree of political opportunism. Fragmentation is also a result of cleavages at the national level.[77] The French political class too is divided over the Corsican reforms, and the Prime Minister has come under criticism not only from the right but also from within the government coalition. A rare clash occurred between Jospin and President Chirac when the latter, in his capacity as guardian of the Constitution, refused to have the Corsica bill put on the agenda of the Council of Ministers meeting of 14 February 2001, following the criticisms of the Council of State. Jospin refused to reconsider the bill and it was discussed the following week.

The controversial nature of the Corsican Question raises serious doubts as to whether the parties in power after the 2002 national elections will have the necessary political will to initiate a revision of the Constitution, especially as they are not bound to it (no mention is made of Phase 2 in the draft law on Phase 1). A victory of the Socialist Party seems indispensable but will not guarantee a smooth process.

5.3.3 Legitimacy of the Corsican Negotiator and of the Agreement

The question of the legitimacy of the negotiators and support for the agreement among the population concerned, especially in the case of high-level political negotiations, is also paramount in ensuring successful implementation. The discussions at Matignon were elite negotiations which did not involve the more moderate nationalists, the mayors and civil society in general. Some questioned the legitimacy of the Corsican negotiators, claiming that nationalists were over-represented in the Corsican Assembly, and advocated dialogue with the two departmental councils instead. The question also arises whether the talks were not radicalized because of the particular configuration of the negotiators; we have seen, however, that the proposals of 20 July 2000 were reached through consensus with all the members of the Corsican Assembly.

Popular support in Corsica for the reforms is probably divided at best: an early poll indicated that 50 per cent were in favour of the government bill, 19 per cent were against and 24 per cent would have abstained had they been asked to vote for it in the Corsican Assembly in December 2000.[78] A popular consultation in Corsica, as requested by the Corsican Assembly, would reinforce the legitimacy of the arrangement (if it succeeds). In any case, a referendum limited to Corsica poses problems of constitutionality for it would amount to recognizing the existence of a distinct Corsican people; one could envisage a non-binding consultation but the Constitution would probably still have to be revised.[79] The nationalists support the idea of a referendum but wish to poll only Corsicans and long-term residents. Other opponents to the reforms have called on the government to hold a referendum in the whole of France or to dissolve the Corsican Assembly and hold new elections; neither option is legally possible.

The French population was strongly divided over the reforms: a poll in July 2000 found that only 46 per cent believed that the measures announced by the government on 20 July would not lead to civil peace in Corsica.[80] According to the same poll, 59 per cent were favourable towards enabling the Corsican Assembly to adapt French laws under the supervision of Parliament (Phase 1) (30 per cent were against); support was much lower for the power to adapt laws without subsequent evaluation by Parliament (Phase 2) with 61 per cent against and only 34 per cent in favour.

5.3.4   Other Factors Related to Economic, Social and Cultural Aspects

The Corsican experience has demonstrated the importance of coupling institutional solutions with the financial means to carry them out. A positive dimension of the 20 July 2000 proposals are the substantial economic development measures and fiscal incentives proposed. Combined with institutional reform, they are very promising. However, they might not be sufficient to remedy the chronic economic and social under-development of Corsica in a context of corruption and clientelism. These phenomena pose a serious threat to the functioning of autonomy and are invoked by opponents to a devolution of legislative power.

5.4   A Timid Attempt to Draw on the Statutes of Overseas Territories

Although unique in the context of Metropolitan France, institutional reforms in Corsica in 1982 and 1991 were inspired by developments in the French Overseas Departments and Territories (DOM-TOM)[81] on three main aspects:

   a) *Separate executive and deliberative bodies.* In 1991, Corsica received separate deliberative and executive bodies, similarly to the institutional set-up in New Caledonia and French Polynesia (both TOMs).

b) *A degree of influence to have a say regarding laws and decrees affecting it.* (a) While Article 26a of the 1991 Statute made consultation of the Corsican Assembly mandatory for draft laws and decrees affecting the island, the opinion which it rendered was non-binding on the government which was not even obliged to provide an answer. (b) Article 26d of the 1991 Statute (which reproduced a provision of the 1982 Statute) enabled the Corsican Assembly to make proposals concerning existing or proposed laws and decrees affecting the island's organization and institutions as well as its economic, social and cultural development. Again, these proposals were non-binding on the government which was not even obliged to react. A similar mechanism was foreseen in the 1984 statute of French Polynesia[82] as well as for the DOM general councils (to whom the right to be consulted on draft laws and decrees had been granted already by the Act of 26 April 1960). According to Michalon, this right to be consulted constituted an embryonic element of self-organization typical of the autonomy of federal entities.[83] In the case of the TOM, however, not only is consultation of the territorial assembly in case of an amendment to their statute mandatory, it is also binding (according to Article 74 of the Constitution).

c) *Minimum measures to preserve the specific identity of the region by protecting the language and culture of its inhabitants.* While institutional reform in Corsica has been innovative within the context of Metropolitan France, it has lagged behind developments in the overseas territories. Especially in New Caledonia and French Polynesia, significant developments have occurred since 1998 which might redefine their relationship with the centre.[84]

With the Matignon proposals, the statute of Corsica will surpass what is currently in force in the DOM (although here, too, developments are occurring at a rapid pace) and constitute a further step in the direction of the statutes of the overseas territories. The evolution of Corsica's statute might also have repercussions for the DOM where reforms are also underway. The DOM are particularly interested in the proposed administrative simplification of Corsica through the abolishment of *both* departments. Indeed, three of them—Martinique, Guadeloupe and Guiana—have called for the replacement of their current institutional structure (a mono-departmental region with a regional council as well as a departmental council) by a single region with a single assembly (no department).[85]

Although the opinions issued by the Corsican Assembly when consulted will remain non-binding, the reforms of 2000 introduce the *right to be informed* of the position of the government and its planned response. This is more than what the DOM have been granted since the Constitutional Council has rejected a proposal to make it mandatory for the Prime Minister to respond to DOM proposals or opinions (Decision no. 2000–435 of 7 December 2000).

Still, unlike New Caledonia and soon French Polynesia, Corsica will not have the power to pass local laws. Indeed, the Congress of New Caledonia *(Congrès du Territoire)*, through its deliberations, can adopt local laws *(lois du pays)* in a number of areas, under the control of the Constitutional Council (such as symbols of national identity; fiscal matters; labour regulations; employment of foreigners; land rights; mineral exploitation; marriages and inheritance; and property rights (see Arts. 99–107 of organic law no. 99–209 of 19 March 1999).

The proposed generalized teaching of Corsican as contained in the document of 20 July 2000 is far from being a sufficient guarantee for the preservation and promotion of the Corsican language (and identity). It is also a weak measure if one looks at other autonomies in Europe where the minority language usually enjoys an official status at least in the region concerned.

However, it was highly controversial for a country where French is the sole language recognized in the Constitution (Art. 2) and was the main instrument of nation-building and continues to play the key role in maintaining the cohesiveness of the French nation.

A concept which already exists in New Caledonia and in other insular regions to protect their specific character[86] and which has been evoked in the Corsican context is that of *regional citizenship* consisting of certain requirements in order to vote and other entitlements. This, however, is yet another sensitive issue, even if it were extended to a broader Corsican community including long-term residents. Furthermore, such measures would necessitate a special derogation from the EU.

5.5 Impact on Mainland French Regions

The Corsican reforms are likely to have an impact on other French regions. Several of them, such as Brittany, the French Basque Country and perhaps also Alsace and Savoie, are also interested in autonomy. Some opponents of autonomy for Corsica also advocate extending the same measures to all French regions to preserve the symmetry of the state. While the other French regions certainly stand to benefit from a greater degree of autonomy in the management of their affairs, to extend the same measures to the mainland regions might jeopardize the whole process of reform in Corsica, as with decentralization in 1982–86. It would also no longer be appropriate to speak of a specific autonomy arrangement in Corsica.[87] The government plans to extend some of the Corsican measures to the other regions, but this only concerns additional areas of competence at present, not the power to adapt national laws.[88]

5.6 Prospects for Durable Conflict Resolution in Corsica

5.6.1   *Have the Root Causes Been Addressed?*

Will the proposed reforms result in a reduction of violence or is it 'too late' for such comparatively mild measures at this stage of the conflict? Have the root causes of the conflict been addressed?

If one accepts the statement that the violence which predominates in Corsica today aims to draw the attention of the authorities,[89] then positive effects should be expected from the Matignon Process. Indeed, although no symbolic concessions were made to satisfy the self-determination claims of a segment of Corsicans (no official recognition of the Corsican people and its language), by treating the Corsican deputies as equal partners in the talks, the government extended recognition to local actors including nationalists. The most positive feature of this latest initiative of the government is perhaps the process of open and transparent negotiations behind it. This constituted a collective learning process reinforcing a cooperative attitude on the Corsican side. The emergence of a consensus amongst the deputies is noteworthy; the efforts of a portion of the nationalist movement to unify and engage in political dialogue should be commended as well.

Still, there are serious doubts that 25 years of violence will cease soon for several reasons. First, a legitimate argument is that violence was seen as having paid off and therefore will be used again. The fragile nature of the so-called nationalist reconciliation also means that violence between rival groups is likely to continue. Violence by radical elements outside the *Unità* initiative seeking to increase their influence with the government or to preserve the status quo from which they derive profit is another concern (although the two presumed leaders of *Armata Corsa*, the main clandestine group opposing the Matignon Process, are now dead).[90] Just as serious is the nationalists' threat to withdraw their support if minimum concessions are not made. A major problem was therefore that two basic demands of the nationalist deputies—clear legislative powers and mandatory teaching of Corsican—are not satisfied, at least not in Phase 1. Even if the proposals are fully implemented (and we have already seen the huge problems concerning Phase 1), it is highly unlikely that Corsica will have the authority to pass specific Corsican laws; even the experimental powers to adapt national laws and decrees are at risk. And it is already clear that there will be no mandatory teaching of Corsican. The nationalist deputies clearly expressed their displeasure over the deviations between the draft law adopted by the National Assembly in May 2001 and the government's original proposals. The issue of 'political prisoners' and 'decorsification' of jobs was also abruptly brought up. In September 2001, after nationalist deputy Talamoni and other nationalists were interrogated in connection with the investigations into Rossi's assassination, *Corsica Nazione*, under pressure by the new nationalist coalition party *Indipendenza* (founded on 13 May 2001 by *A Cuncolta* and three others), suspended its support for the reforms.

Since the precondition of 'durable reestablishment of civil peace' has been set for entering Phase 2, the question is how much violence the government will tolerate. The persistence of terrorist attacks and several murders of nationalists seriously risk the process.

5.6.2 The Economic Dimension

It can only be hoped that the significant economic and fiscal measures proposed by the government will contribute to an improvement of Corsica's economy and infrastructure. While there is un-doubtedly a need for intervention by the centre, responsibility for raising revenues should be in-creasingly shifted to local authorities rather than having them depend on state and other subsidies. Increased financial accountability necessitates increased political responsibility of the local elite. The state should seek to encourage such political maturation by demonstrating trust in the ability of Corsicans to manage their own affairs.

5.6.3 Overall Assessment

The prospects for a successful resolution of the Corsican conflict through the implementation of the Matignon Proposals are mixed due to factors related to the agreement itself as well as unfavourable external conditions. What can be said at this early stage is that very few success factors are present while there are many obstacles. The history of conflict regulation in Corsica does not bode well for autonomy either.

While legal hurdles and the persistence of violence are major concerns at present, the fragile political environment, heightened by the prospect of the upcoming presidential elections, may pose an even greater threat. One year later, following a spate of assassinations of nationalists in Corsica, support amongst the French population had dropped sharply: 57 per cent were against the limited power to adapt French laws in Phase 1.[91] Support for the reforms is probably decreasing also in Corsica.

Predictions regarding the durability of conflict resolution are difficult at this point. Only once the new statute has been established can the chances for durable conflict resolution in Corsica truly be assessed.

According to Nordquist, the fact that the pre-autonomy level of militarization of the conflict was low as well as the fact that the central government is democratic should have increased the chances for settlement of the conflict; still, the durability of the 1991 arrangement was 'low' due to the persistence of violence after the establishment of autonomy.[92] Today, the conditions in Corsica are certainly significantly less favourable than they were 25 years ago for the establishment and functioning of autonomy. Although the degree of militarization of the Corsican conflict is still comparatively low, it has considerably escalated, making any attempt to expand autonomy risky. The hardest test will be the first experimental phase where little is being given by the government yet much is expected from Corsica. Whether Corsica is getting too much or too little autonomy shall probably be known in another ten years.

6. CONCLUSION

6.1 Current Arrangements in Corsica

The current arrangement consists of territorial–administrative autonomy based on the 1991 Special Statute which granted the island distinct institutions from those of the mainland regions and extensive administrative competencies in a wide range of fields. Although this statute was a significant improvement compared to the first arrangement of 1982, many problems persisted. Some related to deficiencies within the arrangement, although external factors such as the political environment and widespread violence represented the most significant obstacles to the resolution of the crisis.

6.2 Most Relevant Characteristics of the Proposed Arrangement

The most relevant characteristics of the arrangement proposed in the document of 20 July 2000 are: administrative simplification resulting in a single Corsican region with no departments; new powers as well as additional competencies; the teaching of Corsican to all children in kindergartens and primary schools in Corsica; and, finally, important economic and fiscal measures to ensure that the expansion of autonomy is accompanied by the necessary resources.

We have argued, however, that it will stop short of granting Corsica true political autonomy with clear legislative powers. If fully implemented, Corsica's current administrative autonomy will be significantly expanded, though remaining under the strict supervision of the centre. An interesting feature will be power to adapt national laws; however, the adaptations which the Corsican Assembly will make through its deliberations will be of an administrative nature and will not constitute specific Corsican laws. When the two departments are abolished, state administration will be reduced while the degree of integration of Corsica into national political structures will probably remain the same.

6.3 Determining Factors in the Outcome of the Talks

A combination of political and economic factors created a favourable context for renewed discussions over Corsica's statute after 1997. These include the nomination of a Socialist Prime Minister, increased calls within Corsica that the government pay due attention to the island's troubles and a process of nationalist unification. Violence appeared to have triggered the whole process, through the assassination of the Prefect of Corsica and a series of bombs, and continued to play a key role throughout the Matignon Process (13 December 1999–20 July 2000).

Determining factors in the outcome of the talks—a set of proposals by the government to the elected representatives of Corsica on 20 July 2000—were the following: this was a compromise, a politically-binding document negotiated with deputies from the Corsican Assembly, including the separatist nationalists aligned with the *FLNC-Canal historique*. The Prime Minister rejected allegations that the nationalists controlled the talks using violence as blackmail and emphasized that the agreement was the result of transparent negotiations with a representative segment of the Corsican political class. The proposals were approved by a majority of the Corsican Assembly on 28 July, a significant result given that it had been strongly divided a few months earlier. The question of support for the agreement within the Corsican population is a concern.

A determining factor in the course that institutional reform has taken in Corsica until now has been that Corsica belongs to a traditionally centralized and unitary state. The fact that Corsica is one of the 22 regions of Metropolitan France has severely limited the extent of reform, for the Constitution sets strict constraints with regard to the territorial organization of the state (constraints which apply to a lesser degree to the French Overseas Territories—TOM). No involvement by international actors has been possible either. The dependence of Corsica on financial support from the centre has been an important argument in favour of continued ties with the French state. However, this does not preclude granting the autonomous region a greater degree of independence in managing its economic affairs.

6.4 Conflict Management Potential

The measures contained in the proposals of 20 July 2000 which do not necessitate a revision of the Constitution are currently being translated into a law on the first, experimental phase (2002–2004) and are due to come into force on 1 January 2002. The drafting process has been less than smooth, mainly due to legal obstacles as well as the opposition of a significant segment of the French political class. Some of the provisions of the government bill, especially those concerning the new powers and the language provisions, were modified by the National Assembly due to concerns that they would be rejected by the Constitutional Council. The Senate chose to entirely delete the provisions on the experimental powers. At the time of writing (November 2001), while efforts were being made to respect the deadline for the law on Phase 1, expectations focussed on Phase 2 (after 2004) and the new statute to be prepared by the parties in power after the national elections in May 2002.

In addition to constitutional and other legal obstacles, due to the persistence of violence, there are legitimate concerns that the precondition of 'durable reestablishment of civil peace' necessary for implementation of the second phase will not be met. This has also caused a decrease in support for the reforms within the French political class and the general population. This will lead to more problems when it comes to revising the Constitution and preparing a new statute.

* * *

The conditions for a functioning autonomy in Corsica are clearly unfavourable. There is widespread political and other forms of violence, a fragile and fragmented political environment, corruption and lack of responsibility of the local political elite, and electoral fraud which represent an important obstacle to democratic government. These problems have often been compounded by the lax attitude of a central government. However, despite these unfavourable conditions, the complexity of the Corsican conflict warrants a comprehensive solution. Autonomy therefore still seems a well-suited, flexible response. While the problems encountered thus far have been significant, it still has the potential to work if the necessary political will is present. As in the past, this presents perhaps one of the greatest obstacles to successful conflict resolution in Corsica.

Despite the widespread scepticism in France, this latest and most significant effort of the French government to resolve the Corsican Question through a specific form of autonomy can still succeed for it has sought to address several of the root causes of violence: it has sought to extend recognition to a segment of Corsican nationalists and proposes additional measures for the development of the island while respecting its specific identity. Whether these measures are sufficient cannot yet be determined. While one must foresee periodic eruptions of violence in Corsica, there are still high hopes that the reforms signal the beginning of a new approach of the government to the Corsican Question and that they will lead to the establishment of mutual trust between the French state and Corsica, thereby forming the basis for a durable resolution of the conflict.

Table 3.1
Final Results of Nationalist Lists in the Second Round of Elections to the Corsican Assembly (1982–99)

Election Year	Nationalist Parties	Share of Votes (Second Round)	# Seats in (Total)
1982	UPC	12.62%	7 (61)
1984	UPC-MCA	11.22%	3 (61) 3 (61)
1986	UPC-MCA	8.97%	6 (61)
1992	*Corsica Nazione* (CN, UPC, ANC) MPA	17% 8%	9 (51) 4 (51)
1998	*Corsica Nazione* (CN)	9.85%	5 (51)
1999	*Corsica Nazione* (CN)	16.77%	8 (51)

Autonomist lists: UPC: *Unione di u Populu Corsu* / Union of the Corsican People

Separatist lists: *Corsica Nazione:*   A pre-electoral coalition formed in 1992 consisting of the separatist CN and ANC and the autonomist UPC; the latter two ran alone in subsequent elections.

MCA (later MPA):   *Muvimentu pà l'Autodeterminazione* / Movement for Self-Determination (political front of the clandestine organization *FLNC-Canal habituel*).

CN: *A Cuncolta Naziunalista* (political front of the clandestine organization *FLNC-Canal historique*)

ANC: *Accolta Naziunale Corsa*

SOURCES: Peter Savigear, "Corsica", in *Contemporary Minority Nationalism*, Michael Watson, ed. (London: Routledge), pp.86–99; Claude Olivesi, "The Failure of Regionalist Party Formation", in *Regionalist Parties in Western Europe*, Lieven de Winter and Huri Türsan, eds. (New York: Routledge, 1998), pp.174–189; John Loughlin and Farimah Daftary, *Insular Regions and European Integration: Corsica and the Åland Islands Compared*, ECMI Report No.5 (Flensburg: European Centre for Minority Issues, 1999), pp.60–61 and 62–63.

Table 3.2
Composition of the Corsican Assembly est. in 1998 (Regional Elections of 15 and 22 March 1998)[93]

Party List	Head of List	Votes (Second Round)	# Seat (Out of 51)
Gauche plurielle	Emile Zuccarelli	33.23%	(16)
DVG *(Mouvement pour la Corse)*	Toussaint Luciani	9.11%	(4)
REG *(Corsica Nazione)*	Jean-Guy Talamoni	9.85%	(5)
RPR/UDF	Jean Baggioni	36.99%	(21)
DVD *(Corse nouvelle)*	Philippe Ceccaldi	10.82%	(5)

Table 3.3
Composition of the Corsican Assembly est. in 1999
(Elections of 7 and 14 March 1999)[94]

Party List	Head of List	Votes (Second Round)	# Seat (Out of 51)
RPR-DL *(Une majorité pour la Corse)*	Baggioni-Rossi	27.29%	17
Gauche plurielle	Emile Zuccarelli	22.70%	11
REG *(Corsica Nazione)*	Jean-Guy Talamoni	16.77%	8
DVG *(Corse–Social démocrate)*	Simon Renucci	9.67%	5
DVD *(Corse nouvelle)*	Philippe Ceccaldi	9.42%	4
DVG *(Mouvement pour la Corse)*	Tousaint Luciani	7.71%	3
DVD *(Un autre avenir pour la Corse)*	Jean-Louis Albertini	6.44%	3

Party Lists:
- *Gauche plurielle* or pluralist left, the national governing coalition consisting of the Socialist Party (PS—*Parti socialiste*), the Communist Party (PCF—*Parti communiste français*), the Citizens' Movement (MDC—*Mouvement des Citoyens,* and the Left Radicals (PRG—*Parti des Radicaux de Gauche*). While the PS is strongly in favour of Jospin's proposals, the PRG is divided and the PC and especially MDC are in opposition.

- **DVG:** *Divers gauche* or left-wing political parties which are not part of the *gauche plurielle* government coalition. *Mouvement pour la Corse* is a centre-left party which supports autonomy. *Corse–Social démocrate* is a citizens' movement, rather than a political party, close to the Socialist Party but not a reliable supporter of the government's reforms regarding Corsica.

- **REG:** *Régionalistes, autonomistes, indépendantistes.*

- **RPR:** *Rassemblement pour la République* (the right-wing Gaullist party of President Chirac and Executive Council President Jean Baggioni).

- **UDF-DL:** *Démocratie libérale* is the right-of-centre coalition party of José Rossi, President of the Corsican Assembly. It is a dissident party of the *Union de la Démocratie française* (UDF). Both support the reforms in Corsica.

- **DVD:** *Divers droite* consisting of *Corse Nouvelle*, a neo-Bonapartist traditionalist party.

- **FN:** *Front National.* France's far-right party has failed to muster the same support in Corsica as in the rest of France.

Table 3.4

Application of Autonomy Success Factors to Corsica

A Success Ingredients*	B Present in Corsica? (Based on 1991 Statute)	C Present in Corsica? (Based on the Proposals of 20 July 2000)
1. A regime of autonomy should be established with the consent of the population to benefit from it.	No	No
2. The regime should be established with the consent of the foreign state to which the autonomous group may have an ethnic or other affiliation.	N.A. (In the 19th century, Italy could have been considered as such)	N.A.
3. The regime should be beneficial for both the state and the population of the autonomous region.	Yes	Yes
4. The local population should be permitted to enjoy the formal or symbolic paraphernalia of self-determination.	No	No (teaching of Corsican to all children is important symbolically, though less so if not mandatory).
5. The division of powers should be defined as clearly as possible.	No	Yes (significant improvement in the law on Phase 1. In Phase 2, following administrative simplification, this task should be easier.)
6. If activities of the central government in spheres that are under its authority directly affect the autonomous region, the local authorities should, if possible, be consulted.	Partially present (Article 26a on the obligation to consult the Corsican Assembly but its opinion is non-binding)	Partially present (see column B)
7. Organ for cooperation between the central government and the local authorities.	No	No
8. Modes and mechanisms for settling disputes between the centre and the local authorities, with a maximum of detail.	Partially present (judicial only)	Partially present (judicial only) Disputes may also be mediated by the Prefect (although he is not neutral).
9. Under certain circumstances it may be preferable to establish the autonomy in stages (gradual transfer of powers and perhaps also the territory involved).	No	Yes Two stages have been defined

A Success Ingredients*	B Present in Corsica? (Based on 1991 Statute)	C Present in Corsica? (Based on Proposals of 20 July 2000)
10. Both the central government and the autonomous authorities are based on democratic regimes.	Partially (because of widespread violence as well as fiscal and electoral fraud in Corsica)	Partially (see column B)
11. Guarantees for the respect of human rights, including the principle of equality and non-discrimination among all the inhabitants. A minority that lives within an ethnic group that has been granted autonomy should enjoy minority rights.	Partially (The Constitution upholds the principles of equality and non-discrimination)	Partially (see column B)
12. A rather similar stage of economic development and standard of living in the autonomous region and in the state as a whole may enhance the chance of success.	No	No
13. If autonomy is established for a limited period, the procedure to be followed at the end of that period should be established. If possible, a list of tentative options to be considered at that stage should be drafted.	N.A. (no further step beyond autonomy is envisaged) for New Caledonia which will gain 'associate state status' in 10–15 years).	N.A. (no further step beyond Phase 2 envisaged, unlike
14. If the autonomy arrangement includes a commitment to certain rules of behaviour, it may be helpful if those rules can be based on international norms.	No (the conflict is internal; no reference to international norms possible)	No (see column B)
15. Prevailing atmosphere of conciliation and goodwill. This condition must be generated by an energetic and sustained effort to explain and to engage in patient dialogue.	Partially	Yes Much effort by both sides, especially by the Prime Minister, to show good will; but does not apply to all actors.
16. Autonomy should be established before relations between the state and the region deteriorate considerably.	Yes (Low level of militarization)	Unclear whether 'too late'. Chances of success might have been greater if these measures had been proposed in 1991.

*   The "success ingredients" are from Ruth Lapidoth, *Autonomy: Flexible Solutions to Ethnic Conflicts* (Washington, D.C.: United States Institute of Peace Press, 1997), pp.199–201.

NOTES

[1]   In this analysis, a definition will be used according to which there must be an autonomous entity with powers of legislation, administration and adjudication in specific areas in order to call it 'political autonomy' as opposed to 'administrative autonomy' which is limited to powers in the sphere of administration. For more on these various concepts, see Ruth Lapidoth, *Autonomy: Flexible Solutions to Ethnic Conflicts* (Washington, D.C.: United States Institute of Peace Press, 1997), pp.49–58; see also Hurst Hannum, *Autonomy, Sovereignty, and Self-Determination. The Accommodation of Conflicting Rights* (Philadelphia: University of Pennsylvania Press, 1996), pp.467–468.

[2]   According to a poll by the weekly *Le Nouvel Observateur* on 4 April 1996, 10% of Corsicans (and 41% of nationalist sympathisers) were in favour of independence. A poll by *L'Evènement du Jeudi*, taken a few days after the murder of the Prefect in February 1998 indicated a slight decrease with 6% of Corsicans in favour of independence. Nationalists claim that support is as high as 25%, based on the combined results of nationalist lists in the first round of elections to the Corsican Assembly (it should be noted, however, that this is not a pure separatist vote for it also includes autonomist and protest votes).

[3]   Jean-Louis Briquet, *La Tradition en Mouvement. Clientélisme et politique en Corse* (Paris: Belin, 1997).

[4]   See the 1999 census by the French National Institute for Statistics and Economic Studies (INSEE) at http://www.insee.fr. The Corsican 'diaspora' on the mainland (350–500,000) is larger than the population of Corsica itself!

[5]   According to a 1982 survey, 96% of the inhabitants of Corsican origin understood Corsican and 86% regularly spoke it (estimates of the European Bureau for Lesser Used Languages at http://www.eblul.org/State/france.htm#Corsican). A poll from 1995 found that 81% of all persons polled understood Corsican and 64% spoke it (in Hervé Guillorel, "La langue corse: histoire et enjeux actuels", *Pouvoirs Locaux* 47, December 2000, p.71). No official statistics are available.

[6]   The 1951 Deixonne Law on the teaching of regional languages excluded Corsican, Alsatian and Flemish on the grounds that they were non-native dialects; the measures of this law were extended to Corsican by Decree no. 74–33 of 16 January 1974 (although not recognizing it as a regional language of France but simply as "*langue Corse*" for it is considered to have a special status under the 1991 Statute). A degree to teach a regional language at the secondary level (CAPES) may be obtained for Corsican as well as for the Basque, Breton, Catalan, Occitanian and French Tahitian languages.

[7]   James Minahan, "Corsica", in *Nations Without States* (London: Greenwood Press, 1996), pp.134–136.

[8]   See Ettori, in Claude Olivesi, "The Failure of Regionalist Party Formation", in *Regionalist Parties in Western Europe*, Lieven de Winter and Huri Türsan, eds. (London: Routledge, 1998), pp.175–176.

[9]   On 21 August 1975, the occupation by the autonomist ARC (*Action régionaliste corse*) of a wine cellar belonging to a *pied noir* settler in Aleria turned into tragedy when the cellar was stormed by the gendarmes and two of them were killed.

[10]   Olivesi, "The Failure of Regionalist Party Formation", *op. cit.*

[11]   In 1990, the FLNC split into two branches: the *FLNC-Canal historique* ('historic' channel), with its political wing *A Cuncolta Naziunalista*, and the *FLNC-Canal habituel* ('usual' channel), represented by the MPA *(Mouvement pour l'autodétermination)*. For a genealogy of nationalist groups, see John Loughlin and Farimah Daftary, *Insular Regions and European Integration: Corsica and the Åland Islands Compared*, ECMI Report No.4 (Flensburg: European Centre for Minority Issues, 1999), pp.62–64.

[12]   According to Briquet, demands to protect the specific Corsican language and culture are therefore not a symptom of a suppressed identity. Recognition of these demands and institutional measures proposed by the government result in fights over credit for these concessions so that reform actually leads to increased conflict between various interest groups (Jean-Louis Briquet, "Le problème corse", in *Regards sur l'actualité* no. 240, April 1998, pp.32–34).

[13]   The Constitution (1958), including the latest amendments, can be found at http://www.conseil-constitutionnel.fr/textes/constit.htm (in French) and at http://www.assemblee-nationale.fr/8/8ab.htm (in English).

[14]   The Constitutional Council ruled that, while the concrete measures which France proposed to implement did not pose any problems, the Charter's preamble and some of its articles were contrary to the principles of indivisibility and equality

(Article 1 of the Constitution) for they would amount to granting collective rights to linguistic groups in France. Article 2 ("French is the language of the Republic", a provision added only in 1992 in the context of European enlargement) constituted another obstacle (see Decision no. 99–412 of 15 June 1999, at http://www.conseil-constitutionnel.fr/decision/1999/99412/comm.htm). A report commissioned by the Prime Minister found 11 regional languages in mainland France and the overseas, including Corsican (Poignant report, *Langues et Culture Régionales*, 1 July 1998, at http://www.multimania.com/insanne/poignant/poignant.html; see also the Cerquiglini report which lists 75 "languages of France" including those spoken by French citizens who immigrated from North Africa (Bernard Cerquiglini, *Les Langues de la France*, April 1999, at http://www.culture.fr/culture/dglf/lang-reg/rapport_cerquiglini/langues-france.html).

[15] The Constitutional Council may be consulted by the President, the Prime Minister, the President of the National Assembly or of the Senate, or 60 members of either. It is composed of nine members, one third of whom are replaced every three years, appointed by the French President and by the presidents of the Senate and the National Assembly. Former Presidents of the Republic are *de jure* life members (see: http://www.conseil-constitutionnel.fr).

[16] Consultation of the Council of State, which consists of about 300 members, is mandatory in the case of draft decrees, ordinances and bills (Constitution, Arts. 37, 38 and 39); its opinion is secret, unless the government chooses to make it public, and non-binding (see: http://www.conseil-etat.fr).

[17] Act no. 82-214 of 2 March 1982 "Statut de la collectivité territoriale de Corse", *Journal officiel de la République française*, 3 March 1982, pp.748–752 (at http://www.journal-officiel.gouv.fr/).

[18] The attenuation of the statute was also due to pressure from the left-radical PRG clan in Corsica.

[19] In its decision of 25 February 1982, the Constitutional Council accepted the specific adaptations proposed for Corsica under the condition that they be limited to the administrative sphere.

[20] See decentralization laws of 2 March 1982, 10 July 1985, and 6 January 1986; see also the law of 7 January 1983 and of 22 July 1983.

[21] Claude Olivesi and Jean-Claude Pastorel, "La nouvelle collectivité territoriale de Corse", in *Regards sur l'actualité*, no. 173 (1991), pp. 33–43.

[22] This motion, which was adopted by 44 votes against 10 (and 1 abstention), offered a broad notion of "Corsican people", including those who had adopted Corsica as their home: "*une communauté historique et culturelle vivante regroupant les Corses d'origine et les Corses d'adoption: le peuple corse*". The Corsican Assembly also called upon the government to adopt a programme for implementing the rights of the Corsican people to the preservation of its cultural identity and the defence of its economic interests (Olivesi and Pastorel, "La nouvelle collectivité territoriale de Corse", *op. cit.*, pp.34–35).

[23] The bill was passed on the third reading by 276 votes to 262, with 38 abstentions and 1 absent. Almost all opposition deputies as well as the PRG and the MDC (Chevènement) faction voted against.

[24] Act no. 91–428 of 13 May 1991 "Statut de la collectivité territoriale de Corse", *Journal officiel de la République française*, 14 May 1993 (sic), pp.6318–6329 (at http://www.journal-officiel.gouv.fr/).

[25] Article 1 read: "The French Republic guarantees to the living historic and cultural community constituted by the Corsican people, a component of the French people, the right to preserve its cultural identity and to defend its specific economic and social interests. These rights related to insularity are to be exercised with respect for national unity, within the framework of the Constitution, of the laws of the Republic, and of the present statute (author's translation)". The Constitutional Council ruled that this article was contrary to the principle of indivisibility of the French people and of the Republic as well as to Article 3 of the Constitution which designates the French people as the holder of national sovereignty (CC Decision no. 91–290 of 9 May 1991). See Helen Hintjens, John Loughlin, and Claude Olivesi, "The Status of Maritime and Insular France: The DOM-TOM and Corsica", in *The End of the French Unitary State? Ten Years of Regionalisation in France (1982–1992)*, John Loughlin and Sonia Mazey, eds. (London: Frank Cass, 1995), pp.125–126.

[26] Two overseas territorial units already had a *sui generis* status of '*collectivité territoriale*': Mayotte, which in a referendum on 11 April 1976 rejected both independence and TOM status; and St.Pierre-et-Miquelon, established on 11 June 1985. Note that other territorial entities of France, such as regions an departments, are also referred to as *collectivités territoriales*.

[27]   Parliament must be informed as soon as possible. The President of the Executive Council together with the Prefect decide on day-to-day business until a new assembly is elected.

[28]   Due to the great number of seats in the Corsican Assembly (61), in the first elections of 8 August 1982, 2,231 votes were sufficient to obtain one seat.

[29]   For more on the balance of political power in Corsica since 1982, see Olivesi, "The Failure of Regionalist Party Formation", *op. cit.*, p.183.

[30]   While there were only two nationalist lists in the 1992 regional elections, there were 6 out of a total of 15 lists in 1998 (as well as two women's lists) and 5 out of a total of 12 lists in the 1999 elections (see Loughlin and Daftary, *Insular Regions, op. cit.*, pp.62–65).

[31]   While the government did react to some recommendations on technical and other issues related to the environment, it rejected proposals concerning linguistic and cultural matters. This mechanism was even weaker than under the 1982 statute where the Prime Minister had 15 days to confirm receipt and inform the Assembly on when to expect a response. In its decision of 9 May 1991, the Constitutional Council rejected a clause which would enable the Corsica Assembly to request that the Prime Minister respond within a certain period.

[32]   See Emmanuel Négrier, "The Changing Role of French Local Government", *West European Politics* 22 (October 1999), 4.

[33]   French political scientists prefer the notion of a "local political/administrative system" to "local government". In order to prevent hierarchical dependencies between the three levels (communes, departments, and regions), powers were transferred *en bloc* according to the subsidiarity principle. The state possesses *a posteriori* legal control over these areas. In addition to Corsica, there are also exceptions amongst the communes (Paris, Lyon, and Marseilles); the departments (Alsace-Moselle, justified by historic reasons) and Île-de-France (Paris region). For more on local autonomy, see Henri Oberdorff, *Les Institutions Administratives* (Paris: Armand Colin, 2000), pp.151–184; on local government, see also the website of the *Direction Générale des Collectivités Locales* (at http://www.dgcl.interieur.gouv.fr/index.html).

[34]   The decentralization laws are cited in footnote 20; on the deconcentration of state administration, see the Act on Territorial Administration (6 February 1992) and the "Deconcentration Charter" (1 July 1992).

[35]   The current President of the Corsican Assembly, José Rossi (DL), is also a national deputy. There has never been a nationalist Corsican deputy or senator in Paris.

[36]   One national deputy is elected for every 100,000 inhabitants. For example, Alsace, also a bi-departmental region but with a population of 1.7 million, has nine deputies and four senators for one department and seven deputies and three senators for the other. Two of the DOM, Guadeloupe (422,496 inhabitants) and Martinique (381,427), have the same representation as Corsica even though they are monodepartmental regions. New Caledonia (196,836) and French Polynesia (219,521) (single entity TOMs) have two national deputies and one senator only. New Caledonia, French Polynesia and the DOMs have an economic and social advisor in Paris which Corsica does not have.

[37]   Between 1971 and 1998, there were 45 political murders in Corsica, of which 21 were claimed by nationalists (Briquet, "Le problème corse", *op. cit.*, p.35). 75% of the 1,172 bomb attacks in 1995 and 1996 were not political but rather attributed to personal settling of scores (Olivesi, "The Failure of Regionalist Party Formation", *op. cit.*, p.187).

[38]   Six different categories of entrenchment of the autonomy arrangement are possible: *regional entrenchment* (where a separate regional reaction is envisaged whenever legislation relating to the autonomy arrangement is amended); *special entrenchment* (special amendment rule for the autonomy provisions in the national constitutional setting), *general entrenchment* (explicit regulations in the national constitution) or *semi-general entrenchment* (through an organic law which may be amended by a two-thirds majority); and *international entrenchment*, including through treaties (Markku Suksi, "On the Entrenchment of Autonomy", in *Autonomy: Applications and Implications,* Markku Suksi, ed. (The Hague: Kluwer Law International, 1998), p.152.

[39]   The complaint was filed by the UPC which had obtained 4.97% in the first round. The UPC list obtained 3.85% in 1999, again failing to make it to the second round.

[40]   A series of recent parliamentary commissions have blamed not only local actors but also the state for insufficient enforcement of the law in Corsica (see the Glavany report on the use of public funds in Corsica of 9 September 1998,

at http://www.assemblee-nat.fr/2/2dossiers.html and two reports from November 1999 on the actions of state security forces in Corsica, at http://www.assemblee-nat.fr/2/2dossiers.html and http://www.senat.fr).

[41] The autonomist UPC and several others refused to join *Unità* because of its ambiguous position concerning political violence in general.

[42] "Mon pari pour la Corse", *Le Nouvel Observateur*, 17 August 2000 (also at http://www.premier-ministre.gouv.fr/fr/p.cfm?ref=4993).

[43] Twenty-eight Corsican representatives attended the meeting on 13 December 1999 including the two senators and four national deputies, the presidents of the two general councils, the President of the Assembly, the President of the Executive Council, as well as two representatives from each of the nine political parties at the Corsican Assembly); the senators and deputies were not present at subsequent meetings.

[44] This was a highly controversial decision for *Corsica Nazione* as it is practically the same organization as *A Cuncolta Naziunalista*, now *A Cuncolta Indipendentista*, which has been the political front of the *FLNC-Canal historique* ever since the other two parties in this pre-electoral coalition formed in 1992 withdrew (see Table 1). *Corsica Nazione* minimally condemned the murder of the Prefect as well as the November 1999 bomb attacks, a condemnation which enabled the Prime Minister to justify its inclusion in the negotiation. Still, *Corsica Nazione* viewed the persons who committed the murder as heroes.

[45] The nationalists oppose what they designate as "*décorsisation des emplois*" which refers to the increased reliance on labour from outside the island. However, this is due to the lack of qualified local personnel, especially during the tourist season. Many politicians stress that to give preference to Corsicans for jobs would be discriminatory.

[46] This outcome was due to Émile Zuccarelli (PRG) (former Minister under Jospin and mayor of Bastia), producing an alternative proposal while a compromise with the nationalists was being sought.

[47] The four organizations which formed the 'new FLNC' included the *FLNC-Canal historique* which claimed responsibility for the December bombs and *Clandestinu* which claimed responsibility for the November bombs.

[48] This document is available at http://www.premier-ministre.gouv.fr/fr/p.cfm?ref=16468 (in French only).

[49] Gérard Marcou, "Déléguer un pouvoir législatifá l'Assemblée de Corse?" Pouvoirs Locaux 47 (2000), pp.113–118.

[50] "Le Gouvernement proposera au Parlement de doter la collectivité territoriale de Corse d'un pouvoir réglementaire, permettant d'adapter les textes réglementaires par délibération de l'assemblée" (*Propositions du gouvernement*, Section 1.C "L'adaptation des normes", subsection 4).

[51] " ... le Gouvernement proposera au Parlement de donner à la collectivité territoriale de Corse la possibilité de déroger, par ses délibérations, à certaines dispositions législatives, dans des conditions que le Parlement définirait, les adaptations ainsi intervenues à l'initiative de l'assemblée devant, comme le prévoit la décision n 93–322 du conseil constitutionnel du 28 juillet 1993 qui affirme la conformité à la Constitution de telles expérimentations, être ensuite évaluées avant que le Parlement ne décide de les maintenir, de les modifier ou de les abandonner" (*Propositions du gouvernement*, Section 1.C "L'adaptation des normes", subsection 5).

[52] The person behind this creative though legally precarious idea was the head of Jospin's cabinet and former general secretary of the Constitutional Council, Olivier Schrameck. The autonomist faction of the Corsican Assembly was not satisfied with the experimental and temporary nature of the proposed mechanism, insisting instead on an irreversible devolution of legislative power as a sign of the government's commitment to reform in Corsica.

[53] "... Le Parlement pourrait ainsi autoriser l'assemblée territoriale de Corse à adapter par ses délibérations, dans certains domaines précisément déterminés et dans le respect des principes qu'il aura fixés, des dispositions législatives déjà en vigueur ou en cours d'examen ...." (*Propositions du gouvernment*, Section 1.C "L'adaptation des normes", sub-section 7).

[54] The Constitutional Council would certainly reject the mandatory teaching of Corsican. (See Decision no. 91-290 of 9 May 1991 that the teaching of Corsican during normal school hours did not contravene the principle of equality so long as it was not mandatory; see also Decision no. 96–373 of 9 April 1996 on the teaching of Tahitian in French Polynesia.)

[55]   There will be two separate recruitment processes to avoid discriminating against teachers who do not speak Corsican.

[56]   On 26 June 1992, the Corsican Assembly had adopted a resolution to grant the Corsican language official status in Corsica. This resolution had no legal or other effects.

[57]   Corsicans are exempted by the 'Miot Decrees' ('arrêtés Miot') dating back to 1801 from paying inheritance taxes. This special regime was due to be abolished in 1999 and then again in 2001. The government had proposed a 10-year transitory period, with full exemption for the first 5 years only.

[58]   A complete file on the drafting process is available on the website of the National Assembly at http://www.assemblee-nat.fr/dossiers/corse2001.asp#accesdossier.

[59]   The Government Bill (*Avant projet de loi modifiant et complétant le statut de la collectivité territoriale de Corse*) is available at http://www.interieur.gouv.fr/actualite/corse/avant_projet.htm).

[60]   It requested a "competency of principle" (rather than exclusive competency) in economic development, tourism, agriculture, fishing, forest management, professional training, the environment, culture and sports. See Paul Silvani, "L'Assemblée de Corse approuve le projet de loi sur le statut de l'île", *Le Monde,* 11 December 2000. The number of shared areas of competence between the state and Corsica would be reduced to education, regional planning and transportation.

[61]   Author's translation. See preamble entitled in the *Avant projet de loi modifiant et complétant le statut de la collectivité territoriale de Corse* (at http://www.interieur.gouv.fr/actualite/corse/avant_projet.htm). This section disappeared from the draft law adopted by the National Assembly and subsequent versions.

[62]   "II.—Dans les matières dans lesquelles elle exerce des compétences, ... et sauf lorsque sont en cause les conditions essentielles d'application de lois organisant l'exercice d'une liberté publique, la collectivité territoriale de Corse peut, dans un but d'intérêt général, apporter aux décrets, pris pour l'application des dispositions législatives régissant ces matières, les adaptations que justifie sa situation spécifique ...." (*Avant projet de loi,* Title I: Organization and Competencies of the Corsican Region, Chapter I: Legal Regime of the Acts of the Corsican Assembly, Article 1, Subsection 3 "Competencies").

[63]   "III.—Lorsque l'Assemblée de Corse estime que les dispositions législatives en vigueur ou en cours d'élaboration présentent, pour les compétences de la collectivité territoriale, des difficultés d'application liées aux spécificités de l'île, elle peut demander au Gouvernement, sur proposition du conseil exécutif, et par délibération motivée, que lui soit conférée par la loi qui en fixe les modalités l'autorisation de prendre par délibération, dans un but d'intérêt général, à titre expérimental, des mesures d'adaptation de ces dispositions législatives" (*Avant projet de loi,* Title I, Chapter I, Article 1, Subsection 3).

[64]   "La langue corse est enseignée dans le cadre de l'horaire normal des écoles maternelles et élémentaires à tous les élèves, sauf volonté contraire des parents ou du représentant légal de l'enfant" (*Avant projet de loi,* Title I, Chapter II, Section 1, Subsection 1, Article 7).

[65]   Although the decisions of the *Conseil d'État* are not usually made public, its principal reservations on the Corsican bill were communicated to the press (see *Libération* of 10–11 and 14 February 2001).

[66]   The version of the government bill submitted to the National Assembly in February 2001 is at http://www.assemblee-nationale.fr/projets/pl2931.asp.

[67]   The text of draft law adopted by the National Assembly on 22 May 2001 (*Projet de loi relatif à la Corse* no. 673) is available at http://www.assemblee-nationale.fr/ta/ta0673.asp.

[68]   "Lorsque l'Assemblée de Corse estime que les dispositions législatives en vigueur ou en cours d'élaboration présentent, pour l'exercice des compétences de la collectivité territoriale, des difficultés d'application liées aux spécificités de l'île, elle peut demander au Gouvernement que le législateur lui ouvre la possibilité de procéder à des expérimentations comportant le cas échéant des dérogations aux règles en vigueur, en vue de l'adoption ultérieure par le Parlement de dispositions législatives appropriées ..." (*Projet de loi no. 673,* Title I, Chapter I, Article 1[4]).

69 "La langue corse est une matière enseignée dans le cadre de l'horaire normal des écoles maternelles et élémentaires de Corse ..." (*Projet de loi no. 673*, Title I, Chapter II, Article 7[1]).

70 The Senate version of the law *(Projet de loi modifié par le Sénat relatif à la Corse no. 3380)* is at available http://www.senat.fr/pl/16-0102.pdf.

71 " ... Les délibérations adoptées par l'assemblée de Corse dans ces conditions seraient, sous réserve de l'exercice des voies de recours devant la juridiction administrative, exécutoires. De valeur réglementaire, elles ne seraient pas soumises à une validation ultérieure obligatoire de la part du législateur" (*Propositions du gouvernment*, Paris, 20 July 2000, Section 1.C. "L'adaptation des normes," subsection 7). See also the clarifications offered by the Prime Minister, *Questions—réponses sur la politique du gouvernement en Corse*, at http://www.premier-ministre.gouv.fr.

72 The Constitution was revised in July 1998 for the New Caledonian reforms, including a local referendum (Arts. 76 and 77); the same method will be used for French Polynesia. It was also used to enable ratification of the Amsterdam Treaty and of the treaty establishing the International Criminal Court. Roland Debbasch, "L'Avenir Institutionnel de la Corse et la Constitution", in *Pouvoirs Locaux* 47, December 2000, pp.94–95.

73 Debbasch, "L'Avenir Institutionnel de la Corse et la Constitution", *op. cit.*, p.96.

74 Thierry Michalon, "Vers l'indispensable autonomie", in *Pouvoirs Locaux* 47, December 2000, p.53.

75 See e.g. the Decision of 9 April 1996 on the organic law establishing autonomy in French Polynesia.

76 See endnote 55 on the 1992 resolution of the Corsican Assembly making Corsican official.

77 There are divisions within both the right and the left concerning the Corsican reforms. Rifts have also appeared between the national and local branches of the RPR whose national president is opposed to autonomy in Corsica while the President of the Executive Council was generally in favour. Divisions are also visible in the Radical Party (PRG) between supporters of autonomy, e.g. the President of the General Council of North Corsica, Paul Giacobbi, and opponents such as Emile Zuccarelli.

78 Louis Harris Institute poll of 600 persons in Corsica taken between 13 and 14 December 2000 (before the bill was 'watered down' by the National Assembly), published in *Corsica*, 3 January 2001.

79 Consultations may be held in the Overseas Territories and Departments since the preamble of the Constitution recognizes the right to self-determination and free expression of the will of the overseas people. However, only in the TOM can a binding referendum be held. In its Decision no. 2000-428 of 4 May 2000, the Constitutional Council accepted that a non-binding consultation be held in Mayotte (the question was whether, based on the agreement of 27 January 2000, Mayotte should become a '*collectivité départementale*', an entity closer to a DOM). It also ruled that any consultation of the inhabitants of a DOM would be non-binding (CC Decision no. 2000-435 of 7 December 2000). Within Metropolitan France, a referendum may only be organized at the national or at the commune level.

80 Nine per cent were unsure. IFOP (Institut français de l'opinion publique) poll of 802 persons, published on 23 July 2000 in *Journal du Dimanche*, cited in *Le Monde*, 25 July 2000.

81 There are four DOMs (*départements d'outre-mer*)—Reunion, Guadeloupe, Martinique and Guiana—established according to Article 73 of the Constitution. Although they were not entitled to a particular organization, their legislative system and administrative organization were adapted to their special situation due to the great distance to the mainland. They became mono-departmental regions of France under the law of 5 July 1972 with a regional as well as a departmental council. They were also granted special competencies in economic development, education, culture and maritime questions (see Act of 2 August 1984). The four traditional TOMs (*territoires d'outre-mer*)—New Caledonia, French Polynesia, Wallis and Futuna, and the French Austral and Antarctic Territories—were entitled to self-administration and a particular organization defined by law, according to Article 74 of the Constitution (see the website of the State Secretariat for Overseas, at http://www.outre-mer.gouv.fr).

82 Under the first autonomy statute of 9 September 1984, the acts of the local Polynesian assembly took effect immediately, subject to the authority of the administrative courts. While the new statute of 12 April 1996 was an improvement, no legislative powers could be granted (see organic law no. 96–312 of 12 April 1996, modified by law no. 96–624 of 15 July 1996 completing the autonomy statute of French Polynesia, at http://www.presidence.pf).

[83]   Michalon, "Vers l'indispensable autonomie" *op. cit.*

[84]   Two laws implementing the Noumea Accords (5 May 1998), one organic and one ordinary, were approved by Parliament on 16 February 1999, following a referendum in New Caledonia on 8 November 1998. This will lead, over a period of 15–20 years, to 'associated state' status through a gradual transfer of powers. Starting in 2014, all eligible voters who have resided for at least 20 years in New Caledonia will be consulted on full sovereignty (for more, see http://www.gouv.nc/organisation.htm). An agreement was reached in 1998 on political autonomy for French Polynesia, making it an 'overseas country' (*Pays d'outre-mer*—POM). An organic law adopted on 12 October 1999 still needs to be approved by the Polynesian Assembly.

[85]   Efforts to simplify the institutions of the DOM and to introduce a single assembly alternating as a regional and a departmental council had failed until now (in its Decision no. 82–147 of 2 December 1982, the Constitutional Council ruled that the DOM could not have a statute different from that of the mainland departments). However, in a new framework law (*loi d'orientation pour l'outre-mer*, 13 December 2000), a series of institutional, economic and social reforms are proposed, including the establishment of a Congress for each DOM consisting of regional and departmental deputies.

[86]   A minimum residency of 5 years as well as citizenship of Finland and a satisfactory knowledge of the local language—Swedish—is required to be able to operate a business, to possess land, or to vote or stand for election in the Åland Islands. The requirements for Caledonian citizenship, which is necessary to be able to vote and also confers privileges in local employment, are 10 years of residency and French citizenship; there are no language requirements. A similar Polynesian citizenship is also foreseen.

[87]   Nordquist defines an autonomous region as "as intra-state territory, which has a constitutionally based self-government that is wider than any comparable region in the state" (Kjell-Åke Nordquist, "Autonomy as a Conflict-Solving Mechanism—An Overview", in *Autonomy: Applications and Implications*, Markku Suksi, ed. (The Hague: Kluwer Law International, 1998), p.63).

[88]   See the report of the Mauroy Commission on Decentralization of December 2000 (at http://www.senat.fr/grp/soc/mauroy.html). The Commission found that the principles of unity and indivisibility of the French Republic were compatible with adaptations to local specificity and recommended that all regions be given additional competencies. The conclusions of the Commission do not presage a major juridical revolution in France. In June 2001, the National Assembly adopted a bill on local democracy, including a short section on decentralization.

[89]   Xavier Crettiez, "Violence et Politique de la Reconnaissance", in *Pouvoirs Locaux* 47, December 2000, pp.58–63.

[90]   *Armata Corsa* had threatened large-scale violence throughout France if the persons responsible for the murder of presumed *Armata Corsa* leader Jean-Michel Rossi in August 2000 were not found, claiming that the FLNC was responsible. One year later, the other leader (and former FLNC chief) François Santoni, was also assassinated.

[91]   However, 67% were in favour of the generalized teaching of Corsican (see the extensive poll published in *Libération*, 22 May 2001).

[92]   Nordquist suggests durability as a useful overall indicator of success of an autonomy arrangement. A 'high' level of durability is assigned if two criteria are fulfilled: (1) If the conflict has subsided militarily after the initiation of autonomy; and (2) If the autonomy has continued to exist on the basis of an operative political document after at least one constitutional change of government in the central state. A 'low' level of durability is assigned when one of these conditions is lacking (Kjell-Åke Nordquist, "Autonomy as a Conflict-Solving Mechanism", *op. cit.*).

[93]   For complete results, see Loughlin and Daftary, *op. cit.*, pp.57–61.

[94]   For complete results, see Loughlin and Daftary, *op. cit.*, pp.57–61.

Overview of Proposals for Minority Self-Governments of Hungarian Minorities in Central Europe

Zsolt G. Pataki

Overview of Proposals for Minority Self-Governments of Hungarian Minorities in Central Europe

Zsolt G. Pataki

A study of the autonomy concepts of the Hungarian national minorities in Central Europe needs to apply a comprehensive analysis of their political strivings and to point out the relations of these communities with Hungary. In a broader sense, this problem may have an impact on the European integration process. The belated nation-state building in Central Europe as well as outbursts of nationalism increasingly gives rise to a tendency towards self-determination by minority communities. Ethnic claims do not tend to disappear as a result of modernization in these countries. On the contrary, the states concerned are more and more forced to take measures for the protection of different ethnic, linguistic, cultural and religious groups in their countries. They may choose from divergent models of ethnic accommodation ranging from all-out integration to models of self-management.

This overview is meant to provide a comparative analysis of different proposals for minority self-governance of the Hungarian minorities in Central Europe, for instance in Slovenia, Transcarpathian Ukraine, southern Slovakia and Transylvania (Romania). Autonomy is treated as a possible form of self-governance, which, in turn, is seen as a form of addressing the needs and aspirations of minority communities within the context of sovereign states.

1. THE HUNGARIAN MINORITIES (COMMUNITIES)

According to the official statistics, in the Carpathian Basin there are about 13.1 million Hungarians, and at least 2.8 million (about 22 per cent of all Hungarians) live in the neighbouring countries. The majority of these people, almost 2 million, live in Romania, in the regions surrounded by the Carpathian Mountains (in historical *Transylvania*, in *Banat* and in the *Partium*), and 700,000 in Slovakia. In *Vojvodina* (Serbia) there may now live about 300,000 Hungarians. Table 3.5 shows the figures of the Hungarian national minorities in the neighbouring countries.

As detailed by the official census data, out of 13,150,000 Hungarians in the Carpathian Basin, 2.8 million still live in Hungary's neighbouring states. The Hungarians in these countries became a minority as a consequence of the Treaty of Trianon (1920), after the First World War. Only the number of Russian minorities—estimated at 15,500,000—exceeds that of the Hungarians; nevertheless, the percentage of the Hungarian minority is much higher (30 per cent) than that of Russians (12 per cent). This could be one of the reasons why the Hungarian minorities in Central Europe represent a principal political challenge for Hungary and for the neighbouring countries, as well as for Europe as a whole. From the point of view of stability in Central Europe, the question of the status of Hungarian minorities remains without any doubt one of the most important ones.

Table 3.5

Hungarian National Minorities in Hungary's Neighbouring Countries
(Population and Percentages)

Country	Hungarians	Year of Census	% in the Country	% in the Total Number of Hungarians
1. Romania	1,620,199	1992	7.1	12.30
2. Slovakia	567,296	1991	10.8	4.30
3. Yugoslavia (Serbia)	385,356	1991	3.93	2.92
4. Croatia	25,439	1991	0.53	0.19
5. Slovenia	9,496	1991	0.48	0.07
6. Ukraine	163,111	1989	0.31	1.23
7. Austria	33,459	1981	0.44	0.25
Total Hungarian minorities	2,804,353	—	—	21.32
Population of Hungary	10,345,000	1992	—	78.67
Total Hungarians	13,149,353	—	—	100.00

SOURCE: Official census data of Romania, Slovakia, Yugoslavia, Soviet Union, and Austria.

Hungarian minorities are present in each neighbouring state of Hungary and they do have a very strong national identity. They resisted any kind of assimilation and reaffirmed their linguistic and educational claims. However, their situation is much different as their status depends on the state they live in. The situation of these minorities is generally better in countries where they represent a low percentage of the population (Austria, Slovenia, Croatia), while their situation is more difficult in countries where they represent a higher percentage of the population (Slovakia, Romania, Serbia).

One may also classify Hungarian minorities according to the importance of geopolitical problems they induce. The first category could then be formed by those Hungarians who have a very strong collective national identity, i.e. in the regions where they are the most numerous—in Transylvania (Romania), in Southern Slovakia and in Vojvodina (Serbia). The mere existence of the largest Hungarian minority communities—the Hungarians of Romania, Slovakia and Serbia—imply a national problem for and within the state they live in. There is thus a 'Hungarian problem' for the governments to solve in these three countries. It seems to be extremely hard for the majority nations to tolerate the existence of another 'nation' on their territory, especially when this minority once belonged to the dominant majority.

The second category is represented by those Hungarian communities having a distinct Hungarian identity and living in a country where the Hungarian problem is not a major political issue. In Austria, Croatia or Slovenia, the demographic weight of Hungarians would not induce a 'national' problem. A borderline case could be made for Hungarians in Ukraine, who number more than 150,000, but represent less than one per cent of the total population.

Moreover, geopolitical considerations play an extremely important role in the context of relations between states and minorities. For the people of Central European nations, the 'national' territories are psychologically important. There are power rivalries in these territories between different geopolitical actors. In fact, there is confusion between a *nation* and a *state*. The latter is sovereign in a well-defined territory. Linguistic areas correspond only exceptionally to national territories—consider the case of Germans (Germany, Austria, Germanic Switzerland, Liechtenstein, etc.) or of Romanians (Romania, Moldova and the Ukraine). The geopolitical representations affect directly the political debates between states (majority nations) and minorities (or co-nations). The objective backgrounds for the political cleavages between co-habiting nations are their different ethnicities, languages, religions, etc., whereas the subjective ones are based on different geopolitical representations which originate from permanent sources of tension between these nations. These result from ambiguous historical memories and from different interpretations of the same territory's history. By taking into account the mutual geopolitical considerations, one may identify the power rivalries controlling these territories. The Hungarian minorities who represent a local majority wish to establish their own self-government system, but the state does not want to leave power to a minority it mistrusts.

Why is there no ETA- or IRA-type terrorist organization among the Hungarian minorities? Was the communist regime's political control too strong, or is terrorism a sensitive point for only democratic societies? None of these questions reach the real issue. First and foremost, there is no longer a Hungarian irredentism or territorial claims in any direction, and that is embodied in Hungarian foreign policy, national security strategy and military doctrine. The foreign and security policy principles are put in the context of Hungary's contribution to European stability. The structure of the foreign and security policy has three main directions, each of them seeking cooperation: European integration, good relations with the neighbouring countries and support for Hungarian minorities abroad. After 1989, Hungary officially declared that the government felt responsible for the well-being of Hungarians abroad. This commitment has been introduced into the Constitution of the Republic of Hungary.[95]

After the democratic changes of 1989–90, the situation of the Hungarian minorities in Central and Eastern Europe improved. Since then, minority organizations have been able to conduct actions on an international level and are able to protest against any attempt towards assimilation. In the democratization process of the Central European countries, the most important achievements included freedom of the press and the almost free self-affirmation of national minorities. Since 1990, the Hungarian communities of Romania, Slovakia, Serbia and the Ukraine have been able to build up their own network of international relations. For them, it is important to be represented at different international fora, such as the Council of Europe, the European Parliament, the OSCE, etc. A sort of mini-diplomacy has been established in the framework of the RMDSZ (Democratic Alliance of Hungarians in Romania) and the MKP (Party of the Hungarian Coalition, Slovakia), whose members are lobbying on the international political scene. For example, in 1993, the RMDSZ became a member of the European Democratic Union (EDU), an international association of conservative parties in Europe.[96] At the same time, the RMDSZ is a member of the Federalist Union of European Nationalities (FUEN), which embraces all European ethnic or national minorities (Catalans, Basques, Corsicans, Germans, Hungarians, Ladins, etc.) and functions as a minority rights protection association.

From an international point of view, ethnic minorities represent an important diplomatic challenge in Europe. In general the Hungarian minorities affect eight states. Although the minority question is not omnipresent in European and world media, the issue may affect the entire continent. The Central and Eastern European countries are halfway towards European integration. All wish to join NATO and the European Union. Consequently, it is evident that those states having national minorities should solve their problems now. Newcomers to the EU and NATO should not import any potential sources of conflict. Hungary has a vested interest in maintaining and developing dynamic and friendly relations with all her neighbours. Hungary's security is further enhanced if her neighbours are and feel secure and *vice versa*.

Making an evaluation of peaceful solutions for the problem of the Hungarian minorities in the region, one may find the following points of interest (the modification of borders is excluded as a solution for this problem not only because of endangering the existing status quo, but also because this type of solution has been clearly rejected by Hungary):

1) *Immigration* of Hungarians to Hungary. This is not a desire of the Hungarian state, but some neighbours unofficially consider it a possible solution. Unfortunately, mass migration is still occurring in the Balkans. New generations are encouraged to believe that their futures lie outside their home state and that emigration is the solution. The best and most skilled working forces and intellectuals therefore leave the country, often leaving for their kin state.

2) *Assimilation* of ethnic Hungarians. This is not a desire of Hungary either. Taking into account the strong national identity of Hungarian communities, this is a possible scenario but with a very low probability.

3) Hungarian *citizenship* for Hungarians abroad has a low probability as well. It is not desired by the neighbouring states. This option was often claimed by certain political groups among the Hungarian minorities and remains to be studied by the government in Budapest. Nevertheless, even though the Hungarian state can grant nationality to its 'nationals', this problem implies not only questions of international law, but also economic questions. For the small-sized minorities like those in Croatia, Slovenia and Austria, this is perfectly feasible, while in the case of Hungarians in Slovakia, Romania, Serbia and the Ukraine it would affect about 3 million people, consequently impacting taxation, employment, social services, military service and other areas.

4) *Regionalization* of the home countries (and later, creation of federal structures) could be a long-term solution. Slovakia and Romania present a good case, but the geopolitical actors and the local people are not prepared and politically ready for promoting this option. Nevertheless, the European Union could give some positive examples in this field; during this decade, the regions have become both politically and economically without doubt more important.

5) Administrative *decentralization* would also be possible, but the geopolitical actors have to be assured that this is by no means a disguised seizure of a portion of the national territory. The devolution process has transformed Corsica into an autonomous region within the French Republic, and this is the case for Scotland as well, and to a lesser

extent, Wales. This scenario is possible in the near future (50 years) even for Slovakia or Romania. The minority communities are perfectly aware of the fact that the implementation of a well functioning administrative decentralization in a democratic state could also mean *de facto* territorial autonomy.

6. *Personal autonomy* (cultural autonomy) could be realized very easily, but at the moment the majority societies and the nationalist forces in Slovakia, Romania and Serbia are against any autonomy. The trouble with this form of autonomy is that in most of the cases it is poorly formulated and wrongly interpreted. Personal autonomy is not based on a concrete territory—it refers to and regroups the persons who are members of a national (or religious) minority, as for example may be the case of the autonomy of the Church within the states. The main fields of personal autonomy are: education, culture, media, preservation of traditions and monument protection, exclusively non-territorial fields.

Generally, the claims of Hungarian communities remain at the limits of cultural autonomy that has no spatial transcription nor territorial implication. The latter concerns only some individuals or some cultural and religious organizations and the media. This form of autonomy does not refer to any precise territory and, consequently, does not put into question the central authority's control on its territory.

As stated, the Hungarian minorities have maintained a strong national identity, regardless of their status in different states. By taking into account geopolitical considerations, one may understand the rivalries of power in controlling these territories. This is even true within the Hungarian minority community. Where they represent the majority, they wish self-administration for themselves, and the state does not want to give up the control and leave it for a minority they mistrust.

In the following parts, we shall describe the status of the Hungarian communities in the states where Hungarians claim cultural and/or territorial autonomy. First, one has to note that the common characteristic of Hungarian minorities is their permanent quest for autonomy. The situation of the Hungarian communities varies from one region (or country) to another, but the common denominator is the rejection of secession and the claim for autonomy. The autonomy concepts of the Hungarian organizations in the Carpathian Basin are based on a common value system and an identical perception of state and law. They also envisage the same objective, namely to secure the collective rights of the Hungarian national minority within an institutional framework, in conformity with European norms and the practices of the developed European democracies.

2. CULTURAL AUTONOMY OF HUNGARIANS IN SLOVENIA[97]

2.1 History and Geography

For centuries following the foundation of the Hungarian state, the territory now belonging to Slovenia, specifically the region between the Hungarian Kingdom and the Styrian–Austrian Principality, was a defence zone settled by Hungarians or in part unpopulated. The Paris Peace Conference, modifying the originally proposed Mura line, drew the Yugoslav–Hungarian border along the watershed of the Mura and Rába rivers. As a result, Muravidék[98] (Prekomurje) became part of Yugoslavia with 15,000 ethnic Hungarians, while the so-called Porabje area remained in Hungary with some 5,000 ethnic Slovenes (and Vends). The Yugoslav (Serbian) army moved into Muravidék only on 12 August 1919. Like in the case of Burgenland (Austria), the decision of the Great Powers was a kind of compensation for the territories inhabited by Slovenes which had been ceded to Italy and left within Austria.

The ethnic Hungarian community inhabits the north eastern part of the country, in a 50-km long and 3 to 15 km wide strip of land along the Slovenian-Hungarian border from Hodoš to Pince, the so-called Muravidék (Prekomurje) region. The Hungarians living in Muravidék can be further divided into two groups or units, the 'Lendva' and the 'Őrség' groups. The Hungarians in the Lendva region live primarily in the villages between Dobronak and Pince, with Lendava (formerly Alsólendva) as its centre.[99]

The Hungarian inhabitants of Hodos (Hodoš), Kapornak (Krplivnik), Domonkosfa (Domanjševci), Szerdahely (Središče), Pártosfalva (Prosenjakovci), Kisfalu (Pordašinci), Csekefa (Čikečka vas) and Szentlászló (Motvarjevci) belong to the group of the Őrség region. Prior to the First World War, these settlements were part of Vas County, with the exception of Szentlászló, which belonged to Zala County. Outside the Muravidék region, a very small number of ethnic Hungarians live in other areas of Slovenia, mainly in cities. The two largest groups of scattered Hungarians are found in Muraszombat and Ljubljana.

The size of the ethnic Hungarian community in Muravidék and its willingness to assimilate is similar to the Hungarians living in Burgenland. A Hungarian-Slovenian joint survey conducted in the mid-1980s indicated disadvantageous economic and infrastructure conditions, growing migration and assimilation in the form of mixed marriages on both sides of the border. Between censuses conducted every ten years, the number of ethnic Hungarians in Slovenia decreased by an average of 13 per cent per decade. The proportion of mixed marriages exceeds 50 per cent, and 80 per cent of those born in these marriages consider themselves Slovenes. In the summer of 1991, the ethnic Hungarians unanimously supported the independence of Slovenia, and they have been playing, with the added support of inter-state agreements, a bridge-building role between the two countries—a role given to them by history.

2.2 Their Legal Status

For the past two decades, compared to the other republics of the former Yugoslavia and the entire region of Central Eastern Europe, Slovenia has provided the most stable legal conditions for minorities, including Hungarians. In its first article, the republic's Constitution of 1974 defined the autochthonous Hungarian and Italian nationalities as state-forming factors. The fundamental law guaranteed special rights not only for individuals (in the section dealing with human and civic liberties), but also for the communities. These can be summarized as follows:

- In those territories inhabited by minorities, the Hungarian and Italian languages are on equal grounds with the Slovenian language;
- Native language education, media, book publication and other cultural practices are guaranteed;
- Relations among the minorities and between the minorities and their mother countries are supported;
- Nationality symbols can be used freely;

- Members of the Hungarian and Italian nationalities may establish cultural and educational self-governing interest associations for the realization of the above-delineated rights.

In March 1975, the Nationality Self-Governing Association of the Mura Region (NSAHM) was established in the two Hungarian-inhabited districts to protect nationality interests. The NSAHM has been successful in combining the representation of its political interests and its cultural functions. It has significant influence in regional and state decisions regarding questions that affect the two Hungarian-inhabited communities.[100]

After becoming an independent state, the Slovenian House of Representatives adopted a new constitution in December 1991. Article 11 of the new Constitution of the Republic of Slovenia guarantees the right to the free use of the native language. Article 61 allows for the "free expression of one's national identity", while Article 64 regulates "the special rights of the autochthonous Italian and Hungarian national minorities". The essence of Slovenia's national minority policy is based on a system of special rights for minorities. This lies in the fact that the minority community enjoys special opportunities in the fields of education, culture, information and contacts with the mother country. These opportunities are also financially supported by the state, directly out of the central budget.

The significant changes on minorities in the Constitution can be summarized as follows:

- neither nation nor group—including the Hungarians—designated as state-forming;
- instead of using the political and legal term 'nationality', the Constitution uses the term 'national community';
- the rights of minorities are expanded to include the right to economic and scientific activity, the right to establish their own kindergartens and schools, and a veto right in decisions affecting the community;
- the new Constitution limits the sphere of influence of the administrative districts (that will be redrawn in the near future anyway)—thus the local minority self-government;
- the new Constitution does not unequivocally refer to previously reciprocal bilingual education.

Similar to the Italians on the coast of the Adriatic Sea, the Hungarian communities have a separate electoral district and succeeded in delegating a representative to each of the three houses of the Parliament. In December 1992, the elections to the House of Representatives proceeded under conditions that were even more favourable. While in the past every citizen of the multiethnic territory voted for the nationality representative, from 1992 on, only the minorities have been allowed to vote. As the previous three-chamber Parliament was reduced to only one chamber and the number of members was reduced to half, the three minorities currently declared to be autochthonous inhabitants (the Hungarian[101] and Italian nationalities and the Roma ethnic groups) could each delegate one representative. More precisely, Article 80 of the Constitution states that "at every election one representative of both the ethnic Italian and Hungarian communities is to be elected into parliament". Both the ethnic Italians and Hungarians have a two-fold right to vote. On the one hand, like every Slovene citizen, they can vote for political parties, while on the other hand they can also elect the representative of their national minority. Thus they assure the democratic election of their deputy in the Parliament.

In difficult situations, the deputies of the national minorities can tip the balance between the two sides. It already happened that the Hungarian representative voted with the left-wing parties, which generally support the preservation of the special rights enjoyed by the nationalities. For this reason, some of the Slovenian right-wing parties have attacked both the Hungarian parliamentary deputy and the representation system based on affirmative action.

Despite the unquestionable good will of the majority, there are deficiencies in the realization of certain minority rights. Although use of the native language is realized in administrative affairs, the posting of public signs and various areas of everyday life, the Slovenian language dominates in business matters. The bilingual school system actually is reciprocal from kindergarten to secondary school: regardless of nationality, the children of the multiethnic region attend these institutions. But the form of education that was introduced three and a half decades ago is not the most efficient; recently introduced reforms serve to strengthen education in the native language. Outside the bilingual territory, the Hungarian language may be studied as an optional subject in secondary school. Hungarian language teacher training is offered at the University of Maribor, and since the late 1970s, many students also receive degrees from higher education institutions in Hungary.

The political conditions for the preservation of the identity of Hungarians in Slovenia are stable (certainly partly because of the stringent human rights criteria that a country must meet in order to be recognized by Europe). In Slovenia, autochthonity is the criterion for the practice of territory-based special community rights.[102] The implementation of the two documents signed by the Foreign Minister of Slovenia in November 1992 is also expected to lead to a further improvement in minority conditions. On the one hand, Slovenia joined the Hungarian-Ukrainian-Croatian declaration on the protection of minorities, and on the other hand, Hungary and Slovenia signed a convention to guarantee collective rights to the Slovenian community in Hungary and the Hungarian community in Slovenia.[103] In addition to providing strong guarantees for the preservation of their identity, the document also provides guarantees in the fields of education, culture, use of native language in public, provision of information, minority research, economic development and participation in decision-making regarding issues affecting the community. The text also includes the prohibition of forceful alteration of the ethnic composition of regions inhabited by minorities. Moreover, the document provides for the establishment of an inter-governmental joint committee to deal with minority issues.

In summary, we can state that the 12,000 Hungarians of Slovenia are able to guide their own fate, and the Slovenian and Hungarian states both provide multilateral moral and material support for the preservation of their identity. In the case of the Hungarians of Slovenia, discriminating concern is necessary, for the community has reached the threshold where assimilation (albeit not forced) can be prevented only by conscious measures.

2.3 Economic Situation

As in so many other places in the Carpathian Basin, minority concerns are mainly economic. In Slovenia, as a border region, the inhabitants have complained about the relative underdevelopment for decades, the Mura region having one of the highest unemployment rates in the country. Due to a lack of professionals, the ability of the population to take full advantage of their rights is also hindered. Moreover, peripheral conditions also lead to the low quality road and railroad infrastructure. Two new border-crossing points that opened last year have given some hope of improvement in this field (and more border-crossing points are planned to be opened in the future). Moreover, the plans for the Trieste–Budapest highway and two international railways (one already built) in this region are also promising.

The Slovenian state, which became independent in 1991, had to make serious efforts in order to build up its market economy despite the fact that economically it was the most successful member of the Yugoslav Federation. But with the collapse of Yugoslavia, Slovenia had lost about 70 per cent of its markets. As a result, a large number of enterprises, including those in Muravidék, went bankrupt while unemployment rates soared and continue to do so.

Muravidék belongs to the group of relatively underdeveloped regions of Slovenia and thus has witnessed significant emigration for decades while unemployment has become increasingly distressing in recent times. A large number of ethnic Hungarians are elderly people who live in villages and cultivate the land formerly privately owned in farmers' cooperatives. The NAFTA enterprise in Lendava,[104] the most important industrial plant in the region, is struggling with serious financial problems. The fate of the enterprise, which provides employment for some 300 ethnic Hungarians, is uncertain. The share of privatized industry and trade is modest, and larger investments can hardly be expected due to the lack of capital and the underdeveloped infrastructure.

Also, due to the lack of capital, only a small number of ethnic Hungarians are able to take advantage of the preferential credit possibilities aimed at creating and supporting the economic base of the indigenous national communities because the cost of loan-related value assessment, mortgage and insurance is too high.

In the past decade, the successive opening of border-crossing points along the Hungarian–Slovenian frontier has been helping this region to catch up with developed Europe. The Slovene–Hungarian railway between Hodoš and Bajánsenye, scheduled for completion in 2002, and the planned European superhighway that would also link the two capitals aim to develop the backward infrastructure and activate cross-border economic ventures.

The governments of the two countries signed an *Agreement on Education, Cultural, and Scientific Cooperation* for 1996 to 1998. Following the preparatory work to renew the agreement, the new Agreement on Education, Cultural, and Scientific Cooperation was signed on 26 November 1999. Since 1986, an *Agreement on Cooperation* has been signed every year between the Hungarian National Self-Government Community of Muravidék and the General Assemblies of Vas and Zala Counties in Hungary. This agreement ensures cooperation opportunities in education and culture at the regional level. The Hungarian–Slovenian agreement on the mutual recognition of degrees has been signed in February 1999. The intents of Slovenia's generous minority policy—which is unique in Central Europe, in that in addition to the preservation of the democratic traditions, it also has incentives for the promotion of a national minority policy—are similar to those of Hungary's minority policy. There are almost as many ethnic Slovenes living in Hungary as ethnic Hungarians living in Slovenia, thus Slovenia's efforts also aim at setting a positive example in the treatment of its minorities.

2.4 Hungarian Self-Government of Muravidék

The Republic of Slovenia is divided into 190 communal self-governments (local authorities). On 4 December 1994, the *Act on the Self-Administration of National Communities*, which guarantees the representation of nationalities in self-governments, went into effect in Slovenia. Following the local elections held on 4 December 1994, some *Communal National Councils* were established in three Muravidék localities, namely in Lendva, Hodoš-Salovci and Muravske Toplice. The elected representatives of these councils set up the 18-member *Hungarian National Self-Administrative Community of Muravidék* (Muravidéki Magyarok Nemzeti Önigazgatási Közösség, MMNÖK). In the same election, the city of Lendava elected an ethnic Hungarian as its mayor. In the local elections held on 22 November 1998, the localities of Hodoš and Dobrovnik, which had opted for self-government in a referendum held on 19 April 1998, elected their representatives and established a nationality self-administrative council. In January 1999, MMNÖK elected its 12-member council chaired by György Tomka, while József Koczon was reelected as mayor of Lendava.

MMNÖK is the association for political representation of the Muravidék Hungarians. It created the cultural and information institutions of the Hungarians in Muravidék, and was a co-founder of the bilingual schools introduced in the area. After the 1999 elections, the MMNÖK's specialized committees (legal, information, cultural-religious, education, economic, agricultural) began to address topical problems. They paid particular attention to the preservation of the native language, national identity, and the material and intellectual heritage of the Muravidék Hungarian community, as well as to the implementation of the special rights guaranteed to minorities by the Constitution in everyday life.

On 12 July 1999, the Council of the *Hungarian National Self-Administrative Community of Muravidék* adopted new statutes and changed its name to *Hungarian Self-Government of Muravidék*. The highest decision-making body is the General Assembly of the Hungarian Self-Government of Muravidék, which has opened a self-government office.

2.5 Education and Culture

Hungarian-language education in the areas of Slovenia having a mixed population has been ensured in the form of bilingual instruction and education ranging from kindergarten to university. Bilingual instruction was introduced in primary schools in 1959. This happened because purely native-language educational institutions had become almost completely empty. Furthermore, graduates of Hungarian-language primary schools did not have the opportunity to further education because the Hungarian high schools in Vojvodina were far away while Hungary was practically sealed off from Slovenia. Bilingual education was introduced in kindergartens two years later, and in high schools starting with the school year 1981–82 under the terms of the law adopted in 1980. In this manner, Slovenia's bilingual educational system was completed.

There are four bilingual primary schools in Muravidék.[105] In bilingual primary schools, Hungarian and Slovene rank equally as languages of instruction, and both are taught at two levels: as a native language and as a second language. Hungarian-language instruction at these two levels is provided up to grade 8, while Slovene-language instruction is given at only one level from grade 5 on. Concerning the use of the two tongues as language of instruction, teachers also try to maintain in every lesson the required 50 per cent ratio for both languages. In the higher grades, this ratio is 70–30 per cent in favour of Slovene language instruction. In the school year 1998–99, a total of 1,087 students were enrolled in the four bilingual schools, and an additional 46 students attended the auxiliary school in Lendava, which also provides bilingual instruction.

The vast majority of the students who graduate from bilingual primary schools may continue their studies at the Bilingual Secondary School in Lendava, with course offerings in high school studies and vocational programs in mechanical engineering, economics and commerce. In the

1998–99 school year, 402 students were enrolled in this bilingual secondary school. There is also a growing interest in high schools located in Hungary.

During the past few years, bilingual education was criticized on many occasions, in particular with regard to the standards of the Hungarian-language instruction. In order to improve the quality of native language education, the appointment of a Hungarian school inspector is needed.

The University of Maribor has had a department for Hungarian language and literature since 1966, and since 1980, a Faculty of Hungarian Language and Literature, which trains teachers for bilingual schools. The faculty has established a close cooperation with the Dániel Bessenyei Teachers Training College in Szombathely, Hungary. There is also a Hungarian language department at the University of Ljubljana.

In 1994, the *Hungarian Cultural Institute of Muravidék* was established to group and co-ordinate the region's approximately 40 Hungarian amateur art performing groups, and to give them professional and methodological guidance.[106] The Hungarian Cultural Institute in Muravidék, besides coordinating the activities of the various cultural associations, organizes a variety of programs to keep alive the ethnic Hungarians' national consciousness. These programs include competitions and quizzes in literature and history, poetry recitals, summer camps on the knowledge of the native language and homeland, theatrical performances, puppet shows, and music and folk dance festivals. Recently, scientific activities have been enhanced, primarily in ethnography, local history, sociology and cultural history. By issuing annually some ten publications on the history, culture and ethnic studies of Slovenia's Hungarians, the Institute plays an indispensable role in redefining the Hungarian community's national self-identity.

The developments and results in the fields of culture and mass media are also remarkable. Several books on literature, local history, political science and art are published annually. Dozens of artistic groups preserve traditions in music, dance and drama, and the exceptionally beautiful scenery has inspired nine contemporary painters and sculptors; the gallery of the Lendava fort has been the location of an internationally renowned artist colony for two decades. The Catholic and Protestant dioceses are characterized by bilingualism, though practically all of the pastors are Hungarian-speaking Slovenians. A weekly paper, two literary-cultural journals, a calendar, seven to eight hours of radio programs daily, a Hungarian television studio and a local television tower that allows for better reception of Hungary's television programs all demonstrate a tolerant, and in fact supportive, national policy. Relations with the kin state have effectively functioned on the individual, municipal, regional, employment, organizational and state levels for years. The complex research that has been carried out by professionals from the Ljubljana and Budapest universities since the mid-1980s in order to uncover the diverse social relations of the minorities inhabiting both sides of the border is a unique form of contact in Europe.[107] The use of national symbols is unhindered.

3. THE HUNGARIAN COMMUNITY IN CROATIA

In December 1918, 6.5 per cent of Hungary's territory, amounting to 21,000 square kilometres, was ceded to what was soon to become the Serbo-Croatian-Slovenian monarchy. According to the 1910 census data, one-fifth of the total 577,000 ethnic Hungarian inhabitants came under the jurisdiction of Croatia and approximately one-twentieth under the jurisdiction of Slovenia, the rest becoming citizens of Serbia. According to the 1991 census data, the Hungarian minority decreased by 200,000, over one-third, and its proportion of the population also changed. Currently, only six per cent live in independent Croatia and two per cent in independent Slovenia. The population of Hungarians in Croatia decreased by four-fifths, and in Slovenia by two-thirds.[108] Now, the total assimilation of these communities can be avoided only if serious measures are undertaken.[109]

Most of the ethnic Hungarians in Croatia (representing about one-third of the total population in the region) have inhabited the northeastern corner of the territory, which had been under Serbian occupation until 1996. The territory inhabited by Hungarians specifically includes the area of the Dráva River, the Baranya Triangle (the region of Pélmonostor/Beli Manaštir)[110] and some eastern Slavonian settlements near the city of Eszék/Osijek. The rest of the ethnic Hungarian population live scattered along the Hungarian border and in large cities.

Regarding their political organization, until the eruption of the Yugoslav civil war in 1991, the Hungarians of Croatia enjoyed more freedom to nurture their national identity than did the Hungarians of Vojvodina. Since 1949, the Hungarians of Croatia have had an independent organization that has striven for a sort of minority cultural autonomy, impossible under socialist rule. Nevertheless, the Association of Hungarians in Croatia (Horvátországi Magyarok Szövetsége, HMSZ)[111] somehow attempted to address issues regarding Hungarian schools, art groups, book publishing, media, language education and relations with the kin-state (Hungary, at that time was under socialist rule as well). Its main tasks were the following:[112]

- realization of equal rights to use one's language in education, culture and public life;
- use of bilingual signs, forms, stamps and publications in official matters;
- support for fostering the native language in kindergartens as well as in elementary and specialized education, and provision of guidance for young persons to attend Hungarian-language higher education;
- development of Hungarian-language information, popularization of the *Magyar Képes Újság* (The Hungarian Pictured Newspaper) and organizing Hungarian-language book publishing;
- development of libraries in regions inhabited by Hungarians and of the central library of the Pélmonostor People's College;
- organizing exhibitions, literary productions and Hungarian film shows;
- organizing theatre guest performances and other cultural programs in the framework of inter-republic and international cooperation; moreover, organizing research excursions and visits to theatres;
- enrichment of the central dance group's equipment and provision for regular rehearsals and performances in the Hungarian-inhabited regions of Croatia and Vojvodina, as well as in Hungary;
- organizing research related to folk culture and local history, publication of research papers, and patronage of the Vörösmart (Zmajevac) museum collection.

These are not far from today's requests. However, since this association was considered unable to fulfil a political interest-protecting role, the Hungarian People's Party of Croatia (Horvátországi Magyar Néppárt, HMNP) was suddenly founded in the spring of 1990, immediately after the first multiparty elections. The central tenet of its platform was to develop the individual and community rights of the Hungarian minority, to develop rural areas and agriculture, and to make efforts in environmental protection. Nevertheless, the failure of the HMNP to become a viable organization is partially due to the eruption of the armed conflict in Yugoslavia in the summer of 1991. One of the focal points of the conflict was the Baranya region where ethnic Hungarians lived in large numbers. This war practically eliminated the institutions of the Hungarians of Croatia and forced its prominent members to flee to Hungary. These institutions are in the process of being regenerated in Hungary: the schools, a weekly paper and the cultural association have already begun to function. The psychosis resulting from life in emigration allowed previously latent contradictions to surface. The Hungarian minority has one representative of the Hungarian population in the Croatian Parliament, the *Sabor*.

The continuous aggression and terror forced a significant proportion of Hungarians in Croatia to flee to either Hungary or Western Europe. The second year of ethnic cleansing in the territory inhabited by Hungarians—territory that was proclaimed the Serbian Republic of Krajina and not recognized by any country—was carried out systematically. According to some estimates, 30,000 Serbs have been relocated in Baranya and Eastern Slavonia. The few remaining Croatian and Hungarian populations continue to experience extreme physical and psychological pressure and economic deprivation; they are either eliminated or decide to permanently leave the land of their ancestors. The functioning of Hungarian-language political, educational, cultural, religious and information-providing institutions has been made impossible under Serbian occupation. The state of the economy, infrastructure, medical provisions and telecommunications was catastrophic—and is increasingly marked by the same symptoms characteristic of the crisis in the new Yugoslavia.

It is not an exaggeration to speak of the situation of Hungarians in Croatia as one threatened by the danger of extinction. The scattered Hungarian communities lack necessary institutions and are consequently in the stages of advanced assimilation, while the communities of Hungarians living *en masse* have been destroyed by the war. (Although both the Hungarian government and the Hungarian society have exerted great sacrifices to provide for the refugees, the loss of homes, properties, possessions and lives will not be soon forgotten.)

After gaining independence, Croatia adopted a democratic Constitution and nationality law. Moreover, Croatia joined the Hungarian–Ukrainian minority-protecting declaration, and it facilitated the establishment of the Hungarian–Croatian minority joint committee in December 1992. Nevertheless, before one-third of the territory of Croatia had not regained its sovereignty, and as long as the conditions for the reestablishment of the original ethnic proportions were not present, every law and convention meant a theoretical possibility only and not a real guarantee for the protection of the identity of minorities. It was not by accident that the public figures and organizations of Zagreb, Dubrovnik and the Hungarian, Croatian and German communities of Vojvodina turned to the world in the winter of 1992–93 to request assistance against the complete elimination of the Hungarian community.[113]

The Constitutional Act on Minorities, adopted in December 1991 and amended in 1992, makes it clear that national and ethnic minorities have the right to cultural autonomy. It ensures the free use of national minority symbols, native-language education, culture, information and publishing activities, and the oral and written use of minority languages in official contacts. The law guarantees national minorities, the number of which exceeds eight per cent of the population, proportional representation in the lower chamber of Parliament. The autochthonous minorities that do not reach this threshold—among them the Hungarians—can elect one deputy each, or a total of five. For those minority communities which, based on the 1981 census, make up more than one-half the local population, the law ensures the establishment of self-governments of special status. These territorially connected villages with special basic rules may form communities based on a cooperation agreement. However, this has not happened to this day in Baranya.

In December 1991, the Republic of Croatia joined the declaration on "The principles of the cooperation between the Republic of Hungary and the Ukrainian Soviet Socialist Republic to ensure the rights of national minorities on their territory". On 16 December 1992, Hungary and Croatia signed a Treaty of Friendship and Cooperation. On 5 April 1995, the Hungarian–Croatian Treaty on Minority Protection was signed in Eszék/Osijek, followed by the setting up of the Hungarian–Croatian Joint Minority Committee in October. At its fourth session held in December 1999, the committee discussed mainly issues related to reconstruction, employment and education. In 1995, the governments of the two countries signed an *Agreement on Educational, Cultural and Scientific Cooperation*. A bilateral agreement on education and science, and a new cultural agreement were signed in April 1999 and July 1999, respectively.

The amended Croatian Constitution, which came into force on 1 January 1998, mentions by name the ethnic Hungarians and, together with other autochthonous minorities, recognizes them as state-constituent factors. In the 1995 elections, one ethnic Hungarian deputy, Sándor Jakab, vice-chairman of the Democratic Community of Hungarians in Croatia (Horvátországi Magyarok Demokratikus Közössége, HMDK), gained a seat in the lower chamber of the Sabor, the Croatian Parliament.

In the April 1997 local elections, the two competing Hungarian organizations, with the candidates of the HMDK running as independents (independent district list) and on the county list of the opposition Croatian Social Liberal Party, clearly won with 13 seats over the candidates of the Hungarian People's Party in Croatia, running a joint list with the Croatian Democratic Community (HDZ). As a result of the elections, Hungarian local representatives hold seats in the representative bodies of Hercegszöllős, Bellye and Tordinci districts. In two of these districts, the representative body elected an ethnic Hungarian as chairman.

In June 1997, the Community of Hungarian Representatives was established, made up of 13 members under the chairmanship of Tibor Szántó, who was elected a deputy later, in the parliamentary elections held on 3 January 2000, as a candidate of the HMDK.

4. AUTONOMY PLANS OF HUNGARIANS IN SLOVAKIA[114]

4.1 History and Geography

In the 8th century, the Great Moravian Empire extended its authority over parts of the western Slavic tribes who lived on the territory of present-day Slovakia. Divided by domestic conflicts, the Empire was not able to survive the attacks of the incoming Hungarian tribes who settled in the Carpathian basin. From then on, the territory north of the Danube River and bordered by the Carpathian Mountains—called in Hungarian Felvidék (Upper Region) or Upper Hungary—was part of the Kingdom of Hungary until the dissolution of the Austro-Hungarian Monarchy in November 1918. The Hungarians settled in the southern river valleys suitable for land cultivation and, starting in the 12th century, Germans moved into the cities. The Slovak population of shepherds and farmers settled in the mountainous areas and in the northern regions, blending in some places with Poles and Ruthenians. From the 16th century on, an increasing number of Hungarians fleeing from the Turks settled in the towns of Upper-Hungary along with Slovaks coming down from the mountains. After the break-up of Hungary into three parts, the capital of the Hungarian Kingdom was moved to Pozsony (Bratislava) in 1541.

As a result of the Trianon Peace Treaty (1920), Hungary ceded to Czechoslovakia an area of 61,633 km² with a total population of 3,517,568 (according to the previous census, 30.3 per cent were Hungarians, 7.4 per cent Germans, 48.2 per cent Slovaks and 12.3 per cent Ruthenians). By 1924, nearly 88,000 persons, the majority of which were dismissed Hungarian civil servants, military officers and dispossessed landowners, moved to Hungary. A network of villages inhabited by Czech and Slovak settlers was established on the estates confiscated in the course of the land reform. The administrative districts were changed on 1 January 1923. The creation of large counties and of a north-south administrative territorial division aimed to ensure that the Hungarian population would have as few areas as possible where it constitutes a majority, and thereby to eliminate the need to give them the right of native-language use. Administratively, the towns were downgraded to the status of large settlements in order to make it possible to abolish their elected self-governments.

Based on the 1991 census, the number of ethnic Hungarians in Slovakia is 567,296, however, the number of Hungarian-speaking people is somewhat larger (608,221). The ethnic Hungarians live in the unbroken southern strip of Slovakia adjacent to Hungary, stretching from Pozsony (Bratislava) to the Ukrainian border. In 523 localities, the number of Hungarians exceed 10 per cent of the population. Among these, Hungarians make up over 80 per cent of the population in 272 localities, and over 50 per cent in 150 localities. Among the districts of southern Slovakia, ethnic Hungarians constitute the majority of the population in Dunaszerdahely/Dunajská Streda (87.23 per cent) and Komárom/Komárno (72.25 per cent).

The main objectives of the Hungarian national minority in Slovakia are the preservation and development of the traditions, language and culture of the Hungarian national community through self-determination within the state borders, and the modernization of the society, economy and public administration. The Hungarians in Slovakia expressed their own political personality through the elaboration of various autonomy concepts: since 1990, the Hungarians of Slovakia have elaborated six different autonomy plans. The idea to establish an autonomous region (self-government) appeared already in 1989 as the Hungarian Independent Initiative (Független Magyar Kezdeményezés, FMK) was founded. Some months later, the 'Együttélés' Political Movement prepared a framework-document for the personal autonomy of Hungarians. The Hungarian Christian–Democratic Movement (Magyar Kereszténydemokrata Mozgalom, MKDM) also prepared a draft, accentuating local autonomy.

In the wake of the 1997 parliamentary elections, the Hungarian political organizations made a fusion under the name of Hungarian Coalition Party (Magyar Koalíció Pártja, MKP) and later, they entered the new government headed by Mikuláš Dzurinda. The issue of public administration represents a high priority for the Hungarian minority in Slovakia. The Slovakian government accepted the concept of public administration reform at its session on 26 June 1999, the essence of which is the establishment of 12 higher-level regional (county) units.[115] In the committee preparing the law, the Hungarians did not participate in spite of the fact that they have a role in government. Hungarians regard this fact as offending the principle of effective participation in public life of minorities, which is especially recommended by international documents in cases concerning decisions that fundamentally influence the life of minorities.

The MKP, as stated in its latest National Council decision, is a supporter of the public administration reform, but it insists on the establishment of a southern county that would contain the currently existing districts of Komárom, Dunaszerdahely, Galánta, Vágsellye, Érsekújvár and Léva (Szenc). Thus the MKP does not object to the public administration and country planning reform but to the fact that the '12 counties version' approved by the cabinet is contrary to the party's proposal and disregards the opinion of the MKP, that is that it rejects the establishment of a county with a Hungarian majority. On the contrary, it would carve up Southern Slovakia in a way that would violate international norms and treaties already signed by Slovakia (e.g. the Treaty between the Republic of Hungary and the Slovak Republic). The Slovakian political parties consider these plans of the Hungarian minority as the first step toward an ethnic autonomy which they cannot accept.

Another very important issue is that of the so-called 'unspecified lands' being under state administration. According to the government program, these lands should have fallen into the hands of local authorities. So far, the government has not kept this promise and it is feared that these lands will remain in state hands. The Hungarian minority is afraid that this may enable a state settlement policy in the course of which ethnic proportions may be modified to the detriment of the Hungarians in Southern Slovakia.

The majority of the Hungarian minority in Slovakia lives in agricultural areas. The proportion of those employed in agriculture is higher amongst the Hungarians than the national average. Hence, the increased interest in agricultural issues places this issue on a prominent place in the politics of the MKP.

5.   AUTONOMY PLANS OF HUNGARIANS IN THE UKRAINE[116]

Transcarpathia, where the Hungarian minority lives, was part of the Hungarian state since the 10th century. It was not, however, a homogenous historical region until the First World War. Throughout the past centuries, the population was at all times a mixed one. During the 13th century, German urban settlers and large numbers of Romanian shepherds began moving into the area. The 18th century witnessed a radical change in the region's ethnic landscape, with the Ruthenian community now making up the majority of the population while a large number of Slovaks and Jews also settled in the area. During the course of the 20th century, as a result of the frequent border changes, Transcarpathia's inhabitants successively became the citizens of five states without ever leaving their homeland. They became Czechoslovak citizens after the demise of the Austro–Hungarian Monarchy as a result of the peace treaties of Versailles, then citizens of Hungary during the Second World War, of the Soviet Union after 1945 and of the Ukraine since 1991. The various states always sought to assert the dominance of their own language and culture on the inhabitants. During the inter-war period, the Hungarians living in Transcarpathia were not able to fully exercise their rights in the civil democracy of Czechoslovakia. During this period, however, the infrastructure of Transcarpathia developed significantly, and the character of the towns changed, in particular with the construction of many public and residential buildings. During the Soviet totalitarian regime, neither the human nor the nationality rights of the region's ethnic Hungarian population were respected. Ethnic Hungarians suffered most during the Second World War and the period of reprisals that followed. Close to 25,000 of them fled to Hungary. At the end of 1944, occupying Soviet troops deported more than 25,000 men aged between 18 and 50, a third of whom never returned from the labour camps. In their place, thousands of ethnic Ukrainians and Russians were settled in cities which previously had a predominantly Hungarian population. In a region of such ethnic diversity, Hungarian culture gradually lost its leading position in the 20th century.

Based on the 1989 census, the population of the Hungarian ethnic community was 163,111. The vast majority of the Hungarian population is concentrated in an area of 12,800 km² in Transcarpathia (Kárpátalja) county. According to official data, 155,711 persons of Hungarian ethnicity live in the Beregszász (Berehove) district *(raion)* (close to 200,000 according to their own estimate), and in parts of the Ungvár (Uzhorod), Munkács (Mukačeve) and Nagyszőlős (Vinohradiv) districts. Isolated ethnic Hungarian communities inhabit the Upper-Tisza region. Ethnic Hungarians live in scattered communities in the valleys of the Upper-Borzsa (Bilke, Ilosva/Iršava), the Upper-Latorca (Szolyva /Svaljava) and the Upper-Ung (Perecsény/Perečin, Nagyberezna/Velikij Bereznij). However, 84 per cent of the Hungarian population is concentrated in a 20 km strip along the Hungarian border. Most Hungarians live in river valleys and in low lands suitable for farming. They usually reside in sparsely populated villages. Among the larger towns, Beregszász (Berehove) is the only one in which Hungarians constitute a very small majority. The Hungarian minority belongs to the Reformed Calvinist Church (100,000), to the Roman Catholic Church (65,000), to the Greek Catholic Church (30,000), and there are also about 2,000 Jews among them.

In November 1991, the Supreme Council of Ukraine adopted a Declaration on National Minorities guaranteeing to every nation and nationality group the right to equal political, economic, social and cultural development, as well as the right to use their native language in every field of social life. The Law on National Minorities adopted in June 1992 guarantees minorities the use of their native language, the right to native-language education, to establish a system of cultural institutions and to national-cultural autonomy. For the most part, the law reinforces all the principles formulated in the Hungarian-Ukrainian declaration on the protection of national minorities signed in 1991. It does not, however, allow for the creation of territorial autonomy by minorities.

After 1989, the Hungarian cultural organizations, primarily the Hungarian Cultural Federation in Transcarpathia (Kárpátaljai Magyarok Kulturális Szövetsége, KMKSZ), provided the framework for the self-organization of the Hungarian ethnic community. Consequently, during the period when the Ukraine became independent, Hungarians played a prominent role in the socio-political life of Transcarpathia and contributed decisively to the success of the local referenda on Ukrainian independence and on autonomy. The KMKSZ, established in 1989, was the first and remains to this day the biggest social interest protection organization of Transcarpathia's ethnic Hungarian community. To serve the community's long-range interests, the statutes of the Federation aim to protect the interests, preserve and cultivate the national culture and traditions, promote native-language education and instruction, ensure the collective rights and shape the national consciousness of Transcarpathia's Hungarians. The program of the KMKSZ sets as a goal the establishment of national minority self-administration, the creation of nationality self-government or territorial autonomy.

As a result of the uncertain situation prevailing in the Ukraine, however, the Hungarian organizations have not been able to achieve any significant success so far in this area. The creation of various forms of autonomy figures among the long-term goals of the Hungarian organizations, but they have different concepts about how to achieve this objective. The KMKSZ has worked out a draft for the establishment and functioning of a national, cultural self-government.

In December 1991, along with the referendum held on Ukrainian independence, two local referenda were held in Transcarpathia: one on the self-government for the region, and the other in the Beregszász district on the establishment of an Autonomous Hungarian District. Even though the vast majority of the population (78 per cent) supported both, the draft bills on Transcarpathia's self-government status and on the Hungarian Nationality District of Beregszász prepared in the wake of the referenda were not accepted at higher governmental levels. In 1993, the Territorial

Council of Transcarpathia had prepared a draft and sent it to the Parliament in Kiev, which has not discussed it yet. A general problem is that the institutional framework of law enforcement and legal competencies have not been properly outlined because of political uncertainty and the frequent modifications of legal regulations.

On 17 December 1992, the representative of the Ukrainian President in Transcarpathia issued a decree on the practical implementation of the Ukrainian language law and of the law on national minorities. The decree stipulates that wherever a national minority constitutes the majority of the population, the language of that national minority may also be used along the Ukrainian state language in state and social organizations, enterprises and institutions. Under the terms of this decree, bilingual signs may be used and national minorities may use their own symbols in addition to state symbols.

The laws and regulations affecting self-governments have been changed and amended several times. In July 1995, the county and local administrations were centralized, thereby transferring the rights of the self-governments to the state administration. Ukraine became a member of the Council of Europe in 1995. At the time of its admission to the organization, it made a commitment to study the European Charter on Local Self-Governments and the European Charter on Regional or Minority Languages for the purpose of their ratification. It further pledged to sign and ratify within one year after its admission to the Council the Framework Convention for the Protection of National Minorities, and to pursue a national minority policy on the basis of the principles laid down in Recommendation 1201 of the Parliamentary Assembly of the Council of Europe.

In December 1999, it submitted a proposal for the creation, in accord with Ukrainian laws, of an *autonomous Hungarian public administration unit* which would include all the compact ethnic Hungarian communities in Transcarpathia, with Beregszász as its seat. The ethnic Hungarians of Transcarpathia are concerned about the possibility that following Hungary's accession to the European Union, it will become more difficult to maintain contacts with the kin-state. Many of them even fear the erection of a new iron curtain at the Hungarian–Ukrainian border. For this reason, they urge Budapest to work out in time some sort of acceptable solution for the ethnic Hungarians living in the neighbouring countries which have fallen behind in the European integration process in order to facilitate their travelling to Hungary. It is with this objective in mind that the KMKSZ (as a participant in the Hungarian Standing Conference) is urging that the Hungarian Parliament adopt a special law on the legal status in Hungary of the ethnic Hungarians living on the territory of Hungary's neighbours.

The Hungarian organizations in Transcarpathia feel that in the last two to three years, there has been a change for the worse in the previously positive minority policy of Ukraine. Measures by local and central authorities aimed at restricting the rights of nationalities, which first appeared gradually and were barely visible, are now appearing in more concrete form in connection with the growth and consolidation of Ukraine's nationalistic institutions of power. Kiev explains that the restrictions imposed on the rights of the nationalities living in the Ukraine and the country's failure to fulfil its obligations accepted in international agreements by saying that the state lacks money to satisfy the demands of the minorities. Until 1999, the Ukrainian state provided no financial support to either the Hungarian or other minority organizations operating in the country. Under the regulations currently in force, minority organizations do not receive any financial support subsidies but may submit applications for the financing of concrete events and programs. The financing of education, however, remains the task of the state, which has resulted in a contradictory situation regarding minority educational institutions.

6.   AUTONOMY PLANS OF HUNGARIANS IN ROMANIA

The Constitution adopted in 1991 and confirmed by a referendum declares Romania to be a nation-state where the official language is Romanian. The Constitution lays down several fundamental minority rights, such as the right of ethnic identity, the right of native-language education, the right of parliamentary representation, and the right to use the native language in court proceedings. However, the use of these minority rights is not sufficiently guaranteed in practice due to inadequate legal regulations.

Since 1991, Romania's national minorities have been calling for the adoption of a *minority law*. The political representation of the Hungarian national community—the Democratic Alliance of Hungarians in Romania (Romániai Magyarok Demokratikus Szövetsége, RMDSZ)—submitted the text of a concrete draft in 1993. The government of that time failed to deal with the proposal despite the fact that upon Romania's admission to the Council of Europe in 1993, the Council's Parliamentary Assembly stipulated such an obligation, which Romania promised to fulfil.

The public administration law adopted in 1994, making the exclusive use of the Romanian language mandatory, represents a setback compared to the situation during the Ceausescu era. The Ciorbea government's emergency Decree 22 of 1997 modified it in principle, allowing the use of national minority languages in public administration (posting of bilingual road signs, for example) in settlements where minorities exceed 20 per cent of the population. However, the implementation of this government decree was long hindered and could not been elevated to the status of law by the Parliament in the period between 1996 and 2000. The public administration law was one of the first laws adopted by the new parliament, elected in 2000.

The education law, which came into force in 1995, legalized the supremacy of the Romanian majority language and culture, restricting the possibilities for native language and church education. The government's emergency Decree 36 of 1997 did remove the anti-minority provisions of the education law, but the new education law passed in 1999 based on that decree includes numerous restrictions in the sphere of minority language education. For example, it does not allow for the re-establishment of an independent, state-funded, Hungarian-language university for the Hungarian national community.

The basic objectives of the RMDSZ are the preservation and development of the traditions, language and culture of the Hungarian national community in Romania through internal determination, and the overall modernization of the society, economy and public administration. The RMDSZ declared wishing to achieve its goals by establishing and consolidating its own educational, cultural and other institutions guaranteeing the preservation of its self-identity. It firmly believes that the problems of the minority community can be solved only within a democratic and lawful framework.

The results of the 1996 elections created a new situation[117] for the Hungarian community in Romania. The participation of its political organization in the government coalition offered new, previously untested opportunities. By coming into a position of political power, the Alliance could participate in the management of the country and attempt to achieve its goals with increased chances of success. The acceptance of the responsibility of coalition governance represents in several respects progress for the Hungarians. The government program, adopted as a result of a compromise, includes (directly or indirectly) important objectives of the RMDSZ such as decentralization, the application of international legal rules and the appropriate modification of the domestic legislation, native language education at the professional and university levels, and adaption of a law on minorities and church affairs.

In proportion to its participation in the coalition government, the RMDSZ has been given important positions in the central and local administrations. After the 1998 cabinet changes, the Alliance again appointed two ministers (health and minority affairs) and six secretaries of state (state council, government secretariat, regional planning, culture, education and agriculture). It also gained essential positions in several central state institutions and has got two posts of prefect, eight deputy prefects and five prefecture directors in county public administration, and held leading positions in county institutions subordinate to the government.

However, these results constitute only the framework that gives ethnic Hungarians in Romania the opportunity to fulfil their rightful needs and aspirations. Obtaining a role in the government represented a step forward in several respects, but in crucial issues (such as the obligations undertaken in the Romanian government program) only partial results have been achieved. In addition, the free use of the mother tongue in public administration and in court and bilingualism in public life and notices is still being hindered. In fact, no education law has been passed. The discriminative education law has been amended, but it still fails to enable the creation of an independent Hungarian state-financed university. The return of church and community property confiscated by the communist regime to their former owners has not taken place. No minority law has been passed.

The RMDSZ achieved significant results in the local elections in June 2000 and consolidated its positions in the local and county authorities. Through the mandates of its county representatives, it became Transylvania's strongest political formation. At the same time, they had sensitive defeats, losing the seat of mayor in Marosvásárhely (Tirgu Mures).

International and bilateral agreements signed by Romania can only partially substitute for the shortcomings of domestic legislation. Among the Council of Europe's documents on minority protection, Romania ratified the Framework Convention for the Protection of National Minorities in 1997, while the ratification of the European Charter for Regional or Minority Languages, signed by Romania in the same year, is still under way. The 1996 Romanian–Hungarian State Treaty lays down the rights needed to protect minority identity and the general principles of related state policy policies. It also validates additional international documents, such as the 1992 United Nations Declaration on the Rights of National or Ethnic, Religious, and Linguistic Minorities, the Copenhagen Document adopted by the Conference on Security and Cooperation in Europe and Recommendation 1201 (1993) of the Council of Europe's Parliamentary Assembly. Even though the Constitution stipulates that international documents signed and ratified by Romania take precedence over domestic laws, their implementation in practice is contradictory and the exercise of the rights contained in these documents is often not possible.

The government that took office in 1996 undoubtedly inherited severe difficulties, primarily of an economic nature. The political parties attach particular importance to the handling of social tensions and regard the minority issue as a secondary question. For historical, emotional and existential reasons, ethnic Hungarians in Romania today feel these problems more intensely and do not consider them as merely of an economic nature. During the current period, the Hungarian community must exercise patience twofold and maintain its trust both in the government and in its own interest protection organization. While it mostly accepts the handling of general economic problems, it has more doubts about the resolution of minority concerns, the latter because of the experiences of not merely 5 but 75 years.

6.1 The Autonomy Plans

The Hungarians in Romania have been striving to express their own political personality through the elaboration of several autonomy concepts. Thus, for them autonomy does not only mean an abstract legal notion but their future, for which it would be worth to stay where they were born, in equality and democracy, after such a long time of oppression.

The idea to establish a self-government appeared already in 1989 when the RMDSZ was founded. Since 1990, the Hungarians of Romania have elaborated about seven different autonomy drafts. One of the key elements of their existence and future in Romania was the elaboration of autonomy drafts and their approval or adoption by the Romanian political elite. This was seen by the Hungarian community as the unique opportunity to make their voice heard and to participate in decisions in matters concerning them.

One of the first 'experiments' were the Autonomy Statutes elaborated by RMDSZ-senator József Csapó, followed by the proposals of Miklós Bakk or the Minority Law by former senator Géza Szőcs, in which he sketched the functional organization of personal autonomy. The most important in the Alliance's autonomy program is the claim for financial autonomy for local communities and public administration. In the authors' view, this could be assured by the enactment of laws regulating the situation of national minorities and which would ensure the free use of the mother tongue in private and public life and in legal matters, the establishment of an independent native language school system on each level and in every form run by the minorities, the establishment of an independent system of cultural institutions, and freedom to maintain contacts and exchange information with the kin state. All of these autonomy drafts evoked negative reactions on the Romanian side.

One may outline three stages in the evolution of the autonomy concepts of the RMDSZ. The first, from 1990 to 1993, could be described as the beginning of the elaboration and as the organizational development, under president Géza Domokos.

The second stage began with the Third Congress of the RMDSZ held in December 1993 in Braşov and ended with the 1996 elections when RMDSZ was invited to the government. In 1993, a political struggle began for the implementation of the autonomy concept. The then RMDSZ was in opposition in the Parliament of Romania, but its parliamentary group began to gain an increasing political influence as the RMDSZ-faction participated in all the internal political and professional debates that affected the citizens of Romania. They did not refer merely to issues regarding only the Hungarian community in Romania. That was the time when the civic society began to separate and differentiate itself from the political scene.

The third stage began in 1996 when the RMDSZ became a member of the governing coalition and had to accept pragmatic compromises. Contrary to the previously generally accepted status of a minority protection union, the RMDSZ then began to behave as a political party.

7. CONCLUSIONS

As we can see, in the relations between states and minorities, often the nation-state perceives the minority's presence as a threat. Since the state identifies itself with the majority and vice-versa, the majority is striving to identify itself with the state and its symbols.

Although the situation of the Hungarian communities varies from one region (or country) to another, there is a common feature in their claims: the *refusal of secession* and the *claim for autonomy*. This is a most delicate issue in the relations between minorities and states, although several examples of minority governance can be found in Europe. As each minority has particular characteristics, one cannot say that there exists any standard for resolving the specific problems appearing in different national contexts.

If we take into account the numerical and political importance of the Hungarian minorities and the complexity of the geopolitical situations that each of them could imply, these minorities form a very rich ensemble and an exceptional field of study for the question of national minorities in Europe. Departing from the idea that Hungarian minorities live in a geographic area that encircles Hungary, we must remark that this is a rather exceptional case. Even if the situation is comparable with the situation of some other minorities in Europe (Albanians, Serbs, Russians, Romanians, Germans, etc.), the conflict between the Hungarian minorities and the states they live in does not imply any open conflict (except for some unique and isolated local ones). Since the battle for maintaining their identity is conducted only on political and cultural level, the only 'arms' they have are political representation (impossible before the democratic changes of 1989–90) and cultural solidarity.

The minority's autonomy (self-government) is one of those political conditions of which the existence or lack can influence the chances of survival of these communities. Our approach assumes the recognition of the fact that the real protection of minorities can only be ensured within a democratic framework. In a well-functioning democracy, with the help of the principle of subsidiarity, the local and regional authorities enjoy a wide degree of autonomy in matters concerning the population under their jurisdiction.

There is a classical European example in Central Europe: the case of South Tyrol, as this region has a special status within Italy, a cultural and territorial autonomy. For the Hungarian minorities, this is a very good analogy since the German-speaking minority of South Tyrol became a minority in the same period as the Hungarians, immediately after the First World War.

A concrete plan in this field is the autonomy-plan elaborated by the Hungarians of Vojvodina (Serbia), which was later considered and adopted by both the Hungarians of Romania and Slovakia. This plan described the possibility of an autonomy structure on three levels, perfectly feasible and in harmony with the European norms, also recommended by several documents of the Council of Europe and OSCE. This meant practically:

1) *personal autonomy*, formulated as self-administration and self-management (government) of the national minorities;

2) *local self-administration with special status* on territories where there is a sizeable national minority population. They should have a special status concerning language use in the local administration, at the juridical instances and other authorities (in order to maintain the national language and identity). This type of autonomy with special status was projected in the Vance-Owen or Carrington plans (for Bosnia-Herzegovina);

3) the third level should be the *classical territorial autonomy*, since it is also remarkable that the local autonomy with a special status is, in fact, a territory-based autonomy.

Coming to a conclusion, we must note that, in fact, there is only one functioning minority self-government for the Hungarian communities, that of Slovenia. The structure and the powers given to the Hungarian minority in Slovenia do not follow any general pattern, but so far it can be described as a flourishing exception and an example for other Hungarian minority communities. In the next lines, we will try to summarize the main characteristics of the cultural autonomy of the Hungarians in Slovenia:

- in the territories inhabited by the Hungarian minority, the Hungarian language is on equal grounds with the Slovenian language;
- native language education, media, book publication and other cultural practices are guaranteed;
- relations among the minorities and between the minorities and their mother countries are supported;
- nationality symbols can be used freely;
- members of the Hungarian national minority community may establish cultural and educational self-governing interest associations for the realization of the above-delineated rights.

Moreover, the Hungarian community has a separate electoral district and thus generally succeeds in delegating a representative to the Slovenian parliament. Not every citizen of the multiethnic territory may vote for the nationality representative: since 1992, only the minorities have been allowed to vote. This minority self-government could be envied by other Hungarian communities.

NOTES

95 According to Article 6 (3) of the Constitution, "The Republic of Hungary feels responsible for the well-being of the Hungarians abroad and facilitates their relations with Hungary...".

96 Other members are the British Conservatives, the French RPR, the German CDU, etc.

97 Some statistical data: Area: 20,251 km², total population: 2,000,000. Ethnic Groups: Slovenes 90.5%, Croats 2.9%, Serbs 2.2%, Bosnians 0.7%, Hungarians 0.5%, Italians 0.3%, others 2.9%. Religions: Roman Catholic (90%), Muslim (0.7%), other (9.3%). Official Language: Slovene; Italian and Hungarian in the areas declared bilingual (Koper, Piran, Portorož on the Adriatic coast, and 33 localities between Muraszombat (Murška Sobota) and Alsólendva (Lendava), respectively). GDP per capita: 9,864 USD, Inflation: 7.9%. Unemployment: 7.9% (1998, ILO). Total foreign investment: 2.2 billion USD (1997). Foreign debt: 4.9 billion USD.

98 Muravidék is the Hungarian name for the *Prekomurje* region of Slovenia, literally meaning the region of the river Mura.

99 These localities are: Dobronak (Dobrovnik), Zsitkóc (Žitkovci), Kámaháza (Kamovci), Göntérháza (Genterovci), Radamos (Radmožanci), Hidvég (Mostje), Bánuta (Banuta), Hosszúfalu (Dolga Vas), Hosszúfaluhegy (Dolgovaske Gorice), Lendva (Lendava), Lendvahegy (Lendavske gorice), Alsólakos (Dolnji Lakoš), Felsőlakos (Gornji Lakoš), Gyertyános (Carpinis), Kapca, Kót (Kot), Csente (Čentiba), Petesháza (Petišovci), Hármasmalom (Trimlini), Völgyifalu (Dolina pri Lendavi) and Pince. These localities were part of Zala County in Hungary prior to 1918 and between 1941 and 1945.

100 For more details see András Bertalan, Székely *A Rábától a Muráig. Nemzetiségek egy határ két oldalán* (Budapest, Püski, 1992), pp.101–113.

101 Out of seven candidates, Mária Pozsonec, who was both supported by political parties and running as an independent, won in the Hungarian-inhabited Mura region.

102 On the differential treatment of 'guest worker' immigrants and the autochtonous Serb and German minority populations, see Imre Szilágyi, "Kisebbségi politika—kisebbségi lét Szlovéniában", in *Társadalmi Szemle* 47 (1992) 6, pp.54–59.

103 "Convention on the Guarantee of Special Rights for the Slovenian National Minority Living in the Republic of Hungary and the Hungarian National Community Living in the Republic of Slovenia", in *Dunatáji Figyelő* 1, 2–3, (November–December 1992), pp.11–13.

104 For example, there were 2,658 registered jobless in Lendava (September 1999), representing 22% of the population able of work, while the total population of Lendava is 12,083.

105 In Lendava, Göntérháza (Genterovci), Dobronak (Dobrovnik) and Pártosfalva (Prosenjakovci).

106 Among the Hungarian associations in scattered communities, the *Sándor Petőfi Society of Ljubljana* and the *Mátyás Society of Nova Gorica* deserve mention.

107 The results of the research have been published in both countries: *Madzari in Slovenci. Sodelovanje in sozitje ob jugoslovansko–madzarski meji* (Ljubljana: Institut za narodnostna vprasanja, 1987), p.618 and *Magyarok és szlovének I-II. Együttélésük és együttműködésük a jugoszláv–magyar határ mentén* (Budapest: Állami Gorkij Könyvtár, 1987), p.739.

108 For more details see Károly Kocsis and Eszter Hódosi–Kocsis, *Magyarok a határainkon túl—a Kárpát-medencében* (Budapest: Tankönyvkiadó, 1992), p.66.

109 For more details see András Bertalan, Székely, "Etnikai folyamatok déli határaink mentén", in *Magyar Szemle*, new series 2 (1992), 2, pp.308–312.

110 Regarding demographic processes in the twentieth century, see György Éger, Rudolf Joó and András Bertalan Székely, Egy horvát–magyar közös nemzetiségkutatás néhány településszociológiai tapasztalata, in *Magyar Tudomány*, 96, 22–26.

111 Known as the Hungarian Cultural and Educational Federation of Croatia until 1969.

[112] Ferenc Merki, "A Horvátországi Magyarok Szövetségének szerepe művelődési életünk fejlesztésében", in *Horvátországi Magyarok Szövetsége Évkönyv 1* (Osijek: HMSZ, 1979), pp.149–151.

[113] József Botlik, "A horvátországi magyarok segélykiáltása: Folytatódik az etnikai tisztogatás", in *Magyar Nemzet*, 13 January 1993, p.5.

[114] Some statistical data: Area: 49,000 km², Total population: 5,274,335 (1991 census), Ethnic groups: Slovaks 86.6%, Hungarians 10.76%, Gypsies 1.44%, Czechs 1%, Ruthenes 0.33%, Ukrainians 0.25%, Religions: Roman Catholic (60.4%), Lutheran (6.2%), Greek Catholic (3.4%), Reformed/Calvinist (1.6%), Greek Orthodox (0.6%), Baptist (0.1%). Spoken languages: Slovak (official state language), Hungarian, Czech, Ukrainian, Ruthenian. GDP per capita: approximately USD 3,500, inflation rate: 13.6%, external debt: USD 11 billion, unemployment rate: 19.1%, total foreign capital investment: USD 1,875,000 (until August 1999).

[115] At the moment, Slovakia is divided into 8 regions: Pozsony (Bratislava), Nagyszombat (Trnava), Trencsén (Trenčín), Nyitra (Nitra), Zsolna (Žilina), Besztercebánya (Banská Bystrica), Eperjes (Prešov), Kassa (Košice), and 79 districts.

[116] Some statistical data: Area: 603,700 km², Total population: 49,900,000 (1999 census), Ethnic groups: Ukrainian (72.7%), Russian (22.1%), Jewish (0.9%), Belorussian (0.9%), Moldavian (0.6%), Bulgarian (0.5%), Polish (0.4%), Hungarian (0.3%), Romanian (0.3%), Crimean Tatar (0.1%). Religions: Ukrainian Orthodox, Ukrainian Greek Catholic, Roman Catholic, Jewish, Islamic. Languages spoken: Ukrainian (state language), Russian and others. GDP per capita: approximately USD 600, GDP annual growth rate: –3% (1999). Inflation rate: 19.2% (January 2000). Foreign debt: USD 11.470 billion. Unemployment: 4% (estimated figure: 20.0%). Amount of unpaid salaries: 7.0 billion Hrivna (USD1.8 billion). Total foreign capital investment: USD 2.815 billion.

[117] In the 1996 parliamentary elections, the UDMR ended up in the fourth place. With a total of 812,653 votes, it obtained 25 mandates (7.24%) in the 343-seat Chamber of Deputies, and with 836,790 votes, 11 mandates (7.69%) in the 143-seat Senate, respectively. In the 1996 municipal elections, the Hungarian community had overall 177 mayors (6.44%), 2,640 local councillors (6.61%) and 137 county councillors (7.97%).

271

Chances for Ethnic Autonomy in Vojvodina: Analysis of the Latest Autonomy Proposal of Hungarian Political Parties in Vojvodina

Tamás Korhecz

Chances for Ethnic Autonomy in Vojvodina: Analysis of the Latest Autonomy Proposal of Hungarian Political Parties in Vojvodina

Tamás Korhecz

1. INTRODUCTION

In the early nineties, political representatives of the Hungarian minority in Vojvodina presented their first concept of autonomy. In the meantime, several other proposals have emerged in public, prepared partly by the various Hungarian minority parties, partly by other regional political parties and movements. The common denominator of all proposals is their ultimate failure, as the Milošević regime rejected them all without discussion.

This study does not seek to decide whether the ethnic-based autonomy or minority self-governance (these phrases will be used as synonyms) is a justified and legitimate means from the standpoint of political theory or philosophy. However, this analysis presupposes that minority self-governance is at least one acceptable, legitimate and just option to be considered for multiethnic societies.

The present study wishes to describe and critically evaluate the most recent, adjusted autonomy concept of the Hungarian political parties in Vojvodina. Besides the interpretation and normative analysis of the text of the autonomy proposal, it will try to determine some factors and conditions on which the success or the failure of the concept, and of minority autonomy in Vojvodina generally, depends.

A short introductory part on the history, demography and minority question in Vojvodina is followed by a discussion of the autonomy of Vojvodina according to the 1974 Constitution and of its current position. In part three, the Agreement on the Political and Legal Frameworks of the Self-Government of Vojvodina and the National Communities of Vojvodina (hereinafter 'Agreement on Self-Government') will be analyzed. The chapter concludes with an analysis of factors and conditions determining the prospects of the Agreement on Self-Government of the Hungarians' autonomy in Vojvodina.

1.1 On the History, Demography and the Minority Question in Vojvodina

The Autonomous Province of Vojvodina (APV), until 1990 the Socialist Autonomous Province of Vojvodina (SAPV), in the northern part of the Federal Republic of Yugoslavia (FRY) and the Republic of Serbia (RS) with its colourful national (ethnic) composition is almost unique in Europe. Vojvodina comprises approximately 20 per cent of the 21.5 square kilometre territory and 19.3 per cent of the population (2.01 million) of the Federal Republic of Yugoslavia (FRY). The 'breadbasket' of Yugoslavia is the most developed part of the FRY,[118] with the lowest rate of illiteracy.[119] In such a relatively small territory various autochthonous national communities have lived side by side for centuries. According to the 1991 census, alongside the Serbs (1,143,723) a substantial number of Hungarians (339,491), Croats (74,808), Slovaks (63,545), Ruthenians (17,652), Rumanians (38,809), Roma (24,366) and Germans (3,873)[120] live in the APV. The largest minority community, the Hungarian, is an autochthonous minority in Vojvodina that has lived for more than a thousand years in this part of the Carpathian basin. This national community speaks the Hungarian language as their first language, and it is culturally part of the Hungarian nation. Its area of settlement consists of a block of neighbouring municipalities alongside the Hungarian border and river Tisza[121]—partly dispersed on isles of settlements with a local Hungarian majority and partly in settlements together with the Serb majority.

The unique ethnic diversity of Vojvodina dates back to the time of Turkish invasion and the multiethnic post-Turkish resettlement of Vojvodina—which was part of the Hungarian Kingdom from its establishment until the Turkish conquest. In 1920, with the Trianon Peace Treaty—under the umbrella of the self-determination of nations—the territory was seized by the newly established Kingdom of Serbs, Croats and Slovenes, despite the fact that South-Slavs together comprised only a minority of the population.[122] Subsequently, as a result of different organized settlement of Serbs in Vojvodina, and the expulsion of the large German population in 1945, Serbs constituted the majority of the population in Vojvodina. After new waves of Serb refugees arrived in Vojvodina in the nineties, their percentage of the population climbed to over 60 per cent.[123]

With different contents, the notion of autonomous Vojvodina has existed for more than one and a half centuries. In the nineteenth century 'autonomous Vojvodina' covered the claims of the Serbs in south Hungary for the territorial autonomy in a Serb Voivodeship;[124] later it evolved in a struggle for regional autonomy within different South-Slav states.

2. AUTONOMY OF VOJVODINA ACCORDING TO THE 1974 CONSTITUTION AND ITS CURRENT POSITION

2.1 Minority Autonomy or Federal Unit—Vojvodina until 1989

Vojvodina gained its autonomy after the Second World War. Alongside the second Serbian province of Kosovo, the autonomy of Vojvodina was gradually enlarged with constitutional reforms in 1953, 1963, 1974 and 1981. Consequently, Vojvodina and Kosovo were almost given equality with the six federal republics of the former Socialist Federal Republic Yugoslavia (SFRY). This process was ended by the Milošević era, when the autonomy of provinces was diminished by extra-constitutional means, such as mass demonstrations and police power.

According to the 1974 Constitutions of the SFRY, the Socialist Republic of Serbia (SRS) and the Socialist Autonomous Province of Vojvodina (SAPV) Vojvodina has substantial legislative,[125] judicial, and executive powers, its own legislature, government (Executive Council), Presidency, Supreme Court, Provincial police, National Bank, etc., similar to all other Yugoslav Republics. It is not clear whether until 1990 Vojvodina was an autonomous province or a federal unit.

Various authors have offered definitions of autonomy. Lapidoth defined political autonomy as follows: "Territorial political autonomy is an arrangement aimed at granting to a group that differs from the majority in a specific region, a means by which it can express its distinct identity".[126] Hannum's definition also stresses the connection between autonomy and the identity of national minorities. He defines autonomy as "a right to be different and to be left alone; to preserve, protect, and promote values which are beyond the legitimate reach of the rest of society".[127] H.J. Steiner provides a more general definition of autonomy for national minorities as "[a] governmental system or subsystems administered or staffed by a minority of its members".[128]

All three authoritative definitions, notwithstanding their differences emphasize that autonomy is genuinely connected with national minorities and their right and powers to preserve their identity. Bearing in mind these characteristics (and notions) of autonomy, one can raise the question whether the SAPV until 1990 was autonomous in the real meaning of the word. There are at least three grounds on which one could defend the position that the SAPV was not an autonomous province, but rather a federal unit. Firstly, as a result of the expulsion of the large German minority from Vojvodina and Yugoslavia since 1945, and the organized settlement of Bosnian and Croatian Serbs to their stead, ethnic Serbs and Montenegrins make up the absolute majority of the population in Vojvodina. Therefore, one can plausibly argue that the autonomy of Vojvodina was not an autonomy of or for any national minorities in Vojvodina but the autonomy of Serbs living in Vojvodina. Moreover, the origin of the idea of 'Serb Vojvodina' is deeply connected with the struggle of the Serbs in South-Hungary for self-government within Austria-Hungary. Secondly, the lack of a representative government, separation of powers, plural elections and civil rights along with the presence of the almighty Communist Party Committees are all factors which might undermine and disqualify the legal and constitutional arrangements that have formally established and guaranteed the autonomy of the SAPV within Serbia and Yugoslavia. Finally, one may argue that the SAPV was a federal unit of Serbia and Yugoslavia, without explicit recognition of its status. According to Article 427 of the 1974 Constitution of the SRS, consent of the Assemblies of the SAPV and Kosovo was inevitable for amending the Constitution of the SRS. Furthermore, the same consent of the provinces was required for the amendment of the federal Constitution.[129] Provincial legislatures elected their representatives to the Federal Assembly and the Presidency[130] as well. If we accept that some authors, like King, take the above-mentioned characteristics as core elements which divide federations and unitary states, the SAPV could be considered a member state of both federal Serbia and federal Yugoslavia, rather than an autonomous province.

2.2 Upheaval of the Old System by the Milošević Regime and the Present Position of the Autonomous Province of Vojvodina

In late 1987, Slobodan Milošević won a narrow victory at the VIII Conference of the Alliance of the Communists of Serbia and began a nationalist campaign against the 1974 constitutional system accusing it of being 'anti-Serb', 'federalising Serbia' and 'providing too many rights for minorities'. The Serb Communist Party launched a populist campaign against the provincial Communist leaderships in Vojvodina and Kosovo. The Vojvodina leadership swiftly crashed under the wave of well-organized nationalist demonstrations of the so called 'anti-bureaucratic' or 'Yoghurt revolution'.[131] Milošević then replaced the old 'autonomous' leadership with nationalist leaders. The new Vojvodina leadership unanimously backed the amendment of the Serbian Constitution, which suspended all relevant powers of the provinces and provided for an extremely centralized state.

277

According to the 1990 Constitution of the Republic of Serbia, Serbia has two autonomous provinces, the Autonomous Province of Vojvodina and the Autonomous Province of Kosovo. Besides this formal recognition, though, the two provinces have few substantial powers, and they completely lost all their legislative and judicial powers.[132] Since 1990, the provincial assembly and authorities were established only in Vojvodina, while in Kosovo they were not even formally established. The best way to demonstrate the level of autonomy of the APV is to look at its annual budget. In 2000, the overall budget of the APV is less than 3 million USD, which is below the similar budget of the municipality of Subotica, and it primarily covers the costs of the Assembly and the salaries of the employees in the provincial administration.[133] The APV has its statute,[134] previously called the Constitution, which lays down the powers of the province defined in the Serbian constitution. The powers of the APV guaranteed in the 1990 Serbian Constitution were often neglected by Serbian laws and regulations, leaving no space for provincial legislation and administration.[135]

3. THE VOJVODINA AGREEMENT ON SELF-GOVERNMENT

3.1 Introductory Remarks

In 1990, the united and at that time only Hungarian political party in Yugoslavia, the Democratic Alliance of Hungarians in Vojvodina (Vajdasági Magyarok Demokratikus Szövetésge, VMDSZ), openly advocated different forms of autonomy and self-government as the best solution for the preservation of the identity and rights of Hungarians in Vojvodina. In 1992, the same party prepared its concept of Hungarian autonomy, which combined ethnic-based territorial and personal autonomy with wide powers and authorities. The concept was neglected by the ruling Serbian political powers as well as by the opposition and the international community. In 1993, a process of division and polarization unsettled the VMDSZ. The party, which was able to successfully collect the majority of the Hungarian votes in different elections between 1990 and 1993[136] was not able to overcome the rivalries among their leaders. In 1994, the majority of the federal and republican deputies, local politicians and mayors, etc., established the Vojvodina Alliance of Hungarians (Vajdasági Magyarok Szövetsége, VMSZ). Following the split into the VMDSZ and the VMSZ, four more minor political parties emerged. The Hungarian political parties fought each other in three elections, practically without forming coalitions: in 1996 (federal, provincial and municipal elections), 1997 (republican), and 2000 (federal, provincial and municipal elections). In all elections the VMSZ was the most successful party, winning the majority of seats in several municipalities and in provincial, republican and federal assemblies. Notwithstanding the notorious rivalry and lack of cooperation, almost all Hungarian political parties unanimously advocate the self-governance of the Hungarian national minority in Yugoslavia and have prepared their proposals toward this end. The space and aim of this study does not allow for elaboration of these documents, but they all argue for a kind of ethnic self-government, and decentralization in the areas of mother tongue education, media and official use of the mother tongue. In other words, political representatives of the Hungarian minority in Vojvodina unanimously claim a form of self-governance and decision-making in areas which are decisive for the preservation of the specific identity of the minority. Finally, in 1998 and 1999 on the initiative of the Hungarian government, the Hungarian minority political parties began consultations in order to reach a consensus and to adjust a united autonomy proposal. The basis of the above-mentioned Agreement on Self-Government was the autonomy proposal of the VMSZ, which was modified upon the proposals and amendments of other political parties. Finally, three Hungarian political parties (Vojvodina Alliance of Hungarians—VMSZ; Democratic Community of Hungarians in Vojvodina, Vajdasági Magyarok Demokratikus Közössége—VMDK; and the Civil Movement of Hungarians in Vojvodina, Vajdasági Magyarok Polgári Mozgalma—VMPM), which can be said to represent the majority of the Hungarian political corpus in Vojvodina, reached an agreement.

3.2 Description of the Major Parts of the Document

The following section summarizes the most important solutions and provisions of the Agreement on Self-Government, primarily focusing on three complementary forms of autonomy (Hungarian personal autonomy, Hungarian territorial autonomy and the autonomy of Vojvodina).

3.2.1   List of Rights

The first part of the document contains a long list of rights of the Hungarian minority community.[137] The official use of the Hungarian language is proposed in all municipalities where Hungarians constitute at least five per cent of the population or in any settlement with 500 ethnic Hungarians. The official use of the Hungarian language in these places entails the right to apply to and receive a reply from all "organs of power and public offices", to have a judicial and administrative procedure conducted in the Hungarian language "at the request of either party", bilingual public signs, the use of personal names in official documents according to the "rules of the Hungarian language" and the publication of all laws and regulations in Hungarian. The Agreement includes the right to mass media in the Hungarian language including "the foundation and management of media organizations" by the minority community. Right to mother tongue education at all levels, including the authority for the Hungarian National Council (Magyar Nemzeti Tanács, MNT) to determine the curricula of those "school subjects, which affect the preservation of national identity". There is also the right to use national symbols alongside "the state symbols of Serbia and Yugoslavia" the right to maintain "contact, without interference, with national communities of the same kin outside" the FRY, and the "protection of monuments and memorial sites" of the national community. Finally, the Agreement establishes the right of the Hungarian community to "the proportional representation in the state organs and administration".

This part of the Agreement also contains a declaratory provision on funding, which provides for the proportional funding of the cultural, media, and educational institutions of the Hungarian community, i.e. 17 per cent (corresponding to the proportion of Hungarians in Vojvodina) of the budgetary funds for these purposes shall be guaranteed for minority institutions.

The proposed list of community rights is not a novelty in many respects. For example, some rights mentioned are already recognized by the constitution of the FRY (such as the right to maintain cross-border contacts, or to display 'national symbols'), others are partially recognized by Serbian legislation (e.g. the right to judicial and administrative procedures being conducted in Hungarian and bilingual public signs), or they were recognized in Vojvodina before 1990 (e.g. proportional representation in state authorities). On the other hand, some of these rights are novelties, e.g. the management of the mass media by the Hungarian community or the determination of part of the school curricula by the Hungarian National Council.

3.2.2   Hungarian Personal Autonomy

The most detailed section of the Agreement on Self-Government relates to the establishment, structure and institution of the so-called personal autonomy model. The Agreement on Self-Government provides that all "national communities" in Vojvodina shall exercise their rights concerning their "mother tongue, culture, education, media in their own language and the preservation of their national identity" by way of personal autonomy for which end they may establish National Councils democratically elected by the national communities themselves. Furthermore, the Agreement details the establishment, structure and powers of the Hungarian National Council. According to the proposal, the MNT shall be elected by "direct, equal, general elections through secret ballot". All persons who are included in the "electoral register of the ethnic Hungarians of Vojvodina" may vote. Inclusion in the electoral register is voluntary. Any Yugoslav citizen may be included upon his/her own initiative, if: a) he/she "declares to be Hungarian"; b) he/she or his/her underage children use the institutions of the personal autonomy; or c) he/she "annually contributes a specified amount to assist their functioning". The Agreement also provides that the direct elections for the MNT will be held when the majority of the number of those casting a ballot for Hungarian political parties in the 1997 Republican parliamentary elections enter "their names on the electoral register", in other words if the register reach the figure of 40–45,000 names. The MNT has its Executive Committee as well.

According to the Agreement, the Hungarian National Council shall have the authority to make decisions in the areas of "public education, culture, the media, the use of all languages on an equal basis, the protection of historical monuments, maintaining cross-border contacts, the use of national symbols, the budget, etc.". The major concrete role of the MNT is that it "shall exercise the rights of founder over state-funded Hungarian institutions ... ensure the funding of public educational and cultural institutions and media organiyations ... elaborate—and ... approve the program for the teaching of Hungarian language and literature, history, musical education, and visual-arts education, etc.".

The Agreement on Self-Government provides for a provisional solution as well. Section 3.5 stipulates that until the final register of Hungarian voters described above is completed, deputies nominated by the Hungarian political parties and elected to the FRY, RS and APV assemblies, and one-fifth of deputies elected to municipal assemblies, shall form the Provisional Hungarian National Council (PMNT). It is noteworthy that the PMNT was established in August 1999 and elected its Executive Committee in the same year. However, these bodies have only symbolic authority, bearing in mind that the amendment procedure necessary for the implementation of the provisions on personal autonomy was not initiated and completed by the authorities of RS and the FRY.

3.2.3   Hungarian District Self-Government (HDSG)

Besides laying down the details for personal autonomy, the Agreement contains a chapter on the establishment of the Hungarian District Self-Government (HDSG). This special territorial unit will include nine municipalities and some settlements bordering this region.[138] The HDSG will have its

"Body of Representatives", elected by the citizens residing in the district, and an Executive Committee elected by the Body of Representatives. The scope of authority and competence of the HDSG will include regional development, regional cooperation, health care, ensuring the conditions for the use of the Serb, Croat and Hungarian languages and national symbols, the exercise of the right of consent in the appointment and dismissal of municipal and district judges, prosecutors, tax authorities and police officials, and social services.

3.2.4   *The Autonomy of the Autonomous Province Vojvodina (APV)*

The Agreement on Self-Government has detailed provisions for the future status of Vojvodina, its powers, procedures and composition of organs. The main bodies of the APV are the Assembly, the Government, the Ombudsman of Minority Rights, the Supreme Court, the Prosecutor's Office and the Constitutional Court (see Section 5). The APV shall have wide legislative and executive powers, among others in the areas of territorial organization, the protection of human and minority rights, minority self-governments, property relations in Vojvodina, the justice system in Vojvodina, internal affairs in Vojvodina, family and heritage law, the position of churches, official language use, social protection, the protection of the environment, the system of information and media, the position of archives, utilities, taxing, etc. (see Section 5.1, 1–14).

According to the Agreement, the Assembly of Vojvodina shall have two councils; the Council of Citizens and the Council of National Communities. The Council of Citizens should be elected on the principle of 'one citizen—one vote' (see Section 5.2.2), while the Council of National Communities should be elected by the national councils of the respective national community (see Section 5.2.3). The main powers of the Assembly are legislation in areas defined by the Constitution of Vojvodina, enactment of the budget, and cooperation with the Assemblies of the RS and the FRY (see Section 5.2.4).

The Assembly decides with majority vote in both councils; however, a special procedure is provided for in the case that a delegation of a national community objects to a decision, because it is considered detrimental to the interests of the respective community (see Section 5.2.6). Following such an objection, a reconciliation procedure begins and the decision can pass only if the majority of the delegation of the national community concerned accepts it consequently. If negotiations fail, a new adjustment procedure can be initiated after three months. In the case of repeated failure, the proposal will be taken off the agenda (see Section 5.2.7). The Assembly shall have a presidency, whose president is elected on the principle of rotation, and the President of the Assembly and the Prime Minister must be of different nationality (see Section 5.2.8.).

The APV shall have a government which holds executive power. All national communities represented in the Council of National Communities shall have at least one representative in the government. The members of the government are proposed by the Presidency of the Assembly by way of consensus, and both councils of the Assembly elect them. The government decides by majority vote, except in cases provided by Section 5.2.6, when the reconciliation procedure provided in Section 5.2.7 shall be applied.

The Agreement on Self-Government provides that the APV shall regulate the official and equal use of minority languages in administration, administrative and court procedures, and furthermore that the ethnic composition of the staff of all authorities shall reflect the ethnic composition of the local or Vojvodina population (see Section 5.3.2).

The Agreement also stipulates that the APV shall have an Ombudsman for Minority Rights, proposed by the Presidency of the Assembly and elected by the Assembly for the term of five years (see Section 5.4).

3.2.5   Other Provisions

In Sections 6, 7, 8 and 9 of the Agreement, one can find different provisions regarding the election of judges and prosecutors, an ethnically balanced local police force, municipal governments and the financing of the institutions provided in the Agreement.

3.3 Analysis of the Major Provisions
of the Agreement on Self-Government

In the following section of this paper basic solutions of the Agreement on Self-Government will be analyzed and commented on. The analysis will focus on the internal normative deficiencies and contradictions of the Agreement and its compatibility with some autonomy proposals and solutions concerning the province of Kosovo and Bosnia-Herzegovina.

It is worth noting that the Agreement on Self-Government in Vojvodina is primarily a political document containing a set of claims and solutions forwarded by the Hungarian political parties to the governments of Serbia and the FRY concerning the constitutional status of the APV and the minorities in the APV. However, the text of the Agreement contains provision like norms regulating the constitutional and legal status of the APV, its organs and the institutions and rights of minorities. Knowing this, the analysis will treat the provisions of the Agreement as legal provisions, notwithstanding the fact that it is neither a draft constitution nor a draft law on minorities.

The part on personal autonomy is worked out in detail in the Agreement, and it is rather coherent as well. The Rambouillet Accord and the counter-proposal of the Yugoslav delegation both contained similar solutions for the national communities in Kosovo, with similar and even wider competencies, with the remark that those provisions lacked details on elections.

The most problematic issue concerning the personal autonomy is the register of voters and the eligibility criteria for it. The criteria laid down in the Agreement are loose and lack objectivity. There are three ways to enter the voting register: (1) by simple declaration of Hungarian ethnicity; (2) by using the institutions of the personal autonomy and (3) by paying donations to the institutions of personal autonomy. All three criteria might raise concerns. First, there is a danger that for various motivations non-Hungarians may register in order to manipulate the work of Hungarian institutions. The second criterion referring to the use of the institutions of the personal autonomy does not make sense at present, because these institutions do not exist. The third one resembles the voting census system used in the early stages of liberal democracies.

Another problem is related to the threshold of 40,000 registered Hungarian voters required to organize elections and establish the Hungarian National Council. Statistically there are 279,000 ethnic Hungarian voters living in Vojvodina, out of a total of 340,000 inhabitants. The democratic legitimacy of an institution that is according to the Agreement responsible for the culture, education and media of the whole community of the province is questionable if it is elected on the basis of an electoral register containing only 40,000 voters.

The second pillar of the minority self-government is the Hungarian district self-government. There are different problems concerning this chapter of the Agreement. Out of nine municipalities included in the Hungarian district self-government, Hungarians do not constitute a majority in at least two. Thus, it may happen that Hungarian political parties lose the elections for the assembly of the HDSG, and this may result in the negligence of the Hungarian interests in the HDSG.

The third pillar of the Agreement—on the future status and institutions of the APV—also contains some problematic solutions. One might object that the ethnic principle is exaggerated in this part of the document, in all institutions of the APV. A special veto mechanism is added to the proportional representation of national communities in the Council of National Communities of the Assembly and the government of the APV. The veto guaranteed to all national communities (to delegations in the Assembly and representatives in the government) concerning all decisions detrimental to the interests of their community (see Section 5.2.6) is absolute. If reconciliation fails, the draft-decision is 'dead'. This solution is problematic for many reasons. First, there is no control mechanism concerning the determination of the interests of a national community. Without it, however, the veto right can at best malfunction and block the whole decision-making procedure. In contrast, the Rambouillet Agreement for Kosovo contains a similar veto right, however with the difference that it contains a mechanism to determine "whether the proposal really hurts the interests of the respective community" and that the veto may be outvoted as well. The mere existence of the Council of National Communities, which participates in the decision-making on an equal footing with the Council of Citizens, entails the danger of majority rule and the neglect of minority interests. Furthermore, according to the Agreement on Self-Government, almost all issues related to the culture and identity of a national community are decided by the national councils alone, and not by the Assembly or the government of APV. Therefore the veto right seems superfluous and can damage the effective decision-making and governing in the APV. A minority veto should be limited and precisely regulated, available only in well-grounded, exceptional cases.

The above-formulated objection seems to be equally valid concerning the composition of the government of the APV. The obligatory representation of all national communities in the government might well limit its the efficiency. Bearing in mind that the Council of National Communities elects the members of the government on the consensual proposal of the Presidency of the Assembly, it is hard to imagine that the interests of a minority might be neglected without explicit ethnic-based representation in the government of the APV.

4. PROSPECTS OF THE HUNGARIAN AUTONOMY IN VOJVODINA

This section of the paper will focus on two related issues. First, what are the chances of minority autonomy in Vojvodina, and what are the factors and conditions influencing the outcome of the struggle for autonomy. Second, on what factors and conditions does the successful implementation of autonomy depend in Vojvodina and in general. In the forthcoming section there will be no specific differentiation in respect of the different autonomy models contained in the Agreement on Self-Government. The reasons for this approach are twofold. Autonomy models have in common that they require recognition of the ethnic principle in governance as antidote for majority rule, therefore the factors determining their establishment and success are more or less similar. Second, the provision and solutions contained in the Agreement are proposals, a basis for bargaining and negotiations with the state, and not definitive solutions to be analyzed as such.

4.1 Factors Determining the Establishment of the Minority Autonomy Arrangement in Vojvodina

One can easily answer the questions raised above: A minority autonomy regime will be established if the representatives of the majority ethnic group, the Governments and Assemblies of the FRY and RS decide to do so. While this answer is certainly true, it is also oversimplified. What is really interesting is to find out which circumstances can 'convince' the leadership of the RS and FRY to establish a system of minority autonomy and to accept the Agreement on Self-Government. Without proposing that the following list is final, this paper will discuss some factors on which the establishment of minority autonomy in Vojvodina depends:
   a)   popular support for autonomy on the side of the minority;
   b)   the will of the Government to establish autonomy for the minority;
   c)   international support;
   d)   the sentiments of the majority population toward the minority and the self-government of the minority;
   e)   the acquired level of minority rights; and
   f)   constitutional traditions and internal structures of power of the state concerned.

4.1.1   Popular Support for the Autonomy Arrangement on the Side of the Minority

When deciding on the position and rights of a minority, any democratic government in Serbia has to take into account the popular will of the respective minority. For any democratic Serb government it will be difficult to ignore the Agreement on Self-Government if a large proportion of the Hungarian population supports it. Bearing in mind that there was no popular referendum on the issue among the Hungarian community in Vojvodina, the only indicator of the legitimacy of the Agreement is the support of the Hungarian political parties. The results of the elections since 1990 reveal that the majority of the Hungarians give their support to Hungarian political parties. The federal parliamentary, provincial and local elections on 24 September 2000 stressed the leading role of the VAH among the Hungarian political parties. The VAH became the largest political party in all eight Hungarian-dominated municipalities and managed to gain 17 seats in the Assembly of the APV.[139]

It is also noteworthy that different systematic studies and opinion polls show that large proportions of the Hungarians in Vojvodina feel that they are not equal with the Serbs. They emphasized discrimination in the field of education (61 per cent), employment (36 per cent) and the use of the mother tongue (33 per cent).[140] On the other hand, ethnic Hungarians rarely mentioned different forms of autonomies as a panacea for their unequal position.[141] However, no far-reaching conclusions can be drawn from these results, because only a small fragment of the citizens have even a basic knowledge of different autonomy arrangements.

4.1.2   The Will of the Government to Establish Autonomy for the Minority

Until the elections of 24 September 2000, and the democratic revolution of 5 October 2000 in Belgrade, the political power of the Milošević Regime was absolutely dominant. The Socialist Party of Serbia (SPS), the Yugoslav United Left (YUL) and the Serbian Radical Party (SRP) had ultimately rejected all Hungarian initiatives for any form of self-government. Either deep silence or vehement hate rhetoric characterized their reaction to various autonomy concepts put forward by the Hungarian political parties. The Agreement on Self-Government also shared this destiny. While the mere announcement and publication of the document was silently received by the power holders, the establishment of the Provisional Hungarian National Council (PMNT) in 1999 generated furious reactions. It was labelled an attack on the territorial integrity of the RS and FRY, and a step toward secession and ghettoization of the Hungarian minority. The orchestrated attacks in pro-government media lacked any objective analysis, usually neglecting even the mere content of the Agreement.

The recent and still ongoing change in Belgrade makes the chances of the Agreement on Self-Government more realistic. In spite of the fact that the leading Serbian opposition parties can also be characterized as nationalist parties sharing similar views on Serb nation-building, recent political developments are promising. At meetings of the major Serb opposition parties and the representatives of minorities, in Vienna and Athens, both sides agreed on the support of different arrangements of autonomy. In Vienna, the Communiqué emphasized that "the self-organization of national communities through adequate autonomy arrangements ... is necessary for the more efficient organization of multicultural communities of citizens of Vojvodina, as well as for democratization of Serbia. Taxes and other financial contributions paid by members of the national community should constitute the financial foundation of their self-organization".[142] A similar formulation was adopted in Athens as well.[143]

It would be exaggerated optimism to believe that the implementation of these points will be without problems under the new democratic government in Belgrade. However, the importance of these agreements is not to be neglected. First, they can serve as a solid basis for the claims of the minorities toward the new government; second, they can make the notion of minority self-government presentable in Serbia. Thus, the concept of minority autonomy, considered taboo not too long ago, might become a legitimate object of political bargaining.

The positive attitude toward autonomy might also be motivated by the fact that the major Hungarian political party, the VAH, was the coalition partner of the anti-Milošević United Serbian Opposition (DOS) in the elections of 2000 and actively contributed to the victory of the opposition. The VAH participates in the government of the APV with three members.[144]

4.1.3   *International Support*

One of the factors determining the chances of an autonomy arrangement in Vojvodina, as well as in general, is the support of the international community. Recent developments in international law as well as in politics are in favour of both: autonomy of minorities as a means for a solution of minority issues in general, and self-government of minorities in Vojvodina in particular.

The Council of Europe's (CoE) 1994 Framework Convention for the Protection of National Minorities and numerous of other international agreements for the protection of national minorities all provide for different forms of self-governance and effective minority participation in decision-making, especially in areas related to the specific identity of minorities.[145] Among these documents, the most recent OSCE document merits special attention. Parallel to this process of international codification in the nineties, the autonomy arrangements received more and more recognition in many states—in old democracies as well as in newly liberated, independent states.[146]

Moreover, there is a detectable shift in Western liberal political philosophy as well, providing a strong theoretical foundation for the autonomy arrangements.[147] Recent developments in Kosovo, notwithstanding the substantial differences between the two problems, also made the autonomy more suitable. It is noteworthy that the UN Security Council resolutions openly advocated substantial self-government for the province.[148] The above-mentioned changes in the nineties all make autonomy cases more legitimate and powerful.

Concerning the struggle for self-governance of the Hungarians in Vojvodina, one can also identify positive developments. Besides the general strengthening of the idea of minority self-governance, the strong support of autonomy by the NATO member and EU candidate Hungary, together with the Bill of the US Senate on Vojvodina, all make the future prospects of the Agreement on Self-Government promising. The strong support of the Hungarian government was clearly formulated in the Final Statement of the Permanent Hungarian Conference in 1999. On the other hand, the above-mentioned Bill of the US Senate on Vojvodina emphasizes the concern of the United States for the rights of the Hungarian community in the FRY and stresses that the proposed arrangements of the Hungarian community have to be considered by the Serb authorities.

All the above developments favour the 'case of self-governance' in Vojvodina. However, it would be a mistake to overestimate the importance of the positive international climate. The examples of Bosnia and Kosovo teach us that the international community is willing to powerfully advocate the self-governance of minorities usually only after interethnic relations have reached the bottom and bloodshed has begun, and when the struggle for moderate autonomy is replaced by a struggle for independence.

4.1.4   Sentiments of the Majority Population toward the Minority
and the Self-Government of the Minority

One of the factors which might help or hinder the chances of an autonomy arrangement is the relationship between the majority population of the state and the respective minority group. One might logically suppose that in the case of strong animosities and negative sentiments between two groups, it might indeed be a risky and unpopular step for the government to accept an autonomy claim from the minority concerned. Autonomy might be considered as an undesirable and superfluous concession to the 'enemy' by the majority.

What is the situation in the RS and FRY in this respect? The few systematic studies available on this topic reveal an ambiguous picture. While they unanimously prove that the Serbs show a substantially less negative attitude and less hatred toward Hungarians than toward Albanians, Muslims and Croats, the attitude of Serbs toward smaller ethnic groups, like Slovaks and Ruthenians, is much more positive.[149] On the other hand, other results show that the Serbs in Vojvodina do not support the autonomy claims of the Hungarians and that they categorically reject to be governed by non-Serbs, which would be the factual consequence of any territorial autonomy arrangements.[150]

4.1.5   Acquired Level of Minority Rights

If we perceive minority self-governance—as Herbert Küpper correctly describes—as the highest level of minority rights and protection, then the present standards of minority protection in the FRY and RS are a factor to be taken into account. It is easier to first implement different instances of minority protection before establishing forms of minority self-governance. Thus, it will most likely be less difficult to establish minority self-governance in minority education if minority education and the right for mother tongue education already exist in a particular state. The opposite is also true: if a minority is not recognized at all or if there is no minority instruction, it is more problematic to establish minority self-governance in education. In the first case, only the reform of the existing system of mother tongue education has to be modified to ensure the management of these institutions by minorities, while in the latter case, the basic preconditions for minority institutions are non-existent.

The Constitution of the FRY contains a number of provisions which guarantee the rights of national minorities and persons belonging to national minorities. The right to education and information in the mother tongue and the official use of minority languages is explicitly recognized.[151] Furthermore, persons belonging to national minorities have the right to cross-border contacts with their co-nationals,[152] to private educational and cultural institutions,[153] and to the use of national symbols.[154] The Constitution of the FRY explicitly recognizes the collective right of national minorities to preserve their identity.[155] The catalogue of minority rights in the Constitution of the RS is much more moderate, merely granting the right to mother tongue education[156] and the official use of minority languages.[157]

The implementation of constitutional rights is more problematic. First, the statutes, regulations and by-laws regulating different areas of minority protection seriously limit the content of the guarantees primarily contained in the Federal Constitution. Second, even these legal rules are often insufficiently enforced in practice.[158] As Várady stated, outright legal discrimination against minorities is a rare phenomenon, while the biased use of the manoeuvring space provided by the sometimes too vague and general Serbian legislation is very common in Vojvodina.[159] The lack of the rule of law and an independent judiciary in Serbia also contribute to the non-enforcement of some minority rights.

Although the constitutional guarantees of minority rights in the FRY are often no more than declarations directed toward the domestic and international public, it would be a strong exaggeration to state that the Hungarian minority in Vojvodina is denied any positive minority protection. Of course, it is more or less a weak version of the sophisticated and developed system of minority protection guaranteed by the Vojvodina legislation before the radical changes made by the Milošević regime in 1988. Still, there are almost eighty primary schools in Vojvodina with Hungarian classes and instruction and dozens of secondary schools as well. There is a province-wide, state-funded 24 hour radio program, and more than one hour per day of TV broadcasting in Hungarian. The only Hungarian daily newspaper, *Magyar Szó*, was founded and is funded by the Autonomous Province of Vojvodina. However, it must be emphasized that the existing number of minority rights is much lower than a decade ago. Some examples will be described below.

In the area of education, the new provisions omitted the right to college and university level education in languages of national minorities, and today, such instruction is exclusively dependent on the approval by the republican government. Mother tongue university entry exams and equal opportunity for minority candidates are not guaranteed either by the new provisions.[160] The number of primary and secondary schools and classes with instruction in minority languages substantially decreased between 1990 and 1998 and so did the total number of minority pupils instructed in their mother tongue.[161] The establishment of private minority schools is not allowed in Serbia,[162] while in public (state) schools the curricula for minority language instruction are a mere translation of the Serb curricula, neglecting the history and culture of the respective minority group.[163] In the

287

official use of languages, restrictions are even more manifest. Until the late eighties, federal and Serbian laws were published in both Albanian and Hungarian. This is no longer the case.[164] Shortly after the adoption of the new 1990 Serbian Constitution, the Constitutional Court declared null and void all acts requiring the knowledge of a minority language.[165] The consequence of this ruling was that the newly appointed public officials were not able to use minority languages in communication with local residents, in spite of the official recognition of minority languages in Serbia. According to the annulled Provincial Act, members of the national minorities had the right to administrative and court procedures being conducted entirely in their own language, from the first instance to the final one.[166] Today, only bilingual procedures are allowed and only in the first instance, with the limitation that the Serbian language shall have the primacy if a party in a procedure asks for a Serbian-language procedure. These limitations swiftly led to complete extinction of procedures in a minority language.

Furthermore, members of the national minorities are greatly underrepresented in many areas of public life. According to the report of the Helsinki Committee for Human Rights in Serbia, Hungarians and Croats are rarely appointed as headmasters of schools, state-owned company directors, etc., and are underrepresented in the administration, courts and police as well.[167] However, it must be noted that before the Milošević era, "the system of national keys" guaranteed proportional representation of minorities in public life. Today, various national minorities are seriously underrepresented in the staff of different state authorities and agencies.[168]

From the above-mentioned facts it is obvious that there are serious setbacks and problems concerning the position of the Hungarian minority in Vojvodina. However, there still are functioning systems of education in the Hungarian language (in elementary education around 79 per cent of Hungarian pupils receive their education in their mother tongue) and of the media in the mother tongue. This may serve as a basis for future autonomy arrangements, notwithstanding current difficulties.

4.2 Factors on Which the Effective and Successful Implementation of a Minority Autonomy Arrangement Depends

This section focuses on the factors and circumstances which may influence the successful and effective functioning of an existing autonomy arrangement, particularly in Vojvodina. Of course, the precondition is that the autonomy arrangement, in our case that of the Hungarians in Vojvodina, is reached and established normatively.

Among the factors on which the success of the implementation of a self-government model depends one can mention the following:

a) well-shaped rules on the division of powers and conflict-resolving mechanisms between the government of the autonomy and central authorities;

b) existing minority institutions and personnel on which the autonomy arrangement can be based;

c) confidence-building measures and protection of local minorities in territorial arrangements;

d) human rights protection and limited representative government within the autonomy; and

e) the administrative structure of the state.

4.2.1 Well-Defined Rules on the Division of Powers and Conflict-Resolving Mechanisms between the Government of Autonomy and Central Authorities

Ruth Lapidoth, in her pioneering book on autonomy, stresses that for the successful functioning of any autonomy arrangement the precise division of competencies between the local and central authorities is inevitably necessary, together with proper reconciliation mechanisms for resolving potential conflicts between these authorities.[169] In a country with weak democratic traditions, this requirement is even more important. This was highlighted, for example, in the constitutional crises of the late eighties and early nineties in Serbia and Yugoslavia. The conflict between Serbia and the Provinces and the subsequent abolishment of the autonomy by extra-legal means on the one hand, and the constitutional stalemate, subsequent crises and the break-up of Yugoslavia on the other, were at least partially the result of the vague constitutional provisions on the vertical division of powers between the Republics and the Provinces, and the Republics and the Federal authorities. The tragic outcome was also worsened by the lack of conflict-resolving mechanisms and provisions. This does not suggest that the break-up of the former Yugoslavia or the abolition of the Provinces in Serbia was primarily the result of insufficient constitutional and other legal provisions, but these factors made the dismantling process easier and harsher.

The Agreement on Self-Government, which is the primary object of this analysis, cannot deserve an outstanding qualification in this respect. There is no precise division of powers between the provincial authorities, national councils and the HDSG in many areas like mother tongue education, official use of the minority language or media, not to mention the division of competencies between the republican and federal authorities on the one side and Vojvodina on the other. Concerning conflict-resolving mechanisms, the situation is even worse. The lack of an effective mechanism in the case of minority veto in the Vojvodina Assembly was mentioned earlier. Additional veto powers are also provided in the Agreement on Self-Government concerning the appointment of prosecutors and judges for the national councils and the HDSG, but mechanisms for the reconciliation of stalemates and conflicts are not laid down.

Of course, it is obvious that the Agreement on Self-Government is not a complete and final document which contains all necessary provisions for the autonomy arrangement. However, the emphasis on the precise division of powers and conflict-resolving mechanisms needs to be taken seriously in the future.

4.2.2 Existing Minority Institutions and Personnel on Which the Autonomy Arrangement Can Be Based

The good functioning of an autonomy arrangement depends on its institutions and personnel. In Vojvodina, the most important institutions, together with the necessary personnel are the Hungarian municipal governments. In five municipalities,[170] Hungarian political parties have been in power since the first multiparty local elections in 1992. These municipal governments have a substantial budget and are founders of various public companies and cultural institutions. The Hungarian politicians have gained substantial managing skills and experience, and have developed cultural institutions and strategies during the last eight years.

Notwithstanding the extreme centralization, in education and culture the experience and staff of municipal governments can serve as a solid basis for the well functioning of a potential autonomy arrangement. The mayors, members of executive boards, deputies of local assemblies and heads of cultural institutions founded by municipalities in these towns are not only ethnic Hungarians, but representatives of the Hungarian community in Vojvodina with democratic legitimacy. They are individuals implementing the policy of the Hungarian political parties.

In this way, municipal governments are important factors in the successful implementation of the Hungarian autonomy in Vojvodina.

It is noteworthy that there are several public media institutions which might also serve as the basis of the autonomy arrangement. The educational system, on the other hand, is not independent. Hungarian-language instruction is organized together with Serb-language instruction in territorial schools, in separate classes. The implementation of the Agreement on Self-Government requires the reform of the existing educational system of the Hungarian minority.

4.2.3 Confidence-Building Measures
and the Protection of Local Minorities in Territorial Arrangements

Autonomy arrangements, especially territorial ones, make the position of the local minority group special and delicate. Thus, for example, through the implementation of the Agreement on Self-Government, the position of the local Serbs in the HDSG and in Vojvodina will become less privileged. In fact, they will be governed by the representatives of the Hungarian minority (HDSG) or will have to share the power at the level of the APV. Even the local Hungarian author István Bosnyák argues that territorial autonomy of the Hungarians in northern Vojvodina will inevitably result in the opposition of local Serbs, therefore it is not a viable solution.[171] In order to make this new situation acceptable to local Serbs, confidence-building measures are needed. These measures, like special school programs emphasizing the need for self-government arrangements in multi-ethnic states, and mutual learning of the language and culture of neighbouring national communities, can make the success of the autonomy more probable. Institutional cooperation and reconciliation of political parties representing the minority and majority, multicultural media programmes and events can also have positive effects.

Special emphasis needs to be put on the protection of minority rights of Serbs living in the territory of the HDSG. Cultural autonomy provided for in the Agreement on Self-Government protects the interests of the local Serb minority in the field of culture. This should be complemented by a limited veto in some areas of decision-making. These measures may lead the local majority to respect the interests of the local minority. The experiences of Hungarian-led municipalities deserve attention, where the Hungarian majority respects the interests of the local minority as well.

4.2.4 Human Rights Protection
and Limited Representative Government within the Autonomy

It is also noteworthy that the provisions for the competencies and division of power need to take into account the basic liberal tenets on representative, limited and democratic government. The separation of powers, an independent judiciary, the rule of law and respect for individual human rights are principles which have to be implemented in all autonomy arrangements. The institutions and authorities of the autonomy are endowed with important public powers that have to be limited and controlled just as the central ones. Without such mechanisms, ethnic autonomy arrangements may become instruments of the tyranny of local ethnic leaders. Therefore, successful autonomy models have to ensure, besides the protection of the national minority from the majority rule and majority nation, the protection of both democracy and individuals from local authorities. This is extremely important in the case of the Hungarian autonomy in the RS, bearing in mind the overall situation in Serbia in respect to democracy, human rights and the division of powers. Unfortunately, the Agreement on Self-Government does not deal with these concerns in sufficient measure. Besides emphasizing that the organs of different autonomies have representative, elected legislative bodies, the Agreement contains no provisions on these issues, or on the level of principles.

4.2.5   Administrative Structure of the State

The chances for the successful and effective implementation of the Agreement on Self-Government, or any other autonomy arrangement, may be better if it fits into the general administrative structure and division of the state. It may be rather difficult to successfully maintain autonomy arrangements in a state which is over-centralized. This might generate tensions and disputes over competencies between the authorities of the autonomy and the central authorities. On the other hand, a decentralized administration may create a stable balance between the units and the centre, regardless of the fact that some units are ethnically mixed. The cases of Canada, Spain and Italy are good example for this case.

If the present over-centralized administrative structure of the RS is left unchanged outside the APV, chances are small for the successful implementation of the Agreement on Self-Government or any other ethnic autonomy arrangement in Serbia.

It is promising that the major political parties within the winning block of the opposition parties (Democratic Opposition of Serbia—DOS) are unanimously in favour of a decentralized Serbia. However, they differ on the question of autonomy and position of the APV and minority self-government.[172]

5.   CONCLUSION

The primary aim of this chapter was to formulate some preconditions for the successful and effective implementation of a Hungarian autonomy arrangement in Vojvodina. The latest autonomy arrangement of the Hungarian political parties in Vojvodina, the Agreement on Self-Government, served as a basis for this analysis. However, the emphasis was on the preconditions of minority autonomy in general—and in Vojvodina in particular—and not on particular solutions forwarded in the Agreement on Self-Government. This emphasis was chosen because the Agreement is primarily a political document of the Hungarian political parties, a one-sided draft proposal articulating claims of the Hungarian minority, and not a final autonomy arrangement resulting from negotiations, compromises and reconciliations between the representatives of the Hungarians and the Serb-dominated state. For this reason, there was less emphasis on an article-by-article description and analysis of the document, and more on the general circumstances and preconditions influencing the chances of minority autonomy in Vojvodina.

The Agreement basically contains three interconnected but still rather independent models of autonomy: Hungarian personal autonomy, Hungarian district self-government; and the model of autonomy for Vojvodina province. Notwithstanding some contradictions and weak points of particular solutions, the document seems to be compact and detailed. The solutions provided in the Agreement are partially borrowed (though not copied) from different documents of the international community (the Rambouillet Agreement, the Constitution of Bosnia-Herzegovina) and from the Serb government dealing with different multiethnic regions of the former SFRY.

Preconditions for the success and effective implementation of an autonomy arrangement in Vojvodina could include well-defined rules on the separation of powers and competencies between the central government and the authorities of the autonomy arrangement, together with mechanisms available for conflict resolution ensuring the success of the autonomy arrangement. Besides well-defined rules, confidence-building measures, protection of local minorities and the restructuring of Serbia proper are all-important preconditions for a successful autonomy arrangement in Vojvodina. Moreover, rules ensuring a limited, representative, rule-of-law government of the autonomy are also necessary.

5.1 The Type of the Draft Arrangement

The Agreement contains three different types of autonomy draft arrangements: personal autonomy with elected National Councils, ethnic territorial autonomy (the Hungarian District Self-Government) and a special territorial autonomy of Vojvodina province with consocietal decision-making mechanisms.

The eventual implementation and success of this draft arrangement primarily depends on the political environment in Vojvodina and Serbia after the revolutionary changes that occurred in the FRY at the end of the year 2000. The defeat of the xenophobic totalitarian regime of Slobodan Milošević has opened the door for negotiations on the Agreement on Self-Government because the VMSZ actively participated in the anti-Milošević democratic coalition. However, the final outcome is not yet visible, and it depends on the political power-struggle in the post-Milošević era. The tradition of positive minority rights, territorial autonomy of the APV and the general decentralization plans and programs of the winning parties are all reasons for optimism. Two recent decisions of the new democratic Vojvodina Assembly on 20 December 2000, initiated by the VMSZ government members, are evidence of the new atmosphere.[173]

5.2 The Most Relevant Characteristics of the Draft Arrangement

The Agreement on Self-Government foresees that the three types of autonomy should be established and implemented within the legal framework of the FRY, RS and APV with constitutional and statutory amendments. Subjects of the draft arrangement are the minority communities in Vojvodina, primarily the Hungarian community, but also other minority communities and, generally, all citizens residing in Vojvodina (Arrangement for the APV). The National Council, as the body of the personal autonomy, is elected primarily by the members of the Hungarian community, on the basis of the special register of Hungarian voters. This body has primary authority in the areas of education, culture and mother tongue media. In this way, personal autonomy is a cultural one as well.

The bodies of the HDSG are elected by all citizens residing on the territory of Hungarian dominated municipalities, and its primary powers are related to official language use, health care, regional planning and the nomination of high state officials working on the territory of the HDSG.

The draft arrangement contains detailed provisions concerning the constitutional status and powers of the APV. The Serb-dominated but multiethnic province would have wide legislative, judicial and executive powers with special rules of decision-making aimed to prevent majority rule and outvoting of the minorities in the APV.

All three types of autonomy are tailored to be an integral part of the state structure, regulated by the Constitution and other laws. The Agreement on Self-Government contains only general provisions concerning the financing of the arrangements. However, the basic idea is that for the purposes of Hungarian minority culture and institutions, 17 per cent of the overall expenditure in Vojvodina should be reserved for cultural purposes.

5.3 The Role of the Draft Arrangement in Ethnic Conflict Management

Bearing in mind that Vojvodina was not afflicted by fierce ethnic conflicts, the primary aim of the draft arrangement is not conflict management but rather the insurance of the full and effective equality of the majority and minority communities and the preservation of the minority identity. The last decade of the twentieth century in Vojvodina was characterized by the ethnic domination of Serbs in all areas of economic and social life, including those directly affecting minority culture, education and information. Therefore, the draft arrangement primarily intends to redress this situation.

Even without public referenda on this issue, one can conclude, from various opinion polls and electoral results, that the majority of the Hungarians living in the region support the solutions proposed in the draft. On the other hand, the reactions of the majority population and political parties vary. There is no serious opposition, at least generally, to the idea of personal autonomy and autonomy of the APV with a special representation. However, the idea of HDSG is treated with wide suspicion by almost all political actors on the Serb political scene. Acceptance of the arrangement will depend to a large extent on how it is conveyed to the public in the Serb media. The reactions of the fragile civil societies in Vojvodina and Serbia toward minority self-government are primarily positive. Recent conferences on minorities in Niška Banja and Subotica, held in late 2000, also confirm this development.

5.4 The Outcome of the Draft Arrangement

It is surely an advantage of the VMSZ draft arrangement that it is a more or less complete document offering three different, well-defined autonomy models with a set of solutions for the protection of minorities and a list of minority rights. The complexity of the document makes it relatively elastic, allowing various solutions to be realized which are not exclusive or interdependent. The proposals of the document could be successfully put into practice in several stages. Moreover, even partial realization of the draft arrangement would achieve the basic goal of the document, ensuring the preservation of minority identity and the effective participation of the minority group in public decision-making, primarily in issues related to culture and identity.

Concerning the problems related to the draft arrangement, one could mention the issues of the democratic legitimacy of the National Councils and the eligibility criteria for the special register of minority voters. The overemphasis on the ethnic principle in the government structure and decision-making in the APV could also be considered superfluous and problematic. Some corrections in this direction, which are not only desirable, but also probable in the course of future negotiations, can make the autonomy arrangement viable and durable as well. Furthermore, the successful implementation requires precise, well-defined legal rules regulating the establishment, powers, competencies and financing of autonomous bodies, as well as the separation of the powers of these bodies from the powers and competencies of state and provincial public bodies. These requirements have not yet been included in the document. However, this was not to be expected from a political document of this type.

NOTES

[118] Vojvodina's participation in the gross domestic product of the FRY is 29%, in agriculture 36%. Source: *Društveni proizvod i narodni dohodak 1996 Statistički Bilten* No 2185 (GDP in 1996), (Belgrade: Federal Statistical Office, 1998).

[119] In Vojvodina, the illiteracy rate is 4.1%, in Central-Serbia 6.8% and in Montenegro 5.9% Source: Svetlana Radovanović ed., *Stanovništvo i Domaćinstva u SR Jugoslaviji prema popisu 1991* (Population and Households in the FRY, according to the 1991 census), Stanovništvo 47 (Belgrade: Federal Statistical Office, 1995).

[120] Figures from Jovan Zelenović ed., *Nacionalne zajednice u Vojvodini* (National Communities in Vojvodina) Executive Committee of APV, Novi Sad, 2000. In 1991, the number of 'undecided' was 182,155, and Yugoslavs 174,295. Presumably the majority of these persons is from ethnically mixed marriages.

[121] Hungarians constitute a local majority in seven municipalities (towns with surrounding settlements): Ada, Bačka Topola (Topolya), Bečej (Becse), Čoka (Csóka), Kanjiža (Kanizsa), Mali Iđoš (Kishegyes), Senta (Zenta), Subotica (Szabadka)—the Hungarian names of the settlements are given in parenthesis. Approximately 55%–60% of all Hungarians in Vojvodina live in these settlements. Károly Kocsis and Eszter Kocsis-Hodosi, *Ethnic Geography of the Hungarian Minorities in the Carpathian Basin* (Budapest: Georgaphical Research Institute Research Centre for Earth Sciences and Minority Studies Program—Hungarian Academy of Sciences, 1998).

[122] Kocsis, Kocsis-Hodosi, *op.cit.*, p.143.

[123] Sasa Kicosev and MihályKocsis, "A menekültek társadalmi-demográfiai aspektusai a Vajdaságban", in *Régió* 9 (1998) 3, pp.63–75.

[124] In 1850, the Austrian Crown established the Serb Vojvodina, with an Austrian governor, without substantial Serb self-government.

[125] According to Article 292 of the Constitution of the SAPV, the province had powers to legislate independently in areas like education, the justice system, media and the health-care system.

[126] Ruth Lapidoth, *Autonomy—Flexible Solutions to Ethnic Conflicts* (Washington, D.C.: United States Institute of Peace Press, 1997), p.33.

[127] Hurst Hannum, *Autonomy, Sovereignty, and Self-determination—The Accommodation of Conflicting Rights* (Philadelphia: University of Pennsylvania Press, 1990), p.4.

[128] Henry J. Steiner, "Ideals and Counter-Ideals in the Struggle over Autonomy Regimes for Minorities", in *Notre Dame Law Review* 66 (1991), pp.1539–1555.

[129] Constitution of the SFRY, Article 398.

[130] *Ibid.*, Article 292 and 321.

[131]   In October 1988, a supposedly 'spontaneous' mass demonstration against autonomy in Novi Sad was organized by the government of Yugoslavia. As the demonstrators, who were brought there by trains and buses, were rewarded with drinks, bread and yoghurt, this incident also became known as the "Yoghurt Revolution".

[132]   According to Article 109 of the Constitution of the Republic of Serbia, the provinces can enact "decisions" within the limits of the Serbian Constitutional and statutory provisions in the areas of "culture, education, official use of minority languages, public information, etc.". and they can "implement" Serbian statutes and acts if such acts provide so. Furthermore, the provinces can enact development plans, which are in harmony with the Republican development plans.

[133]   Budget of the APV, *Službeni List APV* (Official Gazette of the APV) 1/2000.

[134]   "Statut Autonomne Pokrajine Vojvodina", *Službeni List APV* (Official Gazette of the APV) 17/1991.

[135]   According to Article 109 of the 1990 Serbian Constitution, Autonomous Provinces autonomously regualte the areas of education, culture, health care, social protection, etc., in harmony with the Constitution and laws. However, laws and by-laws of the Republic regulated these areas in such a way that they excluded the possibility of the provincial regulation.

[136]   In these elections the united DAHV got between 106,036 and 140,825 votes. Bearing in mind that the total number of Hungarian voters in Vojvodina is below 300,000 and the proportion of those not voting, we can claim that the DAHV was able to collect approximately 50–70% of Hungarian votes. Source: Miroslav Samardžić, *Položaj manjina u Vojvodini* (The Position of the Minorities in Vojvodina (Beograd: Centar za antiratnu akciju, 1998), p.139.

[137]   The document avoids the terms 'national' or 'ethnic minority' and uses the notion 'national communities' instead.

[138]   Next to eight municipalities with a Hungarian majority, it includes the municipality of Novi Kneževac (Törökkanizsa), where Hungarians make up one-third of the population.

[139]   For more details see the Budapoest weekly *HVG*, October 21, p.66.

[140]   Mikloš Biro, *Doživljaj ravnopravnosti pripadnika manjinskih naroda u Srbiji* (Equality of Minority Nations in Serbia), Helsinki Committee for Human Rights in Serbia, July 1996, p.3.

[141]   *Ibid*, p.6.

[142]   Project on Ethnic Relations, Roundtable on Interethnic Relations in Vojvodina, Vienna, Austria, 23–25 September 1999, Communiqué, section 3.

[143]   Project on Ethnic Relations, Roundtable on Vojvodina, Athens, Greece, 14–15 February 2000. Communiqué.

[144]   See more in weekly *Szabad Hét Nap*, 1 November, pp.4–5.

[145]   UN Declaration on the Rights of Persons Belonging to National, Ethnic, Religious and Linguistic Minorities, General Assembly Resolution 47/135, adopted 18 December 1992. UN Doc.A/RES/47/135, Article 2(3), CE Framework Convention for the Protection of National Minorities, Article 15, Recomendation 1201 (1993) of the Assembly of CE, Article 11,OSCE Copenhagen Documents, Paragraph 35.

[146]   Belgium, Canada, Slovenia, Constitution of the Republic of Slovenia, *Uradni List* 33/1991, Estonia, Estonian Act on Cultural, Autonomy for National Minorities, adopted in 26 October 1993, *Riigi Teataja* 71/1993, Moldova, Spain, Northern Ireland, UK.

[147]   Will Kymlicka, *Multicultural Citizenship* (Oxford: Clarendon Press, London, 1995); Lapidoth, *op. cit.* Yael Tamir, *Liberal Nationalism* (Princeton, N.J.: Princeton University Press, 1993), János Kis, *Az állam semlegessége* (Neutrality of the state) (Budapest: Atlantisz, 1997).

[148]   Security Council Resolutions 1160, 1203, http://www.smip.sv.gov.yu.

[149]   Mikloš Biro, *Stavovi građana srpske nacionalnosti prema nacionalnim manjina u Srbiji* (Opinion of the Ethnic Serb Citizens Toward National Minorities), Helsinki Committee in Serbia, July, 1996, pp.6–7 and Srećko Mihailović, *Predstave o nacionalnim manjinama u javnom mnenju Srbije* (The picture of national minorities in the public opinion in Serbia) in

Miloš Macura and Vojislav Stanovčić, *Položaj Manjina u Saveznoj Republici Jugoslaviji* (Position of Minorities in the Federal Republic of Yugoslavia) (Belgrade: SANU [Serb Academy of Sciences and Arts], 1996), pp.424–426.

[150] Vladimir Ilić and Slobodan Cvejić, *Nacionalizam u Vojvodini* (Nationalism in Vojvodina), Ekopres Zrenjanin, 1997, p.183.

[151] Articles 46 and 15, Constitution of the FRY, *Službeni List SRJ* (Official Gazette of FRY) 1/92.

[152] Article 48, Constitution of the FRY, *Službeni List SRJ* (Official Gazette of FRY) 1/92.

[153] Article 47, Constitution of the FRY, *Službeni List SRJ* (Official Gazette of FRY) 1/92.

[154] Article 11, Constitution of the FRY, *Službeni List SRJ* (Official Gazette of FRY) 1/92.

[155] *Ibid.*

[156] Article 32 (4), Constitution of the Republic of Serbia, *Službeni Glasnik RS* (Official Gazette of RS) 1/1990.

[157] Article 8, Constitution of the Republic of Serbia, *Službeni Glasnik RS* (Official Gazette of RS) 1/1990.

[158] Characteristic examples of the non-enforcement of minority rights can be detected in the case of bilingual public signs. According to the Act on the Official Use of Languages and Scripts, *Official Gazette of RS*, 45/1991, Article 19, in all multiethnic regions, public signs should be bilingual and the violator faces fines up to 80,000 dinars (Article 26). Despite clear provisions and high fines, the central authorities, responsible for the implementation of the Act, do nothing to implement and enforce these provisions. On the contrary, they are the number one violators of these provisions, exclusively using monolingual Serb signs. For detailed analysis of the practice, see Tamás Korhecz, *Pravna regulativa višejezčnih natpisa u Republici Srbiji i njihovo sprovodenje u Vojvodini* (Regulation and practice of bilingual public signs in Vojvodina), *GLASNIK: Advokatske komore Vojvodine* (Gazette of the Vojvodina Bar), 11/97.

[159] Várady, *op.cit.*, pp.21–22.

[160] Tamás Korhecz, *The Minority Rights of the Hungarian National Group in Yugoslavia* (Budapest: Minority Protection Association, 1998), p.26–27.

[161] Dr. Lajos Tóth, "A magyar tannyelvű oktatás a Vajdaságban", (Hungarian language instruction in Vojvodina), in Irén Gábrityné Molnár and Zsuzsa Mirnics eds., *Anyanyelvű oktatásunk* (Our mother tongue education) (Subotica: MTT, 1997), pp.40–48.

[162] Law on Elementary Schools, *Official Gazette of RS*, 50/1992, Article 9. Law on Secondary Schools, *Official Gazette of the RS*, 50/1992, Article 11.

[163] Samardžić, *op.cit.*, p.66.

[164] Tibor Várady, "Minorities, Majorities, Law, and Ethnicity: Reflections of the Yugoslav Case", *Human Rights Quarterly* 19 (1997), p.27.

[165] Decisions of the Constitutional Court IU 52/89 and IU 58/89 from 26 April 1990, *Official Gazette of the RS*, 28/1990.

[166] "Zakon o načinu ostvarivanja ravnopravnosti jezika i pisama naroda i narodnosti u određenim organima, organizacijama i zajednicama", (Act on the equality of the languages and scripts of the nations and nationalities in different state organs, organizations and communities), Articles 9, 10, 11, 12 and 13, *Official Gazette of the Socialist Autonomous Province of Vojvodina*, 29/1977.

[167] Helsinki Committee for Human Rights in Serbia, *Report on human rights in Serbia for 1997*, pp.100–102; 110–112.

[168] Samardžić, *op. cit.*, p.152.

[169] Lapidoth, *op. cit.*

[170] Bačka Topola (Topolya), Bečej (Becse), Kanjiža (Kanizsa), Senta (Zenta), Subotica (Szabadka). In the Hungarian-populated municipalities of Ada, Mali Iđoš (Kishegyes), Čoka (Csóka), the Hungarian political parties lost their majority in the period between 1992 and 1997.

171 István Bosnyák, "Minority Local Self-Governments and Difficulties Concern the Establishment of the Personal Autonomy in Vojvodina", *Létünk* 1996, 1–2.

172 In the course of the Conference in Subotica, from 18–20 May 2000, all important Serbian opposition parties (at that time) elaborated their programmes on decentralization and regionalism. The documents were published in a the booklet "Političke stranke i autonomija Vojvodine",(Political Parties and the Autonomy of Vojvodina) (Subotica: Open University-Centre for Multiculturalism, May 2000).

173 The Vojvodina Assembly accepted the draft amendments on the Serbian Official Language Law. The amendments, proceeded to the Serbian Assembly for acceptance, contain several provisions guaranteeing the wide use of minority languages in courts and administration. The second decision guarantees the issuance of bilingual certificates of the Registrar's Office in Vojvodina for the members of national minorities. Daily *Magyar Szó*, 21 December 2000, p.1.

Substantial Self-Administration for Kosovo: From Rambouillet to the Adoption of a Constitutional Framework Document

Marc Weller

Substantial Self-Administration for Kosovo: From Rambouillet to the Adoption of a Constitutional Framework Document

Marc Weller

1. INTRODUCTION

Kosovo is a territory occupying an area of some 10,887 square kilometres. According to a 1990 census, it had a population of roughly 2 million inhabitants, of whom some 88 per cent were estimated to be ethnic Albanians, 8 per cent Serbs and the remaining number divided among small groups of Turks, Vlachs, Goranies, Roma and others. As a result of poverty and repression during the 1990s, between 300,000 and 400,000 ethnic Albanians left the territory, even before the hostilities and the dramatic Yugoslav campaign of forced displacement began in earnest in 1998–99. After the conclusion of hostilities involving NATO in June 1999, over 100,000 ethnic Serbs left the territory, few of whom have returned.

The Yugoslav Federal structure was fundamentally revised in 1974, establishing a complex balancing of public powers among the republics—and also the two autonomous provinces that were contained within Serbia: Kosovo and Vojvodina. The latter enjoyed a quasi-federal status. While their continued appurtenance to the republic of Serbia was confirmed, at the same time the two entities enjoyed all the substantive rights also granted to full republics under the 1974 Socialist Federal Republic of Yugoslavia (SFRY) Constitution, including equal representation in the collective federal Presidency. Like the republics, the autonomous provinces were entitled to a very wide measure of self-government, extending even to limited powers in external affairs and the running of a central bank. The Tito design for Yugoslavia was therefore already one of power-sharing, combining self-government or autonomy of constituent entities with joint representation in collective federal organs. This was underpinned by a doctrine of 'unity and brotherhood', which was meant to reflect the equality of nations, nationalities and minorities.

The doctrine of nations and nationalities is one which has retained some relevance in the post-communist transition, as it still informs the thinking of some actors. Nations were perceived to be ethnic populations that do not possess a kin-state elsewhere (Serbs, Croats, Montenegrins, Macedonians, Bosniaks, Slovenes). They were entitled to full self-government through their own republic and they enjoyed an express right to self-determination, to be exercised through the republics. Nationalities were other large ethnic groups that did possess external kin-states and could therefore be accommodated through autonomy (the ethnic Albanians of Kosovo and the ethnic Hungarians of Vojvodina). Finally, the smaller groups of Turks, Vlachs, Goranies, Roma, etc., were considered minorities—an odious term within this system, as it implied virtual political disenfranchisement, the doctrine of unity and brotherhood notwithstanding.

The conflict in Kosovo progressed from a struggle for identity and control of political power within an autonomous province as part of a federal structure to a genuine self-determination conflict aiming towards secession. This transformation occurred simultaneously with the attempts of Serbia, one of the six constituent republics of the SFRY, to gain political dominance within the Federation. While it still seemed possible to reform the Federation, Kosovo agitated for promotion to the status of a republic. When the Federation dissolved in 1991, Kosovo declared itself independent. In March 1999, as a result of the Rambouillet and Paris conferences, Kosovo accepted, for an interim period, a complex power-sharing arrangement featuring an intricately layered authority from local communes up to the federal level. After the conclusion of hostilities in June 1999, a UN interim administration was established for Kosovo, providing for the gradual transition to autonomous self-government within Kosovo under international supervision. All ethnic Albanian political parties in Kosovo remain committed to independence, whereas UN Security Council Resolution 1244 (1999) confirms the attachment of the international community to Yugoslavia's demand to leave its territorial integrity untouched. A Constitutional framework has been generated, providing for a complex power-sharing regime until this clash of interests can be addressed.

2. THE RAMBOUILLET DRAFT

2.1 The Negotiations

From the summer of 1998 onwards, an attempt was made under the leadership of U.S. mediator Christopher Hill to achieve a political settlement, or interim political settlement, for Kosovo. A number of drafts were presented to the Yugoslav/Serb authorities and to a team of ethnic Albanian delegates, nominated by the unofficial government of Dr Ibrahim Rugova and headed by Dr Fehmi Agani. Yugoslavia took the view that the matter was one relating to the domestic jurisdiction of the FRY. If a settlement with international involvement could be achieved at all, it would need to respect the territorial integrity of the Federation. In fact, such arrangements could only be concluded at the lower level of relations between Kosovo and the Serb Republic (a principle maintained to the last and evidenced by the fact that the Yugoslav delegation at the Rambouillet and Paris talks was presented as a Serb delegation). While it would be possible to strengthen autonomy arrangements, this would need to be balanced by special rights of minority populations. Moreover, all of the ethnic groups in Kosovo should be treated principally equally, enjoying equal representation in political bodies.

The Kosovo delegation took the view that it could accept an interim arrangement, provided it did not prejudice its claim to self-determination and provided there would be a process providing for the ultimate option of independence after the expiry of an agreed interim period. While it was a strong advocate of equal human rights for all groups, it objected to special regimes for minority populations. Kosovo, in particular, was strongly opposed to the assignment of equal political representation of all ethnic groups in the territory, which would have given the 90 per cent ethnic Albanians the same level of representation as each of the minority groups. It argued that in this way the overwhelming majority of ethnic Albanians would only control one voice out of six or seven, turning the majority into a minority in terms of representation.

The Hill drafts that were produced oscillated slightly over time on the issues of the status of Kosovo. At one stage, the express reference to the right to territorial integrity of the FRY was dropped. On the other hand, there was never an affirmation of the right to self-determination for Kosovo. The question about the time frame for the interim agreement was left unaddressed. While there was provision for a comprehensive assessment of the agreement after three years, any changes to the agreement would be subject to a veto of either party. Hence, the situation would have been effectively frozen. There was also the question of the precise nature of a mechanism to review the situation after the three-year period. In the Hill draft the sides would undertake the review, thus apparently removing the internationalized element of the negotiation process at the review stage.

When the Holbrooke Agreement collapsed in January 1999 in the wake of the Racak massacre, the Contact Group, acting with the support of the UN Security Council, summoned the parties to a conference (in fact a 'meeting', to downplay expectations) where they were expected to reach an interim settlement within a period of two weeks at most.

2.2 The Issue of Status and the Basic Distribution of Powers

Before the Rambouillet conference, the Contact Group had established a list of so-called non-negotiable principles. These reflected the FRY/Serb demand that the territorial integrity of the FRY and its neighbouring countries had to be respected. The government of Kosovo had responded that it would be willing to attend the Rambouillet talks, provided a proposed settlement would not prejudice the status of Kosovo, in accordance with the approach that it had adopted in the initial Hill proposals. The first draft of the agreement presented to the conference was in accordance with this idea of leaving out express statements on issues on which no agreement could be achieved. It contained, in what started out as the Draft Framework Agreement, merely a preambular paragraph which recalled the commitment of the international community to the sovereignty and territorial integrity of the FRY. Hence, in signing this text, Kosovo itself would not have had to take an express view in this matter. There was also a reference to United Nations and OSCE principles. As these contain both the rule of territorial unity and the principle of self-determination, this reference was also acceptable to Kosovo, while it provided reassurance to the FRY/Serbia. The Constitution (initially Annex 1) did not contain a preamble and, instead of addressing the status of Kosovo and the legal quality of its relations with the FRY or even Serbia, it focused on a reasonable division of competencies.

When the second draft of the Agreement was presented on 18 February 1999, a preamble had been added which referred to "democratic self-government in Kosovo grounded in respect for the territorial integrity and sovereignty of the Federal Republic of Yugoslavia, from which the authorities of governance set forth herein originate". While the Contact Group attempted to assert that this was an insubstantial addition, it did in fact fundamentally change the nature of the entire interim settlement. To avoid a failure of the Rambouillet process on account of this unilateral change, made without explanation two days before the deadline for signature, the following compromise was in the end adopted:

Desiring through this interim Constitution to establish institutions of democratic self-government in Kosovo grounded in respect for the territorial integrity and sovereignty of the Federal Republic of Yugoslavia and from this Agreement, from which authorities of governance set forth herein originate.

Even as amended, this provision almost led the Kosovo delegation to reject the Agreement. Still, the formulation permitted Kosovo to argue that acceptance of the territorial integrity and sovereignty was limited to the interim period.[174] In any event, this commitment and the legal personality and powers of Kosovo were rooted in the Agreement, rather than in a grant of autonomy by the FRY.

Another important change that had been made in the draft of 18 February related to the assignment of powers. According to Article 1(2) of the initial draft of what then was Annex 1, Kosovo as an entity would enjoy responsibility for "all areas" other than those where authority was expressly assigned to the FRY. Those areas of authority were enumerated exclusively and their exercise was subject to important restrictions and safeguards for Kosovo. In the draft of 18 February, the express presumption in favour of Kosovo authority had been abandoned. Instead, a new paragraph had been added, indicating that Serbia, too, would exercise competence in relation to Kosovo as specified in the Agreement.

The FRY/Serbia strongly insisted on the inclusion of a further provision in the introductory section of the Agreement (formerly the Framework Agreement), stating that the parties would only act within their powers and responsibilities in Kosovo as specified by this Agreement. Acts outside those powers and responsibilities would be null and void. Kosovo would have all rights and powers set forth in the Agreement, in particular as specified in the Constitution. While the FRY/Serb delegation might have intended this provision as a safeguard against creeping jurisdiction by the Kosovo organs, the delegation of Kosovo interpreted it as a helpful confirmation that the powers of Kosovo were indeed based in the Agreement, and not in a sovereign grant of rights by the FRY. In addition, this formulation supported the view that FRY/Serb exercises of powers in relation to Kosovo would be strictly limited to competencies that have been expressly granted to them.[175]

The issue of legal personality for Kosovo as a whole was also clarified in some measure through a provision concerning the communes. One of the difficulties with the initial Hill proposal was its insistence that Kosovo communes would be the basic unit of self-governance in Kosovo and that they would exercise all authority not assigned to Kosovo and not assigned to other Kosovo organs. While the latter element was retained,[176] it was clarified in what was to become Article 1 (8) of Chapter 1 of the final text that the communes were merely the basic unit of 'local' self-government. The insertion of the word 'local' ensured that this provision no longer diluted the overall legal personality of Kosovo as a whole.

2.3 The Kosovo Institutions and their Powers

The principal organs of Kosovo according to the Agreement were the Assembly, the President of Kosovo, the Government and Administrative Organs, judicial organs and the communes.[177] The Assembly was to be composed of 120 members, of which 80 would be directly elected. The other 40 members would be elected by members of qualifying national communities. Communities whose members constitute more than 0.5 per cent of the Kosovo population but less than 5 per cent were to divide 10 of these seats among themselves. Communities whose members constituted more than 5 per cent of the Kosovo population (in fact, only the ethnic Albanians and Serbs) would divide the remaining 30 seats equally.

The draft of 18 February had introduced as an additional feature a second chamber of the Assembly as a result of FRY/Serb pressure. In that Chamber of 100 seats, the Turks, Goranies, Romani, Egyptians, Muslims and any other group constituting more than 0.5 per cent of the population (hence also including the ethnic Albanians and Serbs) would be equally represented. The Chamber would have had the right of consultation in relation to legislative acts of the Assembly, and any of the groups represented within it could have initiated so-called 'vital interest motions' which would amount to an attempted veto of legislation.

The FRY/Serb delegation itself abandoned the concept of the second chamber and instead focused on attempting to strengthen the power of veto of national communities in the Assembly. According to the initial draft and the draft of 18 February, the decision as to which legislative acts would violate the vital interests of a national community and would thus be null and void would have been taken by the Constitutional Court of Kosovo. The Kosovo delegation had grave reservations about the very concept of special powers for ethnic groups, including separate elections according to ethnic criteria. While strongly endorsing the notion of equal rights for members of all ethnic groups, the idea of separate representation appeared to grant to very small groups broad rights of co-decision which were unrepresentative and hence undemocratic. Moreover, the example of ethnic politics in Bosnia and Herzegovina had demonstrated the divisive nature of ethnic organization of a political system. Finally, a legislative system which was subjected to the constant threat of a veto by any ethnic group would result in perennial paralysis.

Despite these concerns, and in view of the strong position of the FRY/Serbia in this matter, the Kosovo delegation endorsed, however reluctantly, the concept of special representation for ethnic groups for the interim period. However, this concession was dependent on a judicial process to check vital national interest motions in the Assembly, in order to avoid an arbitrary use of this procedure leading to constant deadlock in the legislature. The Contact Group disregarded this view and gave way to a FRY/Serb proposal of settling disputes about vital national interest motions outside the judicial system. According to Article 2(8) (c) of Chapter 1, the final Agreement provided that the decision about such motions would be rendered by a panel comprising three members of the Assembly: one Albanian, one Serb, each appointed by his or her national community, and a third Member of a third 'nationality' to be selected within two days by consensus of the Presidency of the Assembly. As the Serb national community was guaranteed a member of the Presidency of the Assembly (in fact, actually the President of the Assembly), it appears that this nominating process itself can be blocked by a factual veto.

Decisions of the Assembly which had been challenged according to the vital national interest procedure were to be suspended in regard to the national community having brought the challenge, pending completion of the dispute settlement procedure. Hence, it might appear as if a Serb veto in relation to Assembly decisions was introduced through the back door. However, as this veto would depend on an abuse of process in frustrating the nomination of the third member of the arbitration panel, the general dispute settlement mechanism attaching to the Agreement as a whole, or the general powers of the Constitutional Court, would probably be brought to bear on a matter of this kind. It should also be noted that the decision on the merits of a vital interest motion, while conducted by a political body, was to be made according to legal criteria.[178]

The substantive powers of the Assembly were reasonably wide, covering most aspects of governance. Importantly, this included the power to set the framework of, and to coordinate, the exercise of competencies assigned to the communes. The first elections in Kosovo were to be held within nine months of the entry into force of the Agreement under international supervision.

The President of Kosovo was to be elected by the Assembly by a majority vote. His or her functions included representation before international, FRY or republic bodies, the conduct of foreign relations consistent with the authorities of Kosovo institutions, proposing to the Assembly candidates for Prime Minister and for the principal courts of Kosovo, etc. The Government, also to be approved by the Assembly, would have general authority for implementing the laws of Kosovo, etc. At least one Minister would have been a member of the Serb national community.

The powers reserved for the communes were narrowed down somewhat in comparison with earlier drafts. However, while there was provision for coordination on a Kosovo-wide basis, the police had to be organized on a communal basis and limited to a ceiling of 3,000 active law-enforcement officers throughout Kosovo. In addition, there was authority in relation to education, childcare, the communal environment and local economic issues.

The judiciary consisted of a Constitutional Court composed of nine judges. At least one judge would have been a member of the Serb national community and five other judges would have been selected from a list drawn up by the President of the European Court of Human Rights. The powers of review of the Constitutional Court were quite wide. They included, but were not limited to, determining whether laws applicable in Kosovo, decisions or acts of the President, the Assembly, the Government, the Communes and the national communities were compatible with the Constitution.

The Supreme Court composed of nine judges, including one member of the Serb national community, would hear final appeals from subordinated courts in Kosovo, including communal courts.

A special feature related to the right of citizens in Kosovo to opt to have civil disputes to which they are party adjudicated by other courts in the FRY, would apply the law applicable in Kosovo. In criminal cases, a defendant would be entitled to have a trial transferred to another Kosovo court designated by the defendant. In effect, this meant that a defendant could opt to be tried in the local court of a specific commune, which would be principally composed of members of his or her ethnic community. In criminal cases in which all defendants and victims were members of the same national community, all members of the judicial council would be from the national community of their choice if any party so requested. A defendant in a criminal case could also insist that one member of the judicial council hearing the case would be from his or national community. This might include judges of courts in the FRY serving as Kosovo judges for these purposes.

2.4 Human Rights and Additional Rights of National Communities

The provisions on human rights were strangely short and undeveloped in the Constitution and the Agreement. There was no listing of fundamental human rights to be applied in Kosovo. Instead, Article 6(1) of the Constitution stated rather generally that all authorities in Kosovo must ensure internationally recognized human rights and fundamental freedoms. As opposed to the Dayton Agreement, which included a long list of human rights instruments identifying what internationally recognized human rights and fundamental freedoms were, the Agreement in Article 6(2) incorporated by reference the terms of the European Convention for the Protection of Human

Rights and Fundamental Freedoms and its Protocols which "shall apply directly in Kosovo". In this way, a very sophisticated body of human rights law, refined over decades of jurisprudence by the European Court and Commission of Human Rights would have been instantly available in Kosovo. The Kosovo Assembly also had the power to enact into law other internationally recognized human rights instruments.

The rights and freedoms established in this way would have priority over all other law. Interestingly, according to Article 6(3), all "courts, agencies, governmental institutions, and other public institutions of Kosovo or operating in relation to Kosovo shall conform to these human rights and fundamental freedoms". This meant that the FRY and republic authorities would also have had to exercise their competencies in relation to Kosovo in accordance with these standards. As the FRY was not a party to the European Convention and its Protocols, this would have placed it in an unusual position.

While the human rights provisions were compact, the additional rights granted to national communities were extensive, but not unlimited. Firstly, these rights were tied to the specific purpose of preserving and expressing their national, cultural, religious and linguistic identities. This was to be done in accordance with international standards and in accordance with human rights and fundamental freedoms.

More controversially, each national community could elect and establish its own institutions— a feature which was feared to give rise to a parallel state structure within Kosovo. However, national community institutions would have to act in accordance with Kosovo law and not take discriminatory action. National communities could arrange for the naming of local names of towns and villages, etc., in the language and alphabet of the respective community, issue information in that language, and provide for education and schooling in that language and culture. Reflecting a spirit of tolerance between communities and respect for the rights of members of all national communities, national communities could also display national symbols, including those of the FRY and Serbia, protect national traditions on family law, arrange for the preservation of sites of religious, historical or cultural importance in cooperation with other authorities, implement public health and social services on a non-discriminatory basis, operate religious institutions in cooperation with religious authorities and participate in non-governmental organizations.

National communities could also enjoy unhindered contacts with representatives of their respective national communities within the FRY and abroad. Access to and representation in the media was guaranteed, and they could finance their activities by collecting contributions from members. Importantly, every person had the right to choose to be treated or not to be treated as belonging to a national community.

2.5 Final Status

The draft presented to the parties at the outset of the Conference restated the concluding provision from previous Hill proposals, providing for amendments to the Agreement to be adopted by agreement of all the parties. Each party was to be entitled to propose such an amendment at any time. However, after three years, there would occur a comprehensive assessment of the Agreement under international auspices with the aim of improving its implementation and determining whether to implement proposals by either side for additional steps.[179] The means of undertaking this assessment and the procedure to be adopted were left unclear.

The Kosovo delegation argued strongly that in accordance with the interim character of the Agreement, provision would need to be made for a further international conference on a final settlement for Kosovo. The decisions of that conference would be based on the will of the people of Kosovo, made manifest in a referendum. The negotiators pointed out that they were not authorized by the Contact Group to adopt language on a referendum. However, even the non-negotiable principles had at least provided for "a mechanism for a final settlement after an interim period of three years". In the dramatic final phase of the conference, it became possible to obtain significant changes to the final provision, in reflection of this wording. The final text of what became Article 1(3) of Chapter 8 reads:

> Three years after the entry into force of this *Agreement*, an international meeting shall be convened to determine a mechanism for a final settlement for Kosovo, on the basis of the will of the people, opinions of relevant authorities, each Party's efforts regarding the implementation of this Agreement, and the Helsinki Final Act, and to undertake a comprehensive assessment of the implementation of this Agreement and to consider proposals by any Party for additional measures.

This wording stops short of actually establishing a mechanism for a final settlement, contrary to what might have been expected in view of the language contained in the non-negotiable principles. However, startlingly, it was accepted that this mechanism shall be established and/or operate, *inter alia*, on the basis of the will of the people.[180] On the other hand, this mechanism would be created by 'an international meeting' the composition and authority of which was not defined. All organs of the international community had consistently ruled out the possibility of independence and thus it would not be surprising if the 'international meeting' held a similar view. These uncertainties were not necessarily entirely removed by the unilateral interpretation offered by the US in a draft side letter, which confirmed that Kosovo could hold a referendum on independence after three years. In any event, that side-letter was in the end not formalized, given the failure of the Kosovo delegation to sign the Agreement by the stipulated deadline at Rambouillet.

2.6 Implementation

The provisions for implementation contained in the Rambouillet text were complex and distributed throughout the interim Agreement. They consisted principally of the introductory section of the Agreement entitled Framework, Chapter 2 on Police and Public Security, Chapter 3 on the Conduct and Supervision of Elections, Chapter 4 (a) on Humanitarian Assistance, Reconstruction and Development, Chapter 5 on the Civilian Implementation Mission in Kosovo, Chapter 6 concerning the Ombudsman and Chapter 7 on "Implementation II", that is to say, military implementation. For reasons of space, it will only be possible to review some of the principal features of this implementation structure here.

2.6.1 Confidence-Building

Upon signature of the Agreement, a ceasefire was to come into force immediately. Alleged violations of the cease-fire were to be reported to international observers and could not be used to justify use of force in response. The status of police and security forces in Kosovo, including withdrawal of forces was to be achieved according to Chapter 7. Paramilitary and irregular forces in Kosovo were deemed incompatible with the terms of the Agreement. The latter provision gave rise to some difficulty, inasmuch as the Kosovo Liberation Army (Ushtria Clirimtare e Kosoves, UCK) did not consider itself a paramilitary or irregular force. However, it was clear that it, too, was addressed through Chapter 7 of the Agreement.

All abducted persons or other persons detained without charge were to be released, including persons held in connection with the conflict in Kosovo. No one was to be prosecuted for crimes related to the conflict, except for persons accused of serious violations of international humanitarian law. Persons already convicted for committing politically motivated crimes related to the conflict were to be released, provided these convictions did not relate to serious violations of humanitarian law obtained in a fair and open trial conducted pursuant to international standards.

The Agreement confirmed the obligation, already contained in mandatory Security Council resolutions, to cooperate with the Hague International Criminal Tribunal for the Former Yugoslavia. This included the obligation to permit complete access to tribunal investigators and compliance with the orders of the Tribunal. This provision was somewhat contested at Rambouillet. Kosovo attempted to strengthen its scope, as did, indirectly, the Tribunal itself. However, in the face of determined opposition from the FRY, a rather short paragraph was adopted which did not greatly improve upon the obligations already contained in the demands of the Security Council.

The parties also recognized the right to return of all persons to their homes, including those who have had to leave the region. There was to be no impediment to the normal flow of goods into Kosovo, including materials for the reconstruction of homes and structures. The FRY would not require visas, customs or licensing for persons or things connected with international implementation.

2.7 NATO-Led Implementation and the Withdrawal of Forces

The military implementation chapter was the most detailed element of the entire accords. The parties would have agreed that NATO would establish and deploy a force (KFOR) operating under the authority and subject to the direction and the political control of the North Atlantic Council (NAC) through the NATO chain of command. However, contrary to much subsequent speculation, a Chapter 7 mandate was supposed to be obtained from the Security Council. Other states would be invited to assist in military implementation. While this was not spelt out, it was envisaged that KFOR would be of a strength of approximately 28,000 troops. It would include a sizeable Russian contingent according to the precedent of IFOR/SFOR in Bosnia and Herzegovina. In accordance with that precedent, KFOR would be authorized to take such actions as required, including the use of necessary force, to ensure compliance with Chapter 7. As opposed to the arrangements of Dayton, it was made clear at the beginning that KFOR would not only be available to ensure compliance with the military aspects of the Agreement, but that it would also actively support civilian implementation by the OSCE and others as part of its original mandate. As in the Dayton Agreement, the mandate of KFOR could have been broadened through further action by NATO, in this instance acting through the North Atlantic Council.

A Joint Implementation Commission would have been established to consider complaints by the parties and other matters. It would have been composed of FRY military commanders and FRY/Serb officials, Kosovo representatives and representatives of the military and civilian implementation missions. The Agreement envisaged that final authority to interpret the provisions of Chapter 7 would rest with the KFOR military commander.

The regular armed forces of the FRY (Vojska Jugoslavije, VJ) would have been subjected to a rigorous regime of redeployment and withdrawal according to fixed deadlines. This included the removal of assets such as battle tanks, all armoured vehicles mounting weapons greater than 12.7mm and all heavy weapons of over 82 mm. Within 180 days of the coming into force of the Agreement, all VJ units, other than 1,500 members of a lightly armed border guard battalion deployed close to the border would have had to be withdrawn from Kosovo. An additional 1,000 support personnel would be permitted in specified cantonment sites. The border guards would have been limited to patrolling the border zone and their travel through Kosovo would have been subjected to significant restrictions. Moreover, the air defence system in Kosovo would be dismantled and associated forces withdrawn, as would be other FRY or Serb forces, including the Ministry of Interior Police (MUP). The MUP would initially be drawn down to a size of 2,500, and be entirely withdrawn upon the establishment of a Kosovo police force within one year. Upon entry into force of the Agreement, all other forces would have had to commit themselves to demilitarization, renunciation of violence, to guarantee security of international personnel, etc. The definition of the term 'demilitarization' had been subject to some discussion, especially as it applies to the UCK. It would have included the surrender of heavy armaments and some small arms.

The military Chapter was accompanied by two Appendices, which were both published along with the Agreement. The claims that they reveal a secret agenda by NATO for the virtual occupation of all of Yugoslavia made some time after the conclusion of the conference are without substance. Appendix A established cantonment sites for FRY/Serb forces. The famous Appendix B established what in other contexts would be the standard terms of a status of forces agreement for KFOR, very much in line with the precedent of IFOR/SFOR in Bosnia and Herzegovina and United Nations peace-keeping operations. A provision which permits transit through Yugoslavia for NATO and affiliated forces falls within these standard terms, although it may have been phrased slightly more broadly than would have been usual. If, as was subsequently claimed, the terms of the Appendix, or this particular provision, were the reason which rendered Rambouillet unacceptable, it remains to be explained why the FRY did not seek clarification or even modification of this provision at the Paris follow-on conference. That conference was exclusively dedicated to negotiations on the implementation aspects of the Agreement, which had not been available at Rambouillet itself.

2.8 Civilian Implementation

The OSCE would have been charged with principal responsibility over the civilian elements of implementation, operating under a Chief of the Implementation Mission (CIM). The implementation mission would monitor, observe and inspect law enforcement activities in Kosovo, which would be established principally at communal level. The Kosovo police force of around 3,000 was to be only lightly armed. The authority of Federal and Serb police would have been very significantly restricted. Importantly, the CIM would have had final authority to interpret the provisions of the Agreement in relation to civilian implementation.

All aspects of civilian implementation would have been coordinated and monitored by a Joint Commission, including Federal, Republic and Kosovo representatives and others, and chaired by the CIM exercising a final right of decision in this rather powerful body. In addition, an ombudsman would monitor the rights of members of national communities and the protection of human rights and fundamental freedoms. Elections were to be held at communal and Kosovo level within a period of nine months from entry into force of the Agreement, once the OSCE certified that conditions had been established for a free and fair ballot. Finally, the Agreement provided for the administration of humanitarian aid and reconstruction principally through the organs of Kosovo, with strong involvement by the European Union. In fact, throughout the conference, the European Union, through its negotiator and through representatives of the Commission, exercised a considerable influence, also and especially in relation to this issue. Great emphasis was placed on careful planning, rapid and non-bureaucratic deployment of resources once needs had been identified, and close cooperation with the beneficiaries of such aid.

3.   RESOLUTION 1244 (1999) AND THE DEVELOPMENT OF THE CONSTITUTIONAL FRAMEWORK

3.1 The Remit of Resolution 1244 (1999)

UN Security Council Resolution 1244 (1999) was adopted on 10 June 1999 by 14 votes to none (China abstaining). The entire text of the resolution is subject to Chapter VII of the United Nations Charter. Preambular paragraph 10 reaffirms the commitment of all UN member states to the sovereignty and territorial integrity of the Federal Republic of Yugoslavia and the other states of the region. In its very first operative paragraph, it addresses the issue of a political settlement, "deciding" that a political solution to the Kosovo crisis shall be based on general principles established in two annexes to the resolution. In addition, the Council authorized the deployment of "international civil and security presences" under UN auspices. The civil presence was to be "controlled" by a Special Representative of the UN Secretary-General. While the military presence established by "member states and relevant international organizations" is to coordinate closely with the civil presence, it is not subject to control by the Secretariat. It enjoys a mandate to enforce the cease-fire, deter hostilities, ensure withdrawals and prevent the return of certain forces. It is also empowered to demilitarize the UCK, ensure public safety and order in the interim, conduct border monitoring, ensure freedom of movement for itself, the civil presence and other international organizations and support, as appropriate, the civil presence.

The civil presence is charged with:
a)   promoting the establishment, pending a final settlement, of substantial autonomy and self-government in Kosovo, taking full account of Annex 2 of the Rambouillet accords (S/1999/648);
b)   performing basic civilian administrative functions where and as long as required;
c)   organizing and overseeing the development of provisional institutions for democratic and autonomous self-government pending a political settlement, including the holding of elections;
d)   transferring, as these institutions are established, its administrative responsibilities while overseeing and supporting the consolidation of Kosovo's local provisional institutions and other peace-building activities;

e) facilitating a political process designed to determine Kosovo's future status, taking into account the Rambouillet accords (S/1999/648);

f) in the final stage, overseeing the transfer of authority from Kosovo's provisional institutions to institutions established under a political settlement;

g) supporting the reconstruction of key infrastructure and other reconstruction;

h) supporting, in coordination with international humanitarian organizations, humanitarian and disaster relief aid;

i) maintaining civil law and order, including establishing local police forces and meanwhile through the deployment of international police personnel to serve in Kosovo;

j) protecting and promoting human rights;

k) assuring the safe and unimpeded return of all refugees and displaced persons to their homes in Kosovo.

Annex 1, to which reference is made, consists of the St. Petersburg G-8 declaration of 6 May 1999, which effectively contained the peace terms that Yugoslavia was invited to accept before a termination of hostilities with NATO could take place. That document refers to an interim administration of Kosovo to be decided by the Security Council and "a political process towards the establishment of an interim political framework agreement providing for a substantial self-government for Kosovo, taking full account of the Rambouillet accords and the principles of sovereignty and territorial integrity of the Federal Republic of Yugoslavia and the other countries of the region and the demilitarization of the UCK".

Annex 2 consists of a ten-point statement presented to the FRY on 2 June 1999 and expressly accepted by it as part of the ceasefire negotiations. It provides for:

• Establishment of an interim administration for Kosovo as part of the international civil presence under which the people of Kosovo can enjoy substantial autonomy within the Federal Republic of Yugoslavia, to be decided by the Security Council of the United Nations. The interim administration to provide transitional administration while establishing and overseeing the development of provisional democratic self-governing institutions to ensure conditions for a peaceful and normal life for all inhabitants in Kosovo (item 5).

• A political process towards the establishment of an interim political framework agreement providing for substantial self-government for Kosovo, taking full account of the Rambouillet accords and the principles of sovereignty and territorial integrity of the Federal Republic of Yugoslavia and the other countries of the region, and the demilitarization of the UCK. Negotiations between the parties for a settlement should not delay or disrupt the establishment of democratic self-governing institutions (item 8).

While there was initially some confusion as to the precise extent of the mandate, and in relation to the progression of events foreseen in the three different instruments to which reference has been made, in practice there has occurred a fairly smooth development. During the period of establishing a UN administration under the first Special Representative of the UN Secretary-General (SRSG), Bernard Kouchner, there were generated processes of involvement through consultation for local politicians and officials in the exercise of public authority. In a second phase, provision was made for limited co-decision, when, early in 2000, the UN administration established a Joint Interim Administrative Structure. This consisted of the establishment of some twenty departments with responsibility for civil administration. These departments were jointly headed by one local and one international official.

This was matched by the holding of municipal elections and the establishment of local structures of self-government at the end of 2000. A third phase provides for conditional self-government, to be realized under the terms of the Constitutional Framework that was put forward in 2001.

3.2 The Constitutional Framework

3.2.1   Origin and Establishment

The Constitutional Framework for Provisional Self-Government was issued on 15 May as United Nations Mission in Kosovo (UNMIK) Regulation 2001/9. That is to say, its legal force is rooted in Regulation 1999/1 (subsequently amended), which vests supreme executive powers and also quasi-legislative powers in the Special Representative of the Secretary-General (SRSG). This power is, in turn, derived from the mandate contained in Security Council Resolution (UNSCR) 1244 (1999). The drafting of the document had caused some friction among the Western members of the Contact Group (the quint) throughout 2000. The United States was attempting to present a draft instrument that was very much based on Rambouillet, although the powers for FRY/Serbia had been significantly reduced in view of the recent conflict and its outcome. Others were arguing that it would be pre-mature to offer any sort of consolidated interim constitution, which would accelerate the process of claims for statehood on the part of the Kosovo majority parties. Instead, there should be issued individual regulations that would, over time, address issues that would normally be contained in a constitutional document.

The debate took a different turn with the appointment of a new SRSG, former Danish Minister of Defence Hans Haekkerup. With amazing speed, and the encouragement of a Presidential Statement of the Security Council, a consultative expert body was established to draft a framework document (at the time the use of the word 'constitution' was not accepted). This body was intended to be fully representative, but was generally boycotted by its Serb representatives. Some of the ethnic Albanian experts also resigned towards the end of the drafting process, when it emerged that the draft texts they had submitted would not be taken as the basis for the venture. Overall, therefore, the text that emerged showed a strong hand of internationalized drafting, through the UN's own legal advisor's office and other international experts, including especially an expert of the Venice Commission. Nevertheless, the ethnic Albanian experts did have influence on the shaping of the document, which eased the process that led all major ethnic Albanian political parties to embrace the document (although with hesitation) as an acceptable interim solution. At the very end of the drafting, an effort was also made to take account of positions of the Serb leadership and to incorporate at least some of them, despite the continued failure to participate formally in the drafting process.

Overall, therefore, an instrument emerged that will most likely fulfil the functions of a constitu-tion for some years to come. There was no democratically legitimized constitutional drafting process, say through a constitutional convention. Instead, the document was internationally established, with the involvement (or in the case of the Serb community, with the possible involvement) of experts. Some of these experts were in fact affiliated with the principal political parties in Kosovo. Hence, local ownership of the drafting process was fairly limited.

On the part of the ethnic Albanian parties, it was possible, at least for the moment, to avoid the appearance of spoilers. Instead of attacking the document, they declared it flawed but acceptable and focused on the upcoming election campaign in order to attempt to fill some of the positions of political power foreseen in the document. The Serb National Council had rejected the instrument and remains a potential spoiler in the establishment of the intended power-sharing arrangement. However, Serb groups did eventually agree to participate in the elections of November 2001.

3.2.2   Status, Structure and the Layering of Public Authority

Kosovo is defined in Article 1(1) as an entity under interim international administration which, with its people, has unique historical, legal, cultural and linguistic attributes. This clause appears to acknowledge that Kosovo is an entity that has 'a people'. If so, then the preambular paragraph which refers to provisional self-government as a step for a peaceful and normal life for all inhabitants of Kosovo, with a view to facilitating the determination of Kosovo's future status through a process at an appropriate future stage which shall, in accordance with UNSCR 1244 (1999), take full account of all relevant factors "including the will of the people", takes on an interesting meaning. The two combined could give rise to a view that Kosovo is a self-determination unit. On the other hand, the entire text is, of course, subject to the superior authority of UNSCR 1244 (1999).

There exists an institutional and a functional layering of authority. The institutional layers of authority are arranged in a comparatively simple way. There are municipalities, the Kosovo-wide layers of provisional self-government and the SRSG. Municipalities are the basic territorial units of local self-government, exercising responsibilities as set forth in UNMIK legislation in force. Hence, as opposed to the Hill draft, the municipalities are no longer the residual source of all public authority not expressly assigned elsewhere.

The Framework also refers to communities and their members. However, as opposed to the Rambouillet draft, there is emphatically no provision for parallel institutions for communities. Instead, these are now defined in terms of traditional minority rights. That is to say "communities of inhabitants belonging to the same ethnic or religious or linguistic group (communities) shall have the rights set forth in this Chapter in order to preserve, protect, and express their ethnic cultural, religious, and religious identities". To this end, they can use their own language, receive education in their language, have access to information in their own language and enjoy equal opportunities, etc. They can also establish associations to promote their community interests, their culture and operate educational institutions. However, the communities are not equipped with institutions that exercise original state powers almost by way of full functional autonomy. Hence, this layer of public authority that was a crucial element of Rambouillet has simply disappeared.

The Kosovo-wide institutions enjoy powers that are specifically enumerated in the Framework. These functions extend to most aspects of public policy. These institutions also have the power to coordinate and supervise the exercise of public powers by the municipalities. This fact, together with the finding in Article 1(1) that "Kosovo is an undivided territory throughout which the Provisional Institutions of Self-Government established by this Constitutional Framework ... shall exercise their responsibilities" clearly subordinates the municipalities to the Kosovo-wide institutions. Hence, there is no original autonomy located within the municipalities, other than specific power of municipal governance assigned in legislation.

A third institutional layer consists of the SRSG who exercise certain "reserved powers and responsibilities" that remain exclusively in his hands:

- full authority to ensure that the rights and interests of Communities are fully protected;
- final authority to set financial and policy parametres and approval of the Kosovo Consolidated Budget and its auditing;
- dissolving the Assembly and calling for elections, especially when other institutions have acted in violation of Resolution 1244 (1999);
- monetary policy;
- control of the customs service;
- appointment, removal and disciplining of judges and prosecutors;
- assignments of international judges and prosecutors and changes of venue of trials;
- international legal cooperation, conclusion and implementation of international agreements, and exercise of foreign affairs powers;
- authority over law enforcement institutions and correctional facilities;
- control over the Kosovo Protection Corps.

While the chapeau to this provision does suggest that these are exclusive powers, several provisions do in fact provide for the exercise of administrative authority in relation to them "in co-operation" with the Kosovo institutions. Hence, it is to be expected that some of this residual authority will be exercised by the Kosovo institutions, up to the point when the SRSG sees a need to intervene. In relation to other functions that are indeed formally exclusive, there is room for consultation and advice before decisions are taken. However, the principle of unchallengeable supreme powers in relation to these issue areas must be noted. Moreover, according to a concluding provision of the Regulation, the SRSG retains a general right to oversee the provisional institutions and its officers and to take appropriate measures whenever their actions are inconsistent with Resolution 1244 (1999) or the Framework.

The unique character of the SRSG's role is also evident in the fact that he can either at the initiative of the two-thirds majority of the Assembly, or at his own discretion, 'effect' changes to the constitutional framework. This provision does, of course, cast some doubt on the character of the instrument as a 'constitution', and instead confirms its *sui generis* character.

3.3 Veto-Mechanisms and Guaranteed Representation

The Kosovo Assembly, the principal legislative organ of provisional self-government, consists of 120 members elected by secret ballot in a nation-wide, single-district vote. One hundred of the seats are assigned proportionally to the votes cast for parties, citizens' initiatives (according to a fixed list system) or individual candidates. Additionally, twenty seats are reserved for "the additional representation of non-Albanian Kosovo communities". Ten of these fall to those declaring themselves as representatives of the Kosovo Serb Community, the others are divided amongst the Roma, Ashkali, Egyptian, Bosniak, Turkish and Gorani communities.

The seven-member Presidency of the Assembly must contain one member representing the Serb community and one member representing another minority community. However, there is no rotating Presidency of the Presidency. Instead the President is nominated by the party having achieved the highest number of votes. There is no provision for representation of other groups through offices of Vice Presidents. The Presidency which manages parliamentary business is invited to attempt to agree by consensus, but failing that, it decides by majority vote.

315

There is also no specific quota for representation in function committees, other than the general exhortation that the membership shall reflect the diversity of the membership of the Assembly. Chairs and Vice Chairs of committees are appointed according to the strength of parties in the Assembly.

A Committee on the Rights and Interests of Communities does exist: it consists of two members from each of the Communities represented in the Assembly (but only one Gorani representative). The Committee can adopt by simple majority a recommendation in relation to draft legislation or other matters.

Decisions of the Assembly are adopted by simple majority of members present and voting (the quorum being 50 per cent for decisions and 33 per cent for debates). Within 48 hours of approval of a law any six members may submit a motion to the Presidency alleging a violation of vital interests of the community to which at least one of them belongs. A motion may be made on grounds that the law or provisions discriminate against a community, adversely affect the rights of the community or otherwise seriously interfere with the ability of the Community to preserve, protect or express its identity.

A conciliatory attempt will be made by the President to put forward a consensus proposal. If that is not possible, a panel consisting of one member of the majority, one representative of the complainants and one presiding individual appointed by the SRSG issue a decision as to a recommendation by simple majority. However, the Assembly remains at liberty to decide to accept or reject the consensus proposal of the Presidency or the recommendation of the panel. An Assembly decision can be reviewed for compatibility with the Constitutional Framework by a special chamber of the Supreme Court.

Overall, therefore, there exists no effective blocking mechanism in the Constitutional Framework. There is also only limited provision for representation of minority groups. While it is confirmed that judges, the police and other public officials shall be fully reflective of the diversity of the population, there is no rigid quota system as part of the Constitutional Framework (implementing legislation may be different). The only concession to quota rules and minority representation is the determination that out of nine ministries that are to be established after the election, two shall be headed by minority representatives, one of them an ethnic Serb.

4.   CONCLUSION

Kosovo has gone through an interesting permutation of constitutional designs, from a (barely) autonomous territory within Serbia to a quasi-federal entity in the 1974 SFRY system. Indeed, it gave itself an independent state constitution at one stage in 1991. Since then, the Hill drafts, but in the most pronounced way the Rambouillet Agreement, provided for an ever more complex fragmenting of public power in Kosovo. This was overcome to a considerable extent in the Constitutional Framework that has now been established for an interim period. This instrument was principally generated by United Nations and other international drafters, although with input from experts representing the majority population. Its authority is based in powers derived from a Chapter VII Security Council resolution. Residual authority remains with the SRSG to a considerable extent, although it remains to be seen to what extent it will actually be exercised in future. It is quite likely that there will emerge an informal process of co-decision between the Kosovo-wide layer of authority and the international layer. On the other hand, power-sharing between the ethnic communities is not supported by a very strong institutional framework, probably as a result of the Bosnian experience. This may result in a withdrawal of ethnic Serb populations to virtual autonomy exercised through the municipalities. While in principle these are subject to control and coordination by the Kosovo-wide institutions, this power will be difficult to exercise in practice, especially if minority communities feel disenfranchised on the Kosovo-wide level.

NOTES

[174] A proposal to entitle Chapter 1 'Interim Constitution' was not adopted. However, given the overall title of the Agreement, the specific reference to the interim period in this preambular provision, and the concluding provisions, this was not seen by the Kosovo delegation as a significant setback.

[175] Federal functions were still expressly, and from the perspective of Kosovo (in the view of the delegation), exhaustively listed: territorial integrity; maintaining a common market within the Federal Republic of Yugoslavia; monetary policy; defence; foreign policy; customs services; federal taxation; federal elections and other areas specified in this Agreement.

[176] See also Article 8(5) of Chapter 1, and the important reference contained therein to Article 2(5) (b) of Chapter 1.

[177] On the national communities and their institutions, see the section which follows.

[178] A vital interest motion shall be upheld if the legislation challenged adversely affects the community's fundamental rights as set forth in Article 7, or the principle of fair treatment.

[179] This formulation actually represented a slight retreat from the final Hill draft, put forward on 27 January, which had referred to a 'procedure' for considering such addition steps to be determined taking into account the Parties' roles in and compliance with this Agreement.

[180] In a dramatic night negotiating session of the delegations towards the very end of the conference, the Kosovo delegation was able to extract from the negotiators an even better formulation, referring to the 'expressed will of the people'. However, this concession was lost when the delegation was not immediately able to sign the final text and when the Contact Group overruled it afterwards.

Governing Post-War Bosnia-Herzegovina

Florian Bieber

Governing Post-War Bosnia-Herzegovina

Florian Bieber

Since the end of the war in late 1995, Bosnia-Herzegovina has managed to maintain its peace through massive international presence, while interethnic political cooperation only recently underwent some substantial transformations. The main goal of the dominant political representatives of the Bosnian Serbs—to separate from Bosnia and bring a significant part of Bosnian territory under its control—has been partly achieved during the war and recognized by the peace accord in the form of the *Republika Srpska* (RS). This entity was, however, required to affirm its commitment to remain part of Bosnia. The ambition of Croat leaders to separate parts of the Herzegovina from Bosnia and join them with Croatia was limited by the creation of a Bosniak[181] and Croat Federation in 1994.[182] The re-creation of joint Bosnian institutions in the Dayton Peace Accords (DPA) restricted the possibility of both Croat and Serb politicians in Bosnia to split up the country. At the same time, the degree of autonomy afforded the entities and the predominance of the war-time national parties merely transformed the military struggle of disintegration into a political struggle over weakening the political centre and reinforcing mono-national territorial autonomy, based on war-time ethnic cleansing.

As a multinational country, Bosnia-Herzegovina has three predominant groups, Bosniaks, Serbs and Croats, all equally recognized by the Constitution as constituent nations of Bosnia. Although Croats constitute less than a fifth of the population, their constitutional status is equal to that of the Bosniaks. Minorities, as defined by the Bosnian legal system, are granted only a limited degree of self-administration. The low degree of autonomy given to minorities, such as Roma, Hungarians, etc., is the result of both their small share in the population and their lack of involvement in the war.

Table 3.6
Population of Bosnia[183]

	Population in 1991 (census)		Population in 1998 (estimate)	
	[in Per cent]	[in Numbers]	[in Per cent]	[in Numbers]
Bosniaks/ Muslims	43.5	1,884,045	46.7	1,465.000
Serbs	31.2	1,358,198	31.4	986,000
Croats	17.4	758,059	14.0	440,000
Others	7.9	340,416	7.9	249,000
Total	100.0	4,340,718	100.0	3,140,000

1. THE EMERGENCE OF POST-DAYTON BOSNIA

While the particular geography of Bosnia led to strong regions, in particular in the case of Herzegovina, the management of ethnic differences in Bosnia before 1992 was limited to non-territorial forms of autonomy. The Ottoman *millet* system, which granted self-governance to the non-Muslim population, applied to Bosnia while it was part of the Ottoman Empire (until 1878) and was adopted in a modified form also by the Austro–Hungarian administration of the province (1878–1918).[184] Inter-war Yugoslavia, on the other hand, paid only little attention to the pre-existing degrees of autonomy in the province and divided Bosnia into several separate administrative units in 1929. Communist Yugoslavia reestablished Bosnia and ensured the so-called 'ethnic key' for the equal representation of the Bosnian nations. This was only achieved in the 1970s with the recognition of the Muslims as constituting a separate nation in its own right. As elsewhere in Yugoslavia, with the notable exception of the two Serb provinces of Vojvodina and Kosovo, the republics constituted the main level of power and the representation of ethnic groups and/or nations.[185]

The demand for territorial autonomy within Bosnia was first raised by the Serbian Democratic Party (SDS) in 1990 and soon thereafter also adopted by the Croatian Democratic Community (HDZ). The call for the establishment of territorial autonomy, backed by the establishment of so-called Autonomous Oblasts (SAO) in 1991,[186] foresaw the creation of small, ethnically homogenous territories which could eventually be linked together in a contiguous territory and joined to the respective 'motherland'. Territorial autonomy, as envisaged by the Croat and Serb political leadership in the early 1990s, did not constitute a political goal in its own right, but rather a transitory step towards secession. The Muslim political elite, represented predominantly by the Party for Democratic Action (SDA), opposed any form of territorial autonomy and favoured power-sharing at the government level of a unitary state.[187]

The war led to the creation of two monoethnic territorial units, the *Republika Srpska* (in 1991–92 and *Herceg-Bosna* (in 1992–93), which both sought to secede from Bosnia. The government of Bosnia-Herzegovina, reduced mostly to its elected Bosniak representatives, exerted its power mostly over the predominately Bosniak lands not under the control of the other two para-states. With the beginning of the war, the central institutions *de facto* ceased to exist and were only re-instated after the war. While the *Republika Srpska* survived the war, albeit with less territory under its control than during the peak of the war, *Herceg-Bosna* was formally dissolved, and the Croat controlled parts of Bosnia, together with the areas under control of the Bosnian government, formed the US-brokered Federation of Bosnia-Herzegovina in 1994.

The different forms of autonomy granted to the three nations of Bosnia are a result of this war-time conflict and include both highly decentralized territorial autonomy and power-sharing at the level of the central government.

Consideration of the institutional infrastructure in Bosnia is frequently limited to the Dayton Peace Accords alone. This definition, however, would exclude other significant centres of power— and subsequently also of (potential) power-sharing.

As the war in Bosnia was based on claims to self-determination by the dominant political representatives of two of the three nations of Bosnia, the settlement is preoccupied with re-constructing a political centre, vested with limited competencies. The Constitution of Bosnia and Herzegovina, annexed to the DPA, thus mostly governs the joint institutions of the state.

The Constitution, just as most of the other annexes to the DPA, tries to combine three conceptions of statehood and peace-building:

First, it is based on the outcome of the war, reflecting the unwillingness of the international community to significantly alter the military and political balance with the use of force.[188] Consequently, the settlement had to make concessions on the basis of military might rather than legitimate demands of the representatives of the national communities.

Second, the DPA sought to establish such a tri-national state, which grants Bosniaks, Croats and Serbs equal protection and ensures political representation and power on the basis of the groups' numerical strength. While a tri-national state with significant powers granted to the national groups does follow from the demands of the Serb and Croat leadership in the early phases of the war, this concept had to establish a political balance which did not equal the military balance during the war: i.e. the largest nation in Bosnia, the Bosniaks, which was the weakest (military) party in (in fact the victim of) the war, had to receive stronger representation in the institutions than their actual military strength would have suggested.

Third, the peace agreement did, although in a limited way, recognize some civic features of the state. The permeation of exclusive group representation throughout the institutional system is extensive. In its references to Bosnian citizens (as opposed to just the three nations), and in its commitment to refugee return, there have been some attempts in the Dayton Peace Accords to reverse some of the consequences of the war and the 'ethnification' of all spheres of public life.

The peace accords had sought to strike a balance between competing demands, such as the demands of the secessionist movements among Croats and Serbs (i.e. the recognition of *Republika Srpska* as a separate entity), demands of the all nationalist parties, including the Bosniak SDA, and, at the same time, to provide space for the development of new political elites who would demonstrate greater willingness than the war-time parties to work with each other and with the international community.

While there has been no formal change to the Dayton Peace Accords since its ratification in late 1995, developments since the signing of the agreement changed the nature of power-sharing in Bosnia. Most significantly, the role of the international actors, especially the High Representative, has been enhanced in recent years. The Peace Implementation Council granted the High Representative the power to remove officials from office and to impose laws. This has affected not only the decision-making process, but also the balance of power between the different political actors in Bosnia, mostly in the form of open support for moderate political parties and a range of measures (e.g. dismissal of officials, banning of parties) taken against nationalist parties.

The origins of the power-sharing arrangement in Bosnia place a burden on its success. Despite the fact that it includes some elements that predate the peace accords and that draw on established institutional mechanisms, such as the presidency system, the current power-sharing in Bosnia is widely perceived as being 'imported' rather than a result of the will of the polity, or at least of the political representatives of national groups.[189] Past practices in power-sharing arrangements suggest that mechanisms which are perceived as 'indigenous' rather than externally imposed have a higher likelihood of success.[190]

2.   POWER-SHARING AND ETHNIC FEDERALISM

The structure of institutionalized power-sharing, as mentioned above, draws on different tools to divide power among different national groups. The two predominant features of the state are: (a) a consociational arrangement at the level of the joint state institutions; mixed with (b) an asymmetric multinational federation.

2.1 Power-Sharing at the Centre

The executive body of Bosnia requires the participation of all three national groups. The institutional system attempts to ensure the representation of Bosniaks, Croats and Serbs, as well as a veto right for all groups on questions of 'vital interest'. While a number of consociational arrangements in multinational states (e.g. Switzerland, Lebanon) are at least in part informal and not an aspect of the constitutional setup, power-sharing in Bosnia is laid down by the Dayton constitution to the last detail.

The highest state organ—the Presidency, which combines representative functions with the foreign policy of Bosnia—embodies equal representation and the veto power for each group. Not only is the ethnicity of the members of the presidency prescribed—one Croat, one Serb and one Bosniak—but the members are also elected by the two entities separately. The Presidency is thus based on territorial and national representation.[191]

The national identity conditions,[192] along with their territorial base, results in political representation that neglects the limited diversity within the two entities (RS and the Federation) and is institutionalized not only on the level of the Presidency, but also in other joint institutions such as the House of Peoples and the Governing Board of the Central Bank.

This double delimitation raises a number of questions. As the main cleavage cutting across Bosnia is doubtlessly ethnicity, as opposed to regional identity, the Presidency members are arguably elected to represent primarily their respective nation and only secondarily their entity. While the war created largely homogeneous entities, some level of diversity has remained both in the Federation and in *Republika Srpska* (RS), which was enhanced by a small number of refugee returns.[193] The electorate of the Presidency members is thus not inherently monoethnic. Theoreticians have debated over the utility of one group participating in the vote for representatives of the other group. Some, like Lijphart, have argued that in a power-sharing arrangement the representative should represent their respective community and any dilution of this principle might undermine their legitimacy and ability to negotiate with other groups' representatives on behalf of their group.[194] Others have countered this argument with the observation that with the co-participation of other groups, the elected leaders might be more moderate than representatives who are selected on a purely monoethnic basis.[195] The reality of the Presidency in Bosnia since 1995–96 suggests that neither of the two interpretations applies in this case: the Presidency members have been generally regarded as legitimate leaders of their respective nation, mostly because they did not moderate their platform to garner minority support. This can be attributed, in part, to the relatively low number of other nations living in the two entities. Instead, the past elections to the Presidency have *de facto* deprived a segment of the population from representation in the Presidency.[196] Serbs from the Federation and Bosniaks and Croats in *Republika Srpska* have thus had no representation of their own in the Presidency.

Rather, they have had to rely on the—frequently inadequate—representation by members of their nation from the other entity. This not only raises questions about the inclusiveness of democratic representation, but it also stands in conflict with the principle of refugee return, which, if carried out, would transform both entities into multinational territories again.

The rigidity of the institutions has been remarked on by the Constitutional Court in regard to the Federation. Its observations do, however, also apply to the level of joint institutions:

> [T]here is at least one striking difference in the electoral mechanisms of Belgium on the one hand, and the federation of BiH on the other, in particular as far as the right

to stand as a candidate is concerned. The Belgian system does not preclude per se the right to stand as a candidate *solely* on the ground of language. Every citizen can stand as a candidate, but has—upon his election—to decide whether he will take the oath in French or in Flemish. It is therefore the subjective choice of the individual candidate whether to take the oath in French or in Flemish and thereby to 'represent' a specific language group, whereas provisions of the Constitution of the Federation of BiH provide for *a priori* ethnically defined Bosniac and Croat delegates, caucus and veto powers for them.[197]

Besides the rigidity of ethnicity in the Presidency, a number of problems can be identified with a presidential system as part of power-sharing in general.[198] A presidential system, even if exercised in the moderated form of a Presidency, personifies ethnicity more than a cabinet-based system, and renders a distribution of power more difficult.

The degree of institutionalization of power-sharing is not as strong in the joint government, although formal regulatory mechanisms to ensure broad representation exist. The Council of Ministers is formed by up to two-thirds from the Federation and one-third from the *Republika Srpska*. In addition, every minister has a deputy from a different national group. As the Chair of the Council of Ministers must be nominated by the Presidency, and he/she and his/her government must be approved by the House of Representatives, there are additional in-built mechanisms ensuring the inclusion of the different national groups in government.[199] Like the Presidency, the competencies of the government are limited, reflected in the small size of the government.

Territory and national group adherence similarly determine the legislature. The parliament consists of two chambers, the House of Representatives and the House of Peoples. The 42 members of the House of Representatives are directly elected by the voters of the entities, with two-thirds of the seats given to the federation and one-third to the *Republika Srpska*. While this chamber of parliament possesses no guaranteed representation for the national group, the House of Peoples, consisting of 15 members chosen by the parliaments of the entities, is constituted by five members from each nation, with the Serbs elected in the RS, the Bosniaks and Croats in the Federation. A veto right granted to the representatives of the three nations protects any group from being outvoted in case a decision is "destructive of a vital interest of the Bosniak, Croat, or Serb people".[200] Due to the assertive role of the international implementing agencies, the national veto has rarely been abused. The High Representative has become the *de facto* arbiter of the legitimacy of such a veto. Blocked decision-making in post-war Bosnia is thus less a result of the veto power—unlike in Bosnia before the war in 1990–91—but rather the result of the electoral successes of uncompromising nationalist parties until 2000, creating a *de facto* stalemate in the chambers of parliament and preventing any substantial decision-making, not only in issues directly pertaining to the sensitivities of the national groups, but also in areas where necessary decisions run the risk of reducing the popularity of the governing parties.

The overall emphasis of ethnic belonging in the executive and legislature of Bosnia ensures a permanent grand coalition of the three national groups. At the same time, the over-institutionalization provides little flexibility in the executive power-sharing.

Among a number of additional difficulties associated with the particular institutional set-up in Bosnia is the near total exclusion of 'others' or 'citizens' from the power-sharing arrangement. The constitution recognizes 'citizens' as a quasi-separate group from the three national groups, while the institutional—just as the political and social—reality ignores the existence of other minorities, citizens of mixed marriages and those not willing or able to identity with the national groups. This group—'citizens'—whose strength is near to impossible to determine, is not guaranteed representation.[201] A legal scholar recently posed the rhetorical question: "Who defends the vital interests of the citizens of Bosnia and Herzegovina"?[202] Until early 2001, the answer to this question would have been nobody. The High Representative did, however, establish two Constitutional Commissions for both entities in January 2001, which are charged with safeguarding the interests of the three constituent nations and the 'others'.[203] Both Commissions contain four members of all four groups and the majority of each group can object to a proposed regulation, law or decision of the entities, if it discriminates against their group. The Commissions are charged with resolving the claim, and, if they cannot agree, refer it to the High Representative. The Commissions, as provisional institutions—pending the incorporation of the Constitutional Court decision on the constituent people in the entities (see above)—thus provide for the protection of citizens who are not members of the three national groups.

2.2 Bosnia as a Multinational Federation

In Bosnia, power-sharing at the centre accounts for only a small segment of the actual power exercised by elected officials. The high degree of decentralization towards the entities has transformed Bosnia into a very loose union. The constitution of Bosnia and the Dayton Peace Accords conspicuously avoid any formal ascription of the nature of the state. In fact, the previous attribution 'Republic' was dropped, resulting in the country's official name being only 'Bosnia and Herzegovina'. The extent of power vested in the two entities would suggest that the country is at least a federation. The term 'federation', however, is already reserved for the 'Federation of Bosnia and Herzegovina' that encompasses fifty-one per cent of the country which is predominantly Bosniak and Croat. Thus, the question arises: what is Bosnia? The Constitutional Court has, for example, compared Bosnia with federal states, suggesting that Bosnia itself is a federation.[204] Most studies of federal systems distinguish between 'federalizing states' (e.g. Belgium) and federations deriving from an agreement between different units (e.g. the U.S. and Switzerland). This distinction not only bears historical importance, but also determines the original (and frequently still primary) level of authority.[205] Bosnia constitutes a curious mixture of both systems. On the one hand, the current state possesses some elements of continuity with the pre-war state and is the legal successor to the Republic of Bosnia and Herzegovina,[206] suggesting a 'federalizing state'. On the other hand, none of the pre-war institutions has been incorporated in the new state, weakening the connection to pre-war and war-time Bosnia.[207]

While the degree of decentralization suggests that Bosnia is *at least a federation*, it is more difficult to determine whether Bosnia might be a confederation.[208] Two factors in particular would suggest that Bosnia is in fact a confederation. First, the fact that one of its constituent units calls itself, and by its structure *is*, a federation, could be viewed as an indicator of the confederal nature of Bosnia. More importantly, the lack of competencies of the joint state in the sphere of defence[209] and the existence of two separate armies of the entities seem to point to a confederal state. A confederation would, however, suggest that the constituting units are in fact dominant and have supremacy over the central authorities. The structure of Bosnia does nevertheless establish the supremacy of the joint institutions over the entities.[210] As a result, Bosnia could be considered a loose multinational federation.[211] In addition to being a highly decentralized federation, Bosnia is also an asymmetric federation from at least two points of view. First, the sub-units are constituted very differently: one is a loose federation consisting of ten cantons and two predominant nations and the other is a (formally) centralized republic of one dominant nation. Second, the existence of a third unit, the district of Brčko provides for asymmetry. Brčko, officially a third separate unit ('condominium') since March 1999 has the same competencies as the two other entities, however, only in coordination with them. As the district formally belongs to both entities simultaneously, it also lacks individual representation in joint institutions.[212] This asymmetry of Bosnia has meant that, in reality, the types of governance in the country vary greatly in terms of power-sharing, but also in other aspects. This poses particular problems to Bosnia that do not apply to other federations, be they based on national or territorial criteria.

In addition, some general questions arise with regard to multinational federations in general. A number of factors seem to put into question the adequacy of a federal system for a multinational setting. The existence of territorialized national groups in the form of federal units frequently creates a fear of secession. In the regional context the demand for a republican status, i.e. being a federal unit, by some Albanians in Kosovo within Yugoslavia in the 1980s was widely perceived as a demand for gradual secession from the state. Similarly, the demands of some Albanian politicians in Macedonia for territorial autonomy and/or federalization of Macedonia have caused such fears among the majority. This fear can be found equally in other interethnic disputes around the world, especially when the demand for federalization is raised at times of high tensions. Even if the potential danger of separation in Bosnia has been reduced by excluding any reference to self-determination of either the nations or the entities in the Constitution, and politically by the international presence, the concept of a multinational federation does not fully address this fear.

Decentralized territorial units that are defined primarily in ethnic terms tend to accelerate the homogenization of these units or, in the case of Bosnia, delay the 're-mixing' of the population. The territorialization of ethnic identity follows the (flawed) assumption that "good fences make good neighbours".[213] The resulting segregation and minimal contact between the nations, however, rather reduces the political and emotional investment of the nations constituting the state and precludes a reconstruction of trust through interaction on an everyday basis. It furthermore reinforces the division of the state's polity. Will Kymlicka has argued that multinational federations encourage centripetal tendencies, which result in a weaker institutional reality than intended in the constitution.[214] As result of this and other deficiencies, Kymlicka has challenged the desirability of multinational federations: "For all these reasons, it seems likely that multinational federalism will be plagued with instability, and may eventually devolve into a confederation or simply break up".[215]

3. CHALLENGES TO THE CURRENT ARRANGEMENT

Few would argue that Bosnia has been governed effectively since the Dayton Peace Accords was signed. Not only has progress in some key areas of governance—such as economic reforms, effective institutions and reconstruction—been limited, but also the degree of successful decision-making between representatives of the different national communities has been minimal. Thus the question is raised whether power-sharing actually did take place in the past five and half years.

This development, combined with the objective need for sustained international intervention in the political process, has led a number of observers to conclude that the power-sharing structure of Bosnia, as instituted in the DPA, is fundamentally flawed.[216] In fact, the weaknesses often attributed to DPA are limited almost exclusively to the Constitution (Annex 4). Proponents of a 'Dayton 2' generally point to flaws in the Constitution, which could be addressed without a change to the overall peace plan.[217]

Furthermore, if one is to identify the weaknesses of the power-sharing system (or/and the absence thereof), it emerges that—the flaws of the constitutional arrangement notwithstanding—most of the difficulties in establishing successful governance in Bosnia are not associated with the power-sharing system embodied in the Constitution, but rather have to do with institutions and mechanisms which either precede or have followed the Dayton Peace Accords.

Thus, an assessment of the power-sharing structure in Bosnia cannot be limited to the institutional arrangement of the Dayton Peace Accords alone. Rather, one has to examine two additional aspects: the functioning of the entities, and the role of the international community.

3.1 Dysfunctionality of the Entities

The entities constitute the level of primary political power in Bosnia. The Constitution of Bosnia explicitly grants them "all governmental functions and powers not expressly assigned in ... [the] constitution to the institutions of Bosnia and Herzegovina".[218] The powers of the entities thus cover most aspects of governance with the exception of some limited areas, such as foreign policy, customs and monetary policy.[219] In addition, the power-sharing at the level of the joint institutions has meant in practice that the political centre is frequently dominated by political representatives whose primary loyalty lies with the entities, the national groups they represent, and often—most importantly—with the nationalist political party they represent.

This power vested in the joint institutions, however, is in no way matched by the competencies allocated to, and real political power exercised by, the entities. Despite their political weight in Bosnia, both the Federation of Bosnia-Herzegovina and *Republika Srpska* have been unable to exercise effective control over their respective territories. Both the Federation and *Republika Srpska* have been internally divided for most of the past five and a half years. In the Federation, the areas in Herzegovina controlled by the HDZ as result of the war were never effectively integrated into the structures of the Federation. The Croatian cantons and army units maintained separate institutional structures with each other and until the end of HDZ-rule in Croatia in January 2000, also with Croatia. The situation was the same during the period between the official dissolution of *Herceg-Bosna* with the establishment of the Federation in 1994 and the establishment of the Croat self-government in March 2001.[220]

In 1997, the OSCE observed in an internal study that the area "in every aspect from military and security matters to business ties, is part of Croatia".[221] Although the change of government in Croatia eventually led to a cessation of funding of these separate institutions, formal and informal institutions remained separate from the Federation, mostly due to the continuing dominance of the HDZ in the Croat-dominated areas of the Herzegovina.

While there was a visible decline in the institutions of *Herceg-Bosna* in 2000, based both on the weakening of the HDZ and the more assertive role of the international implementing agencies,[222] non-federation Croat institutions remained in place. After the HDZ, under the leadership of the then-Croat member of the Bosnian Presidency,[223] declared a withdrawal from the joint Federation institutions in March 2001, both international and domestic observers noted an obvious continuity between the newly-formed Croat self-government and pre-existing structures.[224] The Croat self-government consequently marks in part the acknowledgment of pre-existing structures rather than creation of new ones. The recent political crisis in the Federation thus has only brought to light and exacerbated a pre-existing deficiency of the Federation.

Unlike in the Federation, where the weaknesses are closely intertwined with its decentralization, the dysfunctionality of the *Republika Srpska* is caused by failed political centralization and geo-graphic disintegration. The aim of the Serbian war-time leadership, as evidenced in the name *Republika Srpska*, sought to establish a contiguous territory which would form a joint state with Serbia/Yugoslavia in the future. The establishment of a centralized and unified 'republic' had been one of the primary demands at all peace conferences by the Serbian Democratic Party.[225] The Dayton Peace Accords, however, only partly fulfiled this demand. The territory defined as *Republika Srpska* consists of two territories, linked only by the city of Brčko in northern Bosnia, which was governed by the *Republika Srpska* pending international arbitration. With the decision of the international arbiters in March 1999, the city and the surrounding county have been transformed into a *condominium*, thus removing the only link between the two separate parts of the RS. Not unlike the self-declared Croatian autonomy in March 2001, the arbitration decision revealed a weakness of the entity rather than creating it. The arbitration, which occurred at the same time as the removal from office of the president of the RS, Nikola Poplašen, and shortly before the NATO bombardment of Kosovo began, created considerable opposition on the side of the political elite of the RS.[226] Nevertheless, for a number of years before the Brčko decision, the *Republika Srpska* had already been divided politically, and *de facto* geographically. The split emerged in the course of the dispute between Biljana Plavšić and Momčilo Krajišnik over the degree of cooperation with the international agencies in Bosnia in 1996–97. This conflict effectively ended the control of the RS government over its eastern part. Even after the departure of both Krajišnik and Plavšić from the political scene after the 1998 elections, the government had only limited influence over all of the *Republika Srpska*; in many respects, geography played into the hands of political divisions. In addition, neither the nationalist government, nor the more moderate one of Milorad Dodik, could claim significant economic, social or political progress in the entity.[227]

Two key factors contributing to the dysfunctionality of *Republika Srpska* have been the detrimental role of Milošević and the continued economic and social decline of Serbia in the second half of the 1990s. Furthermore, the division of the political elite of *Republika Srpska* over cooperation with the international community rendered governance more difficult. Although *Republika Srpska* itself does not provide for power-sharing at any level and emphasizes its 'Serb' nature[228] (reversed partly by the Constitutional Court ruling in 2000), the government of Milorad Dodik, and currently that of Mladen Ivanić, has had to rely on the support of Bosniak parties. This form of power-sharing has been largely informal and has allowed for only limited direct participation of non-Serb parties in governance. Their support was mostly based on the interest in avoiding the return of an extreme nationalist government. The provisional electoral law which allowed[229] refugees to vote in their original place of residence has made the political representation of *Republika Srpska* more diverse than its actual population distribution. For example, in the November 2000 elections for the RS Assembly, predominantly Federation-based parties—such as the SDA, *Stranka za BiH* (Party for Bosnia-Herzegovina), SDP and the Croat parties—gained nearly 20 per cent of the vote.[230] While the share of the non-Serb population on the territory of the RS before the war amounted to nearly 50 per cent, the representation of Bosniaks and Croats in parliament at present exceeds the actual demographic distribution. Nevertheless, in the absence of effective decentralization (which would empower more non-Serb or mixed administrations in areas of refugee return), and without any power-sharing mechanisms beyond the coalition between moderate Serb, Bosniak and Croat parties in *Republika Srpska*, it would be misleading to describe the *status quo* as power-sharing.

The Constitutional Court decision of July 2000 could be considered as an important step in improving power-sharing on the level of the entities. The court declared as unconstitutional under the Constitution of Bosnia-Herzegovina parts of the entity constitutions which declared the respective nations to be the constituent nations of the entities.[231] As a result, the entities are forced to change their constitutions so as to include all three nations as constituent nations. While the court decision does not directly affect the institutional set-up of both entities, changes in the nature of governance in both are to be expected once the court decision is incorporated into the entities' constitutions. The provisional constitutional commissions, as outlined above, are a direct result of the court ruling and symbolize the most significant institutional change in Bosnia since the Dayton Peace Accords, leaving aside the augmented role of the High Representative.

3.2 Role of the International Community

Next to the entities the role of the international community provides for a particular challenge to the power-sharing system in Bosnia. The participation of international agencies in the implementation of the peace process has been widely viewed as being crucial in the success of maintaining peace in Bosnia.[232] The role of international organizations was originally intended to facilitate the domestic decision-making process by insuring adequate security for citizens (KFOR, IPTF), creating the economic framework for successful governance (EU, UN), and by promoting democratic and more tolerant institutions and processes (OSCE). Even the High Representative as the most influential international representative in Bosnia was originally limited to facilitate, monitor and report on the civilian aspects of the peace process. One of his prime powers was the final authority of the interpretation of the DPA.[233] In recognition that these powers did not suffice to successfully implement the peace accords, after 1997 the High Representative was equipped with additional powers, which transformed him from a facilitator to an integral institution of the current system of government in Bosnia.[234] Equipped with both legislative and executive powers, the High Representative (HR) has emerged as the most influential institution in Bosnia—and the only one not formally based on power-sharing.

Since this increase in power to the High Representative, the HR's Office has passed over 100 laws and decisions—ranging from the state symbols and license plates to pension funds—and dismissed over 60 public officials from office, including a president of *Republika Srpska* and the Croat representative of the Bosnian Presidency.[235] As a result, Bosnia has gained some attributes of a protectorate since 1997. This followed suggestions of a number of Bosnian intellectuals, who advocated a protectorate to reduce the role of the nationalist parties.[236] Until the post-election coalition-building in the winter of 2000–01, concrete improvements in the system of power-sharing as a result of the increased powers of the High Representative were not visible. The tangible success of the High Representative's increased role has been the passing of significant legislation which would have either been postponed indefinitely or been watered down.[237] The dismissal of public officials could also be interpreted as a success. The case has been made, however, that the successful outcomes notwithstanding, the process in fact has hurt the development of power-sharing structures. As Marcus Cox details, the High Representative's decisions relieve the participants in the power-sharing structures from negotiations and compromises.[238] As a result, "nationalist politicians have often welcomed the High Representative's interventions, which relieve them of the responsibility for difficult political positions".[239] The power-sharing institutions in Bosnia, in addition to their original weaknesses, have been further weakened by the strengthening of international intervention. It is nevertheless important to note that the representatives of the three nationalist parties demonstrated little willingness to engage in serious negotiations even before the enhancement of the HR's role.

Within the layers of governance, international representation is more closely interlinked with Bosnian institutions. The Constitutional Court, the Human Rights Chamber and the Central Bank incorporate significant international participation. The international judges and the Governor of the Central Bank are not representatives of international organizations, but merely appointed by them (the European Court of Human Rights, the Council of Europe and the International Monetary Fund respectively). As such they become 'Bosnian' actors, with the primary advantage of not being a member of one of the three national groups and thus resembling a neutral arbiter and mediator within these institutions.[240] The inclusion of international members into domestic institutions has the advantage of not having to bypass domestic institutions to take decisions. In addition, the process of interethnic negotiations is only slightly impaired.

In examining the nature of the power-sharing mechanisms in Bosnia, it has become clear that the dysfunctional nature of the entities with regard to power-sharing and decision-making, as well as some aspects of the international powers exercised in Bosnia contribute significantly to some key problems of the complex institutional structure of the country. Most of the power in the country is currently exercised by the High Representative or by the entities, both of which have no, or only inadequate, power-sharing mechanisms. At the same time, the nature of the problems prohibits 'quick fixes' to the problems of power-sharing in Bosnia.

4. ALTERNATIVE PROPOSALS FOR GOVERNANCE IN BOSNIA

Both international observers and domestic politicians and intellectuals have argued for a change of the current system of governance in Bosnia. Members of the international community engaged in implementing the DPA have, however, been firm in arguing against changes in the ways the country is governed.

The most fundamental changes were proposed by the *Stranka za BiH* (Party for BiH), led by the war-time Bosnian prime minister Haris Silajdžić. He and his party, now as part of the Alliance for Change, participating in the Federation and joint governments, have advocated a 'Dayton 2' which would change the institutional structure of the country. Most importantly, the party proposed the abolition of the entities or alternatively the introduction of a House of Peoples in *Republika Srpska* which would also represent the other constituent people (and 'others').[241] A similar proposal was raised by Dražen Budiša, president of the Croatian Social-Liberal Alliance, a partner in the Croatian government. Budiša suggested, in the light of the establishment of the Croat self-government in Herzegovina, to transform Bosnia into a Federal State consisting of 12–14 cantons. His suggestion would *de facto* extend the institutional arrangement of the Federation to the whole country.[242] The cantonization of all of Bosnia, as first proposed in the Vance-Owen peace plan in 1993,[243] could provide for a degree of decentralization while decreasing the asymmetry of the state and increase the need for cooperation. The proposal was met with criticism from the High Representative Wolfgang Petritsch, however. Besides the unwillingness to change the Dayton Accords, his criticism related to the origin of the proposal. It was seen as implicit support for the Croat self-government in Bosnia.[244] An additional key problem of such a proposal, despite some obvious merits, is the fact that *Republika Srpska* and the Serb political elite vehemently oppose any such change.

On the other end of the political debate the argument is put forward that what is required are not changes in the structures but rather changes in the practices. This case has been made primarily by the international community which has advocated a more robust implementation of the existing power-sharing structures and an active promotion of moderate political forces into public offices through informal means (e.g. financial and logistical aid, media publicity). This has created a curious situation where multiethnic parties and candidates promoting a more inclusive conception of political processes are discouraged by the structures of the political institutions, but promoted by those who designed and defend them. The reality of these practices has produced mixed results. The open support of the international community for Biljana Plavšić and Milorad Dodik was probably counter-productive both in terms of ensuring public support and also in glossing over fundamental problems of both politicians' records—one an indicted war criminal, the other a politician overseeing economic stagnation and corruption. In other cases, such as the Alliance for Change emerging in the post-election negotiations in the winter of 2000–01, there is a potential for changing the functioning of institutions through a change of power-holders.

However, to tie the functioning of power-sharing to the elected officials holding positions in this system cannot provide answers for the problems of the system, as a return of less cooperative political elites remains possible. It also neglects the basic premises of power-sharing institutions, which are intended to provide an incentive structure for an inclusion of those political actors whose main interest might not be cooperation.

The aforementioned decision of the Constitutional Court has raised some fundamental questions, not only regarding the entities, but also the joint state. Many of the arguments of the Constitutional Court discussed not only the constitutionality of the institutionalization of ethnic dominance, but also their impact on the *quality* of democracy in Bosnia.[245] The criticism of the exclusion of 'others' in the Federation by the Constitutional Court, mentioned above, could be applied similarly to the joint state, where the only difference to the Federation lies in the inclusion of Serbs. 'Others', be they minorities or persons from ethnically mixed marriages, remain excluded from many layers of the power-sharing structure. It is not only the exclusion of segments of the population that needs to be addressed on a state-wide level but also the over-institutionalization of ethnic identities, as detailed by the Constitutional Court with regard to the Federation and the election of officials.[246]

The HDZ-declared Croat self-government has overshadowed and, some argue, hijacked,[247] an emerging constitutional debate in Bosnia about new ways to promote power-sharing. While the new governments, dominated by the Alliance for Change, seem to work more effectively than previous nationalist ones, the need to strengthen existing institutions is widely recognized. Such a project remains highly contentious, and places the three national groups, as well as the multi-national parties, on different sides.[248]

5.   CONCLUSION

As has been demonstrated, some of the key problems with post-Dayton Bosnia have not been related to the degree of autonomy granted to the three national groups, but rather to aspects not addressed in the Dayton Peace Accords themselves or developments which ensued. Nevertheless, the high degree of segmentation of power in Bosnia and the extensive territorial autonomy granted to the three nations pose long-term difficulties for the success of the political arrangement in Bosnia.

Any fundamental revision of the existing Constitution and arrangement in Bosnia is unlikely for two reasons. First, the international community has repeatedly rejected demands for renegotiating the Dayton Peace Accords and penalized Bosnia officials for advocating changes. Second, the demands for alterations by the political elites of the different national communities highlight a continuing lack of consensus over changes. While the Constitutional Court decision, mentioned above, initiated the first major revision of the way the three nations are conceived in the entities, there is currently little or no room for a revision of the joint state powers and institutions. Although the Constitution allows for a revision,[249] the political room for such changes is limited. Any compromise which would resolve some of the problems of the current arrangement thus seems unlikely. Changes to the current system are more likely to be initiated through auxiliary institutions, such as the constitutional commissions, and changes in the election law.

For success with the current arrangement in Bosnia, some changes in the system of government might be worthy of consideration. First, the balance of different group interests evolves over time. As a result, any arrangement governing a divided society requires an in-built mechanism for renegotiation. Not only does the current system lack such a mechanisms for domestic re-evaluation, but any challenge to the current arrangement is considered a threat to peace in the country. Instead the arrangement needs to be reconceptualized as a *process* with clearly determined mechanisms for its development.[250] Second, the current system rests mostly on a combination of territorial autonomy and power-sharing. As the ruling by the Constitutional Court highlights, the autonomy granted to the national groups in the form of territorial autonomy has led to the discrimination of minority groups within the entities. The establishment of levels of personal autonomy instead of or in addition to some layers of territorial autonomy could reduce the nation-based conception of the entities and ensure representation of the nations which find themselves in a minority. Personal, non-territorial autonomy would also allow for a reduction of the rigidity of national representation in the joint institutions. Third, the double delimitation of office holders on a territorial and a national basis would merit reconsideration.

The decision of the Constitutional Court and the constitutional commissions in the respective entities, as well as the more assertive approach of the international agencies involved in the implementation of the peace process, point to a strengthening of civic aspects of the Bosnian system of governance and a reduction of the high degree of monoethic territorial autonomy. This process, being only at the beginning, has already met with the resistance of national parties, as evidenced by the withdrawal of the HDZ from Bosnian institutions during February and March 2001.

Bosnia is indeed paradigmatic for determining an adequate degree of autonomy of national groups without diminishing the quality of democracy. The need to differentiate between the protection of legitimate national and minority rights and unacceptable nationalist demands emerges as a challenge with no easy solution.

NOTES

[181] The paper refers to Muslims (Musilmani) as 'Bosniaks' (Bošnjaci) for the period after 1993–94 when this new term was adopted. The term 'Bosniaks' (Bošnjaci) is not be confused with 'Bosnians' (Bosanci) which denotes inhabitants of Bosnia irrespective of their national origin. See Steven L. Burg and Paul S. Shoup, *The War in Bosnia-Herzegovina. Ethnic Conflict and International Intervention* (Armonk, N.Y: M.E. Sharpe, 1999), pp.195–196.

[182] The official term is the Federation of Bosnia and Herzegovina.

[183] International Forum *Bosnia: The Return of the Refugees and Displaced People as a Precondition for the Survival of Bosnia and Herzegovina*, Sarajevo, March 1999, p. 12.

[184] Austria-Hungary only 'administered' Bosnia from 1878 until 1908, while it remained formally under Ottoman sovereignty. In 1908, the Habsburg Empire formally annexed the province.

[185] According to the Communist conception of the National Question in Yugoslavia, nations were defined as being the six constituent national groups in Yugoslavia (Slovenes, Croats, Serbs, Muslims, Montenegrins and Macedonians), while ethnic groups have their 'motherland' outside Yugoslavia (Albanians and Hungarians). Cf. Pedro Ramet, "Theoretical Models of Yugoslav Nationalities Policy", in *Nationalitätenprobleme in Südosteuropa*, Roland Schönfeld, ed. (München: R. Oldenbourg, 1987), pp.105–123.

[186] Burg and Shoup, *op. cit.*, p.73.

[187] On the institutional and political development of Bosnia in the first half of the 1990s, see Steven L. Burg, "Bosnia Herzegovina: A Case of Failed Democratization", in *Politics, Power and the Struggle for Democracy in South-East Europe*, Karen Dawisha and Bruce Parott, eds. (Cambridge: Cambridge University Press, 1997), pp.122–141.

[188] Extensive bombings of military positions of *Republika Srpska* took place in August 1995. These were the exception rather than the rule in the policy of the West. Despite the confrontational negotiating style of Richard Holbrooke, the countries attempting to end the war in Bosnia were unwilling to enforce a peace settlement with the use of force, as, for example, they did in Kosovo in 1999.

[189] Heinrich Schneider raises the issue of the ratification of the accords and points to the *de facto* exclusion of legislative bodies in the DPA, "Friede für Bosnien-Herzegowina? Das Vertragswerk von Dayton als Herausforderung für Europa", *Integration* 19 (1996), 1, pp.1–2.

[190] Ulrich Schneckener, "Making Power-Sharing Work. Lessons from Successes and Failures in Ethnic Conflict Regulation", *InIIS-Arbeitspapier*, No. 19, 2000.

[191] This is likely to change with the adoption of a permanent electoral law. The OSCE-OHR proposed law still foresees the same double-delimitation, but the Bosnian Council of Ministers has advocated the possibility for Serbs from outside the RS and Bosniaks and Croats outside the Federation to run for Presidency. The draft election law, as proposed by the OSCE-OHR, based on the recommendations of international and domestic legal scholars, is available at http://www.oscebih.org/documents/draftelectionlaw/eng/del-eng.htm.

[192] The Constitutions of Bosnia-Herzegovina or the DPA at large do not attempt to define the membership in the different national communities, allowing—hypothetically—for a Croat, Bosniak, or a candidate of mixed descent to run as a self-declared Serb in the elections for representation of *Republika Srpska* in the Presidency.

[193] In the absence of a post-war population census only rough estimates exist of the population distribution in both entities. According to some estimates, over 110,000 non-Serbs lived in *Republika Srpska* in 1998, which constitutes approx. 12% of the population. In the Federation, some 450,000 Serbs and 'others' lived in 1998, i.e. approximately 17%. These numbers increased substantially in 1999 and 2000. Cf. International Forum Bosnia: *The Return of Refugees and Displaced People as a Precondition for the Survival of Bosnia and Herzegovina*, Sarajevo, March 1999.

[194] Arend Lijphart, "The Power-Sharing Approach", in *Conflict and Peacemaking in Multiethnic Societies*, Joseph V. Montville, ed. (New York: Lexington Books, 1991), pp.497–498.

[195] Donald L. Horowitz, *Ethnic Groups in Conflict* (Berkeley: University of California Press, 1985).

[196] This also applies to other minorities, which do not belong to any of the three nations.

[197] Constitutional Court of Bosnia-Herzegovina, Partial Decision, Case No. U5/98-III (1 July 2000), Para. 120.

[198] See Lijphart, *op. cit.*, pp.497–498.

[199] Art. 5(4), *Constitution of Bosnia and Herzegovina* (1995).

[200] In addition, every vote should include at least one-third of the votes from the territory of each entity. If this is not achieved, a commission of the Chairs (from different national groups) is tasked with finding a resolution. If this yields no result, the decision can be passed, if those opposed are less than two-thirds. Art. IV, *Constitution of Bosnia and Herzegovina* (1995).

[201] Such a representation is difficult to achieve, as illustrated by the first election in Bosnia in 1990. A seat in the Presidency was reserved for 'Yugoslavs'. The seat was, however, won by a member of the SDA (Ejup Ganić), while representatives of multiethnic parties lost. The absence of a clear identity marker poses the danger that such representation might be 'hijacked' by representatives of one national group and used to enhance their strength in relation to others.

[202] Ćazim Sadiković, "Ko štiti vitalne interese gradjana BiH?", *Ljudska Prava* 1 (2000), 3–4, pp.85–88.

[203] OHR Press Release, "High Representative issues Decision establishing interim procedures to protect vital interests of Constituent Peoples and Others, including freedom from Discrimination", 11 January 2001; OHR Press Release, "High Representatives names Members of the Constitutional Commissions of the Entity Parliaments", 7 February 2001.

[204] Constitutional Court of Bosnia-Herzegovina, Partial Decision, Case No. U5/98-I (29–30 January 2000), Para. 32.

[205] Dwight Herpreger, "Distribution of Powers and Functions in Federal Systems", (Ottawa: Government of Canada, Privy Council Office, 1991), available at http://198.103.111.55/aia/doc/english/perspective/constitutional/powers1.html [accessed 19 March 2001].

[206] Art. 1(1), *Constitution of Bosnia and Herzegovina* (1995).

[207] Marcus Cox, *State-Building and Post-War Reconstruction: Lessons from Bosnia, The Rehabilitation of War-Torn Societies* (Geneva: CASIN, January 2001), p.6.

[208] Schneider has compared Bosnia with the European Union, referring to the German Constitutional Court describing the EU as a "Staatenverbund" (Association of States). Heinrich Schneider, "Friede für Bosnien-Herzegowina? Das Vertragswerk von Dayton als Herausforderung für Europa", *Integration* 1(1996), 1, p.4.

[209] Although defence is not listed as one of the competencies of the state (Art. 3(1), *Constitution of Bosnia and Herzegovina* (1995)), "each member of the Presidency shall, by virtue of the office, have civilian command authority over armed forces". Art 5(5)(a) *Constitution of Bosnia and Herzegovina* (1995).

[210] This is enshrined in the Constitution and has been reiterated by the Supreme Court of Bosnia (Case No. U5/98-I (29–30 January 2000), para. 10), see also Omer Ibrahimagić, *Supremacija Bosne i Hercegovine nad Entitetama/Supremacy of Bosnia and Herzegovina over its Entities* (Sarajevo: Vijeće Kongresa Bošnjaka Inteletualaca and Kult B, 1999). This interpretation is not undisputed, especially from politicians and legal scholars from *Republika Srpska*.

[211] This position is, for example, also taken by Cvetan Cvetkovski in his analysis of the Dayton Accords. Cvetan Cvetkovski, "The Constitutional Status of Bosnia and Herzegovina in Accordance with the Dayton Accords", *Balkan Forum* 4 (1996), 2, pp.115–116.

[212] Brčko Arbitration Tribunal for Dispute over Inter-Entity Boundary in Brčko Area, Final Award (5 March 1999), para. 10 & 11. The status of Brčko resembles the role of the District of Columbia within the USA.

[213] As argued more radically by John Mearsheimer and Chaim Kaufman, see for example Chaim D. Kaufman, "When All Else Fails. Ethnic Population Transfers and Partitions in the Twentieth Century", *International Security* 23 (1998), 2, pp.120–156.

[214] Will Kymlicka, "Is Federalism a Viable Alternative to Secession?", in *Theories of Secession*, Percy B. Lehnig, ed. (London and New York, 1998), pp.139–40.

[215]   *Ibid.*, p.141.

[216]   See, for example, the reports of the International Crisis Group.

[217]   See, for example, International Crisis Group, "Is Dayton Failing? Bosnia Four Years after the Peace Agreement", Sarajevo, Brussels, 28 October 1999, p.53.

[218]   Art. 3(3)(a), *Constitution of Bosnia and Herzegovina* (1995).

[219]   The complete list of the joint institutions' responsibilities is listed in Art. 3(1), *Constitution of Bosnia and Herzegovina* (1995).

[220]   Florian Bieber, "Croat Self-Government in Bosnia—A Challenge for Dayton?", *ECMI Brief*, No. 5, May 2001.

[221]   Quoted from Burg and Shoup, *op.cit.*, 377.

[222]   For details, see European Stability Initiative, "Reshaping International Priorities in Bosnia and Herzegovina, Part Three, The End of the Nationalist Regimes and the Future of the Bosnian State", Berlin, Brussels, Sarajevo, 22 March 2001.

[223]   He was dismissed by the High Representative in March 2001 after declaring Croatian self-government.

[224]   *Dnevni Avaz* (Sarajevo), 16 February 2001; Also see International Crisis Group, "Turning Strife to Advantage. A Blueprint to Integrate the Croats in Bosnia and Herzegovina", Sarajevo, Brussels, 15 March 2001.

[225]   See Richard Holbrooke, *To End a War* (New York: Random House, 1999).

[226]   See International Crisis Group, "Republika Srpska—Poplašen, Brčko, and Kosovo: Three Crises and Out", Sarajevo, 6 April 1999.

[227]   Despite the dismal situation in most of the Federation, the economic situation in the RS has been significantly worse. See, for example, *Reporter*, Banja Luka, 28 June 2000.

[228]   For example, the RS Constitution in its preamble refers to the struggle for freedom and independence of the Serb people, and Art. 1 declares the state to be of the "Serb people and of all its citizens".

[229]   The new permanent election law similarly allows for refugee voting in their pre-war residence. Art. 20(8), Izborni Zakon Bosne i Herzegovina, 23 August 2001.

[230]   All election results at http://www.oscebih.org.

[231]   Constitutional Court of Bosnia-Herzegovina, Partial Decision, Case No. U5/98-III (1 July 2000). This decision of the Constitutional Court was probably only possible because it does not have a minority veto. Of the nine judges, five—the three international judges and the two Bosniak judges—voted for, and four—the two Croat and Serb judges—voted against. The decision was welcomed by the Bosniak parties and also the Croat parties, while it was condemned by most Serb parties. Sarajevo: *ONOSA*, 3 July 2000; Baja Luka: *SRNA*, 3 July 2000.

[232]   There has been severe criticism of the role of international agencies and their policies. See for example, David Chandler, *Bosnia. Faking Democracy After Dayton* (London: Pluto Press, 1999).

[233]   Annex 10, DPA (1995).

[234]   At the Conference of the supervisory Peace Implementation Council (PIC) in Bonn in December 1997, the HR was given the permission to remove officials from office who violate the DPA and, if the legislative bodies of Bosnia are unable to do so, to impose laws. Bonn Peace Implementation Conference 1997, "Bosnia and Herzegovina 1998: Self-Sustaining Structures", Bonn, 10 December 1997, available at http://www.ohr.int/docu/d971210a.htm.

[235]   The decisions are listed at the website of the Office of the High Representative: http://www.ohr.int/decisions.htm.

[236]   See for example, Džemal Sokolović, "*Social Reconstruction and Moral Restoration*", in *Reconstructing Multiethnic Societies: The Case of Bosnia Herzegovina*, Džemal Sokolović and Florian Bieber, eds. (Ashgate: Aldershot, 2001), pp.93–106.

237 The successes are very tangible were joint Bosnian license plates proved instrumental in reestablishing cross-entity travel. The property laws enacted by the High Representative also facilitate minority returns.

238 Marcus Cox, *State-Building and Post-War Reconstruction: Lessons from Bosnia, The Rehabilitation of War-Torn Societies* (Geneva: CASIN, January 2001), pp.12–15.

239 *Ibid*, p.14.

240 In addition, none of the international members of these bodies can be from Croatia or Yugoslavia in a further attempt to insure their neutrality. Art. VI, Art. VII, *Constitution of Bosnia and Herzegovina* (1995); Annex 6, DPA (1995).

241 The main electoral slogan of the SBiH was "Bosna bez entiteta" (Bosnia without Entities). See the interview with Silajdžic in *Slobodna Bosna* (Sarajevo), 30 November 1999.

242 *Globus* (Zagreb), 7 March 2001.

243 See Burg and Shoup, *op.cit.*, pp.214–249.

244 *Nacional* (Zagreb), 22 March 2001.

245 This is a frequent objection to consociational democracies in general, see for example Kenneth D. McRae, "Theories of Power-Sharing and Conflict Management", in *Conflict and Peacemaking in Multiethnic Societies*, Joseph V. Montville, ed. (New York: Lexington Books, 1991), p.96.

246 See above and Constitutional Court of Bosnia-Herzegovina, Partial Decision, Case No. U5/98-III (1 July 2000).

247 International Crisis Group, "Turning Strife to Advantage. A Blueprint to Integrate the Croats in Bosnia and Herzegovina", (Sarajevo/Brussels, 15 March 2001).

248 Nurko Pobrić, "Ustavne Reforme u Bosni i Hercegovini—'Za' i 'protiv'", *Ljudska Prava* 1 (2000), 3–4, pp.77–81.

249 Art. 10, *Constitution of Bosnia and Herzegovina* (1995).

250 Florian Bieber, "Consociationalism—Prerequisite or Hurdle for Democratization in Bosnia?", *South-East Europe Review* 2 (1999), 3, pp.79–94.

PART IV

Conclusion

Questions and Answers on Minority-Related Autonomy Issues
(Summary and Comments)
Péter Kovács

■

Minority Governance between Self-Rule and Shared-Rule
Ulrich Schneckener

Questions and Answers on Minority-Related Autonomy Issues (Summary and Comments)

Péter Kovács

Questions and Answers on Minority-Related Autonomy Issues (Summary and Comments)

Péter Kovács

At least sixteen European countries recognize autonomies of minorities in one way or another, either in territories which are inhabited predominantly by a minority or in linguistic communities. These regimes concern at least fifty minorities or linguistic communities in Europe. The following conclusion summarizes the parametres applied to the analysis of both the concept and the actual cases of minority autonomy in Europe.

1. FUNDAMENTAL PROBLEMS OF MINORITY AUTONOMY

It is no coincidence that the European Court on Human Rights passed a historic judgement just before the new millennium. In the case *Serif v. Greece*,[1] the European Court of Human Rights made a courageous step forward: it decided in favour of a minority plaintiff in a case linked to the religious and judicial autonomy of the musulman minority in Greece; an autonomy which originates in the different international treaties contracted after the Balkan wars and World War I. According to these international instruments, the musulman community in Greece was granted the right to elect a 'mufti', i.e. a person who performs both religious and certain judicial functions, especially in civil and matrimonial law. After unilaterally cancelling the election system of muftis in the 1990s, the Greek president appointed a pro-governmental mufti and Mr. Serif, who had been elected by the musulmans of the region according to the international treaties and the previous Greek law, was pursued criminally because of "usurpation of religious symbols", falling under a definite article of the criminal code.

The European Court of Human Rights, however, came to the conclusion that the intervention of the state into religious freedom had trespassed the limits "necessary in a democratic society". Even if the judges in Strasbourg did not think it inevitable to pronounce on the legal validity of the given international treaties, affirmed by the plaintiff but contested by the respondent state, the judgment does not only serve the interests of religious freedom in general, which has a well established jurisprudential background, but also the religious and judicial autonomy of the musulman community in Greece.[2]

What this judgement teaches is that even if minority autonomy is not directly protected by the European Convention of Human Rights, a pre-existing autonomy has such connotations that it cannot be demolished without infringing the ECHR. In sum, the judgement is the victory of the concept of the protection of seized rights.

Apparently, the judgement *Serif v. Greece* is not an isolated verdict but signals the emergence of a new jurisprudential philosophy. In the case *Hassan and Chaush v. Bulgaria,* once again linked to the status of the muftis, the respondent country was condemned because of its arbitrary intervention in the religious autonomy of musulman communities and it was also emphasized that the maintenance of the autonomous existence of religious communities is a *sine qua non* element of the pluralism of a democratic society.[3] If this *dicta* is evidence of a new jurisprudential policy, we can expect far more from the ECHR in the future than in the past when judges were reluctant to rule in regard to minority protection issues.[4]

Minority protection in the different constitutional systems cannot be described by antinomies, as has often been done in the past through the simplistic distinction between individual and collective rights. More often a far more complex system, a large network of different institutions, is established. In the following, a list of central parametres for the description of minority protection is suggested:[5]

 a) the constitutional acceptance of collective rights does not lead in all cases to the acceptance of the collective rights of minorities;

 b) several countries use the collective approach as a specific approach complementing the individual rights of minority members;

 c) collective rights do not correlate with autonomies and *vice versa*;

 d) autonomies can be linked to collective rights, to individual rights, complemented with the collective approach, and they can also be established within the framework of human or minority rights;

 e) the distinction between territorial and personal autonomies is a relative one: the territorial element appears in both types;

 f) cultural autonomy can appear in territorial autonomies as well as in personal ones;

 g) special linguistic regimes can be identified neither with cultural autonomy nor with cultural rights. In reality, these regimes can be conceived as one of their essential elements, but in some countries they may also have been established on the basis of human rights, simply as the result of special preferential administrative considerations;

 h) the question of continuity and the protection of seized rights emerged in a number of cases of former autonomies and resulted in recognition;

 i) actual European constitutional tendencies are not at all opposed to the establishment of different autonomies;

 j) constitutional approaches can go much further than international legal codifications, traditionally more hesitant. Some bilateral and particular international legal arrangements also contain numerous examples of collective rights, autonomies and special linguistic regimes.

2. COMMON PROBLEMS—SIMILAR AND DIFFERENT SOLUTIONS

The authors of the different studies in this book deal with a number of identical problems. However, while it is not surprising that the solutions offered or implemented partly differ according to various experiences, they also often show a number of similarities. Therefore, a comparative approach is particularly appropriate in the analysis of minority autonomies.

2.1 Relationship between Ethnic Tensions and Legal Reforms

It is evident that the establishment of the autonomies presented and analyzed in this book always required considerable constitutional reforms. The Scandinavian and the Hungarian reforms were the result of a peaceful change in the mentality of decision-makers, and the same can be said about a number of newly created autonomies in Europe. The Gagauz study and the Vojvodina proposal, on the other hand, are certainly related to existing conflicts, and Corsica, South Tyrol and the Basque country also make us remember news of explosions and killings, even if the South Tyrolian events now belong to history. However, the picture is much more differentiated: even in Italy, Spain and France, the regionalization or the acceptance of certain forms of personal autonomies concern also territories and communities which were mostly ignored by the media because 'nothing happened' there: Val d'Aosta, Navarra, Catalonia, Breton schooling, German autonomy in Belgium, the Færøe Islands and Greenland in Denmark, the Isle of Man and Guernsey in the United Kingdom, the Friesian islands in the Netherlands, Germany and the Sorb territory, etc.

This means that our vision should not be conflict-centred: ethnic conflict is not a *sine qua non* of an adequate reform. The international community commits an error if it deals only with open conflicts. Moreover, this attitude may radicalize both majority and minority.

2.2 Legitimacy of Assemblies and Electoral Registers

The importance of this issue was highlighted in the study by Brunner and Küpper as well as in the studies on the Scandinavian, Hungarian, South Tyrolean, Slovenian and Vojvodina solutions, reflecting the three logically possible ways.

In Scandinavia, the establishment of the Sami voting register did not cause any major problem. It is based on individual application (i.e. there is no registration against the individual's will) and neither the national law on the protection of personal data nor the memory of historical events prevents the use of the register in the organization of elections where only the concerned community takes part. It is, however, clear that only a part of the Sami community has taken an active part in the registration and the election in the past.

In South Tyrol, the local population recognized that the implementation of the principle of proportionality could easily be realized through a register based on self-identification, even if the question concerns language and not ethnicity.

In Hungary, different national minorities reject the use of a register (either general or electoral). The reason generally invoked is the memory of the post-war partial expulsion of Germans on the basis of the 1941 census. Another reason why in particular the leaders of minority associations and assemblies oppose a minority register is the fear of the discovery of a potential discrepancy between the low number of registered and the high number of estimated members of a community, the latter having served for the calculation of certain state subsidies in past years. The negative aspect of the generous solution is, however, that in the competition of members of the elite of a minority, outsider votes will decide.[6]

In the Yugoslavia of Milošević, after the experiences of Vukovar, Srebrenica and Kosovo, it is understandably not easy for an individual to decide whether to enrol on a nominal list of any kind. During the Tito period and in spite of anti-Hungarian and anti-German massacres in 1945, ethnic affiliation was mentioned without objection in personal identity documents, even if the high number of 'Yugoslavs' probably covered many hesitant people. After the 1990s, once again fear prevailed and the question remains how to organize minority elections under these circumstances. The Scandinavian voluntary register may be a solution: here the direct identity declaration can be substituted by 'participation in schooling' or by voluntary contribution to the budget of minority institutions.

2.3 Territorial or Personal Autonomies?

This book consists of studies on territorial and personal autonomies as well as on a combination of these two types of self-government. They show that two factors are decisive for the establishment of minority autonomies: first, the type of settlement and demographic coordinates of a minority, and second, historical background, traditions and constitutional framework. Nevertheless, the decision is always a political one.

It would be erroneous to say that a territorial autonomy is always stronger than a personal one because the real merits can be found in the competences of power-sharing and the efficacy of their exercise. Nor is it true that a personal autonomy is more acceptable to states, as it allegedly means a smaller threat to territorial integrity.

There are states where several types of autonomies of a different nature complete each other: in Finland, only one-tenth of the Swedish-speaking population lives on the famous Åland islands, but the members of this linguistic minority living on the continent have also been granted an adequate linguistic regime. That is to say, the combination of personal and territorial autonomy elements is not alien to existing minority protection regimes. The future will show whether the mixed institutional framework of the Vojvodina proposal is an optimal one.

2.4 Institutions and Competences

There are common characteristics in all the autonomy regimes analyzed, and also in those omitted. Moreover, these characteristics are very similar in the territorial as well as in the personal autonomies: the crucial element is an elected assembly appointing an organ dealing with executive functions. Cultural autonomy, i.e. the possibility for the minority to organize and run associations and institutions to maintain their traditions and keep their culture, language and history alive has always been the core (a *sine qua non*) of personal autonomies. In addition, there is generally at least a consultative or a co-decisional competence, implying a *de facto* veto right in cases which are particularly important for the preservation of the identity (e.g. the Sami autonomies in Finland, Norway and Sweden; see also the minority regimes in Slovenia or Hungary)

It is not surprising that the same topics also constitute the core of territorial autonomies (Corsica) or a very important part of a larger complex of competences (South Tyrol, Åland, Greenland, the Færøe Islands, etc.). The power-sharing between a territorial autonomy and its state is generally formulated in such a way that all strategic areas such as military, constitutional, legal (especially penal code, commercial code and civil code), judicial, economic and fiscal competencies are the responsibility of the central state.

In the case of legal disputes between central and autonomy authorities either the Supreme Court, the Constitutional Court or an analogue independent body is entitled to pass a decision.

346

If there is no such an *a priori* habilitated institution, it becomes more difficult to settle in a short time disputes linked to differences of interpretation, as we have seen in the cases of the Scottish devolution and the Gagauz autonomy.

2.5 Ongoing Adaptation and Reforms

All the case studies emphasize the importance of small steps, adjustments, and minor or major reforms—either *de lege lata* or *de lege ferenda*. It is hardly possible to set up once and for all well functioning minority autonomy. It should be born in mind that the normal functioning of a state also requires institutional adaptations and legal reforms. The Scandinavian, Scottish, South Tyrolean, Moldavian and Hungarian studies underline that the first step towards autonomy may be a political decision which is later tailored into institutions. The description of competences often lacks precision and either the central government or the autonomy can take the initiative for the necessary legislative reforms. The importance of economic aspects when the transfer of competence is discussed is worth mentioning, as was outlined in the chapter by Grin and Vaillancourt. The financial background is particularly well analyzed in the Gagauz and Vojvodina case studies.

2.6 Dialogue between Majority and Minority

The studies also deal, in different depth, with the importance of a continuous dialogue between majority and minority élite. In the Scandinavian countries, this did not constitute any problems, as dialogue seems to be deeply enshrined in the Nordic tradition. The Scottish and South Tyrolean studies show a progressive metamorphosis in the elites, but the studies on Northern Ireland and Corsica reflect tensions, although in appeasing contexts. The case study on Gagauz also reflected the beneficial influence of dialogue, truly important after an armed conflict, as well as the Vojvodina study, which also emphasizes the necessity of dialogue on all levels.

2.7 International Context

The studies dealing with international legal and geopolitical coordinates have provided a comprehensive picture: there is no universal obligation in international law that is binding upon all states to set up minority autonomies, but no rule of international law prohibits their establishment or their vindication either. The multilateral, universal or regional standard-setting treats this issue as one possible form of the 'effective participation of minorities in the decision-making procedure'. Bilateral treaties can be more explicit in the matter, and in certain exceptional cases, the international community clearly expressed its desire to set up a minority autonomy in a given territory in the interests of international peace and stability.

The international community is also under transformation and there seems to be a growing acceptance of instruments like the subsidiarity principle, enhanced decentralization, regionalization and devolution. The multiplication of existing autonomies can also be explained by the fact that modern states are leaving the classic nation-state concept behind and are not afraid of a major territorial reorganization of their administration: they know that their political and territorial integrity is not endangered.

3.   CONCLUSION

It is clear that minority autonomy is neither a panacea nor a Pandora's box. It is a legal instrument used in a number of countries, based on the division of competences on the national, regional or local level, or between governments and the special representation of a community. Like all legal instruments, it needs regular adaptation: far from being perfect at the beginning, it can constantly be improved once it has been put into practice.

The general assessment of existing autonomies seems to be positive, i.e. they serve the basic idea well: the articulation and the protection of distinct interests of a given territory or a given community and the contribution to the internal stability of states. This is why even if international law (of universal or regional organizations) does not prescribe it as an *erga omnes* obligation, it proposes it as a possible solution, as something already confirmed—according to the terminology of the OSCE or the Council of Europe—in the 'good practice' of a number of states.

NOTES

[1]   *Serif v. Greece*, judgment passed on 14 December 1999.

[2]   For an analysis of the judgement, see Péter Kovács, "Le gain de cause du mufti de Rodopi á Strasbourg", *Civitas Europa* 4 (2000), 1, pp.167–181 and Péter Kovács, *Le droit international pour les minorités face á l'État-nation*, Publicationes Universitatis Miskolciensis, Sectio Juridica et Politica Tomus XVIII (Miskolc: Miskolci Egyetemi Kiadó, 2000).

[3]   Case *Hassan and Chaush v. Bulgaria*, judgment passed on 26 October 2000.

[4]   Belgian linguistic case (3 July 1968), *Tyrer v. UK* (25 April 1978), *Gillow v. UK* (24 November 1986), *Mathieu-Mohin and Clerfayt v. Belgium* (2 March 1987), *Mrs Buckley v. UK* (25 September 1996)

[5]   For more detail, see Péter Kovács, "Individual and Collective Rights in the Constitutional Evolution—a Positivist Approach", Lecture at the Canadian-Hungarian Symposium on national minorities and multicultural policies Budapest, 11–13 September 1995, published in *Dual Images—Multiculturalism on Two Sides of the Atlantic*, Kulcsár-Szabó, ed. (Budapest: Hungarian Academy of Sciences, 1996); Péter Kovács, *International Law and Minority Protection: Rights of Minorities or Law of Minorities?* (Budapest: Akadémiai Kiadó, 2000).

[6]   There were a few examples for the fact that apparently it was more important for someone to become member of any minority self-government than to represent his own minority.

Minority Governance
between Self-Rule and Shared-Rule

Ulrich Schneckener

Minority Governance between Self-Rule and Shared-Rule

Ulrich Schneckener

1. INTRODUCTION[7]

Minority governance is essentially guided by two basic principles: *self-rule* and *shared-rule*. The first holds that minorities should enjoy some kind of self-government—or autonomy—in order to determine their own political, socio-economic and/or cultural affairs. As this volume has shown, the legal and institutional framework as well as the scope of autonomy differs widely from case to case. Generally, territorial autonomies or federal units enjoy more rights and freedoms, in particular with respect to legislation and financial resources, than personal/cultural autonomies. This notwithstanding, both concepts are based on the idea of easing tensions between majorities and minorities by *separation*. In other words: minorities get separate institutions with their own, albeit sometimes rather limited competences and no longer depend entirely on the decisions taken by the majority society. The general assumption is that the more matters are delegated to self-rule bodies, the less will be the need for interethnic cooperation and therefore the potential for conflicts between minorities and majorities. The second principle applies a different logic: shared-rule arrangements aim to foster cooperation between majorities and minorities. By special arrangements both sides are forced to work together and to find compromises. In its broadest sense, shared-rule allows each ethno-national group to be represented in all political bodies and to participate in decision-making processes, be it at the state, regional or local level. The ultimate goal is to ease interethnic tensions by *integration*, thus turning potential opponents into coalition partners.

The main purpose of this article is to explore the interplay between the two principles. Empirically, they are usually applied in combination; depending on the individual case of minority governance the emphasis is sometimes more on self-rule, sometimes more on shared-rule. Power-sharing regimes are often built on self-rule arrangements, be they non-territorial (as in Cyprus from 1960 to 1963) or territorial (as in Belgium since the early 1970s). The same applies *vice versa:* in most cases of self-rule one can find specific shared-rule provisions. Moreover, with respect to territorial autonomies or federal units, shared-rule has an internal and an external dimension: the former refers to the relationship between the dominant regional group and regional minorities (see South Tyrol or Northern Ireland), the latter refers to the relationship between the region as a whole and the state institutions.

Before examining the linkage between self-rule and shared-rule in more detail (see Section 3), it is necessary to introduce the power-sharing model at greater length, since this volume discusses predominantly self-rule arrangements. This will be done in three steps. First, the conceptual framework will be mapped out and differentiated from other measures for ethnic conflict regulation (see Section 2.1). Second, successful and failed European cases of shared-rule will be presented briefly in order to illustrate the empirical applications of the model (see Section 2.2). Third, based on the comparison of these cases, better power-sharing regulations are distinguished from more problematic or even counter-productive ones (see Section 2.3). In conclusion, some general criteria for good minority governance are developed, which are relevant for any kind of conflict regulation, be it based predominantly on self-rule or shared-rule principles (see Section 4).

2. THE POWER-SHARING APPROACH

2.1 Concept and Elements

The key idea of any power-sharing structure is that two or more ethno-national groups (be they numerically in a majority or minority position) have to rule the common polity jointly and to take decisions in consensus. Ideally, no single group can decide important matters without the consent of the other. On the basis of informal or formal rules, all groups have access to political power and other resources. This concept of conflict regulation was prominently shaped during the 1970s by the work of Arend Lijphart, Eric Nordlinger, Gerhard Lehmbruch and others;[8] it is also often called *consociational democracy*, *consensus democracy*, *corporatism* or *proportional democracy*.

Despite the fact that these terms were often used in a synonymous way, they should be treated separately. Lijphart's ideal-type distinction between *majority* and *consensus democracy* could be used as a starting point, the first being characterized by elite competition and changing majorities, the second by elite cooperation and joint governance. In a broad sense, the term consensus democracy applies to each polity where the main parties *de facto* rule together, be it a national or a multi-national environment. *Consociationalism* would be a specific form of consensus democracy, linked to ethnically segmented societies or, rather, to multinational polities, i.e. states or regions in which two or more ethnonational groups live. This definition seems to be more precise than the notions of 'deeply divided societies'[9] or 'plural societies'.[10] In other words: not every form of institutionalized, long-standing, cross-party cooperation within a nation-state should be called consociationalism. This kind of consensus politics is better labelled as *corporatism* or *proportional democracy*. Belgium and Austria can illustrate the difference: Both are considered as classical examples of Western consensus democracy, but both obviously represent two different types of society. Whereas in Belgium power-sharing rules have been necessary to keep two distinct ethno-national groups (Flemings and Walloons) in one polity, in post-1945-Austria two political movements (Catholic conservatism and socialism) of one and the same national group developed a system of power-sharing. According to Lijphart, consociationalism implies both the existence of "segmental cleavages" and elite cooperation, while corporatism just refers to the latter.[11] Consociationalism therefore is more comprehensive, since it describes not only a way of government, but also a specific type of society. In order to distinguish different forms of democracy, one can slightly modify Lijphart's typology (see Table 4.1).[12] Each model should be seen as an ideal-type, since in reality we often observe mixed systems or, at least, some overlapping features, notably between corporatism and centripetal democracy.

Table 4.1
Ideal-Types of Democratic Systems

	Nation-State	Multi-National Polity (State or Region)
Consensus Democracy (elite cooperation)	*corporatism* (proportional or 'depoliticized' democracy) e.g. Austria	*consociationalism* e.g. Belgium, Switzerland, South Tyrol, Bosnia
Majority Democracy (elite competition)	*centripetal democracy* (Westminster-Model) e.g. Great Britain, New Zealand	*centrifugal democracy* (hegemonic control by one group), e.g. Northern Ireland (1921–72)

Furthermore, consociationalism or power-sharing should be better distinguished from other concepts of ethnic conflict regulation.[13] On the one hand, minority rights, transborder regimes, territorial autonomy or federalism can be an integral part of a power-sharing regime, but on the other hand, these models do not necessarily include consociational procedures and instruments. In particular, federalism and consociational democracy share common features, but they are by no means identical concepts.[14] Empirically, they may enforce each other, but in principle, power sharing could also work without federal structures and the other way round. For example, some territorial solutions (such as the Spanish system of Autonomous Communities, Corsica or the British devolution) are hardly characterized by shared-rule at the central level, but rather by allowing regions or ethnic groups a certain degree of self-rule.

In contrast to other modes of ethnic conflict regulation, power-sharing systems typically contain the following institutional arrangements which are either formalized and legally binding or based on informal agreements and unwritten rules:

a) *Power-sharing executive:* The government includes representatives from all relevant groups in society either in the form of a *great coalition* among the main parties, of *all party governments* or of temporary *roundtables*. In each case, it would be decisive to secure "the participation by the leaders of all significant segments".[15]

b) *Proportional representation:* All groups or segments are adequately represented within the executive, the parliament, the legal system and the public service, including the army or state-owned companies (i.e. railways, postal services). This can be assured through a quota system according to the size of the groups, the number of voters or a fixed ratio. In some cases parity would be an option too; one example is the Belgian Council of Ministers which contains an equal number of French- and Flemish-speaking ministers. Often, smaller groups are significantly over-represented in these kinds of key positions.

c) *Veto rights:* Each group has the opportunity to block political decisions by using veto rights. The aim is to foster consensus building and the search for compromises. The right to veto could either apply unrestrictedly to all decisions (absolute veto), it could be conditional and just refer to some Basic Laws or it could just have a delaying effect in order to renegotiate disputed issues.

d) *Segmented autonomy:* Each group enjoys some degree of self-government, they maintain their own elected bodies, institutions and competencies. Only few issues therefore have to be coordinated with other segments of society. This can be organized on the basis of territorial or non-territorial arrangements. The former implies that consociationalism will coincide with a federal-type structure (as, for example, in Belgium, Switzerland or Bosnia), the latter implies that the various groups are organized on the basis of the personality principle, irrespectively of their territorial basis (see Cyprus in 1960–63).

e) *Arbitration:* In case of a dispute, it is necessary to develop mechanisms for conflict settlement. Measures include informal meetings among the group leaders, ombudspersons, formalized mediation committees, independent commissions or special arbitration courts in which all sides are represented.

In one or the other way, all these arrangements have to be present in order to speak about full-fledged power-sharing. In some cases only few elements exist and/or they are merely seen as a temporary matter (such as affirmative action programs). In post-Yugoslav Macedonia (since 1991), for example, a Slav-Macedonian party and an Albanian party always formed a coalition in order to stabilize the tense interethnic situation, but this informal power-sharing at the top level has not been extended to other elements such as systems of representation, veto rights or segmental autonomy. In a number of other European cases, however, all consociational elements were put, or at least attempted to put, into practice. They can serve as empirical material for illustrating benefits and problems with regard to the shared-rule principle.

2.2 Shared-Rule in Practice

The cases chosen here are Belgium (since 1970), South Tyrol (since 1972), Cyprus (1960–63), Bosnia-Herzegovina (1995) and Northern Ireland (1998). The sample thus comprises two success stories (Belgium and South Tyrol), one historic failure (Cyprus) and two recent attempts whose outcome is still open (Bosnia and Northern Ireland).

2.2.1   Belgium (since 1970)

The country is culturally and politically divided into a Flemish- and a French-speaking group. This is mirrored by the establishment of three political regions (Flanders, Wallonia and Brussels) and of three cultural communities (one each for the Flemings, the Francophones and the small German-speaking minority in East Belgium).[16] The road to power-sharing between the two main language groups was largely shaped by two developments: the first process centred on the linguistic and political emancipation of the Flemish community starting at the end of the 19th century and lasting until the late 1960s. As a result of successive language laws the Flemish gradually attained the same constitutional status as the formerly dominant French. This had implications for language use in politics and administration and, therefore, increased the political power of Flemish-speakers. In the course of this process, Belgium became *de facto* subdivided into two monolingual regions (Flanders and Wallonia) and one bilingual region (Brussels). Based on these language areas, the second process of several constitutional revisions (1970, 1980, 1988 and 1993) gradually trans-formed Belgium from a unitary into a federalized state. In doing so, the leading parties (Christian

Democrats, Socialists and Liberals) also reacted to the growing support for regional movements in the 1960s and early 1970s (e.g. *Volksunie*, *Rassemblement Wallon*, the Brussels *Front Démocratique de Francophones*). Consequently, the regions and the communities were established, the first being mainly responsible for socio-economic issues, the second for cultural and educational matters. Moreover, the 1970 reform turned the central institutions into a fully-fledged power-sharing system: the government (Council of Ministers) had to have an equal number of Flemish and French-speaking ministers (the principle of parity), the same rule applied to the highest courts, to the important Permanent Language Commission and to the upper ranks of the army. The Parliament (House of Representatives) was split into two parliamentary language groups, which obtained their own constitutional status and special veto rights in order to prevent major decisions against the will of one side. They also served automatically as Councils for the various communities and regions, before later reforms (1988, 1993) established directly elected regional and communal parliaments.

2.2.2   South Tyrol (since 1972)

The province, long disputed between Italy and Austria, is today composed of two-thirds German-speakers and one-third Italian-speakers. But back in 1948, the province was integrated by the Italian government into the larger region of Trentino-South Tyrol, which turned the German–Italian majority–minority situation on its head. The question of autonomy for German South Tyrolians therefore led to a vigorous conflict between the German-speaking community, largely represented by the South Tyrolian People's Party (SVP), and the Italian side as well as to a dispute between the Italian and the Austrian governments, the latter regarding itself as a 'patron' of South Tyrol. After several years of negotiations between the different sides, the so-called 'package solution' was agreed in 1969.[17] It comprised: (a) a substantially up-graded autonomy for the German-dominated province of Bozen/Bolzano within the overall region ('double autonomy'), institutionalized by the 1972 autonomy statute; (b) a detailed measures for ethnic proportional representation *(Proporz)*, in particular in the public service; and (c) rules for power-sharing in the provincial and regional institutions. The latter implied a joint government (*Landesregierung*) of German- and Italian-speakers according to the number of mandates each group won in parliamentary elections, which usually led to a fairly stable coalition of the SVP and the local branch of the Italian Christian Democrats (DC) before it disappeared from the Italian political scene in the 1990s. While the head of the provincial government *(Landeshauptmann)* may be a German-speaker, one of his two deputies has to be an Italian; at the regional level, the same rule applies the other way round. The two language groups also have to be jointly represented at the top of both the provincial and regional parliament. In these assemblies, each group enjoys veto rights to preserve its interests, in particular as regards financial and budgetary questions. A special feature of the South Tyrolian model is the principle of ethnic proportionality, which literally applies to all public jobs in the province, including state-owned enterprises (in total 25,000). Decades of dominance by the Italian minority came to an end with the special law of 1976, which laid down a number of rules about appointments to public posts. These should ensure a gradual increase in the number of German-speakers until achieving a degree of representation equivalent to their share in the population. According to government sources, this should be achieved in 2002.

2.2.3   Cyprus (1960–63)

Cyprus with its mixed Greek and Turkish population remained under British rule until 1960. In the 1950s the Greek majority (80 per cent) began to demand ever more strongly that the island should be united with Greece (enosis). In turn, the Turkish minority (18 per cent), supported by Turkey, called for a partition of the island (taksim) in case its constitutional status changed. Hence, between 1955 and 1959, the situation in Cyprus escalated into a violent conflict when Cypriot Greek paramilitary groups started to attack both British institutions and the Turkish minority, provoking counter-reactions by the British and by Turkish paramilitary organizations. Finally, in order to solve the crisis, the British government proposed independence for Cyprus. At two peace conferences in Zürich and London in 1959, Westminster and the patron states Greece and Turkey agreed upon an institutional framework for an independent Cyprus which provided for Greek-Turkish power-sharing under the international auspices of the three powers.[18] A special treaty of guarantee ensured their right to intervene in Cypriot affairs in case basic constitutional principles were violated. The power-sharing regime provided for a 'double presidency', a Greek president and a Turkish vice-president, and for a common government in which the Greek side could appoint seven ministers and the Turkish three ministers. The Parliament was composed of 35 Greek members and 15 Turkish delegates. Thus, the Cypriot population was split into two electorates; each person had to declare to which community he or she belonged—a system called "constitutional bi-communalism".[19] Extensive veto rights were given to both presidents and each parliamentary group. In public service, ethnic representation had to follow a quota of 70:30; in the army, the ratio of 60:40 was even more in favour of the Turkish minority. For cultural, religious, educational and local matters, the constitution foresaw two communal chambers as well as a communal court system. But from the very beginning, both sides interpreted the constitution differently and were unable to make compromises: while the Greek side complained about Turkish privileges, the Turkish side saw most regulations as a necessary protection of their rights. Major unresolved disputes concerned the implementation of the ethnic quota for public jobs, the use of veto rights, tax and budgetary policies, the planned army structure and the separation of city administrations as regulated by the constitution.[20] In 1963, the permanent deadlock led to another outbreak of violence between paramilitary groups on both sides, turning the capital of Nicosia into a de facto divided city. At the same time, President Makarios presented his "13 points" for constitutional reform, which would have led to a Greek majority rule. The Turkish side, backed by Ankara, rejected his proposal and left the government. The power-sharing regime had thus failed, the result being a return to violence, a policy of ethnic cleansing and resettlement in order to achieve homogenous territories.

2.2.4   Bosnia-Herzegovina (1995)

The collapse of the Yugoslav federation led to a brutal ethnic war in the former republic of Bosnia-Herzegovina (1992–95). In 1992, Bosnia was internationally recognized as an independent state, but at this stage the internal conflict between the three ethnonational groups (44 per cent Muslims, 31 per cent Serbs and 17 per cent Croats) had already turned violent. Neither Serbs nor Croats accepted Bosnian statehood, and both groups and, in particular, their paramilitary forces were strongly supported by Croatia and Serbia. Extreme human rights violations, torture, rapes, massacres and ethnic cleansing characterized the war, which was used to conquer territory and to destroy all mixed ethnic structures. The international community made several attempts to stop the war, for example, by deploying U.N. peacekeeping forces (UNPROFOR). But all negotiations and cease-fires eventually failed, and the war continued on a smaller scale.[21] In March 1994, external pressure, particularly from the U.S., led to the establishment of a Muslim–Croat federation in order to counter-balance the self-proclaimed Serb *Republika Srpska* (regime of Pale). But only after the Serb side had suffered severe defeats by the combined Croat–Muslim forces and NATO air strikes around the besieged city of Sarajevo in August–September 1995, was the Serb president Milošević and the Pale regime willing to negotiate a peace accord. The Dayton Agreement of 14 December 1995 provided for a new constitutional and territorial structure for Bosnia-Herzegovina. The state was subdivided into two entities, the Serb republic and the Muslim–Croat federation, both based largely on the borders drawn by warfare. Each part was granted its own president, government and parliament as well as substantial competencies in all policy areas (except foreign policy, foreign trade, monetary policy, refugee matters and all-Bosnian infrastructure). Moreover, each entity was allowed to introduce its own citizenship and to maintain special parallel relationships with neighbouring states (i.e. Croatia and Serbia). At the politically weak centre, however, the accord aimed to establish a power-sharing system: each group is represented in the three-member state presidency, the presidents are directly elected and enjoy comprehensive veto rights. In the Council of Ministers, each group holds *de facto* one-third of the posts. The parliamentary assembly is divided into a House of Representatives (42 elected members) and a House of Peoples (15 members delegated by the two entities); in each chamber the Muslim–Croat federation elects or appoints two-thirds and the Serb republic one-third of the deputies. The same quota applies to public posts in the central administration. In order to take a decision in both chambers, it is generally necessary that a majority and in some cases even a two-third majority of each side agree. However, unlike in Cyprus, the international community maintained its high level of involvement by deploying IFOR (later SFOR) and an international police force (IPTF) as a security guarantee. Furthermore, the five members of the Bosnian Contact Group in their role as formal witnesses of the Dayton Peace Accord established a wide range of civil activities in order to mediate or arbitrate between the segments:[22] an EU-appointed High Representative with far-reaching competencies, the OSCE election commission the UNHCR-commission on refugees, an OSCE ombudsperson, a human rights commission, and, finally, three of nine judges at the Constitutional Court have to be neutral (appointed by the European Court for Human Rights).

2.2.5   *Northern Ireland (1998)*

Since the mid-1980s the British and the Irish governments established a joint structure (Inter-Governmental Conference) and developed over time a common platform for solving the Northern Ireland conflict, which was documented by the joint *Downing Street Declaration* (1993) and the *Framework Documents* (1995). While the first established general principles, the second made more concrete institutional proposals for settling the conflict. On this basis, in 1996 all-party talks resumed. After an IRA cease-fire, the Nationalist Sinn Fein party was allowed to join the negotiating table in September 1997. The political wings of loyalist paramilitary groups were also represented. After long-lasting negotiations the talks finally resulted in the *Good Friday Peace Agreement* (10 April 1998), which maps out a new political structure for the province.[23] The Agreement found wide support among the Northern Irish (and the Irish) population in a special referendum on 22 May 1998 where 71 per cent voted in favour. The parties agreed to set up a power-sharing executive with a maximum of ten ministers, in which each party would be represented according to its numerical strength in the parliamentary assembly. The First Minister is to be a Unionist, the Deputy First Minister a Nationalist, and both are elected jointly by the assembly. For certain important questions, the 108 proportionally elected assembly members have to give their consent by way of cross-community voting procedures in order to prevent any majority rule. However, the implementation of the 1998 agreement proved to be rather slow and difficult, mostly because of the dispute on decommissioning arms, which had only been settled in part and in rather vague terms by the accord. While the Unionist UUP demanded to begin disarmament before the executive took office ("no guns, no government"), Sinn Fein (and the IRA) saw the establishment of a government as a precondition for further progress in decommissioning ("no government, no guns").[24]

2.3 Use and Misuse of Power-Sharing

The various cases confirm Lijphart's statement that there exists "no single consociational blueprint".[25] The concept of power-sharing can indeed be realized by various institutional options. In each case, the elements introduced above were implemented in a different manner. However, despite the diversity of regulations, it is possible to make some basic distinctions in order to show which institutional designs proved better than others in attaining the overall goal of elite cooperation.[26]

1) *Formal or Informal Regulations*
   Power-sharing can be based on formalized rules or informal practices: the former is done on the basis of a written constitution, a peace accord or special laws, the latter on the basis of oral agreements or unwritten customs. Switzerland serves as a prime case for informal rules: neither the composition of the government ("magic formula"), the representation of linguistic groups in politics and administrations nor the *de facto* veto opportunities and mechanisms for conflict settlement are strictly formalized. In contrast, the cases chosen here are mostly characterized by written laws, legal guarantees and detailed formal procedures. However, in Belgium, the parity rule at the Council of Ministers received an official constitutional status only in 1970 after having been practiced informally since 1950. Highly formalized are, in particular, the composition of power-sharing governments, the representation of all groups in parliaments, proportional systems for public administration and the division of power between different levels (e.g. regions in Belgium), as well as procedures for veto rights (see Table 4.2). Only in the field of arbitration, informal ways are also occasionally used, often in the form of *ad hoc* roundtables with major party leaders in order to solve concrete problems (see Belgium, South Tyrol). In general, informal arrangements are merely a supplement to already established formal rules. They could be seen as an indication of growing mutual trust, since both sides apparently believe that unwritten agreements will be kept. Informal rules are, therefore, signs of stability and the result of lasting peace.

Table 4.2
Formal and Informal Regulation

	Power-Sharing-Executive	Representation	Veto Rights	Segmental Autonomy	Arbitration
BEL	formal	formal	formal	formal	formal, informal
STY	formal	formal	formal	formal, informal	formal, informal
CYP	formal	formal	formal	formal	formal
BH 95	formal	formal	formal	formal	formal
NI 98	formal	formal	formal	informal	formal, informal

2) *Cabinet or Presidential System*

The power-sharing executive can basically be organized according to a cabinet or a presidential system. The first option implies the establishment of a collegial system which is either in total or in part (i.e. the Prime Minister and its deputy) elected by the Parliament. Ideally, the Cabinet's decisions are based on consensus and will be collectively supported. This model applies to the Belgium Council of Ministers, the South Tyrolian *Landesregierung* and the new Northern Irish regional government. In each case, some kind of formal or informal coalition-building is inevitable in order to gain the necessary majority in Parliament and to represent each group in the Cabinet, as guaranteed by the constitution. Indeed, both Belgium and South Tyrol have traditionally been ruled by formal coalitions between the largest parties on each side. In Northern Ireland, the power-sharing system works differently: Only the *First* and the *Deputy First Minister* (on the same ticket) have to be elected by a *de facto* coalition of a Protestant and a Catholic party; the other Cabinet members, unlike in Belgium or South Tyrol, are chosen autonomously by the parties according to their numerical strength in the Assembly, and here agreements among parties do not seem necessary.

The second option implies a direct popular vote for the head of state (president or joint presidency) whereby each group nominates and elects its own representative. The presidents largely control the composition of the government: Either they directly appoint ministers or they propose their candidates to the parliament. The first procedure applies to Cyprus, the second to Bosnia. In both cases, the Cypriot Council of Ministers as well as the Bosnian state presidency is able to take decisions by simple majority, but the inferior minority can block any legislation by using its veto rights. For example, the Greek members in the Council of Ministers always used their structural majority (seven to three) for decisions, while the Turkish vice-president counter-reacted with his veto. The Council members were not forced to cooperate—unlike in Cabinet systems. The failed attempt of Cyprus demonstrates why generally presidential systems seem to be less suitable for consociationalism than Cabinet systems. The disadvantages are obvious: The leaders (presidents) have strong legal powers and because of popular voting they are closely linked to their own ethno-national group and they do not need any cooperation (coalition-building) with other parliamentary groups in order to enter office.[27]

359

3) *Proportional Representation or Overrepresentation*

The representation of all groups in executive, legislative, judicative and administrative bodies can be organized in two different ways: First, mandates and public posts are distributed according to the principle of proportionality. For public administration, the principle is usually based on a proportional share of the total population. For governmental posts, the number of the groups' representatives or the numerical strength of the parties is also used as a measure. This applies, for instance, to the South Tyrolian and the Northern Irish executive. Second, some regulations are especially designed in order to over-represent the minority at specific posts and ranks. Examples are the principle of parity (widely used in Belgium) or fixed quota systems (such as in South Tyrol or Cyprus).

Both variants are often combined, and as a rule one can state the higher the positions and ranks, the more likely it is that smaller groups are over-represented. This is primarily the case for leading positions in state and government, as the Belgian Council of Ministers, the Cypriot double presidency or the Bosnian presidency may show. But it often also refers to the presidency of the parliament, to high courts and to arbitration commissions as well as to top positions in administration and the military. The composition of parliaments, on the other hand, mirrors the size of the various groups, since elections normally take place on the basis of proportional voting. One significant exception is the failed Cypriot model, where by constitutional rule the Greeks received 70 per cent and the Turks 30 per cent of the seats. Since the Turks made up only 18 per cent of the Cypriot population, they were highly over-represented. Officially, the 70:30 ratio had also to be respected in the Cypriot public administration. But this rule caused a constant quarrel between the two sides: on the one hand, the Greek majority feared the loss of positions and influence, while on the other hand, the Turkish minority insisted upon the rapid implementation of the ethnic proportional representation. Both sides were unable to find a compromise; they could not develop a less static quota system which would not ask too much from the majority population and would also allow for appropriate representation of the minority. In other words, in Cyprus, the problem was not over-representation *per se,* but its strict and overall application. It is therefore important to use this instrument more flexibly and to restrict over-representation to some areas. In general, proportional regulations should not be too rigid, particularly with respect to the public service. At the least, there has to be, unlike in Cyprus, a longer transition period to change the system. An example of a more flexible solution is the 'asymmetric' appointment model in the Belgian public service, i.e. there is no fixed quota for any post and any hierarchical level, but in sum there has to be certain number of both Flemish and French-speakers within the administration. If one group is traditionally strongly represented in one institution or one administrative unit, then it is possible to privilege the other group in other places. Additionally, long-term timetables for the introduction of proportional rules such as in South Tyrol and in Belgium have the benefit that civil servants can usually keep their posts, thus reducing the conflict potential significantly.

4) *Delaying, Indirect or Direct Veto Power*

As regards veto rights, there are again various options: (1) delaying veto; (2) indirect veto; and (3) direct veto. The first type aims at delaying a decision in order to reconsider the matter, often by using a special parliamentary mediation procedure or by referring it to the constitutional court. One example is the Belgian 'alarm bell procedure', introduced in 1970. In Parliament, each language group can stop a draft law if at least three-quarters of the group members sign a resolution. Within 30 days, the Council of Ministers has to search for a compromise and to table a new proposal.[28] In South Tyrol, each parliamentary language group is allowed to call upon the Italian constitutional court, if a law has passed the South Tyrolian *Landtag* or the Regional Council against the will of two-thirds of one language group. This procedure protects the interests of the German minority within the region South Tyrol–Trentino and, in turn, those of the Italian minority within the province of Bozen/Bolzano.[29]

The second type leads to an indirect veto for each group, since specific conditions have to be met in order to pass a legislation in Parliament. In general, the majority of each group has to agree, otherwise the draft law will not pass (principle of double majority). In Belgium, this procedure is institutionalized through the so-called 'community majority law'.[30] For specific, important matters (such as questions of institutional reform), the majority of each parliamentary language group has to approve a piece of legislation and the total number of affirmative votes should be two-thirds of all votes. In South Tyrol, again, the majority of each language group must agree to each sub-section of the yearly budget. Similar, rather complicated regulations can be found in the cases of Cyprus, Bosnia and Northern Ireland.[31] The third type enables groups to declare each matter to be of 'vital interest' and, therefore, to stop any political action directly. An extreme case were the presidential veto rights in Cyprus. The Greek President and the Turkish Vice President had the possibility to block any decision. The situation is similar for the three members of the Bosnian state presidency as well as the deputies of each group in the House of Peoples, which can also put a 'vital interest' mechanism in operation.

The Cypriot experience of mutual blockage, however, demonstrates that veto rights should be restricted in order to prevent their misuse. The first two options are therefore more preferable. They are based on formalized procedures and constitutional barriers, which make it much more difficult to use veto rights in an inflationary manner. These restrictions are necessary since veto rights should foster and not obstruct consensus building.[32] They should serve as a kind of emergency measure for a certain case, limited by constitutional rules. The less often veto rights are used, the better. Their frequent use can be seen as a sign of severe crisis. At best, veto rights develop a preventive effect, i.e. the threat of a veto forces both sides to find a compromise at an early stage of decision-making in order to make any veto unnecessary. This preventive nature can be observed in Belgium or South Tyrol. In both cases, veto rights such as the alarm clock procedure or the budget guarantee are hardly used, but their mere existence seems important for finding compromises.

5) *Territorial or Personal Group Autonomy*
Segmental autonomy is either based on the principle of territoriality or of personality. The former implies federal structures (Belgium) or territorial autonomy (South Tyrol). The latter is, for instance, realized through elected, non-territorial, self-governing communal chambers (Cyprus) or private institutions which obtain certain responsibilities for each community (Northern Ireland). Both options can be combined, as the examples of Belgium and South Tyrol demonstrate. In Belgium, regions coexist with non-territorial (cultural) communities, which have their own institutions and competencies in language, culture and education. In South Tyrol,

the German- and Italian-speakers possess some degree of autonomy in school matters. The advantage of self-rule is that interethnic coordination is limited to policies which are in the common interest of all segments, while in all other cases "decision-making authority is delegated to the separate segments as much as possible".[33]

The successful operation of this element depends less on the question of how many competencies are delegated to the territorial or non-territorial self-rule institutions, but on how the division of competencies between central power-sharing and self-government bodies is organized. Most importantly, it is necessary to avoid a permanent competition and struggle between the two levels of government. In particular, segmental autonomy should not undermine central institutions as it happened in Cyprus, where the communal chambers gained more and more powers while joint decision-making proved to be impossible. Thus, the central and the autonomy levels should be more interlocked, for example by a two-chamber legislature. The more competencies that are delegated to self-governing bodies, the more important cooperation between the two levels becomes in order to prevent centrifugal and destabilizing tendencies.

6) *Political or Juridical Arbitration*
Conflict mediation and settlement mechanisms are of great importance for the functioning of consociationalism. Arbitration can be done by political as well as juridical arrangements. The former includes a wide range of parliamentary and extra-parliamentary measures: informal meetings, *ad hoc* commissions or formalized mediation procedures. The latter refer to high or constitutional courts and to quasi-judicial arbitration commissions, which may give recommendations for compromises as well as binding conclusions. In successful power-sharing regimes, both options coexist. In Belgium, the Permanent Language Commission usually settles conflicts over linguistic rights. For constitutional matters, two juridical institutions serve as mediator and arbitrator: the highest administrative court *(Conseil d'Etat/Raad van State)* and the arbitration court *(Court d'Arbitrage/Arbitragehof)*, the latter dealing in particular with disputes over competencies between the centre and the regions. Moreover, Belgian politics knows a range of other formal or non-informal ways to prevent and to solve conflicts, such as consultation procedures within the Parliament or the special 'advisory committee' representing central and regional institutions.

In South Tyrol, important mediating and arbitrating bodies are the parliamentary arbitration commission (in cases of budget questions), the 'Commission of the Six' for relations between the central and the provincial government and, finally, the local administration court in Bozen/Bolzano. Similarly, the 1998 institutional framework for Northern Ireland provides not only for juridical, but also for political mechanisms: for example, the various committees of the Assembly gained a strong role in the legislation process in order to prevent conflicts at an early stage of decision-making. They are closely linked to the respective ministry, they have control powers as well as the right to initiate draft laws. Whoever governs a ministry, Nationalist or Unionist, has to defend his policy before the committee, in which both sides are represented. Additionally, a *Special Committee* will check each draft law in respect of human rights and equality rights.[34]

The Cypriot and the Bosnian model, however, rely almost entirely on juridical arbitration. Since no softer, more political instruments for conflict mediation and settlement existed in Cyprus, the result was that practically all political disputes were transmitted to the Constitutional Court: between 1960 and 1963 almost 2,000 cases were pending at the Court.[35] The three judges (one Greek, one Turkish and one neutral, external judge) were therefore heavily overburdened and, moreover, in most cases they could not agree and blocked one another. Bosnia may to some extent face a similar juridical deadlock. The lesson from these cases would be to develop and to implement a more advanced procedure for conflict settlement, including the whole range of political bodies. Appealing to the highest court should be the very last resort, and one reserved for purely constitutional questions.

If one compares the different power-sharing regimes (see Table 4.3), it follows that the institutional arrangements of the 1998 Northern Irish Peace Agreement are much closer to the consociational blueprints of the two success cases. The Bosnian framework, however, has some significant similarities with the failed Cypriot constitution, in particular with respect to the presidential system, based on popular voting, and with respect to absolute veto rights.

Table 4.3
Options for Consociational Arrangements

	Executive	Representation: Executive/Legislation	Veto Rights	Segmental Autonomy	Arbitration
BEL	Cabinet system	over-represented/ proportional	delaying/indirect	territorial/personal	political/juridical
STY	Cabinet system	proportional/ proportional	delaying/indirect	territorial/personal	political/juridical
CYP	Presidential system	over-represented/ over-represented	delaying/ indirect/direct	personal	juridical
BiH	Presidential system	over-represented/ proportional	delaying/ indirect/direct	territorial	juridical
NI	Cabinet system	proportional/ proportional	delaying/indirect	personal	political/juridical

Summarizing, it can be said that in order to reduce the potential misuse and to fostering elite cooperation by consociational arrangements, it will be important to acknowledge the following points: (1) Cabinet governments are preferable to a presidential system; (2) proportional rules should be flexible in order to allow suitable representation for each group (particularly in key positions) without demanding too much from the majority group; (3) veto rights should be subjected to conditions on questions of substance and of procedure, and direct and absolute vetoes on each and every political issue should therefore be avoided; (4) segmental autonomy, personal or territorial, should also be limited to specific matters; moreover, there should be an institutional link between central power-sharing and self-governing bodies; (5) it is important to use both political and juridical mechanisms of conflict mediation and settlement.

3.   LINKING SHARED-RULE AND SELF-RULE

The assessment of the power-sharing model and its various options already indicated how shared-rule could benefit from self-rule elements. As stated above, segmental autonomy may reduce the need for cooperation and thus circumvent difficult bargaining processes, since not each and every policy has to be adopted by consensus. The precondition is, however, that segmental autonomy is strictly understood as "minority rule over the minority itself in matters that are the minority's exclusive concern".[36] What *exclusive* means in concrete terms is of course not to be decided by each group on its own, but must be decided jointly by all segments. Moreover, any changes, be it limitations or extensions of self-rule elements, must also be agreed by all groups in order to prevent a situation like in Cyprus, where the unilateral and extensive use of self-rule finally destroyed the overall power-sharing structure.

After having identified the use of self-rule to power-sharing regimes, one may pose the reverse question: what could be the added value of shared-rule elements to self-rule regimes? In order to find out whether and in what way shared-rule could be beneficial, it is necessary to point out some of the typical problems connected with autonomies, be they organized on a territorial or non-territorial basis:

- Governments and minorities are often in conflict about diverging interpretations of already agreed self-rule regulations, laid down in specific minority laws, in an autonomy statute and/or in the constitution. Generally, governments try to understand the guaranteed rights as strictly and narrowly as possible, while minorities pursue a more generous reading of the laws. In most cases, the monopoly of interpretation (executed through the administration, the parliament and the courts) is reserved to the central institutions.
- Governments sometimes simply do not comply with their own commitments towards minority self-rule institutions. They may delay the implementation of certain minority rights, omit to consult minority self-governments or even exclude them deliberately from information; they ignore proposals or initiatives from minorities; they do not deliver the amount of financial or logistic support granted to minority institutions, etc. In particular, regional and local public administrations employ these practices of non-compliance, which frequently undermine self-rule arrangements and thus increase tensions between minorities and majorities.
- In principle autonomies, whichever way designed, do still depend on the juridical and political framework of the state. Unless they serve as federal components, autonomies are legally subordinated to the central institutions. Their rights and competencies can be reduced; they may even be dissolved by a unilateral parliamentary decision.[37] Autonomies usually 'borrow' their legislative and/or executive rights from the state, which implies that any legislation or administrative action made by the autonomies could ultimately be blocked or overruled by the central institutions. In some cases of territorial autonomy (such as South Tyrol or the Åland Islands), the constitution or the statute may set some limits to the state's supremacy and therefore make it more difficult to interfere, but in most instances the autonomies depend largely on the goodwill of the central institutions.
- In terms of finance, autonomies also rely heavily on the state. The vast majority of self-rule regimes has no independent financial resources, but receives regular transfers or funding from the central institutions which have to be negotiated from time to time, sometimes on an annual basis.[38]

- Competency clashes are another prominent area of potential conflict between minority regimes and governments. Competences are often not clearly divided between the different levels of government, in particular when it comes to details. For example, both the state and the autonomy share overlapping competences in the field of education or economic development. In general, the state defines basic guidelines and overall goals to which the autonomies have to adapt their own policies. Sometimes, however, these policies conflict with those implemented by the central administration.
- A particular problem inherent to any territorial self-rule regime is that however administrative borders are drawn in order to create a regional autonomy, there will always be 'internal' minorities. Sometimes they are members of other, non-territorial minorities such as the Roma or Ladin (in South Tyrol) who need special minority protection within the autonomy. But more often they are members of the majority society (or the state's titular nation) such as the Italian-speakers in South Tyrol, the Moldovans in Gagauzia or the Serbs in Kosovo. In particular, the latter situation entails an enormous potential for ongoing conflict, best illustrated by the Kosovo conflict. These groups perceive the self-rule arrangement in favour of special groups (i.e. the German-speakers, Gagauz or Albanians) as a threat to their own identity and seek support from the central government. In turn, the local majority distrusts these groups and their special relationship to the state's institutions. In many places, moreover, these so-called 'double minority' situations create a major barrier for allowing territorial self-rule which would bring the overall minority into the position of a local majority (e.g. Albanians in Macedonia, Hungarians in Southern Slovakia or Russian-speakers in north east Estonia).

These problems exist to varying degrees in each case of autonomy. Obviously, some self-rule arrangements, notably territorial autonomies, have a better legal status and greater political independence than others. But even the most advanced autonomies like South Tyrol, the Færøe Islands, the Åland Islands, Scotland, Catalonia or the Basque Country have to coordinate their policies with the state's institutions to some extent. They still depend on central decision-making, in particular with regard to legal rights and their interpretation, competences, resources and finances.

From the viewpoint of autonomies, however, shared-rule elements may facilitate matters. Their main purpose would be to link self-rule institutions more closely to central decision-making processes, at least when it comes to issues of minority concern. That can be done by different means, either by ensuring sufficient participation at the state level within the legislative, judicative and executive or by special bodies (commissions) in which the autonomies and the state are equally represented, or by a mixture of both alternatives. The first option is typical for federal systems. Each unit is represented at the centre and the government needs their approval for certain measures. This is often institutionalized by a two-chamber legislative (Switzerland, Bosnia) and/or by complicated veto powers for the regions/groups in the parliament (Belgium). A more low-profile variant would be the direct representation of minority self-government institutions within the executive, either at the ministerial level (*Ministry for minority/regional issues*) or at the administrative level (*office or ombudsperson for minority questions*). These governmental or quasi-governmental bodies do not usually have any veto power, but they ensure an early involvement of the minority or the region in the executive's policies. Examples are the unit for Sami issues at the Norwegian Ministry for Communal Affairs or the Hungarian Office for National and Ethnic Minorities. The links are stronger in the Gagauz case where the governor of the autonomy is automatically an *ex-officio* member of the Moldovan government[39] or in the South Tyrolian case where the *Landeshauptmann* can participate in governmental meetings in Rome, when the competences of the province are at stake. The second option, the establishment of permanent commissions for regular region-centre dialogue, can best be highlighted by the example of South Tyrol and the Åland Islands. Both the so-called South Tyrolian *Commission of the Six* and the *Åland Delegation* became the most important bodies for negotiations between regional and central governments. In addition, they often serve as a mechanism for early consultation and information exchange as well as political bodies for dispute settlement.[40] In both cases, decisions have to be taken jointly. Similar inter-governmental bodies exist between regions and the centre in Belgium and, albeit more on an *ad hoc* basis, between Spanish autonomies and Madrid.

Whatever their design, these shared-rule elements, even their soft versions, facilitate cooperation between minority self-governments and the state. Generally, autonomies are institutionally involved in governmental politics and could thus use their influence at an early stage of decision-making in order to safeguard their rights. Conflicts such as those described above on opposing interpretations, non-compliance, legal status, finances and competences can be discussed, mitigated and finally solved over time by the application of standing procedures and within an institutionalized framework, where representatives of the regions/minorities and the central bodies meet on a regular basis. In other words: shared-rule mechanisms could strengthen self-rule, since they improve the minorities' opportunity to defend their autonomy at the state level. From the government's perspective, the combination of both principles has some appeal as well. While autonomies gain influence at the state level, they are at the same time more integrated into the general political framework. In this way they are forced to cooperate and may even develop a broader perspective on the common good for the society as a whole, which would certainly lead to a moderation of their own position.

Beyond the relation between region and centre, shared-rule elements also provide an answer to the problem of 'internal minorities' in the case of territorial autonomy. Regional institutions could themselves be designed in such a way that they allow power-sharing between the various groups. Here again, South Tyrol is the paradigm case; as stated above, both German- and Italian-speakers must be represented in the provincial government and, in accordance with the *Proporz* rule, in all sectors of public services.[41] South Tyrol illustrates convincingly that shared-rule arrangements could compensate a local minority (i.e. Italian-speakers) for conceding self-rule to a local majority (i.e. German-speakers) and could therefore ease fears among "internal minorities". The two principles are combined in order to solve two problems at once: shared-rule for "internal minorities" and self-rule for the region as a whole. Moreover, since Italian-speakers are granted shared-rule on the provincial level, South Tyrol can claim in return at least some limited shared-rule elements at the domestic level. Similar package deals which reflect different levels of government are in principle possible in other cases—such as Kosovo or Southern Slovakia where local power-sharing could be granted to Serbs and Slovaks while allowing self-rule (including some shared-rule provisions) for the Albanian- and Hungarian-dominated regions, respectively.

4. CONCLUSION: CRITERIA FOR GOOD MINORITY GOVERNANCE

As most cases in this volume illustrate, political elites or leaders on both sides play a major role in setting up minority governance regimes. Obviously, their consent is a *condition sine qua non* for achieving an agreement in the first place. But also during the post-agreement phase, success or failure largely depends on whether and how minority and majority elites change their behaviour over time from confrontation to cooperation. Against this general background the institutional design of minority governance becomes an important variable for explaining success or failure. A 'good' design can indeed be supportive of the depicted changes in group leaders' attitudes and behaviours; in short, it can foster constructive learning processes among elites. A case in point again is South Tyrol. In the course of conflict regulation since the early 1970s, all elites gradually changed their former goals and attitudes that had shaped their behaviour and their identity in the 1950s and 1960s. The crucial question therefore is which general criteria can be identified for good minority governance? The following list is by no means exhaustive, but is based on the empirical analysis of various cases and tries to summarize the most important findings. It should be used as a 'checklist' for both self-rule and shared-rule arrangements.

1) *Capability for Solving Implementation Problems*

In the course of implementation each type of regulation necessarily runs into problems, due to the fact that most agreements are deliberately ambiguously formulated. To some extent, ambiguity is inevitable since "ambiguity is the mother of compromise".[42] The consequences are often different interpretations, misunderstandings over rights and duties or attempts by one side to undermine the promises they made in the agreement. This can lead to renewed political tensions and considerable backlashes, in extreme cases even to the resurgence of violence (as in Northern Ireland). The only way out is if both sides (as well as external mediators) consider the implementation phase an integral part of the process of conflict regulation. In more concrete terms: bodies such as expert commissions, all-party talks, *ad hoc* committees and so on, which were primarily set up for the negotiation of an agreement, should be in place for a longer period in order to prevent a crisis during the implementation. Additionally, it is often necessary to set up arbitration procedures, clearing-houses or ombudspersons in order to solve implementation problems.

2) *Openness for Reforms*

A general experience in almost all cases of minority governance is that reforms are necessary. Often regulations prove not to be suitable for solving the interethnic conflicts, or they are simply impractical or lack the necessary financial resources. On the one hand, reforms or readjustments of difficult and lengthy brokered compromises imply certain risks, since the package has to be renegotiated. On the other hand, simply sticking to unworkable regulations may also lead to tensions. Each governance model should therefore be seen as an institutionalized system of ongoing negotiations, which is in principle open for reforms and changes. The parties have to be prepared to evaluate their decisions from time to time and to make new compromises.

3) *Fostering Elite Cooperation Instead of Mutual Blockage*

Generally, self-rule and shared-rule regulations should foster cooperation among the elites and should not be instruments for further confrontation. For example, they have to be designed in such a way that they cannot be misused for mutual blockage. As noted above, this aspect is mainly related to veto rights, which are common in power-sharing and federal regimes. To avoid the use of veto rights, or at least to counter-balance their potentially negative effects, it seems to be helpful to set up cooperative structures, which allow for the early participation of all parties concerned in a decision-making process. Examples are cooperative federalism (Switzerland) or special joint commissions between minority/regional and central institutions (South Tyrol). More generally, as a rule each minority governance regime should be characterized by a balanced mix of self-rule and shared-rule elements in order to avoid two potential pitfalls: on the one hand, a permanent interference by the government into the autonomy which ultimately undermines the purpose of self-rule; and on the other hand, the development of selfish regional or local group elites, who are not interested in any common good or in the state as such. There needs to be institutionalized interplay between minority governance and central institutions. Each level should at least be consulted and informed about the other's plans and actions.

4) *Turning Zero-Sum Games into Positive-Sum Games*
    The solutions have to turn zero-sum situations which are typical for ethnic conflicts into positive-sum games which allow each side, and in particular the political leaderships, to perceive themselves as 'winners'. In other words, the agreements have to fulfil central concerns of both sides, and each concession to the other side should pay off to some extent. This can be achieved in different ways:

    By *implementing preferred arrangements simultaneously*, when each group prefers different institutional solutions. Under certain circumstances this allows the opportunity to introduce both preferred frameworks at the same time. One example is the 1998 Northern Ireland Agreement: Catholics had always demanded the acknowledgement of an 'Irish dimension' through special North–South institutions, while Protestants often perceived those as a first step towards unification. In order to ease Unionist fears, the accord provides for the simultaneous establishment of British–Irish institutions.

    By *exploiting the flexibility of regulations*, i.e. the same instrument can be implemented in different ways thus leaving room for compromise. For example, in the case of Belgium, proportional rules and quota systems offer a wide range of possibilities and options intended to satisfy majority and minority interests.

    By *using the possibilities for reciprocal arrangements*, i.e. regulations are made in such a way that they favour both groups, but on different levels. Rules which may be beneficial for one group at a national level could be helpful for the other group at a lower level (regional, local) and vice versa.

5) *Involving All Conflict Parties*
    Particular regimes of minority governance cannot be isolated from an overall solution which involves the majority society and other minorities, which are either directly affected by territorial self-rule (the question of 'internal minorities') or need a different means of protection (territorial versus non-territorial groups). Furthermore, often the involvement of one or more neighbouring states should be considered, in particular if they see themselves as patrons for special minorities as Hungary does with respect to Hungarians in Slovakia, Serbia or Romania. In complex minority situations such, as in Northern Ireland, South Tyrol or Kosovo, one needs a comprehensive solution which reflects each level of conflict—the inter-state, the centre-regional and the local level. A successful strategy has been the combination of the various models of ethnic conflict regulation. They could stabilize and amend each other. The best example is the solution

for South Tyrol which includes bilateral conflict management at inter-state level (Italy/Austria), territorial autonomy at centre-regional level and power-sharing requirements as well as minority rights for Italian- and Ladin-speakers at the local level.

6) *Timing*
Ethnic conflict regulation has to be well timed. Very often the timing of a proposed regulation is decisive for its success. The further a conflict has escalated, the more preferences, interests and power relations change not only between the groups, but also within the groups. Obviously, in this situation typically 'hard-liners' on each side tend to win ground, while moderates lose popular support. Under these conditions it is often the case that a proposal for minority governance which might have solved the conflict before violence escalated is no longer a viable option. Generally, the majority population has to grant more concessions to stop a violent or terrorist conflict than beforehand. On the other hand, each concession could be perceived by the extremists of the other side as sign of weakness. In short, if concessions come too late, in some cases their peaceful and stabilizing effect may vanish.

The closer agreements and institutional designs come to fulfiling these criteria, the better the functioning of minority governance, be it based primarily on self-rule or on shared-rule. This, in turn, will surely effect the behaviour and attitudes of elites, which in most cases are not characterized by goodwill at the beginning of the process. The more positive their experiences with institutions and regulations are, the better it is for the learning process mentioned above. Moreover, the better politicians from both sides get used to the daily business of cooperation, the easier it will be for them to convince, or at least to marginalize sceptical voices or radical opponents in their own camp, which until today have in many places, be it Northern Ireland, Corsica, Transdnister, Bosnia or Kosovo, the potential to destroy any peace process.

NOTES

[7]   This article is based on results of a larger research project on ethnic conflict regulation, see Ulrich Schneckener, *Auswege aus dem Bürgerkrieg: Modelle zur Regulierung ethnonationaler Konflikte in Europa* (Frankfurt: Suhrkamp, 2002).

[8]   See, Arend Lijphart, "Consociational Democracy", in *World Politics* 21 (1969), 2, pp.207–225; Arend Lijphart, "Consociational Democracy", in *Consociational Democracy: Political Accommodation* in *Segmented Societies*, Kenneth D. McRae, ed. (Toronto: McLelland and Stewart, 1974), pp.70–89; Arend Lijphart, *Democracy in Plural Societies* (New Haven: Yale University Press, 1977); Arend Lijphart, "Consociation and Federation: Conceptual and Empirical Links", in *Canadian Journal of Political Science* 12 (1979), 3, pp.499–515; Arend Lijphart, "Consociation: The Model and its Applications in Divided Societies", in *Political Cooperation in Divided Societies*, Desmond Rea, ed. (Dublin: Gill & McMillan, 1982), pp.166–186; Arend Lijphart, "The Power-Sharing Approach", in *Conflict and Peacemaking in Multiethnic Societies*, Joseph Montville, ed. (New York: Lexington Books, 1991), pp.491–510; Gerhard Lehmbruch, *Proporzdemokratie: Politisches System und politische Kultur in der Schweiz und in Österreich* (Tübingen: Mohr, 1967); Gerhard Lehmbruch, "A Non-Competitive Pattern of Conflict Management in Liberal Democracies: The Case of Switzerland, Austria and Lebanon", in *Consociational Democracy: Political Accommodation in Segmented Societies*, Kenneth D. McRae, ed. (Toronto: McLelland & Stewart, 1974), pp.90–99; Gerhard Lehmbruch "Konkordanzdemokratie", in *Lexikon der Politik*, vol. 3: Die westlichen Länder, Manfred G. Schmidt, ed. (München: Beck, 1992), pp.206–211; Gerhard Lehmbruch, "Consociational Democracy and Corporatism in Switzerland", in *Publius: The Journal of Federalism* 23 (1993), pp.43–60; Eric Nordlinger, *Conflict Regulation in Divided Societies* (Cambridge, Mass.: Harvard Studies in International Affairs, 1972); and Hans Daalder, "The Consociational Democracy Theme", in *World Politics* 26 (1974), 4, pp.604–621.

[9]   Nordlinger (1972), *op. cit.*

[10]   Arend Lijphart, *Democracy in Plural Societies* (New Haven: Yale University Press, 1977).

[11]   *Ibid.*, p.5.

[12]   See Arend Lijphart (1974), *op. cit.,* pp.85–89; (1977), *op. cit.,* pp.104–119, who distinguishes between 'homogenous' and 'plural society'.

[13]   For an overview of different models, see John Coakley, "The Resolution of Ethnic Conflict: Towards a Typology", in *International Political Science Review* 13 (1992), 4, pp.343–358; John McGarry, Brendan O'Leary, eds., *The Politics of Ethnic Conflict Regulation* (London: Routledge, 1993), pp.1–40;

        Ulrich Schneckener, "Regulierung ethnischer Konflikte in Südosteuropa: Die Politik der Anerkennung", in *Internationale Politik* 9 (1999), pp.7–20; and Brunner/Küpper in this volume.

[14]   For the conceptional link of federal and consociational frameworks, see Arend Lijphart, (1979), *op. cit.,* pp.499–515; Kenneth D. McRae "Comment: Federation, Consociation, Corporatism—An Addendum to Arend Lijphart", in *Canadian Journal of Political Science* 12 (1979), 3, pp.517–522; Daniel Elazar, *Exploring Federalism* (Tuscaloosa: University of Alabama Press, 1987), pp.18–26, and Timothy D. Sisk, *Power-Sharing and International Mediation in Ethnic Conflicts* (Washington: United States Institute of Peace, 1996), pp.49–53.

[15]   Lijphart (1977), *op.cit.,* p.31.

[16]   For the Belgian political system, see Arend Lijphart, ed., *Conflict and Coexistence in Belgium: The Dynamics of a Culturally Divided Society* (Berkeley: Institute of International Studies, University of California, 1981); Maureen Covell, "Ethnic Conflict and Élite Bargaining: The Case of Belgium", in *West European Politics* 4 (1981), p.3; Maureen Covell "Possibly Necessary but Not Necessarily Possible: Revision of the Constitution in Belgium", in *Redesigning the State: The Politics of Constitutional Change in Industrial Nations*, Keith Banting and Richard Simeon, eds. (Toronto: University of Toronto Press, 1985), pp.71–94; Maureen Covell, "Federalization and Federalism: Belgium and Canada", in *Federalism and the Role of the State*, Herman Bakvis and William Chandler, eds. (Toronto: University of Toronto Press, 1987), pp.57–81; Kenneth D. McRae, *Conflict and Compromise in Multilingual Societies: Belgium* (Waterloo and Ontario: Wilfred Laumer University Press, 1986); Frank Delmartino, "Regionalisation in Belgium: Evaluation of an Ongoing Institutional Crisis", in *European Journal of Political Research* 16 (1988), 4, pp.381–394; André Alen, "Belgien: Ein zweigliedriger und zentrifugaler Föderalismus", in *Zeitschrift für ausländisches öffentliches Recht und Völkerrecht* 50 (1990), pp.501–544; Saul Newman, *Ethnoregional Conflict in Democracies* (London: Greenwood Press, 1996), pp.57–106.

[17]   For the South Tyrolian solution, see Otto Triffterer, "The Rights of the German Speaking Population of the South Tyrol", in Yoram Dinstein, Mala Tabory, eds. *The Protection of Minorities and Human Rights* (Dordrecht: Martinus Nijhoff, 1992), pp.464–489; Karin Oellers-Frahm, "Die rechtliche Stellung der Minderheiten in Italien", in *Das Minderheitenrecht europäischer Staaten*, vol. 1, Jochen Frowein, Rainer Hofmann, Stefan Oeter eds. (Berlin: Springer, 1993), pp.192–224; Antony E. Alcock, "South Tyrol", in *Minority Rights in Europe*, Hugh Miall, ed. (London: Pinter, 1994), pp.46–55; Rolf Steininger, *Südtirol im 20. Jahrhundert: Vom Leben und Überleben einer Minderheit* (Innsbruck/Wien: Studien-Verlag, 1997); and Rainer in this volume.

[18]   For the Cypriot solution of 1960, see Norma Salem, ed., *Cyprus: A Regional Conflict and Its Resolution* (New York: St. Martin's Press, 1992); Hurst Hannum, ed., *Documents on Autonomy and Minority Rights* (Dordrecht: Martinus Nijhoff, 1993), pp.355–383; Stanley Kyriakides, *Cyprus Constitutionalism and Crisis Government* (Philadelphia: University of Pennsylvania, 1968).

[19]   Stanley Kyriakides, (1968), *op. cit.*

[20]   *Ibid.*, pp.79–103.

[21]   See Marie-Janine Calic, *Krieg und Frieden in Bosnien-Hercegovina* (Frankfurt: Suhrkamp, 1996); and James Gow, *Triumph of the Lack of Will: International Diplomacy and the Yugoslav War* (London: Hurst, 1997).

[22]   USA, Great Britain, France, Russia and Germany were members of the Contact Group.

[23]   For the history of the conflict, see John McGarry, *Explaining Northern Ireland* (London: Blackwell, 1995); John Mc Garry, *The Politics of Antagonism: Understanding Northern Ireland* (London: Athlone, 2nd edition 1996); John Darby, "Scorpions in a Bottle: Conflicting Cultures in Northern Ireland", in *Minority Rights Publication* (London: Minority Rights Publications,

1997); for an analysis of the latest peace process and the Good Friday Agreement, see Stefan Wolff, "Der Nordirlandkonflikt: Minderheitenschutz durch demokratische Institutionen und Volksabstimmungen?", in *Moderner Minderheitenschutz: Rechtliche oder politische Absicherung?* Hans-Joachim Heintze, ed. (Bonn: Dietz, 1998), pp.195–229; O'Leary (1999), *op.cit.*; Jonathan Stevenson, "Irreversible Peace in Northern Ireland?", in *Survival* 42 (2000), 3, pp.5–26 and Gallagher in this volume.

[24] In December 1999 a compromise led to the establishment of the power-sharing executive including ministers from Sinn Fein. But after repeated disputes over decommissioning the British Northern Ireland Minister suspended the regional body in early February 2000 in order to prevent the formal resignation of the First Minister Trimble (UUP). New guarantees by the IRA, however, made the executive's reestablishment in May 2000 possible.

[25] Lijphart (1982), *op.cit.*, p.175.

[26] For the analysis of different institutional options, see also *ibid.*; Sisk (1996), *op.cit.*, pp.27–45.

[27] Lijphart (1991), *op.cit.*, pp.506–507.

[28] Alen (1990), *op.cit.*, p.510.

[29] Oellers-Frahm (1993), *op.cit.*, pp.222–224.

[30] Alen (1990), *op.cit.*, pp.509–510.

[31] In Cyprus, the majority of MEPs of each side had to agree upon questions of communal, tax and election laws (art. 78) and, furthermore, two-thirds of each group had to approve any constitutional reform (art. 182). In Bosnia, any decision can be blocked by the Parliament, if two-thirds of MEPs of one entity (Croat–Muslim federation or *Republika Srpska*) vote against a piece of legislation. According to the 1998 Northern Irish Peace Agreement, cross-community voting is necessary in cases of budget questions and in any other matter, if at least 30 deputies call for it. Cross-community voting can either be done by the 'parallel consent'—or the 'weighted majority'—procedure. In the first case, the majority of Nationalists and Unionists have to agree, in the second case, 60 per cent of all present deputies and at least 40 per cent of each side have to agree.

[32] For the ambivalence of veto rights, see also Lijphart (1977), *op.cit.*, pp.37–38; (1982), *op.cit.*, pp.177–181.

[33] Lijphart (1979), *op.cit.*, p.500.

[34] Other political bodies are a parliamentary *Equality Commission* in order to prevent discrimination, a consultative *Civic Forum* with representatives from politics, economy and trade unions, and a *Human Rights Commission*.

[35] Kyriakides (1968), *op.cit.*, p.82.

[36] Lijphart (1979), *op.cit.*, p.500.

[37] In some cases, a dissolution would presuppose an alteration of the constitution in question. For example, the Sami rights or the autonomy of the Åland Islands are protected by the Finnish constitution.

[38] A prominent exception to this rule is the autonomy of the Basque Country, which has the right to raise its own taxes. In other cases, the situation for self-rule regimes has been improved by the introduction of financial statutes which at least set guidelines for the calculation of the yearly transfer (cf. South Tyrol since 1989).

[39] See the study by Neukirch in this book.

[40] The *Commission of the Six* comprises of three members each from the *Land* and the state. Within the *Åland Delegation* the *Lagting* (the Island's assembly) and the Finnish government are represented by two members each. While in the South Tyrolian case, the commission usually meets only when necessary, the Delegation approves as a standing procedure each provincial law and must decide every year on the financial transfers to the autonomy.

[41] To a much lesser degree, the Gagauz autonomy, too, has some internal shared-rule regulations in order to represent the Moldovan minority; one deputy speaker of the assembly has to be non-Gagauz.

[42] Fen Osler Hampson, *Nurturing Peace: Why Peace Settlements Succeed or Fail* (Washington: United States Institute of Peace Press, 1996), p.221.

Index